q741.503 Worl v.1.
The World encylopedia of
cartoons.

DATE DUE		
DEC 0 3 1996		
DEC 1 7 1996		
SEP 1 7 1997		
APR 1 2002		
MAY 1 5 2003		
JUN 1 7 2004		
JUL 2 1 2005		
AUG 3 1 2009		
NOV 0 8 2009		

JUL 1 8 1980

PEDIA OF CARTOONS

VOLUME 1

Maurice Horn, Editor

Richard E. Marschall, Assistant Editor

1980

GALE RESEARCH COMPANY
in association with

CHELSEA HOUSE PUBLISHERS
New York   London

Project Editor: Joy Johannessen
Art Director: Susan Lusk
Editorial Assistants: Laura Giardina, Frank Lusk, Deborah Weiss, Marion Wood

Library of Congress Cataloguing in Publication Data

Main entry under title:
The World encyclopedia of cartoons.
    Bibliography: p.
    Includes indexes.
      1. Caricatures and cartoons. 2. Comic books, strips, etc. 3. Wit and humor, Pictorial.
I. Horn, Maurice. II. Marschall, Richard. III. Title: Encyclopedia of cartoons.
NC1325.W67   1979b   741.5'03   79-21953
ISBN 0-8103-0183-0

Chelsea House Publishers
A Division of Chelsea House Educational Communications, Inc.
70 West 40th Street, New York 10018

Harold Steinberg, Chairman & Publisher
Andrew E. Norman, President
Susan Lusk, Vice President

Acknowledgments

The editors of *The World Encyclopedia of Cartoons* wish to express their sincere thanks to the following persons: Herbert Block, Mary Beth Calhoun, André Carpentier, Jacky Chalard, Frank Dunay, Franco Fossati, Vasco Granja, Burne Hogarth, Jud Hurd, Jim Ivey, Heikki Kaukoranta, Isidore Klein, Fred Ladd, Eric Leguèbe, Jay Leyda, Ernie McGee, Dušan Makavejev, Nancy Marschall, Alvaro de Moya, Sophie Niestadt, Kosei Ono, André Parinaud, Professor Leonello Ricci, H.F. Broch de Rothermann, John Ryan, Erna Schoaf, Ronald Schwarz, David Smith, Kate Steinberg, Jessie Straut, Ernesto Traverso, Bernard Trout and Russell Young.

We also want to extend our appreciation to the following organizations: ASIFA, American Film Institute, Bibliothèque Nationale, Comic Research Library, Editoriale Corno, Gutenberghus Publishing Service, King Features Syndicate, Macmillan Educational Corporation, National Cartoonists Society, New York Times, Smithsonian Institution, Universal Press Syndicate, Walt Disney Archives, Walt Disney Productions, Warner Communications, Washington Post and Wilhelm Busch Museum.

THE CONTRIBUTORS
Stanley Appelbaum, *Germany*
Bill Blackbeard, *U.S.*
Richard Calhoun, *U.S.*
Clube Português de Banda Desenhada, *Portugal*
Jared Cook, *Japan*
Bill Crouch, *U.S.*
Denis Gifford, *Great Britain*
Maurice Horn, *U.S./France/Eastern Europe*
Pierre Horn, *France*
Serge Jongué, *Canada*
Doug Kendig, *Canada*
Vane Lindesay, *Australia*
Augusto Magalhaes, *South America*
Richard Marschall, *U.S.*
José Muntañola, *Spain*
Maria-Grazia Perini, *Italy*
Jukka Rislakki, *Finland*
Carlo Scaringi, *Italy*
Frederik Schodt, *Japan*
Luciano Secchi, *Italy*
Jørgen Sonnergaard, *Scandinavia*
Sergio Trinchero, *Italy*

Contents

Foreword

The World Encyclopedia of Cartoons is the first book to survey on an international scale the entire cartoon field: caricature, editorial and political cartoons, sports cartoons, syndicated panels and animated cartoons. It examines and evaluates all aspects of caricature and cartooning—historical, ideological, aesthetic, sociological, cultural, commercial. To give unprecedented depth and scope to this undertaking, a team of 22 contributors from a dozen different countries has been assembled, each with personal knowledge and experience of the field (see Notes on the Contributors). The exhaustive data compiled for this book has, for the most part, been obtained firsthand from a reading of the sources and from interviews with cartoonists, animators, editors, publishers and producers. In conjunction with its companion volume, The World Encyclopedia of Comics (Chelsea House, 1976), this encyclopedia constitutes a unique overview of all the cartooning arts; by itself it provides fascinating reading and deep insight into a field that has touched all important phases of human history for the past 200 years.

The core of the encyclopedia is comprised of close to 1,200 alphabetical entries. These are cross-referenced and fall into two classifications: biographical and bibliographical. The biographical entries summarize succinctly the careers of individual cartoonists, animators, editors and producers, with emphasis on their cartoon work, their stylistic, thematic and sociological contributions, their influence on other artists and their cultural significance. The bibliographical entries deal with the works themselves (animated cartoons, cartoon series, weekly or monthly panels, etc.) and contain a brief history, a summary of theme or plot, an evaluation of the place of the work in the history and development of its medium, and a discussion of its adaptation to other media. The entries also include anecdotal material and comparisons that further illuminate their subjects.

To supplement the bio-bibliographical entries, and to give the reader a general perspective on the subject, the encyclopedia also contains a number of informative articles, including an overview of caricature and cartoons, a brief history of humor magazines, a world summary of animated cartoons, a chronology of important events in the history of cartooning, and an extensive glossary of cartooning terms. Together with the entries, these articles make The World Encyclopedia of Cartoons the definitive study of one of the most influential and significant art forms of this century. It is an invaluable tool for historians, sociologists, political analysts, educators and anyone curious about one of mankind's liveliest arts.

For those interested in further research, a bibliography and a number of appendixes are also included. Particularly helpful are the indexes, which provide ready access to additional information on thousands of names and titles not treated in individual entries. Almost a thousand illustrations (some reprinted in a special color section) add visual excitement to the work and constitute the most extensive and representative anthology of cartoons ever assembled. In addition to its value as straight reference work, the text makes for lively, enjoyable and informative reading.

The data contained in The World Encyclopedia of Cartoons covers developments in the cartooning fields through December 1979. It is the intention of the publisher to update, revise and enlarge this encyclopedia at regular intervals.

The Editors

The World in Cartoons

Caricature and Cartoon
Humor Magazines
The Animated Cartoon
From Cartoon to Comic Strip
A World Chronology of Cartoon Art

Caricature and Cartoon:

An Overview

The nature of the cartoon has always been difficult to circumscribe. Most definitions are either too broad (making it impossible to distinguish cartoon from illustration) or too narrow (making appearance on the printed page a sine qua non). It is precisely its protean quality that has made the cartoon such an overwhelmingly popular graphic form. Liberated from the constraints of literalism and slavish representation, it embodies freedom of expression at its simplest and most direct.

The desire to communicate thoughts by drawing predates, of course, written language and may even lie at its origin. Every culture seems to have felt a need for such an eidetic language; in this context any drawing that encapsulates a complete thought can be called a "cartoon." This brief study attempts to retrace the history of the cartoon (and its relative, caricature) in broad outlines and to draw some tentative conclusions.

The origins

In what was possibly the first "how-to" cartooning book ever published, *Rules for Drawing Caricaturas* (1788), Francis Grose wrote: "The sculptors of ancient Greece seem to have diligently observed the forms and proportions constituting the European idea of beauty.... These measures are to be met with in many drawing books; a slight deviation from them, by the predominancy of any feature, constitutes what is called *character*.... This deviation or peculiarity, aggravated, forms *caricatura*." Such exaggeration of forms, already evident in Greece, flourished even more in Roman culture (as some of the bawdier frescoes in Pompei attest) and found expression in a great number of satirical drawings, many of which were displayed during Roman festivals.

The Middle Ages, despite its proclaimed piety, indulged widely in the representation of farcical or satirical themes, even in the churches (the gargoyles are the best-known manifestations of this mocking spirit). Indeed, so prevalent had the trend toward putting comic sculptures in the churches become by the 13th century that Saint Bernard felt called upon to inveigh against the practice. The medieval figures in turn inspired the first satirical engravings of the 15th century, particularly the remarkable drypoint etchings of the anonymous German artist known simply as "the E.S. master," whose works (dating from 1466) include a "grotesque alphabet" that is very modern in outlook. From there the thread leads through Dürer, Bosch, Bruegel, Da Vinci (in his drawings of heads) and Callot into modern times.

"Alexamenos Worshipping His God." This first-century A.D. graffito, found on the Palatine Hill in Rome, satirizes Christian doctrines.

Early Cartooning in Japan

Chōjūgiga ("Animal Scrolls") is a series of four monochrome paper scrolls from Japan's 12th and 13th centuries. It primarily depicts animals engaged in human activities. The scrolls, preserved in the Buddhist temple of Kōzan in the city of Kyoto, were for years attributed to the priest-artist Toba Sōjō (also known as Kakuyu), but present evidence indicates that there may have been more than one artist and that the last two scrolls may actually have been drawn a hundred years later than the first two.

Irrespective of authorship, Chōjūgiga is one of Japan's earliest examples of cartooning, and with its scroll format it almost straddles the line between cartoon and animation. Predating Walt Disney by well over a thousand years, the first scroll is a humorous depiction of rabbits, frogs and monkeys behaving as humans would–swimming rivers, hunting with bow and arrow, praying in mock religious ceremonies. It is the best drawn and consequently the most famous of the four scrolls. The second scroll depicts horses, oxen, chickens, lions, dragons and other fanciful animals, while the third and fourth are mainly humorous scenes of Buddhist priests engaged in competitive games with each other and with laymen.

Unfortunately, if any text ever existed, it has since been lost, and the exact meaning of the Chōjūgiga scrolls is open to question. The most common interpretation is that they are a satire on Japanese society of the Heian period, focusing particularly on the abuses of the Buddhist church of that time, which was notorious for its corruption. Nonetheless, the pictures alone, especially those in the first scroll, are powerful enough to have a universal appeal, and even today they evoke laughter. The artist worked with sumi ink on white paper and had a steady hand and a keen eye; parts of Chōjūgiga are regarded by some experts today as representative of the best in Japanese brush painting. The artist's appreciation of animal shape and motion were uncanny, and in viewing the scrolls one is immediately struck by their realism and fluidity. Chōjūgiga is a designated national treasure of Japan today.

F.S.

CARICATURE AND CARTOON

E.S. Master, letter D from "A Fantastic Alphabet."

Modern caricature

It is customary to ascribe credit for the development of modern caricature to the brothers Annibale and Agostino Carracci. Indeed, they are credited with coining the very word *caricature*, which derives from their *ritrattini carichi* ("loaded portraits") satirizing well-known personages and ordinary individuals alike. The Carraccis, whose caricatural work was done chiefly during the last decade of the 16th century, had been preceded in their experiments by another Italian, Giuseppe Arcimboldo, who painted amazing portraits of legendary beings, using inanimate objects, plants and vegetables to make up his fantastic "composite heads." Arcimboldo, however, labored in semi-obscurity in Prague, while the Carracci brothers' work was widely known and soon imitated. In 1646, using Annibale Carracci's own pronouncements on the subject, A. Mosini in his *Trattato* ("Treatise") established the definition of *caricatura* as the art of following nature's disfigurements in an attempt to arrive at *la perfetta difformità*, "the perfect deformity."

The art of caricature was for a long time the almost exclusive preserve of the Italians, who fielded such redoubtable practitioners as Pier Leone Ghezzi, Giovanni Bracelli and Gian Lorenzo Bernini. Bernini is also credited with bringing the concept to France when he settled there in the middle of the 17th century. The English historian Thomas Browne introduced the term in England, and by the beginning of the 18th century the term as well as the practice of caricature was widespread all over Europe.

Caricature as a graphic shorthand (as distinct from caricature as a well-defined graphic form) was enthusiastically seized upon by many artists who saw it as a liberation from the straitjacket of conventional art rules. Even Rembrandt in his self-portraits indulged this penchant towards mockery and fantasy. The rules of caricature have become firmly codified since the 18th century, and there is a direct line from the Frenchman Raymond La Fage (1656-1690) and the Dutchman Cornelius Dusart (1660-1704) to such modern caricaturists as Miguel Covarrubias, Al Hirshfeld and even Saul Steinberg.

From caricature to cartooning: England

It was the universal acceptance of prints that led to the phased transition from caricature to what would later be called "cartoons," a form no longer devoted simply to cataloguing external human idiosyncrasies, but one with an enlarged field of vision encompassing the whole political, social and cultural scene—indeed, the human condition itself.

William Hogarth, plate from "A Harlot's Progress," 1732.

Thomas Rowlandson, "The Genius's Room," 1806.

Perhaps no artist embodied this vision so completely as William Hogarth (1697-1764). As Werner Hofmann noted in his study *Die Karikatur*, "Leaving aside a few prior attempts to adapt caricature to current events, we must regard Hogarth as the first truly artistic practitioner of this genre, which in the concave mirror of the deformed image encapsulates the vision of life in its entirety." Hogarth is the first artist to whom the term *cartoonist* can be legitimately applied. He was the first to draw humorous scenes without recourse to grossly caricatural effects or physical deformities. Background and detail were sufficient to bring out the humor of his compositions. His effects were primarily dramatic, not graphic, and his aims moral or social when they were not overtly political. He can thus be regarded as the first editorial cartoonist as well as the forerunner (in his series of narrative cartoons) of the comic strip.

The first manifestations of the cartoon in print took the form of the broadside, a single sheet with picture and caption printed together. This in turn led to more specialized prints, of which the copperplate became the most common. Hogarth worked chiefly in this medium, as did most of his followers and imitators.

If Hogarth can be said to have had a direct disciple, it was Thomas Rowlandson (1756-1827), who enlarged the popular audience for the cartoon with his caustic and at times bitter criticism of the inequities of his time, and with his satirical depictions of contemporary fads and foibles. Rowlandson found a kindred spirit in James Gillray (1757-1815), who specialized in mordant attacks on the monarchy and the nobility—at least, until the time of the French Revolution, when his patriotism led him away from social criticism into rabid denunciations of the French peril. (For biographies of Hogarth, Rowlandson and Gillray, see *The World Encyclopedia of Comics*, Chelsea House, 1976.)

In the course of the 18th century cartooning found a function as well as a form. The subject of the cartoonist's pen was now the whole world, and especially society, whose most telling failings the cartoonists felt themselves obliged to represent. A tradition was thus born: for a long time to come, cartooning would be a means of social protest (possibly the most effective yet devised) as well as an art of political persuasion. By linking the resources of traditional art to the immediacy of popular illustration, the English cartoonists struck a responsive chord with even the least sophisticated audiences. The lesson was not lost on other Europeans: soon the cartoon was one of the most potent weapons in the political battles of the 19th century.

The spread of the cartoon

The techniques of cartooning slowly spread outside England, although the term *cartoon* was in limited use among artists and only became generalized in the 1830s. In Germany Daniel Chodowiecki began his contributions to the Berlin almanacs around 1770 (and later to the Göttingen almanacs) with satirical and

Francisco Goya, "Till Death . . . ," from "Los Caprichos," 1824.

CARICATURE AND CARTOON

Honoré Daumier, "The Orchestra While Tragedy Is Being Played," 1852.

political drawings and commentaries on contemporary German society. His work was carried on by J.H. Ramberg, who had studied in London and who further spread the tradition of the Hogarthian cartoon in Germany. Cartoons even penetrated Russia in the early years of the 19th century, when Polish-born Aleksander Orlowski settled in St. Petersburg after fleeing from Prussian-occupied Poland because of his anti-Prussian cartoons.

Louis Boilly and Philibert Debucourt transferred the techniques of the English cartoonists to France in the waning years of the French monarchy. After an eclipse during the revolutionary and Napoleonic periods, cartooning in France found a definite footing with the drawings of Carle Vernet, which blazed the way for a recognizable French cartooning style whose most celebrated practitioner was Honoré Daumier. Cartooning did not find favor with the despotic monarchy in Spain, however; only in 1799, when the regime relaxed its grip slightly, could Goya have his *Caprichos* published. Goya's powerful depiction of the wretched human condition, his sardonic humor ("black humor" before its time) and his use of jarring imagery proved decisive in the 19th-century transformation of European cartooning into an art of protest.

Outside Europe cartooning developed fastest and most significantly in the American colonies. American cartoonists (most of them remaining prudently anonymous) took to attacking with mounting savagery the privileges of the British Crown. Their cartoons were not all political, however. Some reflected the purely domestic concerns of the colonists; others were homiletic in tone and didactic in nature. But the indisputable fact was that cartooning was flourishing in 18th-century America, and its most famous practitioner was that man-of-all-talents Benjamin Franklin. Unlike the English cartoons that inspired them, the American versions gave less importance to purely artistic considerations (draftsmanship, composition, perspective) and concentrated more on the main

John T. McCutcheon, 1920. © Chicago Tribune.

point of the argument. This predilection for the "punch line" marked American cartooning from its inception and contributed in no small measure to its phenomenal growth in the 20th century.

Cartoons became established in Latin America towards the middle of the 19th century (although there were sporadic attempts in the early years of the century). The initial impulse came mainly from immigrant Spanish and Portuguese cartoonists; in Argentina, however, there was a strong French influence, chiefly due to the presence of two expatriate French cartoonists, Henri Meyer and Henri Stein.

The art of the cartoon was brought to China by the British in the 1840s and penetrated into Japan after the opening of the country in 1867. Faithful to their approach to modernization, the Japanese then endeavored to learn the new techniques from representatives of the two dominant powers in the field of cartooning at the time: an Englishman, Charles Wirgman, and a Frenchman, Georges Bigot.

"Join or Die," Ben Franklin's famous 1754 cartoon.

The editorial cartoon

For a long time political cartooning (and editorial cartooning generally) was at the very heart of the fledgling medium. The time-honored cliché "A picture is worth a thousand words" never rang so true as during the latter part of the 18th century and most of the 19th, when competing doctrines and ideologies battled fiercely for the minds of people who were still largely illiterate. The potency of the cartoon lay in its ability to make a point sharply and quickly, without the semantic ambiguities inherent in the written word. Nowhere was this lesson as quickly grasped and enthusiastically applied as in 18th-century England and 19th-century France.

Hogarth was, if not the first, certainly the foremost artist to engage in explicit social criticism. His attacks on the English class system mounted in savagery as the century wore on, and his advocacy of social change found a powerful echo on the Continent in later years. Rowlandson redefined political cartooning as less concerned with ultimates and more narrowly focused on topical issues with his jibes at the aristocracy, the Cabinet and sometimes the Crown.

The British, who are rightly credited with inventing the social protest cartoon, did a complete about-face after the French Revolution and the Napoleonic Wars. Some of the greatest English cartoonists of the 19th century (George Du Maurier, John Leech, John Tenniel), while sniping at the more egregious shortcomings of the British social and political system, expressed a broad agreement (indeed a smug satisfaction) with the established order. In current times this conservative tradition is best represented (ironically enough) in the Soviet Union, where cartoonists are asked to uphold the existing order and content themselves with satirizing its more trivial or ridiculous aspects.

The tradition of social protest inherited from Hogarth was carried on most effectively in 19th-century France. Daumier towers over French (and world) cartooning in his embodiment of the cartoonist as prophet. His messianic fervor in the promotion of social change made him a feared figure in French politics, and his example was emulated by a host of talented cartoonists (Gavarni, Grandville, Monnier, Traviès and others).

By the middle of the 19th century, then, European political cartooning was set on two widely divergent paths. On the other side of the Atlantic, it took a slightly different course. Political cartoons played a part in the turmoil leading to the American War of Independence. Paul Revere was especially outspoken in his denunciations of British rule, and Franklin's famous "Join or Die" cartoon epitomized the colonists' plight in one telling image. In the 19th century American cartoonists fell into raucous political argumentation and were often guilty of blind partisanship. Their power was demonstrated when Thomas Nast almost single-handedly destroyed the Tweed Ring in the early 1870s and when Bernard Gillam helped defeat James G. Blaine in the presidential election of 1884. As the century rushed on, however, a new breed of editorial cartoonist came to prominence. More skeptical, less prone to knee-jerk reactions, they injected a welcome dose of evenhandedness into cartooning by attacking all comers; Homer Davenport and John McCutcheon can be counted among this group. Eventually the trend grew as American newspaper cartoonists, thanks to the generalization of the syndicate system, freed themselves to a large extent from a party (or publisher's) line.

It would be futile to go into the evolution of editorial cartooning throughout the 20th century; suffice it to say that the pattern set in the preceding century has, with minor exceptions, held fast to this day. For all practical purposes, editorial

CARICATURE AND CARTOON

The Angels of Peace Descend on Belgium

One of David Low's famous World War II cartoons. © London Evening Standard.

cartoonists can be grouped in two categories: the ideologues (whether of the right or the left) and the agnostics. The former are generally more persuasive, but the latter are usually funnier and more often tellingly accurate.

The humor cartoon

The humor or gag cartoon is a relative newcomer to the cartooning firmament. The drawings and scenes of the early cartoonists were often funny, but they also tried to make a social, political or moral point. Certainly, versatile artists like Gavarni in France, Leech in England, Heinrich Hoffmann in Germany or David Claypool Johnston in the United States were capable of turning out a funny drawing without being too self-conscious about its ultimate meaning, but humor cartoons as a generally accepted genre can be said to have originated in the 1860s.

The birth and flowering of the gag cartoon can be directly traced to the growing popularity of illustrated magazines (a detailed study of humor magazines follows the present survey). Magazine editors discovered that entertainment was more likely to attract a readership than were polemics, and at the turn of the century there arose a new generation of cartoonists. Men like A.B. Frost, T.S. Sullivant, Caran d'Ache and Shisui Nagahara, to mention a few, may have come from different backgrounds and traditions, but they all aimed to amuse first and foremost.

This emphasis on entertainment led to a reexamination of the role of humor in the cartoon, and graphic humor came under the scrutiny of sociologists, philosophers and even a few artists. There was also a resurgence of caricature in cartoons, a technique that had been neglected by the socially conscious cartoonists of the 19th century, who leaned heavily on realism. Simplification of line (already apparent among American cartoonists of the early 20th century) bred increasing stylization, just as the paring down of lengthy captions resulted in growing terseness. One has only to compare the elaborate and prolix "he/she" cartoons of Charles Dana Gibson to the bare, almost wordless drawings of James Thurber to see the astonishing distance covered in a few decades.

Though the taboos and prohibitions of governments and editors alike once restricted the freedom of humor cartoonists, there is now no subject they cannot deal with. In their treatments, the gag cartoonists range all the way from gentle, middle-class fun (Syd Hoff in the United States, Jacques Faizant in France and Orla Getterman in Denmark are a few examples among many) through the raucous humor of the likes of Albert Dubout, George Price and Gerard Hoffnung to the sardonic black humor of Chaval, Ronald Searle, Charles Addams, Chumy-Chumez and Toshio Saeki.

Albert Dubout. © Dubout.

A world of cartoons

While the chief trend in 20th-century cartooning has been towards the fusion of the form as a universal language, a strong opposite current toward specialization of theme or subject has also been evident. There have always been cartoons addressed to a single issue (such as the cartoons of Louis Raemakers during World War I and those of David Low during World War II); there are also groups of cartoons centering on the universal themes—women, fashion, money, medicine, etc.—dear to satirists of every country and every era. In recent times, with the growing number of specialized magazines, cartoons aimed exclusively at stamp collectors, yachting enthusiasts and racetrack devotees have appeared. Of all the special interests reflected in cartoons, however, sports remains the most enduring.

There has been a scattering of sports cartoonists abroad, but the breed is most impressively represented in the United States. In the late 19th and early 20th centuries no American newspaper of any size was without its regular sports cartoonist, usually warming up for better things. Some, like Willard Mullin and Tom Paprocki, remained in the field and became household names, but sports was usually regarded by cartoonists as a springboard to a wider audience: T.A. Dorgan, Robert Ripley and Rube Goldberg are among the cartoonists who started on the sports pages. Today the field has narrowed to a few syndicated cartoonists.

The cartoon series is almost as old as the cartoon form itself: Hogarth, Daumier, Gavarni and others all saw the advantage of having their drawings sequentially issued over a period of time, either as separate plates or in successive magazine

Yvan Le Louarn ("Chaval"). © Paris-Match.

TURF TERROR · · · · · · · · · · · · · · by Pap'

Turf Terror

A sports panel by Tom Paprocki ("Pap"). © AP Newsfeatures.

CARICATURE AND CARTOON

A Journal of the Cartooning Arts: Cartoonist PROfiles

Cartoonist PROfiles, a quarterly magazine, was founded in February 1969 by Jud Hurd. From 1965 to 1969 Hurd edited the newsletter of the National Cartoonists Society and later that organization's magazine, the Cartoonist. With Cartoonist PROfiles he launched his own magazine, and during the ten years since, it has been the only regularly issued U.S. publication devoted exclusively to articles about cartoonists in all branches of the profession—syndicated comic strips, magazines, advertising, sports and political cartoons, comic books and animation. Drawing on his years of experience in the various fields of cartooning, Hurd usually sits down with a longtime cartoon acquaintance and talks shop in order to produce the PROfiles stories. So, as a rule, the information comes directly from a currently active cartoonist rather than from research relying on previously printed material.

The magazine's readership consists of professional cartoonists, young people aspiring to the profession, syndicate editors, newspaper feature buyers, collectors and public libraries, as well as school and college libraries. There are currently subscribers in more than twenty-five countries, in addition to the United States. Because the magazine and its editors take no stand as to the artistic status of the cartoonists reviewed, Cartoonist PROfiles does not completely fulfill the function of an aesthetic journal. It nevertheless constitutes the most comprehensive record of the state of American cartooning today.

M.H.

"Citizen Smith," a daily panel by Dave Gerard. © Register and Tribune Syndicate.

numbers. From this practice derives the modern-day panel feature, a cartoon published in regular daily, weekly or monthly installments in the pages of newspapers or magazines. These panels encompass a wide range of styles and topics. They can be grouped around a common theme (*Side Glances* and *Metropolitan Movies* in the United States, *La Vie en Images* in Canada), a social type (Rube Goldberg's *Lunatics I Have Met*, Pont's *British Character*), a recognizable locale (*Right Around Home* in the United States, *St. Trinian's* in Britain), a single protagonist (Ted Key's *Hazel*, Jean Bellus's *Clémentine Chérie*) and sometimes nothing more than the artist's own style and concerns (Giampaolo Chies's *Monodia*, Guillermo Mordillo's *Crazy Crazy*). In fact, panels need not be cartoons at all, as Ripley's illustrative *Believe It or Not!* demonstrates.

In their periodicity, their use of a permanent cast of characters, their utilization of speech balloons, many panels constitute a bridge between the cartoon and the comic strip. Even closer to the strip in format is the magazine series, a genre pioneered in Europe in the mid-19th century by such artists as Adolf Schrödter (*Herr Piepmeyer*), Nadar (*La Vie Publique et Privée de Môssieu Réac*) and J.F. Sullivan (*The British Working Man*). These series (varying in duration from a few weeks to many months) used a multi-panel format with a lengthy running text underneath each panel; they can be considered the direct forerunners of the comic strip. The form was further refined and generalized by the American humor magazines of the turn of the century. Some of the most prominent cartoonists of the time tried their hands at cartoon series, among them J.M. Flagg, who created *Nervy Nat*. F.B. Opper, who drew *The Suburban Resident* in *Puck*, and C.W. Kahles, who did *The Yarns of Captain Fibb* for *Judge*, later became recognized masters of the comics.

We are now approaching a field where the boundaries between the cartoon proper and the comic strip become blurred. Many cartoonists use a typical multi-panel comic strip layout to extend the point they are making, while gag strip artists sometimes condense their strips into one cartoon panel. In those countries (Japan, Italy) where the comics represent the predominant form of graphic expression, practically no distinction is made between the cartoon and the humor strip.

In his autobiography, *Drawn from Memory* (1950), John McCutcheon wrote, "The cartoon differs from any other picture in that the idea alone is the essential requirement, whether it is meant to inform, reform, or solely to amuse. This idea should be brought out with directness and simplicity, in such a way that people will know it is a cartoon and not a work of art. It has little to do with beauty or grace; it has much to do with strength and uniqueness. It is a peculiar form of art for a peculiar purpose, and presupposes the ability to say things trenchantly, humorously, or caustically, in terms of line."

A 1906 cartoon by Frederick Opper combining the traditions of caricature, cartoons and comics (not to mention literary criticism).

James Ensor, "The Good Judges," 1894.

CARICATURE AND CARTOON

This extract from William Hogarth's "Analysis of Beauty" (1753) seems a fitting summation to the aesthetic debate on the art of cartooning.

Like every self-respecting country, Turkey will divide her people into two classes: those who work and those who watch others work.

A 1908 cartoon by Juan Gris.

McCutcheon's definition is very important in that it represents the majority view of practicing cartoonists (particularly American cartoonists) on their art. It is, however, fallacious on several levels. It ignores the origin of the cartoon in art history. Hogarth, Rowlandson and Daumier were artists of the first rank who happened to work primarily in the cartoon idiom. Closer to us, many of the leading figures of modern art have also been cartoonists: Juan Gris, Jacques Villon, Heinrich Kley, John Sloan—the list could go on and on. More important, the cartoon works of artists like James Ensor, Félicien Rops and Saul Steinberg are considered, and rightly so, works of art. What McCutcheon fails to consider is that if the cartoon has "little to do with beauty or grace" as these are taught in academic art schools, so has most modern art. Artists and cartoonists have learned different lessons, or more precisely, have applied different interpretations to the lesson taught by the masters of the Renaissance: that under the surface order of the world there lurks a frightening disorder of forms. While painters and sculptors have drifted into ever simplified abstraction in their search for "pure form," cartoonists have engaged in ever wilder depictions of the human figure. They represent the allegedly absent but actually very much alive figurative tradition in 20th-century art.

Maurice Horn

From Hokusai's "Shashin Gwafu." In this drawing, Hokusai blends the traditions of Japanese art, Western art, and the art of the cartoon into a single visual statement.

Humor Magazines:

A Brief History

The humor magazine, more than any other medium, has contributed to the universal acceptance and wide popularity of the cartoon. The cartoon—and to a lesser extent caricature—has been tied to the print media from the earliest beginnings. The broadsheets carrying Hogarth's *Rake's Progress* or *Marriage à la Mode* were only a prefiguration of things to come; in the 18th century the proliferation of almanacs in Europe and North America further established the cartoon form as an integral part of print publications. At the same time, caricatures and cartoons began to be collected in albums (an early form of the modern cartoon anthology): in London in 1740 Arthur Pond published *25 Caricatures*, an album of prints after Ghezzi, the Carraccis, Raymond La Fage and others. Towards the end of the century albums reprinting the work of a single author (such as Rowlandson or Gillray) began to make their appearance.

In the meantime contemporary gazettes used the new graphic medium sparingly. Text in the early newspapers predominated overwhelmingly, with only an occasional woodcut (not necessarily humorous) thrown in for good measure. It soon became apparent that a new vehicle would be needed to absorb the work of the cartoonists, whose ranks had swelled considerably in the course of the century.

Gustave Doré, "Musical Evening," 1855.

Early humor magazines

Like the cartoon, the humor magazine also found its modern roots in England. The forerunners of this new development were the gossip sheets that flourished all over England at the end of the 18th century. The *Political Register*, the *London Magazine* and the *Town and Country Magazine* were among the titles of these publications. In order to circumvent the draconian libel laws of the time, they soon fell into the habit of adding a telling illustration to their innuendos, thus giving birth to the modern concept of the magazine cartoon.

After the turn of the century, the second generation of gossip magazines became noticeably more sophisticated, and their cartoons more acerbic as well as more artistically executed. The best known of these publications were the *Satirist, Town Talk* and, foremost among them, the *Scourge*, an avowedly political monthly whose chief claim to immortality was the cartoon work of George and Robert Cruikshank, better known to their readers under their *nom de plume*, "Tom and Jerry." The younger of the two, George, was the more innovative, and his name is one of the most important in cartooning history. As stated in *The World Encyclopedia of Comics* (Chelsea House, 1976), "George Cruikshank was the last cartoonist of note to follow in the footsteps of Rowlandson and Gillray, and provided the link between the 18th-century school of violently contrasted etchings and the realistic style of *Punch* wood engravings. . . .(He) continued and consolidated the work of the early English cartoonists, contributing further innovations to the medium."

Young Gentlemen in the Dress of the Year 1798

More humor magazines came to the fore after the end of the Napoleonic Wars, such as the *Humorist, Life in London* and *Life in Paris*, and they further contributed to the universalization of the magazine cartoon in Britain. More important, their success spawned imitators on the Continent and especially in France, where the cartoon medium was to find its most fertile ground.

Le Charivari and the French school of cartooning

Charles Philipon may well be called the father of the modern magazine of humor and caricature. In 1830 he founded *La Caricature*, taking advantage of the newly introduced lithographic process. *La Caricature* was strongly political (in its pages Philipon himself attacked King Louis-Philippe, and his drawings of the king as a "pear-head" are classics), and as a result it was shut down by the authorities; but a sister publication that Philipon had launched in 1832 under the title *Le Charivari* (a *charivari* was a noisy student demonstration) endured and became a paragon of humor publications.

Le Charivari, although strongly oriented towards the left, was less openly political than *La Caricature*. Manners, mores and customs were as keenly observed as policies and institutions were satirized. *Le Charivari* became a platform for cartoonists and artists, and for almost half a century it dominated the

A magazine caricature by George Cruikshank, 1821.

MANNERS·AND·CVSTOMS·OF·Yᵉ·ENGLYSHE·IN·1849·

Yᵉ FASHONABLE·WORLDE·TAKYNGE·ITS EXERCYSE IN HYDE·PARKE·

Richard Doyle in "Punch."

Paul Gavarni, "Thomas Vireloque."

field in France, as every cartoonist of distinction flocked to its pages. Its success prompted Philipon to embark on more publishing ventures; he founded *Le Journal pour Rire* (which later became *Le Journal Amusant*) and revived *La Caricature* (at first calling it *Provisoire*) in 1837.

In Philipon's journals there reigned an atmosphere of artistic freedom and heady experimentation that was conducive to the cartoonists' best efforts. Daumier created his first acknowledged masterpieces for its pages, Gustave Doré took his first steps there, and the contributions of such artists as Gavarni, Grandville, Henri Monnier, Charles Traviès and others greatly helped to make cartooning an art. The artists' seriousness of purpose was often reflected in their drawings, which were more figurative or romantic than humorous. The sting lay in the captions, in the loaded dialogues that provided an ironic or bitter counterpoint to the seeming amiability or respectability of the visual goings-on (Daumier's gun merchant surveying with unconcealed glee a battleground strewn with corpses represents the epitome of this approach).

Only after reading the captions could the reader discover that the drawings were just as subversive (and possibly more so) in their subtlety and their shock value. Figures were only slightly distorted (but in a telling way, as when one of Daumier's characters extended his hand unobtrusively yet unmistakably for a bribe); and faces revealed upon examination all varieties of vice (greed, stupidity, arrogance, lust, philistinism, opportunism, pettiness, servility), which their bourgeois owners tried vainly to conceal under a show of hypocritical dignity. The object of the French cartoonists' scorn was the triumphant middle class (King Louis-Philippe himself was proud to be called *le roi bourgeois*), which was savagely satirized in the form of stock figures: Monnier, for instance, created the character Joseph Prudhomme, while Traviès focused on his misshapen Mayeux.

Satirical magazines flourished in the two decades from 1835 to 1854. Often cartoonists founded their own journals: Gavarni launched *Le Journal des Gens du Monde* in the late 1830s, Daumier and Philipon teamed up to create *Le Robert-Macaire*, and Nadar brought out the short-lived *La Revue Comique* (1848-49) while he was still in his twenties. At mid-century French cartooning was at its zenith, and its practitioners enjoyed worldwide fame and recognition.

Punch and the British tradition

Philipon's journals soon found an echo in the rest of Europe and especially in the British Isles, where humor publications were already well established, as we have seen. In 1830 there appeared the London *Monthly Sheet of Caricatures* (also called the *Looking Glass*), a close imitation of *La Caricature*. During the 1830s it was followed by more magazines of the same ilk, such as *Figaro in London* (soon giving rise to *Figaro in Birmingham*, *Figaro in Sheffield*, etc.), the *Devil in London* and *Punchinello*, all of them closely copying the French magazines, down to the minutely detailed style and the use of lithographic printing.

These magazines enjoyed a raucous, somewhat freak success for more than a decade, until a more typically British publication emerged in 1841: *Punch*, founded by the prolific publicist Henry Mayhew. Subtitled "the London Charivari," *Punch* first went in for the same sort of social criticism that was prevalent in French cartoon magazines; soon, however, it found its role as the upholder of the British Empire and the English way of life, at the same time sniping at its most glaring shortcomings. Its tone was one of good-natured ribbing and gentlemanly fun, as befits a slightly sarcastic member of the family. *Punch* was undeniably part of the Victorian establishment, whose leading lights delighted in being caricatured (but ever so courteously) in its pages. *Punch*'s practitioners of the gentle rebuff included such luminaries as John Leech, one of the more political, and especially Richard Doyle, father of Arthur Conan Doyle. It was Doyle who designed *Punch*'s famous cover, and Leech is credited with having popularized the term *cartoon* in his 1843 "Cartoons for the Walls of the Houses of Parliament." In later years other talented artists were added to the ranks of *Punch*, such as John Tenniel, Charles Keene and the quintessential *Punch* cartoonist, George Du Maurier.

After the 1850s, at the same time that French cartooning was peaking, *Punch* was entering its most glorious phase. It had become, in fact, a school for the British nation, holding up to it a set of values and attitudes that prevailed almost until the British Empire began to dissolve. The magazine editors themselves were conscious of this fact and in 1856 announced in a mock-serious tone that

Scene: Westminister Bridge.
Time: Two on a foggy morning.
Reduced Tradesman (to a little party returning home): "Did you want to buy a good razor?"

John Leech, 1853.

The Sacred Elephant: This animal is sure to win,
if it is kept pure and clean, and has not too heavy a load to carry.
Thomas Nast in "Harper's Weekly."

HUMOR MAGAZINES

The Goose that Lays the Golden Eggs.
Democratic politician (to Workingman):
"Kill the Goose and get all your eggs at once."

Bernard Gillam in "Judge," 1888.

they held "a lively belief that the world will feel the benignant influence of MR. PUNCH's teaching through its civilised and regenerated rules. In the meantime the Briton will be... proud... that MR. PUNCH as the Schoolmaster, is Abroad."

Throughout the 19th century *Punch's* preeminent position remained assured, despite the efforts of other publications to rival it in the field of cartooning. Over the decades many humor journals came to life, such as *Fun, Judy* and *Tomahawk* (the most politically radical of the lot, advocating, among other things, the establishment of a republic), but they could not compete and were soon forgotten. The same fate awaited *Vanity Fair* (founded in 1868), notwithstanding the brilliant cartoons of its two most distinguished contributors, "Ape" (Carlo Pellegrini) and "Spy" (Leslie Ward), and its tone of sophistication and worldliness. To the solidly middle-class Britons who were the readers of newspapers and magazines, *Punch* was an institution almost as hallowed as the monarchy.

The 19th century in cartoons

To the public of the 19th century the cartoon was the most popular art of the times. It was propagated in countless magazines whose circulation soon extended throughout Europe and to many other parts of the globe as well. Politically, sociologically and in almost every other way, the century is best illustrated through the drawings of the thousands of cartoonists who plied their trade in its midst.

Humor magazines flourished all over Germany from the 1840s on. In 1844 the *Fliegende Blätter* was founded in Munich and over the years became a hospitable haven for all varieties of graphic artists. In its pages Wilhelm Busch published some of his most celebrated series; Adolf Oberländer developed his comic pages there, and it also boasted the cartoons of Carl Spitzweg and Moritz von Schwind. The *Fliegende Blätter* introduced a whimsical style of drawing and an innovative technique of graphic narration that would evolve into the comic strips of the late 19th century. Other German-language humor journals of note before the 1890s were the Berlin-based *Kladderadatsch* (founded in 1848), the Munich-based *Punsch* (the most political in its outspoken anti-Prussian cartoons) and *Kikeriki* (Joseph Keppler published his first cartoons there), *Der Floh* and the *Wiener Witzblatt*, all published in Vienna. The German school of cartooning thus established itself alongside the French and British schools.

The rest of Europe was not long in following suit. In Spain there appeared *El Sol* and especially *Don Quijote*; in Italy *Il Fischietto, L'Arlecchino* and *Don Perlino* were the more notable publications; and humor journals sprang up in Prague (*Humoristické Listy*), Budapest (*Ustökös*), Warsaw (*Mucha*) and Amsterdam (*Notenkraker*), among many other places. The ferment was felt even in Russia, with the founding in the 1850s of *Svistok* (1859-65) and *Iskra* (1859-73), two satirical magazines that sometimes made fun of Russian institutions, but without questioning their legitimacy.

From Europe the humor magazine format migrated to the Americas. In the United States it remained largely unexploited until the 1870s, cartoons instead appearing mainly in almanacs derived from the English tradition and in such

"By Jove! it is slippery."

A Slippery Day
"Oh, hang these slanting pavements!"

"A man does have to have command of his feet on these bad spots."

An 1883 multi-panel cartoon by A.B. Frost.

periodicals as *Leslie's Illustrated* and *Harper's Weekly*. (The remarkable flowering of American humor magazines in the last third of the 19th century will be treated in a separate part of this essay.) In Latin America the influence came from Spain and Portugal, and to a lesser extent from France (in Argentina, however, the leading humor publication of the time, *El Mosquito*, was founded in 1863 by a Frenchman, Henri Meyer, and later edited by another Frenchman, Henri Stein).

The British tradition was upheld in the most far-flung provinces of the empire, even traveling to Australia, where the *Melbourne Punch* appeared in 1855 and *Table Talk* in 1885. There was also a *Punch in Canada*. After the opening of Japan, there was inevitably a *Japan Punch*, founded in 1857 by the English-born Charles Wirgman, and mainly read by Englishmen in Japan. Japanese-language humor magazines soon followed, among them *Nipponchi* (1874), *Marumaru Chinbun* (1877) and *Tobae* (1888). By the last decade of the 19th century the humor magazine was an established institution in almost all parts of the globe.

The American humor magazines

American cartooning experienced a renascence after the Civil War, and a number of humor magazines on the European model sprang up across the land. Titles included *Frank Leslie's Budget of Fun*, *Wild Oats*, *Jolly Joker*, *Phunny Phellow*, *Yankee Notions* and *Phunniest Kind of Phun*; all of them were short-lived.

It took Austrian-born Joseph Keppler to establish the first long-lasting, genuinely American humor magazine. It was called *Puck*, and after several false starts, it began publication in German in 1876, adding an English version the next year. The success of *Puck* was assured when it went into full-color reproduction a few years later, thus adding sparkle and dazzle to the cartoons. These were contributed primarily by Keppler himself, who later added James Wales and F.B. Opper to his staff. In its early years *Puck* was chiefly a magazine of political opinion, and its fervor reached a pitch every four years during presidential elections (its notorious campaign against Blaine is recounted elsewhere in this encyclopedia). *Puck*'s popularity continued unabated throughout the 1880s as more talented cartoonists were added to its ranks, among them C.J. Taylor, A.B. Frost, Louis Dalrymple, E.W. Kemble and Michael Angelo Woolf. By the end of the decade the magazine had achieved a balance between political concerns and purely humorous subjects, a mix that was subsequently retained.

Spurred on by *Puck*'s success, more humor magazines began to appear: *Chic, Truth, Tid-Bits, Rambler, Wasp*, etc. They all soon vanished from the scene with the exception of *Judge*, which started publication (as *The Judge*) in 1881. *Judge* relied on its cartoonists even more than *Puck*, which also employed some good humor writers. Its editors were able to gather a fine staff, including Wales (who came over from *Puck*), Frank Beard, Thomas Worth, Grant Hamilton and Frank Bellew. The contents were too close to *Puck*'s, however, and it was decided to reorganize the publication. Bernard Gillam was brought over from *Puck*, *Judge* took on a Republican hue (*Puck* had Democratic leanings), and the late 1880s witnessed a resurgence in *Judge*'s sales and popularity.

Judge was soon followed (in January 1883) by *Life*, the brainchild of architect and illustrator John Ames Mitchell. The new magazine was an unmitigated disaster for the first several issues, but Mitchell persisted and *Life* began to turn a profit after a few years. In contrast to its competitors, *Life* had no color pages, depending on its staff of writers and above all on its cartoonists to attract a readership. Its early artists included Palmer Cox, F.G. Attwood, W.A. Rogers and C.G. Bush, all excellent draftsmen. It was, however, a young newcomer to the profession who made *Life*'s fortune: Charles Dana Gibson, who sold his first cartoon to the magazine in 1886 and soon established himself as one of America's leading cartoonists.

By 1890 the trinity of *Puck*, *Judge* and *Life* had achieved unchallenged preeminence in the humor field. Their outlook, at first inspired by the English, French and German schools, had become typically American; the style and the tone of their cartoons were distinctly indigenous. With their emergence, the United States took its place in the front rank of world cartooning.

The golden age of the cartoon: 1890-1914

The decades around the turn of the century witnessed an extraordinary surge in the number, quality and popularity of humor magazines and of cartoons generally. There were literally hundreds of cartoon publications flourishing all

The Power of the Human Eye

E.W. Kemble in "Puck," 1895.

HUMOR MAGAZINES

Studies in Expression: When women are jurors.
One of the famous Gibson Girl cartoons drawn by Charles Dana Gibson for "Life" at the turn of the century.

over the world, and they reached unheard-of heights of success. Of necessity this study will limit itself to the more popular or distinguished of these publications.

Nowhere was there greater demand for graphic humor than in Paris. The years following the establishment of the Third Republic had seen a flowering of new publications which now reached maturity. *Le Rire, La Vie Parisienne, Le Journal Amusant, Gil Blas, Le Chat Noir* and *Le Courrier Français* were the most celebrated, but there were countless others. In their pages, exceptionally talented cartoonists like Jean-Louis Forain, Caran d'Ache, Alexandre Steinlen and Adolphe Willette gave free rein to their fantasies and convictions. In addition, some of the greatest artists of the time often contributed (sometimes pseudonymously) to these journals, including Toulouse-Lautrec, Jacques Villon, Felix Vallotton, Jules Pascin, Kees van Dongen and Juan Gris. The most impressively artistic of all the magazines was *L'Assiette au Beurre*, which in the course of its ten-year existence (1901-12) featured the work of the most illustrious names in the profession and also gave such newcomers as the Czech František Kupka and the Greek Dimitrios Galanis a start.

L'Assiette's most outstanding rival in these years was *Simplicissimus*, which had been founded in Munich in 1896. *Der Simpl* (as it was affectionately known) was not as radical as its French counterpart, but it nonetheless ran into difficulties with the authorities on a few occasions. Some remarkable cartoonists worked for the publication: T.T. Heine, Bruno Paul, Eduard Thöny, Rudolf Wilke, Heinrich Zille and Heinrich Kley are probably the best known. *Der Simpl* also attracted talent from other countries, artists like the Norwegian Olaf Gulbransson, the Czech Alfred Kubin and the Austrian Ferdinand von Reznicek. Other humor magazines also flourished on German soil, among them *Jugend, Pan* (both employed many of the *Simplicissimus* artists) and *Ulk* (which published the first cartoons of Lyonel Feininger), in addition to the established periodicals of earlier periods.

In England *Punch* was enjoying one of its richest periods. To its prestigious roster of talented artists were added the likes of Bernard Partridge, Harry Furniss, Phil May, Leonard Raven-Hill and Max Beerbohm. Together they wove a scintillating tapestry of British life, all the way from May's slum shenanigans to Beerbohm's upper-class snobberies. Comic papers proliferated in this period, the most notable being *Comic Cuts* and *Illustrated Chips* (both born in 1890) and *Larks* (1893).

Black humor by "Siné." © Siné.

After the Orgy: "Give a belch, Ted, poverty tears my heart out!"

A 1926 George Grosz cartoon that seems to announce the horrors to come. © Simplicissimus.

(where Siné held sway) was a forerunner of the genre, which is best represented today in the pages of *Hara-Kiri* and *Charlie* (J.M. Reiser and Gébé are two of its mainstays). Italy has *Il Male*, and Spain *Hermano Lobo*. Their counterpart in England is *Private Eye*. The form never caught on in the United States, with the possible exception of the *National Lampoon*, where black humor is definitely a minority trend, drowned in torrents of sophomoric pranks, bad taste and scatology.

The state of the humor magazines today is as uncertain as the future of Western civilization, but it is safe to assume that a form that has been able to weather all the calamities of the 20th century will survive, no matter what happens next.

Maurice Horn

Humor Cartooning in Russia: *Krokodil*

Krokodil began publication in 1922 as the humor supplement to the weekly newspaper Rabochaia Gazeta ("The Workers' Journal"). The Communist party editor and humor writer K.S. Eremeev was its founder and first editor. Humor writing was the weekly's forte, but it is for its cartoons that Krokodil is best known. In its pages appeared the works of such talented Soviet cartoonists as D.S. Moor, Mikhail Cheremnykh, Boris Efimov, Deni and Kukryniksy. In 1932 its success prompted Pravda Publishing House (its parent company) to issue Krokodil as an independent publication three times a month, and it has continued in that format ever since.

The Soviet Encyclopedia states that "Krokodil played a large part in establishing the principles of Soviet satire." These principles preclude any criticism of the Soviet government, the Communist party and established policies. Krokodil's humor, according to one of its own editorials, is aimed at "exposing bourgeois ideology and imperialistic reactionism." At the domestic level it pokes fun at the shortcomings and absurdities of Soviet life and bureaucracy, thereby providing an inoffensive safety valve for the citizenry's grievances. Over the years, two directives aimed at insuring that Krokodil would not overstep its bounds were issued from on high: "Decree of the Central Committee on the Magazine Krokodil" (1948) and "On the

Shortcomings of the Magazine Krokodil and the Steps Needed to Eliminate Them" (1951).

M.H.

Humor Cartooning in Denmark: *Hudibras*

A Danish magazine inspired by the examples of the New Yorker and La Vie Parisienne, Hudibras was founded by Siegfried Cornelius and Asger Jerrild in 1943. From the start it was a forum for young, talented Danish cartoonists at a time when German censorship had cut off all contacts between Denmark and the outside world.

Hudibras (which comes out on the 13th of each month) had more ambitious aims than it could sustain for long. After the war it brought the newest trends in French and American humor to Scandinavia—spiced with what in those benighted times was considered pornography. In a cheerful, relaxed, broad-minded style, it blazed the way for changing views on sexual mores. It is still published monthly, but it no longer carries on the proud tradition of the 1940s. Hudibras today is merely a collection point for stale jokes, but as an institution and as the springboard for many talented Scandinavian cartoonists, its importance cannot be ignored.

J.S.

In the rest of Europe there were such innovative publications as *Cu-Cut!*, *L'Esquella de la Torratxa* and *Es Quatre Gats* (the young Pablo Picasso published his first drawings there) in Barcelona, and *Madrid Cómico* (where Juan Gris made his debut); Italy had *L'Asino* and *Il Travaso*, Switzerland *Nebelspalter*; even Russia had its first satirical magazine in decades, the short-lived *Zhupel*, which appeared for one year after the abortive revolution of 1905.

In the United States *Puck*, *Judge* and *Life* were thriving. The talent that was in evidence in their pages was never to be surpassed, not even in the heyday of the *New Yorker*. *Puck* could boast L.M. Glackens, J.S. Pughe, Rose O'Neill, Will Crawford and A.Z. Baker; *Judge* had Emil Flohri, Victor Gillam, T.S. Sullivant and James Montgomery Flagg (who created *Nervy Nat* there), not to mention Johnny Gruelle and Zim; while the staff of *Life* included Hy Mayer, "Chip" Bellew, Harrison Cady and of course Gibson, whose "Gibson Girl" was sweeping America. Art Young also worked for these magazines, but he gave the best of himself in his drawings for the *Masses* (1911-17), a radical publication that also attracted John Sloan, Boardman Robinson and George Bellows.

Humor magazines were spanning the globe in an unprecedented outburst of creativity—*Grip* in Canada, *D. Quixote*, *O Malho* and *O Tagarela* in Brazil, *Caras y Caretas* and *Don Quijote* in Argentina, *Cómico* and *La Tarántula* in Mexico, the *Rambler* (where Norman Lindsay first appeared) in Australia and *Tokyo Puck* in Japan, to name some of the more notable. This brilliant epoch (of which the cartoons were often a reflection) came to an end with the opening shots of World War I, never to return.

Good Advertisement: "I used your soap two years ago: since then I have used no other."
Harry Furniss in "Punch," 1884.

Between the wars

In the course of the hostilities most humor magazines either disappeared or became shrilly patriotic (such was the case with *Simplicissimus* and *Punch*). The few publications that were born in this period reflected the grimness of the times; none survived, with the exception of the iconoclastic *Le Canard Enchaîné*

After the Strike: "Glad to see you back . . . so you're the fellows who wanted to starve us out!"
Alexandre Steinlen in "L'Assiette au Beurre," 1901.

Art Young in "The Masses."

in Paris. *Puck* lived its last years in the shadow of the war, and it is fitting that its star cartoonist from 1917 until its demise in 1918 was the Dutch artist Louis Raemakers, whose savage anti-German cartoons helped swing American opinion to the side of the Allies.

The end of the war provided a general release and an outburst of renewed optimism and jollity. In France such magazines as *Le Rire* and *La Vie Parisienne* experienced a rebirth of creativity (before turning more and more into "girlie" magazines). In England *Punch* replenished its stable of talented cartoonists with the likes of Frank Reynolds, George Belcher, Heath Robinson, Rowland Emett and C.K. Bird ("Fougasse"). *Simplicissimus*, with George Grosz as its leading artist, continued on a more somber course in Germany, and even in Fascist Italy there was a flowering of new humor publications such as *Bertoldo* before Mussolini cracked down on cartoonists. In the Soviet Union *Krokodil* made its appearance in 1922.

The greatest activity in the field took place in the United States. *Vanity Fair*, which saw the light of print in the early 1920s, boasted the work of Miguel Covarrubias, Ralph Barton and John Held. This was also the time of *Ballyhoo* and *College Humor* and, with such memorable creations as *Hazel, Butch, Little Lulu* and *The Mountain Boys*, of an explosion of cartoon humor in such established publications as the *Saturday Evening Post, Collier's, Esquire, Look* and *Liberty*.

The most important magazine in the field, however, proved to be the *New Yorker*, founded by Harold Ross in 1925. While not a humor magazine in the strict sense (most of its prose is deadeningly humorless, and its style of reporting arch if not downright fatuous), the *New Yorker* changed the tone and tenor of the magazine cartoon. "The *New Yorker*," Ross announced in messianic tones, "will be a magazine which is not edited for the old lady in Dubuque," and his cartoonists reflected the sophisticated, irreverent aims of the magazine. The drawings of Carl Rose, James Thurber, Charles Addams and above all Peter Arno were symbolic of a time and a mood that managed to last (at least in pages of the *New Yorker*) well into World War II.

The Depression left the *New Yorker* relatively unscathed but played havoc with the rest of the magazines. *Life* ceased publication and sold its title to Time, Incorporated, in 1936, though *Judge* managed to limp along, a ghost of its former self, into the late 1940s. In Germany, in Italy, in Japan, the dictators clamped down on humor, while the rest of the world waited joylessly for the storm to break.

Strong Attachment
A Kukryniksy cartoon from "Krokodil."

The current scene

Many of the magazines that had weathered the Depression did not survive the war. In France the humor publications were turned into vehicles of Nazi and anti-Semitic propaganda or disappeared one by one into the long night of the German occupation. In Italy *Bertoldo* was soon gone; and in Germany *Simplicissimus* and the hoary *Kladderadatsch* both stopped publication in 1944.

After the end of the war there was a concerted effort all over the world to go back to the old magazine format, with varied results. Revived versions of *La Vie Parisienne* and *Simplicissimus* did not last long. *Punch* continued a seemingly unflappable career, bringing to the fore such new talent as Ronald Searle, Gerald Scarfe and "Anton" (all of whom it often had to share with the upstart *Lilliput*). In the United States the *New Yorker* suffered a marked decline in quality after the death of Ross in 1952. Its new cartoonists (such as Dana Fradon, Frank Modell and Jack Ziegler) are a talented lot, and Saul Steinberg is in a class by himself, but the vaunted *New Yorker* humor is now largely unfocused, and its themes have been allowed to grow increasingly stale.

The new development in magazine humor has come in the form of the black humor magazines, a trend that developed fully after the 1950s. In France *Bizarre*

Secondhand Shop: Military and courtly goods are being disposed of cheaply.
Heinrich Kley in "Simplicissimus," 1918.

The Animated Cartoon:
A World Summary

This encyclopedia provides the first comprehensive survey of cartoon animation throughout the world. Although there have been prior attempts at a worldwide history of the form, the results have always been fragmentary and largely inaccurate. Their fault lay in trying to fit the history of the animated cartoon (and of its extensions, the silhouette, cutout, painted and collage films) into the general history of the movies. The animated cartoon is part of the cinema in only a superficial and mechanical way—because it is preserved on film stock and usually projected onto a screen. Its aesthetics, however, differ markedly, and sometimes radically, from those of the film. Unlike the live cinema, animated films are created manually, prior to the photographic process; they are *reproduced*, not created on film. The animated cartoon derives not only etymologically but also artistically, historically and conceptually from the cartoon and the comic strip. This point was made in *The World Encyclopedia of Comics* (Chelsea House, 1976) but bears reiterating here. In the term *animated cartoon*, *cartoon* is the operative word, *animated* only the qualifier.

The origins

Man has tried from time immemorial to animate images. The first efforts gave rise to the Chinese shadow theater, early flip books and, closer to us, the magic lanterns of the 17th and 18th centuries. In the course of the 19th century, as the phenomenon known as persistence of vision came to be scientifically understood, it was inevitable that inventors would try to construct a device producing the optical illusion of movement. In 1834 W.G. Horner, a British watchmaker, invented the zoetrope, a revolving drum with slits allowing a spectator to look at moving images within the device. Horner had been preceded, however, by the Belgian scientist Joseph Plateau and his phénakistiscope (or phenakistoscope), a viewing device that was fitted with mirrors, and through which passed drawings painted on a cardboard disc. This 1832 invention allowed more realistic animation effects than had hitherto been achieved and is now regarded as the first successful try at genuine animation. (In 1974 the Japanese animator Taku Furukawa paid Plateau a deserved homage in the form of an animated color cartoon simply called *Phenakistoscope*.)

The French inventor Emile Reynaud took the process one step further with his praxinoscope; he was also the first to organize animation into a spectacle, in 1892 opening a special theater, the Théâtre Optique, where he projected a show completely consisting of skits enacted with animated drawings. His invention, however, could not keep pace with the rapid development of the movie camera, and on the level of simple entertainment, he found himself unable to compete with the trick films of Georges Méliès. Thus, the optical simulation of movement had apparently led to a dead end.

The heroic period: 1906-1918

Despite Reynaud's efforts, it therefore seemed inevitable that animation should go in the direction of the moving picture. The reproduction of images by the movie camera was much more reliable than the results achieved through mechanical means, and Méliès's films had shown that an almost infinite variety of tricks could be accomplished through judicious cutting and editing. It fell to J.S. Blackton, who was both a newspaper cartoonist and a filmmaker, to consummate the marriage between the cartoon and the cinema; with the making in 1906 of the first cartoon film, *Humorous Phases of Funny Faces*, he indisputably earned the title "father of modern animation."

Blackton's discovery—"one turn (of the camera crank), one picture"—was also being explored in Europe at about the same time. In England Walter Booth made the 1906 *Hand of the Artist* (in which a hand is seen tracing a figure that later comes to life) and other film cartoons. The most important cartoonist of this early period, however, was the Frenchman Emile Cohl, who made over two hundred films between 1908 and 1918 and created *le fantôche*, the first hero of a cartoon film series.

In 1912 Cohl went to New York in recognition of the fact that leadership in film animation was passing from France to the United States, thanks to the enthusias-

Frames from an early animated cartoon by Emile Cohl.

THE ANIMATED CARTOON

These cave drawings found near Tassili-n-Ajjer in the Sahara desert capture the essence of motion in an uncanny way.

tic efforts of pioneers such as Blackton, J.R. Bray, Earl Hurd, Raoul Barré (a Canadian working in New York) and, above all, Winsor McCay. It was the public showing in 1914 of McCay's *Gertie, the Trained Dinosaur* that crystallized the diffuse aspirations of the early animators. Cohl, who was there along with every other cartoonist in New York, later reported the event in these terms: "On the stage, in front of the screen, McCay stood, in evening dress, whip in hand. He started a little speech; then, going back to the screen, like a lion tamer he gave an order to the beast, which came out from behind the rocks. Always under the command of the tamer, it gave an exhibition of acrobatic skill; the dinosaur jumped, danced, uprooted trees and finally took a bow in front of the wildly applauding audience."

McCay's cartoon proved that animation had the potential to become a genuine art form. Just as important, other American animators sought ways of making it a viable commercial enterprise as well. The key was to reduce the tremendous amount of labor involved in a few minutes of screen animation. Gradually,

"Autour d'une Cabine" ("Around a Cabin"), an early animated cartoon by Emile Reynaud.

"Gertie the Trained Dinosaur," Winsor McCay's trailblazing animated film. © Winsor McCay.

economies were realized through the introduction of technical innovations like the peg system, cel transparency, in-betweening and rotoscopy, which dramatically cut the costs of producing an animated cartoon. So did the generalization of the studio system, with its rational organization of work and its consistency of output. The first true animation studios were established by Bray and Barré in the mid-1910s. W.R. Hearst, always attracted by new media, formed the short-lived International Film Service in 1916. Others (Pat Sullivan, W.A. Carlson, the Fleischer brothers) soon followed. Despite some competition from Europeans (Cohl in France, Dudley Buxton in England, Victor Bergdahl in Sweden) the American animators seemed to have taken the lead in the budding field.

The studio system had its commercial corollary in the star system (also adopted from the film industry). Animation's "stars" were either borrowed from the newspaper comics (the Katzenjammer Kids, Krazy Kat, Mutt and Jeff) or developed by studio artists (Colonel Heezaliar, Bobby Bumps, Dreamy Dud). In either case their function was to establish the immediate rapport of recognition and familiarity between the cartoon and its audience. Thus was the concept of the cartoon series firmly entrenched in commercial practice.

Towards an art of animation

The early cartoons were of course silent. To convey dialogue, they had recourse to the word balloon, a device borrowed from the comic strip. After 1918, however, these balloons were gradually abandoned in favor of intertitles (borrowed from the movies), which could be more easily translated for sales to foreign markets—a recognition of the growing internationalization of the animation medium, its practitioners and its public following World War I.

World War I also proved that the animated cartoon had definite advantages over live-action films in the teaching of new skills and methods: Bray, Hurd, the Fleischers, all honed their craft by making instructional films for the armed forces, as did Buxton and Anson Dyer in England and Benjamin Rabier in France. There was now an extraordinary flowering of animation filmmaking throughout the world: if American animators were still the most productive, they were no longer unchallenged.

France and England remained two hotbeds of activity, the former with the winsome cartoon fables of Rabier and the witty confections of O'Galop, the latter with the achievements of Dyer, Buxton and especially G.E. Studdy, who created

Otto Messmer's "Felix the Cat." © King Features Syndicate.

Aleksandr Ivanov's "Zay and Chick."

the successful canine character Bonzo. Even more striking was the burst of creativity in the USSR following the appearance of the first Soviet cartoon, Aleksandr Bushkin's *Soviet Toys* (1924). Nikolay Khodataev, Aleksandr Ivanov, Ivan Ivanov-Vano, Mikhail Tsekhanovsky and the Brumberg sisters were among the innovative artists working in the Soviet Union in the 1920s. Animation also came to Japan, spearheaded by the pioneering efforts of Sanae Yamamoto; and Aurel Petrescu founded the Romanian animation industry almost single-handed in 1920. There were animators at work in Germany, Italy, Spain, Argentina, China, everywhere.

In the United States the animated cartoon was enjoying unprecedented popular success. By the 1920s production was booming; in addition to the established series (*Mutt and Jeff, Colonel Heezaliar*), there were new characters coming to the fore. Max Fleischer brought the bouncing Ko-Ko the Clown to the screen, Paul Terry was moderately successful with Farmer Al Falfa, and J.R. Bray was constantly trying out new characters, such as Dinky Doodle, while continuing the cartoon adventures of such earlier Hearst favorites as the Katzenjammers and Krazy Kat. None was as successful, however, as Pat Sullivan's *Felix the Cat* series, ably animated and directed by Otto Messmer. Felix was the indisputable screen cartoon star of the 1920s, as well as the first widely merchandised cartoon character.

Parallel with commercial production, avant-garde animation was springing up all over Europe. The Dadaists and later the Surrealists enthusiastically embraced the medium of animation as they had earlier embraced the medium of film. Experimental animation especially flourished in Germany in the hands of Viking Eggeling, Walter Ruttmann, Hans Richter and Julius Pinschewer, among others. The most seminal animated film, however, proved to be Fernand Léger's *Ballet Mécanique* (1924), which was later called "the ultimate poem of motion."

The innovations wrought by the experimental animators were not lost on the commercial cartoonists. On the threshold of sound, the silent cartoon had achieved a harmonious equilibrium of action, imagery and symbol that was as accomplished as anything in the contemporary cinema. (The most dramatic and convincing illustration of this development is Ronald Schwarz's remarkable screen compilation of silent cartoons, *Early American Cartoons 1900-1920*.)

Walt Disney and the era of sound

Most of the early animation activity in the United States centered on the East Coast. Laboring in Los Angeles, a young cartoonist named Walt Disney was turning out such silent series as *Alice in Cartoonland* and *Oswald the Rabbit* when he became convinced that sound animation was the only way his studio could forge ahead of the competition. There had been a number of American and European experiments (some of them successful) in bringing sound to the

"The Prize Dance," a 1920 cartoon produced by the Bray studio. © Bray Studios.

Mickey Mouse in "Shanghaied," 1934. © *Walt Disney Productions.*

animated cartoon, but Disney produced the first cartoon with a synchronized sound track: "Steamboat Willie," the first *Mickey Mouse* cartoon. Upon its release in 1928, it caused as great a sensation as *Gertie* had more than a decade earlier. The following year, not content to rest on his laurels, Disney brought out *Skeleton Dance*, the first of his *Silly Symphonies*. He later produced the first animated cartoon entirely shot on color film stock (earlier efforts had been hand-colored) and crowned his studio's achievement with the release in 1937 of *Snow White and the Seven Dwarfs*, the first successful feature-length animated film. This period was indeed "the reign of Disney."

There has been a tendency in recent times to downgrade Disney's personal role in the success of his studio. Granted that he left most of the actual animation work to others (notably to the talented Ub Iwerks), the decisions at the studio were chiefly his, if not his alone. He was the one with the vision to constantly innovate and diversify. Under his guidance, his studio attracted the most brilliant and talented artists and writers; the characters they created—Mickey, Donald Duck, Pluto, Goofy—were the equals of any Hollywood star. Not only were the Disney cartoons wildly popular (many of them outdrew the feature films they shared the bill with), but they were also outstanding in style and content. It is no coincidence that Disney won every Academy Award in animation from the inception of the category in 1932 until 1940. A major share of the credit for all these achievements must go to Disney himself.

The effects of the Disney revolution were felt throughout the world, but chiefly in Europe. The commercial studios in England and France could not withstand the competition, while the animators in the Soviet Union were instructed to slavishly copy the American style and methods. Outside the United States the field was left pretty much to individuals, such as the New Zealander Len Lye and the Canadian Norman McLaren working in Britain, Alexandre Alexeieff and Berthold Bartosch in France, and Kenzo Masaoka in Japan. In Germany, Oskar

THE ANIMATED CARTOON

Betty Boop coming out of the inkwell. © *Max Fleischer.*

Fischinger began his research on sound and color animation, and Pinschewer pursued his in Switzerland.

With the exception of Mary Ellen Bute and a few other experimenters, U.S. animation remained the sole province of the cartoon studios. The success of the Disney shorts had created a demand for cartoon shorts to play alongside live features, and several former Disney employees set up their own production units: Hugh Harman and Rudolph Ising produced *Bosko* and the Happy Harmonies cartoons, and Ub Iwerks created *Flip the Frog,* among other series, before returning to the Disney fold. Among earlier animators, Walter Lantz was turning out *Oswald the Rabbit* (taken over from Disney) and *Andy Panda* cartoons. Leon Schlesinger, the most enterprising of the new producers, was intent on turning out a cheap version of the Disney product. ("Disney can make the chicken salad," he is reported to have said. "I wanna make chicken shit.") In the course of the years he assembled a cast of cartoon characters (Porky Pig, Bugs Bunny, Daffy Duck) and a team of animators (Friz Freleng, Bob Clampett, Chuck Jones) that were later to rival Disney's.

Sound brought a new dimension to cartoons. It added dialogue, music, sound effects, characterization and punctuation to the visual goings-on. It also added costs, however, and almost spelled disaster for the older East Coast studios. Sullivan had died, Bray had left animation entirely, and Terry barely survived with his Terrytoons. The only one to hold his own in the 1930s was Fleischer; his diminutive cartoon vamp, Betty Boop, was a favorite of the public, while his *Popeye* cartoons vied in popularity with those of Disney. Encouraged by his success, Fleischer decided in the late 1930s to challenge Disney on his own ground—the animated feature—and this eventually led to his downfall.

Feature animation

Snow White was not the world's first animated cartoon feature. A 60-minute cartoon, *El Apóstol,* had been released in Argentina as early as 1917. In 1926 Lotte Reiniger had produced *The Adventures of Prince Achmed,* but it was a silhouette film, not a cartoon. In the 1930s stirrings were felt all over the world—in France, England, Italy, the Soviet Union, Japan, Argentina—but the various efforts at full-length animation either were left incomplete or received only limited distribution. The success of *Snow White* changed all that.

An animated feature (generally defined as 60 minutes or more in duration) differs from a cartoon short not only in terms of length, increased production costs and expanded manpower but also, and more fundamentally, in aesthetic terms. Because of its time frame, a feature requires greater integration of the parts with the whole, and therefore a sharper definition of the characters, a more consistent story line and a heavier reliance on cinematic (as differentiated from animation) techniques. The feature cartoon is infinitely closer to the live cinema in style, narrative and dramatic technique than is the cartoon short, and is probably as close as the cartoon will ever come to film. Disney understood this: he planned *Snow White* as if it were a live feature, with separate direction of his cartoon "actors" and camera treatment of the various "shots."

Disney enjoyed for a long time a near monopoly on feature cartoon filmmaking. He refined and perfected his technique in *Pinocchio* (1940), *Dumbo* (1941) and *Bambi* (1942). *Fantasia* (1940) marked a departure for the studio in that it was commercially unrewarding but artistically successful. By the late 1940s the Disney studio had the formula down pat and was able to turn out feature after feature without interruptions, even after Disney's death in 1966. Fleischer was the only other American producer to turn to feature animation: in 1939 *Gulliver's Travels* was completed in his new Florida studio. It was moderately successful, but the 1941 *Mr. Bug Goes to Town* was a disaster, leading to the takeover of the Fleischer studio by Paramount. It was a long time before another American studio (UPA with *1001 Arabian Nights* in 1959) challenged Disney's supremacy in the field.

Disney's undisputed dominance also inhibited the growth of theatrical feature cartoons in the rest of the world (though a full-length animated cartoon was made for propaganda purposes in Japan in 1943). A few dates suffice to prove the point: the first Soviet feature (*The Hunchbacked Horse*) came out in 1948, as did the first two Italian features. France followed in 1950 with *Jeannot l'Intrépide*, and the British *Animal Farm* was released only in 1954. As the 1950s rolled along, Disney's grip on the public relaxed and more features came out. Today animated features are produced in many of the countries of the world.

A frame from "Pinocchio." © *Walt Disney Productions.*

THE ANIMATED CARTOON

"Gerald McBoing Boing." © UPA.

The golden age of American animation: 1940-1959

Film historians are fond of referring to the 1930s as "the golden age of American animation," but the period should more properly be called "the golden age of Disney," with the other studios (except Fleischer) riding on his coattails. The two decades following the 1930s, by contrast, saw an explosion in both quantity of output and excellence of execution from almost all the cartoon studios as Disney's leadership in the animation field slowly slipped away. The first cracks appeared in the early 1940s, underlined by the symbolic loss of the Oscar in 1940 (to Ising's *Milky Way*) and the bitter animators' strike in 1941. In feature animation Disney remained supreme, but in the short subject department his rivals slowly began to overtake him in popularity, style and invention.

At Warner Brothers, animation directors were displaying a verbal wit, visual outrageousness and outlandish humor that the more sedate Disney animators were unwilling to match. At MGM Joe Barbera and Bill Hanna's *Tom and Jerry* cartoons were out-Disneying Disney in lavishness of production and excellence of draftsmanship, while Tex Avery was creating a much-admired style of animation based on frenetic pacing and endless gag building. At Columbia Frank Tashlin was developing the trailblazing *Fox and Crow* series, while Walter Lantz created Woody Woodpecker for Universal. Even Terry emerged from his somnolence with two winning creations: Supermouse (later renamed Mighty Mouse, to Disney's everlasting annoyance) and Heckle and Jeckle.

In the 1950s the upstart UPA (United Productions of America) came to the fore and established itself by contradicting all the tenets of animation filmmaking taught by Disney (to add insult to injury, UPA was chiefly staffed with Disney defectors). UPA gave free rein to the imagination and talent of its directors (John Hubley, Pete Burness and others), who responded with some of the most innovative cartoons ever produced and created such outlandish characters as the nearsighted Mr. Magoo and the weird-sounding Gerald McBoing Boing.

At the same time, independent producers felt free to establish their own styles and to pursue their own research, thus bridging the gap between commercial and experimental animation. The most notable were John Hubley (who had left UPA in the mid-1950s) and his wife, Faith, and Gene Deitch (director of animation for Terrytoons/CBS), who created memorable, if isolated, works of animation. Avant-garde cartoon filmmaking was also on the rise, with Robert Breer perhaps the most talented of the experimental animators.

In the late 1950s television definitively replaced movie theaters as the main outlet for animated cartoons. The cheapened standards of TV animation (limited movement, paucity of backgrounds, sloppy draftsmanship, tedious repetition) spelled the end of the golden age of animation.

"Tom and Jerry." © MGM.

"The Devil on Springs."

"The Devil on Springs." © *Barandov Studio. In the post-World War II period, many animators attempted to explore the nature of totalitarianism. Jiří Trnka's "The Devil on Springs" (1946) examined the evils of Nazism, while the 1954 "Animal Farm," based on George Orwell's novel, focussed on the Stalinist variety.*

"Animal Farm." © *Halas and Batchelor.*

Animation: a universal language

World War II disrupted the distribution and production channels of animated cartoons, but the resultant constriction of the world market also brought some benefits. The war created a huge domestic demand for propaganda and instructional cartoons, especially in the United States, Canada, Britain, the Soviet Union and Japan. It also shielded most countries from United States competition, which in turn gave rise to a great many national centers of production operating in isolation, a situation that lasted well into the 1950s. By the end of that decade animation had thus become a worldwide medium of expression.

Animation made its greatest strides during this period in Britain, where the animation unit of the General Post Office (established in the 1930s) had molded a good many young animators. Several studios were formed, chief among them Halas and Batchelor, which was responsible for the first British animated feature, *Animal Farm*, and for many other creations. The Halas and Batchelor studio is today one of the oldest animation units in existence. Perhaps even more startling was the creation almost from scratch of a Canadian animation industry centered around the National Film Board. Its most celebrated practitioner is Norman McLaren, but it also fostered such talents as George Dunning and Grant

John Hubley, "The Hat." © *Storyboard, Inc.*

THE ANIMATED CARTOON

giov. 5 APRILE

merc. 11 APRILE

mart. 17 APRILE

merc. 25 APRILE

mart. 1 MAGGIO

Osvaldo Cavandoli, "La Linea." © Cavandoli.

Munro. In France animation in the 1940s and 1950s was dominated by two men: Paul Grimault and Jean Image. Grimault was the better craftsman and produced some remarkable cartoons, but Image was the better organizer and achieved greater popular success with cartoons unabashedly patterned on the Disney formula.

The Soviet Union, despite an enormous output, was by this time mired in sterility. The earlier animators were still active but largely contented themselves with repeating the same themes over and over again. Not so the Eastern European countries, especially Czechoslovakia, where a flourishing animation industry had been developing since the war around Jiří Trnka (better known for his later puppet films). Trnka and other Czech animators (Bretislav Pojar, Eduard Hofman, Jiří Brdecka) brought a new freshness and a more exuberant style to the animated film, and the genial Karel Zeman has also distinguished himself. Poland also developed a remarkable group of animators that included Witold Giersz, Wladyslaw Nehrebecki and, above all, Walerian Borowczyk and Jan Lenica. Romania had Ion Popescu-Gopo, and a brand-new cartoon industry sprang up in Bulgaria under the tutelage of Todor Dinov.

In the 1950s Japanese production came out of the doldrums, and a number of new studios (Nihon Dōga, Toei Dōga) were established. China also enjoyed a rebirth of animation, spearheaded by the Wan brothers, who carried on their work even under the Japanese occupation and later nurtured a new generation of Chinese animators.

By the end of the 1950s all sorts of cartoons were being produced in almost every part of the world—Italy, Spain, Latin America, Belgium, Scandinavia. Most remarkable of all was the rise of animation in Yugoslavia, where a group of young newcomers revolutionized the art of cartoon filmmaking and founded what came to be called the "Zagreb school." The leader in these developments was Dušan Vukotić, the author of *Cowboy Jimmy*, *Concerto for Sub-machine Gun* and *Ersatz*, the first foreign cartoon ever to win an Oscar.

One world of animation

In the last 20 years two major trends have surfaced in animation: the emergence of the *auteur* and the growing internationalization of the industry. The latter is dramatically symbolized by those artists who have voluntarily expatriated themselves, such as Gene Deitch, who has permanently settled in Prague, and Lenica and Borowczyk, who have consistently worked in Western Europe; but it is also evidenced by the increasing number of animated film co-productions and by the constant flow of animators from one country to another. Moreover, there is a growing tendency in countries with high labor costs (chiefly the United States) to contract production to studios located in less expensive countries.

The *auteur* has become the dominant figure in the animation medium, except among the studios busily engaged in churning out animation footage on an assembly line basis, mostly for television (Hanna-Barbera in the United States and Jean Image in France are two prime examples). There has been such an abundance of gifted animators in recent years that only a few of the more exalted can be cited here. Without a doubt Borowczyk (*Le Jeu des Anges*, *Le Théâtre de M. et Mme. Kabal*) and Lenica (*Adam II*, *Ubu-Roi*) are the two towering figures of contemporary animation and the creators of what might be called "animation of the absurd." In contrast, the Australian Bob Godfrey (*The Do-It Yourself Cartoon Kit*, *Great*) and the Canadian Dick Williams (*The Little Island*, *Love Me Love Me Love Me*), working in England, have created cartoons in the burlesque tradition of the early animators.

Buffoonery and slapstick are the keys to the animation work of the Italian Bruno Bozzetto (*The SuperVIPS*, *Allegro Non Troppo*), while the Japanese Yōji Kuri revels in black humor and sadistic themes. John Hubley (who died recently) and Ernest Pintoff (who no longer does animation work) were the most prominent *auteurs* in the United States. Only the Yugoslavs have preserved a semblance of cohesion (although their work has been declining lately), with Vukotić and such artists as Vatroslav Mimica, Borivoj Dovniković and Nedeljko Dragić trying to keep the Zagreb school alive.

Another striking feature of the last two decades is the increase in the number of animated features being released. Every country seems intent on bringing out at least one full-length cartoon. The audience for such films has been considerably broadened with the introduction in recent times of "adult cartoons," notably Osamu Tezuka's *A Thousand and One Nights* (1969) and Ralph Bakshi's *Fritz the Cat* (1972).

Yōji Kuri, "Au Fou." © *Kuri.*

Experimental animation is also going strong in many places. Stan VanDerBeek (United States), Piotr Kamler (France), Osvaldo Cavandoli (Italy) and Taku Furukawa (Japan) are perhaps the best-known artists working in this mode. The lines between regular, experimental and underground animation are becoming more and more blurred, however, as the tendency towards one world of animation, conceptual as well as geographical, asserts itself. This tendency has been furthered by the proliferation of international animation festivals. While such festivals perform a useful function in bringing animators from all parts of the world together, they have also done a grave disservice by giving out a plethora of awards that have become as meaningless as they are numerous.

The outlook for the animated film has never been rosier: the medium is now widely accepted as a legitimate art form, it has been gaining a wider and wider public, and its boundaries have been extended farther and farther with the discovery of new applications (the latest being the computer). To animators and observers alike, the horizons seem truly unlimited.

Maurice Horn

Dušan Vukotić's "Cowboy Jimmy." © *Zagreb Film.*

From Cartoon to Comic Strip:
A Pictorial Survey

In the second half of the 19th century, cartoons were organized into progressively more complex sequences of drawings. Such sequences were early antecedents of the comic strip, which evolved into an independent and distinct art form in the early years of the 20th century. Representative examples of this transition process follow.

Lothar Meggendorfer, "Intermission," ca. 1875.

FROM CARTOON TO COMIC STRIP:

Caran d'Ache, "The Arkansas Trapper's Mistake," ca. 1875.

FROM CARTOON TO COMIC STRIP:

7

8

FROM CARTOON TO COMIC STRIP:

1

2

5

6

Caran d'Ache, "The Cow Who Watched Trains Go By," ca. 1875.

Frank ("Chip") Bellew, "The Tail Maketh the Dog," ca. 1880.

Frank ("Chip") Bellew, "An Explosive Hug," ca. 1880.

A. B. Frost, "The Fatal Mistake," 1884.

1.

2.

3.

4.

5.

6.

7.

8.

9.

10.

11.

FROM CARTOON TO COMIC STRIP:

Adolf Oberländer, "The Duel with the Fashionable Pointed Shoes," ca. 1885.

Alexandre Steinlen, "Love Story," ca. 1885.

A World Chronology of Cartoon Art

From the Renaissance to the Present

1563

Giuseppe Arcimboldo starts painting the first of his "composite heads."

1590-1600

The brothers Annibale and Agostino Carracci give birth to the term *caricature* with their *ritrattini carichi* ("loaded portraits").

1600-1700

Caricature as a genre flourishes in Italy, France, Germany, England and the Low Countries.

1734

William Hogarth publishes *A Harlot's Progress*.

1735

W. Hogarth publishes *A Rake's Progress*.

1745

W. Hogarth publishes *Marriage à la Mode*.

1754

Benjamin Franklin publishes "Join or Die," widely regarded as America's first national cartoon, in the *Pennsylvania Gazette*.

Francisco Goya, "Old Man on a Swing."

Guiseppe Arcimboldo, "Fire," 1566.

"The Tammany Tiger loose — what are you going to do about it?"

A Tammany cartoon by Thomas Nast, 1871.

1784

Thomas Rowlandson's first cartoons appear in England.

1788

Francis Grose's *Rules for Drawing Caricaturas* is published in London.

1790-1815

James Gillray publishes his series of patriotic and anti-French cartoons.

1799

Francisco Goya's *Los Caprichos* is published in Spain.

1809

T. Rowlandson produces his most famous cartoon series, *The Tour of Doctor Syntax.*

1814

The first volume of *Hokusai Manga* ("Hokusai's Cartoons") is published in Japan.

1829

Grandville's *Les Métamorphoses du Jour* is published in Paris.

1830

Charles Philipon founds *La Caricature* in Paris.

1831

Honoré Daumier is jailed for his caricatures of King Louis-Philippe of France.

1832

C. Philipon starts *Le Charivari* in Paris.

Joseph Plateau invents the phénakistiscope in Belgium.

1835

The first Currier and Ives lithographs are published in the United States.

1841

Punch magazine is founded in England as "the London Charivari."

A WORLD CHRONOLOGY

Scenes of Family Life No. 2:
"Papa, what do you want to be when you grow up?"

A cartoon by T.T. Heine for "Simplicissimus" in its first year, 1896.

1843
John Leech's "Cartoons for the Houses of Parliament" are published in *Punch*.
1844
Grandville's *Un Autre Monde* is published in France.
The *Fliegende Blätter* is founded in Munich.
1846
The first U.S. comic weekly, *Yankee Doodle*, is established in New York.
1848
Le Musée Philipon is published in Paris.
Kladderadatsch starts publication in Berlin.
1851
The Lantern, a humorous weekly, is started in New York, with Frank Bellew listed as one of the founders.
1857
Charles Wirgman founds *Japan Punch* in Tokyo.
1859
Vanity Fair (first version) is published in New York.
The satirical magazine *Iskra* starts publication in Russia.
1863
El Mosquito is established in Buenos Aires by Henri (Enrique) Meyer.
1868
Vanity Fair is founded in London.
1870
Thomas Nast's first Tammany cartoons start appearing in *Harper's Weekly*.

1874

Funny Folks is established in London.

La Caricature (third version) is founded in Paris by Albert Robida.

1877

The English-language version of the comic weekly *Puck* is published in the United States.

The *Maru Maru Chinbun* starts publication in Japan.

1881

Judge is founded in the United States (as *The Judge*).

1883

Life magazine appears in New York.

1884

Bernard Gillam's "Tattoed Man" series of cartoons appears in *Puck*.

Ally Sloper's Half-Holiday is started in England.

Don Quijote is established in Argentina.

1890

Comic Cuts and *Illustrated Chips* start publication in London.

1892

Emile Reynaud opens his Théâtre Optique in Paris.

"We're not the ones who stink the most, Missus!"

Cover by Adolphe Willette for "L'Assiette au Beurre" in its first year, 1901.

A WORLD CHRONOLOGY

Cover for "Marc'Aurelio" by Gioacchino Colizzi ("Attalo"). © Marc'Aurelio.

1896
Albert Langen founds *Simplicissimus* in Germany.

1898
Caras y Caretas is published in Argentina.

1900
J.S. Blackton releases his *Enchanted Drawings*.

1901
L'Assiette au Beurre begins publication in Paris.

1902
The "Teddy bear" is created by C.K. Berryman.

1904
The comic weekly *L'Illustré* (later changed to *Le Petit Illustré*) is started in Paris.

1905
Rakuten Kitazawa starts *Tokyo Puck* in Japan.

1906
J.S. Blackton's *Humorous Phases of Funny Faces* is released in the United States.

1908
Emile Cohl starts his long career in animation in France.

1912
J.R. Bray produces his first animated cartoon, *The Artist's Dream*, in the United States.

1914
J.R. Bray starts his famous animation series *Colonel Heezaliar*. Winsor McCay's *Gertie, the Trained Dinosaur* is given its first public showing.

Louis Raemakers begins his famous series of anti-German cartoons in the Netherlands following the outbreak of World War I.

1915
Earl Hurd creates *Bobby Bumps* in the United States.

1917
El Apóstol, the first full-length animated cartoon, is released in Argentina.

1918
Robert Ripley conceives his first *Believe It or Not!* panel.

The first professional association of cartoonists, the Manga Kourakukai, is organized in Japan.

1920
Walt Disney produces his first work of animation, the Newman Laugh-O-Grams, in Kansas City.

1922
The first Pulitzer Prize for cartooning is awarded to Rollin Kirby.

The Soviet humor magazine *Krokodil* is founded in Moscow.

1923
Max Fleischer produces an animated film called *The Einstein Theory of Relativity*.

1924
Fernand Léger's animated *Ballet Mécanique* is shown in France.

The first Soviet cartoon, *Soviet Toys*, is produced by A. Ivanov and A. Bushkin.

1925
The *New Yorker* magazine is founded by Harold Ross.

1926
Lotte Reiniger's *Die Abenteuer des Prinzen Achmed* is released in Germany.

1928
The first *Mickey Mouse* cartoon, "Steamboat Willie," is exhibited in the United States.

1929
Walt Disney releases *Skeleton Dance*, first of the *Silly Symphonies*.

The first Soviet sound cartoon, M. Tsekhanovsky's *Posta*, is produced.

1930
Betty Boop makes her first appearance.

Marc'Aurelio magazine is started in Italy.

1932
The first Academy Award for a short subject (animation) is given to Disney's *Flowers and Trees*.

"Ersatz," Dušan Vukotić's Oscar-winning cartoon. © Zagreb Film.

Berthold Bartosch's *L'Idée* is released and subsequently banned in France.
1933
Max Fleischer adapts *Popeye the Sailor* to animated cartoons.
1937
The first Walt Disney animated feature, *Snow White and the Seven Dwarfs*, is released.
1938
Bugs Bunny makes his first appearance in "Porky's Hare Hunt."
1939
The first *Tom and Jerry* cartoon, "Puss Gets the Boot," is released by MGM.
1940
Walt Disney's *Fantasia* opens to mixed reviews.
1941
Frederick ("Tex") Avery starts his association with the MGM animation studio. Animators strike the Walt Disney studios.
1943
Hudibras starts publication in Denmark.
1944
Both *Kladderadatsch* and *Simplicissimus* cease publication within days of each other (September).
1945
Stephen Bosustow founds United Productions of America (UPA).
1946
The National Cartoonists Society (NCS) is organized in New York.
1949
UPA releases the first *Mr. Magoo* and *Gerald McBoing Boing* cartoons.
1952
MAD magazine is started in New York.
Biographic Films is founded by Bob Godfrey and Keith Learner in London.
1953
Paul Grimault's *La Bergère et le Ramoneur* is released in France.
1956
The animation unit of Zagreb Film is established in Yugoslavia.
1959
Stephen Becker's *Comic Art in America* is published in New York.

A WORLD CHRONOLOGY

"Fritz the Cat." © Steve Krantz.

1961

Dŭsan Vukotić's *Ersatz* becomes the first foreign cartoon to receive an Academy Award for animation.

1962

David Low is knighted by the Queen of England.

1966

The City Museum of Cartoon Art opens in Omiya, Japan.

1969

Cartoonist PROfiles starts publication in the United States.

1971

An exhibition called Le Dessin d'Humour is organized by the Bibliothèque Nationale in Paris.

1972

The first X-rated cartoon, *Fritz the Cat*, is released.

1974

The Museum of Cartoon Art opens in Greenwich, Connecticut (later moving to Rye, New York).

1975

The Cartoon Museum opens in Orlando, Florida.

1976

The *World Encyclopedia of Comics* is published in New York.

1978

A Saul Steinberg retrospective is held at the Whitney Museum in New York.

1979

Herbert Block ("Herblock") receives his third Pulitzer Prize

A Silly Symphony: "The Tortoise and the Hare." © Walt Disney Productions.

Alphabetical Entries

Aa

ABBEY, EDWIN AUSTIN (1852-1911) American cartoonist, magazine artist and painter born in Philadelphia, Pennsylvania, on April 1, 1852. Edwin Abbey drifted from seminary to a variety of art-related activities: study, engraving, antique collecting. On December 3, 1870, his first published drawing appeared: "The Puritans' First Thanksgiving," a full page in *Harper's Weekly*. The next year Abbey joined the staff of Harper Brothers as an illustrator under Charles Parsons (with whom he was soon to collaborate on drawings) and C.S. Reinhart, and with A.B. Frost, Howard Pyle, W.A. Rogers, Winslow Homer, Gray-Parker and others.

As Willam Murrell points out, many of these artists, especially in their first years on the staff, doubled as rough-sketch artists and cartoonists. The cartoons in *Harper's Weekly* and *Monthly* appeared in the back pages and were often unsigned. Sometimes poems were illustrated, and occasionally humorous series (early strips) ran.

Abbey soon graduated to more dignified stature, however, and became the preeminent artist in American pictorial literature. As Homer depicted the everyday lives of Americans, Abbey introduced readers to the past few centuries of the English-speaking people. He became recognized as a fine artist and was *the* greatest American illustrator before Pyle (indeed, Pyle's sense of history seems strongly derived from his senior).

After a leave from Harper, study in England and freelance work for *Scribner's Monthly*, Abbey in the mid-1880s produced the finest pen-and-ink work of his early career: illustrations for Herrick's poems "She Stoops to Conquer" and "Old Songs." In the context of a time when photoengraving had just been introduced and was being lovingly refined, his work of this period stands as delicate, thoughtful and masterful.

About this time Abbey moved to England, where he spent most of the rest of his life; he sought to be close to the elements of his inspiration, the trappings of old England. However, he still continued to work on American projects, including the Boston Public Library, for which he painted the mural *The Quest of the Holy Grail*; the state capitol of Pennsylvania; Knickerbocker Hotel in New York; and Harper's Shakespeare series in 1905, in which the greatest pen-and-ink work of his later career appeared.

A member of the National Academy, the Royal Academy, the Legion of Honor and other groups, he died on August 1, 1911, in his studio in Chelsea. In 1921, a definitive biography was published in two volumes by Scribner's (and Methuen in England): *Edwin Austin Abbey, Royal Academician. The Record of His Life and work*, by E.V. Lucas.

R.M.

ABENTEUER DES PRINZEN ACHMED, DIE (Germany) Lotte Reiniger's *Die Abenteuer des Prinzen Achmed* ("The Adventures of Prince Achmed") falls midway between the animated cartoon and the silhouette film. It was created by cutting silhouettes out of black paper and photographing them frame by frame. It took Lotte Reiniger, assisted by Karl Koch (her husband) and a team of animators made up of Walter Ruttmann, Berthold Bartosch and Alexander Karadan, fully three years to complete this 65-minute film, which was released in 1926.

The story line for the feature was based on tales from the *Arabian Nights*. Fired by his love for a beautiful princess, Achmed, a poor little tailor, goes in search of the Magic Lamp and with the help of the White Spirits defeats the evil Djinns and the monstrous Afreets. As befits a fairy tale, the little tailor, now hailed throughout the land as "Prince Achmed" for his prowess, marries the princess at the close.

The story, simple and straightforward, was told with a great deal of spontaneity and charm. The figures were skillfully animated and seemed to move with ease in a setting of Oriental splendor with more than a touch of art deco design. A modern-day version of traditional shadow theater, the film did not set a trend among cartoon filmmakers. A new color version of *Prince Achmed* made by Primrose Productions on directions by Lotte Reiniger was shown on British television in 1954.

M.H.

"Die Abenteuer des Prinzen Achmed." © *Lotte Reiniger.*

ABLITZER, ALFRED G. (1889-1968) American artist born in Brooklyn, New York, on July 4, 1889. "Al Zère" (as he is better known), of Alsatian lineage, decided at the age of 12 to be a cartoonist and attended evening art school as a youngster. He later studied at Brooklyn's Adelphi College Art School and, after World War I, at the Sorbonne. At 15 he made his first sale to *Judge* and was soon contributing there, to *Puck* and to the *Brooklyn Eagle*. For the *Eagle*, as a staffer, he created the comic strip *Buttons and Fatty*, which ran for years under a succession of artists, including M.E. Brady.

During the war he served as business manager and cartoonist for the American Expeditionary Force magazine *The Martian* and won awards for his work in its pages and for his posters. In the postwar months he traveled across Europe, sending back sketches to several American magazines. By this time Zère had a mature and breezy style, with lush pen lines delineating character and action.

Zère was one of the first cartoonists to mine the rich lode of material in America's suburban exodus; he also pioneered several "little man" themes, such as the henpecked simp who is married and harried. In the 1920s and 1930s this became a standard device in comics and humorous literature, but Zère masterfully defined the genre in such features as *Man the Master*, a panel for the *Evening Post* (which he joined in 1920) and *So This Is Married Life*, a strip for the *New York Journal* (which he joined in 1924). He married at this time the daughter of Hearst's multitalented art editor, Al Biederman.

Through the 1920s Zère also drew frequently for *Judge* and contributed editorial cartoons to labor newspapers. Thereafter he drew various features for smaller syndicates and busied himself with sculpture, at which he was accomplished. (He had spent two years in Africa seeking inspiration for his handsome plaques and busts.) Titles include: *Flossie*, which ran in 85 newspapers starting in 1935 for the Bell Syndicate; *Ella the Maid; Two Orphans; You've Got Something There*, a Hatlo imitation; and two World War II features—*Rookie Joe*, a panel for United Feature, and *Jerry, Junior Air Warden* for Bell. The widowed Ablitzer ended his full career living near the famous Niederstein's Restaurant in Queens Village, New York, which was operated by his new wife, the former Adelaide Lardon. He died on November 11, 1968.

It remains for Zère to be recognized more fully for his liberation of cartoons from stylistic stiffness and for the affirmation of married and suburban themes in the comics. His cartoons and comics stand out even today as fresh, lively treatments of what have become American stereotypes, thanks in part to him.

R.M.

ADDAMS, CHARLES FRANCIS (1912-   ) American cartoonist born in Westfield, New Jersey, on January 7, 1912. Upon completing high school, Charles Addams attended Colgate University for one year (1929-30) and spent another at the University of Pennsylvania (1930-31). He then bade the academic grind adieu and enrolled in the Grand Central School of Art in New York City, where, according to his established custom, he spent one year (1931-32). This completed his formal schooling; Addams was ready to embark upon his art career, and in 1935 his cartoons began appearing regularly in the *New Yorker*, the magazine with which he has become most closely identified. Such has been the popularity of his work for this magazine that he has joined the select group of cartoonists who have had television series built around their characters. Indeed, *The Addams Family* enjoyed wide popularity as a prime-time network sitcom from 1966 to 1968.

Exhibitions of Addams's work have been mounted at the Fogg Art Museum in Cambridge, Massachusetts, the Rhode Island School of Design Museum, the Museum of the City of New York, the University of Pennsylvania Museum and the Metropolitan Museum of Art in New York City (as part of the War and Print exhibitions). His published work, in addition to his representation in the *New Yorker* albums, includes the collections *Drawn and Quartered* (1942); *Addams*

"The makers of Sun-Glo Toilet Soap bring you an entirely different type of quiz program."

Charles Addams. © The New Yorker.

and Evil (1947); *Monster Rally* (1950); *Home Bodies* (1954); *Night Crawlers* (1957); *Dear Dead Days* (1959); *Black Maria* (1960); *The Groaning Board* (1964); *The Charles Addams Mother Goose* (1967); *My Crowd* (1970) and *Favorite Haunts* (1976).

Even to those unfamiliar with *The Addams Family* from television, a reading of these titles suggests that Addams is very much the black humorist. And so he is. Besides the outré members of the Addams family, one frequently encounters in his work skeletons, assorted demons, various monsters and depraved humans, and one recurrent, round-headed, evil-looking little man whose resolutely antisocial behavior seems to mark him as the cartoonist's graphic representation of the id.

Yet Addams is more than a macabre wit. There is, for example, his innocently childlike fascination with the notion of smallness—a preoccupation that gives rise to small, scholarly men living inside computers, eskimos building ice-cube igloos in refrigerator freezer compartments, musicians hauling their tiny instruments up into Muzak boxes, and cardinals in bird feeders (the kind of cardinal, that is, that might one day become history's smallest pope). Addams also devotes some attention to the upper realms—not equal time, perhaps, but then, why alter a winning formula? Thus, the sculptor of an angel figure calls upward out of his open studio window after his departing model to confirm the next sitting time, and a small, hovering cherub squeegees the stained-glass lights of a cathedral tower. Addams is finally capable of a whimsy that at its best ranks him with his late colleague Thurber—as in the cartoon of da Vinci being asked about a Mondrian-like geometric canvas found by a visitor browsing through his assorted altarpieces and portraits. "That?" answers the master. "Oh, that's nothing. Just something I was fooling around with." (That Leonardo, Addams seems to be saying; as if he weren't satisfied with anticipating the SST!)

For his work, Addams has been honored with the Yale Humor Award (1954) and—not surprisingly, given his more than nodding acquaintance with drafty old mansions—with a special award from the Mystery

Writers of America (1961). And if it is a mark of his worldly success that he collects vintage automobiles, it seems rather more in character that he also possesses a notable collection of arms and armor.

R.C.

ADVENTURES OF THE CLOTHESLINE
See Bugville Life.

ADVICE TO THE MENTALLY FEEBLE (U.S.) Throughout his career Charles Dana Gibson—who always insisted on being called a cartoonist and not a caricaturist, social artist or some other supposedly more polite euphemism—delighted in the depiction of embarrassing moments, uncomfortable situations and awkward interludes. This device made possible the fullest exploitation of his talent for capturing expression and emotion. Though love themes seemed to be what was expected of Gibson, it can be argued that his most successful creations are those that document the realm of the *faux pas,* startling discoveries and strong personality studies/contrasts. He developed this genre—one which was copied by many, even down to George Herriman's newspaper panel *Embarrassing Moments* in the 1930s—around the turn of the century and used it strongly in the succeeding years in *Life* and *Collier's.*

Only in 1912, after his self-imposed exile to Europe and temporary abandonment of pen and ink, did Gibson give this theme a title, and it was an amusing one: *Advice to the Mentally Feeble.* The series of double-page cartoons in *Life* began on December 12, 1912, and featured mainly the trials of dealing with bores, unexpected guests, wealthy relatives and the naive placed in unfamiliar situations. He relied on a favorite theme of young girls marrying rich old men with "By All Means Marry for a Home" and "Sleep Whenever You Can; It Will Protect Your Talking." "Go Back to the Stable As Soon As Possible" focused on a boor, while "Go Down to the Street" and "Keep Out of Politics" dealt with amateur stockbrokers and politicians, respectively.

The cartoon series, actually a burlesque of etiquette manuals and guides to propriety, ran intermittently through the 1910s. In 1920 a similar series, *People We Can Do Without,* ran in *Life.*

R.M.

AESOP'S FABLES (U.S.) Paul Terry started his cartoon series *Aesop's Fables* (also known as *Aesop's Film Fables* and sometimes simply as *Fables*) in 1921. The first one was "The Cat and the Mice," and true to the series title, it followed the ancient tale of the mice trying to decide who would hang a bell around the cat's neck. The series continued with more fable adaptations, but starting in the mid-1920s, it was enlarged to include any subject under the sun. There were fairy tales like "Red Riding Hood" (1931), familiar Bible stories ("Noah Had His Troubles," 1925), prehistoric jokes ("Bonehead Age," 1925) and cartoon musicals ("Mad Melody," 1931). After the mid-1930s the series became indistinguishable from other catchall series at Warners or MGM.

Aesop's Fables was first distributed by Pathé Exchange (1921-31), then by RKO Pictures (1931-33) and finally by the Van Beuren Corporation. It was merged into Terrytoons in the late 1930s and disappeared as an independent title.

Although not quite distinguished, *Aesop's Fables* provided some fine moments of entertainment in its

"Aesop's Fables." © Paul Terry.

early days. The coming of sound proved fatal, however, as Paul Terry never made up his mind about the direction he wanted the series to take. Among the more notable directors of the *Fables* were Frank Moser, Eddie Donnelly and Terry himself.

M.H.

AGE OF HANDBOOKS, THE (U.S.) The year 1886 saw the first inklings of *Puck* magazine's change from a primarily political-satire magazine to one more genteel, focusing on social subjects. Perhaps the shift was due to the pressure applied by the success of *Life* (which was by design a social commentary magazine), or to the changing times, or to the business office's entreaties that partisanship offended half the potential audience—or to all three factors. In any event, *The Age of Handbooks,* which ran between February 24 and May 12, 1886, is also representative of another transformation, that of Frederick Burr Opper from a gadfly to a sage social commentator. *The Age of Handbooks* was the first sustained series, drawn in a sophisticated illustrator's style, in which he examined the harebrained fads and silly mores of his day.

This series was a lampoon of compendia—those promise-all how-to books that still plague us today. Opper was already employing his lifelong cartoon formula of zeroing in on something slightly daffy, stretching it to a bit more ridiculous length, depicting an inevitable complication and reminding us in the end that many commonplace things are really quite useless or pretentious.

The first panel—they all ran in single panels in black and white—dealt with a deluded Sunday painter whose monstrosity on canvas was the proud result of reading *How to Become a Perfect Portrait Painter in Two Hours.* The succeeding weeks chronicle the mishaps generated by advice from the following handbooks: *Manual of*

Ain't It a Grand and Glorious Feelin'?

"Ain't It a Grand and Glorious Feelin'?" © New York Tribune.

Infants' Diseases and Their Cure; The Complete Sportsman's Guide; How to Avoid the Perils and Pitfalls of a Great City; The Parlor Joker and Humorist; The Graceful Guide to Dancing; The Young Housekeeper's Infallible Cookbook; The Handbook of High-Toned Etiquette; The Peerless Parlor Prestidigitateur; The Doctor Dispensed With, or Every Man His Own Physician (in which a fellow can't figure out whether he has heart disease, chronic dyspepsia or St. Vitus's dance); The Rhyming Dictionary, or the Poet's Guide to Immortal Song; and The Peerless and Perfect Horse-Trainer's Handbook.

Opper's newfound art style combined well with his formula for what were twisted logical extensions of everyday elements. All was fair game to him. The device was used constantly in Puck in the following 13 years, though seldom in series format, and led the way to similar examinations of life by Rube Goldberg, Milt Gross and others.

R.M.

AIN'T IT A GRAND AND GLORIOUS FEELIN'? (U.S.)
Ain't It a Grand and Glorious Feelin'? is among Clare Briggs's most fondly remembered slice-of-life newspaper panels. It appeared in sequential form (usually six panels to the page) on an irregular basis, alternating with such other Briggs creations as When a Feller Needs a

Friend and The Days of Real Sport. There was no continuing cast of characters.

Ain't It a Grand and Glorious Feelin'? started appearing in the New York Tribune around 1917 (although the concept had undergone a dry run as early as 1912 under another title in the Chicago Tribune). The panel celebrated those small, everyday moments of serendipity that come as a sharp relief after a moment of fright, embarrassment or frustration. Thus, "ain't it a grand and glorious feelin'" when some housewife discovers that her lost wallet was found at the grocer's, or when some poor bookkeeper goes to bed with a clear mind after the error in his books has been rectified? The feature addressed itself directly to the reader ("When you've been reading about a terrible kidnapping, . . ." Briggs would intone in the beginning, for instance) and always concluded on an upbeat note. Grand and Glorious Feelin' was tremendously popular during the 1920s, a decade whose mood it seemed to match perfectly, and the title became a popular catchphrase of the time.

After Briggs died in 1930 the panel was discontinued, although some newspapers would reprint it occasionally. Long runs of the feature have been republished regularly over the years in cartoon anthologies, as well as in collections of Briggs's works.

M.H.

AISLIN
See Mosher, Christopher Terry.

AKASEGAWA, GENPEI (1937-   ) Japanese avant-garde artist and cartoonist born in Yokohama, Japan, in 1937. After graduating from high school in Nagoya, where he was able to major in art, Genpei Akasegawa entered art school in Tokyo but quit in his third year. From 1958 to 1963 he entered artworks in the Yomiuri Independente exhibit. In 1960 Akasegawa and some friends formed the Neo Dada group, whose name reflected his budding sense of humor and parody. Then, in 1963, at the peak of this phase, he began "wrapping" art and also making imitation thousand-yen notes and burning them in public. At the same time, though not completely seriously, he drew cartoons for magazines such as *Doyō Manga* and *Asahi Sonorama*.

Akasegawa achieved his greatest notoriety in 1965, when he was indicted on counterfeiting charges stemming from his period of experimentation with imitation money. After a five-year trial he was given a three-month prison sentence, suspended for a year. He then became serious about cartooning and did a parody series for *Gendai no Me* ("Modern Eye") in 1969, just at the climax of Japan's student unrest; it dealt with riot police and student radicals, among other things. A rather long comic called *Ozashiki* ("The Living Room") ran in the magazine *Garo* in May 1970. In March 1971 his series *Sakura Gahō*, which ran in the *Asahi Journal*, embarrassed the publisher to the point of recalling it from the newsstands.

Genpei Akasegawa is one of Japan's more provocative cartoonists. His art, in fact, has often been a happening in its own right, and he constantly uses parody to a maximum effect to create humor and a personal political statement. He is an admirer of Yoshiharu Tsuge and often does parodies of his work. Books by Akasegawa include *Obuje of Motta Musansha* ("Proletarian Who Had an *Objet*").

F.S.

AKI, RYŪZAN (1942-   ) Japanese cartoonist born in Ito, Shizuoka Prefecture, Japan, in 1942. Ryūzan Aki's career has been amazingly varied. Upon graduation from junior high school he worked as a fisherman for several years. He then worked for the local post office, and began drawing cartoons for the post office newsletter on the side.

In 1965 he sent several cartoons to *Bessatsu Shukan Manga Times* (a weekly comic). Around the same time, according to one source, he read a short story by Gogol that so influenced him that he quit his job and moved to Tokyo to make his debut as a professional cartoonist. He actively contributed to comic books such as *Doyō Manga* and *Manga Tengoku* in this period and in 1969 achieved considerable popularity with series like *Ryūzan no Gera Gera Baka* ("Ryūzan the Laughing Fool") and *Oh! Jareezu*. In 1971 he won the 16th Shogakkan award for cartoons for *Oyabaka Tengoku* ("Paradise for Doting Parents") and *Gyagu Oyaji* ("Gag Daddy"); in 1975, he received the Bungei Shunju award for cartoons, a reflection of his broad popularity.

Aki's comics fall into a genre known in Japan as "nonsense." His characters generally possess such bizarre countenances that one almost has to look twice, yet they are drawn with clear, simple lines. He revels in reversing human logic and emphasizing the absurd in a black humor style that is absolutely unique. As comic critic Kosei Ono points out, Aki is a sort of Oriental Don Martin. Two of his most representative works are *Ryūzan no Fuzakketta Sekai* ("Ryūzan's Crazy World") and *Aki Ryūzan no Issen Mai* ("One Thousand Pictures by Ryūzan Aki").

F.S.

AKIYOSHI, KAORU (1912-   ) Japanese cartoonist born in Tokyo, Japan, in 1912. After graduating from high school, Kaoru Akiyoshi joined the Shinei Manga Gurūpu ("New Sharp Cartoon Group") in 1934 but soon switched to the Shin Mangaha Shudan ("New Cartoonists' Group"), which was founded to give new artists greater access to Japan's newspapers and magazines. As a member of the Shin Mangaha Shudan, Akiyoshi began to draw for Hidezo Kondo's cartoon publication, *Manga* ("Cartoon"). It was there that he introduced the prototype of his best-known work, *Todoro Sensei* ("Professor Thunder"), but the strip did not become a hit until after World War II.

After the end of the war, Akiyoshi drew for *Van*, one of the most popular humor magazines then appearing. Most of his cartoons of this period were bits of social satire and glimpses of the difficult era of postwar reconstruction. Akiyoshi also contributed to such postwar publications as *Comet* (1946), but most of these, including *Van*, were short-lived enterprises, and Akiyoshi eventually rejoined Hidezo Kondo when he revived the wartime magazine *Manga*. Akiyoshi brought back *Todoro Sensei*, and this time it became an instant success with the public.

The popularity of *Todoro Sensei* had a lot to do with the timing of its presentation. Its humor was derived from the contrast between the main character's traditional ways and the modernization that was going on about him. Professor Todoro was always dressed in traditional Japanese kimono, and his very appearance suggested conservatism. The other characters, however, were always preoccupied with the fashions and fads of the present. The encounters between old and new in *Todoro Sensei* reflected the rapid changes in postwar Japan. It skillfully captured the spirit of the times, and a faithful following as well. *Todoro Sensei* ran from 1948 to 1950 in *Manga* and was then picked up by the *Yomiuri* newspaper, where it enjoyed a long and successful run.

Akiyoshi was also an active contributor to children's cartoon magazines such as *Kodomo Manga Shimbun* ("Children's Cartoon News"), for which he drew *Tara-chan* from 1946. *Tara-chan* was a typical six-to-eight-panel cartoon strip that was cast in the mold of "nonsense" cartoons. The strip primarily contained silly gags and pranks whose sole purpose was to amuse young readers. The *Kodomo Manga Shimbun* and its imitators, the *Kodomo Manga Times* and *Junior Shimbun*, performed a valuable service, because there were very few children's readers available in the years just after the war. Many Japanese of the postwar generation have expressed their gratitude for these cartoon books, which helped sharpen their reading skills.

J.C.

ALAJALOV, CONSTANTIN (1900-   ) American cartoonist and painter born in Russia in 1900. Constantin Alajalov studied at the University of Petrograd but left for the United States in the aftermath of the Russian Revolution and ensuing war and civil war. His progress as an artist in his new country was steady, and all the more impressive when one considers that he was going against the artistic temper of the era. Starting out in the 1920s, with the various postimpressionist movements at full tide, Alajalov was (and remains) true to the classical mode in style and technique. Yet he has coupled this traditionalism with a wit that has enabled him to find commercial outlets for works that might otherwise have languished in the dark corners of galleries and lofts. Ultimately, it has gained him consideration as a serious artist.

His formal credits include commissions to do murals for the S.S. *America* and to paint *The Hands of Leonard Bernstein* (1967). His paintings are included in the permanent collections of the Brooklyn Museum, the Philadelphia Museum, the Museum of Modern Art in New York City and the Dallas Fine

ers for the *New Yorker* and the *Saturday Evening Post* (the heartland's answer to the *New Yorker*). He has also done illustrations for many books and national magazines. One of Alajalov's cartoons, reproduced in the *New Yorker*'s 50th-anniversary album, exhibits a wonderful fusion of excellent technique with an infectious sense of humor: two graceful antelopes, noses raised haughtily in the air, prance across a field before the friendly advance of a bulky, hairy fellow-ruminant. "Good lord!" remarks one to the other. "Here comes that impossible yak again."

But Alajalov is noted less for his cartoons than for the comic painting he has done for magazine covers—painting which tells little anecdotes at the same time that it represents subjects or places. On this level Alajalov must be appreciated not only as a witty craftsman, but as a man who never forgets the nature of the audience to whom he addresses a particular work. Thus, *New Yorker* readers are treated to scenes

"Alan Ford." © *Editoriale Corno.*

Arts Museum. He has been represented in many national exhibitions and has had one-man shows in Hollywood, New York City, Dallas, and Wichita, Kansas. He has also designed sets for the Michael Mordkin Ballet Company. He is currently a member of the faculty at the Phoenix Art Institute and also teaches at Archipenko's Ecole des Beaux-Arts.

The commercial side of his art has included a bit of cartooning for the *New Yorker*, as well as many cov-

from the stage of the Metropolitan Opera House while *Saturday Evening Post* subscribers encounter the homier environment of the local soda fountain.

Alajalov's published work as an illustrator includes *The George Gershwin Songbook, Our Hearts Were Young and Gay, Nuts in May, Bottoms Up*, and Alice Miller's *Cinderella*.

R.C.

ALAN FORD (Italy) *Alan Ford*, created in 1969 by Max Bunker (Luciano Secchi), was one of the most spectacular successes among Italian comics of the 1970s (see *The World Encyclopedia of Comics*, Chelsea House, 1976). In 1977 it was adapted to television for the *Supergulp, Fumetti in TV* program; the three stories that were presented—"Gommaflex, il Bandito della Faccia di Gomma" ("Gommaflex, the Rubber-Faced Bandit"), "Il Caso dei Prosciutti Scomparsi" ("The Case of the Vanished Appetizers") and "Ipnos"—were especially scripted by Max Bunker and drawn by Paolo Piffarerio. All three centered on the hapless special agent Alan Ford and his TNT group of gumshoes. They were pitted against Gommaflex, a gangster who, because of cell mutation, was able to transform himself into any person, animal or inanimate object.

In 1978 Alan Ford returned to the TV screen in four new adventures. This time the protagonist and his associates had to deal with Superciuk, a bandit also known as "the alcoholic menace" because of the superpowers he acquired through guzzling liquor. The success of these stories led to the undertaking of an *Alan Ford* series of 13 animated cartoons, executed by Paolo Piffarerio under the direction of Guido De Maria.

M.H.

ALEXANDER, FRANKLIN OSBORNE (1897-) American cartoonist born in St. Louis, Missouri, in 1897. F.O. Alexander was educated at Northwestern University and the Chicago Academy of Fine Arts; night schools and correspondence courses completed his cartoon training. In World War I he served in Europe with the Camouflage Engineers.

Alexander took over the *Hairbreadth Harry* comic strip upon the death of its creator, C.W. Kahles, in 1931; he continued writing and drawing the strip until its demise in 1939. He then tried two strips of his own—*Finney of the Force* and *The Featherheads*—and drew editorial cartoons for United Feature Syndicate before becoming staff political cartoonist of the *Philadelphia Bulletin* in 1941. He is now retired.

Following Kahles was a tough act. Alexander added his own flavor to *Hairbreadth Harry*, modernizing the gags and artwork but losing the almost surreal wackiness that the great Kahles achieved in his last few years. As a political cartoonist Alexander was conservative and drew in a handsome, uncluttered

F.O. Alexander, humorous Christmas card.

brushstroke style shaded with careful, clean crayon additions on pebbleboard.

R.M.

Alexandre Alexeieff, "Le Nez." © Alexeieff.

ALEXEIEFF, ALEXANDRE (1901-) French animator and producer born in Kazan, Russia, on April 18, 1901. Alexandre Alexeieff went to Cadets School and later attended the Naval Academy in St. Petersburg. He emigrated to France in the aftermath of the Russian Revolution, settling in Paris in 1919. There he studied painting and design, and embarked on a promising career as a book illustrator and stage designer.

In 1933 Alexeieff saw Fernand Léger's fabled avant-garde film of animation *Ballet Mécanique*, and under this influence he made a cartoon short, *A Night on Bald Mountain*, using Modest Moussorgsky's music. This film was based on Alexeieff's famous "pin-board technique"—patterns and images created by means of rows of pins fastened to a board and moved either mechanically or by hand. Turning his attention to puppets, Alexeieff then produced *La Belle au Bois Dormant* ("Sleeping Beauty") to music by Francis Poulenc. He also made numerous cartoon commercials for products ranging from perfume to underwear.

During World War II Alexeieff went first to England and then to the United States. With the help of his second wife, Claire Parker (whom he had married in 1941), he experimented further with the pin-board technique and made several films for the National Film Board of Canada, the most notable being *En Passant*, a delightful romp through Canadian folk songs. Returning to France after the war, Alexeieff again took up commercial animation but later made three impressionistic films with Georges Violet: *Fumées, Masques* and *Nocturnes* (1951-54).

Alexeieff then came back to the pin-board, producing *Le Nez*, ("The Nose," 1963), a film version of Nikolai Gogol's famous tale of a man haunted by his own nose. Turning to Moussorgsky's music once more, he directed *Pictures at an Exhibition*. Dreamy, almost ethereal, this last effort was greeted almost as much with incomprehension as with praise when it was released in 1971. Alexeieff has been the recipient of countless honors over the years; his cartoons (he prefers to call them "animated engravings") have won many international awards. He himself has been called "the Einstein of animation," and he has been a perennial member of juries at animation festivals around the world.

M.H.

Asmo Alho. © *Alho.*

ALHO, ASMO (1903-1975) Finnish cartoonist born in Helsinki, Finland, on August 2, 1903. Asmo Alho might well be the most prolific cartoonist who ever worked in Finland. His gag cartoons and comic strips were published by many large magazines, and he also did some political cartooning. He was active until his death, and his works are still being published regularly.

After finishing school in 1923, Alho went to work for Otava, the big publishing company, doing layouts and artwork. He mainly designed the covers and layouts of the books and magazines published by his company, and to further his knowledge he traveled to Denmark and Germany in 1929. He later worked on the newspaper *Uusi Suomi*, and until 1969 for the large magazine publishing concern Yhtyneet Kuvalehdet, where he became head of the art department.

Alho illustrated a widely used alphabet book and produced several of the most beloved children's books in Finland, some in collaboration with the noted poet and ethnographer Martti Haavio (among them *Porsas Urhea* and *Little Red Riding Hood*). Starting in 1933, he also drew some of the longest-running comics (with academician Mika Waltari writing verse for *Kieku and Kaiku*).

Alho's cartoons were regularly published in *Joulukärpänen, Pippuri, Radiokunntelija, Kotiliesi* and *Suomen Kuvalehti*. He also did advertising work and was president of the Union of Graphic Illustrators. He wrote two books, *Tutustumme Helsinkiin* ("Getting to Know Helsinki") and *Helsinki Ennen Meitä* ("Helsinki Before Us").

After retirement Alho sometimes taught seminars for young cartoonists. The man behind the work remained largely unknown to the general public, however. The Finnish Comics Society awarded him its highest honor, the Puupäähat, just before his death in Helsinki in 1975.

J.R.

ALICE IN CARTOONLAND (U.S.) When he left Kansas City for Los Angeles in 1923, Walt Disney brought with him a copy of his latest effort, *Alice's Wonderland*, a partly animated, partly live-action short. Among the people who saw his sample was Margaret Winkler, an independent distributor, who commissioned a series of cartoons (to be called *Alice in Cartoonland*) from Disney later that same year.

With the help of his brother Roy, Walt Disney set to work with alacrity and in a few months in 1924 turned out six *Alice* cartoons (for which he was paid fifteen hundred dollars apiece). The returns, however, were disappointing, and Charles Mintz (who had married Margaret Winkler earlier that year and taken over the business) asked the Disney brothers to discontinue production. In desperation Disney sent for his former Kansas City partner, Ub Iwerks; Iwerks, an accomplished draftsman, is credited with putting the series back on its feet. Thus propped up, *Alice in Cartoonland* continued on its way until late in 1926, when everybody agreed that the series had played itself out (after a run of some fifty separate titles).

Alice in Cartoonland was not very distinguished. Its live action was rudimentary, the parts being played by neighborhood kids (Virginia Davis was the first Alice, later replaced by Margie Gay), its gags feeble, and the drawing stiff, even after the addition of Iwerks. It represents, however, Walt Disney's first successful venture into animation, and it allowed him to refine his animation and storytelling techniques. It also provided him with the nucleus of his animation team (made up of himself, his brother Roy, Iwerks and three more associates from his Kansas City days, Rudolph Ising and Hugh and Walker Harman).

M.H.

"Alice in Cartoonland." © *Walt Disney Productions.*

ALLEGRO NON TROPPO (Italy) To produce a full-length animated film entirely based on musical works might sound like a hopeless gamble after *Fantasia*; yet that is exactly what Bruno Bozzetto attempted with *Allegro Non Troppo*, released in 1976.

As could be expected, the animation content was as much of a mixed bag as the musical program. The

The "Prelude to the Afternoon of a Faun" sequence of "Allegro Non Troppo." © Bruno Bozzetto.

ALLEN, T.S. (ca. 1870-1930) American cartoonist born in Fayette County, Kentucky, around 1870. T.S. Allen was raised in Kentucky, attended James Kane Allen's school, was a classmate of William H. Walker (later a stablemate at *Life* magazine) and graduated from Transylvania University in Lexington, where he studied classical languages. In the 1890s Allen moved to New York, where his father had established a law office, and worked there as a clerk. He moonlighted as an author and joke writer for magazine cartoonists and eventually sketched his own drawings to accompany his breezy captions.

Allen's style—obviously untutored, but showing shrewd native talent—was as flippant as his light jokes. He was among the first cartoonists to break away from the rigid illustrators' look of magazine cartoons and was perceived as the American Phil May. Thematically, many of Allen's single-panel cartoons dealt with street urchins and working-class or immigrant subjects.

When the very first Sunday supplements were issued, in the days when there were as many text jokes and panel cartoons as strip series, T.S. Allen was a prominent fixture on both the *World* and Hearst sections. Otherwise *Life* was his major outlet well into the 1910s.

R.M.

wittiest (and shortest) piece showed a bunch of uncouth louts first falling in step with, and later rebelling against, their would-be "leader," to the lusty strains of Dvorak's *Slavonic Dances*. Bozzetto's animation for Debussy's *Prelude à l'Après-Midi d'un Faune* was conventional, with a ridiculous satyr in hapless pursuit of a cute young nymph; and his recreation of man's evolution from the earth primeval (to the rhythm of Ravel's *Bolero*) looked too much like a copy of Disney's prehistoric sequence in *Fantasia*. The closing piece—depicting a barren, desolated urban landscape seen through the eyes of a starving alley cat, and set to the music of Sibelius's *Valse Triste*—was probably the feature's most gripping, as well as most original, moment.

The live-action skits connecting the different segments of animation were sophomoric and poorly acted, and the film also suffered from the lack of a live score (the music was culled from records). All in all, *Allegro Non Troppo* was markedly but not disgracefully inferior to *Fantasia*. (It should be noted that the film received first prize at the 1977 Sydney Film Festival.)

M.H.

ALLEY, CALVIN LANE (1915-1970) American artist born in Memphis, Tennessee, on October 10, 1915. Cal Alley was raised in an artistic environment—his father, J.P. Alley, drew editorial cartoons for the *Memphis Commercial Appeal* and created the *Hambone* panel—and attended the American Academy and the Chicago Academy of Fine Arts in 1935-36. For two years thereafter Alley was a cowboy and sketch artist in Arizona and Texas. In 1939 Alley became editorial cartoonist of the *Kansas City Journal* and remained there until its demise in 1942. He then held a similar position on the *Nashville Banner* until 1945, when he joined his father's paper, the *Memphis Commercial Appeal*, as editorial cartoonist. Here he remained until his death on November 10, 1970.

His wife: "Do you know, John, this is the first time I've really enjoyed riding in this thing since you got it."

T.S. Allen, 1909.

Calvin Alley, "The Ryatts." © The Hall Syndicate.

The younger Alley, along with his brother Jim, inherited the Bell Syndicate panel *Hambone's Meditations* in 1934. Their method of working was largely unknown to the general public: they alternated weeks, drawing it in a virtually indistinguishable style. The stereotyped title character, a philosophical "darky," no matter how sympathetic, sage and harmless, was nevertheless deemed offensive by many in the race-conscious 1950s, so the panel died in 1954.

That same year Cal Alley began a family comic strip, *The Ryatts*, modeled on his own home life. Picked up by the Hall Syndicate, it premiered in October 1954 in 24 papers and soon, thanks to its empathy, engaging drawing style and thematic appeal, ran in several hundred papers. In 1967, because of ill health and the crush of daily editorial cartoon production, Alley relinquished the strip to Jack Elrod, who also assists on the *Mark Trail* strip for the successor syndicate, Field.

Alley had an extremely attractive, old-time pen-and-ink drawing style reminiscent of his father's and the Chicago Tribune school's. He very seldom used crayon shading. In politics he was a conservative.

R.M.

ALLEY, JAMES PINCKNEY (1885-1934) American cartoonist born near Benton, Arkansas, on January 11, 1885. J.P. Alley was educated in the public schools of Benton and in 1916 became the cartoonist for the *Memphis Commercial Appeal* in Tennessee; he was to remain there until his death.

Besides his editorial cartoons, which were drawn in the popular mid-South style of Carey Orr and Billy Ireland, Alley drew the widely enjoyed and long-running *Hambone's Meditations*. This syndicated panel about a rural black's observations was in the tradition of Josh Billings and other cracker-barrel humorists; Hambone's commonsense aphorisms were quoted frequently and collected in book form in 1917 and 1919 (McClure, and later Bell, was the distributor in newspapers). Alley also wrote and illustrated *Distinguished Folks* in 1928.

Alley died on April 16, 1934; his sons J.P., Jr., and Cal continued *Hambone*, and Cal was later to draw editorial cartoons in Memphis and Nashville.

R.M.

ALONSO, JUAN CARLOS (1886-1945) Argentine cartoonist and painter born in El Ferrol, Spain, on July 6, 1886. Juan Carlos Alonso came to Argentina in 1899 with his parents. He studied art in Buenos Aires and started his career as a cartoonist around 1905. He first worked for *Caras y Caretas*, then went over to the humor magazine *Plus Ultra*. He contributed many cartoons and illustrations to *Plus Ultra*, becoming its most noted collaborator. In the 1920s he became the director of the magazine.

Alonso was also a noted painter who specialized in genre scenes and picturesque compositions. He exhibited widely, not only in Argentina but also in France,

James Alley, "Hambone's Meditations," ca. 1900.

Italy and Spain, and won first prize at the 1933 Santa Fe Salon. He was named a Knight of the Royal Order of Alfonso XIII and made a member of the Royal Academy of his native Galicia (a province of Spain). He died on February 15, 1945, in Buenos Aires.

A.M.

ALTAN, FRANCESCO TULLIO (1943-   ) Italian cartoonist and illustrator born in Treviso, Italy, in 1943. Francesco Altan left for Brazil after finishing his art studies in Italy; while in Latin America, he contributed cartoons and comic strips to a great number of publications. Returning to his native Venetia in the early 1970s, he freelanced for various Italian magazines.

Altan enjoyed his first success with Trino, a kind of bungling demiurge busy with the creation of the world on orders of an omnipotent boss, himself not quite sure of his intentions. This story first appeared in the monthly *Linus* in 1974 and was later collected in book form. It contained nothing irreverent, but it displayed Altan's wit and irony and indulged in some good-natured ribbing of famous characters from the past, a feature it shares with his political cartoons. These often focus on workingmen—an important aspect of Altan's satirical work, and one common to many other contemporary Italian political cartoonists. Where Chiappori, for instance, pillories the men in power, Altan makes his point indirectly, through the seemingly genuine and spontaneous comments of assembly-line workers: this is a means of putting the political cartoon in a simpler, more immediate context.

Altan is also an illustrator who, in the pages of *Il Corriere dei Piccoli* and in children's books, depicts fabulous and fantastic worlds midway between unreality and poetry. Both in his political cartoons and in his children's stories Altan always displays the same sparse style, without frills and somewhat *naïf*.

C.S.

ALVARUS

See Cotrim, Alvaro.

AMARAL, CRISPIM DO (1858-1911) Brazilian cartoonist born in Olinda, in the state of Pernambuco, Brazil, in 1858. Crispim do Amaral showed an early predisposition toward art, and his parents sent him to Pernambuco (now Recife) to study under the French painter Léon Chapelin. Amaral's artistic career started in 1876, when he designed sets for the stage, first in Pernambuco, then in Manaus. Towards the end of the 19th century Amaral moved to Paris, where he worked as a designer and also contributed cartoons to several French publications, notably *L'Assiette au Beurre*.

Amaral returned to Brazil in 1901, briefly staying in Pernambuco, then permanently settling in Rio de Janeiro in 1902. He pursued a flourishing career as a set designer and as a cartoonist, working variously for *O Malho* (of which he was the first art director), *A Avenida* (a magazine he founded in 1903 and ran until 1905), *O Pau* and finally *O Século*. He died in Rio in 1911.

Crispim's brother, Amaro do Amaral (1873-1922), was also a cartoonist.

A.M.

"No, no, nurse! The tranquilizer is for ME!"

Bradley Anderson, "Marmaduke." © National Newspaper Syndicate.

ANDERSON, BRADLEY (1924-) American cartoonist born in Jamestown, New York, on May 14, 1924. Brad Anderson sold his first cartoon to *Flying* magazine in 1940, while still in high school, and continued to freelance cartoons until he was drafted in 1942. After three years in the navy during World War II, Anderson enrolled at the University of Syracuse and continued to draw cartoons, for the *Syracusan Magazine*.

Upon graduation in 1951 Anderson worked in the university's audiovisual department, contributing a number of cartoons to such publications as the *Saturday Evening Post* and *Collier's* all the while. In 1953 he decided to devote himself to cartooning full time, and the following year he created *Marmaduke*, a newspaper panel about a Great Dane and the havoc caused by his well-meaning but catastrophic exertions.

Brad Anderson is a competent, if somewhat dull, draftsman who is able to achieve some moments of inspired lunacy in the course of *Marmaduke*. He fails, however, to give as good an account of himself in his newest feature, a comic strip titled *Grandpa's Boy*.

M.H.

ANDERSON, MARTIN (1854-1918?) British cartoonist born in Leuchars, Fife, Scotland, in 1854. The caricaturist who signed his work "Cynicus" was the last of the long line of independent graphic satirists who made social, political and topical attacks through the medium of the colored print, a British tradition dating back to Gillray and Hogarth.

Martin Anderson received a local education, then attended Madras College in St. Andrews. After school he went to Glasgow as an apprentice to a designer and attended the Glasgow School of Art as an evening student. His first cartoon ("The Transit of Venus") was published in the magazine *Quiz*, and he obtained a job as staff artist on John Leng's *Dundee Advertiser*.

He came down to London in 1891, converting a fish-and-chips shop at 59 Drury Lane into a studio. From there, under the imprint of the Cynicus Publishing

Company, he produced a long series of caricature plates, hand-colored, which he sold as separate sheets, cards and, occasionally, in book form. His caricatures and topical or political cartoons attacking or commenting on matters of the immediate moment were captioned with couplets, and although crude in technique and basic in style, they continued the tradition of the old satirists, becoming quite popular. He returned to Scotland and set up a studio in Tayport, where, aided by a staff of women colorists, he produced cartoon postcards in series. Anderson died during or shortly after World War I.

Books: *The Satires of Cynicus* (1890); *The Humours of Cynicus* (1891); *Symbols and Metaphors* (1892); *The Fatal Smile* (1892); *Social and Political Cartoons* (1893); *The Blue Button* (1896); *Selections from Cynicus* (1909); and *Who Shall Rule, Briton or Norman* (1911).

D.G.

An opener: "Excuse me, miss.
Would you permit me to afford you some shade?"

Oskar Andersson ("O.A.").

ANDERSSON, OSKAR EMIL (1877-1906) Swedish cartoonist, better known as O.A., born in Stockholm, Sweden, on January 11, 1877. In the tradition that a number of Swedish cartoonists, led by Albert Engström, started in the satirical magazines *Søndagsnisse* and *Strix*, O.A. stands out with a special radiance. Actually, he was Engström's greatest competitor among cartoonists, but his early death at his own hands meant that he was not to be popular among his contemporaries; rather, it is later historians who have discovered his outstanding qualities.

He was a cartoonist of the restaurants and the salons, especially; the backs of menus served as his drawing pad, and with his elegant looks one could have taken him for the son of a rich man, an officer or a rising politician. His self-portrait, which hangs in the National Museum in Stockholm, confirms the impression of a highly gifted, elegant artist. Had he had the desire and the will, he could have become one of the world's great portrait painters. But he felt he was misunderstood and sought refuge in cartoons in order to make ends meet; nobody saw his greatness. Typical of his art and mentality was the cartoon of an office clerk who says, "I'd like to ask permission to have the afternoon off." "For what purpose?" asks his fat employer. "I intend to commit suicide," he answers. Andersson did indeed commit suicide on November 28, 1906.

The young O.A.'s drawings, scattered among Stockholm's small restaurants, have become classics: his captions are familiar quotations, his abbreviations and technique of omissions were trend-setting, his feel for composition was brilliant. (For a description of O.A.'s career as a comic strip artist, see *The World Encyclopedia of Comics*, Chelsea House, 1976.)

J.S.

ANDY PANDA (U.S.) With the popularity of Oswald the Rabbit fading fast as the 1930s wore on, Walt Lantz had the task of finding a new cartoon character who would prove attractive to moviegoers. After trying out several other animals (such as a pup, a mouse and a duck) Lantz finally settled on a cuddly little panda bear named Andy Panda who made his appearance around 1938. Every hand at the Lantz studio seems to have worked on the *Andy Panda* series, James Culhane and Alex Lovy being the most notable.

Andy was a well-intentioned, not overly bright creature, and he always managed to get involved in various scrapes with other animal characters. In "Nutty Pine Cabin," Andy tried to put up a log cabin in the woods, only to be thwarted at every turn by all kinds of forest animals; in "Meatless Tuesday," he went out to catch a rooster for supper, but the hardy fowl proved too strong and crafty for him. One of the best entries in the series, "Poet and Peasant," starred Andy as the conductor of the Hollywood Washbowl Orchestra in a raucous rendition of Franz von Suppé's famous overture, amid complete chaos and mayhem.

Andy Panda was popular enough to last into the 1960s, although with diminishing invention and wit. In the cartoons of the later period (by which time he had acquired a girl friend, Miranda), Andy's role became smaller and smaller. In "Fish Fry," for instance, he was relegated to playing second banana—to a goldfish, yet!

Andy Panda was featured in comic books from 1943 to 1962, and in 1973 Gold Key started releasing a new *Andy Panda* title.

M.H.

"Andy Panda." © Walter Lantz.

ANGOLETTA, BRUNO (1899-1954) Italian cartoonist born in Belluno, Italy, in 1899. From an early age Bruno Angoletta showed a talent for drawing, and he sold his first cartoons to the humor magazine *L'Asino* when he was not yet twenty. He later collaborated on *Pasquino* and *La Tribuna Illustrata*. In 1921 he staged Shakespeare's *Romeo and Juliet* and also illustrated several books and designed book covers. After drawing a number of pages for the weeklies *La Domenica* and *Il Giornalino*, Angoletta went over to *Il Corriere dei Piccoli* in 1928, creating for that magazine many comic strips, among them the famous *Marmittone*. Other Angoletta strips include *Il Professor Tubo*, *Girometto*, *Pancotto*, *Pampan della Micragna*, *Calogero Sorbara* (1930) and *Centerbe Ermete* (1934-41).

During the 1930s and early 1940s Angoletta also contributed cartoons to a great number of publications, such as *Girotondo*, *Novella*, *Donna*, *L'Ardita* and *Il Balilla*, the Fascist youth organization newspaper, for which he created at the time of the Ethiopian war the two famous fez-topped twins Romolino and Romoletto. He also drew many anti-British and anti-American cartoons during World War II. After the defeat of Fascism, Angoletta went into a long period of silence, from which he emerged in 1950 to collaborate on Giovanni Guareschi's newly created satirical weekly, *Il Candido*. Angoletta's cartoons appeared in its pages until his death in Milan in 1954.

M.G.P.

ANIMALAND (G.B.) "*Animaland* Cartoons created in Britain by David Hand: Gay, Lovable, Laughable and Brightly-Coloured." This was how the first fully studio-backed series of animated cartoons to be produced in the

United Kingdom was advertised in the trade press on Monday, December 13, 1948. Gaumont British Animation had been set up by the millionaire flour miller Joseph Arthur Rank as part of his campaign to fill the screens of his British cinemas (the Odeon and Gaumont circuits) with British films of every kind, from features to newsreels, shorts, documentaries and, of course, cartoons.

In charge of the project was David Hand, hired from the Walt Disney organization, where he had been a top producer for many years. The studio was created in a country mansion, Moor Hall, in the village of Cookham, Berkshire, and Ralph Wright was made story supervisor. Their initial trial releases were very short cartoon commercials for Spa toothbrushes (for which they invented *Sparky*) and Rowntree's cocoa (for which they created *Coco and the Bear*). They also produced a sing-song short for Rank's Saturday morning children's clubs, called *Bound for the Rio Grande*. Two series were then planned, *Animaland* and *Musical Paintbox*, and releases alternated from 1948 to 1950.

The first *Animaland* release was *The Lion* (1948), directed by Bert Felstead from a script by Pete Griffiths. Music was by Henry Reed (as it would be for the series), and the story was narrated by radio character-actor Richard Goolden. As an old professor, he studied the life and habits of "Felis Leo" from cubhood to maturity, finally getting eaten for his pains! *The Cuckoo* (1948) was funnier, introducing a fat hero who was indeed "cuckoo." *The House Cat* (1948), written by Reg Parlett and Nobby Clark, again featured Goolden as narrator, this time with songs by The Radio Revellers to brighten the proceedings. *The Platypus* (1949) introduced two funny birds, Katie and Kobber Kookaburra, as well as the

Bruno Angoletta, caricature.

hero and heroine, Digger and Dinkum Platypus. *The Ostrich* (1949) told the life and times of Oscar and was the last of the somewhat formal—certainly as far as titles go—series. A change of policy produced a deliberately

Kid Kelly and his dog Jip in "The Animated Grouch Chasers,"
1915. © Thomas A. Edison, Inc. and La Cinémathèque
Québécoise.

created cartoon star, Ginger Nutt the Squirrel, who
starred in the remaining four releases (see the entry
"Ginger Nutt"). Director for the series was Bert Felstead,
and animators included Stan Pearsall, Ted Percival, Bill
Hopper, John Wilson and Chick Henderson, with backgrounds by George Hawthorne and Betty Hansford.

D.G.

ANIMATED GROUCH CHASERS, THE (U.S.) *The Ani-*
mated Grouch Chasers is the collective title of a series of
cartoons produced by the French-Canadian cartoonist
Raoul Barré for Edison Company in New York. Conceived according to the technique of animation on paper,
this series of thirty-odd cartoons was subdivided into
eleven thematically related films, all released within the
single year 1915: *Cartoons in the Kitchen* (April 21),
Cartoons in the Barber Shop (May 22), *Cartoons in the*
Parlor (June 5), *Cartoons in the Hotel* (June 21), *Cartoons*
in the Laundry (July 8), *Cartoons on Tour* (August 6),
Cartoons on the Beach (August 25), *Cartoons in a Semi-*
nary (September 9), *Cartoons in the Country* (October 9),
Cartoons on a Yacht (October 29) and *Cartoons in a*
Sanitarium (November 12). Structured along the line of
"Chinese boxes," these films blend animation and live
action: the sudden appearance of a comic book titled *The*
Grouch Chaser signals the start of the animation after a
burlesque introduction played by live actors.

In addition to a series of animated fables featuring a
group of insects (notable among them Ferdinand the fly
and his "flyancée"), Barré created three heroes for his
cartoons: Kid Kelly, Hercule Hicks and Silas Bunkum.
The crafty owner of a boardinghouse, Silas is pictured as
a potbellied teller of tales whose absurdity invariably
gets him thrown out of the local general store by his
outraged audience. Silas philosophically crowns each of
his evictions with the resigned comment "Folks don't
believe nothing no more!" In contrast to Silas, Hercule
Hicks is a henpecked little man who escapes from his
redoubtable wife by means of dreaming. His intense
oneiric activity gives rise to some interesting animation
effects, like the dream balloon taking up the entire
screen. The mischievous Kid Kelly is unquestionably the
most interesting of the three characters. *Cartoons on a*
Yacht, in which Barré satirizes office employees, and
Cartoons in the Country both highlight the complicity

between Kid Kelly and his sidekick, the larcenous dog
Jip.

Several innovations were brought to bear on *The Ani-*
mated Grouch Chasers: depth of field ("Suburbanite
Life," "Kid Kelly Has a Lollypop"), use of moving backgrounds ("Hicks in Nightmareland"), foreground effects
("Kid Kelly's Bathing Adventures"). In this respect the
series, although badly dated, represents a giant step in
terms of organization of labor and announces the immi-
nent industrialization of American cartoon film production.

S.J.

ANTHONY, NORMAN (1893-1968) American cartoonist
and editor born in Buffalo, New York, in 1893. Norman
Anthony studied art at the Albright Art Gallery in
Buffalo after worshiping at the pages of *Puck*, *Judge* and
Life as a boy. In 1910, he sold his first cartoon to *Life* and
for ten years thereafter freelanced as a cartoonist and
editor on such papers as the *Lamb*, a short-lived Wall
Street sheet.

As a cartoonist he was always weak; his strength was
in gags. His cartoons sold on their humor, and in the
early 1920s, the struggling *Judge* hired him as an idea
man—often to write captions for artwork accepted on its
visual merits and without gags! He analyzed *Judge's*
problems—too much text, very little real humor—and
put in a bid to reform the magazine. On November 17,
1923, one of his concepts was tried, an advertising
lampoon number, and was a wild success. Immensely
funny (and foreshadowing his later *Ballyhoo*, and even
MAD magazine), it assured him a name on the masthead
and an editorship beginning with the December 8 issue.

Anthony literally revolutionized American cartooning. The he-she captions were out, irreverence was in;
new artists like Dr. Seuss, S.J. Perelman and Jefferson
Machamer were discovered; lampoon issues appeared
frequently; and honest, belly-laugh humor was king.
Slapstick, puns, ethnic humor, sophisticated drollery,
political satire—all romped through *Judge's* pages. As he
discovered artists, writers, entertainers and the like—
including such names as Jimmy Durante and Pare
Lorentz—he raised the circulation from thirty thousand
to more than a hundred thousand a week.

His efforts attracted the attention of the *Life* owners,
smarting from *Judge's* success and the efforts of Harold
Ross at the new *New Yorker*. (Ross was a protégé of
Anthony's in 1924 on *Judge*; they didn't see eye to eye on
percentage of text or style of humor.) *Life* offered
Anthony $35,000 a year and ten percent of the profits. He
switched in 1929, but all the promises made by *Life's*
Charles Dana Gibson, after Anthony's radical changes in
the magazine's format, were broken, and Anthony was
out of a job (he later successfully sued for breach of
contract).

Soon he conceived an idea that George Delacorte at
Dell Publishing brought out as a magazine: it was truly
an early *MAD*, only zanier. The magazine, *Ballyhoo*, had
a bright patchwork-quilt cover, was wrapped in cel-
lophane and contained the wildest ad lampoons and
bawdiest jokes the country had seen. The weekly print
runs sold out—first 150,000 copies, then 300,000...
600,000...1,000,000...1,500,000...2,000,000. It was a
national craze and spawned a score of imitators within a
month. Anthony backed the *Ballyhoo Revue* on Broadway, starring a newcomer named Bob Hope; the critics
panned it, but it was a moderate success.

The *Ballyhoo* craze died after six years. Anthony tried

other magazines—*Manhattan, Mr., Helzapoppin, Der Gag*, the *Funnybone*—a radio show (*The Village Grocery*) and several books, including *The Drunk's Blue Book*, illustrated by Otto Soglow, and *What to Do Until the Psychiatrist Comes*. His autobiography, a Rabelaisian journey through his successes, failures, women and binges, was entitled *How to Grow Old Disgracefully*. Anthony, a comic genius who left a huge mark on American cartooning and humor, died on January 21, 1968.

R.M.

ANTON (G.B.) "Anton came into being in 1937, and we—brother and sister—have been partners since then. But please don't ask us how it works out." This explanation served to introduce *Anton's Amusement Arcade*, the first collection of Anton cartoons, published in 1947 to mark the first decade of this unique collaboration between Harold Underwood Thompson and his sister Beryl Antonia ("Anton" is an abbreviation of her middle name). Percy V. Bradshaw, interviewing this "double act" for his *Lines of Laughter* (1946), considered their mutual understanding uncanny. "They each scrawl their loose shading on to figures and backgrounds in precisely the same way. I am convinced that if the sister did the rough sketches and the brother the finished drawings (instead of the other way around), the results would be just the same."

Time proved the acute Bradshaw right: the brother dropped out, but Anton continued until Antonia's death in June 1970. In addition to the aforementioned *Anton's Amusement Arcade*, several more Anton books were published, including *Streamlined Bridge* (1947), *Low Life and High Life* (1952) and *Entertaining Singlehanded* (1968).

D.G.

APA

See Elies i Bracons, Feliu.

APE

See Pellegrini, Carlo.

APÓSTOL, EL (Argentina) Many countries claim to have been first in the feature-length cartoon sweepstakes, but *El Apóstol*, a 60-minute cartoon produced in Argentina as early as 1917, seems to take pride of place. El Apóstol ("The Apostle") was Argentine president Irigoyen, who had recently assumed office and was then at the peak of his popularity. Adapted from a book by Alfredo de Laferrere, the film depicted the president leaving in a dream for Mount Olympus, where he was given Jupiter's thunderbolts to destroy the corrupt politicians and vice barons of the republic. The president and his ministers were actually portrayed on the screen by means of drawings based on photographs—a kind of rotoscopy.

The film was produced and directed by Frederico Valle, with Diogenes Taborda and Quirino Cristiani as assistant directors and key animators. From all accounts *El Apóstol* was an intriguing and revolutionary movie; unfortunately for posterity, the negative was destroyed in a studio fire in the 1950s, and no copy has been located so far.

"I'm happy to say the danger is passed."

Anton. © Lilliput.

(President Irigoyen was the subject of another Argentinian cartoon feature in 1931. He was then satirized as a tired old man who had run out of ideas. The title of the film was *Peludopolis*, and it was produced, written and directed by Quirino Cristiani, a veteran of the earlier—and kindlier—*El Apóstol*.)

M.H.

ARA MA OKUSAN (Japan) *Ara Ma Okusan* was a four-panel Japanese cartoon that ran in the *Yomiuri* newspaper during the early 1930s. It was drawn by Senpan Maekawa, who was born in Kyoto in 1889. Maekawa was a well-known *Yomiuri* newspaper artist who was fond of working-class themes and fumbling types. *Ara Ma Okusan* centered on a middle-aged housewife who was partial to the common Japanese exclamation "Ara Ma!," which she repeated with great frequency; hence the title of the cartoon, "Mrs. Ara Ma." Her husband was an artist, and they had one son. In short, they were a typical middle-class family that Maekawa's readers could easily identify with.

Reflecting the economic hardships of the 1930s, *Ara Ma Okusan* frequently took up the topic of the need for frugality. In fact, this was the main source of humor in the cartoon. Mrs. Ara Ma was a lover of the arts and a perpetual do-gooder. The cartoons often revolved around the conflict between her desire to go to the movies, visit museums or help out a friend in need and her recognition that her family's budget did not allow such extravagances. Her plight was the same as that of millions of Japanese, and Maekawa's gentle treatment of Mrs. Ara Ma's situation gained him a loyal following.

Ara Ma Okusan is somewhat reminiscent of Maekawa's earlier work *Awate no Kuma-san*, in which much of the humor is also derived from the interesting predicaments of a well-meaning housewife. *Ara Ma Okusan* is most significant, however, because it was the last cartoon series that Maekawa drew before he retired to spend the rest of his life making woodblock prints.

J.C.

ARCADY, JEAN
See Brachlianoff, Arcady.

ARCIMBOLDO, GIUSEPPE (1527-1593) Italian artist and caricaturist born in Milan, Italy, in 1527. Giuseppe Arcimboldo (or Arcimboldi) was a pupil and disciple of Leonardo da Vinci. He worked on the Milan cathedral, and in 1562 he went to Prague as titular portrait painter to the imperial court. For 27 years he indefatigably depicted the faces, tastes and manners of the emperors Ferdinand I, Maximilian II and Rudolph II, and their wives, children and retainers. For his services he was made a margrave. He returned to his native Milan toward the end of his life and died there in 1593.

Arcimboldo was remembered as the inventor of a "color keyboard," but his work was for a long time relegated to obscurity. He was rediscovered after World War I by the Surrealists, who regarded his fantastic paintings as one of the links in the chain leading to surrealism. Arcimboldo's "composite heads" can also be seen as both a statement on the art of caricature and an attempt to transcend it; his grotesque animals are forerunners of one of the more fertile trends in cartooning. Obviously Arcimboldo was not a cartoonist in the strict sense, and his favorite medium was oil, not pen and ink. He has nonetheless left us a legacy upon which to ponder, and echoes of his work can be found in some of the research carried on by modern cartoonists like Saul Steinberg and Michel Folon.

M.H.

Gone with the Wind . . .

Antonio Arias Bernal. © Arias Bernal.

ARIAS BERNAL, ANTONIO (1914-1960) Mexican cartoonist born in Aguas Calientes, Mexico, in 1914. Antonio Arias Bernal was taught to draw by his mother, an amateur artist. He was a fighter against injustice from the earliest age: his first cartoon of note, published when he was 15, savagely attacked the minister of education of his native state of Aguas Calientes. In 1933 Arias Bernal moved to Mexico City, studying briefly at the Academy of San Carlos. His cartoons, which *México al Día* published regularly from 1935 on, created a sensation. He helped found the satirical magazines *Vea, Don Ferruco, El Fufurufu* and others, and his works appeared in such publications as *Hoy, Mañana, Todo* and *Siempre*, as well as in the daily newspapers *Excelsior* and *El Universal*, among others.

Arias Bernal was already a legend when World War II broke out. He relentlessly attacked Latin American dictators, fascist and Nazi regimes, and demagoguery and corruption at home. His books of cartoons were distributed in the hundreds of thousands throughout Latin America by the U.S. Office of the Coordinator of Inter-American Affairs. In 1952 he received a Maria Moors Cabot journalism award from Columbia University for his "distinguished contribution as an artist . . . toward the advancement of friendship in our hemisphere."

Antonio Arias Bernal died of cancer in Mexico City on December 31, 1960.

M.H.

Giuseppe Arcimboldo, "The Vegetable-Man," 1590.

ARISTIDES, OTHON (1932-   ) French cartoonist of Greek origin born in Paris, France, in 1932. Othon Aristides—better known under his *nom de plume,*

"Fred"—embarked upon a cartooning career soon after graduation from high school in 1950. During the 1950s he contributed countless gag cartoons to the French publications *Ici-Paris* (where his first cartoon appeared), *Le Rire* and *Le Journal du Dimanche*, as well as to *Punch* in England and *Quick* in Germany.

When the satirical monthly *Hara-Kiri* was founded in 1960, Fred was among its first collaborators. There, in addition to his cartoons, he drew his first comic strips, *Les Petits Métiers* ("Odd Occupations"), *Tarsinge l'Homme Zan* ("Tarape the Zanman") and the poetic *Le Petit Cirque* ("The Little Circus").

In 1965 Fred went over to the weekly *Pilote*, where he created *Philémon*, a marvelously inventive fantasy strip, and contributed a number of full-page cartoons depicting topical subjects and contemporary situations. Fred is also a prolific scriptwriter and lyricist. The awards and distinctions he has received as a cartoonist are many and richly deserved. One of the most imaginative and wittiest cartoonists on the French scene today, Fred can be counted on to spring even more (felicitous) surprises on his readers in the future.

M.H.

ARMSTRONG, HAROLD BARRY (1902-   ) Australian cartoonist born in Paddington, near Sydney, in March 1902.

It was not without considerable anguish that some Australian newspapers finally adopted comic strips and cartoons in their pages. But during the mid-1930s a gradual increase in strips and cartoons, along with the introduction of political cartoonists, resulted in every metropolitan newspaper competing for circulation with these novel features.

Of the sedate newspapers, the *Argus*, one of Melbourne's oldest (founded in 1846), was published every

"Tell that to the Marines."

H.B. "Mick" Armstrong. © The Argus.

morning for 90 years before it accepted its first and only political cartoonist—Harold Barry ("Mick") Armstrong. "I was not so much appointed," Armstrong has said, "as insinuated into the *Argus*, where my cartoons were mixed in and buried among photo-pictures."

Harold Barry Armstrong—Mick is a family nickname—was the son of a teacher at Sydney High School, who later was the first headmaster of Wagga High School, which Mick Armstrong attended. He completed his education at Orange High School in New South Wales. Mick Armstrong's first published contribution in the *Bulletin* was drawn when he was a 16-year-old high school student. When he left school he worked in Orange as a survey-draftsman with the New South Wales Lands Department for nine years, continuing to submit his self-taught drawings to *Smith's Weekly*, the *Bulletin*, *Aussie* (a wartime soldier-produced magazine which went into civilian life in the 1920s) and other publications, steadily building a reputation as a cartoonist.

In 1931, cartoonist Tom Glover of the Sydney *Sun* recommended Armstrong as his stand-in while he was on holiday. In 1932, Armstrong joined the Melbourne *Herald* at a wage of £17 ($34) a week, a princely sum for those times. He turned out illustrations, political cartoons on the leader page, and for about a month in 1934 drew the *Ben Bowyang* comic strip—a feature still running in the *Herald* since its introduction more than 40 years ago. He was offered a position as a political cartoonist with the *Star* evening newspaper in 1935, but after its failure he was placed on the *Argus* staff in 1936 (the *Argus* had owned the *Star*).

It was at the *Argus* that Armstrong's flair and potential proved him a top-class political cartoonist. His cartoons appeared prominently featured on the leader page in the

Let's laugh a bit.

Othon Aristides ("Fred"). © Aristides.

"Have you read any good books lately?"

Peter Arno. © The New Yorker.

late 1930s, through the war years and up until the *Argus* ceased publication in 1957. Not surprisingly, most of Mick Armstrong's best work was produced during World War II. He was a "grand-manner" cartoonist, making much use of labeled, symbolic figures such as "Peace," "Prosperity," or "The Spirit of Anzac."

One of his wartime cartoons was reproduced on 25,000 flags and sold during an army march through the Melbourne streets—and the original drawing, titled "I've Got a Date," showing a determined Australian "Digger" thumbing at a picture of Hitler, was auctioned and sold for £115 ($230). Mick Armstrong's cartoons enjoyed enormous popularity during the war years and later; he could with satisfaction swell his clippings book with examples of his work published in overseas newspapers and journals.

For the interested collector, Armstrong had ten books of his cartoons published: *Cartoon Cavalcade* (the *Star* cartoons, 1935), *Cartoon Cavalcade No. 2* (1936) and the wartime volumes *Havoc, Mein Kranks, Army Stoo, Blitzy, Stag at Bay, Taxi!, War Without Tears,* and *Civvy Symphony.* Today Armstrong produces cartoon strips and features for various house journals and illustrates educational books for children.

V.L.

ARNO, PETER (1904-1968) American cartoonist and writer born Curtis Arnoux Peters in Rye, New York, on January 8, 1904. Peter Arno was the son of a prominent family whose head was at the time a justice of the state supreme court. Raised as the typical scion of aristocratic lineage, he attended Hotchkiss Preparatory School and then went on to Yale. Despite his upbringing, it soon became apparent to the young man that his destiny lay in the field of show business. He played the banjo and piano and was part of a band at Yale. It only seemed natural to him that he make use of these talents in a professional way, so he dropped out of school in 1923, organized a band (which for a time featured a young vocalist named Rudy Vallee) and set off for New York City—a world of smoky speakeasies, hot jazz and even hotter flappers. About this time he

changed his name to Peter Arno (allegedly to avoid embarrassing his family with the somewhat outré career he had chosen) and plunged into the life of a Jazz Age bohemian.

Tall, urbane and handsome, Arno was the very image of the aristocratic Fitzgerald hero fascinated by the underworld. Unlike Fitzgerald's characters, however, Arno was not destroyed by his fascination but instead used it (and his frequent annoyance with the New York demimonde) as material for his cartoons. Thus, for 43 years he mixed his visions of life—high and low—with color and vigor and spread them out on the pages of the *New Yorker*, to which he'd sold his first drawing in 1925, thereby launching a wholly unlooked-for career.

Arno had no formal training in art, but his inspirations were of the noblest sort—Rouault and Daumier, with strong elements of Picasso-Braque postimpressionism—and he was a disciplined craftsman, gay-blade image notwithstanding. He worked from idea to cartoon by first making some rough sketches in an easy medium like charcoal or pencil and then taking five minutes to a half hour to concentrate his efforts on the principal figures—facial expressions, postures, etc. Backgrounds were filled in later, and the finished cartoon—generally a bold, broad-lined watercolor—was produced from this rough.

Arno was above all an urbanite (if Harold Ross's little old lady from Dubuque ever *had* looked at the *New Yorker*, Arno's work would have been as likely as anything to cause her to shake her head and cluck over wicked city ways). Crowded speakeasies, scantily clad flappers, exotic dancers, boors, fools and drunks were the elements of his work. Yet he always maintained that he was able to portray that environment so well because it made him angry to see so much energy and intelligence wasted in the pursuit of dubious pleasure. Whatever the inspiration, the product was certainly one for which there was a demand among *New Yorker* readers. Ten years after selling his first drawing to Ross for ten dollars, Arno was reputedly commanding a thousand dollars per cartoon.

Besides cartooning and illustration work, Arno maintained an interest in music, and he wrote and produced a number of reviews. He also served as a writer and screen consultant to Paramount Pictures. He wrote voluminously, contributing articles, fiction and newspaper feature material to a wide range of publications, including the *Saturday Evening Post, Harper's Bazaar, American Magazine, Cosmopolitan, London Opinion,* the *Tatler* and the *Bystander.* His art has been exhibited in New York, Paris and London. Arno died in New York City on February 22, 1968, after a long illness.

Books: *The Whoops Sisters* (1927); *Peter Arno's Parade* (1929); *Peter Arno's Hullabaloo* (1930); *Peter Arno's Circus* (1931); *Peter Arno's Favorites* (1932); *For Members Only* (1935); *Man in the Shower* (1945); *Sizzling Platter* (1949); and *Hell of a Way to Run a Railroad* (1957).

R.C.

ARNOLD, KARL (1883-1953) German cartoonist and painter born in Neustadt, near Coburg, Upper Franconia, on April 1, 1883. The son of a democratic member of Parliament, Karl Arnold long preserved his liberal views in life and art, although circumstances forced him into the directorship of the Munich satirical magazine *Simplicissimus* between 1934 and 1936, when it was under the thumb of Hitler.

Arnold studied under Stuck and others at the Munich Academy, and in 1907 he began his long association with *Simplicissimus*. He also contributed to *Jugend* and *Lustige Blätter*, visited Paris in 1910, became a founding member in 1913 of the artistic group known as the New Munich Secession and, as a soldier in the German-occupied French city of Lille, illustrated the *Liller Kriegszeitung* ("Lille Wartime Newspaper") from 1914 to 1917. In 1917 he became a profit-sharing partner in *Simplicissimus*.

During the 1920s Arnold traveled to Berlin (many of his *Simplicissimus* cartoons of that period were submitted from there) and to several other European cities. In the course of his work for *Simplicissimus* his style shifted from strong dependence on shading and hatching to reliance on pure linear contours, and his model for this was obviously George Grosz. Arnold also extensively adopted Grosz's seamy subject matter of selfish bourgeois and disowned proletarians, especially in his Berlin reportage, but in Arnold everything is softened and relatively commercialized. As an observer of Munich, Arnold noted the antidemocratic leanings of the bulk of the population and warned against Nazism from its inception.

Other publications for which Arnold worked were the Zurich humor magazine *Nebelspalter* and the Copenhagen *Aftenbladet*. He was also known as an illustrator of books; an edition of the works of meistersinger Hans Sachs with Arnold's drawings was especially successful. Late in his life he published an album called *Der Mensch Ist Gut–Aber die Leut San a Gsindl* ("Man Is Good—But People Are a Bunch of Crooks"). During the 1940s Arnold's health failed him, and he had less and less to do with the operation of *Simplicissimus*. He died in Munich on November 29, 1953.

S.A.

ARTIS GENER, AVELÍ (1912-) Spanish cartoonist born in Barcelona, Spain, in 1912. Avelí Artis (better known under the pseudonym "Tisner") studied art at the Fine Arts School in Barcelona. His first drawings were published in the early 1930s in the satirical weeklies *L'Esquella de la Torratxa* and *Papitu*. From August 1933 to July 1936 he published cartoons in the *Bé Negre*, the most politically radical magazine of the time. Prior to the Spanish civil war, Artis had cartoons running regularly in such newspapers and publications as *Diari Mercantil*, *L'Opinió*, *La Publicitat* and *La Rambla*. During the war, together with other cartoonists and writers, he managed to keep *L'Esquella de la Torratxa* going. At the same time he drew cartoons for the lesser-known magazines *Gracia-Ramblas* and *Merida*.

At the end of the civil war in 1939, Artis was interned in a concentration camp in France, from which he escaped to Mexico. There he worked for several magazines published for exiled Catalans, the most important being *La Nostra Revista*. During that time he also wrote a novel, *556 Brigada Mixta*, dealing with the civil war. In 1965 Artis returned to Barcelona, and he is currently publishing a daily cartoon in the newspaper *Tele/Express*. In 1972 he won the Catalan literary contest of San Jordi.

As a cartoonist, Tisner (as he still signs his work) uses a bitter, clear and politically radical humor. His style is more modern and abstract than that of other cartoonists of his generation. He characteristically uses people to

Citizens of Munich discuss Hitler's propaganda.

Karl Arnold, 1922. © *Simplicissimus.*

symbolize such things as nations, freedom or tyranny, much as the cartoonists of the 19th century did.

J.M.

ARTUR, J.
See Bevilacqua, José Artur.

ART YOUNG'S INFERNO
See Hell.

ARU MACHIKADO NO MONOGATARI (Japan) *Aru Machikado no Monogatari* ("Story of a Certain Street Corner") was the first animated film production of the legendary but now defunct Mushi Productions; it was released in November 1962. One year and 12 million yen (approximately $34,000) were required to make this full-color 38-minute film, but today it represents something of a classic in Japanese animation.

Produced by Osamu Tezuka with a small staff, *Aru Machikado no Monogatari* was an experiment in creating quality animation without following the usual Disney formula of using prodigious amounts of money and personnel (which were unavailable anyway). The result is a uniquely lyrical work that has been characterized by some as antiwar, but which Tezuka prefers to describe as representing the vitality of life. Like Disney's *Fantasia*, it is entirely set to music, and it has received several awards.

As the title implies, the setting is a street in a city of an unspecified nation. The film opens on an autumn afternoon, and the details of the peaceful street—a balloon seller, a little girl and her teddy bear, a group of house mice—are all charmingly depicted. The focus then shifts to a wall of posters, the pictures on which are themselves animated in time to the music: a young violinist plays to a ballerina. Suddenly, however, the world changes. The posters are torn from the wall and replaced with those of a dictator; war comes, and the town is destroyed. Nonetheless, in the end spring arrives, and life emerges triumphant from the ashes—a favorite theme of Tezuka's.

Aru Machikado no Monogatari is a work of universal appeal that, by emphasizing music and images, transcends both time and culture. Tatsuo Takai was in charge of the music, and he used the entire Tokyo Philharmonic Orchestra.

F.S.

"Aru Machikado no Monogatari." © Mushi Productions.

ASMUSSEN, ANDREAS (1913-) Danish cartoonist born in Ordrup, Denmark, in 1913. Andreas ("Des") Asmussen was born into an academic, artistic environment. His brother Johan is a well-known lawyer; his youngest brother is the world-famous jazz violinist Svend Asmussen. A cartoonist and illustrator, Des made a name for himself, as did so many other illustrators in the 1930s, in *Magasinet*, a supplement to the daily *Politiken*. He got his great following during the German occupation, when the need for artists to express themselves freely in words and pictures was greater than ever before—or since. Lack of fuel literally made people move closer together—and gave the cartoonists an opportunity to illustrate this intimacy. Blackouts during the occupation (1940-45)—and what might follow—were also excellent topics on which to base cartoons. The underground magazine *Muldvarpen* ("The Mole") nourished talents which were given freer rein than in the "legal" political yearly booklets. And Des's line drawings got an extra dimension when used satirically.

As an illustrator of short stories in Danish weekly magazines (*Hjemmet* and *Søndags B.T.*) and of book covers, Asmussen gradually became internationally known, and he has made remarkable contributions to, among others, the *Saturday Evening Post*, where his artistic drawing style, far closer to the French than to the true Danish tradition, resembles character humor.

Among the batch of young talents who blossomed in the Danish humor magazine *Hudibras*, Des Asmussen is without a doubt the most aesthetic. To him the drawing is more important in a cartoon than merely providing a pretty illustration to a good gag. The joy of drawing always shines through and has placed him today in the elite of acknowledged illustrators—from the lightest humorous novels (his *Woodhouse* book covers are unsurpassed) to anniversary booklets for top banks and public institutions.

J.S.

ASTÉRIX (France) In 1959 René Goscinny (writer) and Albert Uderzo (artist) created *Astérix*, a comic strip depicting the exploits of a feisty little Gaul able to hold Julius Caesar's legions at bay virtually singlehanded. The strip became an international success, and it was inevitable that it should be transposed into the animated cartoon medium.

In 1967 Belvision produced *Astérix le Gaulois* ("Astérix the Gaul"). The feature had been intended for television but was released theatrically at the last minute. The animation, done by Nic Broca, André Paape and Henri Verbeeck among others, was crude, and the story was clumsily adapted from the original. This was followed in 1970 by the far more successful *Astérix et Cléopâtre*, which was animated with more verve and spirit than the first film. In 1973 Dargaud, publisher of the *Astérix* comic strips, broke with Belvision. A new animation studio, Idéfix, was formed under the direction of Henri Gruel and Pierre Watrin, and it released a third *Astérix* feature in 1975, *Les Douze Travaux d'Astérix* ("The Twelve Labors of Astérix"). This was not an adaptation, but the development of an original story by Goscinny and Uderzo. The result, however, proved disappointing.

Having been produced under the overall supervision of the creators, the *Astérix* cartoons remained faithful to the original concept. They were, on the whole, entertaining, although they contributed little to the art of animation.

M.H.

ATAMANOV, LEV KONSTANTINOVICH (1905-) Soviet animator and producer born in Moscow, Russia, on February 21, 1905. Lev Atamanov graduated from the First State School of Cinematography in 1926. One of the pioneers of Soviet cartoon animation, he worked first in Armenia, where he directed the early sound cartoon *Crossroads* (1931) and produced *The Dog and the Cat* (1938) and *The Magic Carpet* (1948), two features combining strong elements of regional folklore with a style almost slavishly derived from Disney's.

In 1949 Atamanov was appointed head of the All-Union Animated Cartoon Film Studios; as such, he has been the man most responsible for the sorry state of modern Soviet animation. While some of his productions, such as *The Yellow Stork* (1950), *The Golden Antelope* (1954), *Dog and Cat* (second version, 1955),

"Astérix." © *Dargaud.*

The Snow Queen (1957) and The Bench (1968), have been fairly well-crafted features and have won some prizes, it can be said that most of the Soviet output still lags far behind in style, imagination and inventiveness, and has quite a way to go before matching the brilliant achievements in such Eastern European countries as Yugoslavia, Czechoslovakia and Poland.

M.H.

ATTALO
See Colizzi, Gioacchino.

ATTILIO
See Mussino, Attilio.

ATTWELL, MABEL LUCIE (1879-1964) British cartoonist and illustrator born in London, England, on June 4, 1879. Creator of the most cuddly, lovable little children in picture books, postcards, dolls, toys, advertising and comic strip art, Mabel Lucie Attwell is still a household name in the United Kingdom. The continuing stream of books featuring Attwell's familiar style of full-color pictorial stories is, in fact, continued under her name by her daughter, Peggy, for her original publisher, Dean.

Mabel Lucie Attwell was educated at Cooper's Company School, then studied painting and drawing at the Regent Street Art School and Heatherley's Art School, London. Her first folio of watercolor sketches of fairies, babies and animals was left with an unenthusiastic art agency but sold almost immediately. The teenage artist struck a chord with the sentimental Victorians, and she never had to look for work again. Her chubby kiddies appeared in magazines for both children and adults, on many series of picture postcards, nursery china and pottery, textiles, handkerchiefs, toys and almost every kind of merchandise.

A few regular characters emerged from the multitude—Diddums, who became a best-selling doll; the Boo-Boos, charming little baby gnomes; and others. She also illustrated many editions of popular children's books—Charles Kingsley's *Water Babies*, Hans Christian Andersen's *Fairy Tales*, Grimm's *Fairy Tales*, *Peter Pan*—and executed many posters, including one of the first for London's Underground Railway. She summed up her style: "I see the child in the adult and then I draw the adult as a child." Attwell died in Cornwall on November 13, 1964.

Books: *Peeping Pansy* (1919); *Peter Pan and Wendy* (1921); *The Boo-Boos* (1921); *Lucie Attwell's Alice in Wonderland* (1922); *Lucie Attwell's Annual* (1922-57); *Rainy Day Tales* (1931); *Quiet Time Tales* (1932); *Rockabye Tales* (1931); *Great Big Midget Book* (1934); and innumerable others.

D.G.

ATTWOOD, FRANCIS GILBERT (1856-1900) American artist born in Jamaica Plain, Massachusetts, on September 29, 1856. Francis Attwood enrolled at Harvard with the class of 1878 and, although he left without a degree after three years, contributed more to the school than many others with sheepskins. He founded—with E.S. Martin, John T. Wheelwright, Edmund M. Wheelwright and Frederick J. Stimson (J.S. of Dale)—the *Harvard Lampoon* and was its chief artist for years, even after he was no longer a student. While on the *Lampoon* staff, he was responsible for two satirical series that were later published in book form and achieved wide notice: *Rollo's Journey to Cambridge* and *Manners and Customs of Ye Harvard Student*. At Harvard he was the official artist of the Hasty Pudding Club.

Even when he drew professionally, Attwood took art instruction, in the late 1870s and early 1880s, under Dr. William Rimmer and at the Boston Art Museum school. In 1883 he joined other Harvard alumni in establishing a grown-up *Lampoon*: *Life* magazine, the first issue of which contained Attwood's work. Here he was a mainstay until his death, and his work was an integral part of the magazine's character. In January 1887 he began his monthly page of drawings that summarized current

Lev Atamanov, "Dog and Cat."

events—a feature that remained, in the hands of Frederick T. Richards and later Charles Sykes, into the 1920s. Attwood also became a busy book illustrator and contributed cartoons, illustrations and decorations to the pages of the early *Cosmopolitan* magazine.

Attwood drew elaborate, almost miniature-style cartoons in a wispy but confident manner. In his *Life* years his anatomy was sound, and he employed a unique form of toning and crosshatching; his focal figures received delicate, dark shading for emphasis. He died at his birthplace on April 30, 1900.

R.M.

AUERBACH-LEVY, WILLIAM (1889-1964) American caricaturist, painter, etcher and author born William Auerbach in Brest-Litovsk, Russia, in 1889. His parents adopted the surname Levy after they emigrated to the United States when he was five.

His artistic ability was recognized by a teacher in the elementary school he attended in New York City's Lower East Side, an urban ghetto for many recent immigrants of the period. With the teacher's help William Auerbach-Levy was enrolled at the youthful age of 11 in the National Academy of Design. During high school he was

Alliance Art School. By the time he was 25, his caricatures had earned him fame, and his career was established. A prize-winning painter and etcher, Auerbach-Levy received a Guggenheim Fellowship in 1929 for one of his paintings. His work was traditional in style, as he thought modern art had little merit.

His caricatures appeared in numerous publications including the *New Yorker, Collier's, Theatre Arts, Vogue, Vanity Fair, McCall's,* and *Ladies' Home Journal.* Originally he drew for the old *New York World,* but after the demise of that newspaper he was closely associated with the drama page of the *New York Post* and the *Brooklyn Eagle.* In 1948, assisted by his wife, Florence Von Wien, he summed up his career in *Is That Me? A Book About Caricature.* The book is a classic on the subject and contains sections about his career, along with a brief history of caricature and instructions on how to draw caricatures. A reviewer noted that William Auerbach-Levy had, with caricature, "the same indisputable authority as Freud on sex, Tilden on tennis, or Fanny Farmer on cookery."

"It's the first quick impression that counts," said William Auerbach-Levy. He cautioned students, "Good draughtsmanship is indispensable. . . . Caricature is an art of simple line, so faults in drawing are not easily

Tony Auth. © The Philadelphia Inquirer, The Washington Post Writers Group.

noted as much for his checkers playing as his art. At age 15 he won the citywide public school checkers championship. In later years he was a regular among checkers players at the outdoor tables in Washington Square Park in Greenwich Village, where he lived most of his life.

Following graduation from City College in New York, he won an art scholarship to Paris. Upon his return to New York he joined the faculty of the National Academy's School of Fine Arts and the Educational

concealed." His own style was a masterpiece of the economical use of line, resulting in drawings with power and dignity. He emphasized the need for drawing for the specific type of reproduction used in a publication. For newspaper reproduction he recommended "pure black line or solid black tone" with some use of benday dot patterns for shading. Thousands of William Auerbach-Levy caricatures were published over his long and prolific career: not only famous people in the theater, but

"Un Autre Monde."

in the fields of literature, sports, politics, and finance.

He died of a heart attack at age 75 on June 30, 1964, in Ossining, New York.

B.C.

AUTH, TONY (1942-   ) American cartoonist born in Akron, Ohio, on May 7, 1942. Tony Auth moved to California with his family in 1949. He was raised in Los Angeles and majored in biological illustration at UCLA, graduating in 1965. While in college, Auth contributed to campus publications, and even after graduation he drew for the campus *Daily Bruin;* his cartoons were syndicated by Sawyer Press. He was the chief medical illustrator at Rancho-Los Amigos Hospital from 1965 to 1971, when he became editorial cartoonist for the *Philadelphia Inquirer.*

Auth's handsome style is one of understatement and economy of line. He presents his powerful concepts in a horizontal format and shades with mechanical tones. In 1975 he received a Pulitzer Prize and a Sigma Delta Chi award, and he won the Overseas Press Club award in 1975 and 1976. Auth is syndicated by the Washington Post Writers' Group.

R.M.

AUTRE MONDE, UN (France) Grandville's *Un Autre Monde* ("Another World") came out in 36 installments published in the course of the year 1844. Unlike other books illustrated by Grandville, *Un Autre Monde* used already existing cartoons for which the prolific writer Taxile Delord provided an improvised narrative.

Un Autre Monde probably represents the epitome of Grandville's cartoon work. As Stanley Appelbaum says in his introduction to *Bizarreries and Fantasies of Grandville* (New York, 1974), "*Un Autre Monde* is the work in which Grandville's oneiric leanings re-

ceive fullest expression (leading to his adoption by the Surrealists as one of their multitude of spiritual progenitors and giving psychoanalytically minded art critics a field day)." Indeed, there is a host of disturbing and even frightening images in this work: demons cavorting under a full moon, animals disguising themselves as human beings, threatening objects and strange excrescences coming out of the earth; but there is also a multitude of finely observed social and psychological details, from the anglomania of the upper classes to the general passion for carnivals and merry-go-rounds. The attitudes, the institutions, the morals and the passions of the reign of Louis-Philippe are depicted with an unfaltering pen and a somewhat jaundiced eye.

Un Autre Monde ranks high in Grandville's canon. Its concerns and visions are probably closer to our own time than to the mid-19th century. Drawings from *Un Autre Monde* have been used over and over again in publications throughout the world, cumulatively contributing to the posthumous fame and mythical reputation of their author.

M.H.

AVERY, FREDERICK BEAN (1908-   ) American animator born in Taylor, Texas, on February 26, 1908. Frederick Bean ("Tex") Avery, a distant relative of the notorious Judge Roy Bean, "the law west of the Pecos," went to North Dallas High School and graduated in 1927. After a summer course at the Chicago Art Institute and several unsuccessful attempts at creating a newspaper strip, Avery moved to California in 1929. The following year he joined Walter Lantz's animation studio as an in-betweener and later was promoted to full animator status. (Some of the cartoons he worked on during this period include

F.B. ("Tex") Avery, "Who Killed Who?" © MGM.

Ham and Eggs, Elmer the Great Dane and *Towne Hall Follies.*)

In 1935 Avery moved over to the Warner Brothers studio. During his stay at Warners he directed a number of *Porky Pig* cartoons ("Picador Porky," "Porky the Wrestler," and especially "Porky's Duck Hunt," in which the character of Daffy Duck first appeared, are among the more notable). He was also the artist most responsible for the definitive characterization of Bugs Bunny in the 1940 "A Wild Hare." Other notable Avery-Warners cartoons include *The Penguin Parade* (1938), *Thugs with Dirty Mugs* (1939) and *Cross Country Detours* (1940).

Tex Avery's most creative period came after he had moved over to MGM in 1942. The first cartoon he directed at his new studio was *The Blitz Wolf*, a retelling of the "Three Little Pigs" fable in the context of the Allied fight against Hitler (who appears as the Big Bad Wolf). This was followed by the creation of Avery's most lovable character, Droopy the Dog, who made his first appearance in the 1943 "Dumb-Hounded." Droopy proved more popular than such other Avery characters as Screwy Squirrel, and the two bears, George and Junior.

Avery's fame rests primarily on a number of cartoons which depend less on characterization than on inexhaustible gag building and frenetic action. These include *Who Killed Who?* and *Red Hot Riding Hood* (both 1943), *Bad Luck Blackie* (1949) and, above all, *King-Size Canary*, a 1947 cartoon involving a cat, a mouse, a dog and a canary grown to giant size, which is widely regarded as Avery's masterpiece.

In 1954 Avery left MGM for a short stint back at Lantz (where he directed four cartoons). He has been directing and producing advertising cartoons (including, ironically, the Bugs Bunny Kool-Aid commercials) for Cascade Studios ever since 1955. Looking back on his career in the course of a 1971 interview, he declared, "I do miss the theatricals, but I'd never go back to them."

Tex Avery has been hailed as one of the most gifted and imaginative of American cartoon directors. He has been called "a Walt Disney who has read Kafka" by some critics and blasted for the violence of his cartoons by others. Walter Lantz once admiringly stated, "The thing about Avery is that he can write a cartoon, lay it out, time it, do the whole thing himself." No Avery cartoon ever received an Oscar (an oversight for which the Academy has been castigated time and again), although several of his films were nominated. Avery has been honored at a number of international film festivals, and in 1974 he received the Annie Award for Best Cartoonist from ASIFA.

A book-length study of Avery's career, Joe Adamson's *Tex Avery: King of Cartoons*, was published in 1975 by Popular Library.

M.H.

AZIMZADE, AZIM ASLAN OGLY (1880-1943) Soviet cartoonist born in Novkhany, near Baku, in Azerbaijan, Russia, on May 7, 1880. The son of a village craftsman, Azim Azimzade had no formal art education, but he exhibited a flair for cartooning and caricature at an early age. His first cartoons, about local politics and everyday incidents, were published in such humor magazines as *Molla Nasreddin* and *Mazali*. (According to Azimzade's biographer, M. Nadzhofov, this marked the beginning of Azerbaijani graphic humor and satire.)

In 1914 Azimzade illustrated a collection of satirical poems by A. Sabri (one of the founders of *Molla Nasreddin*) entitled *Khop-Khopname*, and this spread his reputation beyond the borders of Azerbaijan. After the Russian Revolution, Azimzade contributed a great many illustrations to books and magazines, at the same time continuing to draw cartoons. His most notable works are: *Characters of Old Baku* (1937); *Ramazan Among the Poor* and *Ramazan Among the Rich* (both 1938); and the savagely satirical *The Fuehrer's Trophies* (1941) and *The Crow in Peacock Plumage* (1942).

A member of the Communist Party of the Soviet Union since 1923, Azimzade has received many honors and distinctions from the Soviet regime, including the title People's Artist of the Azerbaijani Soviet Socialist Republic (1927). He died in Baku on June 15, 1943.

M.H.

Color in Cartoons
Plates 1-21

(Plates 22-39 follow page 222.)

Color in Cartoons

Although the print cartoon is generally considered a pen-and-ink medium (as it largely is), color has also played a role in its development. The plates of 18th-century cartoonists were hand-colored, often by the artists themselves; in the 19th century chromolithography became the vogue. Modern-day printing and reproducing methods make it easier than ever to publish color cartoons. Color, though not unimportant, is not essential: it can enhance a composition or bring out some telling detail, and of course it adds to our aesthetic enjoyment; but it seldom contributes to the main point of the cartoon, which is one of the reasons it is so rarely used in editorial cartoons.

In animated cartoons, on the other hand, color adds immeasurably to the basic appeal of movement. As in print cartoons, color in the early animation films was done by hand, painted on the cels; only in the 1930s was a color film stock of sufficient reliability and fidelity perfected. Since then, color in animation has come into widespread use: color sets the scene, etches the characters in sharper detail, and rhythmically accompanies the action. Without color the animated cartoon would lose some of its attributes of fantasy and poetry. Indeed, present-day animation is the product of its three basic elements: motion, form and color.

The illustrations in this section have been selected on the basis of representativeness, as well as on purely aesthetic grounds.

1. "Alan Ford". ©Editoriale Corno. The Italian comic strip "Alan Ford" was adapted for television in 1977, and again in 1978, in a series of cartoons executed by Paolo Piffarerio, under the direction of Guido De Maria. So successful were these adaptations that they spawned a collection of 280 trading cards reproducing frames from the cartoons. Here are a few of these cards.

2. Karl Arnold. ©Simplicissimus. Arnold began his long association with "Simplicissimus" in 1907. In the course of his work for the magazine, his style shifted from strong dependence on shading and hatching to reliance on pure linear contours, as in this example dating from 1925. Arnold was also a keen observer of Munich life and of its smug bourgeoisie.

3. Lev Atamanov, "The Golden Antelope." Atamanov is one of the pioneers of Soviet animation. In 1949 he was appointed head of the All-Union Cartoon Film Studios in Moscow, and as such he has been the man most responsible for the current state of Soviet animation. "The Golden Antelope" (1954) is one of Atamanov's best efforts, and a fairly well-crafted feature.

4. Anselmo Ballester, "Rita Hayworth as Gilda." ©Columbia Pictures. Ballester's drawings are not just figures on publicity posters but are really portraits, barely caricatured and charged with evocative expression. This poster, representing a scene from "Gilda," is one of the artist's most famous interpretations.

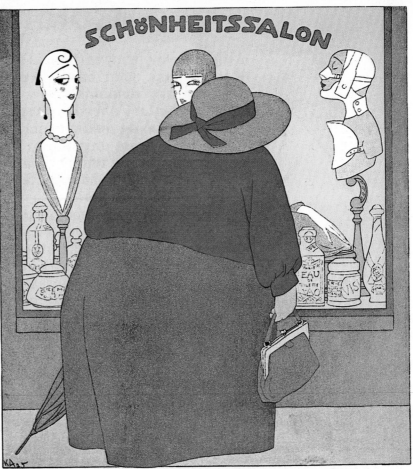

2   How Can I Stay Young and Beautiful? "We women are spared nothing!"

4

Some of the Reasons Why Money Is Scarce in the United States

This is the average foreigner's idea of a typical street-scene in Paris, ——

and in London,

and in Amsterdam, ——

and in Madrid, ——

and in New York, ——

whereas, as a matter of fact, a typical street-scene in any one of them is very much like this.

5. Frank Beard, cartoon for "Judge." Beard was one of the most prolific cartoonists working for American humor magazines during the second half of the 19th century. For "Judge" he drew some very striking, handsome and sophisticated lithographic cartoons, of which this is one.

6. "Believe It or Not!" ©King Features Syndicate. Originally started as a sports feature by Robert Ripley in 1918, "Believe It or Not!" was soon venturing as far afield as geology, history, botany and numismatics. The first feature of its kind, "Believe It or Not!" has enjoyed tremendous popularity for over half a century, presenting "facts" that dwell heavily on the bizarre, the absurd, the incredible and the outlandish.

7. C.K. Bird ("Fougasse"). ©Fougasse. Fougasse, as he signed himself, evolved one of the most individual and recognizable styles in England. His handwritten lettering, as exemplified in this multi-panel cartoon of the 1930s, also became extremely well known.

10

8. Milan Blažeković, "Gorilla Dance." ©Zagreb Film. One of
the most famous practitioners of the fabled "Zagreb school"
of animation, Blažeković taught himself cartooning. He
directed some of the wittiest of the Zagreb cartoons, of which
"Gorilla Dance" is probably the best known.

9. Valentina and Zenayeda Brumberg, "Fedya Zaytsev." A
sister team of Soviet animators, the Brumbergs have been
among the most prolific film cartoonists in the Soviet Union.
They have often dealt with fairy tales and other material
directed at children. "Fedya Zaytsev" is one of their most
enchanting features, and it has received many awards in the
Soviet Union and in the West.

10. Bugs Bunny and his cartoon companions, as drawn by
Chuck Jones. ©Warner Brothers. The nonchalant rabbit with
the Brooklyn accent is one of the most celebrated creations in
animated cartoons. Along with his stablemates, Daffy Duck,
Porky Pig and others, he was the protagonist of some of the
fastest and wittiest cartoons ever produced by an American
studio.

The Photographer: ''Now—SMILE!''

11. E. Simms Campbell, ''Cuties.'' ©King Features Syndicate. Campbell specialized in drawings of beautiful women. In the panel ''Cuties,'' which he drew from 1943 to the time of his death in 1971, the gag was secondary to the depiction of the gorgeous creatures promised by the title. Color greatly added to the appeal of Campbell's basic premise.

12. Miguel Covarrubias, caricature of Mussolini, 1928. ©Life. The style of Covarrubias's caricatures was very distinct. He used a geometric and sculptural line to define the mass and features of his subjects. For all their stylization, however, his heavy renderings were full of vigor and enthusiasm. Covarrubias's most important work was done in the United States in the 1920s and 1930s.

13   Something in a Name. Mr. Horse-fly: "Hang it all! Just 'cause my name is Horse-fly that fool poet insists on using me as a horse."

13. Gus Dirks, drawing for "Judge." In his cartoons Dirks dealt exclusively with insect and small animal life; he was a leader in that very popular turn-of-the-century genre. He utilized confident pen strokes and achieved shading effects with short lines combining to give his cartoons texture and pattern.

14. "Donald Duck." ©Walt Disney Productions. Created in 1934, Donald rapidly rose to unprecedented heights of popularity and was soon eclipsing Mickey Mouse as the star of the Walt Disney studios. His character—cantankerous, ornery and irascible—was established from the first and was further developed in scores of movie cartoons from the 1930s to the 1950s.

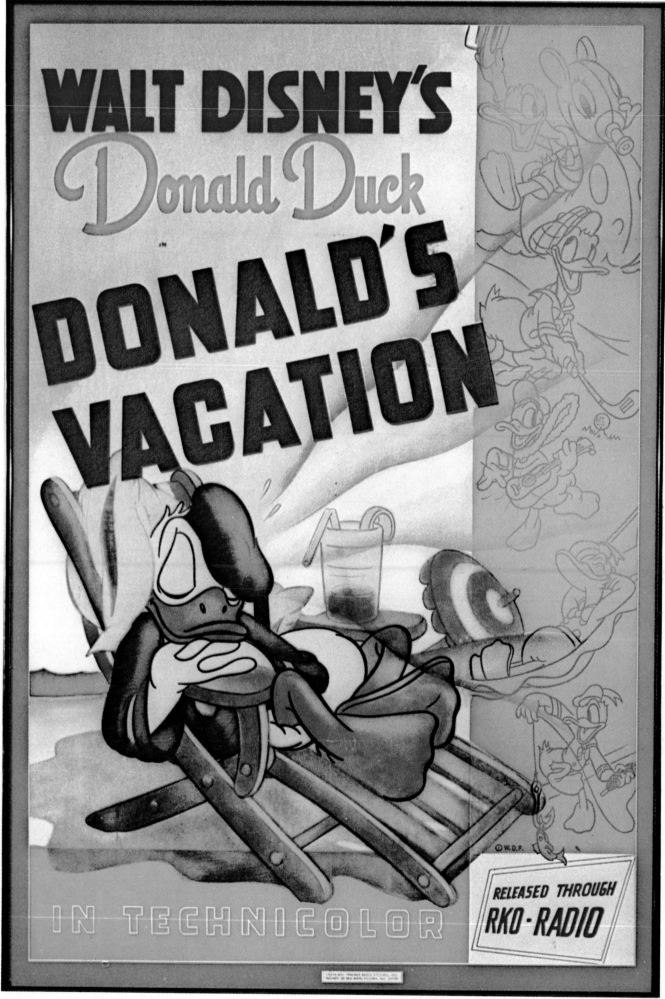

WHAT IS AN "ARYAN"?
HE IS HANDSOME
AS GOEBBELS

15. *Boris Efimov, World War II poster. Efimov is one of the most popular cartoonists in the USSR, as well as one of the most mordant. His popularity reached its peak during World War II; he is best noted for his savage depictions of the Nazi leaders, especially Josef Goebbels, whom he never tired of lampooning.*

16. *Abel Faivre, cartoon for "L'Assiette au Beurre." Faivre, a son and brother of physicians, liked to draw biting cartoons satirizing doctors. The most famous of these were executed for a special issue of "L'Assiette au Beurre" (1902) in which Faivre gave free rein to his sardonic humor.*

17. *"Fantasia." ©Walt Disney Productions. "Fantasia," a full-length animated feature, is considered by most critics to be Disney's single most stunning achievement. Intended as a marriage between animation and the musical arts, the film is a forceful and masterly statement blending music, rhythm, movement and color in one cohesive work.*

16

17

James Montgomery Flagg

18. James Montgomery Flagg, caricature of Theodore Roosevelt. Although Flagg gained his greatest notability as a poster artist, he had earlier made his mark as a distinguished and forceful cartoonist for "Judge" and "Life." Flagg displayed an overwhelming sincerity in his work and had a flair for showmanship.

19. "Fluffy Ruffles." Wallace Morgan's "Fluffy Ruffles" was a verse-captioned, multi-panel Sunday page about a woman so stunningly beautiful that she proved too disconcerting to susceptible males to hold a job. It began in 1907. Fluffy Ruffles was so winningly drawn, and her outfits so stylish, that she was accepted from coast to coast as a weekly symbol of what young American womanhood should emulate.

20. Peter Foldes, "Je, Tu, Elles." ©ORTF. Peter Foldes was one of the most fascinating of modern animators. His works have received the highest praise and have been just as vehemently criticized. This is a frame from "Je, Tu, Elles," one of his last works, which blended animation and live action.

21. Jean-Louis Forain, painting. Forain's cartoons were drawn in a caustic and even cruel style that earned him the nickname "Juvenal of the pencil." He was also a talented painter who, in 1879 and 1880, exhibited some of his canvases alongside those of the Impressionists, many of whom admired his work.

20

21   Artists and Model

Bb

BABA, NOBORU (1927-   ) Japanese cartoonist, comic book artist and children's book illustrator born in Sannohe, Aomori Prefecture, Japan, in 1927. After graduating from junior high school, Noboru Baba was caught up in the wartime draft and served in the Imperial Navy Air Corps. When peace finally came, he tried his hand at pioneer farming in mountainous Iwate Prefecture, but gave up after a year and returned to his home, where he worked as a substitute teacher. At the same time he began studying art. On the side, Baba drew signs and posters for theaters, and in 1948 he worked as an artist for a U.S. military base near Hachinohe. In addition to drawing posters, he began experimenting with cartoons, and in 1949, at the urging of children's book expert Shigeru Shiraki, he left for Tokyo to seek his fortune.

Baba began his cartoon career drawing for educational magazines put out by Shogakkan for children, and he received considerable attention with works such as *Posto Kun* ("Young Post") and *Yama Kara Kita Kappa* ("Kappa from the Mountains"). In 1956 his *Būtan*, which ran in *Yoni Bukku* ("Children's Book") from 1954 to 1957, won him the first Shogakkan award for children's cartoons. Būtan was a cute little piglet who was always involved in a variety of adventures, but it was his mild-mannered misfit character that accounted for his appeal among children. Most of Baba's works at this time featured animals as main characters.

In 1958 Baba joined the Manga Shudan (Cartoonists Group) and made a transition to adult comics, producing popular works such as *Chokkusen Bāsan* ("Straight Ahead Granny"), *Makkana Dorobo* ("Crimson Thief") and *Roku San Tengoku* ("Elementary and Junior High School Paradise"). Today, in addition to creating adult comics, Noboru Baba remains active in the illustration of children's books. His *Juippiki no Neko* ("Eleven Cats") is something of a classic and won him yet another award.

F.S.

BACH, FERDINAND-SIGISMOND (1859-1952) French cartoonist, watercolorist and lithographer born in Stuttgart, Germany, on August 15, 1859. Better known as Ferdinand Bac, he started his cartooning career in 1880 by contributing first to *La Caricature* and *La Vie Parisienne* and then to *Le Rire* and *Le Journal Amusant*.

Many of his fine, even elegant illustrations depicting the Parisian life of the 1880s and 1890s were published in albums, the better known being *Femmes Honnêtes!* ("Honest Women!," 1885), *La Femme Intime* ("Intimate Woman," 1894), *Le Triomphe de la Femme* ("The Triumph of Woman," 1899) and *Le Paradis Terrestre* ("Earthly Paradise," 1903). He illustrated his own books as well, among them *La Volupté Romaine* ("Roman Pleasures," 1922) and *Jardins Enchantés* ("Enchanted Gardens"), and wrote numerous books on history, travel, biography.

Ferdinand Bac died on November 18, 1952, in Compiègne, where he had lived in retirement since the late 1920s.

P.H.

Renate Bachem, fantasy drawing. © Bachem.

BACHEM, RENATE GABRIELE (1916-   ) German cartoonist, illustrator, painter, printmaker and designer born in Düsseldorf, Germany, on May 17, 1916. After studying with her father, a painter descended from a famous old Rhineland publishing family, Bele Bachem (as she is best known) attended the Arts and Crafts School at the Schlesischer Bahnhof in Berlin (1934-37). From 1937 to 1939 she drew for the women's magazines *Die Dame, Elegante Welt* and *Die Neue Linie* and did book illustrations. During the war her art was considered degenerate, and she was not permitted to exhibit or publish, although her important career as a stage designer began with a 1943 production. In the late 1940s, living in Munich (as she still does), she contributed drawings to the resuscitated *Simplicissimus* then being published.

Her first illustrated book of the postwar period, *Manege-Zauber* ("Circus Magic"), was published in 1954. The individual drawings in it, some in watercolor and some in pen, are separately dated between 1942 and 1947 and represent a broad span of years during which

Bachem's style approached full maturity. Already in evidence are the strong influence of Chagall, Klee, Grosz and the Surrealists (Bachem herself cites many more influences, from North Indian painting to Magnasco); the theatrical use of space, with "sets" and "props"; and the theme of odd, isolated people in out-of-the-way situations, epitomized by the nomadic circus performer. The people have the unsettling, wide-eyed stare that is practically a Bachem trademark. But the pen work is still more spiky and tentative than it later became.

In 1959 Bachem did the text as well as the pictures for *Magisches Taschentuch* ("Magical Handkerchief"), a cheerful disquisition on the use of handkerchiefs and related cloths through the ages. Because of the nature of the subject, most of the illustrations are cartoonlike versions of great works of art in many media from ancient times to the present. The renderings, which attest to her wide-ranging knowledge of art history, have all the winsomeness that generally characterizes her work, and the feminine-fashion subject suits her to a tee. The 1960 volume *Ausverkauf in Wind* ("Clearance Sale of Winds") contains original fantasy stories and her most intriguing pictures up to that time. In these surrealistic pen drawings there is real anguish and disquiet. The draftsmanship is skillful in the extreme, and it is clearly a matter of the artist's taste (and not a fault in technique) that even this fine book suffers from a tinge of greeting-card cuteness; the male figures are nearly as wasp-waisted and curvaceous as the female. This tendency is largely overcome in her later paintings.

The startlingly versatile Bachem has also done murals, calendar art, posters, textile and porcelain design, film animation and illustrations for the *Arabian Nights*, texts by Latin and Chinese authors, and other books. In the 1960s and 1970s painting and printmaking have occupied most of her time, and she has had numerous successful exhibitions in Germany and elsewhere in Europe.

S.A.

BAIRNSFATHER, BRUCE
See Old Bill.

BAKER, ALFRED ZANTZINGER (1870-1933) American cartoonist born in Baltimore, Maryland, on January 4, 1870. "Baker-Baker" (as he became known from his monogrammed signature of two *B*s back to back) was educated in private schools and studied art at the Charcoal School of Baltimore, the Académie Julian and the Ecole des Beaux-Arts in Paris.

Baker pursued serious art and was exhibited at age 23 in the National Academy (later exhibitions were sponsored by the Société des Artistes Français and the Salon des Artistes Humoristes), but he joined the staff of *Puck* in 1898. As a cartoonist he did not confine his work to one outlet, and at the turn of the century Baker was appearing frequently in the pages of *Puck, Judge, Life, Scribner's, Harper's, Century* and *St. Nicholas*. His books include *The Moving Picture Book* (1911), *The Moving Picture Glue Book* (1912) and *The Torn Book* (1913). His innovations—such as die-cutting and 3-D drawings with glasses—are surpassed in the children's book genre only by those of the imaginative Peter Newell.

A.Z. Baker stated that he was influenced by French and Japanese cartoons (indeed, he often worked Japanese motifs into his drawings), but whatever the influences, it must be recorded that his work was among the freshest and cleverest of American cartooning at the turn of the century—and retains these characteristics even under modern scrutiny. He rejected the fine-line illustrator's style then threatening to stifle freedom of line and rendered his cartoons—which were almost exclusively animal gags—with a lush brush line, shaded in crayon on a coarse board. He had a delightful and visually agreeable sense of design and anatomy; his funny animals romped with animation among the stolid society drawings in the magazines. In this sense he helped forge a new spirit of amiable looseness in American magazine cartooning and was soon in the company of such men as Art Young, Leighton Budd and Hy Mayer. He died in 1933.

R.M.

BAKER, JULIUS STAFFORD (1869-1961) British cartoonist born in Whitechapel, London, England, in 1869. Julius Stafford Baker, who created the most enduring characters in British comics, was the nephew of John Philip Stafford (1851-99), painter and cartoonist for *Funny Folks*, who taught the boy to draw and paint theatrical scenery. As a boy, Baker appeared on the music hall stage as "Vidocq, the Child Caricaturist." He began to freelance cartoons to the weekly comics and magazines quite early, and was perhaps the first British humorous artist to set out to follow the American cartoonists' style.

In 1891, he created Hooligan, an Irish laborer, and featured him in a weekly panel in *Funny Folks*. The "cod" Irish (or "Oirish") dialogue in the captions caught on with the public and made the character extremely popular. In 1897, he produced a similar series for the *Garland*, featuring Schneider, a funny German.

Baker was one of the first British cartoonists to sell his work in the United States, his cartoons of tramps appearing regularly in *Judge* from 1895 through 1899. For the weekly comic *Illustrated Chips* he created a large humorous panel called *Casey Court* (May 24, 1902), modeled on R.F. Outcault's *Yellow Kid* panels (see *The World Encyclopedia of Comics*, Chelsea House, 1976). This series ran to 1953. On April 16, 1904, the *Daily Mirror* ran its first strip, *Mrs. Hippo's Kindergarten*, in which Tiger Tim appeared. This character is now the oldest in British comics, and it is still running in *Jack and Jill*.

Baker transferred his character to the *Playbox*, a children's supplement to *The World and His Wife* (1904), *New Children's Encyclopedia* (1910), *Playbox Annual* (1912), and the weekly *Rainbow* (1914). Other cartoons he created included *Billy Smiff's Pirates* and *Buzzville*, two panels in *Puck* (1904); *Dr. Ding Dong* in *Woman's Life* (1904); *Swiss Family Robinson* in *Jester* (1904); *Stone Age Peeps* in *Chips* (1904); *Hans the Double Dutchman* in *Comic Home Journal* (1904); *Inventions of Pat* in *Nuggets* (1905); *Playtime at the Zoo* in *Sunday Circle* (1905); *Comic Cuts Colony* in *Comic Cuts* (1910); *Mrs. Jumbo's Junior Mixed* in *Southend Graphic* (1911); *Addums Academy* in *Merry and Bright* (1913); *Ragg's Rents* in *Merry and Bright* (1915); *Little Nigs of Tiny Town* in *Rainbow* (1915); *Prehistoric Pranks* in *Funny Wonder* (1919); *Nutty and Sam* in *Red Letter* (1919); *Dr. Croc's College* in *Sunday Fairy* (1919); *Jacko* in *Children's Newspaper* (1919); *Silas and His Circus* in *Wizard* (1924); and *Sambo Sue and Jolly Golly* in *Sunbeam* (1928).

His son, Julius Stafford Baker II, was born in 1904 and

A.Z. Baker, "A Dire Threat," 1904.

was trained by his father to become his assistant and to take over his strips and panel series. Baker II also drew many strips of his own, signing them "B.S.B." to avoid confusion with his father, whose style he imitated perfectly. Baker II became the official war artist for the Royal Air Force in World War II, resuming his strip career after demobilization. The elder Baker died in September 1961, at age 92. Baker II retired from commercial cartooning and is currently in the antique trade. His son, Julius Stafford Baker III, works in printing. However, *his* son, Julius Stafford Baker IV, is still too small to show artistic talent!

D.G.

BAKER-BAKER
See Baker, Alfred Zantzinger.

BAKHTADZE, NAKHTANG (1914-) Soviet animator born in what is now Soviet Georgia in 1914. The film studios in Tiflis, Georgia, are among the most important producers of animated cartoons in the Soviet Union, second only to the Moscow studios; yet these cartoons are rarely shown abroad, or even outside Georgia. Nakhtang Bakhtadze is probably one of the most gifted and best known of Georgian animators (he is an Honored Artist of the Georgian Republic), but information is spotty and hard to get, and his

career can be documented only through sporadic showings of his films at international festivals and through the interpretation of Russian commentators.

Bakhtadze studied art in local schools, and in 1933 he went to work in the animation department of Georgia Film in Tiflis. He seems to have mainly contributed layouts and designed backgrounds until the 1950s, when he was given credit as an animator on *Nedjenka* (1950), *Jaffana* (1952) and *The Poor Man's Happiness* (1954). He made his directorial debut in 1952 with *Zuriko and Meriko*, in collaboration with K. Mikabadze, another fabled Georgian animator of

Nakhtang Bakhtadze, "Adventures of Samodelkin."

97

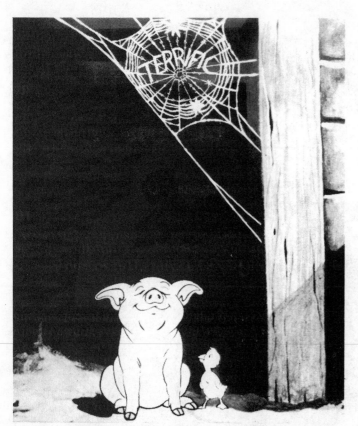

Joseph Barbera (and William Hanna), from the animated version of "Charlotte's Web." © *Hanna-Barbera Productions.*

whom surprisingly little is known. Other films that he directed include *Kursha* (1954), *After the Whistle Blows* and the satirical and much-praised *Narcissus* (1964). Bakhtadze has also been directing a series of animated shorts starring a plucky little hero, Samodelkin, beginning with the 1958 *Adventures of Samodelkin.*

Bakhtadze often uses Georgian themes and stories for his cartoons. The few that have been shown in the West exhibit a fluid style and a lively sense of humor and situation, particularly the witty *Narcissus.*

M.H.

BAKSHI, RALPH (1938-) American animator born in the Brownsville section of Brooklyn, New York, on October 29, 1938. After studies at Thomas Jefferson High School, Ralph Bakshi attended the Industrial Arts School, graduating in 1956. In the late 1950s and early 1960s he worked at CBS-Terrytoons on such series as *Heckle and Jeckle* and *Mighty Mouse.* (Later Bakshi confided, "I spent years drawing mice from every imaginable angle.") From there he went on to Famous Studios-Paramount, where he directed countless *Casper the Friendly Ghost* and *Little Audrey* cartoons, among others. During that same period Bakshi also animated Peter Max's commercials.

When Famous Studios closed in 1967, Bakshi went into partnership with Steve Krantz, whom he had met several years earlier. Their first venture was *Fritz the Cat,* a cartoon feature Bakshi directed from Robert Crumb's original stories and drawings. Produced by Krantz, the picture was released in 1972. The success of *Fritz* prompted the duo to follow suit with *Heavy Traffic* (1973), a funny-sad chronicle of life in New York's slums. Striking out on his own, Bakshi then produced the sometimes brilliant, often disappointing *Coonskin* (1974) and the ill-starred *Wizards* (1977), a nebulous saga of times long

forgotten, on which a number of comic book artists (Mike Ploog, Gray Morrow, Jim Starlin) labored to little effect. His latest work of animation, *Lord of the Rings,* came out at the end of 1978.

Ralph Bakshi occupies a somewhat ambiguous position in today's animation world. Neither *Fritz the Cat* nor *Heavy Traffic* has elicited the kind of unanimous acclaim that he has obviously been craving. His visuals are often dazzling, but he seems to lack a strong story sense, and he appears unsure of his direction. Yet Bakshi is one of the more original artists at work in the animated cartoon medium, and more should be heard from him in the future.

M.H.

BĂLAŞA, SABIN (1932-) Romanian animator born in the Carpathian region of Romania on July 17, 1932. Sabin Bălaşa studied at the N. Grigorescu Institute of Art in Bucharest, graduating in 1954. He worked first as a cartoonist for various Romanian publications and also had a promising career in book illustration.

In the early 1960s Bălaşa gravitated toward animation while continuing his work as a graphic artist. The films he directed and often drew himself were shown sporadically throughout the 1960s and 1970s. The story lines were often cryptic or nonexistent; notable among his films are *The Drop* (1965), *The Wave* (1966) and *Fascination,* which won the 1968 silver prize at the Mamaia Festival. Bălaşa tried to tell a more coherent story in his 1971 science fiction cartoon *Return to the Future,* but again the refinement of the settings and the brilliance of the design were offset by a muddled script. In recent years Bălaşa has gone into experimental and abstract animation, a field for which he seems best suited.

M.H.

BALLESTER, ANSELMO (1897-1974) Italian caricaturist, cartoonist and poster designer born in Rome, Italy, of a Spanish father, in 1897. Anselmo Ballester contributed theatrical caricatures to Rome newspapers while still a teenager. One of the best-known personalities in the world of show business, he never set foot on a movie set; yet he depicted every known star of silent and sound pictures in his 34 years as a movie poster designer, a career which he started in 1913.

Whether he dealt with Charlie Chaplin or Marlene Dietrich, Marlon Brando or Mary Pickford, Ballester's drawings were not simple publicity posters but really portraits, hardly caricatured and charged with evocative expression. He turned them out at the rate of a hundred a year and did thousands in the course of his career. Italo Mussa wrote that Ballester captured in the expression of Douglas Fairbanks, say, or Betty Grable, "the invisible mood of the plot." His sketches, some four thousand of them, reveal a desire to zero in on the imagination and fantasies of the spectator. "I must suggest," the artist once said. "The rest is up to the movie."

In 1944, at a time when war was over for half of Italy, the humor weekly *Il Pupazzetto,* finding too little to laugh about, transformed itself into a comic magazine. The front page featured Ballester's *Lo Scimmiottino d'Oro* ("The Golden Ape"), a story full of violence, adventure and heroism, which perhaps represented the sum of Ballester's experiences as an interpreter of popular dreams. He also drew a few car-

"Now we drink for sorrow, little brother, because they've dissolved our Duma.
But when we have a new Duma, little brother, we'll drink for joy."

Ernst Barlach. © *Simplicissimus.*

toons in the period following the war, but his heart remained with the movies. Just before his death in 1974, Ballester confessed, "With so many porno films, one doesn't rightly know what to draw."

S.T.

BARBERA, JOSEPH ROLAND (1911-) American animator and producer born in New York City in 1911. Despite a flair for drawing, Joe Barbera decided after high school to become a banker, and he attended the American Institute of Banking. He briefly worked as an accountant for a law firm but found himself out of a job at the start of the Depression. After trying unsuccessfully to begin a new career as a magazine cartoonist, he became associated with the Van Beuren studio in 1932, working as an animator and scriptwriter, notably on the *Tom and Jerry* series (which featured two zany human characters in all kinds of weird situations).

In 1937 Barbera went west and joined the newly formed MGM cartoon unit, first as a scriptwriter, then as an animator. He teamed up with William Hanna the following year to direct *Gallopin' Gals*; the association proved mutually satisfying, and in 1939 Barbera and Hanna collaborated again on "Puss Gets the Boot," the first entry in the *Tom and Jerry* series. (While the title was probably inspired by the Van Beuren characters, the protagonists in this one were a cat and a mouse, and very different from their namesakes.) The *Tom and Jerry* car-

toons went on to dizzying success, and from 1939 on the professional career of Joe Barbera became inseparable from that of William Hanna (see the entry "Hanna, William" for further information).

M.H.

BARLACH, ERNST (1870-1938) German sculptor, printmaker, author and cartoonist born in Wedel, in the Lower Elbe region, on January 2, 1870. The son of a country doctor, Ernst Barlach studied at the Hamburg School of Applied Art (1888-91), at the Dresden Academy (1891-95) and in Paris (1895-96). Back in Hamburg, he worked for a few years in conjunction with the successful sculptor Carl Garbers; the two executed numerous private and civic commissions in a grandiose style. In the same years Barlach, a remarkable draftsman, submitted many drawings to the Munich art magazine *Jugend*, pliantly adapting to several of the styles then in vogue, especially art nouveau (he later felt that he had to rid himself of this "pernicious" influence).

Shortly after the turn of the century, although already in his mid thirties, Barlach found himself aesthetically and psychologically at sea. He lived for awhile in his small hometown, taught at a little school of ceramics while filling ceramic commissions himself, and moved in and out of Berlin, a major art center but no spiritual home for him. Finally, in August and September 1906, he visited one of his brothers, an engineer practicing in

Kharkov, Russia. This trip is usually seen as a turning point in his life. The Russian peasants—in his eyes simple, majestic, religious—decisively turned his thoughts to a spare, monumental style. Even the loose and ample Russian peasant smock was to reappear constantly as a garb for his drawn or sculpted figures.

In 1907 and 1908, still in need of funds, Barlach sent several drawings chiefly on Russian subjects to *Simplicissimus*, where they were published with glib, rather unamusing captions. Important as his brief association with this Munich magazine is in retrospect, it was unhappy for him—although at the time there were few other publications where he could freely express the sympathy for the poor and contempt for their oppressors that he managed to convey in some of his *Simplicissimus* work.

Late in the century's first decade, Barlach's financial worries were eased by the Berlin art dealer and publisher Paul Cassirer, and his rich career really took wing. His cartooning days were over, for he turned to other forms of expression. His work in wood, bronze and other media places him securely among the great sculptors of the century. As a woodcut artist, too, he has few equals, and his lithographs are of high quality. Amazingly, from 1912 on, a parallel career in literature—and at a high level—opened up for Barlach. His harsh but powerful expressionistic plays were performed when new and have been revived since World War II (Barlach's art, both visual and verbal, was uncongenial to the Nazis). He also wrote a brief autobiography in 1928.

From about 1910 on, Barlach resided chiefly at Güstrow in the Mecklenburg region. He died at Rostock on October 24, 1938.

S.A.

BARLETTA, SERGIO (1934-   ) Italian cartoonist born in Bologna, Italy, on November 20, 1934. At the age of 23 he started his freelance career with contributions to such

"Aunt Claire asked you a question, dear.
Are you the pitcher or the catcher?"

Perry Barlow. © *The New Yorker.*

publications as *L'Illustrazione*, *Fotografia* and *Graphic Designer*, later becoming the art director of a number of magazines and also working for ad agencies.

Between 1960 and 1976 Barletta devoted himself exclusively to the graphic arts, producing magazine illustrations as well as political cartoons. In 1968 he created a comic strip, *Mr. Manager*, which was scheduled to appear in the weekly *Rinascita*; the magazine editor turned it down, however, because of its leftist orientation. It then was picked up by Italy's first underground publication, *Cabalá*, where it remained until the magazine folded in 1975; it has since been appearing regularly in the pages of the monthly *Eureka*.

Barletta has also contributed political cartoons to the German magazine *Pardon* since 1973, and some of his cartoons have appeared in *Fortebraccio* and *Hara-Kiri*, starting in 1974. Barletta, who has been compared to Jules Feiffer in his unrelenting examination of modern reality, has had many of his satirical cartoons collected in four books: *Homo* (1967), *Uno* (1971), *D.C.* (1976) and *Clericus* (also 1976). Recently the artist has also been active in the field of painting and has had several exhibitions in galleries in Rome and Milan.

L.S.

BARLOW, PERRY (1892-1977) American cartoonist born in McKinney, Texas, near Dallas, in 1892. Perry Barlow, who was most famous for his many *New Yorker* cartoons and covers, was raised on his family's farm and spent his boyhood in Texas. He traveled to Illinois to attend the Art Institute of Chicago and there was part of a remarkable class that included Helen Hokinson and Garrett Price, also destined to be *New Yorker* greats. He met his wife, Dorothy Hope Smith, at the art school; she later became a famous portraitist of children best known for drawing the baby on the Gerber trademark.

Around 1920 the Barlows moved to New York, and he began a career of freelance cartooning and illustrating. At the Art Institute of Chicago he had discovered he was color blind, so his color work, featuring soft muted pastels, was done by his wife (and after her death by watercolorist Catherine Barr). As success came the family joined the growing artists' community of Westport, Connecticut.

James Geraghty, art editor of the *New Yorker* from 1939 to 1973, has commented that Perry Barlow was "a quiet, shy, aloof man" but still "a great artist with children." The *New Yorker*'s editor, William Shawn, regarded Barlow as "one of our three or four most prolific people." Ironically, although he had an opportunity to publish an anthology of his cartoons, Barlow was always lukewarm on the project, and no anthology exists. From the 1920s until the early 1970s, however, his cartoons appeared in a variety of magazines, including the *Saturday Evening Post* and *Collier's*. Fortunately the general cartoon anthologies of such magazines contain generous samplings of his works.

Barlow's cartoons have a loose, sketchy style and soft, understated wash. Children were a favorite theme in his cartoons, which were usually geared more for a chuckle than a belly laugh and always displayed a refined, educated sense of humor. His accomplishments as a *New Yorker* cover artist helped set the style of the magazine, along with covers by Peter Arno, Helen Hokinson and others. A Barlow cover was a humorous cartoon that needed no caption and captured some of the joy of living that appears to a cartoonist with an eye for it. Today, when the *New Yorker*'s covers are often devoted to de-

"Barney Bear." © MGM.

sign sans humor, one can appreciate Perry Barlow's gentle cartoon covers all the more.

He died of natural causes at his Westport home on December 26, 1977, at age 85.

B.C.

BARNEY BEAR (U.S.) Barney Bear, the prototypical dumb bear (indeed, in one cartoon Barney is handed a business card reading "Joe Scarecrow—special rates for dumb bears") made his debut in the 1939 "The Bear That Couldn't Sleep," in the course of which the rotund and slightly obfuscated plantigrade grew more and more desperate in his efforts to silence a variety of forest animals seemingly bent on disrupting his peaceful slumber.

"The Bear That Couldn't Sleep" was made by Rudolph Ising and started a trend. MGM, the producers, felt encouraged enough to turn out more *Barney Bear* shorts, which they alternated with the more popular *Tom and Jerry* series, also born around this time. The pattern hardly varied over the years: as other animals take advantage of Barney's gullibility, the bear becomes aware he is being put upon and then lashes out at his tormentors, usually with unhappy results. In "The Impossible Possum," Barney vainly tries to chase an obdurate opossum

For a Christmas Dinner . . .

Raoul Barré, first French-Canadian comic strip, 1902. © La Presse.

away from his honey tree and finally ends up demolishing his own cabin. In "Cobs and Robbers," in a futile attempt to get back at the crows who feed on his corn, Barney burns down his entire cornfield. And in "Barney's Hungry Cousin," the hapless bear falls victim to his relative's ravenous appetite and superior wits—the ultimate disgrace.

The *Barney Bear* shorts were directed in the fast-paced, crisp style of the MGM school of cartooning by such stalwarts as Dick Lundy, Michael Lah and Preston Blair. Barney's personality remained somewhat undefined, however, and he never transferred to other media the way Tom and Jerry did. When MGM closed down their animation studios in 1957, the *Barney Bear* series was discontinued. However, the slow-moving, slow-witted bear still occasionally appears on television in the course of *The Tom and Jerry Show*.

M.H.

BARRÉ, RAOUL (1874-1932) French-Canadian cartoonist born in Montreal, Quebec, on January 29, 1874. Raoul Barré studied art at the Mont St.-Louis Institute in Montreal; moving to Paris in 1891, he attended courses at the Ecole des Beaux-Arts and the Académie Julian. He also started contributing cartoons to such humor publications as *Le Rire* and *L'Assiette au Beurre*; his caricatures in the satirical *Le Sifflet* were especially noteworthy.

From 1898 to 1902 Barré stayed mainly in Quebec. In 1901 his album of satirical reminiscences, *En Roulant Ma Boule* ("Bumming Around"), was published in Montreal. In 1902 he created what is regarded as the first Canadian comic page for the Montreal daily *La Presse*. During this period Barré also contributed numerous drawings and illustrations to such publications as *La Revue Nationale, La Revue des Deux-France* and *Le Monde Illustré*.

Settling in New York in 1903, Barré for a time kept his ties with the Montreal daily *La Patrie*, to which he contributed two comic strips. *Les Contes du Père Rhault*, a feature in the tradition of *The Katzenjammer Kids*, ran from 1906 to 1908; and, under the pseudonym "Varb," Barré also drew *A l'Hôtel du Père Noé* (1913), the French version of *Noah's Ark*, which he had created the preceding year for McClure Newspaper Syndicate.

In 1909 Barré got involved for the first time in the animation field. From 1910 to 1913 he made advertising films in collaboration with W.C. ("Bill") Nolan. In 1913 he founded the Raoul Barré Studio, the first animation unit organized along commercial lines. Among other famous beginners, the young Pat Sullivan first learned the secrets of his trade with Barré. Barré perfected the "peg system" in 1914 and contributed a number of other technical innovations to the craft of animation. In 1915 he realized one of the first film cartoon series, *The Animated Grouch Chasers*, for Edison, and shared with Frank Moser and George Stallings the production of Tom Powers's *Phables* (also known as *Joys and Glooms*).

Founding with Thomas Bowers the Barré-Bowers Studio in 1916, Barré produced the famous series of *Mutt and Jeff* film cartoons for the next three years. Personal and financial disputes between the partners led to Barré's withdrawal in 1919. He then devoted himself to advertising and illustration. In 1926-27 he came back to animation, notably working on Pat Sullivan's *Felix the Cat* series. Plagued by ill health, Barré returned to Montreal at the end of the 1920s. He resumed his painting activities and briefly drew caricatures and illustrations for his son-in-law's publication, *Le Taureau*, under the pseudonym "E. Paulette." Barré died on May 21, 1932, before he was able to make his planned comeback in animation.

A study of Barré's oeuvre, *Barré l'Introuvable* ("Barré the Unfindable") by André Martin, was published in Ottawa in 1976. The following year an exhibition of Barré's graphic works was organized by the International Pavilion of Humor in Montreal.

S.J.

BARTON, RALPH (1891-1931) American cartoonist, caricaturist and critic born in Kansas City, Missouri, on August 14, 1891. The young Barton studied art in Paris before entering the cartooning profession in 1910 with early work in *Judge* and *Life*.

Due no doubt to his youth, Barton's early work seems to have received its stylistic impulses from impressions of others: trendy European styles of the prewar days and American advertising art, particularly that of Laurence Fellows. Actually, his early work was consistent and

The Seven Infallible Signs of Senility. Diagram showing the average age at which man begins to sputter and fume about:

| Modern Art | Modern Youth | Modern Books | Modern Dress | Modern Dancing | Modern Inventions | Modern Anything |

Ralph Barton. © *Liberty.*

BARRETO, BENEDITO BASTOS (1897-1947) Brazilian cartoonist and newspaperman born in São Paulo, Brazil, in 1897. Better known as "Belmonte," Benedito Barreto started his career as a humor columnist in the second decade of the century, creating, among other things, the popular character Juca Pato, a pompous know-it-all, in the São Paulo newspaper *Fôlha da Noite*. In 1912 he drew his first professional cartoons for the magazine *D. Quixote*; he later contributed more cartoons to *Carêta* (starting in 1922), *O Cruzeiro*, *Revista da Semana* and the humor publication *Fon-Fon!*, where he also doubled as writer and art director. In 1936 he started a cartoon campaign against the Nazis in the *Fôlha da Manhã* of São Paulo, and these cartoons were reprinted in newspapers all over South America. Belmonte also did book illustration, notably for *Povos e Trajes de América Latina* ("Peoples and Costumes of Latin America") and *História do Brasil para Crianças* ("The History of Brazil for Children").

Belmonte's cartoons were collected in book form under the titles *Angústias de Juca Pato* ("The Anxieties of Juca Pato," 1926), *O Amor Através dos Séculos* ("Love Through the Centuries," 1928) and *No Reino da Confusão* ("The Kingdom of Confusion," 1939). His humor columns (illustrated by himself) were also collected in the anthologies *Assim Falou Juca Pato* ("Thus Spake Juca Pato," 1933) and *Idéias de João-Ninguem* (1935).

Belmonte died, covered with honors and distinctions, in 1947 in São Paulo.

A.M.

handsome in an extremely stylized way (the young John Held, Jr., among others, drew similarly).

Soon his work was seen in many magazines—particularly *Vanity Fair* and *Smart Set*. In 1915, Barton was sent to Paris to cover the war for *Puck* and dispatched some witty and sophisticated copy and art about the effects of the war on the Parisian café set.

In the early 1920s, Barton was extremely influential in the field of caricature. His cartoon work had now lost the early willowy, fashion-catalog appearance and was rendered in confident pen lines and richly graded gray tones. His double-page caricatures graced the pages of *Vanity Fair*; news spoofs lightened both *Judge* and the

Berthold Bartosch, "L'Idée," © *Bartosch.*

New Yorker; illustrations appeared in *Cosmopolitan* and *Women's Home Companion;* and book contracts were many. For a time Barton also was drama editor for *Life.*

Included among Barton's many humorous book illustrations are the following titles: *Nonsensorship* by Heywood Broun, George S. Chappell et al. (1922); *More Letters of a Japanese Schoolboy* by Wallace Irwin (1923); *Science in Rhyme Without Reason* (1924); *Gentlemen Prefer Blondes* by Anita Loos (1925); *Droll Stories* by Balzac (1925); *But Gentlemen Marry Brunettes* by Anita Loos (1928); and his own popular history of the United States, *God's Country* (1929).

A chevalier of the Legion of Honor (1927), Barton died a suicide on May 10, 1931.

R.M.

BARTOSCH, BERTHOLD (1893-1968) Czech animator and artist born in Bohemia, then a crown land of the Hapsburg empire, in 1893. From 1911 to 1913 Berthold Bartosch worked as an apprentice and draftsman for an architectural firm in Vienna. He studied architecture and fine arts in Vienna from 1913 to 1917 and there became interested in film through his association with Professor E. Hunslik, director of the Cultural Research Institute. With Hunslik's sponsorship he opened an animation studio for educational films, first in Vienna (1918-19), then in Berlin.

In Berlin Bartosch met Lotte Reiniger and worked on some of her silhouette films, including *The Ornament of the Lovestruck Heart* and *The Adventures of Prince Achmed.* He also made several advertising films for Julius Pinschewer in Zurich. At the same time he produced a number of animated films of his own, often on political or social themes. Of these, *Communism, Animated Cards* (both 1919), *The Battle of Skagerrak* (1922) and *The Occupation of the Rhineland* (1925) are the best known.

Bartosch married in 1930 and settled in Paris. There he made the film for which he is most famous, the 30-minute *L'Idée* ("The Idea"), based on a book of woodcuts of the same title by the Belgian artist Frans Masereel. In it Bartosch used every possible kind of animation (cutout figures, drawings, collages), as well as a score by Arthur Honegger, to tell the allegory of the Artist who tries to lead the workers in their fight against Church, State and Capital with the help of the eternal Idea (represented as a nude woman). The film, released in 1932, was soon banned as scandalous, and Bartosch had to close down his studio. *L'Idée* is now regarded as a landmark in the history of animation.

In the 1930s Bartosch subsisted by working on advertising cartoons. In 1940 he fled the Nazi invasion and went into hiding. After the war he again made a few advertising films but mainly concentrated on his paintings, which were exhibited (although not widely) in galleries in Europe and America. He died in 1968.

M.H.

BASSET, GENE (1927-) American cartoonist born in Brooklyn, New York, on July 24, 1927. Gene Basset studied at the University of Missouri, Brooklyn College (where he received a B.A. degree in design), Cooper Union, the Pratt Institute and the Art Students League. He drew for the *Honolulu Star-Bulletin* in 1961 and 1962 and then switched to Scripps-Howard political headquarters in Washington, D.C. He became chief political cartoonist for the chain's *Washington Daily News*, and

"Come on in, I'll treat you right. I used to know your Daddy."

C.D. Batchelor, Pulitzer Prize-winning cartoon, 1937. © New York Daily News.

from there his cartoons were distributed to the Scripps-Howard papers. In 1972, and after the *News* folded, Basset was syndicated by United Feature Syndicate.

Basset's style seems at once derivative and startlingly original; there is something of the zaniness of *MAD* magazine in his concepts, and his lines are very loose without being sketchy or superfluous. He draws in the now-standard horizontal format on doubletone paper.

Brian Basset, the cartoonist's son, joined the staff of the *Detroit Free Press* as editorial cartoonist in 1978.

R.M.

BATCHELOR, CLARENCE DANIEL (1888-1978) American Pulitzer Prize-winning cartoonist born in Osage City, Kansas, in 1888. C.D. Batchelor attended local public schools and Salina (Kansas) High School before studying at the Chicago Art Institute from 1907 to 1910.

His first drawings were on chalk plate for the *Salina Journal.* In 1911 he was hired by the *Kansas City Star* but fired six months later. He then worked briefly with his father on a railroad and began freelancing for *Puck, Life* and *Judge* magazines. He traveled to New York around 1912 and was variously employed on the *New York Mail* (whose practice it was to solicit talent from around the country), the *New York Tribune* (where he was to return intermittently) and the *New York Journal,* where he remained for four years as a staff artist and occasional political cartoonist. He became the political cartoonist of the liberal *New York Post* (1923-31) and drew a panel, *Once Overs,* for the Ledger Syndicate during that time.

In 1931 he joined the staff at the *New York Daily News*

Joy Batchelor, "Ruddigore." © Halas & Batchelor.

and became its chief editorial cartoonist. The *News* at first supported the New Deal, but the paper and its cartoonist eventually grew disenchanted with liberalism and bureaucracy to the point that their political complexion changed; Batchelor wound up his career, after retiring from the *News* in the early 1970s, on the staff of the *National Review*, a journal of the political right. He died at his Connecticut home in 1978.

His Pulitzer Prize in 1937 was a powerful plea against what was already shaping up, for those who wished to see, as a European conflagration with American involvement. Batchelor's strong cartoons were drawn with irony, a moralizing viewpoint and direction; with labels and captions written on scrolls, they have the appearance of documents. In effect, with his crisp style and strong ideas, they are proclamations in cartoon form.

Batchelor's style is one of lilting brushstrokes graced by wisps of shading. He always had a firm grasp of anatomy and composition; he definitely relied on a newspaper artist's portraiture rather than caricature. One of his most effective series, running for years in the *News*, was *Inviting the Undertaker*, telling arguments mainly against reckless driving that won him many public service awards.

R.M.

BATCHELOR, JOY (1914-) English animator born in Watford, England, on May 22, 1914. After art school Joy Batchelor worked in design, creating everything from lampshades to fashions for *Harper's Bazaar* and *Queen*. Fascinated by animation, she took a job with Denis Connolly, one of the independent animators of the prewar period, and worked on *Robin Hood* (1935) and a cartoon featuring a koala bear. Moving to British Animated Films for the color short *Music Man* (1938), she met John Halas.

After completion of the film, the pair went to Hungary and attempted to set up their own studio, but the political climate and the lack of financing brought them back to England. Halas contributed cartoons to *Lilliput*, the pocket humor magazine, while drumming up potential customers for commercial advertising. Soon they were Halas and Batchelor, producing short theatrical commercials in color for the J. Walter Thompson Agency: *Carnival in the Clothes Cupboard* for Lux soap (1941), *Train Trouble* for Kellogg's Corn Flakes (1943) and *The Big Top* for Rinso (1944). They got married in 1941 and in the same year made their first entertainment short, *The*

Pocket Cartoon. (For further information on Joy Batchelor's career see the entry "Halas, John.")

D.G.

BAUER, ROLF PETER (1912-1960) German cartoonist born in Konstanz, Germany, in 1912. The son of an architect, Rolf Bauer moved to Munich with his family when he was 11. By the time he was 19, he was already submitting sports cartoons to such newspapers as the *Münchener Abendblatt* and the *Neue Augsburger Zeitung*, and his reputation in this field was extremely high in the 1930s. His interest in sports was more than merely graphic, however, for Bauer became the tennis champion of Bavaria. Later in the 1930s, without abandoning sports as a cartoon subject, he turned increasingly to celebrity caricatures, especially of theater and film personalities.

In 1939 he became a soldier, but even in the barracks and at the front he continued to draw. About this time he also created a children's book called *Hupfauf der Gummiball* ("Hopup the Rubber Ball"). After the war he found that his Munich home had been bombed out, so he lived by the Tegernsee for awhile.

In 1946 he published a book of original pictures and verse that he had completed in 1943, *Das Spiel um die Meisterschaft* ("The Championship Game"). Here, with a large number of amusing vignettes, he did for German soccer something similar to what Ernest L. Thayer (more briefly and minus the pictures) had done for American baseball in "Casey at the Bat." Other Bauer books based on sports are *Das Grosse Spiel* ("The Big Game") and *Spiel, Satz und Sieg* ("Game, Stake and Victory").

After the war his work with celebrity caricatures became paramount. Two collections of this kind of material are *Im Konzertsaal Karikiert* ("Caricatured in the Concert Hall") and *Flimmerstars und Fürstlichkeiten* ("Stars of the Flicks and Royal Personages"). After Bauer's untimely death in 1960 at the age of 48, an excellent posthumous volume, *Unterwegs Karikiert* ("Caricatured Along the Way"), gathered together a sizable number of his gentle, likable and genuinely funny caricatures. Bauer also did film posters and television graphics.

S.A.

BAXTER, WILLIAM GILES (1856-1888) British cartoonist born in America in 1856. W.G. Baxter was the creator, or rather recreator, of Ally Sloper, the first great British comic strip hero (see *The World Encyclopedia of Comics*, Chelsea House, 1976). Remarkably little has been written about this giant of the popular pen, perhaps because little is known. And what little has been written is largely inaccurate. His initials stand for William Giles, according to his death certificate, and not William George, as claimed in the only major piece of writing about him ("A Great Comic Draughtsman" by W.G. Thorpe, in *Print Collectors Quarterly*, February 1938). Nor did he create Ally Sloper (as claimed in the same article); rather, he recreated him from the original cartoons by Charles Henry Ross and his wife, Marie Duval.

Commissioned by publisher-engraver Gilbert Dalziel to draw a new series of front-page cartoons featuring Ally for the new weekly comic *Ally Sloper's Half-Holiday*, Baxter exaggerated the simple hack cartoon figure into a

Poor Pa summoned to Windsor: "My wretched Father, having, as usual made himself supremely ridiculous in the House of Commons, Her Majesty thought fit to summon him to Windsor, when, upon making a proper apology, he was taken out for a drive. He sat behind, and, I am told, made a great impression."

W.G. Baxter, "Ally Sloper's Half-Holiday," 1886.

monstrous, grotesque Micawber of the lower classes, complete with ever-expanding family (Queen Victoria's Jubilee produced a topical offspring, Jubilee Sloper!). Although Baxter only worked a short while on *Half-Holiday*, his version of Ally Sloper prevailed throughout English comic history, first continued by W.F. Thomas and revived in the original image in 1976 for *Ally Sloper* magazine by Walter Bell, who learned to draw Sloper at Thomas's elbow in 1920.

Baxter came to live in Buxton, Derbyshire, England, when still a child. As a teenager his sketches of local notables earned him admiration and a small living. John Andrew Christie, a provincial publisher, noticed Baxter's work, and when he started a new Manchester satirical weekly, *Momus*, he hired the 22-year-old artist as his chief (and only) staff cartoonist. The first issue, published March 7, 1878, had a caricature of the dean of Manchester on the cover, and for the second Baxter drew the mayor. Number 5 featured Baxter's first comic strip, *The Perils of Our Streets*. Baxter became joint editor of *Momus*, and when the paper folded in 1883, he went to London to try his luck as a freelance newspaper artist. His first cartoon for *Ally Sloper's Half-Holiday* appeared in number 10 and showed Lord Randolph Churchill at the Henley races. Three weeks later, his first cartoon of the "new" Sloper appeared: "Sloper the Friend of Man," page 1, number 13, July 21, 1884. With the special extra edition of *Alley Sloper's Christmas Holidays*, Baxter truly flowered: he executed superb double-page center spreads of Christmas with the Sloper family.

He died on June 2, 1888, at age 31, of, it is said, alcohol and tuberculosis. He left £286 to his wife, Eleanor. His image of Ally Sloper, produced in merchandise galore, is now immortalized in the annual Ally Sloper awards presented to the top British comic artists. His books include *Fifty Sloper Cartoons* (1888), *Elijer Goff's Complete Works* (1889) and *Strange But True* (1889).

D.G.

BEAR (G.B.) "Caution, Keep Out of Reach of Children!" reads the warning notice on the cover of *The Posy Simmonds Bear Book*, published in 1969. The charming cartoon on the cover shows a slightly sly bear smiling at a slightly embarrassed child. Turn the page, and the drawing is repeated with the "adults only" caption: "Aren't you going to sleep with me tonight?" And it is Bear saying it, not Girl! This book of saucy, even shocking (for 1969) cartoons featuring a teddy bear the likes of which Christopher Robin never knew, a girl, a doll and a rabbit with a decidedly phallic carrot, took a new look at the well-loved nursery characters of old, giving them a Permissive Age twist that really could not offend, so sweetly were they drawn.

Posy Simmonds, their equally sweet creator, says with a smile, "It's all in the mind." The phrase is echoed by Bernard Shrimsley, editor of the daily tabloid the *Sun*, in his introduction to a paperback reprint of *Bear*. It was Shrimsley who, spotting the first Simmonds book, signed her to produce a daily cartoon panel entitled *Bear by Posy*. The series began in the first revamped *Sun*, November 17, 1969, and continues to delight daily.

Rosemary Simmonds, nicknamed "Rosy-Posy," hence "Posy," was born on August 9, 1945, in Cookham Dean, Berkshire. Educated at Caversham, she studied painting at the Ecole des Beaux-Arts in Paris, and graphics at the Central School of Art in London. Her first published cartoons, "little excrescences" she calls them, were thumbnails for the *Times* woman's page and *New Society*. Since 1974 she has been featured regularly in the *Guardian* and also teaches illustration at Middlesex Polytechnic. Her books include *Posy Simmonds Bear Book* (1969), *Bear by Posy* (1974) and *More Bear* (1975).

D.G.

BEARD, DANIEL CARTER (1850-1941) American cartoonist, illustrator, outdoorsman and organizer born in Cincinnati, Ohio, on June 21, 1850. Dan Beard moved with his family to Covington, Kentucky, and as a boy studied art with his father, a portrait painter. He followed his brother, Frank Beard (a cartoonist with the Leslie publications), to New York and from 1880 to 1884 studied at the Art Students League.

In 1882 his first illustrated article, "How to Camp Without a Tent," appeared in *St. Nicholas* magazine, and he was soon one of America's major freelance cartoonists and comic illustrators, drawing for *Life* and many other publications. He was certainly Mark Twain's favorite, working on some of Twain's most notable books.

Beard's style was tight and tended toward the realistic, although he could achieve flights of fancy and had a real decorative sense. His cartoons were always executed neatly but boldly. As his career progressed and his interests became focused, his subjects increasingly followed the outdoors themes.

"Uncle Dan" Beard was the organizer of the Boy Scouts of America, a distinction that has sometimes obscured his achievements as a comic artist. In 1878 he began organizing boys in outdoor activities, and his first published article and first book, *The American Boys' Handy Book* (appearing in 1882), dealt with this theme. It was in 1905, when he was editor of *Recreation* magazine, that he undertook full-scale organization of the group that was to become the Boy Scouts.

For many years he was national scout commissioner, an honorary vice-president of the BSA, and chairman of its National Court of Honor. The year before his death, fifty thousand Boy Scouts gathered before him at the New York World's Fair to sing happy birthday to "Uncle Dan." At the time of his death he was still drawing and writing; he produced a monthly illustrated article for *Boys' Life* for years. At his funeral, honorary pallbearers included Franklin Roosevelt, Charles Dana Gibson and

Theodore Roosevelt, Jr. Among a host of honors dedicated to his ideals, the Daniel Carter Beard Medal for Boys of Kentucky, endowed for a hundred years, is a special one. He died at his home, Brooklands, in Suffern, New York, on June 11, 1941.

Books: *Little People and Their Homes in the Meadows, Woods and Waters* (1888); *A Connecticut Yankee in King Arthur's Court* by Mark Twain (1889); *The American Claimant* by Twain (1892); *The One-Million Pound Bank Note* by Twain (1893); *Journey into Other Worlds* by John Jacob Astor (1894); *Tom Sawyer Abroad* by Twain (1894); *Following the Equator* by Twain (1897); *The Hat and the Man* (1906); and his autobiography, *Hardly a Man Is Now Alive* (1939).

R.M.

Sir Max Beerbohm, "The Rare, the Rather Awful Visits of Albert Edward, Prince of Wales, to Windsor Castle," ca. 1895.

BEARD, FRANK (1842-1905) American cartoonist born in 1842, brother of illustrator Dan Beard. Eight years his brother's senior, Frank Beard took off on his cartooning career like a rocket. When only 18, he drew a cartoon, "Why Don't You Take It?," that was published by Currier and Ives lithographers and distributed by the Republicans as a campaign document; one hundred thousand were ordered, and the cartoon also graced envelopes.

During the Civil War, Beard was a special artist for *Harper's Weekly* and contributed cartoon ideas for the back page between assignments on the battlefronts. In the 1870s Beard was one of the most prolific cartoonists for the various short-lived comic papers like *Phunny Phellow*, *Wild Oats* and the Leslie comic magazines. One

of his most important acts was his kind sponsorship of and advice to young Frederick Burr Opper in the early 1870s; Opper was influenced by Beard's techniques and helped by hours of unselfish guidance.

Beard returned to lithography when *Judge* was founded in 1881. For that Republican paper he drew some very striking, handsome and sophisticated material; sadly, he and the magazine parted ways when the Republicans took an actual financial interest in the sheet and Bernard Gillam and Zim (Eugene Zimmerman) headed up a restructured art staff in 1886.

Frank Beard is credited with being the originator of the chalk-talk, a widely popular form of public entertainment for a generation; cartoonists wore a second hat as stage comics when they entertained with lightning caricatures, sketches and humorous patter. Beard traveled the Chautauqua circuit for 17 years.

The serious—and substantial—side of his talent is revealed by the fact that Beard was for years a professor of fine arts at Syracuse University. Eventually, he gave up politics but not cartoons and joined the staff of the *Ram's Head*, a Chicago religious publication. For it he championed, via cartoons, the cause of temperance. A collection of his religious and temperance cartoons, *Fifty Great Cartoons*, was published by the Ram's Horn Press in 1899. Beard died in Chicago of a cerebral hemorrhage on September 29, 1905.

R.M.

BEERBOHM, SIR MAX (1872-1956) British caricaturist and essayist born in London, England, on August 24, 1872. Henry Maximilian Beerbohm was educated at Charterhouse School and Merton College, Oxford. His elder half-brother was Herbert Beerbohm Tree, the eminent actor-manager of the Victorian stage. An enthusiastic sketcher from the age of seven, he published his first caricature (of Rudyard Kipling) in his school magazine, the Horsmunden *School Budget*. His literary abilities developed at Oxford and blossomed professionally in the controversial magazine *Yellow Book* (1894). Two years later his first collection of cartoons, *Caricatures of 25 Gentlemen* (1896), was published. Cartoonist E.T. Reed introduced the volume: "Since 'Ape' there has been no-one with such an awful instinct for the principal part of a man's appearance. He is a psychologist in drawing if ever there was."

Caricatures signed "Max" appeared in the *Strand Magazine*, and in 1899 he was appointed drama critic of the *Saturday Review*. In 1910 he left England for Rapallo, Italy, where he made his home for the rest of his life. He occasionally returned to England for exhibitions of his color work (Leicester Galleries in 1913 and 1921) and for witty broadcasts for the BBC, particularly during World War II. He was knighted in 1939 and died in Rapallo on May 20, 1956.

Books: *Caricatures of 25 Gentlemen* (1896); *The Happy Hypocrite* (1897); *The Works of Max Beerbohm* (1897); *More* (1899); *More Theatres* (1903); *Caricatures* (1904); *Poets Corner* (1904); *Max Beerbohm in Italy* (1906); *Book of Caricatures* (1907); *Yet Again* (1909); *Last Theatres* (1911); *Second Childhood of John Bull* (1911); *Zuleika Dobson* (1911); *Christmas Garland* (1912); *50 Caricatures* (1913); *The Guerdon* (1916); *Seven Men* (1919); *And Even Now* (1920); *Herbert Beerbohm Tree* (1920); *Survey* (1921); *Rosetti and His Circle* (1922); *A Peep into the Past* (1923); *Things New and Old* (1923); *Observations* (1925); *The Dreadful Ogre of Hay Hill* (1928); *The Stuffed Owl* (1930); *Works and*

More (1930); *Heroes and Heroines of Bitter Sweet* (1931); *Lytton Strachey* (1943); *Mainly on the Air* (1946); *Seven Men and Two Others* (1950); *Around Theatres* (1953); *A Variety of Things* (1953); *Max's Nineties* (1958); *The Incomparable Max* (1962); *Max in Verse* (1964); *Letters to Reggie Turner* (1964); and *The Bodley Head Max Beerbohm* (1970).

D.G.

BEHRENDT, FRITZ (1925-   ) Dutch editorial cartoonist born in Berlin, Germany, on February 17, 1925. By the early 1960s, with his drawings printed in such far-flung publications as the *Algemeen Handelsblad* and *Vrij Nederland* in his adoptive country, *Die Welt* and the *Süddeutsche Zeitung* in Germany, *Der Nebelspalter* and *Weltwoche* in Switzerland, the *Svenska Dagbladet* in Sweden, the *Shimbun* in Japan, the *West Australian* and the *New York Herald-Tribune*, Fritz Behrendt was the world's best-known Dutch journalist, with a readership of some fifty million.

In 1937, when Behrendt was 12, his family left Germany for political reasons. From 1943 to 1945 he studied at the Amsterdam School of Applied Art and in 1948 was a guest student for one semester at the Academy in Zagreb, Yugoslavia. He started working for the Amsterdam publications *Algemeen Handelsblad* and *Vrij Nederland* in the early 1950s. In 1958 he moved from Amsterdam to the nearby town of Amstelveen, and in 1962 he began a monthly television series of "graphic commentary." Behrendt, a Dutch citizen, has also done posters and book illustrations.

His album *Ondanks Alles* ("In Spite of Everything," late 1962 or early 1963) contains 100 political drawings done in a pleasant cartoon pen style with many benday areas. The subject matter is of both local and international import, and there is also some mild social commentary—on frantic weekend pleasures, the inroads of motorcycling, the prevalence of television viewing, etc. Other Behrendt albums include *Geen Grapjes, a.u.b.* ("No Jokes, Please") and *Kijken Verboden* ("No Peeking").

Politically speaking, it may be suggested that Behrendt's unusually widespread popularity is connected with the comfortable, traditional majority position he adopts—unlike most of the major Dutch and German editorial cartoonists, who have tended to join the intellectual opposition of their period. Behrendt's clear-cut defense of American actions and his condemnation of Russian policies might not be out of place in any conservative Midwestern paper. And, although many postwar European cartoonists have been surprised at the emergence of the Third World as a power to be reckoned with, Behrendt's cartoons on the subject seem to contain a special tinge of resentment that this should have come to pass.

S.A.

BELCHER, GEORGE FREDERICK ARTHUR (1875-1947) Cartoonist, etcher, painter, R.A., born in London, England on September 19, 1875. Educated at Berkhampstead School, George Belcher studied art at the Gloucester School of Art, becoming an exhibitor at the Royal Academy from 1909. His first cartoon accepted by *Punch* appeared in 1911, and he was a regular contributor to *Tatler*, *Vanity Fair* and other top periodicals.

His cartoon work was executed in charcoal at amazing speed, capturing Cockney and working-class life to perfection. He prowled the streets with his sketchbook and was adept at persuading characters who caught his eye to accompany him to his studio for more formal sittings. His colorful portraits were of the common man (and woman, especially charwoman) rather than of social notables; his common cornet player rendering "I dreamt that I dwelt in marble halls" was a popular classic. His jokes were basically illustrations of dialogue gags, more often supplied to him than created. It is reported that he often failed to understand these joke scripts and once made nonsense out of a gag by changing its setting from a fishmonger's shop to a greengrocer's because "there's a very good greengrocer's near my home"! He died on October 3, 1947.

Books: *The Lighter Side of English Life* (1913); *Characters* (1922); *Odd Fish* (1923); *Taken from Life* (1929); *The Table in a Roar* (1933); and *Potted Char* (1933).

D.G.

BELIEVE IT OR NOT! (U.S.) One week before Christmas a long time ago, *New York Globe* sports cartoonist Robert L. Ripley was trying to devise a way to fill up the blank space that was his daily assignment. He suddenly decided to draw a series of weird sports happenings around the world—such as the Canadian who ran the 100-yard dash backwards, the Frenchman who stayed underwater for 6 minutes 29.2 seconds, the Australian who jumped rope 11,810 times, etc. Thus, on December 18, 1918, was *Believe It or Not!* born.

Ripley went on drawing his sports oddities for the *Globe* until the paper closed in 1924. He then moved over to the *New York Telegram* and later to the *Post*, which started to syndicate his panel nationally. By that time *Believe It or Not!* no longer confined itself to sports but was venturing as far afield as geology, history, botany and numismatics. In 1929 King Features Syndicate picked up the panel and gave it worldwide distribution (and fame).

The first feature of its kind, *Believe It or Not!* has enjoyed tremendous popularity for over half a century. Its facts—dwelling heavily on the bizarre, the absurd, the incredible and the outlandish—are not always accurate (every critic has a favorite error or fallacy from *Believe It or Not!*, be it the flight time of Lindbergh's solo journey over the Atlantic or the distance from Earth to the sun), but this never fazed Ripley. Good newspaperman that he was, he knew that unadorned facts and bare statistics make for poor copy, and his aim was to entertain, not to enlighten. Indeed, much more accurate fact panels, such as John and Elsa Hix's *Strange As It Seems* and R.J. Scott's *Did You Know?*, have not even approached the success of Ripley's feature.

The popularity of *Believe It or Not!* prompted Ripley to become the national curator of odd facts and freak happenings, with a radio program, numerous motion pictures, books, lectures and even a string of wax museums. All this activity left him scant time for drawing, and the *Believe It or Not!* panel was ghosted by many other hands from the 1930s on. Eventually Paul Frehm became the exclusive artist on the feature, and he later took it over completely, signing it after Ripley's death in 1949. Under Frehm's guidance the format of *Believe It or Not!* has changed very little since that time.

M.H.

BELLEW, FRANK HENRY TEMPLE (1828-1888) American cartoonist born in Cawnpore, India, on April 18, 1828. Frank Bellew, born of an English family, came to

THE *ELEVENTH* COMMANDMENT CAN BE FOUND IN — John : Chapter 13 - Verse 34

A new commandment I Give unto You, That ye love One another

RIPLEY's **Believe It or Not!**

PASQUALE STANISLAO MANCINI ITALIAN FOREIGN MINISTER ~ 1882 ~ WAS OFFERED A HALF SHARE IN THE OCCUPATION OF EGYPT BY GLADSTONE BUT *REFUSED* BECAUSE ITALY HAD NO NEED OF COLONIES!

SIGNATURE OF G.B. SHARP New York

HOLY DOLLAR OF PRINCE EDWARD ISLAND

IN ORDER TO PREVENT THE EXPORTATION OF SILVER DOLLARS THE GOVERNOR ORDERED THE CENTER PUNCHED OUT — THUS MAKING THE COINS — UNACCEPTABLE OUTSIDE OF THE ISLAND

CATS PERSPIRE ONLY THRU THE PADS ON THEIR PAWS!

OPTICAL ILLUSION by F.M. BRICKLEY St. Paul, Minn.

GUARDIAN OF THE DEAD SULTAN! on the Field of the Blackbirds — Kossovo, Serbia.

WHEN SULTAN MURAD II WAS ASSASSINATED IN 1389 — HIS BODYGUARD WAS SO HEARTBROKEN OVER HIS NEGLIGENCE IN NOT GUARDING THE SULTAN BETTER THAT HE TOOK A VOW OF ATONEMENT BY DEDICATING HIS FAMILY TO GUARD THE DEAD — AND FOR THE LAST 552 YEARS A DIRECT DESCENDANT OF THE ORIGINAL GUARD HAS BEEN IN CONTINUOUS ATTENDANCE BEFORE THE TOMB OF MURAD

"Believe It or Not!" © King Features Syndicate.

America from England in 1850 and immediately embarked on a career in cartooning and humorous illustration.

Settling in New York City, he contributed cartoons to the new illustrated monthlies, most notably *Harper's*, and to the *Illustrated American News* and children's books. He was founder of cartoon and humor magazines like the *Lantern*, *Vanity Fair* and *Nick Nax*; he contributed frequently to sheets like the *Fifth Avenue Journal*, *Wild Oats* and the various Leslie comic papers. In the 1870s he was a mainstay of the *New York Graphic*, the first illustrated daily in America, a paper that relied heavily on cartoons and often featured them on its front page.

Bellew wrote and illustrated *The Art of Amusing* in 1866, an interesting treatise on his craft. He died, still active, in New York City on June 29, 1888. His son, Frank P.W. Bellew, was just then gaining fame as a cartoonist, signing his work "Chip," evidently in deference to and in honor of his father.

Bellew was as important to his field—the magazine panel cartoon, which he practically created—as Nast was to the editorial cartoon. Bellew was among the earliest and most prolific of woodcut cartoonists, and his subjects ranged from politics to social comment. He was one of the first celebrities among cartoonists, one who broke the bonds of anonymity and whose signature (a triangle) became as famous as the names of writers who shared magazine space with him. Among his most famous cartoons is the caricature of Abe Lincoln after his 1864 victory: "Long Abe a Little Longer." His contribution to cartoon iconography is highlighted by the 1872 rag doll baby, a Frankenstein's monster that taunted the Greenbackers.

What sustained Bellew through this period—a time span in which he could trace his career from a lonely pioneer cartoonist to a veteran viewing the progress of others such as Thomas Nast, Joseph Keppler and Frederick Opper—was the fact that he was good. His humor is typical of the period but still contains spontaneity and imagination. His drawing—and this is evident especially in the period of photoengraving—is supple and agile. He was more than a plotter who let the wood engraver make him look good—he was a gifted composer, a masterful caricaturist. To him belongs the mantle of father of American cartooning, and a resurrection of his work is deserved and long overdue.

R.M.

BELLEW, FRANK P.W. (ca. 1860-1894) American cartoonist, son of pioneer cartoonist Frank Bellew, known by his pen name "Chip" (as in "chip off the old block"). Obviously overshadowed by his father's long and distinguished career, Chip nevertheless made his own mark with an entirely different style. His father, a pioneering and prominent woodcut cartoonist, was identified with the tight, mechanical crosshatch look necessary for woodcut reproduction. With the advent of photoengraving, most artists used the new freedom merely to copy the look of the earlier process. Chip was among the first to simplify, to drop details and shading, to round his outlines; the characters in his drawings were cartoon figures, not stiff, illustrated models with captions beneath. Hence he formed an important link between two vital schools of American cartooning.

Chip is also significant on his own merits, as his work was enormously popular over his brief, decade-long career. His best-liked subjects were kids and dogs; these personae filled a world of wisecracks, pranks, bad puns and pantomime adventures. Before his death in November 1894, Chip developed a technique of parodying ancient friezes, mixing historical and contemporary subject matter cleverly but without the charm of his dog-and-kid cartoons. He drew mostly for *Life*, which published a posthumous collection, *Chip's Dogs*, through R.H. Russell in 1895.

R.M.

BELLUS, JEAN (1911-1967) French cartoonist born in Toulouse, France on July 22, 1911. After finishing his secondary studies at the Lycée Arago in Paris, Jean Bellus went to work as a bank clerk. Three years later (1933) he started cartooning and contributed thousands of drawings mainly to such periodicals and newspapers as *France-Dimanche*, *Le Figaro*, *Jours de France* and *Ici Paris*.

Although his first album, *Humour Verboten!* (1945), seemed a prelude to a satirist's career, dealing as it did

Frank Bellew ("Chip").

with POW camp life, most of his other cartoons show a more gentle popular humor. Bellus indeed has created the prototypical 20th-century middle-class Frenchman and his family: a bald, roly-poly, middle-aged man (not without resemblance to his creator); his plump and charming wife; and Clémentine, his daughter—the star of the series—a vivacious and lovely young woman typical of the younger generation. Whether riding with one of her many boyfriends, dancing until the early hours of the morning or kissing in the dark, she is viewed by her parents with characteristic broad-mindedness and indulgence. These cartoons, which depict the daily events, joys and worries in the life of an average French family, have been released as albums: *Clémentine Chérie* ("Clémentine Chérie, the Rage of Paris," 1955), *Oh! Clémentine* (1963), *Une Famille Bien Française* ("A Very French Family," 1966) and *Vivre avec Son Temps* ("To Live with the Times," 1967).

"That does it. In new francs, I am no longer a millionaire."
Jean Bellus. © *Bellus.*

Jean Bellus suffered a heart attack in the summer of 1966 but continued to work until November of that year. He died at his home in Paris on January 14, 1967.

P.H.

BELMONTE

See Barreto, Benedito Bastos.

BELTRAME, ACHILLE (1871-1945) Italian illustrator and cartoonist born in Arzignano, near Vicenza, Italy, on March 19, 1871. Achille Beltrame studied art at the Brera Academy, in his youthful days winning a number of awards and competitions. Later he decorated several buildings in Turin and Milan. Beltrame's name is indissolubly tied to the weekly *La Domenica del Corriere*, the covers of which he drew from the beginning weeks of this century to the closing weeks of World War II.

At a time when the objectivity of the camera was gradually supplanting the news drawing, Beltrame, instead of giving a detached account of events (assassinations of crowned heads, shoot-outs between bandits and the forces of order, bloody strikes, earthquakes, shipwrecks, trench warfare, etc.), drew them as the public wanted them to appear, adding dignity and virility to the happenings. As Dino Buzzati astutely observed in his preface to *Trieste e il Carso*, a collection of Beltrame's World War I drawings, the artist's truth, often objectively inaccurate, was "truer" than the camera's truth in that it gave the reality of movement where photography only recorded the immobility of things.

Beltrame also tried his hand at cartooning and caricaturing, but these activities pale in comparison to his achievements in the illustration field. He died on February 19, 1945, covered with honors. Newspapers heralded his death with headlines like this one: "For 46 Years He Illustrated the World." He indeed illustrated the world, perhaps in a rhetorical form, but always with humanity and optimism.

S.T.

BEN BOWYANG (Australia) A god's-eye view of Australian graphic humor today reveals that Australia is the last remaining country in the world celebrating her rural origins in comic art.

Al Capp's *Li'l Abner* and his since-vanished *Long Sam* are reminders of the American rural theme. But in Australia at present, five professional cartoonists are busy drawing humor with such rural and outback themes. Since the mid-1850s successive generations of cartoonists and humorists have reinforced the traditional stereotype of the "country dweller" with particular characteristics and ways of living, a stereotype that has become legendary. Continuing this "backblocks" theme made popular first by the *Bulletin*, then by *Smith's Weekly*, the Melbourne *Herald* introduced *Ben Bowyang*, also known in some states as *Gunn's Gully*.

The hayseed Ben, together with his corpulent mate Bill Smith and the mean Scots shopkeeper Wilson, has provided the fun in this daily feature since October 1933. No less than seven artists have drawn the strip, by and large preserving its rural flavor. Sam Wells was the first artist to delineate the character, but it was the gifted cartoonist Alex Gurney who first drew the feature,

followed by Daryl (now Sir Daryl) Lindsay, Mick Armstrong, Keith Martin, Alex McCrae (whose tenure lasted for 25 years) and Bevyn Baker. It is currently being done by Peter Russell-Clarke, who took over in December 1969.

V.L.

BENGOUGH, JOHN WILSON (1851-1923) Canadian cartoonist and journalist born in Toronto, Ontario, on April 7, 1851. John Bengough grew up in Ontario and, after finishing school, worked in a local law office for a short time. Instead of going on to a legal career, Bengough started working as printer's devil and at age 20 went to the Toronto *Globe* as city reporter. Enrolling in evening classes at the Ontario Society of Artists, he developed his artistic skills and at the same time began learning about the ease and accuracy of lithographic reproduction.

At 22, Bengough left the *Globe* and founded the weekly magazine *Grip*. From May 1873 until September 1892, he edited and did most of the writing and illustrating for this successful publication. Political scandal broke out during its first year and gave *Grip* a theme which led to immediate increases in circulation. Bengough's cartoons attacked most current views, sparing only those he championed himself—the single tax, women's suffrage, antivivisectionism and prohibition of alcohol and tobacco. Working before the era of newspaper photographers and widely recognized public figures, Bengough portrayed the basic features of his subjects, using them to express what he considered to be their essential nature. At times his drawings were quite cruel, but they were also very influential. His friends credited him with contributing to the defeat of the Conservative government in the 1896 federal election.

"Help! Save me! I'm drowning! Glub! Glub!"

Stanley and Janice Berenstain, "It's All in the Family. © McCall's.

"La Bergère et le Ramoneur." © Les Gémeaux.

Bengough's career included cartoon work for various other Canadian and English newspapers. His books include cartoon collections, political treatises and poetry. Starting in 1874, he gave illustrated lectures and chalk-talks. For more than forty years he sketched and spoke on political and moral subjects across Canada, the United States, the United Kingdom, Australia and New Zealand. He declined to run for Parliament for the Prohibition party but was an alderman for a term in Toronto starting in 1907. He died on October 2, 1923. In the 1950s a bronze plaque commemorating him was set up in Toronto. He was the second Canadian journalist to be so honored.

D.K.

BERENSTAIN, JANICE

See Berenstain, Stanley.

BERENSTAIN, STANLEY (1923-   ) American cartoonist born in Philadelphia, Pennsylvania, on September 29, 1923. Educated at the Philadelphia Museum School of Industrial Art and the Pennsylvania Academy of Fine Arts, Stanley Berenstain served as a medical artist with the army before teaming up with his wife, Janice, to draw cartoons. Around 1950 this was not uncommon; Vi and George Smith and Linda and Jerry Walter had formed cartooning teams as well.

The Berenstains drew humorous covers for *Collier's*, a newspaper feature called *Sister*, and the long-running *It's All in the Family* for *McCall's* and later *Good Housekeeping*. In 1962 the couple began designing cards and calendars for Hallmark. They have produced a score of books, mostly featuring their regular magazine family characters. Titles include *Are Parents for Real?* (1971), *What Dr. Freud Didn't Tell You* (1971), *How to Teach Your Children About Sex* (1972), *Lover Boy* (1972) and *Bedside Lover Boy* (1972).

The couples' insights into and depictions of suburban living are as telling as any produced in the comics. A frenzied, laughing atmosphere pervades their cartoons, which are drawn in simple, flowing lines and usually colored in one or two flat shades.

R.M.

BERGÈRE ET LE RAMONEUR, LA (France) Following their success with *Le Petit Soldat*, Paul Grimault and André Sarrut (founders and partners of Les Gémeaux

animated studio) decided in 1947 to bring out a full-length animated cartoon on a story by Jacques Prévert, itself derived from a Hans Christian Andersen tale, *La Bergère et le Ramoneur* ("The Shepherdess and the Chimney Sweep"). Technical difficulties, production delays and a legal fight between the two partners plagued the film, and when it finally came out on May 30, 1953, both Grimault and Prévert expressed their public disapproval of the final version of the cartoon.

The story takes place in the fictional kingdom of Tachykardia, ruled by a ruthless tyrant. The shepherdess and the chimney sweep are relentlessly hounded by the king's secret police, then imprisoned and humiliated. They escape with the help of friendly animals led by a strange bird wearing a silk hat, a frock coat and spats. The music, moody and expressive, is by Joseph Kosma, and some of the most distinguished actors of the French cinema lend their voices to the characters, including Pierre Brasseur (the bird), Serge Reggiani (the chimney sweep) and Anouk Aimée (the shepherdess).

Despite its checkered history, *La Bergère et le Ramoneur* fared well with the public. It did not do well with the critics, however, and it signaled the end of Grimault's innovativeness in the field of the cartoon. It is France's finest full-length animated film and, although flawed, a milestone in the history of film animation.

M.H.

BERNARDINI, PIERO (1891-1974) Italian cartoonist, illustrator and painter born in Florence, Italy, on June 23, 1891. Piero Bernardini started his career as a painter (his self-portrait hangs in Florence's Galleria degli Uffizi), but as he himself wrote in his autobiography, "I have used more paper than canvas, more ink than varnish."

Piero Bernardini, illustration for Alphonse Daudet's "Tartarin of Tarascon." © UTET.

In sixty years of feverish activity Bernardini collaborated on some fifty different magazines and newspapers, among them *Il Corriere dei Piccoli, Le Grandi Firme, La Voce, La Gazzetta del Popolo, Il Ballilla, Il Travaso* and *La Lettura*. In addition to his humorous drawings, Bernardini illustrated over one hundred fifty books in the course of his long career, including fables, fairy tales and novels by Rudyard Kipling, Charles Dickens and Jules Verne. He also illustrated a number of textbooks and occasionally designed a few posters.

The Italian writer Bruno Cigognani was the first to single out Bernardini as an acute observer of human nature in his caricatures. Augusto Calabri wrote in 1926, "Man is to Bernardini the most important object. Man in his gestures and his clothes more than man in his face and his sentiments." Whether criticizing or exalting them, Bernardini indeed observed his fellow men, not through their physiognomies but through an investigation of their gestures. He would synthesize these gestures on paper in a few nervous lines. His style was elegant and discontinuous, as Paola Pallotino observed.

Bernardini died in October 1974, in the midst of a multitude of books and drawings. He said toward the end of his life, "I've consumed gallons of ink, truckloads of paper. The pencils I've used up would top in height any television antenna."

S.T.

© 1976 by NEA, Inc.

"This is planet Earth. Remember, we should not breathe its air, drink its water or eat any of its junk foods!"

Jim Berry, "Berry's World." © NEA.

BERRY, JIM (1932-   ) American editorial cartoonist born in Chicago, Illinois, on January 16, 1932. Jim Berry, the creator of a new type of editorial-page social commentary cartoon, *Berry's World*, received his art training from the Famous Cartoonists Course of Westport, Connecticut. Prior to that, his education was received at the University School in Shaker Heights, Ohio, Dartmouth College (two years) and Ohio Wesleyan University, where he minored in art and earned a degree in business administration in 1954.

In 1957, after various odd jobs, Berry joined Altamira Productions, an animation studio, where he mastered all phases of animation. His *Berry's World*, when introduced at the Newspaper Enterprise Association (NEA) in 1963, was something new in the field of editorial cartooning, even in its media: Berry uses pencils and felt-tip pens, working with originals the same size or smaller than their reproductions.

Berry's success led to a preeminent position at NEA: a comic strip creation, *Benjy*, based on a recurring tramp character in the panel, was separated from the NEA sales package and sold on its own. With art by Bill Yates (signing himself Yale), however, it was short-lived. Berry's commentary is sharpest in his comfortable panel format.

The politically independent cartoonist was three times voted the Best Syndicated Panel Cartoonist by the National Cartoonists Society (NCS) and twice received the NCS Best Special Feature award. Berry was awarded the National Headliners prize in 1967 for "consistently outstanding editorial cartoons."

R.M.

BERRYMAN, CLIFFORD KENNEDY (1869-1949) American Pulitzer Prize-winning cartoonist born in Kentucky in 1869. C.K. Berryman undoubtedly acquired a penchant for cartooning from his father, who used to amuse his 11 children by drawing funny pictures. Berryman's first job in art was with the U.S. Patent Office in Washington, D.C., delineating patent entries for $30 a month. When a cartoon submitted to the *Washington Post* paid $25, his career was chosen. Berryman joined the staff of the *Post* as an editorial cartoonist in 1891; in 1907 he switched to the *Washington Star*, then a larger paper, and remained there until a stroke felled him in his office on November 17, 1949. (His last wish was to live long enough to prevent the pall his death would have cast over Washington's Gridiron Dinner. He died on December 11, 1949, several hours after the dinner.)

Berryman is remembered as a Washington institution. His cartoons were largely without malice, and his caricatures were belabored, betraying a lifelong amateurish tint to his work. He took stands—sometimes very determined—but his primary thrust was toward gentility. He always drew with pen and ink and relied on the crosshatch.

His most famous cartoon contribution to Americana came in 1902, on the subject of one of Theodore Roosevelt's bear hunts. After a hard day with no luck, a misguided guide brought a bear cub on a rope for TR to bag; he sent the man away in disgust. Berryman depicted the incident and began including the little bear as a mascot in his TR cartoons; in a day when almost every cartoonist had a mascot, the "Teddy bear" struck the public. On the basis of the president's popularity, the bear was mass-produced and became an essential element of childhood. Berryman, its originator, never realized a cent from its success.

Among Berryman's other honors was his presidency of the Gridiron Club; he was the first cartoonist to hold the position.

R.M.

BERRYMAN, JAMES (1902-1976) American Pulitzer Prize-winning cartoonist born in Washington, D.C., on June 8, 1902. The son of *Washington Star* cartoonist Clifford Berryman, Jim Berryman studied at George

Wonder how long the honeymoon will last?

Clifford Berryman. © *C.K. Berryman.*

Washington University and at the Corcoran Art School, and began his career as a reporter on the New Mexico *State Tribune* in 1923. He joined his father's paper as a staff artist the next year, after returning to Washington because of his mother's illness; he contributed general art and retouching work. In 1931 he was promoted to editorial art and illustration, continuing in that department for two years, when he became a sports cartoonist; Berryman also drew for the *Sporting News* between 1934 and 1941.

On May 29, 1935, Clifford Berryman suffered a stroke at his drawing board with his Memorial Day cartoon half finished. Jim finished the cartoon and intermittently drew political cartoons thereafter. He became a full-fledged substitute in 1941, and in 1944 his three cartoons a week were picked up by King Features Syndicate. He retired in the late 1960s and died in 1976.

Berryman was also a magazine illustrator and wrote and illustrated articles on arms for sport and hunting. He was an honorary lifetime member of the National Rifle Association and for years was art director of their publications. His drawing style was more polished than that of his father; he was both a better draftsman and a better advocate. His political cartoons, Republican and conservative mostly, were stronger and more incisive.

The Berrymans form the only *père et fils* act to cop Pulitzers.

R.M.

Jim Berryman. © *Washington Star.*

BERRY'S WORLD (U.S.) In 1963 editorial cartoonist Jim Berry started a new daily panel for the Newspaper Enterprise Association simply titled *Berry's World* (a Sunday feature was later added).

A syndicate press release once termed *Berry's World* "a satirical, sociopolitical cartoon," and it does indeed lampoon (or at least mildly spoof) topical events and personages in the news. Berry has declared that he was "highly influenced by the British cartoonists in their approach and by the *New Yorker* cartoonists in their style." The cross between the two is not without merit (as when President Nixon suddenly appears on his daughter's television set, unctuously intoning, "I come to you on White House closed-circuit TV to tell you I've vetoed your request for an increased allowance, Tricia"). The resemblance to editorial cartoons is further enhanced by Berry's use of one-line captions under the drawings.

In his Sunday feature, on the other hand, Berry uses a freer approach (as well as balloons for dialogue), bringing it closer to the comic strip. He also occasionally breaks down the Sunday *Berry's World* into several interrelated panels, often on a given theme ("Berry's World Goes to San Francisco, to Los Angeles," etc.).

M.H.

BERTHELOT, HECTOR (1842-1895) French-Canadian cartoonist, newspaperman and humorist born in Trois-Rivières, Quebec, on March 4, 1842. Hector Berthelot is justly regarded as the founding father of cartooning in the province of Quebec. Save for a stay in Quebec City (1861-65) and another in Ottawa (1865-70), Berthelot worked almost exclusively in Montreal.

Berthelot made his debut in 1861 as a translator and reporter for the liberal newspaper *Le Pays*. He also worked during that year for *La Guêpe*, *L'Ordre* and *Le Courrier de St-Hyacinthe*. He broke into cartooning in 1863. His first drawings were published anonymously in the humor publication *La Scie*, where they appeared until 1865. From 1874 he did investigative reporting for a number of Canadian newspapers, including *Le Bien Public*, *Le Courrier de Montréal*, the *Star*, *La Patrie*, *Le Monde*, *La Presse* and *La Minerve*.

In 1878 Berthelot decided to devote all his time to his humor magazine, *Le Canard*, founded in 1877. From a circulation of 500 at its inception, *Le Canard* jumped to 10,000 in a few months. This phenomenal success (which spawned innumerable imitators) was due almost entirely to Berthelot, who was the author of most of the cartoons that appeared unsigned in the pages of the magazine. Berthelot's most original creation was Baptiste Ladébauche. Père Ladébauche ("Pops Debauchery") appeared officially for the first time in November 1878. One of the most famous characters in French-Canadian cartooning, Ladébauche was successively drawn by Racey, Joseph Charlebois (1904-05) and especially Albéric Bourgeois, who was to immortalize him.

In 1879 Berthelot left *Le Canard* (which he had sold the preceding year) to found *Le Vrai Canard*. This publication was renamed *Le Grognard* in 1881 and *Le Violon* in 1886 before reverting to the original name, *Le Canard*, in 1893. Berthelot died in September 1895. *Le Canard*, which proved to be his most memorable contribution to cartooning, survived him by a number of years.

S.J.

BERTHIAUME, ROLAND (1927-) French-Canadian cartoonist born in Montreal, Quebec, on December 12, 1927.

Better known as "Berthio," Roland Berthiaume attended Ste. Marie College (now the University of Quebec) in Montreal before embarking on a commercial art career. After attending night classes at the Montreal School of Arts, Berthiaume spent a year in Paris (1951-52).

In 1953 Berthiaume started his career with editorial cartoons in the weekly *L'Autorité du Peuple*, also contributing occasionally to such publications as *La Semaine à Radio-Canada* and *Le Travail*. He finally found his métier with the cartoons he published in the political weekly *Vrai*. There Berthiaume was responsible for two pages of cartoons, usually four in number, dealing mainly with city problems. Berthiaume collaborated on *Vrai* from its inception in October 1954 to its demise in May 1959. He then went to the Montreal daily *La Presse*, where until 1967 he contributed *Drôle de Journée* ("Some Funny Day"), a column in the form of caricatural drawings and cartoons commenting on daily happenings.

In 1967 Berthiaume returned to editorial cartooning, first for the daily *Le Devoir*, then for the pro-independence daily *Le Jour* (1974-76) and finally for *Montréal-Matin*. He has also worked for several news magazines (*Time*, *MacLean's*). Two collections of his caricatures have been published: *Un Monde Fou* ("A Mad World," 1961) and *Les Cent Dessins du Centenaire* ("The One Hundred Drawings of the Centennial," 1967).

Like Robert La Palme, Berthiaume has always been concerned with form as well as with content. He was the first Canadian cartoonist to engage in caricature with a social thrust. Twice a winner at the International Salon of Caricature in Montreal (1964 and 1966), Berthiaume was the recipient of the Olivar Asselin Journalism Award in 1973.

S.J.

BERTHIO
See Berthiaume, Roland.

BERUSAIYU NO BARA (Japan) *Berusaiyu no Bara* ("The Rose of Versailles") is a fictionalization in comic book form of the life of France's Marie An-

Return from Quebec: Ladébauche, astride the "Duck," gets himself towed by three steamships of the Richelieu and Ontario Company.

Hector Berthelot, first appearance of "Le Père Ladébauche," 1878.

The National Renovation

Roland Berthiaume. © *La Patrie.*

toinette. It was serialized weekly in *Margaret*, a young girls' magazine, from 1972 to 1973. Created and drawn by the talented woman artist Ryōko Ikeda, it is regarded as a classic of the genre known in Japan as *shōjō manga* ("young girls' comics"). As a comic book, it has no parallel in the Western world in either length or scope. It consists of over fifteen hundred pages (sold today as several paperback or hard-cover volumes) and could be more aptly characterized as literature. While not a work of cartooning in the strict sense, *Berusaiyu no Bara* deserves recognition for its ground-breaking attempt to open hitherto unexplored fields to talented cartoonists and graphic artists.

Berusaiyu no Bara is a fascinating mix of French and Japanese cultural values. Oscar François de Jarjayes is a beautiful woman who, amusingly, always wears men's clothes and is the captain of the palace guard. She is so stunningly beautiful/handsome, moreover, that not only men but also the court ladies swoon over her. Oscar, Marie Antoinette, and Marie Antoinette's lover Hans Axel Fersen are the central characters, and their continuous romances and infatuations are skillfully woven into the context of unfolding French history and the divided loyalties created by the Revolution. In the end Marie Antoinette loses her head, of course; Oscar is killed while storming the Bastille with a troop of rebel soldiers, and Fersen is stoned to death by a mob in his native Sweden. Save for Oscar, nearly all characters are historical, Ikeda having studied French history in school and used Stefan Zweig's book *Marie Antoinette* as a major reference. The genre, however, demands a heavy emphasis on romance, and as a result both the graphics

and the story line are syrupy at times. Nonetheless, the overall work is gripping.

Berusaiyu no Bara was the first "girls'" comic in Japan to break outside a schoolgirl readership. In 1974 it was dramatized and presented by Japan's unique all-female performing group, Takarazuka, under the direction of Ichio Hasegawa. The play was a smash success and captured the imagination of all Japan. A film version scheduled for release in 1979 is being produced on location in France with Mataichiro Yamamoto in charge of direction.

F.S.

BETTY BOOP (U.S.) Betty Boop was first created as a dog character by Grim Natwick and appeared as the girl friend of the equally canine Bimbo in the *Talkartoons* series produced by Max and Dave Fleischer for Paramount. She was featured in "Dizzy Dishes," "Barnacle Bill," and other cartoons through 1930.

Betty Boop finally came into her own with "Betty Co-Ed," when she shed her doggy identity. Natwick later recalled this transformation: "She (Betty) started out as a little dog with long ears, but the rest of her was extremely feminine. After a few pictures the long ears developed into earrings, and she was nothing but a cute little girl." Betty's figure was modeled after Mae West's, and her singing style on that of Helen Kane (the "Boop Boop a-Doop Girl"), who sued Max Fleischer but lost. (Betty's actual voice was, after several women tried the characterization, that of Mae Questal, who also impersonated Olive Oyl.)

"Betty Boop." © *Max Fleischer.*

On the screen Betty was a tiny but resolutely feminine vamp who threw kisses and hearts at the audience, lifted her skirt and batted her long eyelashes in suggestive provocation. Her success was nothing short of fabulous: there were more than one hundred *Betty Boop* cartoons produced (including ninety in the official *Betty Boop* series). Among the most noteworthy are the 1932 "Stopping the Show" and "Betty Boop for President," the 1933 "Boilesk" (which was banned in Philadelphia), "Betty Boop's Birthday Party" (1933), "Red Hot Mama" (1934), "Betty Boop and the Little King" (1936), the 1937 "Zula Hula" and the Oscar-nominated "Riding the Rails" (1938). In all of them Betty Boop sang and danced her way through a variety of farfetched plots, in a surreal world of anthropomorphized clocks, flowerpots, toy trains and furniture.

A wave of puritanical attacks (mostly from women's clubs) against the Betty Boop persona, and a costly strike in 1937, persuaded Fleischer to drop the *Betty Boop* cartoons (whose popularity was waning, anyway). They came to an end in 1939 with the defiantly titled "Yip, Yip, Yippy!"

Betty Boop was made into toys and dolls in the 1930s, and in 1934, King Features Syndicate started distribution of *Betty Boop*, a newspaper strip (drawn by Bud Counihan). After a long eclipse, a Betty Boop craze has been building in the 1970s, with revivals of the old cartoons on television (with color added by a special process), countless toys, T-shirts, and tote bags, as well as a number of Betty Boop cartoon festivals held in the United States and abroad.

M.H.

BEVILACQUA, JOSÉ ARTUR (1880-1915) Brazilian cartoonist and illustrator born in Fortaleza, Ceará, Brazil, in 1880. After completing his high school studies, José Bevilacqua went to Rio de Janeiro in 1900 to attend the National School of Fine Arts. From 1901 to 1906, under the pen name "J. Artur," he collaborated as illustrator and cartoonist on the Rio publications *O Malho, A Avenida, Revista da Semana* and *O Papagio*. In 1907 he took a position as a drawing teacher in an Acre high school, remaining until 1910, when he decided to return to his home state of Ceará.

More Space Outside

Herluf Bidstrup. © *Bidstrup.*

Bevilacqua moved from Ceará to Belém in 1913 and worked for the newspaper *Província de Pará* for awhile. Back in Rio the next year, he resumed his collaboration on *Revista da Semana* and also drew cartoons for *El Imparcial*. A sick and troubled man, he returned to Granja, in his native Ceará, for the last year of his life. He died in Granja in 1915.

Almost a forgotten figure for over fifty years, Bevilacqua has been rediscovered of late, and his work is now being evaluated in a new light. He is hailed today as one of the pioneers of Brazilian cartooning.

A.M.

BIDSTRUP, HERLUF (1912-) Danish satirist and social cartoonist born in Copenhagen, Denmark, in 1912. His subject matter, when not directly political and topical, is human and social weakness, the constant conflict between pretext and reality: pretense, conceit, bureaucracy, etc.

With abstract satire as a base, he developed himself into a political chastiser of the first order. As "house cartoonist" at the morning paper *Socialdemokraten* (1936-45), and at the magazine *Kulturkampen*, his unsentimental drawings (trimmed Prussian necks, fat, self-satisfied collaborationists) became so provoking that the censors demanded he be dismissed. His underground cartoon of a public urinal where a German officer stands alone in the middle of eight receptacles while a long line of Danes waits in a far corner to use one is world famous. After some years as an underground cartoonist—and when the illegal communistic *Land og Folk* became the official daily for the Danish Communist movement after the Liberation in 1945—he became the daily's "house cartoonist." During the 1950s he produced first-rate caricatures and satires, merciless toward opponents, scathing and biting (his signature, "Bid," an abbreviation of his surname, means "biting").

In the 1960s and to the present his political aim has become more blatant, and his impression of the blessings of communism versus capitalism is rather stereotyped. He is still drawing factory owners with top hats, fur collars and moneybags in their hands, while the workers are young, with determined expressions and fists ready for a fight. His cartoons are printed in hundreds of newspapers behind the iron curtain. He has received the Lenin prize and various other Eastern European honors for having kept his political line unbroken and active.

J.S.

BIGNARDI, SECONDO (1925-) Italian cartoonist and animator born in Modena, Italy, on April 1, 1925. Secondo Bignardi graduated in 1943 from the Adolfo Venturi Art School in Modena and then went to the Bologna Art Academy, graduating in 1949.

Bignardi started in animation as early as 1948, drawing the backgrounds for two full-length animated films by Paolo Campani, *Alí Califfo di Bagdad e Dintorni* ("Ali Caliph of Baghdad and Suburbs") and *L'Asino e la Pelle del Leone* ("The Donkey and the Lion's Hair"). In 1950 he became a member of Campani's permanent staff, and along with Angelo Benevelli, he inked the numerous comic strips that Campani (under the pseudonym "Paul") was then supplying for the Argentinian publisher Civita of Buenos Aires. Notable among the many features Bignardi dealt with are *Misterix, Tita Dinamita, Bull Rockett* and *Ted Patton*. At the same time, first as background man and later as director and head animator,

Bignardi worked for Paul Film, the animation studio founded by himself, Campani, Max Massimino Garnier, Angelo Benevelli and others.

In 1962 Bignardi moved to Milan, where he worked as chief animator and director at the Cartoon Film studio, alongside Jimmy Murakami, Harry Hess, George Singer and other well-known American animators. In 1963 he became the director of the animated cartoons produced by Union Film, and in 1965 he decided to return to Modena to work for himself. Putting to good use his vast knowledge of the animated field, Bignardi has produced hundreds of advertising cartoons and has also made a number of entertainment films, among them *Alan Ford* and *Corto Maltese*, produced for Italian television. He has also worked with Guido De Maria on the first series of *Nick Carter* cartoons, also for television. In 1978 his twelve-minute cartoon, *Sandrone, la Pulonia é Sgorghello* ("Alex, the Toilet Is Plugged Up"), was greeted with much acclaim.

M.G.P.

BIJLSMA, RONALD (1934-   ) Dutch animator born in Rotterdam, the Netherlands, in 1934. After graduation from the Netherlands Academy of Arts in 1955, Ronald Bijlsma first worked in stained glass and etching. In 1957 he turned to animation and joined Marten Toonder Studios, working on such forgettable productions as the *Tom Poes* series. In the early 1960s Bijlsma worked with Jim Hiltz at the Cartoon Center in Hilversum, producing some of the wittiest cartoons ever shown on Dutch television.

In 1966 Bijlsma founded his own company, Animated Films, and his first independent production was the very short *The Duel*, a violent, frenetically paced cartoon that was released in 1967. In 1968 came *In the Void*, an innovative color film that Bijlsma painted directly in gouache, followed the next year by *Planet of Peace*, a satire on science fiction, the generation gap, totalitarianism and well-meaning but hollow pacifism. In 1970 Bijlsma collaborated with the Hungarian István Belai on the lighthearted *Parada*, which has been his last entertainment film to date. His efforts are now directed mainly toward producing commercial and promotional films and spots. He has been widely hailed as Holland's most original cartoonist.

M.H.

BILEK, FRANZISKA (ca. 1915-   ) German cartoonist and illustrator born in Munich, Germany, around 1915. Franziska Bilek started drawing for *Simplicissimus* in 1936, when she was a student of about twenty at the Munich Academy, and she was in her later twenties when her first illustrated books were published.

The title of one of her albums, *München und Ich* ("Munich and I," 1969), could serve as a motto for the bulk of her production, which might be even more precisely characterized as "I and Munich." Unabashedly catering to local patriotism and the tastes of the less sophisticated Munich citizenry, one book after another celebrates the city's annual festivities, special customs and amusements (Carnival, finger wrestling, the zoo) and street scenes (construction work, hookers), but each volume turns into an even more detailed celebration of Franziska Bilek. Depicting herself as a small, unprepossessing hausfrau, she draws in a conventional cartoon style much diluted from that of her teacher Olaf Gul-

Secondo Bignardi, promotion piece.

Franziska Bilek, "Medusa at the Hairdresser's," 1943. ©
Simplicissimus.

bransson (her *Künstlervater*, as her ads for *München und
Ich* put it, exploiting his friendship for her long after his
death). She subjects herself to numerous slapstick misadventures—her first Carnival ball, her first attempt at
rock 'n' roll—or describes her appearances on local radio
and television, her wonderful old apartment house, her
hobbies, and so on.

Franziska Bilek worked for *Simplicissimus* until 1943,
during its clouded last years, and then turned to book
illustration. A late *Simplicissimus* cartoon by her,
"Medusa at the Hairdresser's," points toward the realm
of her early book *Der Heitere Olymp* ("Humorous Mount
Olympus"), in which the Greek gods are shows as ordi-
nary folk. In 1944 Bilek treated antiquity once again in
her illustrations for Lucian's *Hetärengespräche*
("Dialogues of Courtesans"), but the same year saw her
resolutely embracing her cult of Munich with *Das Kann
Nur München Sein* ("That Can Only Be Munich"). Other
volumes (some with text by her) include *Vom Brettl
Unserer Tage* ("On the Cabaret of Our Day," ca. 1946),
Franziskas Blumenstrauss ("Franziska's Bouquet"),
Franziska Bileks Heitere Welt ("Franziska Bilek's
Humorous World"), *Mir Gefällts in München* (" I Like It
in Munich," 1958) and *Bayrischer Jahrmarkt* ("Bavarian
Fair," ca. 1960).

S.A.

BILIBIN, IVAN IAKOLEVICH (1876-1942) Soviet cartoonist, illustrator and designer born in Tarkhovka, near
St. Petersburg, Russia, on August 16, 1876. Ivan Bilibin
studied art in Munich in 1898, then in St. Petersburg
from 1899 to 1904, first with I.E. Repin and later at the
Academy of Arts. He started his cartooning career in
1905 with regular contributions to the satirical
magazines *Adskaia Pochta* and *Zhupel*. His caricatures
and lampoons of czarist society brought censure upon
him, and several of his cartoons were banned from publication. In addition to his cartooning, Bilibin also illustrated books and taught at the Society for the Encouragement of Fine Arts.

Bilibin took no direct part in the Russian Revolution.

In 1920 he left the Soviet Union, first for Egypt, then for
France, where he pursued his career as a book illustrator.
Returning to Russia in 1936, Bilibin became a professor
at the Leningrad Academy of Art. He created the "Bilibin
style" of book illustration, relying heavily on the discipline of the cartoon, and also designed sets and costumes for theater and opera. Although his contributions
were fewer in later years, he never quite abandoned
cartooning, and his drawings sporadically appeared in
Pravda and other Soviet publications.

Bilibin died on February 7, 1942, during the siege of
Leningrad. A book-length study of his career by I.N.
Lipovich was published in Leningrad in 1966.

M.H.

BILLON, DANIEL (1927-   ) French cartoonist born in
Paris, France, on July 7, 1927. After completing his
college studies Daniel Billon started his career in 1948 as
a cartoonist on the French women's magazine *Filles de
France*. Moving to Editions Vaillant a little later, he
contributed a large number of illustrations to the
magazines *Vaillant* and *Caméra*.

Billon's career really took off in 1967, when he joined
the cartooning staff of the weekly (now monthly)
magazine *Pilote*. There he contributed a great many
single-panel cartoons on topical subjects, as well as
countless illustrations. At the same time Billon continued to freelance cartoons to such humor publications
as *Marius* and *Le Hérisson*, and he created several comic
strips as well, all of them short-lived. Billon is also noted
for his children's book illustrations, as well as for his
magazine covers.

Billon's style is competent, perhaps a little too tight,
but excellent in its craftsmanship. (Daniel Billon's
father, Pierre Billon, was also a cartoonist and the creator
of countless short-lived humor strips in the 1940s and
1950s.)

M.H.

BILLY BROWN OF LONDON TOWN (G.B.) "I trust you'll
pardon my correction/That stuff is there for your protection!" The rhymed admonishment came from a neatly
dressed, bowler-hatted office clerk and was addressed to
his traveling companion in a London omnibus. The
windows were covered with a close-weave netting
designed to prevent splintering and shattering during an
air raid, and it was the special delight of London
travelers to peel this adhesive away from the glass. *Billy
Brown of London Town* was created by London Transport to prevent this curious habit, and the artwork was
executed by David Langdon. The character caught on,
and his comical couplets and cartoon messages continued throughout the war and after. There was even a
Noel Coward song that went, "Mr. Brown of London
Town had a job to do, thought he'd see it through, and he
did it too. . . .'"

David Langdon, a cartoonist who had come up in
Punch just prior to World War II, somehow made a
specialty of creating comic cartoons out of London's
transport system: tubes, buses, railway trains and their
personnel seemed special bait to him and were (and still
are) a regular source of amusement for him and his
readers. As a flying officer in the war he added the RAF,
its airplanes and personnel, to his gallery, becoming its
special spokesperson in humor. He illustrated a number
of popular handbooks on RAF slang and a strip, *Joe*, in
the *RAF Journal*, which he edited from 1945.

His style, always simple, is distinctive and popular, and he claims to have invented the "open mouth" in gag cartoons. He was born on February 24, 1914, and worked in the architects' department of the London County Council from 1931 to the war. His first cartoon was published in *Time and Tide*, and he has been contributing a strip of topical gags to the *Sunday Pictorial*, now the *Sunday Mirror*, for many years.

Books: *Home Front Lines* (1941); *It's a Piece of Cake* (1943); *All Buttoned Up* (1944); *Meet Me Inside* (1946); *Slipstream* (1946); *The Way I See It* (1947); *Let's Face It* (1951); *Look at You* (1952); *Wake Up and Die* (1952); *All in Fun* (1953); *Laugh with Me* (1954); *More in Fun* (1955); *Funnier Still* (1956); *Little Cabbages* (1956); *Banger for a Monkey* (1957); *Puff and Wuff* (1957); *Langdon at Large* (1958); *I'm Only Joking* (1960); *Punch with Wings* (1961); *Best of Mikes* (1962); *How to Play Golf and Stay Happy* (1964); *David Langdon's Casebook* (1969); and *Über Allies* (1969).

D.G.

BIMROSE, ART (1912-   ) American editorial and political cartoonist born in Spokane, Washington, on March 18, 1912. Art Bimrose graduated from high school and took a job arranged by his father with the Southern Pacific Railroad. But he left the job to attend the San Francisco Art Institute and follow his first love, comic strips and cartoons. When he left art school to enter the profession, he landed a job as a staff artist on the *Portland Oregonian*. This was in 1937, and Bimrose handled everything from retouching photos to drawing cartoon spots. In 1947, when the paper's cartoonist retired, Bimrose became chief editorial cartoonist, a position he

"Do Be Careful Boys," a Biographic cartoon film.© Biographic.

retains as of this writing. His cartoons are syndicated by the *Oregonian*.

Bimrose's style is a handsome blend of pebbleboard shading and benday tones. His early interest in comics is evidenced by his humorous style and resultant gentleness. This nonpartisan, independent cartoonist is the recipient of Freedoms Foundation awards for 1952, 1961 and 1965.

R.M.

BIOGRAPHIC CARTOON FILMS (G.B.) "A British Film Made with British Labour." The closing caption to *The Do-It-Yourself Cartoon Kit* (1961) capped a riotous six-minute send-up of all that animation holds dear. Ironically, the gag, which burlesqued the famous wartime end-title to the prestigious Ealing Studios productions, covered up an equally fierce and patriotic determination to prove that British animators could create and produce cartoon films to equal anything the rest of the world could offer. And despite the constant cost-cutting and corner-cutting that British animators have suffered throughout their seventy-year history, whether their backers have been film companies or television organizations, it is thanks to such small pockets of resistance as Biographic Cartoon Films that Great Britain continues to be recognized and to win awards throughout the world of animation.

Biographic was formed by Bob Godfrey and Keith Learner in 1952 as a spare-time reaction to the dullness of their animation work for the Larkins Studio. Laboring by day on diagram films, by night, working in Godfrey's basement, they produced *The Big Parade*. Their second film, *Watch the Birdie* (1953), a triumph of limited animation, won the Ten Best award of the *Amateur Cine World*, the leading home movie magazine. On the strength of this 16mm production they were commissioned to make a commercial for Gillette razor blades, on the proceeds of which they moved to 11 Noel Street, Soho. There they hit the build-up period prior to the opening of Independent Television in England; on the first night the first cartoon commercial transmitted was a

Still Trying

Art Bimrose. © The Oregonian.

Biographic production for Crompton Parkinson lamps (1955). Commercials for television have continued to be the outfit's main production line, ranging from a Quaker macaroni 15-second job animated over a single hectic weekend to the longest-running series, Esso Blue, which began in 1959 and has won a number of awards.

Their first entertainment work was inserts and sequences for the Michael Bentine television comedy series *After Hours* (1956), which led to the Spike Milligan/Dick Lester series *A Show Called Fred* and *Son of Fred* (1956), and the BBC Bentine series, *It's a Square World* (1957). These segments, made at less than cost, attracted attention to the new company. Vera Linnecar and Nancy Hanna, colleagues from the Larkins Studio, were invited to join the expanding company in 1957, and a large, old house was taken over on Dean Street, Soho. In 1960 came the company's first American commission, commercials for Olde Frothingslosh Stale Pale Ale of Pittsburgh, Pennsylvania. Biographic also entered entertainment cartoons with Bob Godfrey's personal production, *Polygamous Polonius*, in 1960. It was selected for a Royal Film Performance. Godfrey followed with *The Rise and Fall of Emily Sprod* (1962) and *The Plain Man's Guide to Advertising* (1963).

In 1963 the group split into individual animators to handle their own personal films. Biographic 1 (Nancy Hanna) made *Aquarius* (1963), an abstract space journey; Biographic 2 (Keith Learner) made *Goldwhiskers* (1964), about a "James Bond" mouse; Biographic 3 (Vera Linnecar) made *Springtime for Samantha* (1965), a "little girl" cartoon; and Biographic 4 (Bob Godfrey) made *Alf, Bill and Fred* (1964). Godfrey left to set up on his own, leaving Learner, Linnecar and Hanna to continue Biographic. *Do Be Careful Boys* (1965), their first three-handed cartoon, won a British Film Academy award for its humorous handling of safety advice from the Fruit Producers Council. The women have been the most productive in entertainment cartoons: *Quodlibet* (Hanna, 1968), *The Trendsetter* (Linnecar, 1970) and *A Cat Is a Cat* (Linnecar, 1971). All three directed *I'm Glad You Asked That Question* (1970) for the Gas Council and their longest cartoon to date, *I'm Sorry You've Been Kept Waiting* (1976), a 16-minute instructional cartoon sponsored by IBM. Biographic has also animated titles for the feature films *Inn for Trouble* (1960), *The Road to Hong Kong* (1962), *Hand of Night* (1966), and *The Ghost Goes Gear* (1966). Their main line continues to be television commercials, and they are proud of their claim to being the first British animation company organized to produce animated TV commercials.

D.G.

Reginald Birch, "If They Reined In Their Horses," 1895.

BIRCH, REGINALD BATHURST (1856-1943) American artist born in London, England, on May 2, 1856. Reginald Birch grew up in San Francisco and received his art training at the Art Academy of Munich, Germany. In 1881, Birch began to illustrate for the popular illustrated monthlies and to focus his work on the children's magazine *St. Nicholas*, originally published by Scribner's, later by the Century Company. Birch soon became about the most published illustrator in the United States, contributing to all the magazines of these firms as well as to *Harper's, Collier's, Youth's Companion* and *Life*; for his children's drawings he earned the title "the Children's Gibson"; he illustrated nearly two hundred books, including his most notable, *Little Lord Fauntleroy*, by Frances Hodgson Burnett. His drawings for the latter influenced a generation of boys' clothes—ultimately worn by Buster Brown.

His cartoons, principally in *Life* and the back sections of the monthlies, often dealt with society subjects. Birch looked the upper-class type and obviously moved in those circles. His style was always bold and handsome, a precise knowledge of anatomy and skillful use of pen-and-ink crosshatching resulting in arresting and lively representations. In later years his line grew thicker—though not stiffer—and exactitude and detail gave way to economy and exaggeration. His illustrations of Edward Lear's nonsense rhymes are classics of the genre.

Besides the many books for which he drew, a collection of story excerpts and illustrations of fifty years of work was published as *Reginald Birch—His Book* by Harcourt Brace in 1939.

R.M.

BIRCHANSKY, LEO (1887-1949) Russian-American cartoonist born in Odessa, Russia, in 1887. Lev (Leo) Birchansky studied art at a private school in his native Odessa. In 1907 he became the editorial cartoonist and later the art director of *Odesskaia Novosti*, one of the city's leading newspapers, and he continued in these positions until 1917. He then took part in the Russian Revolution and published sketches depicting scenes of the revolution.

In 1922 Birchansky left the Soviet Union for western Europe and later came to the United States, finally settling in New York. There he freelanced cartoons and illustrations, also illustrating books in Russian by his fellow émigrés. He worked for 12 years (1931-43) in the art department of the *New York News*. In 1943 he moved to Miami, where he worked for various local publications as a cartoonist and illustrator. He died in Miami on March 8, 1949.

Leo Birchansky was a noted political cartoonist in his native Russia, but his style of cartooning never found favor in the United States. His career spanned two continents and two vastly different political systems, and this fact makes his contribution worthy of acknowledgment.

M.H.

BIRD, CYRIL KENNETH (1887-   ) British cartoonist born on December 17, 1887. Cyril ("Fougasse") Bird was the Isaac Pitman of British cartooning: he was the first to invent and use a visual shorthand. His early cartoons in *Tit-Bits* and other weeklies just after World War I are average. But during the 1920s he evolved a dot-and-dash code of cartooning that by the 1930s was

C.K. Bird ("Fougasse"), World War II cartoon. © *Fougasse.*

Philip Bissell, "Obliging Ted." © *Bissell.*

one of the most widely recognized individual styles in England.

Fougasse studied at Cheltenham College, obtaining his bachelor of science degree. He studied cartooning by mail through Percy V. Bradshaw's Press Art School until going to war in 1914. In 1916 he was invalided out after having been shot in the spine at Gallipoli and crippled for life. He began to assault magazines with cartoons, signing himself "Fougasse," the name of a small French land mine. Bradshaw, with whom he continued to study, sold Fougasse's first cartoon to *Punch* in 1917, and a destiny was created. Fougasse became the art editor of that famous weekly in 1937 and was appointed full editor in 1949. He retired in 1953 but kept busy by writing his definitive "Survey of Modern British and American Humorous Art," *The Good Tempered Pencil.*

His shorthand style and handwritten lettering became extremely well known (and liked) through his advertising work (Pyramid handkerchiefs, etc.) and his many war posters for the Ministry of Transport and others (1939-45). He often lectured on cartooning and humor on radio and the club circuits and was one of the pioneers of the school of cartooning that believed humor to be more important than art: "It is really better to have a good idea with a bad drawing than a bad idea with a good drawing."

Books: *A Gallery of Games* (1921); *Drawn at a Venture* (1922); *So This Is Golf* (1923); *A Book of Drawings* (1926); *The World's Workers* (1928); *E. and O.E.* (1928); *P.T.O.* (1930); *Southern Ways and Means* (1931); *Fun Fair* (1934); *Aces Made Easy* (1934); *You Have Been Warned* (1935); *Exploring the Avenues* (1936); *Luck of the Draw* (1936); *Drawing the Line Somewhere* (1937); *Stop or Go* (1938); *Jotsam* (1939); *The Changing Face of Britain* (1940); *And the Gatepost* (1940); *Running Commentary* (1941); *The Little Less* (1941); *Dear Turley* (1942); *Sorry No Rubber* (1942); *Fougasse Painting Book* (1942); *Just a*

Few Lines (1943); *Family Group* (1944); *Home Circle* (1945); *A School of Purposes* (1946); *You and Me* (1948); *Us* (1951); *The Neighbours* (1954); *The Good Tempered Pencil* (1956); *Wall Pictures* (1957); *Between the Lines* (1958); *Ballet Exercises* (1960); and *Guided Composition* (1961).

D.G.

BIRDSALL, TIMOTHY (1936-1963) British cartoonist born in Cambridge, England, in 1936. Timothy Birdsall, who signed himself "Timothy," was not only a brilliant and witty political cartoonist on paper, he was a budding and engaging television personality, the first cartoonist to fully use his talents "live." A rocketing career was tragically cut short when he died suddenly of leukemia at the age of 27.

Birdsall came down to London from Cambridge in 1960 and was immediately taken on by the *Sunday Times* to draw the front-page "Little Cartoon." He satirized the newspaper as the *Sunday Tome* in one of his brilliant burlesques for the satirical weekly *Private Eye*, for which he became a regular contributor from 1962. The same year he was appointed political cartoonist of the more serious weekly *Spectator*. With more time and space to play with, his drawing style expanded to become fantastically detailed in the rococo traditions of Ronald Searle, Rowland Emett and Michael Ffolkes. But his wit was always more barbed than his mentors'. He illustrated books, including Michael Frayn's collection *The Day of the Dog*; in a different vein, he drew 49 pictures of theaters for *London Theatres* by Raymond Mander and Joe Mitchenson. A book of his own creation, *This Book Is Good for You*, was never completed due to his illness, but his rough page layouts were printed in a collection of his work, *Timothy*, published as a tribute in 1964.

In the last few months of his life, Timothy became one of the team of young satirists who took the world to pieces every Saturday night on BBC television in Ned Sherrin and David Frost's series *That Was the Week That Was* (1963). For his weekly spot he developed a totally new, live, on-camera cartooning technique, with drawing and commentary linked in one inseparable five-minute flow of spontaneous comedy. His sudden death at the height of his success (June 1963) shocked the British nation.

D.G.

BISSELL, PHILIP (1926-) American cartoonist born in Worcester, Massachusetts, on February 1, 1926. Phil Bissell was a cartoonist on his high school monthly magazine; graduating in 1944, he went directly into the army. Back in civilian life, he studied in a Boston art school on a GI bill for two years. In 1948, after completing his studies, he went to work for the *Boston Traveler*, first as a copy boy, then as a cartoonist drawing sports, entertainment and editorial cartoons. But Bissell's heart was set on sports exclusively, and when he learned in 1953 that the *Boston Globe* was looking for a new sports cartoonist he applied for the job and was accepted. Bissell drew sports cartoons (and an occasional editorial cartoon) for the *Globe* with such gusto that he soon gained national recognition. In 1965 he resigned from the *Globe* and started his own syndicate. He later joined the staff of the *Worcester Gazette*, and in 1975 he became the sports cartoonist of the *Boston Herald-American*.

Bissell has also contributed many cartoons and illustrations to magazines, mostly on sports subjects, and he originated the insignia of the New England Patriots. He has won many awards in the sports cartoon category, and his works are on permanent display in the basketball, football and baseball halls of fame.

M.H.

J.S. Blackton, "Humorous Phases of Funny Faces," 1906.

BLACKTON, JAMES STEWART (1875-1941) American cartoonist and filmmaker born in Sheffield, England, on January 5, 1875. J.S. Blackton came to the United States as a child and started his cartooning career on Joseph Pulitzer's *New York World.* In 1896 he was the subject of an early Edison short titled *Blackton, The Evening World Cartoonist.* Fascinated by the new medium of film, Blackton, in partnership with others, established the Vitagraph Company. Among the early films he directed were "historical reconstructions" such as *Tearing Down the Spanish Flag* (1897) and *The Battle of Santiago Bay* (1899).

In 1900 Blackton produced *Enchanted Drawings,* an early attempt at animation, in which inanimate objects appeared to jump on the screen (the method is called "pixillation"). Blackton next produced what is probably the first genuine animated film, *Humorous Phases of Funny Faces* (1906), in which he discovered the formula of "one turn, one picture," a process still followed today. With this innovation the animated cartoon became irrevocably tied to the camera. Other animated films followed: *The Haunted Hotel* (1907), *Princess Nicotine, True Life, The Magic Fountain Pen,* etc.

In the period following World War I Blackton went back to England to try and recoup his fortunes (he had been ousted from Vitagraph in a bitter power struggle), and there he made several elaborate but unsuccessful live-action features, *The Glorious Adventure* and *Passionate Quest* being the most notable. Upon his return to the United States several years later, Blackton could not find work in the changed climate of the early "talkies." He spent the rest of his life exhibiting his silent films at country fairs, attired in the costume of a turn-of-the-century filmmaker. Blackton died in utter obscurity and poverty in Hollywood on August 14, 1941.

One of the forgotten figures of the early cinema, James Stewart Blackton can be called the father of film animation. His work, in both the animation and the live-action fields, is worthy of rediscovery and reevaluation.

M.H.

BLANCHOT, GUSTAVE (1885-1968) French cartoonist, illustrator and publisher born in central France in 1885. Drawing first for small magazines, he became, under the pen name "Gus Bofa," assistant editor of *Le Rire,* one of the most important humor journals of the 20th century. During World War I, he published *La Baïonnette.*

Bofa also published many albums, such as *Chez les Toubibs* ("At the Medicos'," 1918), *Malaises* (1930), *La Symphonie de la Peur* ("The Symphony of Fear," 1937), and *Slogans* (1939), in which his sophisticated but bitter taste was balanced by a certain comic zaniness. He illustrated dozens of works, from Courteline (1923), *Don Quixote* (1926-27) and Thomas De Quincey (1930) to Edgar Allan Poe (1941), wrote a fine and witty book of "literary and extraliterary theses" (1923) and founded with Jean-Gabriel Daragnès the Salon de l'Araignée. Despite all these accomplishments, however, Bofa is best remembered for a poster he designed for a coal and wood company. It showed a poor fellow condemned to burn at the stake who exclaims, on seeing the excellent quality of the wood and coal briquettes, "Vous me gastez!" ("You're spoiling me!").

Gustave Blanchot died in 1968.

P.H.

BLASHFIELD, ALBERT DODD (1860-1920) American cartoonist and illustrator born in Brooklyn, New York, on July 30, 1860. A.D. Blashfield's brother, Edwin H. Blashfield, was a famous muralist, and the family was an artistic one. Educated at the Brooklyn Collegiate and Polytechnic Institute and the Alexander Military Institute, Blashfield received art training from the Art Stu-

"Going down?"

Albert Blashfield, 1906.

dents League in New York. In the early 1890s, Blashfield joined the staff of *Life* and became a fixture there until his death. A personal favorite of *Life*'s founder and editor J.A. Mitchell, Blashfield was to illustrate several of Mitchell's books, including *The Pines of Lory* and *The Last American*.

Blashfield's major contribution was his delineation of *Life*'s cupid. Thousands of these beings floated through *Life*'s pages throughout Blashfield's tenure there (although he also drew occasional gag cartoons as he had done, crudely and on a freelance basis, before joining *Life*). His drawing style was one of most comfortable and friendly in all of cartooning; gentle, rounded lines were softly shaded by precise, willowy highlight and shadow lines. His work was striking, handsome and never frilly for all its charm. His covers for *Life* betrayed a masterful command of pastel shades, and his decorative work on title pages and in-house ads is a delight to behold.

Blashfield died at the age of 59 on February 7, 1920.

R.M.

Milan Blažeković, "Largo." © Zagreb Film.

BLAŽEKOVIĆ, MILAN (1940-) Yugoslavian cartoonist and animator born in Zagreb, Yugoslavia, in 1940. Milan Blažeković taught himself the art of cartooning by visiting the neighboring studio of Zagreb Film. In 1959 he joined the famed studio as an assistant animator, later graduating to head animator on such films as *Twist Again* (1964). He also animated and occasionally directed many of the cartoons in the *Slučaj . . .* and *Inspektor Masku* series. In the 1960s he became noted for his witty mini-cartoons, of which he directed more than a score.

After directing *Gorilla Dance* (1968) under the close supervision of Dušan Vukotić, Blažeković produced in 1970 his first independent cartoon, *The Man Who Had to Sing*, a droll saga of a little man who went through life singing off-key, to the annoyance and downright hostility of his neighbors. He followed this success with the equally amusing *The Collector* (1972) and did one of the cartoon sketches of *Man the Polluter* (1975). His forte, however, remains the mini-cartoons, and he continues to contribute a goodly number of them. Blažeković is also noted for his gag cartoons, which have appeared in such humor publications as *Kerempuh* and *Rajvitak*.

M.H.

BLECHMAN, ROBERT O. (1930-) American cartoonist and illustrator born in Brooklyn, New York, in 1930. R.O. Blechman attended Oberlin College,

graduating in 1952. He started freelancing cartoons two years later in New York City, and his work appeared in the *New York Times*, *Look* and *Graphis*, among other publications.

Blechman is best known, however, for his work in animation. While not an animator himself, he designs the stories upon which the animation is based and works closely with the animators. His first signal success in the field came in 1957, when he did the drawings for Gene Deitch and Al Kouzel's acclaimed *The Juggler of Our Lady*. In the 1960s Blechman opened his own graphic studio and started providing hilarious advertising cartoons for print media as well as for TV. His "talking stomach" ads for Alka-Seltzer and "attack of the car" ads for Volvo have become fabled examples of witty TV commercials. Blechman occasionally returns to entertainment animation, as with *The Emperor's New Armor*, which he did in 1969 with Kouzel. His latest effort, *No Room at the Inn*, is a wry retelling of the Nativity story; it was shown on public television in 1978.

Blechman has also illustrated a number of books in his well-recognized, wiggly, amorphous style. A much-imitated cartoonist, he has taught a course in humorous art at the School of Visual Arts in New York City since 1960, and he occasionally lectures on his craft at college campuses around the country.

M.H.

BLIX, RAGNVALD (1882-1958) Norwegian satirical cartoonist born in Oslo, Norway, on September 12, 1882. Ragnvald Blix was one of Scandinavia's, and maybe the world's, greatest satirical cartoonists. He studied in various places throughout Europe, making a name for himself in Paris with his caricatures of the Louvre's art treasures. Among his greatest admirers was Mark Twain, who introduced him to the German satirical magazine *Simplicissimus*.

His real breakthrough occurred in Copenhagen and Oslo (1919-21), where he published *Exlex* ("Outlaw"), the first inter-Scandinavian magazine of quality. Here, world-famous cartoonists such as Adolf Hallman and Oscar Jacobsson ("Adamson") later made their debuts. World politics was the target of their sharp-witted pens, and Blix was one of the first to see the Nazi danger in Germany in the years between the wars. His devastating satire of Hitler's and Mussolini's dictator-states was frequently quoted in the world press.

When Norway was occupied by the Germans, Blix moved to Sweden, where *Göteborgs Handels- och Sjöfarts Tidning* secured him as their most talented employee, under the pen name "Stig Höök." Although

R.O. Blechman, "No Room at the Inn." © PBS.

When the Socialists come: —"The new members of government are here, Your Majesty. May I show them in?" —"Yes, but through the servants' entrance."

Ragnvald Blix. © *Simplicissimus.*

Sweden officially was neutral, it was Stig Höök's cartoons that showed the Swedish view of the Germans to the outside world, and as they were smuggled out of Sweden they found their way into the underground press of other countries. Classic is the cartoon about Vidkun Quisling's audience in Berlin, where he greets *der Führer* with a *"Heil"* and says, "I am Quisling!" *"Jawohl,"* says Hitler, "and your name, please?" Seeing Blix's cartoons 20 years after his death confirms the belief that he was a master and possibly never will be surpassed by others in the accuracy of his caricatures and the sharpness of his captions.

J.S.

BLOCK, HERBERT LAWRENCE (1909-   ) American cartoonist, Pulitzer Prize winner and author born in Chicago, Illinois, in 1909. "Herblock" is undoubtedly the most famous signature in cartooning. The son of a Chicago chemist, Herblock won a scholarship to the Chicago Art Institute at the age of 12. Thereafter he briefly attended Lake Forest College before becoming editorial cartoonist for the *Chicago Daily News* in 1929, at age 20.

Five years later Herblock became the syndicated cartoonist for the Newspaper Enterprise Association, winning a Pulitzer there in 1942. He then joined the army to produce GI information material. In 1945 he returned to civilian life to become the *Washington Post*'s political cartoonist, with a charge to be simply as brilliant and freewheeling as he could. What happened is virtually legend—Washington, the paper and Herblock were suited to each other, and Herblock became the most influential cartoonist of his time. His impact was felt as much in his profession—where a generation of imitators followed—as throughout the country, where politicians

nervously opened their morning papers to see if they'd been scored or spared by Herblock that day.

His cartoons were widely syndicated by the Hall Syndicate and its successors. Herblock has opposed a wide array of enemies, including Senator Joe McCarthy, Richard Nixon, and the iconographic Mr. Bomb, while drawing in a conventional vertical format with crayon shading. Today especially, his roots in the label era of cartooning sometimes show, but he remains a prime exponent of devastating partisanship, uncompromising advocacy and brilliant presentations.

As personally modest and friendly as his work is brutal, Herblock is a celebrity who shies from public appearances. Many collections of his work have appeared, including *Herblock Looks at Communism* (1950), *The Herblock Book* (1952), *Herblock's Here and Now* (1955), *Herblock's Special for Today* (1958), *Straight Herblock* (1964), *Herblock's State of the Union* (1972) and *Special Report* (1974). His first Pulitzer has been joined by two more (1954 and 1979), and he has also won four Sigma Delta Chi awards, the National Cartoonists Society Reuben, the National Headliners Club award and the Heywood Broun award for 1950.

R.M.

BLONDEAU, GEORGES (1929-   ) French cartoonist born in Villeneuve-Saint-Georges, a suburb of Paris, France, in 1929. After his high school studies, Georges ("Gébé") Blondeau became an industrial draftsman for the French railway system. He published his first cartoons in the house organ of the company. In 1958 Blondeau left the railways for a career as a freelance cartoonist under the pseudonym Gébé (the phonetic

Herbert Block ("Herblock"). From "Herblock Special Report," W.W. Norton & Co., Inc., 1974. © *Herblock.*

Georges Blondeau ("Gébé"),"The Arrival of the Chestnut Vendor." © Gébé.

rendition in French of the two initials of his name). He has since contributed countless cartoons to such publications as *Paris-Presse*, *Le Journal du Dimanche*, *Arts*, *Pilote* and *Bizarre*. Gébé's most consistent body of work, however, has been done for the satirical weekly *Hara-Kiri*, for which he created the weird character Berck. Gébé is now the editor of *Hara-Kiri Mensuel* (the monthly version of the magazine), and he continues to work for other publications.

Gébé is one of the most imaginative (and one of the most representative) artists of the new school of French cartooning. His dark humor has a disturbing, even neurotic tone, and he crowds his compositions with strange contraptions, eerily disjointed backgrounds and a motley assortment of bizarre, threatening characters. He is the poet of the squalid, the tawdry and the horrible, and his sardonic drawings exude a leering, unsettling quality.

M.H.

BOBBY BEAR (G.B.) "Bobby, a small brown bear, has been my pet ever since I met the jolly little fellow playing in the street." So claimed "Aunt Kitsie" in her editorial introduction to the 1924 edition of *Bobby Bear Annual*. The truth, of course, is slightly different. Kitsie Bridges created *Bobby Bear* for the Children's Corner of the new daily paper published by the Labour party, the *Daily Herald* (although Bobby, of course, in no way reflected the politics of his proprietors!). Bobby appeared in the first issue of the new newspaper on March 31, 1919, in fact predating the more famous *Rupert Bear* in the *Daily Express* by 20 months (see *The World Encyclopedia of Comics*, Chelsea House, 1976).

The original format of the feature was a single panel cartoon illustrating a serialized story, and this gradually expanded pictorially, first to two panels, then to a proper comic strip of four. The first artist was Dora McLaren, who was followed by "Meg" (1930), Wilfred Haughton (1933), and Rick Elmes (1939). The cast of the series included Mother and Father Bear, the adopted orphan Maisie Mouse, Ruby Rat, Aunt McMouse, Percy Porker the Pig and Dr. Deer, the teacher.

In the first paperback publication, *The Daily Herald Bobby Bear Book* (1920), Bobby himself wrote: "I must say it is a very grate privlidge for me to have a rele book ritten about miself, but I have alwaze been a very forchnit little bear, tho I have my trubbles." A Bobby Bear Club was formed, with an enamel membership badge and club song (written by "Tomfool"), and by 1931 there were four hundred thousand members. The annual reprints went into hardback from the 1932 edition, and the books continued to be published long after the feature was dropped from the newspaper. The *Bobby Bear Annual* was published from 1922 to 1943.

D.G.

BOBBY BUMPS (U.S.) Pioneer animator Earl Hurd created his best-known character, Bobby Bumps, in 1915. Bobby was a mischievous little boy clearly inspired by R.F. Outcault's highly popular comic strip character Buster Brown. The resemblance was evident in the little hero's physical appearance, the initials of his name and the fact that Bobby, like Buster, had a bulldog for a companion—named Fido in this case.

In the early entries of the series, such as "Bobby Bumps and His Goat Mobile," "Bobby Bumps' Detective Story" and "Bobby Bumps' Hypnotic Eye" (all 1916), Hurd seemed content to spin routine stories around Bobby's pranks, often played on his parents or his little companions. The cartoons became wilder and wilder as the series progressed, however. The year 1918 is indicative in this respect, as Hurd moved from the banal antics of "Before and After" to the more outlandish "Bobby Bumps and the Speckled Death" before finishing the year with the almost surrealistic "Bobby Bumps Puts a Beanery on the Bum." The 1919 "Bobby Bumps' Film Company" pulled out all stops, blending live action and animation, alternately using word balloons and intertitles and even having the animated characters talk back to the director.

The *Bobby Bumps* series was discontinued in the early 1920s, thus ending one of the more curious experiments in commercial animation.

M.H.

BOBBY SOX
See Emmy Lou.

BOEVOI KARANDASH (USSR) Boevoi Karandash ("The Militant Pencil") was the name of a Leningrad group of artists and writers who banded together to produce a number of political posters (usually in broadsheets) and several collections of cartoons during the days of the Finno-Russian War (1939-40). They took on special importance during World War II, and especially in the course of the Leningrad siege, during which their posters and cartoons kept the morale of the population high despite the rigors of the blockade. The Boevoi Karandash collective has included at one time or another the artists V.I. Kurdov, I.S. Astapov, G.N. Petrov, G.S. Vereiskii, V.A. Serov and N.A. Tyrsa, and the writers V.M. Saianov and N.S. Tikhonov.

Boevoi Karandash dispersed in 1945 at the end of the war. However, another group of the same name formed in 1956, and they have since issued a number of satirical posters and cartoon collections on topical themes dealing not only with international issues but with situations of everyday Soviet life as well.

M.H.

BOFA, GUS
See Blanchot, Gustave.

BOILLY, LOUIS LEOPOLD (1761-1845) French painter, engraver and caricaturist born in La Bassée, in northern France, on July 5, 1761. Louis Boilly received his art education from his father, the wood-carver Arnould Boilly, who wanted his son to become a house painter. In 1775 the young Boilly went to live with one of his relatives in Douai, where he perfected his talents. Moving to Arras in 1779, he painted over three hundred portraits before settling in Paris in 1784.

Boilly became famous at age 27 as a painter of love scenes and portraits. During the French Revolution he almost lost his life because of a series of satirical drawings of revolutionary leaders, but he soon regained his position with a number of patriotic and political paintings. Boilly survived the Directory, the Empire, the Res-

toration and three revolutions without losing his footing. His paintings and engravings remained popular through every change of political regime, though the artist himself stayed poor throughout his life.

Boilly is best known for his satirical drawings, and especially for his *Grimaces*, a series of grimacing heads which he drew over the years and grouped allegorically, often round a didactic or moralistic theme (i.e., "Avarice," "Sloth," "The Perils of Ignorance"). He has been hailed as an acute observer of his times and a forerunner of the French school of social criticism.

Boilly died in Paris on January 4, 1845. Several of his children were also artists, notably Julien-Léopold (1796-1874), Edouard (1799-1854) and Alphonse (1801-1867).

M.H.

BOJESEN, BO (1923-   ) Danish artist born in Aabenrå, Denmark, on March 22, 1923. As the permanent satirical cartoonist at the Copenhagen daily *Politiken* for almost thirty years, Bo Bojesen has established himself as Denmark's number one caricaturist, considered among the world elite of satirical artists. His line is clean, his caricatures accurate and incomparably funny.

Each year he draws three to four panels a week as commentaries on the politics, happenings and whims of

Louis Boilly, "Thirty-five Heads."

the day. His captions are as hard-hitting as his drawing style. Every year a collection of that year's best Bo Bojesen drawings is published. He is also an active book illustrator.

J.S.

In Rothenburg, Germany, there are plans for establishing a degree in humor: "Will Herr Rumpelmayer please attend the lectures more regularly so that he can keep pace with his fellow students!"

Bo Bojesen. © Bojesen.

BOLEK I LOLEK (Poland) *Bolek i Lolek* is one of the most popular series of Polish animated cartoons. It was started in the early 1960s by Wladyslaw Nehrebecki for Polish television. Bolek and Lolek, the two little heroes of the series, are mischievous young boys whose natural curiosity and sense of fun lead them into many adventures and discoveries. They often daydream their way into wild fights against Indians, perilous descents into waterfalls and horse rides into the countryside.

Bolek i Lolek has been a hit with children (and their parents) ever since its inception. The fun is controlled and seldom violent, the direction very professional, and while the appeal is to young children, there are some nice pieces of animation that can be enjoyed by adults. (In the United States the cartoons can be seen on *The Polish Hour*, broadcast by WBTB-TV in Newark, New Jersey, among other stations.)

The success of the TV show prompted the release in 1975 of a full-length animated feature, *Around the World with Bolek and Lolek*, in which the two venturesome boys followed in the footsteps of Phineas Fogg, Jules Verne's famous globe-trotter. This Bielsko-Biala production was directed by Nehrebecki, assisted by Leszek Mech, and provided some eighty minutes of innocent fun reminiscent of simpler and less troubled times.

M.H.

BOLLES, ENOCH (1883-1976) American cartoonist and cover artist born in Boardman, Florida, on March 14, 1883. Enoch Bolles was raised in Florida and Newark, New Jersey, as his family changed residences with the seasons. Following an early interest in art, he studied at the National Academy of Design and at the Art Students League, where Robert Henri was a teacher.

Bolles's first job was with the Hammerschlag Company, a firm that designed packages and labels for various products. Around 1913 he began to contribute to *Judge* and its sister publication, *Film Fun*. Most of his work was in oil and consisted of illustrated puns; the cover was nearly always his showcase, and he devoted himself to boy-girl themes. One of his first pieces for *Judge* became his most popular: "Steady Work," which sold for years as a print. In the 1920s Bolles began to expand his markets and extended the illustrated puns to the realm of the pinup—*Film Fun*, still, and *Spicy Stories*, *Tattle Tales*, *Gay Broadway* and *Breezy Stories*. Almost all this work was done anonymously or signed by an occasional *EB* monogram. He also worked in advertising, with Famous Fain, Best Foods and cigarette companies as his major accounts.

In 1938 Bolles was felled by a stroke and retired to a rest home, where he continued to paint for his own pleasure and that of his friends. He died on March 16, 1976.

Over the years, Bolles was one of the most prolific cover artists in his field. He continued his work on *Film Fun* long after *Judge* sold control, into the days when future *New Yorker* cartoonist Chuck Saxon edited the pinup mag. His work was realistic and shone with personality, and among his distinctions was a bronze medal awarded by the National Academy of Design.

R.M.

BONZO (G.B.) The canine star of the only fully developed, fully animated series of cartoons made in Great Britain during the silent film period was Bonzo. "Who put the pepper in the Tom Cat's milk?" asked a popular song called "How's Bonzo," the chorus of which concluded, "He's the pet of everybody. Gee, is he a clever Study!" This last was a cunning pun on the name of Bonzo's creator, George Ernest Studdy, one of the best-known British cartoonists of his day.

Studdy was born in Devon, England, on June 23, 1878, and tried both engineering and stockbroking before becoming a cartoonist. He churned out illustrations for the early boys' story papers, and for the weekly comic *The Big Budget* he created several regular strips, including *Professor Helpemon* (1903). By the outbreak of World War I he had risen to the status of caricaturist-cartoonist for the *Sketch*, a glossy weekly for which he executed full-page wash "plates." During this time he debuted in animation: for Gaumont he produced a series of three short cartoon films, *Studdy's War Studies*, which were released monthly from December 1915.

After the war he created Bonzo, almost by chance. Drawing weekly cartoon plates about dogs, his favorite characters, he found that one spotty pup kept recurring and finally christened him Bonzo. Soon Studdy realized he was on to a good thing and began to exploit his bull pup hero in all kinds of merchandise. The idea of a cartoon film series came through Gordon Craig and his New Era Films. No fewer than 26 were made for fortnightly release from October 1924 to January 1926, under the production supervision of William A. Ward. (Little is known of "Billy" Ward, save that he passed his

"Bonzo." © G.E. Studdy.

last years drawing Disney serials for *Mickey Mouse Weekly* (1937) and various strip series for *New Funnies* (1940) and other Gerald G. Swan publications.)

The first Bonzo was rapturously received by the trade press: "Although the action is exceedingly funny, there is still more humour in the extraordinarily expressive face and body movements of the mischievous pup. The subtlety of some of the effects is, in fact, remarkable." Some of the cartoons have been preserved in the National Film Archive, and considered in context with average American animation of the period, they are fully comparable.

Not all the titles are known, but some are: "Playing the Dickens in an Old Curiosity Shop"; "Bonzolino"; "Detective Bonzo and the Black Hand Gang"; and "Tally Ho Bonzo." Scriptwriter on several was Adrian Brunel, who became a noteworthy director of feature films. Animators were Percy Vigas, H. McCready, M. Matheson, H. Brian White, M. Jork, Marjorie Drawbell, Charles de Mornay, P.G. Tobin, Kevin Moran, S.G. Castell and Sid Griffiths. The series was supported by a weekly comic strip in *Tit-Bits*, which ran from February 6, 1926. This was followed by a daily and Sunday strip, produced for syndication in the USA.

Books: *Fishing* (1914); *The Studdy Dogs Portfolios* (1922); *The Bonzo Book* (1922); *Bonzo's Star Turns* (1923); *Uncle's Animal Book* (1923); *Bonzo Painting Book* (1924); *Bonzo's Country Holiday* (1925); *Bonzo's Seaside Holiday* (1925); *The Bonzo Book* (1925); *Lucky Bonzo* (1926); *Sportsman Bonzo* (1927); *Bonzo at the Party* (1927); *Bonzo's Little Trip* (1927); *Sea Breezy Bonzo* (1927); *The New Bonzo Book* (1927); *The Bonzoloo Book* (1929); *Bonzo and Us* (1931); *Bonzo's Happy Day* (1932); *Bachelor Bonzo* (1932); *Bonzo's Happy Family* (1932); *Bonzo's Bran Pie* (1932); *Bonzo's Little Holiday* (1932); *Bonzo's Leap Year* (1932); *Bonzo Colouring Book* (1934); *Bonzo Great Big Midget Book* (1934); *Bonzo's Annual* (1934); *Bonzo's Laughter Annual* (1935); *Bonzo Annual* (1936); *Bonzo's Story Book* (1940); *The Jeek* (1940); and *Bonzo Annual* (1950-51).

D.G.

BOOTH, FRANKLIN (1874-1948) American artist born in Carmel, Indiana, in 1874. A major factor in the new sophisticated look achieved by *Life* magazine in the early 1920s, Franklin Booth nonetheless was born on a farm. He studied the work of the great cartoonists and illustrators, and without knowing that woodcutting was the only method of reproduction and that it was one step removed from an original drawing, he mastered by lonely study the flow and composition of minute woodcut elements.

Staying with this style, he glorified pen and ink as much as did Charles Dana Gibson. Rich textures, vivid tones, lush contrasts: all these he achieved with pen and ink by meticulous handling of line work. He became a noted book illustrator and decorative artist; in his striking work in *Life* he decorated articles and poems and executed handsome covers in line and color. Booth died in 1948.

Books: *Lady Geraldine's Courtship* by Elizabeth Barrett Browning (1907); *The Boys of the Old Glee Club* by James Whitcomb Riley (1907); *Riley Roses* (1907); and *A Hoosier Holiday* by Theodore Dreiser (1916).

R.M.

BOOTH, GEORGE (1926-   ) American cartoonist born in Fairfax, Missouri, on June 28, 1926. George Booth graduated from Fairfax High School in 1944 and enlisted in the Marine Corps. After basic training at Camp LeJeune, he was assigned to a Corps printing operation as a result of some previous experience in lithography. It was during this assignment that his talent for caricature was noticed by his commanding officer. Shortly thereafter, he was transferred to Washington, D.C., and assigned to the staff of the *Leatherneck*, the Corps newspaper, as a cartoonist.

After his discharge he entered the Chicago Academy of Art, but upon the outbreak of the Korean conflict he was recalled to active duty. Once again he was assigned to the *Leatherneck*. Discharged a second and final time, he enrolled in the Corcoran School of Art in Washington, D.C., before moving to New York, where he completed his education at Adelphi University on Long Island. Booth worked for a New York-based communications firm for eight years before deciding in the early 1960s to try his hand as a freelance cartoonist. This gamble paid off when he landed the prestigious position of staff cartoonist at the *New Yorker* and set about familiarizing readers of that magazine with his memorable dogs, cats and people.

Like all the most interesting cartoonists, Booth not only has a distinctive style but also a particular cosmos to which he returns again and again for the raw stuff of his humor. His comic talent is thus accented by the element of familiarity he introduces through the recurrent use of certain images: the dogs and cats; a lower-class philosopher who thinks best in the bathtub; the neo-Goldbergian inventions; the fiddling Granny and her ensemble; and the miserable old couple in a cluttered, deteriorating flat, forever exchanging the most unlikely observations. Booth's selection of images, along with his highly idiosyncratic rendering of them, creates a sense of *déjà vu* which makes his already funny drawings even more hilarious.

Booth is an exceptionally collectible artist, to date having published two volumes of his work, taken mainly from the *New Yorker*. They are *Think Good Thoughts About a Pussy Cat* and *Rehearsal's Off* (1978).

R.C.

BOOTH, WALTER R. (18—?-19—?) British cartoonist, animator, conjuror, film producer, director, writer, actor, comedian, special effects creator and mystery man of British films. For a man who did so much in the pioneering period of the British cinema, it is extraordinary how little is known about Walter R. Booth. Between 1899 and 1916 Booth created, scripted, directed and sometimes acted in literally hundreds of short comedy and fantasy films, most involving some kind of photographic trick work, some including the animation of his own drawings. Many of his films were made for R.W. Paul, an early producer who acknowledged Booth in a 1936 address to the British Kinematograph Society: "With the valuable aid of Walter Booth and others, hundreds of humorous dramatic and trick films were produced in the studio." A veteran cameraman, F. Harold Bastwick, wrote in 1938: "I was lucky enough to start my career as a cameraman (in 1908) with W.R. Booth, a pioneer producer and genius at trick photography. He was originally with Maskeleyne and Cook (magicians) at the Egyptian Hall, so was literally steeped in the art of illusion."

Booth applied the art of the stage magician to the motion picture in much the same way that Georges Méliès did in France. His film methods ranged from the simple trick of an inverted camera in *Upside Down or the Human Flies* (1899) to the more elaborate techniques of the science fiction picture *The Airship Destroyer* (1909). His first use of animated drawing was in *The Devil in the Studio* (1901), closely followed by *The Famous Illusion of De Kolta* and *Artistic Creation. Political Favourites* (1904) used an undercranked camera to show Booth caricaturing 6 contemporary politicians in 280 feet of film.

Then Booth joined the Charles Urban Trading Company, and for this American pioneer in London he produced the first fully animated cartoon made in England, *The Hand of the Artist* (1906). This was made in the style of J. Stuart Blackton's *Humorous Phases of Funny Faces* and showed Booth's hand drawing a Coster and his Donah, who then danced the cakewalk, among many other "living cartoons." *Comedy Cartoons* came a year later and was more elaborate: "The most amazing and amusing magic, mirth and mystery film ever published!" Booth used animation occasionally thereafter but never again made a film that was purely cartoon.

D.G.

BORDALLO PINHEIRO, RAFAEL (1846-1905)

Portuguese cartoonist born in Lisbon, Portugal, on March 21, 1846. Rafael Bordallo was born into a family of artists—his father, brothers and sons distinguished themselves in engraving, painting, sculpture, drawing, and the decorative and ceramic arts. He studied at the Academy of Fine Arts from 1868 to 1874. At first attracted to dramatic acting, he performed in the Garrett Theatre but soon abandoned this career. After his marriage in 1866, Bordallo began drawing and illustrating anecdotes. He started caricaturing in 1870 with a lithograph called "O Dente da Baronesa." In the same year he published the album *Calcanhar de Aquiles*, in which great literary personalities of the time were satirized, and started *O Binóculo*, a magazine of theatrical criticism, of which four numbers were issued. In 1870 and 1871 he sold seven pages of *A Berlinda*, a series of humorous notes of social events. In 1872 Bordallo published an album totally illustrated in comic strip form, thus becoming the creator of the Portuguese comic strip. Titled *Apontamentos Sobre a Picaresca Viagem do Imperador de Rasilb pela Europa* ("Notes on the Roguish Voyage of the Emperor of Rasilb Through

Taking Advantage of His Gift

Rafael Bordallo Pinheiro, 1880.

Europe"), it was a satire on the Brazilian emperor, and it went through three printings.

In 1875 Bordallo started the magazine *Lanterna Mágica*, where for the first time the typical figure of the poor and exploited Portuguese, "Zé Povinho," appeared; in 1876 he published the *Album de Caricaturas-Frases e Anexins da Língua Portuguesa*. Meanwhile he published several independent lithographs and three volumes of the *Almanaque de Caricaturas* (1874-76), where he returned to the comic strip format. Also in 1876 he emigrated to Brazil, where he often worked for the magazines *Besouro* (1976), *Mosquito* (1877) and *Pst* (1879). Following a mysterious brawl in which he was stabbed, Bordallo returned to Portugal in 1879. Thereafter several illustrated anecdotes, caricatures and comic strips that gave him even greater fame appeared in *António Maria* (1879), *Album das Glórias* (1880), *Pontos nos Iis* (1885) and *A Paródia* (1900); he drew for the latter until his death on January 23, 1905. It is remarkable to find in some of his cartoons produced after 1880 the use of balloons and onomatopoeia. Iconic signs can be found as far back as 1874.

Bordallo participated widely in the illustration of books, magazine covers, and decorated menus, apart from hundreds of separate lithographs and his sketches of the first Portuguese artistic posters. He also worked for the *Illustración Española y Americana* and the *Illustración de Madrid*, two Spanish magazines, and from 1873 for the *Illustrated London*

News. He directed the construction of the Portuguese pavilion in the Paris Exhibition of 1889, where he displayed some of his ceramics, the main artistic activity of the final phase of his career. There is a museum in Lisbon that bears Bordallo's name; here the several branches of his work, including drawings, caricatures, illustrated newspapers, lithographs and ceramics, are exhibited.

C.P.

BORNSTEIN, MARGUERITA (1950-) Brazilian cartoonist and animator born of Polish parents in Sydney, Australia, in 1950. Marguerita Bornstein's parents took her to Brazil in the mid-1950s. One of the brightest stars in Brazilian cartooning, she had her first drawing published at age nine. Signing simply with her first name, she soon found herself working for major newspapers and magazines in Brazil and winning prizes left and right. She went to Australia in 1970, did drawings, worked for Australian television and had her first experience with drawing animated cartoons. Since her return to Brazil in 1973, she has contributed cartoons on a regular basis to the daily *Jornal do Tarde* and the weekly *Manchete*.

Marguerita is also an internationally known cover designer who has done covers for *Graphis* and *Design*, among other publications. She is equally proficient in the animation field and has directed several animated cartoons for British television (*How to Make Your Child Schizophrenic* is perhaps the best known).

A.M.

BOROWCZYK, WALERIAN (1923-) Polish animator and filmmaker born in Kwilcz, Poland, on October 21, 1923. After studying at the Polish Academy of Fine Arts, Walerian Borowczyk became a painter and graphic artist. His works were frequently exhibited in Poland and abroad. In the late 1950s Borowczyk struck up a friendship with Jan Lenica; working together in 1957 and 1958, they made three animated films of considerable merit: *Once upon a Time*, *Love Requited* and *Dom* ("House").

In 1958 Borowczyk left for Paris. There he made *L'Ecole* ("The School," 1958), about a soldier engaged in absurd maneuvers, followed by *Les Astronautes* (1959), a work that mixed animation and live action. Also typical of Borowczyk's preoccupation with the absurdities and horrors of modern society are *L'Encyclopédie de Grand' Maman* ("Grandma's Encyclopedia"), a spoof of Victorian learning methods; *Le Jeu des Anges* ("The Game of Angels," 1964), a terrifying allegory of the concentration camp universe; and *Renaissance*, an exercise in live-object animation.

In 1963 Borowczyk introduced the slightly sinister couple Mr. and Mrs. Kabal in his cartoon *Le Concert de M. et Mme. Kabal*. He followed this with his first feature film, released in 1967, *Le Théâtre de M. et Mme. Kabal*, in which he elaborated further on the games of cruelty, repression and frustration engaged in by this repellent couple. Since the late 1960s Borowczyk has only sporadically worked in animation, concentrating instead on live-action films (*Goto, l'Ile d'Amour* and *Blanche*, for example).

Walerian Borowczyk is one of the most significant animators of the postwar era. His innovative and thought-provoking films have been honored with a number of awards and distinctions at movie festivals around the world.

M.H.

Marguerita Bornstein, "How to Make Your Child Schizophrenic." © *TV Globo.*

BOSC, JEAN (1924-1973) French cartoonist, poster designer and animated cartoon director born in Nîmes, France, on December 30, 1924. After his military service in France and Indochina, Jean Bosc joined the weekly magazine *Paris-Match* in 1952 and contributed cartoons to other publications as well (*Punch, Esquire, France-Observateur*). Many of his drawings have been published in the albums *Gloria Viktoria, Homo Sapiens, Mort au Tyran* ("Death to the Tyrant"), *Les Boscaves* ("Bosc's Fools," 1965), *Si De Gaulle Etait Petit* ("If De Gaulle Was Short," 1968), and *La Fleur dans Tous Ses Etats* ("Two Flowers," 1968).

All his cartoons show absurd and often cruel incongruity, portraying look-alike, almost interchangeable long-nosed men and children who wait on long lines or walk in funeral corteges or interminable parades. Bosc's long stint in the army is probably responsible for the strong antimilitaristic slant in his work, with officers depicted as heartless fools, sometimes reduced to beribboned and bemedalled jackets only, and privates seen as inoffensive, mechanical dunces forever performing menial and useless chores. Bosc also directed a few animated cartoons: *Le Voyage en Boscavie* ("Travels in Bosc Country"), which won the Emile Cohl Prize in 1959, and *Le Chapeau* ("The Hat").

Like Chaval, Bosc saw no escape from the absurdity of the human condition: in 1973, at 49, he killed himself in Antibes, on the French Riviera. That same year, the

Walerian Borowczyk, "Le Théâtre de M. et Mme. Kabal." © *Les Cinéastes Associés.*

Jean Bosc. © Bosc.

Wilhelm Busch Museum in Hanover, Germany, held a two-month exhibit of his work, along with that of Chaval and Sempé.

P.H.

BOSKO (U.S.) Bosko, a bright little black lad, was created by Hugh Harman and Rudolph Ising in a 1930 cartoon short titled "Bosko, the Talk-ink (sic) Kid," released by Warner Brothers. Harman and Ising, busy working on other cartoon concepts, left the subsequent *Bosko* cartoons in the hands of other Warner animators, notably Friz Freleng and Robert McKimson. Early entries in the series (included under the overall Looney Tunes banner) were "Bosko's Dizzy Date," "Bosko the Speed King" and "Bosko's Knight Mare," all released in 1933.

When Harman and Ising left Warners for MGM they took their creation with them. They gave the character more scope, directing him in a number of charming cartoons such as "Bosko's Parlor Pranks" (1934) and "Bosko's Easter Eggs" (1937). These were very much in the Mickey Mouse tradition, with Bosko getting into all kinds of predicaments and having only his wits to get him out of trouble. Bosko's appearances became rarer and rarer as the 1930s wore on, and he finally bowed out around 1940. (*Bosko* should not be confused with a similar-sounding series, *Bosco*, which featured a pup by that name and ran in the 1940s.) A *Bosko* newspaper strip, drawn by Win Smith, ran briefly in the mid-1930s.

M.H.

BOSUSTOW, STEPHEN (1911-   ) American animator and film producer born in Victoria, British Columbia, Canada, on November 6, 1911. Stephen Bosustow won first prize in a watercolor contest while he was still in grammar school. At the age of 11 he was taken by his parents to Los Angeles, where he attended Lincoln High School. After graduation in 1930 he played drums with local bands and held a variety of odd jobs.

In 1932 Bosustow started his career in the animation field as an assistant to Ub Iwerks on *Flip the Frog*, moving over the next year to Walter Lantz's studio as an in-betweener on the *Oswald the Rabbit* series. Bosustow's next big move was to the Walt Disney studios, where he remained for seven years, from 1934 to 1941, leaving in the aftermath of the famous Disney strike. After a short stint as head of production control for Hughes Aircraft Company and a brief try at making slide films for industrial purposes, Bosustow founded Industrial Film and Poster Service in 1941, making films for government agencies and corporations. In 1944 his cartoon short *Hell Bent for Election*, made for the United Auto Workers on behalf of Franklin Roosevelt's presidential campaign, won him fame and recognition.

Changing his corporate name to United Productions of America (UPA) in 1945, and with the help of other talented refugees from the Disney studios (John Hubley, Peter Burness, Bob Cannon, Bill Hurtz), Bosustow started revolutionizing the art of American cartoon filmmaking. *Robin Hoodlum* (1947), nominated for an Academy Award, was the first UPA release to attract popular and critical attention. Bosustow abandoned active filmmaking after *Swab Your Choppers* (1947) to devote himself to his duties as president and chairman of the board of UPA. As a producer, Bosustow initiated the highly successful *Mr. Magoo* and *Gerald McBoing Boing* cartoon series. He allowed his directors great freedom of expression, and this resulted in such masterpieces as *Rooty Toot Toot* (1952), *The Tell-Tale Heart* and *Unicorn in the Garden* (both in 1953).

In 1961 Bosustow sold his interest in UPA. He has since devoted his time to producing travel and educational films, although he released an entertainment cartoon, *Joshua in a Box*, in 1970, and also produced the Oscar-winner of that year, *Is It Always Right to Be Right?*

The most influential cartoon producer after Disney, Stephen Bosustow helped create a new style of cartooning, sharp, sparse and witty, which has come to be known as "the UPA style."

M.H.

BOUCQUEY, OMER (1921-   ) French animator born in Dunkirk, in northernmost France, on August 17, 1921. After studying drawing in high school, Omer Boucquey worked as an animator for advertising films. In 1942 he created the character Choupinet, a feisty little boy living in medieval times. Choupinet helped build the cathedrals, settled the fighting between rival barons and even

"Bosko." © Harman-Ising.

took on the devil himself in a series of nicely animated, wittily constructed cartoons, the 1945 "Choupinet aux Enfers" ("Choupinet in Hades") being the most notable.

After World War II, Boucquey asserted his position as one of the leading new French animators with *Troubadour de la Joie* ("Troubador of Joy," 1949)and the enchanting *Les Dessins S'Animent* ("Drawings Spring to Life," 1952). Since this effort, however, discouraged by the shrinking market for theatrical cartoons, Boucquey has devoted most of his not inconsiderable talent to the making of advertising and commercial shorts. From time to time he has gone back to making entertainment cartoons, as with the recent *Drôles de Croches* ("Funny Quavers"), in which musical notes come to life in a frenzy of movement and sound.

M.H.

BOUREK, ZLATKO (1929-) Yugoslav cartoonist and animator born in Slavonića Požega, Yugoslavia, in 1929. Even before his graduation from the Zagreb Art Academy in 1952, Zlatko Bourek had been contributing cartoons to Yugoslav magazines, notably the humor and satirical publication *Kerempuh*. He joined Zagreb Film in 1955, working as a background designer for many of the cartoons directed by Dušan Vukotić (*Cowboy Jimmy*, *The Playful Robot*), Boris Kolar (*The Boy and the Ball*, *Boomerang*), Vatroslav Mimica (*Happy End*, *The Egg*) and others.

In 1961 Bourek directed his first animated cartoon, *The Blacksmith's Apprentice*, for which he also wrote the script. This was followed by the stunning, if gruesome, *I Videl Sem Daljine Meglene i Kalne* ("Far Away I Saw Mist and Mud," 1964), a chronicle of the Turkish atrocities against the Croats in the 16th century. Bourek was now one of the most acclaimed of Zagreb animators, and he reinforced his position with a long string of distinguished works, including the folkloric *Dancing Songs* (1966), the grim *Captain Arbanas Marko* (1967) and the charming, pop-art-inspired *Schooling* (1970). Bourek also worked on the *Profesor Balthasar* series, and in 1966 he directed a live-action film, *Circus Rex*. In the 1970s his work as a director of animated cartoons has somewhat diminished, although *The Cat*, which he wrote and directed in 1971, showed him at his peak. He also directed one of the cartoon sketches of the 1975 Canadian-Yugoslav production *Man the Polluter*. His latest effort, the ten-minute cartoon film *Ručak*, was released in 1978.

Bourek is a master of form and color, and his cartoons have a distinctive, art-oriented flavor to them. They have earned him many prizes and awards, at Belgrade, Oberhausen and Mamaia, among other places.

M.H.

BOURGEOIS, ALBÉRIC (1876-1962) French-Canadian cartoonist born in Montreal, Quebec, on November 29, 1876. Albéric Bourgeois won first prize at his graduation from the Montreal School of Fine Arts in 1899; the following year he left for the United States to pursue his studies at the Boston School of Art. During his stay in Boston he contributed a number of cartoons to the *Boston Post* and painted the murals of the now-destroyed Boston Opera House.

In 1903 Bourgeois was enticed back to Montreal by the publisher of the daily *La Patrie*. In addition to drawing political cartoons for the paper, he also created the first regular newspaper strip in Quebec, *Les Aventures de Timothée* (1904). In 1905 Bourgeois joined the staff of the major Montreal daily, *La Presse*, where he was to remain for over fifty years. Bourgeois's variety and versatility (he would indifferently pass from editorial cartooning to comic strip work from one week to the next) testifies to the freedom granted the artist. Bourgeois created a number of comic strips for the paper, notably *Les Aventures de Toinon* (1905-08) and *Les Fables du Parc Lafontaine* (1906-08). At this time, however, he was looking for a more flexible format that would provide greater scope for his energies.

Bourgeois found his niche with *En Roulant Ma Boule* ("Bumming Around"), a feature centered on the character Baptiste Ladébauche. If, in the editorial cartoons that he published in *La Presse* from 1909 on, Bourgeois still used stereotypes such as John Bull, Uncle Sam or the Soviet bear, he was entirely original in his reinterpretation of Ladébauche, first created in 1878 by Hector Berthelot. In Berthelot's mind, the vindictive Père Ladébauche ("Pops Debauchery") was only a polemical tool; Bourgeois, transforming him into a sly patriarch, forged a character in whom the French-Canadian community was able to recognize itself.

In February 1905 Bourgeois took over the *Père Ladébauche* newspaper strip from Joseph Charlebois. Blending text and illustration, he arrived at a definitive format in 1911. The feature, whose title derives from a famous folk song, rapidly became an institution and today represents an irreplaceable document of the political, social and cultural life of Quebec. Aside from Ladébauche himself (to whom he gave a woman companion, Catherine), Bourgeois invented a number of Québécois types such as Marie Scapulaire or Père Gédéon. He published a collection of his *Ladébauche* texts and drawings toward the end of the 1920s.

Bourgeois brought Ladébauche to the stage as early as 1906, and he adapted *En Roulant Ma Boule* into a musical show in the 1930s. He was also a cabaret performer,

Zlatko Bourek, "The Cat." © *Zagreb Film.*

Albéric Bourgeois, "En Roulant Ma Boule." © La Presse.

and in 1932 he produced a humorous radio serial, *Joson Josette*, that lasted for seven years. Bourgeois retired in 1957 (the last installment of his feature appeared on March 23) and died on November 17, 1962. Forgotten for almost twenty years, he was rediscovered through his comic strip work. In 1977 the Montreal Museum of Fine Arts organized a traveling exhibition devoted to Bourgeois's political cartoons and drawings.

S.J.

BOVARINI, MAURIZIO (1934-) Italian cartoonist and illustrator born in Bergamo, Italy, on July 31, 1934. Maurizio Bovarini went to Milan with his parents while

Thomas Bowers, "The Bowers Movie Book." © Harcourt, Brace & Co.

he was still a child. He is self-taught, and his love for drawing led him into a cartooning career. His first works in this field were published in the French magazines *Siné-Massacre*, *Bizarre* and *Adam*, starting in 1962. In 1969 Bovarini became the editor of the Italian edition of *Hara-Kiri*, the French satirical magazine; and between 1963 and 1970, his cartoons were exhibited in international group shows held in Milan, Rome, Paris, Berlin and Montreux, Switzerland.

Bovarini authored a cartoon book, *Ricco Ridens*, in 1970 for Edizioni Morgan, and in 1972 the same publisher brought out Bovarini's hilarious spoof, *Ultimo Tango a Fumetti* ("Last Tango in Comics"). Since then Bovarini has mainly been doing comic strips, such as *Philadelphia Killer* and *Kariplo* for *Linus*. In 1974 he was one of the authors featured in an anthology of horror comic strips, *Il Piacere della Paura* ("The Pleasure of Fear"), and in 1975 he started his collaboration on the comic monthly *Eureka*.

Bovarini is one of the best contemporary Italian cartoonists, noted as much for his violent, incisive drawing style as for the antiestablishment themes he likes to deal with. He has won many cartooning awards, including the Unità prize at Reggio Emilia (1964) and first prize at the Tolentino Biennial (1967).

M.G.P.

BOWERS, THOMAS (1889-1946) American cartoonist and producer born in Cresco, Iowa, in 1889. Tom Bowers was born into a traveling circus family, and he appeared in a tightrope act at the age of six. During the next ten years he performed in circus acts and stock companies. Bowers also had a talent for drawing, and it was during his years on the road that he perfected it, drawing circus posters and painting signs and later murals.

In 1905 Bowers secured a job as a cartoonist on the *Chicago Tribune*, later going over to the *Chicago Star*. Moving east in the 1910s, he became the editorial cartoonist of the *Newark News* and later went into the budding field of animated cartoons. In 1916 he founded, with pioneer animator Raoul Barré, the Barré-Bowers Animated Cartoon Studio, which produced the *Mutt and Jeff* shorts under contract to Bud Fisher. The association, by all accounts, was not a happy one, and late in 1918 or early in 1919 Barré accused his partner of financial irregularities and broke with him. Bowers continued to produce the *Mutt and Jeff* cartoons until the mid-1920s, despite a later dispute with Fisher, again over alleged manipulation of funds.

After leaving the animated cartoon field, Bowers went into writing and illustrating books (*The Bowers Movie Book*, 1923), puppet animation, and later live-action comedy, producing under the name Charley Bowers Comedy Corporation. He also drew cartoons for the *Jersey City Journal*. In 1941 he suddenly became ill and had to stop working (his wife took over for awhile). He died at St. Joseph's Hospital in Paterson, New Jersey, on November 24, 1946.

A colorful personality sometimes referred to as "the modern Baron Munchausen," Tom Bowers was well remembered by all who met him. He epitomized the entrepreneurial spirit of the early days of the animated cartoon.

M.H.

BOZZETTO, BRUNO (1938-) Italian cartoonist and animator born in Milan, Italy, on March 3, 1938. After finishing high school in Milan, Bruno Bozzetto attended the Milan School of Law but did not complete his studies. In 1958, out of his love of drawing, he started on his cartooning career with an animated short titled *TAPUM la Storia delle Armi* ("TAPUM the History of Weapons"), which won a number of awards in festivals around the world. Thus encouraged, Bozzetto went on to produce more shorts, including *The History of Inventions* (1959), in the same vein as TAPUM; *Alpha Omega* (1961); *The Two Castles*, a much acclaimed fantasy spoof; *Ego* (1969); and *Pickles* (1971).

Bozzetto has also produced three feature-length animated films: *West and Soda*, a 1965 western spoof; *VIP, Mio Fratello Superuomo* ("VIP, My Brother Superman"), a hilarious account of the life and times of a family of superbeings (1968); and the musical *Allegro Non Troppo* (1976). Bozzetto is also the creator of the *Mr. Rossi* series, a group of about a dozen twenty-minute cartoons produced for Italian television; he is also active in the advertising cartoon field and has sporadically produced a number of comic books, usually adapted from his films, with the help of his three chief collaborators, Guido Manuli, Maurizio Nichetti and Giancarlo Rossi.

The most prolific and the best known of all Italian animators, Bozzetto has been the recipient of countless awards, from foreign and Italian organizations alike. His latest cartoon film was the ten-minute short *La Piscina* ("The Swimming Pool," 1978).

L.S.

BRAAKENSIEK, JOHAN (1858-1940) Dutch political cartoonist, illustrator and painter born in Amsterdam, the Netherlands, on May 24, 1858. At the turn of the century, Johan Braakensiek was considered in other European countries to be the outstanding Dutch political cartoonist. Some of his own countrymen later complained of his very careful academic draftsmanship (less a valuable rarity than now!) and his tendency to think in terms of visual clichés for nations, political parties and supernatural beings (few editorial cartoonists avoid this altogether). Nevertheless, his solid artistic merits and the obvious popularity that kept him before the public for at

Queen Victoria washes her hands of responsibility on seeing the Boer War casualty lists.
Johan Braakensiek.

least forty years make his position in Dutch cartooning history unassailable.

Braakensiek studied at the Amsterdam Academy from 1876 to 1881. Soon he was drawing for the publication *Het Politienieuws*, and he later contributed to many other magazines, but he found his real niche when *De Amsterdammer Weekblad voor Nederland* was founded in 1883. For decades Braakensiek did one large and one small drawing for each weekly issue. Over the years he covered not only events in Dutch politics (such as the menace, in liberal eyes, of Dr. Abraham Kuyper's severely Calvinist party), but also every important occurrence in Europe and the world (he published an album consisting entirely of his cartoons on the Spanish-American War). Pathos was a frequent ingredient in his work, so that he was especially effective on such topics as the plight of the poor at home in the Netherlands, the injustice done to Dreyfus in France and the situation of Oom Kruger's people in South Africa during the Boer War.

Illustration was another important part of Braakensiek's oeuvre. He did pictures for numerous books, including works by Justus van Maurik, editor of *De Amsterdammer*. Early in his career he did a great deal of documentary drawing and was noted for his ability to render street life and characters. His much-admired pictures for Klikspaan's book *Studententypen* are in this vein. He also did genre paintings.

Braakensiek died in Amsterdam on February 27, 1940. Other artists in his immediate family were his father, Albertus, and his brother, Albertus Berend.

Bruno Bozzetto, "The SuperVIPS." © Bozzetto.

S.A.

BRACHLIANOFF, ARCADY (1912-   ) French animator and producer born in Sofia, Bulgaria, on January 12, 1912. After graduating from art school in Sofia, Arcady Brachlianoff moved to Paris in the 1930s. He soon joined a commercial animation unit and became an assistant animator under the name "Jean Arcady." The studio produced animated ads for showing at intermissions in movie theaters, and Arcady soon animated and later directed some of the wittiest cartoons, such as the one for La Pie Qui Chante, a candy manufacturer.

After World War II Arcady became a naturalized French citizen and opened his own animation studio; there he produced some of the finest French animated cartoons of the 1940s and 1950s by judiciously blending traditional and experimental elements. *Kaléidoscope, Guitares* and *Mouvement Perpétuel* ("Perpetual Motion") are some of the notable Arcady cartoons of the period. His *Prélude pour Voix, Orchestre et Caméra* ("Prelude for Voice, Orchestra and Movie Camera," 1959) earned the Special Award at the 1960 Annecy Festival. Arcady further explored the fusion of sound and image in *L'Ondomane* (1962).

Animation is not only an art, however, but also an industry; Arcady's animated cartoon production is still overwhelmingly devoted to advertising and commercial films. His work in this field is often witty and always distinctive.

M.H.

Design for a Union Station
Luther Bradley, 1907.

BRADLEY, LUTHER DANIELS (1853-1917) American cartoonist born in New Haven, Connecticut, on September 29, 1853. Luther Bradley moved with his family to Chicago in 1857 and received his early education at Lake Forest Academy and Northwestern University; he attended Yale University until 1875, when he began to work in his father's real estate office.

In 1882 wanderlust and illness—apparently he was sick of ledger work—combined to lure Bradley on a round-the-world cruise. On his Australian stopover he was inadvertently stranded. He became interested in newspaper work and was soon contributing cartoons—having until then shown no particular interest in or talent for drawing—to *Australian Tidbits* (later the Australian *Life*) and the Melbourne *Punch*, where he eventually drew cartoons, wrote criticism and edited the paper for a year. His cartoons achieved worldwide republication.

The elder Bradley became gravely ill in 1892, and his son returned to America from Australia the following year. In Chicago he freelanced and illustrated two children's books, originally penned for his own nieces and nephews:*Wonderful Willie: What He and Tommy Did to Spain;* and *Our Indians: A Midnight Visit to the Great Somewhere-or-Other.* The drawings are stunning masterpieces of fantasy using period poster effects. In the late 1890s Bradley attached himself to the *Journal* and *Inter-Ocean*, both of Chicago, before becoming art director and cartoonist of the *Chicago Daily News;* his first editorial cartoon there appeared on July 5, 1899. Bradley's cartoons ran mainly on the front page, and the pioneering *News* comic section was among his editorial responsibilities.

Luther Bradley's editorial cartoons achieved wide circulation and respect. Using careful but lush and textured shadings, he developed a reserved style in which the sophistication of execution mirrored the maturity of comment. He was regarded as a statesman of the drawing board for his fairness and reasoned partisanship—a difficult reputation to attain with John McCutcheon down the block. Bradley's cartoons were uniformly horizontal; he and Ole May of the *Cleveland Leader* were virtually alone in utilizing such a format at that time.

It has been recorded, incorrectly, that Bradley was the only American cartoonist to oppose the United States entry into the Great War. American cartoonists were divided into two camps: out-and-out jingoes like W.A. Rogers, and those who expressed the horrors of war, urged preventive or preparatory arming and highlighted the offenses of both sides. Bradley was certainly not alone in the latter category, but he was perhaps the most eloquent in illustrating his arguments. While he called attention to the British naval outrages that were easily as offensive as German activities against the United States prior to 1917, he also urged vigorous rearmament programs. Bradley was a Republican, and was honestly exasperated with President Wilson's policy of vacillation and appeasement. He rejoiced at armed retaliation against Mexico. One of Bradley's most popular series had Uncle Sam showing to young people paintings that illustrated lessons to be derived from American history.

Bradley, truly a statesman-cartoonist, died at his home in Wilmette on January 9, 1917, four months before the American entry into the war. Rand McNally published a posthumous collection, *Cartoons by Bradley*, later that year. His own cartoon lessons deserve to be reintroduced to America.

R.M.

BRADSHAW, PERCIVAL VANNER (1878-1965) British cartoonist born in Hackney, London, England, in 1878. Percy V. Bradshaw, who signed his cartoons and strips "P.V.B.," was educated at Aske's School and Hatcham. At the age of 14 he became a clerk in an advertising agency and sold his first cartoon to the *Boy's Own Paper*,

Bismarck, in retirement, plagued by interviewers.

Gustav Brandt, 1890.

his favorite childhood reading, receiving half a guinea from the editor, G.A. Hutchinson. This success prompted his transfer to the agency art department, and with evening art study at Goldsmith's and Birkbeck, he was able to freelance full-time at the age of 18. One of the Alfred Harmsworth comic publications sponsored a competition through the *Artist* magazine to find new strip cartooning talent. The first prize of five pounds for a sketch of a jester's head was won anonymously by Percy Bradshaw. Cartoon contributions for the Harmsworth periodicals began to flow; *Home Chat* and the *Sunday Companion* published Bradshaw's work, and finally he won a post on the art staff of the *Daily Mail*.

Bradshaw began writing to back up his drawing, and his first contribution in this field, 20 lines for the *Daily Graphic*, brought him a check for one shilling and eightpence—which he never cashed! Then came a series of articles about cartooning, "Black and White Drawing as a Profession," which ran in the *Boy's Own Paper*. So much correspondence came in to him—questions, sample drawings, requests for advice and criticism—that Bradshaw was inspired to create The Press Art School (1905). Organizing this pioneering correspondence course in cartooning from his home in London, Bradshaw soon had a success on his hands. His first pupil was Leo Cheyney, who capped a considerable career as a cartoonist by creating the familiar trademark figure Johnnie Walker for the whiskey of that name. The cartoonists who sprang from Percy V. Bradshaw's course were legion: Ern Shaw, Peter Fraser, W.L. Ridgewell, Alan D'Egville, Bertram Prance, "Fougasse" (Cyril Bird) and many more.

Other important Bradshaw contributions include the foundation of the London Sketch Club on April 1, 1898, with Phil May, Tom Browne, John Hassall and Dudley

Hardy; the publication of 20 portfolios under the blanket title *The Art of the Illustrator* in 1918 (Frank Reynolds, Harry Rountree, Warwick Reynolds, Lawson Wood, Heath Robinson, Dudley Hardy, H.M.Bateman, Bert Thomas, etc.); and the major monthly series *They Make Us Smile*, which ran in *London Opinion* through the 1940s. In 1936 he published a special six-lesson supplement to his course, *Caricature and Humorous Drawing*, written by the contemporary stalwarts of the art, Tom Webster, H.M. Bateman, Bert Thomas, J.A. Shepherd, Alfred Leete and "Poy" (Percy Fearon).

Bradshaw's own artwork grew less frequent over the years; in 1930 he was working part time with Royds' Advertising Agency, and in 1933 as the London sales organizer to Sun Engravings, a printer in Watford. He died on October 13, 1965, at age 87, leaving a small fortune of £25,000 and an enormous legacy as a cartoonist. He probably did more for the furtherance of the art than any other English cartoonist.

Books: *Art of the Illustrator* (1918); *Art in Advertising* (1925); *Fashion Drawing and Designing* (1936); *I Wish I Could Draw* (1941); *They Make Us Smile* (1942); *Marching On* (1943); *Draw for Money* (1943); *Nice People to Know* (1944); *I Wish I Could Paint* (1945); *Lines of Laughter* (1946); *Seen in Perspective* (1947); *Come Sketching* (1949); *The Magic of Line* (1949); *Water Colour Painting* (1949); *Water Colour* (1952); *Sketching and Painting Indians* (1956); and *Brother Savages and Guests* (1956).

D.G.

BRANDT, GUSTAV (1861-1919) German cartoonist born in the free city of Hamburg on June 2, 1861. Like Wilhelm Scholz, whose principal successor he became, Gustav Brandt had a career completely dedicated to the Berlin satirical magazine *Kladderadatsch*. In the early decades of the magazine's history, that is, from 1848 to about 1880, Scholz worked almost unaided, but in his old age a pleiad of fresh talent moved in for longer or shorter stints. Franz Jüttner and Arthur Wanjura, for instance, arrived about the same time as Brandt but soon left the staff, whereas Brandt (always just one artist among many on the magazine) kept contributing up to the time of his death early in 1919.

Brandt, who had thought he wanted to paint, studied at the academies of Düsseldorf and Berlin but went right from art school to a desk at *Kladderadatsch*. His contributions, which began in 1884, at first consisted of full pages in the supplement containing a host of vignettes on a given general topic (something like a Nell Brinkley page). His draftsmanship was brilliant, bustling and snappy from the very first, and he soon worked these vignette pages into interesting allover compositions (such as the 1890 page about the interviewers crashing the privacy of Bismarck's retirement).

By the turn of the century, however, Brandt had become a specialist in celebrity caricatures. These appeared in *Kladderadatsch* under the heading of *Unsere Zeitgenossen* ("Our Contemporaries"), a series that was continued by others after Brandt's death. (An anthology album by the same name was published separately in 1902.) For his caricatures, which spoofed prominent Germans and other Europeans, Brandt generally used full-length figures with little or no background, the figures themselves being carefully shaded and modeled, with the faces finely rendered. Eduard Fuchs, a historian of humorous art, declared early in this century that Brandt was the greatest living German caricaturist and the first one of world rank. In the 1910s a contributor to the Thieme-Becker (artists' lexicon) flatly stated that Brandt was the outstanding artistic talent on *Kladderadatsch* in his generation—an opinion difficult to dispute.

In his last years Brandt, who also did posters for *Kladderadatsch*, was obviously fascinated by the great artists of the Munich *Simplicissimus* and drew full-page cartoons that are too strongly reminiscent of Gulbransson, Heine and Thöny but are nevertheless at a comparable technical level.

S.A.

BRANSOM, PAUL (1885-1979) American cartoonist and illustrator born in Washington, D.C., in 1885. Paul Bransom left school at 13 to work on technical drawings for the Patent Office. He enjoyed sketching at Washington's National Zoo, and his familiarity with the natural world led to his first work in cartooning.

In 1903 Gus Dirks committed suicide, and the Hearst papers needed someone to continue his very popular feature, *The Latest News from Bugville.* Young Bransom was the replacement for the Sunday cartoon, and he continued the bugs-and-small-animal doings for nearly a decade. Seeking more "serious" work, Bransom set up a studio at the lion house of the Bronx Zoo on breaks from the *New York Journal.* His portfolio of animal art became respectable enough to impress several magazine art directors, and his career as a magazine and book illustrator was launched.

Bransom gave his cartooning influences as T.S. Sullivant and Walt Kuhn, who used to draw little bird cartoons for *Life.* He also admired the work of Charles Livingston Bull and followed Gus Dirks's delightful style very closely throughout his association with *Bugville.* With Bull, Bransom was probably the consummate animal illustrator in the American school. He died on July 12, 1979.

Books: *Kings in Exile* (1909); *Neighbors Unknown* (1910); *The Call of the Wild* by Jack London (1912); *Children of the Wild* (1913); *The Wind in the Willows* by Kenneth Grahame (1913); *The Secret Trails* (1916); *Over Indian and Animal Trails* (1918); *An Argosy of Fables* (1921); *Jungle Babies* (1930); and *Just-So Stories* by Rudyard Kipling (1932).

R.M.

BRAUN, CASPAR (1807-1877) German cartoonist born in Aschaffenburg, Bavaria, on August 13, 1807. Although Caspar Braun's draftsmanship was never first-rate, his services to German humorous art as printer and publisher as well as cartoonist are immeasurable. He studied art at the Munich Academy under Peter von Cornelius, the developer of so many graphic talents, and was preparing to become a historical painter with a special interest in such subjects as romantic landscapes peopled by highwaymen. However, the great book illustrations of the French cartoonist Grandville attracted him to the field of wood engraving—then highly developed in Paris but practically unknown in Germany. Braun went to Paris in 1838, met Grandville and was introduced by him to the master wood engraver Henri Brevière, with whom he proceeded to study.

Back in Munich, Braun went into partnership with court councillor Dessauer to create a wood-engraving printshop (the Xylographische Anstalt) that soon made a name for the excellence of its illustrated books. In 1843 Dessauer sold his share to a Leipzig businessman named Friedrich Schneider (1815-1864), and thus one of the

Eisele and Beisele find peasants planting roadside trees hurriedly and carelessly because a bigwig's visit is expected.

Caspar Braun.

greatest publishing firms in the history of graphic art was established: Braun and Schneider of Munich. On November 7, 1844, Braun and Schneider issued the first number of the *Fliegende Blätter,* the most important German magazine of pictorial satire and humor until the founding of *Simplicissimus* in 1896 (both magazines continued publication until the 1940s). Among the artists who worked for the *Fliegende Blätter* and Braun and Schneider's other famous publication, the *Münchener Bilderbogen,* were Busch, Oberländer, Spitzweg, Pocci, Schwind, Hengeler, Stuck and a host of others.

In the first years of the *Fliegende Blätter,* years of political unrest culminating in the events of 1848, Braun himself was represented by several important contributions. His series *Des Herrn Barons Beisele und Seines Hofmeisters Eisele Kreuz- und Querzüge durch Deutschland* ("The Travels All Over Germany of Baron Beisele and His Tutor Dr. Eisele") was a sharply satirical commentary on the political and social shortcomings of

Santa Monk: "Great Caesar's ghost! What the Dickens do they take me for? A moving van?"

J.R. Bray, 1908.

many regions. He also drew a series featuring the antagonism of the democratic agitator Wühlhuber and the dismayed reactionary Heulmeier, who eventually emigrated to America, and contributed other items about communists, produce-market manipulators and various characters in the news. Braun helped guide the fortunes of his enterprise until his death in Munich on October 22, 1877.

S.A.

BRAY, JOHN RANDOLPH (1879-1978) American cartoonist, animator, producer and businessman born in Addison, Michigan, on August 25, 1879. J.R. Bray studied at Alma College in Michigan in 1895-96 but soon decided upon a career in cartooning. In 1901 he joined the *Detroit News* as a cub reporter and cartoonist. Moving to New York in 1903, he worked first for the *Brooklyn Eagle*, then went on to a successful freelance career as a regular contributor to *Judge, Life* and *Harper's*. For *Judge* he created the popular cartoon series *Little Johnny and His Teddy Bears* (1903-10); he also drew a comic strip, *Mr. O.U. Absentmind*, for McClure Newspaper Syndicate.

Bray became involved in animation in 1911. After working for almost a full year, he brought out his first animated cartoon, *The Artist's Dream*, in 1912 (in his *Who's Who* biography, he claimed somewhat disingenuously that it was *the* first animated cartoon). In collaboration with another animation pioneer, Earl Hurd, he formed the Bray-Hurd Processing Company in 1914. Later that year he also founded Bray Studios, for which he created his innovative cartoon series *Colonel Heezaliar*, releasing first through Pathé and later through Paramount. In addition, Bray produced four animated films a week for Paramount, including Hurd's *Bobby Bumps*, Max Fleischer's *Out of the Inkwell* and Paul Terry's *Farmer Al Falfa*. By the early 1920s, however, Bray had completely abandoned animation work to concentrate on production and business matters. "I could have gone on being just a cartoonist," he stated in a 1925 interview, "but I chose to tackle the business job because I believed it was another Big Chance."

In the 1920s the Bray studio continued to turn out cartoon films (*Colonel Heezaliar, Lampoons, Dinky Doodle, Hot Dog Cartoons*, etc.), but Bray had already shifted his emphasis to documentaries and technical films (a trend that began in World War I when he produced instruction films for the U.S. Army). In the 1930s he produced the Goldwyn-Bray Pictographs and a series of comedy shorts, the *McDougall Alley Comedies*, whose title was clearly inspired by R.F. Outcault's early cartoon panels. More instruction work for the army followed during World War II. In recent years the studio has been producing documentary, safety, health and travel films for schools and television, many narrated in French and Spanish as well as English. Bray himself remained active well into his eighties. Only in 1963 did he step down as president of Bray Studios (to become its chairman of the board); he retired in the late 1960s to a nursing home in Bridgeport, Connecticut, where he died in October 1978, several months short of his 100th birthday.

J.R. Bray is one of the most important figures in early animation. His work proved pivotal in the rational organization of the American cartoon film industry. His technical contributions to the field are many; he pioneered the transparency cel process and

the photographed background, among many other innovations. He received a citation for patriotic services in 1956 and a special mention for his early work in the field at the World Retrospective of Animation held in Montreal in 1967.

M.H.

BRDECKA, JIŘÍ (1917-) Czechoslovakian animator born in Hravice, Bohemia, Czechoslovakia, on December 24, 1917. Jiří Brdecka attended the University of Prague, where he studied art history from 1936 until the university was closed by the Nazis in 1939. During World War II he pursued a career as journalist and art critic, and in 1940 he wrote a parodic novel, *Limonadovy Joe* ("Lemonade Joe"), which was turned into a stage play in 1964.

Brdecka started his long association with animation in 1943 at the Prague Cartoon Film Studio, which he joined as a scriptwriter. After World War II he wrote the scripts for some of Jiří Trnka's cartoons, and in 1947 he directed his first animated film, *Love and the Dirigible*, a period piece about a lover eloping with his sweetheart aboard an airship. Moving over to the Barandov Studio, also in Prague, Brdecka again worked mainly as a scriptwriter on most of the cartoons turned out by the studio. These included most of Trnka's films, notably *The Devil on Springs* and *The Czech Year*.

Brdecka returned to film directing in 1957 with *How Man Learned to Fly*, a comic look at aviation, followed by *Attention, Clementine* (1959) and *Our Red Riding Hood* (1960). *Man Under Water* (1961), another look at one of man's inventions, the submarine, and *Sentiment and Reason* (1962), a rather sophomoric contrast between the traditional and the romantic viewpoints, were not very successful. However, Brdecka rose to the ranks of first-rate animators with *Gallina Vogelbirdae* (1963), a light and lyrical tale of a paper bird and its wild flights of fancy. Since then Brdecka has become one of the most prolific animators in Czechoslovakia. *Minstrel's Song* (1964), *The Deserter* (1965), *Why Do You Smile, Mona Lisa?* (1966), *Hunting in the Forest* (1967), *The Power of Fate* (1969), *Metamorpheus* (1971), *The Logger* (1974) and *The Miner's Rose* (1975) are among his more notable efforts.

Jiří Brdecka is one of the most respected names in international animation. He has won many prizes and awards in his own country and in film festivals around the world.

M.H.

BREER, ROBERT (1926-) American animator and painter born in Detroit, Michigan, on September 30, 1926. Robert Breer studied painting at Stanford University and moved to Europe in 1949. He exhibited his paintings in many group shows in Europe. Breer became interested in animation in the early 1950s and produced his first films, *Form Phases I* and *Frame by Frame*, in 1952.

Encouraged by the reception of his first efforts, Breer continued his explorations into animated forms with such outstanding abstract films as *Form Phases II-V* (1955-56), *Jamestown Baloos* (1957) and *Blazes* (1961). Of the more representational (but hardly less baffling) *A Man and His Dog out for Air* (1958), the artist said in an interview: "This film, like most of my films, begins in the middle and goes toward the two ends...." His early works, as well as more recent films such as *Horse over*

Robert Breer, "Fist Fight." © *Breer.*

including *Le Petit Soldat* ("The Little Soldier") and *La Bergère et le Ramoneur* ("The Shepherdess and the Chimney Sweep").

After a short stint as a freelancer, Bressy joined the staff of Opera Mundi (one of France's largest press syndicates) in 1952. Since that time he has been turning out cartoons and comic strips for a variety of French and Belgian publications. His contributions include comic strip adaptations of Sax Rohmer's *Fu-Manchu* (1962) and other popular novels, as well as the condensation in strip form of several Walt Disney movies (*Mary Poppins* being the most memorable).

Bressy has been the recipient of a number of distinctions, including the 1972 Best Cartoonist Award given by the French Union of Newspaper Cartoonists.

M.H.

BRÉTECHER, CLAIRE (1940-   ) French cartoonist born in Nantes, a town in western France, in 1940. Claire Brétecher, who describes herself as the daughter of "a bourgeois family with no money," was educated in a Catholic convent and later studied fine arts. After failing to get a job as an art teacher, she went to Paris in the early 1960s. She started her cartooning career in 1964 with the weekly magazine *Record*, to which she contributed spot cartoons and illustrations as well as a short-lived comic strip, *Molgaga*, about a court jester.

Moving to the Belgian weekly *Spirou* in 1968, she drew two new but unsuccessful comics, *Les Gnan-Gnans* (a kid strip) and *Les Naufragés* ("The Castaways"). Her first success came in 1969 with *Cellulite*, a hilarious comic strip about a homely spinster princess, which was created for *Pilote*. Brétecher received further recognition when the intellectual magazine *Le Nouvel Observateur* asked her to create a weekly satirical strip for them. This turned out to be *Les Frustrés* ("The Frustrated Ones"), a savage, brilliant, often bitter indictment of modern civilization and the whole human race.

Claire Brétecher is the only European woman cartoonist whose professional fame is equal to that of her male colleagues. She is a writer, an illustrator and an editor as well as a successful cartoonist. She has received many distinctions and awards, and her fame has reached American shores: her cartoons have appeared in *Esquire* and *Ms.* magazine, and she was the subject of a 1977 article in the *New York Times*. A collection of her cartoons titled *The National Lampoon Presents Claire Brétecher* was published in New York in 1978.

M.H.

Tea Kettle (1963), *BLP 3* (1970) and *Fuji* (1974), have increasingly come to be recognized as original and innovative works of art.

Breer returned to the United States in 1959. In addition to his work as an animator he continues to paint and also creates kinetic sculptures. His work in the field of experimental animation has earned the Creative Film Foundation Award twice (in 1957 and 1961), as well as the Bergamo Festival Award in 1960 and the Max Ernst Award in 1969.

M.H.

BRESSY, ROBERT (1922-   ) French cartoonist and animator born in Avignon, in southeastern France, on September 5, 1922. Robert Bressy studied at l'Ecole des Beaux-Arts in Paris and upon graduation joined the animation studio of Les Gémeaux, under the direction of Paul Grimault and André Sarrut. There, from 1946 to 1949, he worked on most of the Gémeaux projects,

BRITISH CHARACTER, THE (G.B.) That which we call "the British character"—the modes, the manners, the class structure, the life-style—had no finer depicter during the 1930s and 1940s than the cartoonist who signed himself "Pont." The weekly panels under that title in *Punch* still come alive on the page, preserving for all time that which the British (and the rest of the world) regard as "British." "A tendency to put off until the last minute," "A disinclination to sparkle," "An ability to be ruthless": these captions alone speak truth, without the brilliantly drawn and hilarious illustrations that are inseparable from them.

"Pont," a pseudonym reduced from *Pontifex Maximus*, disguised Gavin Graham Laidler, A.R.I.B.A. He was born on July 4, 1908, in Jesmond, Newcastle upon Tyne, the son of a painter and decorator. He was educated at the local preparatory school and then at

José Carlos de Brito e Cunha, model drawings for "Lamparina" series. © *O Tico-Tico.*

Trinity College, Glenalmond, Perth. He preferred caricaturing the school's staff to compulsory games, and also studied at the London School of Architecture. In 1930 he started a strip for *Woman's Pictorial*, *The Twiff Family*, running it for seven years before it was taken over by Fred Robinson. In 1932 he illustrated the Christmas catalogue for the Glendenning wine merchants, and in August of the same year a long run of rejection slips was broken by the appearance of his first cartoon in *Punch*, titled "An Uninterrupted View of the Sea."

His first episode in the *British Character* series appeared on April 4, 1934: "Adaptability to Foreign Conditions" showed the impeccable English playing a rubber of bridge in the African bush. In 1937 a new weekly, *Night and Day*, lured him, or tried to. Editor E.V. Knox quickly signed him for *Punch* on that paper's first exclusive contract. He died quite suddenly, of poliomyelitis, on November 23, 1940, at 32 years of age.

Books: *The British Character* (1938); *The British at Home* (1939); *The British Carry On* (1940); *Pont* (1942); *The British Character* (1956); and *Pont* (1969).

D.G.

BRITISH WORKING MAN, THE (G.B.) "The British Working Man, by Someone Who Does Not Believe in Him" began his comic strip career by driving a nail into the top of a post, an act that took him so long that he was bearded by the time he abandoned the task because he was too old for the job! The six-picture incident filled half a page of *Fun*, dated August 14, 1875. The following week, when "Phase Two, Piece-work" took place (the Working Man builds a house that falls down), the strip occupied a full page, and it continued to do so for 17 weeks. The Working Man was replaced by the British Domestic and the British Bumpkin and the British Thief, and ever onwards. The artist, "J.F.S.," had carved an original niche that would in later years be profitably occupied by Pont's *The British Character*.

James Francis Sullivan, one of the first British cartoonists to employ strip technique with consistency, was born in 1853. His publishers, the brothers Dalziel, wrote, "He was a student at South Kensington when he first forwarded sketches for our inspection. We at once availed ourselves of his drawings." The Dalziels published *Fun*, a comic weekly rival to *Punch* (and a far livelier, indeed better, publication), and its editor, Tom Hood, used "Jasef" (as Sullivan often signed himself) a lot. Sullivan also drew for *Tom Hood's Comic Annual* and ran a feature called *The Queer Side of Things* in George Newnes's *Strand Magazine*. He drew with a hard line and indeed took a hard line against the people and things that annoyed him: bureaucrats, navvies, servants, shopkeepers. His revenge on human stupidity was often grotesque, fantastic, even ugly. But his was the style of his time, and he was experimenting with a very new form, the strip cartoon. He died in 1936, long after his heyday, at the age of 83.

Books: *The British Working Man* (1878); *The British Tradesman* (1880); *Among the Freaks* (1896); *Belial's Burden* (1896); *The Flame Flower* (1896); *Here They Are* (1897); *Here They Are Again* (1899); *The Great Water Joke* (1899); *Queer Side Stories* (1900); and *Glimpses of English History* (1901).

D.G.

BRITO E CUNHA, JOSÉ CARLOS DE (1884-1950) Brazilian cartoonist born in Rio de Janeiro, Brazil, in 1884. After art studies in Rio, José de Brito started his career as a cartoonist on *O Tagarela* in 1902. Alternately using pen-and-ink, crayon and etching techniques, "J. Carlos" (as he signed his works) became one of the most prolific and admired cartoonists in Brazil.

J. Carlos's long career spanned almost half a century, with contributions to all the major publications in Brazil. From 1902 to 1921, his most fecund period as a cartoonist, he worked successively or simultaneously for the following Rio magazines: *O Tagarela* (1902-03); *A Avenida* (1903-04); *O Malho, Século XX, Leitura para Todos* and *O Tico-Tico* (1905-07); *Fon-Fon!* (1907-08); *Carêta* (1908-21); *O Filhote da Carêta* (1910-11); *O Juquinha* (1912-13); and *Revista da Semana, Revista*

Nacional and *Eu Sei Tudo* (1918-21). In this same period he also found time to contribute cartoons, illustrations and caricatures to magazines published outside Rio, such as *A Cigara, A Vida Moderna, Illustração Brasileira, Cinearte, D. Quixote, A Noite, A Hora* and others.

In 1922 J. Carlos was appointed art director for all the publications of the *O Malho* group, a position he retained until 1930. In the 1930s he drew comic strips for *O Tico-Tico*, where he created the characters Melindrosa and Almofadinha. In 1933 he published a children's book, *Minha Babá*, which he wrote and illustrated himself. In 1935 he returned as the regular cartoonist of *Carêta*, to which he contributed countless cartoons, caricatures and illustrations until the time of his death in Rio in 1950.

J. Carlos received many awards and honors for his work. An anthology of his cartoons was published by the Ministry of Education just before the artist's death, and a posthumous exhibition of his works was organized some months later.

A.M.

BROOKS, CHARLES GORDON (1920-   ) American political cartoonist born in Andalusia, Alabama, on November 22, 1920. Chuck Brooks was educated in local public schools and attended Birmingham Southern College, which he left in 1941 to attend the Chicago Academy of Fine Arts. In Chicago his teacher, Vaughn Shoemaker, taught him editorial cartooning.

Brooks enlisted in the army and won four battle stars for action in such campaigns as Normandy. After the war he freelanced in Chicago for a year, married and returned to Alabama, where he became editorial cartoonist on the *Birmingham News* in 1948. He remains there today as one of the South's strongest political cartooning voices.

Traditional-style figures and conventional crayon shading have been Brooks's visual forte throughout his career. In concepts he is strong and has always vigorously upheld the Southern point of view. One of his frequent themes, and one most tellingly presented, was of Northern hypocrisy during the desegregation years. Politically, Brooks is an independent with definite Republican-conservative leanings.

"You can rest easy—they'll be running the CIA from now on!"

Charles Brooks. © *The Birmingham News.*

"Brother Juniper." © *Field Newspaper Syndicate.*

Brooks has won ten Freedoms Foundation awards, the Sigma Delta Chi Distinguished Service Award in 1960 and the Grover C. Hall Award for Excellence in Alabama Journalism from Troy State University in 1974. He also edits annual compilations of the best American editorial cartoons.

R.M.

BROTHER JUNIPER (U.S.) "I wish I had a whole forest of Junipers," St. Francis of Assisi is said to have punned about a short, kindly colleague. This historical anecdote inspired Father Fred McCarthy, art editor of the *Friar* magazine, to create *Brother Juniper* in 1953. This panel cartoon about a monastery's well-meaning cook attracted notice outside Franciscan circles, and in 1957 Doubleday collected the gentle, clever gags into a book. In December 1958 Publisher's Syndicate of Chicago introduced *Brother Juniper* as a daily panel.

Brother Juniper features other regular characters, but most, like the tall Brother Superior, are unnamed. The dog, Bernard, does have a name and is a fixture of the panel, as are cute conventions like Juniper's car with stained-glass windows. All in all, it is a warm, whimsical world that McCarthy, now laicized, has created. His art style is competent, appropriate and witty. In recent years the gags have appeared a bit obtuse at times because of a ridiculous syndicate preference that McCarthy recaption old gags instead of drawing new ones. The panel, which has never been transformed into a Sunday version, has been collected in book form several times and is now distributed by Field.

R.M.

BROWN, BUCK (1936-) American cartoonist born in Morrison, Tennessee, in 1936. After high school Buck Brown served in the air force and upon his discharge settled in Chicago. There he joined the Chicago Transit Authority and worked as bus driver from 1958 to 1963, meanwhile attending Wilson Junior College, from which he received an associate of arts degree. Moving on to the University of Illinois, he obtained his B.F.A. in 1966.

The extent to which Brown's job as a bus driver provided him with an appreciation for human foibles can only be surmised, but it can be said that Chicago was during these years a good place to be a young apprentice cartoonist with a risqué sense of humor and a healthy attude toward sexual topics—Chicago being the home (since 1953) of a magazine devoted to celebrating precisely these new "virtues." Capitalizing on his assets, Brown was soon a regular contributor to *Playboy*, as well as to *Esquire* and other male-oriented magazines. By 1970, he was sufficiently well known in Chicago to be named one of Chicago's ten most outstanding young men by the local chapter of the JayCees. The same year he wound up a two-year term as a member of the President's Task Force on Youth Motivation—an appointment probably less whimsical than it sounds.

In his approach to cartooning, Brown recalls Peter Arno—at least as one imagines that Arno, freed of Rossian restraints, might have painted—even to the bold signature figured along the border of each work. With their vivid colors, each of Brown's pieces is a complete, full-page picture, including central characters, supporting characters and a finished, detailed backdrop—a virtual showcase of the caricaturist's art. He likes to spoof period pieces and exploit topical situations, and his subjects range from French aristocrats of the 18th century to young modern swingers to dirty old men and women of any era—all appropriately endowed.

Unlike many "stag-magazine" artists, Brown rarely descends to the use of crude captions, preferring to let his pastels do the titillation. And titillate they do, as in the assault by a bespectacled, moustachioed supermarket manager on a Junoesque young housewife-shopper, amidst a tumbled display of toilet tissue. Captioned "Mr. Whipple, please! Don't squeeze the shoppers," the piece is a masterful exploitation of one of Madison Avenue's sillier attempts to merchandise a commodity that by itself inspires the scatologist in all of us to snicker.

As Jackie Gleason's Ralph Cramden character might have observed with some envy, not many bus routes lead to the destination achieved by Buck Brown.

R.C.

BROWN, ROBERT (1906-   ) American cartoonist born in Pennsylvania in 1906. Robert ("Bo") Brown attended the University of Pennsylvania, graduating in 1928. He planned on a career as an attorney and was a law school student when the *Saturday Evening Post* accepted one of his drawings; he renounced forthwith the perquisites of the "Philadelphia lawyer" to become a gag cartoonist, a vocation he has been pursuing successfully ever since. Working in ink, lines and washes, Brown calls cartooning a "relaxing" profession and claims to do his best work when he is tired.

Brown's style is adequate to his purpose but hardly distinctive, being a derivative mélange of the early 20th-century styles upon which he was raised. His gag lines are generally acceptable, but much of his humor is topical and without noticeable bite or recurrent imagery, and so does not stand up as well as the humor of the greatest of his contemporaries—artists like Peter Arno or George Price. When he avoids the topical and exploits the cliché, Brown is at his best.

For example, in a late-1940s panel a prospective customer points angrily to his children, sitting rapt before the console radio, and exclaims to the television salesman who has dropped by to make a pitch, "You mean I'll even have to *look* at Oatsy-Woatsies?" In this case, Brown proved rather prophetic, for it was precisely "Oatsy-Woatsy"-supported television programming that ultimately killed off the mass-circulation general-interest weeklies like the *Post* and *Look* that provided the main market for his bland, middle-of-the-road art and humor.

R.C.

"I wonder what Herb is up to now?"

Robert ("Bo") Brown. © Brown.

BROWNE, CHRISTOPHER KELLY (1952-   ) American cartoonist born in South Orange, New Jersey, on May 16, 1952. The son of cartoonist Dik Browne, Chris Browne was raised in Connecticut and lists his only formal artistic training as one month at the Philadelphia College of Art. He had his first cartoon published by the YMCA when he was 13: a Christmas card design distributed regionally by the organization. He entered the cartooning field in 1970 with the help of his father's associates, assisting Dick Hodgins in slide and filmstrip preparations, and penciling for Frank Johnson on such comic books as *Barney Rubble* (Charlton) and *Bullwinkle* and *Road Runner* (Gold Key). For two years he pursued such work, until the elder Browne began producing *Hagar the Horrible*, which debuted in February 1973. Since then he has played an active role in the strip, writing gags, assisting on art chores, and penciling *Hi and Lois* for a stretch as well.

Apart from his work with his father, Browne's independent career and individual style, not to mention his zany sense of humor, mark him as one of the upcoming generation's brightest talents. In 1974 he was associate editor of the *Funny Papers*, a short-lived but highly innovative tabloid that utilized reprints of classic comics and new work by underground artists; while there, Browne created the *Mr. Nostalgia* strip. Since 1976 he has drawn regularly for the *National Lampoon* (spots and parodies including *Funny the Bunny*), and since 1978 for *Playboy*, where his creations included *Benny Juice, Born Toulouse,*

Valentina and Zenayeda Brumberg, "Puss in Boots."

Tom Morrow, *The Kinky Report* and *Cruiser*, a gibe at the Playboy philosophy. He also made sales to *Head* and *Esquire* magazines.

Browne's style is either a handsome refinement or a sympathetic caricature of the "Connecticut school" big-foot look, depending on his thematic material. He tends toward economical simplicity, well-spotted blacks and a wild, anarchical humor that seems even wilder when set against his reserved drawings.

R.M.

BRUMBERG, VALENTINA (1899-   ) and ZENAYEDA (1900-   ) A sister team of Soviet animators, both born in Moscow, Russia, in 1899 and 1900 respectively. Valentina and Zenayeda Brumberg studied art in Moscow and were drawn into animation in the mid-1920s. In 1925 they were part of the collective that turned out some of the earliest Soviet cartoons. Their first solo film appears to have been *The Young Samoyed* (1929), the adventures of a plucky little seal-hunter in the Arctic.

After the Brumbergs joined the newly created Soyuzmult'film in 1935, their career picked up. They directed a great number of animated films, including the excellent *Tale of Czar Duranda*, a 1935 effort in which they joined forces with Ivanov-Vano, *The Tailor Hare* (1937) and a rather nicely animated version of *Puss in Boots* (1938); there followed *Little Red Riding Hood* (also 1938), *Ivashko and Baba Yaga* (both 1939). Like many other animators and filmmakers, the Brumberg sisters devoted most of their talents during World War II to turning out patriotic films, though they did succeed in making a 1943 entertainment short, *Tale of Czar Zoltan*. The period after the end of the war witnessed a flurry of activity, starting with the whimsical *Lost Certificate* (1945), and culminating in the enchanting and much-awarded *Fedya Zaytsev* (1949).

The 1950s and 1960s were a time of intense activity for the sisters. Notable among their many films of this period are *The Night Before Christmas* (1951), *Flight to the Moon* (a classic theme of science-fiction animation, 1953), *Stepa the Sailor* and *The Island of Mistakes* (both 1955), *Great Troubles* (1961), *Three Fat Men* (1963), *The Brave Little Tailor* (1964), *Golden Stepmother* (1966), *The Little Time Machine* (another science fiction effort, 1967) and *The Capricious Princess* (1969). Little has been heard from the Brumbergs in the last ten years, and it is assumed that they are in retirement. They were reported as still living at the time of this writing.

The Brumberg sisters have been among the most prolific animators in the Soviet Union. Their subjects have often been fairy tales and other material directed at children, but they have managed to remain fresh and reasonably innovative. Their work has been widely seen in the West and has received a fair share of awards and honors.

M.H.

BRUNHOFF, JEAN DE (1899-1937) French cartoonist, writer and painter born in Paris, France, on December 9, 1899. Jean de Brunhoff studied painting in Paris, and he later became a pupil of Othon Friesz. He was commissioned to do several paintings for industrial corporations and also started contributing cartoons and drawings to French magazines such as *Excelsior* in the mid-1920s.

Jean de Brunhoff and his wife Cécile enjoyed telling tales to their two sons, Laurent and Mathieu. One day Cécile told the children the fabulous story of a little elephant in a big forest. Elaborating on this premise, Jean de Brunhoff wrote and illustrated his first children's book, *L'Histoire de Babar le Petit Eléphant* ("The Story of Babar the Little Elephant"), which was published in Paris in 1931. The first story was so well received and successful that it was soon translated into several foreign languages (including English) and spawned four more *Babar* books, published between 1932 and 1936. That same year de Brunhoff was commissioned to decorate the children's dining room of the *Normandie* ocean liner. At the same time, *Babar* was scoring a hit in New York and running serially in the London *Daily Sketch*.

Amid all the acclaim, Jean de Brunhoff died suddenly, of a heart attack, in October 1937. The two books he was then working on, *Babar en Famille* ("Babar Among His Family") and *Babar et le Père Noël* ("Babar and Santa Claus") were completed by his editor, in collaboration with de Brunhoff's brother Michel, and published in 1938 and 1939 respectively.

M.H.

BRUNHOFF, LAURENT DE (1925-   ) French cartoonist and writer born in Paris, France, on August 30, 1925. The son of famed *Babar* creator Jean de Brunhoff, Laurent de Brunhoff was literally raised in the company of Babar, the little elephant, and his friends: his father would tell him the stories and show him the drawings before the *Babar* books went to press. Laurent himself would often sketch Babar for his own amusement. After the death of his father in 1937, Laurent de Brunhoff went on to complete his studies at Lycée Pasteur; in 1945 he decided to devote himself to painting and studied art at the Académie de la Grande Chaumière.

Partly for fun and partly to continue a family tradition, Laurent de Brunhoff decided to write a *Babar* book. Titled *Babar et ce Coquin d'Arthur* ("Babar and That Rascal Arthur"), it was published in 1946. Success was again immediate, and Laurent de Brunhoff went on to write many more *Babar* stories. At the same time he continued with his painting and had his works exhibited in galleries from Paris to New York. He also contributed cartoons to such publications as *Paris-Match* and *Elle*, and he created the character of Serafina the Giraffe in the 1950s. The *Serafina* books never attained the popularity of the *Babar* series, however. His latest effort, *The One Pig with Horns* (1979), is also a non-Babar book.

Laurent de Brunhoff has traveled to the United States

Laurent de Brunhoff, "Babar." © L. de Brunhoff.

many times to promote his books, and he helped design as well as write the *Babar* animated cartoon special directed by Bill Melendez and first seen on American television in 1968.

M.H.

BUBBLE AND SQUEAK (G.B.) Bubble, the Cockney taxi driver, and Squeak, his brand-new baby cab that walked rather than rolled on wheels, were the first postwar "series characters" in British cartoon films. Named after the traditional British dish "bubble and squeak" (a mixture of cooked potato and cooked cabbage fried in a pan), they were created by George Moreno, Jr., during his active service in France as an American GI.

Moreno had worked for the Max and Dave Fleischer Studios before America's entry into World War II, and a chance wartime meeting with a British soldier, Richard A. Smith, led to the two men forming a private company to promote and produce British animated cartoons. They called themselves British Animated Productions, and produced their first seven-minute short in Smith's office in Walthamstow, London. It was called *The Big City* (1947), and it introduced Bubble and Squeak. Rather rough-and-ready in style and technique (perhaps not surprisingly), the animation showed more than a little trace of the rubbery Fleischer school. Moreno wrote, produced, directed and animated, with some assistance from Harold F. Mack.

Fun Fair followed, and Bubble and Squeak visited the holiday fairground on Hampstead Heath and won a golden horn. *The Old Manor House* (1948) was a departure from the series: it introduced Colonel Rat (voice, Jon Pertwee) and his pet monster, Frankie Stein. The colonel also starred in *Loch Ness Legend* (1948). *Home Sweet Home* was the last Bubble and Squeak adventure, and it introduced a "baby car" called Squeaker. By this time B.A.P. cartoons had developed a decided style, but without big studio backing the venture collapsed. After a period drawing strips for the children's weekly *TV Comic* (*Polly Copter*, etc.), and drawing *Bubble and Squeak Annual* (1950-52), Moreno formed his own company, Moreno Cartoons, to produce animated commercials for television. Talent on the Bubble and Squeak series included: Harold Mack (direc-

tor), Hugh Gladwish, Pamela French, Jimmie Holt, Fay Thompson (animation), Claude A. Lipscombe (layout) and José Norman (music).

D.G.

BUDD, CHARLES J. (1859-1926) American cartoonist born in South Schodack, New York, on February 14, 1859. C.J. Budd received art training from the Hudson River Institute, the Pennsylvania Academy of Fine Arts and the Art Students League. Budd entered the art field in Philadelphia in 1885 as a magazine and children's book illustrator. In 1890 he moved to New York, becoming a regular contributor to *Life* magazine in 1894, after winning a contest illustrating quotations. He drew for *Life* until 1917, and briefly for *Harper's Weekly*—through the influence of *Life*'s editor E.S. Martin—in 1912 and 1913. In retirement Budd ran a successful business manufacturing artistic gifts. He died in March 1926.

The main contribution of C.J. Budd to cartooning was his innovation of combining photographs and realistic wash drawings, mostly for caricature effects. When he worked in pen and ink, his figures were somewhat stiff, and his style, though fully competent, was never quite polished. His work in wash, however—even without the photographic gimmicks—was self-assured and realistic. His humor cannot be branded any better or worse than many of his fellows'; and like other *Life* artists of his period he dabbled in social commentary.

R.M.

BUGS BUNNY (U.S.) There have been almost as many cartoonists claiming the distinction of having created Bugs Bunny as there were ancient Greek cities vying for the honor of having been Homer's birthplace. *The World Encyclopedia of Comics* (Chelsea House, 1976) unraveled the mystery thus: "The creation of the wise-cracking rabbit (under producer Leon Schlesinger, releasing through Warner Brothers) was done in stages with contributions by many studio employees. The genesis was in a *Porky Pig* film, 'Porky's Hare Hunt,' directed by Ben ('Bugs') Hardaway and Cal Dalton, based on a story by Bob Clampett (1938). The hare, quite unlike the final Bugs, proved popular and warranted another film. 'Hare-um Scare-um' was done by the same directors.... Another version appeared in "Presto Change-o," directed by Chuck Jones. In 1939 ... two more films were assigned: 'Elmer's Candid Camera,' directed by Jones; and 'A Wild Hare,' directed by Fred ('Tex') Avery."

In Avery's cartoon the rabbit used for the first time the famous catchphrase "What's up, doc?" and later got his name—Bugs Bunny. More than any other director, Avery was responsible for the development of the Bugs Bunny persona—a feat all the more remarkable in light of the fact that he directed only three more cartoons: "The Heckling Hare," "Tortoise Beats Hare" and "All This and Rabbit Stew." All of Bugs's personality traits were already in evidence: the flippant attitude, the disjointed walk, the jaunty demeanor and the all-pervasive assertion of superiority. A star was born, and it remained for other hands (Avery having left for MGM in 1941) to bring him to full glory.

Bugs Bunny was at his best when resisting the encroachments of some aggressive type, and the animators had fun matching him against each and every character in the Schlesinger/Warner Brothers stable. The bumbling Elmer Fudd had been Bugs's most constant foil ever since "Elmer's Candid Camera," and the "wascally wabbit" (as the exasperated Elmer called Bugs) thwarted his every attempt at shooting him in such gems as "A Wild Hare," "Wabbit Twouble," "Rabbit Seasoning," "Rabbit Fire" and "Duck, Rabbit, Duck." (In the last three, Daffy Duck and Bugs Bunny kept confusing Elmer about just what hunting season it was—duck or rabbit.) Bugs and Fudd, however, were best partnered in two musical entries in the series, "Rabbit of Seville" and the irrepressible "What's Opera, Doc?"

Bugs's declared foe, the diminutive, gun-toting and foul-tempered Yosemite Sam, appeared for the first time in "Hare Trigger" (1944), in which he was outsmarted at every turn by the cunning rabbit. He reappeared time and again in countless cartoons, such as "Hare Lift," "Mississippi Hare," "Southern Fried Rabbit," and especially "Rabbitson Crusoe," a glittering little gem featuring Bugs and Yosemite stranded on a desert island in the vicinity of a ravenous shark.

Bugs also contended with lesser fry such as the irascible opera singer of "Long Haired Hare," the feckless mobster of "Bugs and Thugs," the inept vampire of "Transylvania 6-5000" and the supremely silly Tasmanian devil of "Devil May Hare." In 1958 the fearless rabbit finally won an Oscar (for "Knighty Knight Bugs"). Bugs Bunny's most perfect moment, however, had occurred nine years previously when, in the opening sequence of "Frigid Hare," he bounded, with beach towel and sunglasses, upon the icy wastes of the North Pole and incredulously exclaimed, "So, this is Miami Beach?"

Virtually every animator in the Schlesinger and Warners studios worked on *Bugs Bunny*; in addition to that of Avery, the work of Chuck Jones, Friz Freleng, Robert Clampett, Robert McKimson and Frank Tashlin must be singled out. They raised the character of Bugs Bunny to mythical proportions and made the rabbit into the most celebrated cartoon creation next to Mickey Mouse and Donald Duck. Credit for Bugs's extravagant success is also due Mel Blanc, who gave the bunny his inimitable nasal voice and street-wise Brooklyn accent.

"Bugs Bunny." © *Warner Brothers.*

The popularity of Bugs Bunny spilled out to other media. In 1941 he started his career in comic books, and the following year a *Bugs Bunny* Sunday page started syndication. Bugs has also been the star of countless commercials, notably those directed by Tex Avery for Kool-Aid, and he still appears on reruns of *The Bugs Bunny Show* and in many TV specials.

M.H.

BUGVILLE LIFE (U.S.) In the pages of adult humor magazines around the turn of the century—in the days when that term did not mean pornography, and as distinct from the humor columns of children's magazines like *St. Nicholas*—animal and insect cartoons were quite common. In *Puck*, *Judge* and *Life*, interspersed among savage political broadsides and biting social commentary, was a goodly number of purely cute and lightweight gags about outdoor creatures in human situations. That they were simply entertaining takes nothing away from the competence or cleverness of these creations; indeed, some brilliant artwork highlighted this widespread theme, and the public appreciated the material greatly.

Perhaps the foremost exponent of this school was Gus Dirks, and his cartoons and series can serve here as representative. *Bugville Life* was his series for *Judge* in the late 1890s and featured the doings of busy colonies of insects and small animals in real-world situa-

Yule-log in Bugville: "Come on Billy. Hurry up and help me carry it. This cigarette will make the best Yule-log ever."

"Bugville Life."

tions. The drawings were distinguished by Dirks's remarkable pen work and shadings and were collected in a book (with verses by veteran humorist R.K. Munkittrick) published by *Judge* in 1898. Dirks also drew this type of material for *Puck* and *Life* before he was lured away by Hearst to do Sunday comics in 1903.

Dirks was by no means alone, and when he left *Life*, Walt Kuhn was already establishing himself as a consistent delineator of bird life. Kuhn continued his back-of-the-book panel cartoons for *Life* right through his organizational efforts in behalf of the famous Armory Show. He published a book, *A Little Bird Told Me*, in 1908. Imitating Kuhn was "Lang" (Louis Lansing Campbell, according to the best available research), who later drew birds in *Adventures of the Clothesline* for *Puck* in the 1910s. Harrison Cady drew a series of stunningly detailed *Beetleburgh* cartoons for *Life*. T.S. Sullivant, of course, often concentrated on animal subjects, and C. Barnes and Larkin were among a host of others. One of the most prolific was A.Z. Baker (Baker-Baker, who often signed his cartoons with a double *B* monogram). His animals were easily the funniest, rendered in a style of such freedom that they seem out of place in the more rigid turn-of-the-century milieu.

The animal and bug cartoon went out after World War I, when the general mood seemed more sophisticated and/or cynical and talking animals seemed out of place. But in the first two decades of the 20th century, a random sampling of 10 magazine cartoons was bound to include several animal subjects, whether those listed above or Kemble's frogs, Frost's cats and goats, Carl Anderson's pups or E.G. Lutz's mice.

R.M.

BULL, CHARLES LIVINGSTON (1874-1932) American cartoonist and illustrator born in 1874. Charles Livingston Bull is considered the foremost depicter of animals in American illustration. His animals and birds, even in cartoons, were never caricatured or exaggerated; rather cartoonists' shorthand techniques (bold outlines, dropped backgrounds, etc.) were employed for breezy poster effects. His series in *Life* in the 1920s contrast with Sullivant's delineations of fauna but are striking cartoons nonetheless. Bull variously used crayons and wash for his shadings.

No doubt Bull's expertise grew from his taxidermy skills; as a youth he skinned pelts for Ward's Museum in Rochester, New York. Later, when employed by the Smithsonian Institution in Washington, D.C., he attracted the notice of Theodore Roosevelt. The president admired Bull's skills as an artist and taxidermist and, in fact, Bull later mounted many of Roosevelt's bird specimens for the Smithsonian. Like Paul Bransom, another cartoonist-illustrator of animals, Bull learned much from studious observation at the Bronx Zoo. And like Ding Darling, another cartoonist-conservationist, Bull was active in work to preserve dwindling species of birds.

Books: *The Kindred of the Wild* (1902); *The Call of the Wild* by Jack London (1903); *Denizens of the Deep* (1904); *The Race of the Swift* (1905); *Before Adam* by Jack London (1907); *Haunters of the Silences* (1907); *Old Crow Stories* (1917); and many others.

R.M.

BULLWINKLE SHOW, THE (U.S.) Producer Jay Ward, writer Bill Scott, and directors Bill Hurtz and Peter Burness teamed up to create *Rocky and His Friends*, a television animated series that first aired on NBC in 1958. This was a weird mock-adventure program relating the exploits of resourceful Rocket J. Squirrel (alias Rocky) and dumb Bullwinkle Moose, both of Frostbite Falls, Minnesota, and their unending struggle against sinister Boris Badenov and his scheming female assistant, Natasha Fatale. The show, initially telecast on Saturday mornings, proved so popular with children (and their parents) that the network later rescheduled it for an evening slot, rechristening it *The Bullwinkle Show* (in recognition of the star status that the goofy moose had attained in the meantime).

The Bullwinkle Show was actually made up of several segments, only one of which featured the continuing adventures of Rocky and Bullwinkle. There was in addition a north-of-the-border tale recounting the harebrained exploits of Dudley Do-Right of the Royal Mounted Police as he tried to collar the snarling, top-hatted Snidely Whiplash and to save his girl friend, the blond Nell Fenwick, from the villain's clutches. Another popular segment was "Fractured Fairy Tales," which joyously demolished such traditional tales as "Little Red Riding Hood" and "Sleeping Beauty."

In 1964 the network cancelled *The Bullwinkle Show* and it went into syndication. In the early 1960s, and again in the 1970s, there was a *Bullwinkle* comic book. Al Kilgore, who drew the first comic book version, was also responsible for the short-lived *Bullwinkle* newspaper strip (1962-64).

The Bullwinkle Show was a highly entertaining work which managed to overcome the "limited animation" techniques that have usually proved the bane of TV animated cartoons. Its success was due to clever direction, imaginative plot lines, irreverent dialogue and excellent voice characterizations by such luminaries as William Conrad, Charlie Ruggles, June Foray and Hans Conried.

M.H.

BURCHARD, FRANZ (1799-1835) German cartoonist and printmaker born at Fellin in what was then Livonia (now the Latvian Soviet Socialist Republic) on February 22, 1799. Franz Burchard worked under the pseudonym "Dörbeck" and is best known by that name.

In 1816 Dörbeck began to study the art of engraving in St. Petersburg, the European capital nearest to his native region, and got a job there working in the Russian government bank as an engraver of legal tender. After the death in 1820 of his first wife, a native of St. Petersburg, he moved to Riga, where he worked as a commercial engraver and portraitist. Marrying again in Riga, he traveled on in 1823 to Berlin, where his chief artistic development took place. In Berlin, Dörbeck continued to engrave portraits, but he also extended his range to engraved and lithographed illustrations for historical and medical books and such works of fiction as *Robinson Crusoe*.

His importance in the history of cartooning rests on commissions he received from the active art-publishing firm of Gropius—which also patronized Schadow and Hosemann—for humorous scenes of everyday life in Berlin. For such Gropius print series as *Berliner Witze* ("Berlin Jokes") and *Berliner Redensarten* ("Berlin Sayings"), Dörbeck did numerous color pen lithographs on such subjects as street and market scenes, domestic servants, small storekeepers and householders, student jollity, trades and occupations, conveyances (for the series *Berliner Fuhrwerke*) and the like. His drawing style, some-

Copyright©Jay Ward Productions 1976

"The Bullwinkle Show." © Jay Ward Productions.

what roughhewn but extremely energetic, was exactly right for this subject matter, the common denominator of which was the glib, wide-awake and never-to-be-bested character of the population of Berlin. Dörbeck's influence in this area on the young Menzel, on Hosemann—and, through him, on Zille—was incalculable. His work is always featured prominently in anthologies of old Berlin humor and in illustrated cultural and social histories of Berlin.

Beginning in 1832, Dörbeck worked on a series completely dedicated to student life and called *Album Academicum*. He died in his native town at the early age of 36, on October 2, 1835.

S.A.

BURCK, JACOB (1904-   ) American cartoonist and Pulitzer Prize winner born in Bialystok, Poland, in 1904. When he was ten, he and his family emigrated to America to join his bricklayer father. He was educated in the Cleveland public schools and attended the Cleveland School of Art. In 1930 Burck studied at the Art Students League under Boardman Robinson and Albert Sterner, whose protégé he became. At this time he aspired to fine arts, but both his mentors were cartoonists, and Burck was a strong partisan whose entry into cartooning was made even easier by the desire for work during the Depression.

He was a radical leftist and worked for the *Daily Worker* and *New Masses*. Whitaker Chambers, in *Witness*, recalls that Burck's 14th Street studio was a hangout for radicals and artists. Shortly after the publication of his anthology of cartoons, *Hunger and Revolt* (with deluxe editions sold in a very bourgeois manner), he was invited to Russia by the Soviets to execute murals. He returned to the United States disillusioned with communism. He was offered a position as political cartoonist for the *St. Louis Post-Dispatch* in 1937, and a year later he transferred to the *Chicago Times*, now the *Sun-Times*, where he is still chief cartoonist.

Burck's work, especially the cartoons drawn in his radical prime, is squarely in the tradition of Boardman Robinson, Robert Minor and the original *Masses* cartoonists. He obviously had an ax to grind but was more than gifted in his presentations. Stylistically, he was the heir of Robinson, Minor and Fred Ellis. When his radicalism waned, so did much of his punch, although his Pulitzer was well deserved in 1941 for his devastatingly poignant comment on war. Today his artwork is sharply simple and abbreviated, but his ideas and humor are fresh.

R.M.

BURIED TREASURE (U.S.) In the late 1920s a group of prominent New York cartoonists (reportedly including Winsor McCay, George McManus and Bud Fisher) got together and, as a prank, decided to collaborate in the making of one of the few (and possibly the first) pornographic animated cartoons. This short feature came to be known as *Buried Treasure*.

Buried Treasure is less remarkable, however, for its subject matter—the sexual adventures of an extravagantly well-endowed little man by the name of Everready Hardon (*sic*)—than for the quality and imagination of its animation. The process was characterized by a lusty, outrageous humor—a kind of graphic equivalent of the ribald tales of Petronius and Rabelais. Laughter at Everready's sustained but inept efforts at sexual fulfillment far overwhelms the incongruous and, to some, obscene shenanigans. As Professor Rabkin observes in his study of the stag film, *Dirty Movies: An Illustrated History of the Stag Film, 1915-1970*, "*Buried Treasure* is consistently amusing because it fully exploits the power of animation to delineate a logic photography can only suggest: when men are led by (sex), they have problems as well as pleasures."

An oddity among underground movies, *Buried Treasure* is probably the only film of its kind worth mentioning.

M.H.

BURNESS, PETER (1910-   ) American animator born in Los Angeles, California, on June 16, 1910. In the early 1930s Peter Burness worked for the Harman-Ising animation unit, later switching to the Amédée Van Beuren studio (where the *Little King* cartoons were among his more notable efforts). He finally came to rest in the late 1930s at the Disney studio and later at MGM (where he worked on many of the *Tom and Jerry* cartoons). His work all that time remained largely uncredited and unnoticed.

Burness finally came to prominence in the 1940s as one of the original founders of United Productions of America, grouped around Stephen Bosustow. He worked on a number of early UPA cartoons but gained fame with the Mr. Magoo series, to which he was the most prolific contributor. He directed such Magoo classics as "Bungled Bungalow" (1949), "Trouble Indemnity" (1950), "Captains Outrageous" (1952), "Magoo Goes

"If I should die before I wake."

Jacob Burck, Pulitzer Prize-winning cartoon, 1941. © Chicago Times.

Peter Burness, "Destination Magoo." © UPA.

West" (1953), the hilarious "When Magoo Flew" and the classic "Destination Magoo" (both 1954), "Stagedoor Magoo" (1955) and "Magoo's Puddle Jumper," which earned him an Academy Award in 1956.

When UPA began to falter in the late 1950s, Burness joined the Jay Ward organization, most notably as a director on the witty and very popular *Rocky and His Friends* (later retitled *The Bullwinkle Show*) from 1958 to 1964. In recent years Burness has made a great number of animation commercials as well as a few TV specials. He is widely acknowledged as one of the masters of the "limited animation" technique, which he has perfected to a high degree of sophistication and polish.

M.H.

BUSH, CHARLES GREEN (1842-1909) American cartoonist and illustrator born in 1842. C.G. Bush studied fine arts in Paris under Bonnat and followed a dual career in painting and illustrating upon his return to America. American magazine illustration being what it was in the 1860s, and given Bush's famed sense of humor, it was natural that he would turn to the new art of social cartoons. For *Harper's Weekly* he produced a series of complicated, involved double-page cartoons on topics of the day. When the *New York Daily Graphic* was established on March 4, 1873, Bush's cartoons appeared from the first several issues; he was, therefore, a pioneer in the American daily cartoon, along with other *Graphic* artists like C.J. Taylor, W.A. Rogers, E.W. Kemble, Gray-Parker, Livingston Hopkins, Michael Angelo Woolf, A.B. Frost and Walt McDougall.

Bush was one of the earliest and most frequent contributors to *Life* magazine during its first year (1883). By this time—and because of the advent of photolithography—his style was well established and mature. As New York dailies began to use daily political cartoons, he became, with McDougall, a pioneer in that field, drawing for the *New York Telegram* and the *New York Herald*. A series of notable and forceful local cartoons attracted attention in 1895; he evidently relished lambasting corrupt political bosses Thomas Collier Platt, Richard Croker and David Bennett Hill.

Bush's new fame resulted in an offer from Joseph Pulitzer to join the staff of his *New York World*. Here the veteran drew his most sophisticated political cartoons—although stylistically he was just as biting and polished a generation earlier. Bush finished his career with the *World* and died in New York in 1909. His most amusing cartoons and, regrettably, virtually the only ones for which he is remembered today, were of Theo-

Charles Bush, 1887.

BUSHKIN, ALEKSANDR IVANOVICH (1896-1929) Soviet animator born in Kiev, in the Ukraine, Russia, on April 1, 1896. Aleksandr Bushkin showed an early disposition for art and drawing, and in 1919 he graduated from Kiev Art College. In 1922 he founded the first Soviet animation workshop, at the Moscow State Film Studios, under the guidance of Dziga Vertov; the following year he co-directed (with Aleksandr Ivanov) the first Soviet film cartoon, *Soviet Toys*, released in 1924.

For the rest of his short life Bushkin turned out a number of artistically distinguished cartoons, often of a political or didactic nature, including *Yumoreski* ("Humoresques," 1924), a group of three separate political cartoon films; *Sluchay v Tokio* ("Incident in Tokyo," 1924); *Kar'yera Makdonal'da* ("MacDonald's Career"), a satire on the British prime minister, in 1925; and *What the Peasant and Worker Should Know About the Soviet Union*, a flag-waving, morale-building lesson in civics, Soviet style. Bushkin also wrote several newspaper and magazine articles about the craft of animation, and in 1926 he authored a book-length study of the medium, *Tryuki i Mul'tiplikatsiya* ("Trick Films and Animated Cartoons"). His untimely death on June 5, 1929, at age 33, cut short a brilliant and promising career.

M.H.

BUSINO, ORLANDO FRANCIS (1926-) American magazine gag cartoonist born in Binghamton, New York, on October 10, 1926. Orlando Busino wanted to be a

Aleksandr Bushkin, "Humoresques."

dore Roosevelt during his presidency. Bush's Roosevelt was always in his Rough Rider costume and was frequently portrayed in keeping with Joseph Pulitzer's Democratic policies.

Bush's style marks him as one of the most talented cartoonists ever to touch pen to paper in America; his current obscurity represents a tragic loss to scholars and fans of the art alike. Perhaps only in the forgotten work of Joe Donahey of a later generation can another sad parallel be found. C.G. Bush was fecund and technically awesome; he was the first cartoonist of his generation to employ conscious physical exaggeration and distortions to his creations—no mean feat when there are absolutely no artistic precedents. In this regard he was definitely the artistic father of A.B. Frost, whom he preceded and later worked side by side with for several years. Frost's artistic gymnastics are well known today, and he inspired many cartoonists himself, but his mature work always resembled that of Bush, whose classical training obviously stood him in good stead: for the best exaggeration is based on a thorough knowledge of anatomy and other fundamentals.

The delightfully wispy lines of Bush's art led the reader's eye through comically distorted scenes. Figures were agile and constantly in motion, the reader's perspective down at the figure's feet but up at the face—all combining for a friendly, zany atmosphere. Bush's world was as consistent and competent as T.S. Sullivant's or George Herriman's, and fully as personal. It is to be hoped that a major reprinting of his work will take place in the near future.

R.M.

"You're getting warmer."

Orlando Busino. © *Busino.*

cartoonist from the time he started drawing, at about nine years old. As a youth he idolized the drawing in Elzie Segar's *Popeye* and the work from the Walt Disney studios, which he, like most kids, thought was done entirely by Disney himself.

Orlando Busino graduated from high school just at the end of World War II. He entered the United States Army and served from 1945 to 1947. In high school, cartooning for the student newspaper and yearbook had been important to him, and he was able to do some cartooning in the military. He continued his education under the GI bill after his tour of duty, earning a fine arts degree from the State University of Iowa in 1952. While at college he contributed cartoons to the *Daily Iowan*. As the result of high scores achieved in a competitive test for former GI's, Busino was able to continue his studies in art at the School of Visual Arts in New York City. During the day he worked in the advertising department of the Macmillan Company, book publishers.

In 1954 Orlando Busino decided to freelance magazine gag cartoons. "I was very lucky and sold on my first try," he says. He had taken ten cartoons to the *Saturday Evening Post,* and they bought one. Sales to *Colliers'* and *American Magazine* soon followed. His entire freelance career has been with general readership magazines doing mostly family humor. "I draw a big nose and big foot type cartoon and enjoy it," he says. Cartoons about children, animals, men from Mars, married life, doctors and all the standard themes for general readership have consistently received a fresh and humorous treatment from Orlando Busino. *Ladies' Home Journal, Family Circle, Good Housekeeping* and other women's magazines have steadily published his work. For seven years he has drawn *Gus*, a monthly panel cartoon about a big white shaggy dog, for *Boys' Life* magazine, the national magazine of the Boy Scouts of America. Both King Features' *Laugh-a-Day* and McNaught Syndicate's *Funny World*, syndicated gag-a-day panels, publish innumerable Orlando Busino cartoons.

Although he regularly sold to *True* and *Argosy* magazines several years ago when they were the leading cartoon market for men's adventure magazines, Busino admits he doesn't seem to think up risqué gags, so he's never submitted work to *Playboy*. Hallmarks of his cartoons are a clean, strong design and outline in the drawing. A light wash or benday dot pattern is used for shading, depending on whether his market is a magazine or newspaper. Unlike some cartoonists, Orlando Busino is a traditionalist who believes the picture has to be

funny, and not just the gag line. He has won the National Cartoonists Society's award for Best Magazine Gag Cartoonist three times.

B.C.

BUTE, MARY ELLEN (1914?-   ) American animator and film director born in Houston, Texas, at the start of World War I. Mary Ellen Bute began her career in the early 1930s with Lewis Jacobs and then married the cinematographer Ted Nemeth, with whom she made a long series of abstract animated films, starting with the silent *Synchrony* (1934). She later set her films to music. Her most important pictures of the 1930s, all in black and white, are: *Rhythm in Light*, set to Edvard Grieg's "Anitra's Dance" (1936); *Synchrony No. 2*, set to Richard Wagner's "Evening Star" (1937); and *Parabola*, set to Darius Milhaud's *La Création du Monde* (1938).

In 1940 Bute added color to her musical experiments in motion with *Escape*, set to J.S. Bach's Toccata and Fugue; this was followed in 1941 by *Spook Sport*, a film set to Camille Saint-Saens's "Danse Macabre," which Norman McLaren animated. Increasingly Bute turned to live-action film, first documentaries and later features, such as *Finnegan's Wake* and *The Skin of Our Teeth*, only occasionally going back to animation (*Color Rhapsody*, 1958, is one such exception).

Mary Ellen Bute used objects as well as cutouts and drawings in her animation films, but her experimentation with light, color and music was later widely transposed to the medium of traditional animation.

M.H.

BUXTON, DUDLEY (189-?-19—?) "They're British, quite British, you know!" was the jovially patriotic catch line to the advertisement for the first Tressograph Cartoons (producer, H. Tress) in November 1914, "drawn by the eminent lightning cartoonist, Dudley Buxton." Buxton, a familiar signature to humorous cartoons in the pictorial periodicals of the day, produced a series of three *War Cartoons* half-reelers during November 1914, then the following spring joined the Cartoon Film Company at 76 Wardour Street, London (proprietor, J.A. Clozenberg). There he worked in tandem with Anson Dyer, producing alternating editions of a series entitled *John Bull's Animated Sketch Book*. This ended with number 21 in November 1916, despite Buxton's delightful, if unauthorized, use of Charlie Chaplin as his "star"! Buxton's sense of humor often outshone Dyer's, although from

Mary Ellen Bute, "Spook Sport." © *Bute.*

time to time his skill shone in his choice of subject, such as the sinking of the German battleship *Blucher* (which preceded Winsor McCay's *Sinking of the Lusitania* by three years).

In 1917 Buxton joined Kine Komedy Kartoons, run by Frank Zeitlin, and *The Devil's Little Joke* was the first of eight short films he produced there. Unlike the *John Bull* series, these were not made up of short cartoon items. Rather they told a story, and one, *Ever Been Had?*, is preserved in the British National Film Archive. It is a humorous, even satirical, story of the Man in the Moon coming down to meet the Sole Surviving Englishman. In between the jokes Buxton creates a superb sequence of science fiction warfare. More famous, however, was Buxton's dramatic reconstruction of real warfare, *The Raid on Zeebrugge* (1918).

After World War I, Buxton's sense of comedy returned, and he created several series of cartoons, all sadly short-lived: *The Cheerio Chums* (1919), *Bucky's Burlesques* (1920), and *The Memoirs of Miffy* (1920), which actually had a daily newspaper strip syndicated to some local English newspapers. One of the Miffy series, *Running a Cinema* (1920), is in the National Film Archive and marks a stage in the evolution of British cartoon filmmaking. Gone is the old cutout system; it is replaced by the American cel technique. Gone, too, are the deliberate jokes and captions, replaced by fast-moving visual gags.

In late 1924 Buxton launched what was to be his last series, *Pongo the Pup*. Six short cartoons were made as items in the magazine film series *Pathé Pictorial*, which alternated with Sid Griffith's established series *Jerry the Troublesome Tyke*. The first was *Pongo Arrives*, followed by *Pongo's Day Out, Pongo Gets a Meal, Pongo at the Rodeo, Pongo Cheers Up the Goat Family* and *Pongo Catches the Crossword*, a cartoon comment on the craze of the day. This series marks the last trace of Buxton on the animation scene. He appears not to have survived the transition to sound.

D.G.

Cc

CADY, WALTER HARRISON (1877-1970) American cartoonist and illustrator born in Gardner, Massachusetts, on June 17, 1877. Harrison Cady received no formal art training, but Parker Perkins, a local marine painter, introduced the youngster to art, and the elder Cady took his son on innumerable hikes, thereby instilling a love of nature in the future cartoonist.

After the death of his father Harrison Cady moved to New York to pursue a career in art; the 19-year-old boy arrived with $19 in his pocket. He made an early sale to *Harper's Monthly* (the subject matter—a gnome, tiger lilies and bugs—was precisely the type with which he was identified throughout his career) and soon was a staffer on *Truth* magazine and a news sketch artist for the *Brooklyn Eagle*. By the late 1890s his work was a regular fixture in the pages of *St. Nicholas* (it was at the staff's suggestion that he removed the "Walter" from his signature), and his cartoons—intricate pen-and-inks as well as pleasant wash drawings—were soon also appearing in the *Saturday Evening Post, Country Gentleman, Ladies' Home Journal* and *Good Housekeeping*.

There were three phases to Cady's career: strips, book illustrations and magazine cartoons. His first work in comics was a jungle strip for the *Philadelphia Press* in 1905, and for 29 years his *Peter Rabbit* strip ran through the Herald-Tribune Syndicate. As an illustrator he achieved his greatest fame—which endures today—for his work on hundreds of Thornton W. Burgess children's books and newspaper columns. The *Mother West Wind* and *Peter Rabbit* series were two of the umbrella titles under which several generations of children were enchanted, a real reflection of the warm personal friendship between author and artist, and a tribute to their skill at weaving animal fantasy tales. In the magazine field, *Life* was Cady's principal cartoon outlet for two decades into the middle 1920s; editor J.A. Mitchell said approvingly, "I like men who see things that aren't there."

Cady's cartoons were remarkable for their overwhelming detail work. Literally thousands of tiny crosshatch lines composed his invariably large drawings (either full- or double-page cartoons), imparting an almost photographic shading quality when taken as a whole. His subjects fell into two quite disparate categories: pleasant, amusing bug and animal jokes, many of them set in Beetleburgh (the running title for the cartoons with no recurring characters); and vicious anti-Jewish polemics on matters pertaining to immigration, business practices, etc. The latter ran primarily in *Life* from the turn of the century to the mid-1910s, a time when ethnic slurs were the stock-in-trade of many cartoonists.

Meticulous shading and unfettered concept presentation combined to make Cady one of the most interesting cartoonists of his time. As his later work still lives in reprinted Burgess books, so should his early work be rediscovered; his artistic visions were impressive and fiercely personal. The later work was as simplified as the earlier work was detailed. Thin lines and careful shading patterns gave way to thick outlines and broad open areas of white (a change dictated, perhaps, by self-inflicted eyestrain). The colors in some of the illustrations in the Burgess books are among the handsomest and most soothing ever to grace cartoon illustrations.

Cady is remembered also as a distinguished, cultured conversationalist and friend, and a member of many clubs and societies, some of which exhibited his ventures into oils and watercolors. He won the Palmer Memorial Prize from the National Academy and exhibited at the Pennsylvania Academy and the Chicago Art Institute. He had one-man shows at the Salmagundi and Pleiades clubs, as well as at the Macbeth, Kleeman and Currier galleries and the Rockport Art Association. His etchings are in many museum collections as well.

Cady retired from active work in his seventies and died, much honored, on December 9, 1970, at the age of 93. His very special talents and insights have made him immortal. The world of fantasy, the realm of friendly animals, the pastel home of magical happiness, was his domain; he was one of the lucky few who retained the special childhood vision of that world—and the rest of us are the luckier for his charming depictions of it.

R.M.

"Hurrah! The first potato vine is up!"

Harrison Cady.

CAJETAN
See Elfinger, Anton.

"But, honey, I haven't got a girl in every port.
I ain't BEEN in every port!"

E. Simms Campbell. © *New York Journal-American.*

CAMPBELL, ELMER SIMMS (1906-1971) American cartoonist born in St. Louis, Missouri, on January 2, 1906. The son of an assistant high school principal, Elmer Campbell was known as Elmer to his friends and as E. Simms Campbell professionally. He began showing an interest in art at about the age of four, and was undoubtedly encouraged by his mother, who herself painted watercolors. When Campbell was 14, his family moved to Chicago, Illinois. He graduated from Englewood High School there and attended the University of Chicago briefly. He knew art would be his career and switched to the Chicago Institute of Fine Art, from which he graduated.

In 1932 and 1933 he lived with his aunt on Edgecombe Avenue in the Harlem section of New York City. He studied at the Art Students League under George Grosz during the day and drew for *College Comics,* a humor magazine, at night. Although extremely talented, Campbell was a black American and as such was no stranger to discrimination in his early efforts to sell his work. In a 1966 interview in *Ebony,* he said, "Oh, I could always draw, but I was a failure as an artist 'til I became a successful dining car waiter."

Campbell was 27 years old when his big break came in the spring of 1933. He got his chance through a combination of talent, luck and the recommendation of famed cartoonist Russell Patterson. A new magazine named *Esquire* was starting up. Arnold Gingrich, one of the founders of *Esquire,* had hoped to use art by Patterson, whose drawings of beautiful women were almost as famous as the Ziegfeld Girls. At the time Gingrich could offer only $100 per featured cartoon, and Patterson declined his offer. However, as Gingrich remembered in his memoir of *Esquire's* early days, "He did have a

suggestion; that is, he did—if I didn't 'draw the color line.' I said I didn't."

Gingrich needed color cartoons for *Esquire's* debut issue. E. Simms Campbell solved his problem. After visiting Campbell at his aunt's apartment, Arnold Gingrich had an armload of finished color cartoons and rough idea sketches. The debut issue of October 1933 contained 13 color cartoons, a good portion of which were by E. Simms Campbell or were worked up by artists such as John Groth and George Petty from Campbell idea sketches. *Esquire* was an instant success, and Gingrich credits the color cartoons with a significant contribution to that success.

Although dated January 1934, the second issue of *Esquire* appeared on December 5, 1933, the day Prohibition was repealed. It also marked the debut of Esky on the cover of *Esquire.* This popeyed, white-moustached, large-nosed admirer of female beauty was created by E. Simms Campbell. His cartoons also appeared in the old *Life, Judge, Collier's,* the *Saturday Evening Post,* the *New Yorker, Playboy, Cosmopolitan* and *Redbook.* King Features Syndicate distributed his daily panel *Cuties* from about 1943 until his death. The panel featured beautiful women and a gag.

Early in his career a friend had told Campbell that if he specialized in drawing beautiful women, he'd always have work. It was advice he took to heart. Beautiful women were his favorite subjects. One of his most famous creations was a continuing series in *Esquire,* and later *Playboy: Sultan and Harem* cartoons. The sultan, a short, rotund, jovial sort more in love with food and toys than sex, was always surrounded by his harem. The series was published as a full-page color cartoon rich both in the intensity of the bright orange tones Campbell favored and in lush odalisques.

E. Simms Campbell changed from pen and ink to pencil and watercolor with ease. His drawing had a spontaneity that often made the gag secondary. His color cartoons were painted and not just line drawings with color dropped in between the borders. Although he did illustrate such work as black writer Langston Hughes's *Popo and Fifna,* Campbell mostly cartooned the world of high society, nightclubs, expensive wine, women and song. Ironically, many admirers of his work are often surprised to learn he was black.

His work did not elicit a belly laugh as much as a chuckle and the sincere gratitude of male readers who didn't know much about art but knew what they liked. Throughout Campbell's work, the women portrayed in sensuous watercolors and line drawings were usually white. This prompted *Negro Digest* to ask in a 1951 article on Campbell, "Are Black Women Beautiful?" Occasionally, he did draw dark-skinned women, but they were usually Polynesian and not black.

For the last 14 years of his life until shortly before his death, E. Simms Campbell lived in Neerach, Switzerland. The expatriate life in Switzerland proved ideal, as he told *Ebony* in 1966. "Out here in this little off-the-wall village we don't have to prove nothin' to nobody.... Nobody bothers us unless we invite them in, and nobody gets mad because we're out here living in their community. Man, I can walk into any joint I want to out here and nobody starts looking as if they're thinking, 'Ugh, there's a nigger in here.' "

E. Simms Campbell left Switzerland after the death of his wife, Vivian, in October 1970. He returned to White Plains, New York, where on January 27, 1971, he died after a brief illness.

B.C.

CANFIELD, WILLIAM NEWTON (1920-   ) American cartoonist born in Orange, New Jersey, on October 8, 1920. "Bil" Canfield studied at the American School of Design in New York in 1940 and 1941 before taking a job as sports cartoonist for the *Morning Telegraph and Racing Form* in New York (1941-46). An admitted follower of the style of Bill Crawford, Canfield secured a job as sports cartoonist on Crawford's paper, the *Newark (N.J.) News*, in 1946 and continued in that position, and as staff artist, until Crawford left for the Newspaper Enterprise Association in 1960. In 1972 the *News* folded, and Canfield became editorial cartoonist of the *Newark Star-Ledger*. He also draws editorial cartoons for the *Red Bank (N.J.) Register* under his wife's maiden name, Lev.

Canfield's earlier tight style and careful crosshatching and crayon shading have given way to a hurried, informal look that includes shading with broad strokes of the brush over doubletone paper. His cartoons exude movement and emotion and are generally liberal-Democratic in political content.

R.M.

CANNON, ROBERT (1910-1964) American animator born in San Bernardino, California, in 1910. Bob Cannon started his animation career in 1934 as an assistant to Bob Clampett and Chuck Jones at the Leon Schlesinger studio. He began as an in-betweener but later worked as a full-fledged animator on a number of *Porky Pig* cartoons, especially "Porky's Duck Hunt" (1937), which marked the first appearance of Daffy Duck. In the 1940s Cannon moved over to Walt Disney, where he worked on some of the *Mickey* and *Donald* shorts. In 1945 Cannon helped found United Productions of America (UPA) and became its vice-president. He directed some early UPA cartoons, *Fear* and *The Brotherhood of Man* (the latter in collaboration with Stephen Bosustow), in the mid-1940s, at the same time continuing to do animation work for MGM and Disney (his name appears on the credits for *Melody Time* as late as 1948).

Cannon finally gained fame and recognition in 1949 with the creation of Gerald McBoing Boing, the little boy who could not talk but made noises through his nose. *Gerald McBoing Boing* won the Academy Award in 1950, and Cannon went on turning out more *Gerald* cartoons. In 1952 he created another child character, Christopher Crumpet, who turned into a chicken when he threw a temper tantrum; the *Christopher Crumpet*

Robert Cannon, "Madeleine," from Ludwig Bemelman's story. © UPA.

cartoons were never as popular as his earlier creation, however. Aside from his work on the *McBoing Boing* and *Crumpet* series, Cannon also directed a number of outstanding cartoons, including *Madeleine* (from Ludwig Bemelmans's story) and *Willie the Kid* (both 1952); *Fudget's Budget, Ballet Oop* and *Little Boy with a Big Horn* (all 1954); and *Department of the Navy* (1958). After the breakup of UPA in the late 1950s, Cannon went into commercial work and also taught animation at San Fernando College. He died in Northridge, California, on June 5, 1964.

M.H.

CAO, JOSÉ MARÍA (1862-1918) Argentine cartoonist born in Lugo, Spain, in 1862. José María Cao was apprenticed at age 15 to a manufacturer of porcelain in Gijón, Spain, where he became a designer. In 1884 he went to Madrid to further his art studies. He immigrated to Argentina in 1886 and settled in Buenos Aires. In the years immediately following, under the pseudonym "Democrito II," he collaborated on a number of Argentine magazines as a political cartoonist. His best work was done for *Don Quijote, Caras y Caretas* and *Fray Mocho*.

A great admirer of the French cartoonist Nadar, Cao often resorted to morality plays in comic strip form. His cartoons would tell a little fable (often in verse) in which the regular characters were replaced by well-known personalities in business or government. He also often used black silhouettes on white backgrounds to make his point and contributed many more innovations to the Argentine cartoon scene. He died in Buenos Aires in 1918.

A.M.

CAPTAIN PUGWASH (G.B.) "Captain Pugwash had three particular belongings: (1) His plank (for walking); (2) His compass (for navigating); (3) And a Very Special Box (invariably locked)." Thus was the "bravest, most handsome pirate in the Seven Seas" introduced in the first issue of the weekly comic *Eagle* (April 14, 1950), along with his wife ("who was far more terrifying than Pugwash"), his ship (*The Black Pig*) and, in due course, Cut-throat Jake (his deadly enemy). Later came the cabin boy Tim, who was smarter than Pugwash and his crew put together. It was Tim, really, who thwarted the entire British navy under Admiral Sir Splycemeigh Maynebrace!

The original strip, taking up two rows on one-third of a page, ran only 19 weeks before it was dropped. But its writer and artist, John Ryan (who continued in *Eagle* with *Harris Tweed, Extra Special Agent*), put the Cap'n into mothballs, reviving him later for a television series. This series of short cartoon films for children, *The Adventures of Captain Pugwash*, was simply drawn and produced in the cutout style of early animation. But good editing and construction prevented it from becoming boring, and the series continues intermittently to this day. Ryan still draws and produces the strip. It reappeared in *Swift* in 1958, then turned up in *Playland* in 1974, and is currently in *Pippin in Playland*.

Books: *Captain Pugwash* (1957); *Pugwash Aloft* (1958); *Pugwash and the Ghost Ship* (1962); *Pugwash in the Pacific* (1973); and *Captain Pugwash Annual* (1975).

D.G.

CARAN D'ACHE
See Poiré, Emmanuel.

Albert Carmichael. © New York World.

CARLOS, J.
See Brito e Cunha, José Carlos de.

CARMICHAEL, ALBERT PETER (1890-1917) American cartoonist born in Albany, New York, on December 13, 1890. Albert P. Carmichael started his cartooning career with the *New York World* when he was not yet 17. Among his co-workers on the *World* art staff were Gus Mager, Jack Callahan and George McManus, whose style Carmichael greatly admired and endeavored to emulate.

Carmichael contributed a great many cartoons and spot illustrations to the columns of the *World,* as well as a number of panels and comic strips, including *Jay Jones and His Camera, So English* and *Why Be Discontented* (all 1907), *The Adventures of Sonny and Sue* (1908), *Our Funny Language* (a panel dissecting the idiosyncrasies of the English language), *Dr. Spook's Explorations* (1909), *Rosie, the Joy of New York Life* (1911) and a funny takeoff on the vagaries of contemporary life, *Everybody's Doing It!* (1912).

Carmichael is best noted for his continuation of McManus's *The Newlyweds,* which he took over in 1914, and for his sophisticated daily strip, *The High Cost of Loving,* which he began in the same year. He also did a series of editorial cartoons characterized by an imaginative combination of photographic collages and pen drawings. Carmichael died on February 3, 1917, from complications of an appendicitis operation, at the age of 26.

Albert Carmichael's style was characterized by a deft, witty and uncluttered line which he adopted from McManus. His later cartoons show him in greater control of his work, with added individuality and expressiveness. Despite his untimely death, Carmichael remains one of the minor glories of the cartooning world.

M.H.

CARTER, ROBERT (1875-1918) American cartoonist born in Chicago in 1875. Robert Carter began his newspaper career in Chicago, where he chronicled some of the major murder trials of the day as a sketch artist. He attracted the attention of William Randolph Hearst, who brought him to New York around 1910 to work for the *New York American.* There he drew giant half-page cartoons to accompany the editorials of Arthur Brisbane. He later switched to the Progressive *Globe* and then to the *Sun.* In late 1916, he moved to Philadelphia and drew for the *Press* until his untimely death at the age of 44, on February 28, 1918.

Carter was at the forefront of his field during the 1910s, and it was the consensus of his peers and the newspaper profession in general at the time of his death that he was destined to be one of America's great cartoonists. An examination of his work bears out this contention. Carter drew in bold, slashing brushstrokes, yet without the harshness of, say, W.A. Rogers. His knowledge of anatomy and composition made nearly every cartoon a powerful message. He seldom pulled his punches, and his cartoons—supporting Roosevelt, attacking Wilson, furthering the war effort—place his regrettably small body of work squarely in the tradition of Nast, Keppler and Davenport.

R.M.

CARUSO, ENRICO (1873-1921) Italian tenor and American cartoonist born in Naples, Italy, on February 25, 1873. Enrico Caruso began to sing locally at age 11 and debuted in opera in 1894. He sang four seasons in La Scala before touring Europe to great acclaim. He was also a tremendous success in America after debuting at the Metropolitan Opera in New York on November 23, 1904. He made his home in Florence but spent much time in America, becoming, incidentally, one of the first great recording stars.

Caruso was also a talented caricaturist who captured his subjects on menus, envelopes and from memory. His fame as a cartoonist spread until, in 1907, he began contributing weekly caricatures for the Italian-language paper *La Follia di New York*—a schedule he maintained for years, although he declined salary. He died on August 2, 1921.

Caruso had a definite eye for characteristics and for translating a personality to paper. With his fame he had some of the world's best subjects pose willingly, and the informal circumstances of execution were evidenced by the rough media used in drawings. He was less polished as an artist than as a singer but could have achieved fame and respect on the basis of his cartoons alone. He is reported to have been offered a $50,000-a-year contract

Enrico Caruso, self-caricature as Pagliacci. © La Follia.

to draw for the *New York World*; for his work he must be recognized as America's first true caricaturist in the modern sense. A collection of Enrico Caruso's caricatures was published by *La Follia di New York* in 1916 and reprinted by Dover Books in 1977.

R.M.

CASPER (U.S.) Casper, a sprightly little spirit who had come from the netherworld to make friends with humans, was introduced in 1945 in "The Friendly Ghost," produced by Famous Studios, Paramount's animation arm. The cartoon was released under the Noveltoons title reserved for one-shots and features. It proved quite popular, however, and before the end of the 1940s several more *Casper* cartoons had been released, including "There's Good Boos Tonight" (1948) and "A-Haunting We Will Go" (1949).

The first *Casper* cartoons were directed by old hands I. Sparber and Seymour Kneitel and animated by Otto Messmer and Bill Turner on scripts by Joe Oriolo and Sy Reitt; Frank Gallop provided the voiced-over narration. By the start of the 1950s the series had acquired its permanent cast of characters: Wendy the Good Little Witch, Nightmare the Ghost Horse, the villainous Ghostly Trio, etc. The series rapidly lost whatever charm it had possessed in its beginning, however, and it was strictly aimed at a juvenile audience. It finally folded, along with Famous Studios, in the 1960s.

In the meantime *Casper* had been adapted to the comic book medium, first by Jubilee, then by St. John and finally by Harvey, which made it into a huge success. After Paramount sold the rights to the *Casper* cartoons to Harvey, these were successfully released to television under the Harveytoon banner.

M.H.

CASSELL, JONATHAN H. (ca. 1875-1940) American cartoonist born in Nebraska City, Nebraska, around 1875. John Cassell, as he became known (although he signed his work "Jno. Cassell") was educated at Doane College of Crete, Nebraska (1892-94). He studied art at the Art Institute of Chicago and began drawing cartoons for the *Ram's Horn* in that city; the magazine was a religious publication for which Frank Beard had drawn.

In the 1890s Cassell began freelancing to *Puck*, *Judge* and *Life* magazines and illustrating for popular monthlies and books. Around 1913, when the *New York World* lost Macauley and Minor as editorial cartoonists, Rollin Kirby and Cassell replaced them on the evening and morning editions, respectively. Though Cassell was eclipsed by Kirby, he was a respectable and forceful cartoonist in his own right. He drew vicious anti-Hughes cartoons in 1916 and generally supported the Democratic cause. When the *World* went to a single edition, Cassell left and, changing his political allegiance, drew editorial cartoons for the *Brooklyn Eagle*.

Cassell had a handsome crayon line and shaded his drawings neatly. There was much animation in his figures, and he had a way of endowing his targets with squint-eyed, dour expressions. He died in 1940.

R.M.

CASTANYS I BORRÁS, VALENTÍ (1898-1965) Spanish cartoonist born in Barcelona, Spain, in 1898. Valentí Castanys's first cartoons were published throughout the late 1910s and early 1920s in such Catalan humor magazines as *El Sr. Daixonses i la Sra. Dallonses*, *El*

"Casper the Friendly Ghost." © Harveytoons.

Senyor Canons, *En Patufet*, *El Bé Negre* and *La Veu de Catalunya*.

Castanys is best known for his contributions to the magazine *Xut*, which he directed for 15 years (1922-36). During that period he was not only the publication's chief cartoonist and illustrator but one of its most important literary contributors as well. At the same time, he regularly contributed cartoons and comic strips to the illustrated magazine *Papitu* under the name "Eufemio Rodriguez." In addition he founded a humor magazine specializing in film spoofs and in 1937 wrote *Barcelona-Hollywood*, dealing with movies and filmmaking. During the Spanish civil war Castanys went to France and later to Italy. When the war ended in 1939, he returned to Spain, working as a cartoonist and comic strip artist and later founding a sports magazine, *El Once*.

From 1925 until the time of his death in Barcelona in 1965, Castanys was one of Spain's most celebrated cartoonists. The fictitious places and characters he created (La Familia Sistacs, Succesors de la Viuda Pasturet, Gafarro en Comandita, Rafeques i Companya, Picamoixons, Masrampinyó, etc.) have become so popular that they are now referred to in everyday conversation. Perhaps the best testimony to Castanys's creative genius as a cartoonist is his *El Pais de Sidral* ("The Land of Sidral"), a science fiction strip based on a utopian country.

J.M.

CAVALLI, RICHARD (1923-   ) American cartoonist born in New York City in September 1923. Dick Cavalli exhibited strong talents for cartooning during his school days in Brooklyn. Drafted into the army after his graduation from high school, he served three years in the infantry and the air force. Discharged in 1946, he studied art on a GI college bill, first at the School of Industrial Arts, and later at the School of Visual Arts.

Cavalli started freelancing cartoons in the late 1940s with such success that a 1956 *Writer's Digest* article described him as "having risen to the top faster than any other cartoonist in the business." That same year Cavalli created *Morty Meekle*, a situation comedy strip later

157

"I don't understand it. Why didn't he marry both of them?"

Richard Cavalli. © *This Week.*

turned into a kid strip, for the Newspaper Enterprise Association service. Retitled *Winthrop*, the feature is still being done by Cavalli today.

Dick Cavalli is best known for *Winthrop*, but the innumerable gag cartoons which he contributed to *Collier's*, the *Saturday Evening Post* and other magazines were often funnier and certainly more pungent.

M.H.

CAVANDOLI, OSVALDO (1920-   ) Italian animator born in Maderno del Garda, Italy, in 1920. Osvaldo Cavandoli is a self-taught artist who started his career in the early 1940s, settling in 1946 at the animation studio of the Pagot brothers. In 1948, along with Nino and Toni Pagot, Osvaldo Piccardo and Carlo Bachini, he completed *I Fratelli Dinamite* ("The Dynamite Brothers"), a feature-length cartoon begun in 1942 (the original drawings for the film had been destroyed in a bombardment).

In the 1950s, after working on theatrical cartoons that were well received critically but disastrous at the box office, Cavandoli devoted himself to the production of advertising cartoons to be shown during film intermissions. In 1970 he directed a number of animated mini-films of a few seconds' duration, such as *L'Amore E la Fine* ("Love Is the End") and *Attenti*

Osvaldo Cavandoli, "La Linea." © *Cavandoli.*

alle Colombe ("Beware of Doves"). The critics have recently "discovered" Cavandoli and have showered him with countless awards at Italian and foreign film festivals.

Cavandoli's fame is founded above all on the recent cartoons titled simply *La Linea* ("Line") followed by a numeral (there are to date eight *Line* cartoons). The technique involves running a simple line along the film, shaping it at given intervals into various objects, people or animals. The effect is startling and was further enhanced when Cavandoli introduced color. Of the *Line* cartoons, Ralph Stephenson wrote: "They are engaging little comedies, perfectly drawn, full of humor and in a unique style which should be capable of development." The cartoons have been seen on television and have given rise to a series of *Mr. Linea* comic books, in which Cavandoli indulges in linear variations that cannot be shown over the prudish Italian television networks. *La Linea* is a genial, unusual creation that allows its author to confront his one-dimensional hero with all the obstacles surrounding him, thus establishing a man-object rapport—which, as Buster Keaton has taught us, is a permanent love-hate relationship.

S.T.

CECCON, SILVIUS PETRUS CLAUDIUS (1937-   ) Brazilian cartoonist born in Garibaldi, Rio Grande do Sul, Brazil, in 1937. While he was still a child, Claudius Ceccon's parents moved to Rio de Janeiro, where their son received his art education. His first job was doing page layouts for *O Cruzeiro*. In the mid-1950s he started doing spot drawings for *O Cruzeiro*, as well as illustrations to short stories published in the magazine *A Cigarra*.

Claudius (as he is professionally known) began his cartooning career in 1957 on the daily *Jornal do Brasil*, first as a general cartoonist, then as the newspaper's political cartoonist, a position he held from 1961 until 1965. That year Claudius became the regular cartoonist for the magazine *Manchete*, and some of his most pungent cartoons have been published in its pages.

A prolific worker, Claudius has also contributed cartoons to most major Brazilian publications (*Diário Carioca, Revista da Semana, Mundo Ilustrado, Senhor, Fairplay, Correio da Manha, O Jornal*, etc.), as well as to foreign publications (the *New York Times, Life, Paris-Match* and *Stern*, among others). He has had a number of his cartoons collected in book form, and he has received many awards, both Brazilian and foreign.

A.M.

CEM
See Martin, Charles Edward.

CESARE, OSCAR EDWARD (1885-1948) American cartoonist born in Linkoping, Sweden, in 1885. Oscar Cesare studied art in Paris, then moved to America at the age of 18 and continued his art studies in Buffalo. He took his first jobs in Chicago and worked for several newspapers, including the *Tribune*, for which he drew dramatic sketches. Moving to New York, Cesare drew editorial cartoons for several papers, including the *World*, the *Sun*, the *Post* (after Munsey bought the *Sun* in 1916 and banished cartoons from its pages), *Harper's Weekly* and the *New York Times*. He also worked for the *Sun* magazine, and it was for the *New York Times Magazine* that he did much of his notable work.

For the dailies Cesare drew in a remarkably free and seemingly slapdash style, a whirlwind combination of loose brushstrokes and thickly applied grease crayon; the results looked more like the studies of a fine painter than the finished products of a daily editorial cartoonist. In a day when fellow cartoonists were using crayons to liberate the form from the tight pen-and-ink style, Cesare took things further; his busy cartoons were widely admired as fine examples of composition and rendering. His liberal concepts were translated lucidly, and his work was generally free of captions and labels. For the weeklies he drew in wash and gained much fame with the *Times* as an interviewer-sketcher. His most famous interview was with Lenin in 1922; he also visited General Billy Mitchell, Orville Wright and Benito Mussolini.

Cesare was married briefly in the 1910s to Margaret Porter, the daughter of O. Henry. *One Hundred Cartoons by Cesare*, a collection dealing mostly with war-related issues, was published in 1916 by Small, Maynard. Cesare died at the age of 63 at his home in Stamford, Connecticut. Lamentably, his brilliant work is largely forgotten today.

R.M.

CHAM

See Noé, Amédée de.

CHARLES, WILLIAM (1776-1820)
American cartoonist born in Edinburgh, Scotland, in 1776. William Charles set himself up in his native city as a printmaker and caricaturist but was chased from the country for the

"When the President kicks Congress he's not kicking his dog; he's kicking his People's dog."

Oscar Cesare. © New York Times.

—"The light bulb was invented by our people, Yablochkov and Lodygin" —"Yes, but the Americans invented the idea that Edison invented it!"

Mikhail Cheremnykh. © Krokodil.

viciousness of his personal attacks and his scatological humor.

He moved to the United States in 1805, adopted the style of James Gillray and worked as a printmaker and caricaturist in New York (until 1814) and Philadelphia (1814 until his death on August 29, 1820). He had ample opportunity during the War of 1812 to mete out revenge to his former countrymen, and the first great sustained series of American cartoons flowed from Charles's pen, savagely attacking the British, their allies, their troops and their king.

Charles also occupies an important place in the history of American humorous illustration. He drew for the *American Magazine of Wit* (1808), illustrated *Pinkerton's Travels* (1810-12) and was one of several artists to illustrate *The Travels of Doctor Syntax*. Charles pioneered the use of line stipple and aquatint and during his career worked as a bookseller and stationer as well.

R.M.

CHARLIE BROWN

See Peanuts.

CHAVAL

See Le Louarn, Yvan.

CHEREMNYKH, MIKHAIL MIKHAILOVICH (1890-1962)
Soviet cartoonist and graphic artist born in Tomsk, Russia, on October 30, 1890. Mikhail Cheremnykh graduated from the Moscow Institute of Painting, Sculpture and Architecture in 1917. He was active during the Russian Revolution and the ensuing civil war. In 1919 he founded the Orkna Rosta ("Windows of the Russian News Agency"), which turned out propaganda posters of current events, and he himself contributed many noted posters of the era.

In 1922 Cheremnykh became one of the founders of the satirical weekly *Krokodil*, to which he contributed innumerable cartoons over the years. During World War II he went back to poster designing and created a number of powerful anti-Nazi images. In addition to his cartooning and poster work, Cheremnykh found time to illustrate books by famous Russian authors, including Saltykov-

—"My dear lady . . . so sweet . . . a little kiss . . . for God's sake."
—"Your father had me already this morning . . ."

Guillaume-Sulpice Chevalier ("Paul Gavarni").

Shchedrin, Krylov and Chekhov. He was also a professor at the Surikov Art Institute in Moscow from 1949 until his death on August 7, 1962.

Cheremnykh was a member of the USSR Academy of Arts, and a People's Artist of the Russian Federated Republic. He was the recipient of many honors and awards, including the Stalin Prize in 1942.

M.H.

CHEVALIER, GUILLAUME-SULPICE (1804-1866) French cartoonist, watercolorist and lithographer born in Paris, France, on January 13, 1804. Better known under the pseudonym "Paul Gavarni," Guillaume Chevalier studied at the Conservatoire des Arts et Métiers while selling some of his paintings. His first success came at 20, when his *Etrennes de 1825: Récréations Diabolico-Fantasmagoriques,* a volume of lithographs, was published by Blaisot. In 1829, during a land-surveying tour in southwestern France and the Pyrenees, he painted a landscape, *Cirque de Gavarnie,* which gave him his pseudonym. His drawings, full of elegance and wit, caught the attention of the press magnate of the July Monarchy, Emile de Girardin, who published many of Gavarni's fancy-dress costume studies in the newly founded *La Mode* (1830); they appeared as well in *L'Artiste* and *La Silhouette.*

The year 1837 marks an important date for Gavarni because he went to work for *Le Charivari,* where he was allowed to exercise his elegant style and charming irony to the fullest on his favorite subjects—street urchins, bohemians and the foibles and adventures of women, whether sophisticated, low-class or of easy virtue. *Fourberies de Femmes en Matière de Sentiment* ("Women's Deceptions in Matters of the Heart," 1837-40), *La Boîte aux Lettres* ("The Mailbox," 1837-39), *Les Lorettes*

(1841-43) and *Le Carnaval* (1846) are the most important series of that period.

After the death of his mother and an unhappy marriage, Gavarni went to England and Scotland (1847-51), where he depicted the plight of the poor with bitter and compelling realism, mainly for the *Illustrated London News.* On his return to France he abandoned his portrayal of dandies to show, in *Masques et Visages* (1852-54), ugly old men and women in their dirty, vulgar getup, and to satirize, often bitingly, the profiteers of the Second Empire. These cartoons have been published in series like *Les Propos de Thomas Vireloque* (1851-53), with its philosophical beggar, *Les Partageuses* (which may be translated as "The Gold Diggers," 1852), *Bohèmes* (1853) and *Histoire de Politiquer* (1853-54).

Although he became famous, Paul Gavarni never overcame the pessimism caused by social and political conditions both in Paris and London. He died in Paris on November 24, 1866, at the age of 62, leaving behind more than twenty-seven hundred lithographs and over five thousand drawings and sketches. Gavarni's art, while not as powerful as Daumier's, was graceful, polished and light and was much praised by Balzac, Delacroix, Baudelaire and Gautier, who called it "as profound and cynical as Swift or Voltaire."

P.H.

CHIAPPORI, ALFREDO (1943-   ) Italian cartoonist born in Lecca, Italy, in 1943. Alfredo Chiappori studied at the State Art Institute in Fano under the guidance of the sculptor Edgardo Mannucci. After graduation in 1965, he tried his hand at painting but returned to his hometown in 1967, taking up a teaching position at the local high school. It was then that he drew his first political cartoons.

In 1968 Chiappori created *Up il Sovversivo* ("Up the Subversive"), a political comic strip, for the monthly magazine *Linus.* It was collected in book form in 1970, the same year he started contributing political cartoons to the left-wing magazine *Compagni.* In 1972 Chiappori published a book of comics titled *Alfreud,* and the next year he came out with *Vado, l'Arresto e Torno* ("I Go, Arrest Him and Come Back"), in which Up commented on the wave of terrorism that had descended upon Italy. The book established Chiappori as one of the most acute political observers of the Italian scene.

In collaboration with Fortebraccio, a political writer for the Communist daily *L'Unità,* Chiappori authored another book derisively called *Il Belpaese* ("The Fair Country") and started a cartoon column of the same title for the weekly *Panorama.* In 1975 he published another volume of political comic strips, *Padroni e Padrini* ("Bosses and Godfathers"), in collaboration with Oreste del Buono. He also contributes weekly political cartoons to the Rome daily *Paese Sera.* At the same time Chiappori continues to devote a good portion of his talent to painting.

L.S.

CHIES, GIAMPAOLO (1947-   ) Italian cartoonist born in Bologna, Italy, on January 26, 1947. Giampaolo Chies decided to go into cartooning after finishing his high school studies. He started his career in 1968, drawing *Virus Psik,* a comic strip about a somewhat extravagant woman psychiatrist, on texts by Max Bunker (Luciano Secchi). He then drew a great number of cartoons and illustrations for the monthly magazine *Eureka*.

In 1971 Chies moved to Milan and briefly worked as an animator for Gamma Film. Later that year he resumed the *Virus Psik* strip and also created a monthly cartoon panel, *Monodia* ("Monody"), in which he gave free rein to his absurdist humor. In these somewhat disquieting cartoons, strange objects float in the air, mechanical women nurse real-life babies, and robots weep or bleed. The air of eerie unreality is further enhanced by the total absence of captions or dialogue. Chies is currently working on a comic book adaptation of *Pinocchio*, scheduled for publication in 1979.

L.S.

CHILLY WILLY (U.S.) In 1953 Walter Lantz attempted to duplicate the roaring success of his red-crested woodpecker, Woody, with a bird of a different plumage—the black-attired Chilly Willy, a penguin.

Chilly Willy was a sad-faced little creature who lived in the icy wastes near the Pole and whose main occupation in life was the continuous search for food and shelter. Fighting off dumb dogs, moronic polar bears and benumbed humans, the indestructible little penguin would resist all attempts to kick him out of trappers' cabins, Eskimos' igloos and scientists' weather stations. No less dogged in his intent to secure food, Chilly Willy would hijack a boatload of fish or mooch a meal of dog food with the single-mindedness of despair. There was a touch of pathos in the *Chilly Willy* series that one rarely found in other animated cartoons of the period.

As with all his products, Walter Lantz released the

Giampaolo Chies, "Monodia." © *Editoriale Corno.*

"Chilly Willy." © *Walter Lantz.*

Chilly Willy cartoons through Universal until production was halted in 1973. Among the directors who worked on the series were Alex Lovy, Jack Hannah, Sid Marcus, Paul J. Smith and especially Tex Avery, who realized two of the best entries in the field, "I'm Cold" and "The Legend of Rockabye Point" (the latter nominated for an Academy Award in 1955).

Chilly Willy can still occasionally be seen on television in *The Woody Woodpecker Show*.

M.H.

CHIP

See Bellew, Frank P.W.

CHIP 'N' DALE (U.S.) Chip and Dale were relative newcomers to the Walt Disney menagerie of funny animals. They made their debut in 1946 in a *Pluto* cartoon titled "Squatter's Rights" (nominated for an Academy Award), in which they bedeviled the simpleminded dog.

Chip and Dale were two resourceful chipmunks whose penchant for pranks and larceny often caused them to run afoul of an enraged Donald Duck. In "Donald Applecore," for instance, they laid waste to Donald's apple orchard; in "Chips Ahoy" they commandeered Donald's model boat for a cruise down a park basin; and in "Up a Tree" they turned the tables on lumberjack Donald trying to cut down their tree.

The redoubtable chipmunks never ran out of enemies. Trying to steal eggs, they had to disguise themselves as baby chicks in order to avoid the fury of a mother hen ("Chicken in the Rough"), and they even faced up to Disney's all-purpose cartoon villain, Pegleg Pete, playing a bank robber in "The Lone Chipmunks." While the chipmunks enjoyed the bonds of mutual friendship, they would occasionally have a falling out, as when they vied against each other for the affections of the fickle *chanteuse* Clarice in "Two Chips and a Miss."

The *Chip 'n' Dale* theatrical shorts were discontinued in the late 1950s. The two irrepressible chipmunks continue to be seen, however, on the Disney TV program in

Chip 'n' Dale in "Up a Tree." © *Walt Disney Productions.*

specials such as "The Adventures of Chip 'n' Dale" and "Mixed Nuts"; there was even a spirited song composed for these occasions ("I'm Chip—I'm Dale").

M.H.

CHŌ, SHINTA

See Suzuki, Shūji.

CHODOWIECKI, DANIEL (1726-1801) German illustrator, printmaker and painter born in Danzig (now Gdańsk, Poland) on October 16, 1726. In his astonishingly fruitful career, Daniel Chodowiecki supplied a wealth of visual imagery and inspiration to his generation and those that followed. His specifically humorous works, although drawn academically and comprising only a part of his total production, entitle him to be considered the father of German cartooning in the 19th and 20th centuries.

Chodowiecki's father, a merchant who also painted miniatures, died when Daniel was 14. Three years later the young man was sent to Berlin to work for an uncle who taught him how to paint miniature portraits on parchment for application to snuffboxes and similar bric-a-brac. By 1754 he and his younger brother, Gottfried, were established enough to set up on their own as painters on enamel. In 1757 Daniel began painting in oils (this proved to be a weaker sideline and dropped out after the 1770s) and, most important, etching. He was eventually to etch over two thousand images on nearly a thousand copperplates, nine-tenths of this output coming after 1773.

Besides documentary illustration (of human types for the works of the phrenologist Lavater; of trades and occupations for the encyclopedia of the educator Basedow) and illustrations for countless novels and almanacs, Chodowiecki tirelessly depicted the everyday bourgeois world around him with all its small sorrows and joys, its sentimentality and its fun (never boisterous in his pictures, but genuine all the same).

As a careful observer of reality and as the single most prolific delineator of life in Berlin, Chodowiecki is the precursor of such cartoonists as Schadow, Dörbeck, Hosemann and Zille. The gluttony of a Berlin picnic is expressed in a famous 1775 print, "The Pilgrimage to Französisch Buchholz." A series of five prints entitled *The Law-Abiding Citizens of Berlin*

Wallfahrt nach Frantzöst. Bucholz   *gezeichnet von D Chodowiecki in Berlin*

Citizens of Berlin well supplied for a picnic.

Daniel Chodowiecki, 1775.

concerns a new city ordinance about leashing dogs. Foolish fashions, gossiping servants, ill-matched couples and the like abound in his pictures. His images of the *Aeneid* are important examples of the parodies of antiquity that cropped up here and there in that sternly neoclassical period.

Chodowiecki became a member of the Berlin Academy in 1764 and its director in 1797. He was also a major art collector, owning 146 paintings and some 10,000 prints and drawings. He died in Berlin on July 2, 1801.

S.A.

CHUMY-CHUMEZ

See González Castrillo, José María.

CLAMPETT, ROBERT (1910?-   ) American animator and producer born in San Diego, California, around 1910 (his exact birthdate is a closely guarded secret). Bob Clampett moved in childhood to Hollywood, where he received his schooling. While in high school he drew a comic strip for the *Los Angeles Times*, and after graduation he went on to study at the Otis Art Institute in Los Angeles.

Clampett joined the animation unit of Rudolph Ising and Hugh Harman in 1931. There he worked on the early Looney Tunes and Merrie Melodies that were turned out for distribution by Warner Brothers. When Harman and Ising left Warner, Clampett joined the studio Leon Schlesinger was forming to continue the Warner Brothers cartoons. Clampett received his first directorial assignment in 1936, when he did a cartoon sequence for a Joe E. Brown picture called *When's Your Birthday?* (that same year he also tried in vain to produce a cartoon series of his own based on E.R. Burroughs's John Carter stories).

Clampett's star rose in the following years with a number of imaginative *Porky Pig* cartoons such as "Porky's Badtime Story" and "Porky in Wackyland." He also helped assure the solid success of the Bugs Bunny character in such entries as "What's Cookin', Doc?," "Falling Hare" and "Corny Concerto" (featuring Bugs at his most obnoxious during a Johann Strauss recital). In the late 1940s Clampett was one of the trio of directors who propelled the Warner cartoons to unheard-of popularity. In addition to the many *Bugs Bunny, Porky Pig* and *Daffy Duck* shorts he directed, he did such ground-breaking cartoons as *Horton Hatches the Egg* (from a Dr. Seuss story), *Tin Pan Alley Cats* (a wild and raucous musical parody) and the morale-boosting *Russian Rhapsody*, also known as *The Gremlin from the Kremlin.* He also introduced Tweety Pie the canary in the 1942 "A Tale of Two Kitties."

Clampett left Warner in 1946, worked briefly for Columbia and then formed his own studio, turning out animation commercials. In the late 1940s he created the highly successful puppet show *Time for Beany* for television. Beany and his friends, Captain Huffenpuff and Cecil the Seasick Sea Serpent, became favorites of the public and lasted in syndication well into the 1960s. At present Clampett still takes his puppet characters on tour, turns out a few animation commercials, and lectures on college campuses. He has received many awards, including three Emmys and an Annie Award from ASIFA. His work has been studied and analyzed by scholars in the field of ani-

Bob Clampett, "Horton Hatches the Egg." © *Warner Brothers.*

mation who recognize him as one of the outstanding craftsmen of the form.

M.H.

CLARK, JAMES ALFRED (1886-   ) American cartoonist and illustrator born in Eustis, Florida, in 1886. James Clark was raised in Springfield, Massachusetts, and studied art at the Connecticut League of Art Students in Hartford. While studying and working on early jobs, he fell under the artistic influence of fellow artist René Vincent, a Frenchman—and friends dubbed Clark with the nickname "René," which stuck.

Clark was in the forefront of the field of illustrators when the markets shifted from the popular monthlies to the weeklies. In the late 1910s he drew for the comic weeklies and appeared frequently in *Judge* in the early 1920s. His cartoons were marked by simplicity of line and masterful spotting. His decorative drawings in *Judge* were often complemented by a single-tone shade of color.

After the mid-1920s the bulk of his work was in advertising, a field which he led in both influence and awards. Here he showed that watercolors were also his domain, although he never abandoned his restrained but striking pen-and-ink work. Clark won many awards from the Art Directors Club and ultimately became president of his advertising agency, Calkins and Holden.

R.M.

CLARKE, ROBERT JAMES (1926-   ) American cartoonist and illustrator born in Port Chester, New York, on January 25, 1926. Raised in the neighboring town of Mamaroneck, New York, Bob Clarke was always interested in cartooning as a child and got his first break by winning a high school art contest. The prize was the opportunity to help Robert Ripley on his syndicated comic strip, *Ripley's Believe It or Not!*

During 1943 and 1944, Bob Clarke did research and some spot art and lettering on Ripley's *Believe It or Not!* Upon graduation from high school he immediately enlisted in the army. World War II in Europe was winding down, and Clarke was assigned to Germany and *Stars and Stripes*, the armed forces newspaper, as art editor in 1945. He returned to the United States as a civilian in 1946 but spent the year recovering from illness contracted while in the military. In 1947 he began working for a Madison Avenue advertising agency, and when he left agency work to freelance in 1955, he was an art director at Dancer, Fitzgerald and Sample.

Bob Clarke got his chance to join the *MAD* magazine group of freelance cartoonists as a result of the Bill Gaines and Harvey Kurtzman split in 1955. *MAD* needed some new cartoonists, and the information was passed on to Clarke by his friend from army days and fellow cartoonist Gill Fox. Samples were submitted and accepted. A two-page story entitled "Motorists Beware" was Bob Clarke's first artwork published in *MAD*.

With *MAD* his cartoons have often illustrated parodies of advertising, a natural for him given his years of ad agency experience. Generally he considers himself to be "a troubleshooter," illustrating pieces that don't fit the special talents of other *MAD* artists. Bob Clarke's style emphasizes controlled line drawing and is considerably tighter than many of the other *MAD* artists'. The end result is a sophisticated look based on line rather than wash tones.

Besides his work for *MAD*, Bob Clarke has done straight and humorous illustration for many trade journals such as *Fleet Owner*, *Electronics* and *Data Communications*. He's done a series of humorous covers for *American Legion* and cartooned for *Fortune* magazine. Clarke has also illustrated four original *MAD* paperback books that do not reprint material previously published: *MADvertizing* by Dick DeBartolo (1972); and *MAD's Turned On Zoo* (1974), *MAD Jumble* (1975) and *More MAD About Sports* (1977), all by Frank Jacobs.

B.C.

CLAUDIUS
See Ceccon, Silvius Petrus Claudius.

CLAY, EDWARD WILLIAMS (1799-1857) American cartoonist born in Philadelphia, Pennsylvania, on April 19, 1799. Edward Clay was a midshipman under Commodore Perry in the War of 1812 and later studied law, being admitted to the bar in Philadelphia in 1825. Clay became an etcher, engraver and cartoonist in Philadelphia (1825-36) and New York City (1837 to about 1840), after which he deserted the artist's craft to become a public servant, holding such jobs as clerk of the Delaware orphan's court.

During his career as a cartoonist Clay was one of several artists responsible for introducing the lithograph as a cartooning medium; his most famous cartoon is of a devastated Andrew Jackson in the wake of the Peggy Eaton scandal. "Rats Leaving a Falling House" was judged one of the most effective and professional cartoons of early 19th-century America by several critics.

Clay published volumes of his cartoons and produced *Life in Philadelphia* and *Sketches of Character* (both in 1829). He contributed to Child's *Views of Philadelphia* and was remembered as a merciless caricaturist. While in New York he drew his cartoons for the firm of Henry R. Robinson, a prominent lithographer and printmaker. Clay died on December 31, 1857, in New York City.

R.M.

CLAY, JOHN CECIL (1875-ca. 1930) American cartoonist and illustrator born in Ronceverte, Greenbrier County,

West Virginia, on April 2, 1875. John Clay was educated at the Friends School in Washington, D.C., and received art training at the Students League of Washington (1895-96) and New York's Art Students League (1897-98).

Clay, in the late 1890s, became a frequent contributor to *Life* and in 1899 broke into the illustration market with a sale to the *Saturday Evening Post*. Among his books are *In Love's Garden* (1904), *Portraits of Celebrated Actresses* (1905), *Portraits of Celebrated Authors* (1906) and *The Lovers' Mother Goose* (1907).

Perhaps "Vanity" is Clay's most famous cartoon. Originally drawn for *Life*, it shows a high-fashion lady at her dressing mirror; the mirror and its reflection, upon studied observation, give the effect of a human skull. It has been reprinted in the millions and is still sold today, even in Times Square souvenir shops. It is fitting that Clay is remembered by this cartoon, because it is characteristic of his output—he often dealt with society in a moralistic and melancholy way. His renderings were in wash—here he was in the vanguard of the school *Life* nurtured through the 1890s and the early years of this century—and careful pencil shadings. In these techniques he was a master.

R.M.

The principal characters of "Clémentine Chérie." © Jean Bellus.

CLÉMENTINE CHÉRIE (France) Clémentine, the daughter of a middle-aged, middle-class couple, made her debut in the weekly magazine *Jours de France* in the early 1950s. The creation of French cartoonist Jean Bellus, she has had a successful career for more than a dozen years.

A comely, vivacious and charming brunette with a Jean Seberg haircut, Clémentine seems to spend most of her time dancing at parties, gossiping with girl friends, buying things and in general having no graver worries than how to put off an eager beau or catch the eye of an indifferent one. She represents the modern though not fully liberated young woman, and her bald, rotund father and plump mother regard her tolerantly, even permissively, reacting to her adventures in a manner more amused than shocked.

Of the thousands of well-drawn, humorous Clémentine cartoons, often enhanced by color, a few hundred have been issued in albums and translated. The last one, *Vivre avec Son Temps* ("To Live with the Times"), was published in 1967, the year Bellus died.

P.H.

COBEAN, SAM (1917-1951) American magazine gag cartoonist born in Gettysburg, Pennsylvania, in 1917. Sam Cobean was raised in Altoona, Pennsylvania, and attended the University of Oklahoma. Following college he worked for the Walt Disney studios and other motion picture companies in Hollywood. He joined the U.S. Army Signal Corps during World War II and while in the army met Charles Addams, already well known as a *New Yorker* magazine cartoonist. The two men became close friends, and Addams encouraged him to submit cartoons to the *New Yorker*. By 1944 Cobean's cartoons were a regular feature there.

Sam Cobean's most famous cartoon image, variations of which extend throughout all his published work, was based on the idea that ever since women began wearing clothes, men have been trying to visualize how women would look without clothes. His X-ray-eyed heroes' thought balloons showed any woman who passed by in the nude. This international masculine pastime was first published in the *New Yorker* in June 1945. Scores of variations on the theme followed. For example, a man passes a woman modeling a dress before a triple mirror in a clothing store. The man's thoughts conjure up four nude views of her—front, back and both sides. In another a man passes by four bathhouses at the beach, and his thoughts show four beautiful unclad women changing into swimsuits. Another recurring theme Cobean used was the young, presumably unwed mother with her child in her arms being turned away from home, dogs, children, artists, models and bars.

Cobean drew easily with economy of line. Besides the *New Yorker*, his cartoons were published in the *Saturday Evening Post* and *Collier's*. His cartoons have a

Neg Cochran, "The Worry Wart." © *NEA.*

spontaneous, unlabored look to them. Some gray wash and black areas were used in the design, but in general he preferred minimal use of these techniques in favor of simple line drawing.

In 1950 a collection of his *New Yorker* cartoons, *Cobean's Naked Eye*, was published in both hardback and paperback editions. The collection was the cartoon-book best seller of the year. Then, on the night of July 2, 1951, Sam Cobean's brilliant career was tragically ended. The Jaguar sports car he was driving crashed into the rear of another car near Watkins Glen, New York, and Cobean was killed instantly. He was 34.

Shortly after Cobean's death, Charles Addams said, "I hope he knew or at least suspected that he will be long remembered as one of the great comic artists of all time." An anthology, *The Cartoons of Cobean*, was published in 1952. The book was edited by Saul Steinberg, with a foreword by Charles Addams. In 1954, the fledgling *Playboy* magazine also paid posthumous tribute to Sam Cobean's cartoons.

B.C.

COCHRAN, NEGLEY (1913-   ) American cartoonist born in Oak Park, Illinois, on August 27, 1913. After studies at Western Reserve University and the Cleveland Institute of Art, Neg Cochran worked in the advertising office of a Cleveland department store. In 1936 he joined the staff of the Newspaper Enterprise Association (NEA) in Cleveland. (His father, Negley Cochran, was an NEA editor and had discovered many budding cartoonists.) Soon thereafter Cochran started assisting J.R. Williams on the daily *Out Our Way* panel, and especially on the Sunday page, which featured the adventures of the Willett family. Cochran stayed close to Williams's style and made the *Willetts* family strip into an endearing chronicle of domestic life in mid-America.

When Williams died in 1957, Cochran took over the daily *Out Our Way*, which he continued in his typically gentle, unobtrusive manner until his retirement in 1975. A solid, dependable craftsman, Neg Cochran is one of the unsung heroes of the daily newspaper panel, a medium that has remained neglected for too long.

M.H.

Sam Cobean. © *Anne M. Cobean.*

Gioacchino Colizzi. © Attalo.

COELHO, EDUARDO TEIXEIRA (1919-   ) Portuguese illustrator and cartoonist born in Angra do Heroísmo, Azores Islands, on January 4, 1919. E.T. Coelho went to Lisbon at the age of 11 to attend a commercial course. He published his first drawings, some short, naive anecdotes, in the weekly *Sempre Fixe* in 1936. He improved rapidly and produced some very good illustrations at the beginning of the 1940s in *Colecção de Aventuras, Senhor Doutor, Engenhocas e Coisas Práticas* and *Filmagem.* Starting in 1943 in the magazine *O Mosquito,* he achieved total mastery in the illustration of novels of historic, modern or fantastic characteristics.

It was also for *O Mosquito* that Coelho drew his first comic strips, among which *Os Guerreiros do Lago Verde, O Grande Rifle Branco, Os Náufragos do Barco Sem Nome, O Feitiço do Homem Branco* and *O Falcão Negro* deserve mention. His masterpieces, however, are *Trilogia das Mouras* ("Trilogy of the Moorish Women"), *O Caminho do Oriente* ("The Far East Path"), *A Lei da Selva* ("The Law of the Jungle") and the comic strip versions of some of Eça de Queiroz's stories. Coelho also had drawings published in daily newspapers (*O Século, Diário de Notícias*), magazines (*Portugal Ilustrado, Auditorium*), books (*Caminhos da Terra Santa, Lições de Ginástica Infantil, A Nossa Pátria*), and on the covers of volumes of the *Biblioteca dos Rapazes* and the *Biblioteca das Raparigas.* A great part of his work was also published in the Spanish magazine *Chicos.* For the festivities directed in 1947 by Leitão de Barros to commemorate the 800th anniversary of the reconquest of Lisbon from the Moors, Coelho did the models, sketches and drawings included in the illuminations of the allegoric messages.

Because of the restrictions imposed by the Portuguese press on the expansion of his art, Coelho emigrated in 1953 and worked for publishers in England, France and other countries. The characters he created after that date derive from the Viking era (Ragnar, Bjorni, Eric le Rouge), the Middle Ages (Robin des Bois, Le Furet, Yves le Loup) or other periods (Davy Crockett, Till l'Espiègle, Cartouche, Wango). In Portugal he sometimes signed simply *ETC,* whereas in France he mainly used the pseudonym "Martin Sièvre." Among his most recent works are some chapters of *Histoire de France en Bandes Dessinées* (under the signature Eduardo Coelho) and documentaries about Italian armory.

Coelho's early style—with its thin, sinuous line and long, dynamic figures weaving in a spiral composition—prompted the Spanish artist Emílio Freixas to call him a "poet of line" (in *Lecciones de Dibujo Artístico*). This initially clear and fluent style has gradually become more static and detailed, as can be seen in the work Coelho has done since his departure from Portugal. In 1973 he received the Best Foreign Illustrator award at the Lucca Festival. Coelho, who presently lives in Florence, Italy, is married and has a daughter.

C.P.

COHL, EMILE
See Courtet, Emile.

COLIZZI, GIOACCHINO (1894-   ) Italian cartoonist born near Rome, Italy, in 1894. After completing his studies, Gioacchino Colizzi (better known under the pseudonym "Attalo") joined the State Railway Authority as an accountant for the planning office in Rome. He had always loved to draw as a hobby, and he sent some of his cartoons to the humor and satirical magazine *Serenissimo* in 1920. These were accepted, and Attalo continued to contribute cartoons to the publication until it was suspended by the Fascist authorities in the late 1920s. Colizzi, who did not want to lose his civil service post, then judged it prudent to switch from cartoons to movie posters.

When the humor magazine *Marc' Aurelio* started publication in the 1930s, Attalo was among its first cartoonists. Federico Fellini, who was writing a column for the magazine at that time, recalls, "Attalo very seldom came to the magazine. . . . The captions were sent to the railway office for him to illustrate." Among the characters made famous by Attalo's cartoons are "the ugly Genoveffa," always chasing after her elusive lover Gastone, and especially "the barfly who told his friends," whose boasts were always deflated in the cartoons.

The cartoons Attalo has drawn for the pages of *Marc' Aurelio, Marforio, Pasquino, Il Travaso* and others number over ten thousand; the most famous are those on the theme of "the easygoing war" (waged with cork-guns and water pistols). Fellini was inspired by Attalo's depictions of old Rome when he made his movie *Roma*, thus paying a deserved homage to his former co-worker.

S.T.

COLL Y COLL, JOSÉ (1923-   ) Spanish cartoonist born in Barcelona, Spain, in 1923. José Coll graduated from art school and started his career in the 1940s as an illustrator. In 1948 his first cartoons were published in the magazine *La Risa*, followed by more cartoons in most major Spanish publications. Coll's most important work appeared in the comic weekly *TBO*, where, starting in 1953, he had an average of four cartoons or comic strips running in each issue. Since the late 1960s, however, his output has been decreasing.

Coll's characters move with incredible elasticity: they shrink, bend, spring back like rubber dolls, but always retain their verisimilitude. Coll creates a highly personal, original and coherent universe. The "gags" do not arise from the characters themselves, but from the situations in which they are placed, and the cartoons are almost completely silent. Coll is a master of visual and sequential organization, and his success is due to the particular attention he pays to landscapes and backgrounds, his carefully delineated graphics and his respect for perspective, which is unusual among cartoonists.

J.M.

COLONEL HEEZALIAR (U.S.) John Randolph Bray created *Colonel Heezaliar* in 1914 for Pathé Exchange. The colonel, a short, middle-aged, rotund man, was modeled after the character of Baron Munchausen, and his adventures were a variation on the tall tale; he got himself into all kinds of predicaments from which he escaped by extraordinary means (tying together the tails of a couple of lions or getting out of quicksand by grabbing the feet of overflying geese, for example). The colonel, with his never-ending wild animal hunts in the remotest parts of

"Colonel Heezaliar." © *Bray Studios.*

the globe, is also said to have been a lampoon of Theodore Roosevelt.

"Colonel Heezaliar in Africa" seems to have been the first cartoon in the series. J.R. Bray directed most of the early cartoons in an adequate if somewhat stilted style (the 1916 "Colonel Heezaliar Wins the Pennant" and "Colonel Heezaliar Hobo" are two good examples). In the 1920s Bray left the responsibility for the series to Vernon Stallings, who directed the best-remembered of the cartoons, such as "Colonel Heezaliar and the Ghost," "Colonel Heezaliar Detective" and "Colonel Heezaliar in the African Jungles."

The advent of sound was fatal to the series, which was discontinued in the late 1920s. Its importance lies not only in the fact that *Colonel Heezaliar* was one of the earliest cartoon series ever produced, but also in that it was the first successful American series of animated films based on an original cartoon character.

M.H.

COME ON STEVE! (G.B.) "Come on, Steve!"—the cry of the crowd at prewar racetracks as champion jockey Steve Donoghue rode for yet another win—formed the ready-made title to a weekly strip drawn by Roland Davies. Steve, a cheerful cart horse, began his adventures in the *Sunday Express* on March 6, 1932, and became the first British newspaper strip character to appear in sound cartoon films.

In 1935 Davies taught himself animation from available books, and with a camera that cost him 18 shillings, he set up a small studio in his country kitchen. Seven months later he had a somewhat primitive and jerky silent cartoon, but on the strength of a showing the minor British distributor Butcher's Films agreed to back him for a series in sound. With one or two professional animators and some students from the Ipswich Art School, Davies completed his first sound cartoon, the black-and-white *Steve Steps Out*, in 1936. It was not trade-shown until December of that year, by which time two additional, better cartoons had been completed: *Steve of the River* (a burlesque of the Alexander Korda feature film based on Edgar Wallace's *Sanders of the River*) and *Steve's Treasure Hunt*.

We're coming to it: —"Oi hear they do be sindin' messages now widout woires er poles. Faith, it's wondherful toimes we're livin' in, Dinnis!" —"It is, Moike. Shure, th' way things is goin' we'll be able t' thravel widout lavin' home, wan av thim days."

John Conacher.

Davies, addressing the Ipswich Rotarians, stated, "A film could be produced in about eight weeks by (the) staff of 43, and . . . except for twelve artists, (the) staff consisted of local boys and girls, practically all products of the Ipswich School of Art."

Steve's Cannon Crackers came in April 1937 and *Steve in Bohemia* and *Steve-Cinderella* in May. The first two films were published as picture-story paperbacks by The Children's Press.

D.G.

CONACHER, JOHN (1876-1947) American cartoonist born in 1876. Around 1907 John Conacher's drawings began to appear in *Life;* they were "semi-cartoony" but promised polish because of their controlled lines and grasp of composition and anatomy. By 1912 Conacher was a polished illustrator-type cartoonist, and his work was showcased in *Life* and *Judge.* He never did covers and only occasionally strayed to do straight illustration for the popular monthlies. Unlike fellow cartoonists such as Angus MacDonall who dabbled in washes and sentimental pieces, he remained loyal to pen and ink and to purely humorous cartoons.

His cartoons dealt with absurdities, contradictions and character delineations. His mature style was wonderfully realistic and detailed. Several of Conacher's cartoons were widely circulated, particularly one in *Judge,* a double-page cartoon done after Lindbergh's transatlantic flight in 1927. By the 1930s Conacher had retired from cartooning; the day of the illustrative cartoon was over. Conacher died in Rowayton, Connecticut, on December 14, 1947.

R.M.

CONRAD, PAUL FRANCIS (1924-   ) American cartoonist born in Cedar Rapids, Iowa, on June 27, 1924. Paul Conrad grew up in Ding Darling country and claims that for years he hardly knew there was such a thing as a cartoonist other than Ding. With this influence, after a five-year hitch in the army, he studied art at the University of Iowa and graduated with a B.S. degree in art. Shortly thereafter, in 1950, he joined the *Denver Post* as political cartoonist. His work attracted wide attention for its cleverness and sharp commentaries. He was syndicated weekly by the Hall Syndicate and later by the L.A.

Times Syndicate until the *Times* itself picked him up in 1964. He has remained in Los Angeles since.

Conrad has won a gaggle of awards, including Pulitzers in 1964 and 1971; the Sigma Delta Chi awards for 1962, 1969 and 1971; and the Overseas Press Club award in 1969. He has lectured on cartoons and been reprinted widely.

His style is reminiscent of Ding's but has a striking individuality that especially stands out during the post-Oliphant era. Conrad has even retained, like Herblock, the integrity of the vertical format and crayon rendering. His concepts are among cartooning's most forceful, and his drawings display an amazingly consistent quality. The *Post* and *Times* are both independent Republican papers, but Conrad's views have usually been to their left.

R.M.

CONTES À REBOURS (France) Richard Peyzaret (who was later to sign "F'Murr") started his collaboration with the weekly *Pilote* with *Contes à Rebours* ("Wrong-Way Tales"), a hilarious series of parodies which first appeared, appropriately, on April Fool's Day in 1971.

In these artfully addled tales (usually spread over one or two pages), F'Murr took a resolutely revisionist view of folk stories. Thus the Big Bad Wolf was pictured as the fall guy (fall beast?) in a power play between Red Riding Hood and her eager grandmother, Cinderella was depicted as a sobbing little hypocrite who blamed her poor stepsisters for her own shortcomings, and so on. The artwork, slapdash and falsely naive, provided an appropriate graphic counterpoint to the sardonic commentary.

Contes à Rebours ran only for a short period and was discontinued on December 28, 1972. It is apparent that the series bewildered many of the readers of *Pilote* during its short existence, but it also won F'Murr a small but devoted coterie of fans and admirers. All the tales were later collected into a book published by Editions Minoutchine in Paris.

M.H.

". . . Drunk? . . . Of course I'm not drunk!"

Paul Conrad. © *Los Angeles Times.*

COONTOWN SKETCHES (U.S.) On July 13, 1899, E.W. Kemble began a regular series of cartoons based on life in an impoverished black rural community for *Life* magazine. The series ultimately came to be called *Coontown Sketches*.

Fully half of Kemble's output at this time consisted of black-oriented cartoons, and his handling was expert, sympathetic and wildly funny. Many of the situations in the cartoons were based on high-society themes or fads of the day transferred to the black milieu. Some were rendered in pen and ink, giving free rein to Kemble's masterful crosshatching, but some were executed in wash—a then-recent innovation for magazine reproduction—and are handsome comic masterpieces.

The *Coontown Sketches* series continued for several years, with the cartoons collected in *Coontown Sketches*, *Coontown's 400* and *Kemble's Coons*.

R.M.

CORDEIRO, CALISTO (1877-1957) Brazilian cartoonist and painter born in Niteroí, a suburb of Rio de Janeiro, Brazil, in 1877. Calisto Cordeiro did his first painting at age 13 while working as an apprentice at the Casa de Moeda (the mint) in Rio. In 1898 his first cartoon was published in *O Mercurío* under the pseudonym "Klixto," by which he has since become known.

For over thirty years Klixto contributed cartoons to all major publications in Rio, such as *O Riso, D. Quixote, Carêta, Fon-Fon!, A Caricatura, A Semana Illustrada, Gazeta de Notícias* and *O Cruzeiro*. In the early 1900s he was instrumental in the founding of no less than four magazines: *O Malho, Avança, Degas* and *O Tagarela*.

From 1913 on, Klixto created carnival themes and costumes for one of the carnival associations in Rio. He received a multitude of honors, including the bronze medal (1916) and later the silver medal (1954) of the National Salon of Fine Arts. He was a member of the National Academy of Art, and his works were displayed in many exhibitions throughout Brazil. He was also highly regarded as a painter, poster designer and poet.

Klixto's drawings display an elegance of line that excludes the baroque and the grotesque. He showed a predilection for depicting members of café society, easy women and barflies in ironical but compassionate compositions that often recall the themes dear to Toulouse-Lautrec. He died in São Paulo in 1957.

A.M.

CORNELIUS, SIEGFRIED (1911-   ) Danish cartoonist of international renown born in Copenhagen, Denmark, on April 20, 1911. The son of opera singer Peter Cornelius, Siegfried ("Cosper") Cornelius debuted as a jazz musician in the 1930s. He later began to draw almost surrealistic cartoons that editors thought too naive and stereotyped. As he could not find a market, he founded the humor magazine *Hudibras* in 1943, together with Asger Jerrild. There, his and other young artists' cartoons—lightly frivolous, sometimes pornographic—settled with the prudery and narrow-mindedness of the middle class by proving that one can be naughty without being dirty.

Cornelius worked closely with Jørgen Mogensen (forming the famous "Moco" signature which combined the first two letters of their surnames) and moved to Nice, where together they drew the comic strip *Alfredo* (*Moco* in the United States). Each cartoonist delivered three of the six weekly strips, but they were almost indistin-

Siegfried Cornelius ("Cosper"). © PIB.

guishable from each other. Most characteristic of Cornelius, however, is his daily panel *Cosperier*, syndicated to 80 European dailies. Within its limitation of crazy nonsense and sex, *Cosperier* has founded a humorous tradition that is still alive. Also worth mentioning are his Sunday page, *Mr. Mox*, and his one-column panels syndicated under the pen name "Pollux" by PIB, Copenhagen.

Cornelius's humor, which at the outset was based on an untranslatable play on words, is sometimes very tough (for example, a father to his child: "No, I don't know where the little kids come from—and if I knew, I would send you back!").

Cornelius has made countless theater decorations for Copenhagen revues and cabarets and done book covers and magazine illustrations. He and Virgil Partch are kindred souls. He moved to Rome towards the end of 1950 and lived in Venice until 1973. He is now working in Copenhagen.

J.S.

CORNET I PALAU, GAIETÁ (1878-1945) Spanish cartoonist born in Barcelona, Spain, in 1878. Gaietá Cornet studied engineering at the University of Barcelona, but he never pursued an engineering career. His first cartoons were published in *L'Esquella de la Torratxa* at the turn of the century. In 1902 he became the director of *Cu-Cut!*, a magazine gravitating towards the conservative Catalan party, La Lliga Catalana. It was in this magazine that Cornet realized his best work in terms of both quantity of output and quality of draftsmanship. When *Cu-Cut!* ceased publication in 1912, Cornet went on to contribute cartoons to such publications as *En Patufet, Virolet, L'Esquitx*, and most importantly, *La Veu de Catalunya*, where he openly expressed his politically conservative views.

Cornet's drawings are as clear and straightforward as is his humor, based on the life-styles, customs and stereotypes that he found around him. His lines are often moralistic and didactic in tone and intention. He died in Barcelona in 1945.

J.M.

CORREIA DIAS DE ARAÚJO, FERNANDO (1893-1935) Brazilian cartoonist born in Pantoja, Portugal, in 1893. Fernando Correia Dias studied art at the University of

Gaietá Cornet.

Coimbra in Portugal. Starting in 1912, he regularly contributed cartoons to the magazines *A Rajada* (Coimbra), *Aguia* (Porto) and *Illustração Portuguêsa* (Lisbon). In 1914 he went to Rio de Janeiro to organize an exhibition of his works that included not only cartoons and illustrations but also ceramics and caricatural characters carved in wood. The success of his exhibition made Correia Dias decide to stay in Rio, and he soon found himself very much in demand. For the next 20 years he tirelessly contributed cartoons and illustrations to most major Brazilian magazines (*O Pais, Fon-Fon!, D. Quixote, Illustração Brasileira, Revista da Semana, Brazilian American,* etc.) and newspapers (*O Jornal, O Radical, Diário de Notícias, O Globo*).

Correia Dias also illustrated many books by Brazilian authors, as well as a revamped version of *The Arabian Nights.* He was active in newspaper circles and managed a printing plant for a time (1916-17). He died a suicide in Rio de Janeiro in 1935.

A.M.

CORY, J. CAMPBELL (1867-ca. 1925) American cartoonist born in Waukegan, Illinois, on September 11, 1867. J.C. Cory was educated in Waukegan and began cartooning in New York in 1896. His style was breezy, with slashing, thick-and-thin pen strokes held together by beautiful areas of precise, old-fashioned crosshatching; he and Fred Morgan of the *Philadelphia Inquirer* were probably the last great crosshatch political cartoonists. Throughout his career the doctrinaire Democrat drew for many of America's largest newspapers and magazines, including the *New York*

World and *Harper's Weekly.*

Cory's significance lies in his enterprising approach to cartooning, however. He was a self-starter, almost a vagabond, who worked in many formats, experimented with the business end and was a pioneer syndicator. As a publisher, he put out the *Great West* monthly in 1907-08 and the *Bee,* an oversized chromolithographed humorous weekly, during the Spanish-American War. In 1912, beginning a practice that was to continue for two decades, he became a paid cartoonist for a political party; the Democrats supplied Cory cartoons to any paper that could use them. Soon afterward, in the early days of large-scale syndication, Cory started a syndicate, distributing his own cartoons and those of others. He ran a correspondence school and published books teaching the elements of cartooning, including *Cory's Hands* and *The Cartoonist's Art.* Active in other spheres as well, Cory was a prospector, miner, champion balloonist, pioneer aviator, big game hunter, sportswriter and athlete.

Cory was responsible for helping many youngsters into professional cartooning careers. Charles Kuhn was one, and Cory's niece, Fanny Y. Cory, was another; just after she had her first work published in *St. Nicholas,* she became a featured contributor to the *Bee,* and her uncle boosted her early work through newspaper syndication as well.

R.M.

COSPER
See Cornelius, Siegfried.

COSSIO, CARLO (1907-1964) Italian cartoonist and animator born in Udine, Italy, on January 1, 1907. The Cossio family moved to Milan, where the young Carlo grew up and went to school. After first working as a graphic designer, he went into animation with his brother Vittorio in 1928, at the urging of the painter

. . . said the game chick to the old Rooster.

Campbell Cory, 1919.

Carlo and Vittorio Cossio, "Zibillo e l'Orso." © Fratelli Cossio.

Bruno Munari. From 1928 to 1931 the Cossio brothers produced a number of advertising shorts. In 1932 they released *Zibillo e l'Orso* ("Zibillo and the Bear"), a silent animated short which is a milestone in Italian animation.

In 1937 the Cossio brothers embarked on a grandiose experiment: to produce in full color, on stereoscopic 70-mm film devised by the engineer Gualtiero Gualtierotti, the tale of chivalry *La Secchia Rapita* ("The Stolen Bucket") and H.G. Wells's fantastic novel *The Time Machine*. The films did not find a distributor, however, and the two artists returned to their activities as comic strip cartoonists. During World War II, together with Luigi Giobbe, the brothers produced an animated short titled *Pulcinella e i Briganti* ("Punch and the Brigands"), which made children's eyes "open in wonder," as one critic wrote. After the success of this cartoon Carlo Cossio made a sequel without his brother, but again in collaboration with Giobbe: *Pulcinella e il Temporale* ("Punch and the Storm"), with music by Derevitzky.

The difficulty of finding a market for animated cartoons in Italy again drove the brothers to the comics, and Carlo Cossio successfully worked for the weeklies *L'Intrepido* and *L'Audace*. In 1954 he went back to animation briefly, designing the titles for the film *Giove in Doppio Petto* ("Jove in a Double-Breasted Suit"). He died of cancer in Milan on August 10, 1964. (For further information about Carlo Cossio's career in the comics, see *The World Encyclopedia of Comics*, Chelsea House, 1976.)

S.T.

COSSIO, VITTORIO (1911-   ) Italian cartoonist and animator, younger brother of Carlo Cossio, born in Udine, Italy, in 1911. Like his brother, Vittorio Cossio grew up in Milan, and like him he started work as a graphic designer. When Carlo decided to devote himself to animation towards the end of the 1920s, Vittorio, who was already a fine draftsman, agreed to join him; the two brothers thus became pioneers of Italian animation.

The Cossio brothers, with Bruno Munari as designer, produced several advertising shorts between 1928 and 1931. On his own Vittorio directed two shorts in 1931, *Tango dell' Amore* and *Tango del Nomade*, based on songs popular at the time. In 1932

the Cossio brothers brought out *Zibillo e l'Orso* ("Zibillo and the Bear"), an open imitation of John Foster's and Frank Rufle's *Tom and Jerry* cartoons, but the film and its characters met with utter indifference.

The Cossio brothers then went back to the comics. Vittorio, who had previously collaborated on *Rin-Tin-Tin*, *Primarosa* and *Il Corriere dei Piccoli*, took over the comic strip *Furio Almirante* in 1941; in 1945 he created *Raff, Pugnio d'Acciao* ("Raff, the Iron-Fisted"), his most notable success in the field. In the meantime he had gone back to animation, producing *Pulcinella* with his brother in 1941. A fire destroyed the Cossio studio in 1943; after that date Vittorio returned to animation only twice: in 1954, when he and his brother designed the titles for the movie *Giove in Doppio Petto* ("Jove in a Double-Breasted Suit"), and in 1958, when he directed, in collaboration with Luciana Pensuti, the Andersen fable *The Magic Flintlock*.

At age 67, Vittorio Cossio continues his career as a cartoonist, book illustrator and painter, also finding time to manage a publishing company with youthful vigor.

S.T.

COTRIM, ALVARO (1904-   ) Brazilian cartoonist and caricaturist born in Rio de Janeiro, Brazil, in August 1904. After studying art and drawing in high school and college, Alvaro ("Alvarus") Cotrim sent his first cartoons in 1925 to *A Pátria*, which immediately accepted them. From that moment he became one of Brazil's most popular and respected cartoonists.

Alvarus has been justly mentioned as the Brazilian caricaturist par excellence. His style was influenced in the beginning by contemporary European, and especially French, cartoonists, but he soon found himself, and his signature is as distinctive as his cheerful attitude to life. He is famed for his caricatures of personalities in politics and the arts, which appeared from 1927 on in *Para Todos* and *Vamos Ler!* He also drew cartoons for *Diário de Notícias*, *Diário da Noite* and *A Noite Illustrada*. He later also did political cartoons for publications like *A Manhã*, *Critica* and *A Granada*.

Alvarus has had his works exhibited in many shows and has received a great many awards and honors. His cartoons have been reprinted in books like *Hoje Tem Espetáculo* ("There Is a Show Today," 1945) and *Alvarus e os Seus Bonecos* ("Alvarus and His Characters," 1954).

A.M.

COUNIHAN, NOEL JACK (1913-   ) Australian cartoonist and caricaturist born in Melbourne, Australia, in 1913.

Master cartoonists like Honoré Daumier, Olaf Gulbransson, Will Dyson and Ralph Steadman, among others, have demonstrated that satire succeeds totally when expressed from a definite point of view. Noel Jack Counihan in fact works from two uncompromising points of view—as a person he stands for socialism and the cause of the working man, as an artist he pursues the practice and discipline of sound draftsmanship with no shortcuts to drawing.

Today a nationally recognized painter, printmaker and lithographer, Counihan began a career in journalism in 1935 during the Great Depression, when, after seeing an exhibition of Counihan's pencil portraits, the editor of the Melbourne *Argus* commissioned him to draw a

Noel Counihan, caricature of Australian prime minister Ben Chifley. © Counihan.

weekly caricature for that newspaper. During this dreadful and difficult period his caricatures of prominent national personalities were being published in the *Bulletin*, and his drawings also appeared in the weekly magazine *Table Talk* and the Melbourne *Sun* newspaper.

The first political cartoons Counihan drew also date from this period. In 1935 he began cartooning for the Communist party newspapers *Worker's Weekly* and *Worker's Voice* and for trade union publications.

In 1943 Counihan started submitting a weekly cartoon for the *Guardian*. His antifascist cartoons and those attacking political corruption and defeatism on the home front were powerful features and continued through the war years until early 1949, when he departed for Europe. His post on the *Guardian* was taken over by the greatly talented and ideologically committed Ambrose Dyson, son of a *Bulletin* cartoonist and nephew of the London *Daily Herald's* world-famous cartoonist, Will Dyson. On his return to Melbourne in 1951, after travel and study in Europe, where his work was published in Prague, Warsaw, Budapest and London, Counihan joined with Ambrose Dyson back on the *Guardian*. He relinquished his feature cartooning in 1958 to again travel and paint full time.

Counihan's development as a cartoonist and caricaturist was influenced by a number of artists, including George Finey, whose astonishingly virile caricatures were featured in *Smith's Weekly*. Early in his career Noel Counihan had also discovered the fine satirists and caricaturists of the celebrated German publication *Simplicissimus* and the dramatically presented full-page cartoons of the American William Gropper in the radical journal *New Masses*. Counihan was later to meet and travel through Poland with Gropper in 1949.

A collection of his *Guardian* work, *60 Counihan Cartoons*, was published in 1946; in 1974 he was distinguished by the publication of his biography by the Melbourne University Press.

Noel Counihan was among the last of the notable cartoonists to draw for the left-wing press in Australia—a list which included Syd Nicholls, Claude Marquet, Tom ("Tac") Challon, Ambrose Dyson and George Finey. The art of caricature as Will Dyson, David Low and Finey practiced it is gone; there is no longer an outlet for it in Australia today. In recent years, however, the enterprising Australian publisher Lloyd O'Neil commissioned Counihan to prepare two sets of caricatures to highlight two volumes of published reminiscences of Australian celebrities. A selection of these superb caricatures is now in the Ballarat Fine Art Gallery collection. And a magnificent series—comic portraits of Australian authors (in a private collection)—has been bequeathed to the Australian National Library in Canberra.

Art critics, gallery experts and his fellow brush practitioners agree that Counihan's brilliant comic portraiture has established his place for all time in the master class.

V.L.

COURTET, EMILE (1857-1938) French cartoonist and animator born in Paris, France, on January 4, 1857. Emile Courtet was first apprenticed to a jeweler, but he liked drawing, and he made many sketches of his co-workers and, after he was drafted into the army, his fellow soldiers. Back in civilian life in 1878, he became a pupil of the famous cartoonist André Gill. Taking up the *nom-de-plume* "Emile Cohl," he embarked on a successful career as a cartoonist, his work appearing in such leading French magazines of the day as *Le Rire* and *La Vie Parisienne*. In 1885 he added photography to his many endeavors.

Cohl joined the Gaumont movie studios in 1907 as the director of trick films in the manner of George Méliès. His first effort at animation took place in 1908 with a series of cartoon shorts featuring a timid but resilient character known as *le fantôche* (literally, "the puppet"), often drawn in white ink on black backgrounds. His first animated film was *Fantasmagorie*, followed by *Le Cauchemar du Fantôche* ("The Puppet's Nightmare"), *Un Drame Chez les Fantôches* ("A Drama Among the Puppets") and others. In 1908 he also directed *Le Baron de Crac*, an animated version of the adventures of Baron Munchausen.

Among Cohl's enormous output from 1908 to 1918, mention should be made of *Les Joyeux Microbes* ("The Jolly Microbes"); *Transfiguration*; *Castro à New York* and *Le Subway* (both made in the United States);

Emile Courtet ("Emile Cohl"), "Un Drame Chez les Fantôches."

Metamorphoses; Flambeau Chien Perdu, about the misadventures of a stray dog; *Bonne Année 1916* ("Happy New Year 1916"); and *Le Tour du Monde en 80 Minutes* ("Around the World in 80 Minutes"), an enchanting spoof of Jules Verne's novel.

From 1912 to 1914, Cohl was in New York working with George McManus on a series of *Snookums* animated cartoons, based on McManus's successful comic strip, *The Newlyweds*. Cohl's last notable work of animation was another adaptation of a popular comic strip, Louis Forton's *Les Aventures des Pieds-Nickelés*, which he realized in 1918 in collaboration with the noted French cartoonist Benjamin Rabier.

Ruined by World War I, Emile Cohl stopped making films in 1918; until 1923 he labored in obscurity on commercial cartoons for theatrical release. Destitute and out of work, he spent the last years of his life in a home for the aged at Orly, near Paris. There, in a freak accident, his long white beard caught fire, and Emile Cohl died of his burns on January 27, 1938.

Cohl left behind him an enormous legacy that has not been adequately assessed to this day. Along with J.S. Blackton and Winsor McCay, he can be regarded as one of the discoverers of the art of animation. In *Animation in the Cinema*, Ralph Stephenson summed up Cohl's achievements in these words: "Cohl had a fertile imagination, and a sharp sense of the comic.... The pace of his films never flags and they are packed with the fantastic invention appropriate to the cartoon world.... His gags today are as fresh as when he made them."

M.H.

COVARRUBIAS, MIGUEL (1904-1957) Mexican cartoonist, author and artist born in Mexico City, Mexico, in 1904. Miguel Covarrubias's highly stylized caricatures of famous contemporaries earned him an international reputation while still a young man. Covarrubias was born and raised in Mexico City, and his father was a politician well connected in the national government. His family was affluent, and his artistic talents blossomed although he never went to art school. His father's connections got Covarrubias his first job as a draftsman with a federal bureau producing maps. Bored on the job, he began drawing caricatures that he soon sold to Mexico City newspapers. By age 18, Miguel Covarrubias was a syndicated cartoonist in publications from Cuba to Buenos Aires.

His caricatures earned him the patronage of the celebrated poet Juan Tablada. A government grant was arranged for the young Covarrubias to spend six months in New York City studying art. In 1923, he arrived in New York City, but instead of studying art, he immediately began selling his own to *Vanity Fair* and other magazines. Among his most famous caricatures early in his career were the Prince of Wales, Charles Chaplin and John D. Rockefeller, Sr. An anthology of his work, *The Prince of Wales and Other Famous Americans*, was published in 1927. Covarrubias enjoyed the high life of New York City of the 1920s. He frequented the Harlem nightclubs then in vogue, and in 1927 a second book, *Negro Drawings*, was published.

The style of his caricatures was distinct. His line was geometric and sculptural in defining mass and features of his subjects. However, for all the stylization, his heavy lines were full of vigor and enthusiasm. His most famous group caricature was done in color for *Vanity Fair* in 1933. It showed an impudent and fanciful version of Franklin D. Roosevelt's first inauguration as president.

Miguel Covarrubias, caricature of Rudolph Valentino. © Covarrubias.

Plump, with a dark complexion, Covarrubias lived abroad more than he lived in Mexico. He was the model of the talented, cultured gentleman with financial security. His interests in painting, lithography, anthropology and archaeology eventually overshadowed his interest in drawing caricatures. In 1937 *Island of Bali*, Covarrubias's drawings supplemented by photographs taken by his wife, was published. The next year an edition of *Uncle Tom's Cabin* illustrated by Covarrubias was published. *Mexico South*, a history of the Olmec Indians, was published in 1946.

He returned to Mexico and taught art at the National Anthropological School. He later became director of dance for the National Institute of Fine Arts. But he continued to paint; his panels decorate numerous public buildings in Mexico. *Eagle, Jaguar, and Serpent*, a survey of Indian art of the Americas, was published in 1950 and was his last important book.

On February 2, 1957, at the age of 53, Covarrubias died in Mexico City of septicemia, a kind of blood poisoning. In honor of his accomplishments, his body lay in state at the National Museum of Anthropology and History prior to his funeral.

B.C.

COX, PALMER (1840-1924) American cartoonist and poet born in Granby, Province of Quebec, Canada, on April 28, 1840. As a boy, Palmer Cox worked in a railroad office in California. After it became clear that a trainman's life was not for him, he lived in San Francisco from 1863 to 1875 and cartooned for local publications, including the *Golden Era* and *Alta Californian*.

In 1875 Cox moved to New York City, set up a studio, and began to gain a reputation as an illustrator of children's books and for his animal drawings. He drew for the first issues of *Life*, lending it critically needed quality, along with other nascent talents like E.W. Kemble and Oliver Herford. But Cox's real success came about this time in the pages of *St. Nicholas* magazine, with *The Brownies*. In the poems and cartoons—crammed full of dozens of his little characters—he managed to create a separate world. *The Brownies* was

Palmer Cox, "The Brownies and the Tide."

enormously successful and spawned 13 books and a host of merchandising items.

Cox remained a lifelong bachelor, but his studio was filled with portraits of children and he corresponded with many of his young fans. After leaving his New York studio, he returned to rural Quebec and settled in Brownie Castle in Granby—the mountains around which are said to have inspired the Brownie legends. Cox died on July 7, 1924, in his 84th year.

Cox's drawing style, especially for *The Brownies* but throughout all his work, was detailed and precise. It was crosshatched, whether manifesting itself in seriocomic animals or romping Brownie snow scenes. Here was a cartoonist, the reader must conclude, who loved his work and all his characters; there was great humor and warm affection in the smallest detail—which, when Brownies were concerned, often constituted a major point of interest! His originals are about the size of the printed work, so his dedication and working method-ology must have been akin to an etcher's. The Brownies, of course, are classic cartoon creations and began a wondrous heritage that continued through the *Kewpies* and *The Teenie Weenies*.

Books: *Squibs of California, or Everyday Life Illustrated* (1875), republished as *Comic Yarns* (1889); *Hans von Pelter's Trip to Gotham* (1876); *How Columbus Found America* (1877); *That Stanley* (1878); *The Brownies, Their Book* (1887); *Queer People* (1888); *Queer People with Wings and Stings* (1888); *Queer People with Paws and Claws* (1888); *Another Brownie Book* (1890); *The Brownies at Home* (1893); *The Brownies Around the World* (1894); *The Brownies Through the Union* (1895); *The Brownies Abroad* (1899); *The Brownies in Fairyland* (1895); *The Brownies in the Philippines* (1904); *The Palmer Cox Brownie Primer* (1906); *Brownie Clown in Brownie Town* (1907); *The Brownies' Latest Adventures* (1910); *The Brownies' Many More Nights* (1913); and *The Brownies and Prince Florimel* (1918). A three-act play based on the Brownies was also produced in 1895.

R.M.

CRANE, FRANK (1856-1917) American cartoonist, cousin of author Stephen Crane, born in Rahway, New Jersey, in 1856. A graduate of the New York Academy of Design,

Crane became a staff cartoonist for the *New York World* in the early 1890s, and ultimately its art editor. He then moved to the *Philadelphia Press* in the same capacity, supervising such later greats in the fields of cartooning and illustration as Everrett Shinn, John Sloan, William Glackens, James Preston and F.R. Gruger.

Crane returned to New York as cartoonist for the *Tribune* and later switched to the *Herald* (as art editor) and to the *Times*; the *Boston Herald* also ran his cartoons and strips. Among his strips were *Willie Westinghouse Edison Smith, Muggsy* and *Uncle Dick's Contraptions.* Crane drew panel cartoons for *Life* around the turn of the century as well. He died at his home in New Rochelle, New York, on October 26, 1917.

Crane's style was broad and humorous, full of anima-tion, technically similar to Walt McDougall's. His car-toons had an appearance that suggested, according to the taste of the observer, either crudity or native humor.

R.M.

CRAWFORD, ARTHUR (1867-1922) American writer and agent born in Montreal, Canada, on July 2, 1867. Arthur Crawford was graduated from the Royal Military College of Kingston, Ontario, in 1883, and began a career on the stage; he acted throughout Canada until 1896. He then moved to New York and, after a feeble attempt at cartooning, hit upon a system that suited his talents and in a major way shaped the course and content of American magazine cartooning for a generation. Crawford became an idea man, providing cartoonists with gags or themes for their drawings. At the same time—a time when cartoon markets were burgeoning and many artists eschewed humbling personal visits to editors' desks—he became an agent of sorts, submitting portfolios of cartoons to the various cartoon markets.

His success is attested by the many cartoonists' signatures followed by the caption "+A.C." giving credit to the originator. Sometimes half the cartoons in an issue of *Puck, Judge* or *Life* would bear Crawford's mark. His fecundity was amazing, and his ideas spanned the "he-she" gags to the single-caption era. He also pioneered the full-page theoretical cartoons later popularized by Gluyas Williams, Forbell and Rea Irvin.

Crawford committed suicide on November 14, 1922. Whether the resultant absence of his enormous influence was responsible for the advent of the new humor of the 1920s and the so-called one-line caption or merely coincided with the new era is probably beside the point. In terms of sheer production, the pen of Arthur Crawford played as large a role in shaping America's conception of humor as any other man's. The years 1900 to 1922 should rightly be called the Crawford era.

R.M.

CRAWFORD, WILL (1869-1944) American cartoonist born in Washington, D.C., in 1869. Will Crawford's first art assignments were for the *Newark* (N.J.) *Call* and then the *New York World*. His first major cartoons appeared in the pages of the old *Life* magazine when he was in his mid-twenties.

In the mid-1890s cartooning styles were relaxing. Crawford, with Sullivant and Hy Mayer, was the first since Frost and Bush to test distortion and exaggeration; most American cartoonists were slavishly sticking to "realism" or copying Gibson.

Crawford was soon drawing full-page cartoons for *Life*. He did series (*Historical Bits* was one—later historical illustrations for *Puck* in the mid-1910s were factual rather than satirical) and complicated genre drawings. Crawford's style was one of marvelously crosshatched understatement. There was motion, but it was arrested. He managed a blend of realism and caricature and spotted his figures in an impressive way that led the reader's eye through the cartoon as a guide would conduct a museum tour. There were seldom solid blacks in his cartoons; thin, spiny lines would combine for crosshatch and shading effects of incredible visual variety.

By the middle of the first decade he was a major fixture in *Puck*, perhaps due in large part to his friendship with Joseph Keppler, Jr. Crawford drew some brilliant double-page spreads in color, although his political attempts were shallow. After Keppler sold his interest in *Puck*, Crawford remained for some time but ultimately left and, in temporary semi-retirement, joined Keppler in the West to live among and work on behalf of Indian tribes—whose welfare and way of life became a consuming interest of the two cartoonists. Crawford died in Nutley, New Jersey, in 1944.

In addition to his numerous cartoons and magazine illustrations, Crawford illustrated many books, where his work can be (and deserves to be) discovered today: *Jack Morgan, A Boy of 1812* (1901); *Pigs Is Pigs* (1907); *The Great American Pie Company* (1907); *The Mystery* (1907); *Skunny Wundy and Other Indian Tales* (1926); *Paul Bunyan and His Great Blue Ox* (1926); *A Narration of Col. Ethan Allen's Captivity, Containing His Voyages and Travels* (1930); and *Long Remember* (1934), among many others. Whether the illustrations were straight or in cartooning style, the wispy, textured elements of Will Crawford's work were always in evidence.

R.M.

CRAWFORD, WILLIAM H. (1913-   ) American political and sports cartoonist born in Hammond, Indiana, on

"May I carry your books?"

William H. Crawford. © *NEA.*

March 13, 1913. Raised in Germantown, Pennsylvania, Bill Crawford took the W.L. Evans correspondence cartooning course and studied at the Art Institute of Chicago. He was graduated from Ohio State with a fine arts degree after studying sculpture under Hoyt L. Sherman.

Study in Paris followed at l'Académie de la Grande Chaumière, under Lucien Fontanarosa and others, for fine arts and drawing. Returning to the United States, he freelanced cartoons before taking a job on the art staff of the *Washington Post*. Later he switched to the *Washington Daily News*, where he cartooned for two years in the sports and editorial departments. Harold Talburt, chief political cartoonist of the *News*, informed Crawford of an opening on the *Newark* (N.J.) *News*, which Crawford applied for and won. That was in 1938, and among his assignments was drawing one editorial cartoon a week to relieve Lute Pease. Eventually he took over the full-time political chores—as well as contributing sports cartoons, news features and theatrical caricatures. In 1962, when John Fischetti left the Newspaper Enterprise Association, Crawford moved over under editor Boyd Lewis. For years, as America's most widely circulated editorial cartoonist, he drew six a week, eventually reducing his load to five a week and then two a week; he retired in 1977.

Crawford, originally a liberal Democrat, has an amazing versatility of talents, including photography, the classical viola and especially sculpture. He has done many portrait busts and, on the lighter side, fashioned the National Cartoonists Society Reuben award from a Rube Goldberg sketch. He has illustrated 20 books, won the Best Editorial Cartoonist award three times, and has several Freedoms Foundation and National Headliners Club awards to his credit.

Crawford's style displays exceptional verve and competence; all his figures are distorted and exaggerated but technically correct and balanced. He drew on a very large scale, and his prime work shows a feeling of scope and great, arresting composition. His shading, before he switched to Craftint in the 1970s, was with a free and slashing crayon. Crawford's work from the 1930s to the early 1950s was among the strongest produced in America—he is just one of the many outstanding artists who somehow evaded Pulitzer recognition. His work deserves to be anthologized.

R.M.

CRÉATION DU MONDE, LA (France) In 1945 French cartoonist Jean Effel (François Lejeune) started a series of humorous cartoons based on the Book of Genesis. Collectively called *La Création du Monde* ("The Creation of the World"), they depicted God as a bearded and well-meaning old fussbudget who brought forth the sky, stars, water, etc., only after much prodding from his high-spirited retinue of angels. His old adversary, Satan, was always lurking in the shadows, trying to turn each of his creations into a disaster. The cartoons enjoyed incredible success and were later collected into a series of five books, *Le Ciel et la Terre* ("The Sky and Earth"), *Les Plantes et Animaux* ("The Plants and Animals"), *L'Homme* ("Man"), *La Femme* ("Woman") and *Le Roman d'Adam et Eve* ("The Romance of Adam and Eve").

In 1956 Barandov Studio in Prague produced a full-length animated cartoon of *La Création du Monde*. It was directed by Eduard Hofman from a screenplay by noted cartoonist (and former ambassador to France) Adolph Hoffmeister. The film was very successful, both artisti-

"La Création du Monde." © *Jean Effel.*

cally and commercially, and received many awards. In 1974 a sequel, *The Tribulations of Adam and Eve*, also based on Effel's drawings, was produced by the Czech studio.

M.H.

CROCKETT, GIBSON MILTON (1912-   ) American political cartoonist and painter born in Washington, D.C., on September 18, 1912. After graduation from high school, Gib Crockett visited the art department of the *Washington Star* to show his sketches, thereupon beginning a 41-year association with the paper. His only art training—other than what he was to acquire on the job—was an unfinished cartoon correspondence course. His early influences were Dorman H. Smith and Willard Mullin.

He advanced at the *Star* from apprenticeship in spot cartooning, human interest sketches and sports cartoons to editorial and political cartoons. It was in 1948, the year before Clifford Berryman's death, that Crockett began on the editorial page, at first at the rate of one a week, as relief for Jim Berryman.

Crockett is an accomplished painter and a member of several painting societies in the Washington area. He has had exhibitions of his paintings and received a U.S. Treasury medal for war work, as well as Freedoms Foundation awards and a National Headliners award for his cartoons. Crockett, an independent-leaning Republican, draws in the portraiture school of cartooning; he employs likenesses of his subjects rather than the frequent use of caricature itself. His shading medium was usually crayon until, in recent years, he switched to a single-tone wash. For years his work was syndicated by King Features Syndicate.

R.M.

CUMMINGS, MICHAEL (1919-   ) British political cartoonist of the Beaverbrook newspaper group, brought in to give some serious commentary contrast to the often knockabout comedy of their principal cartoonist, Carl Giles. Michael Cummings was born in Leeds in 1919, the son of A.J. Cummings, a political columnist who became the political editor of the *News Chronicle*. Educated at The Hall, Hampstead, and Gresham's School, Norfolk, he studied art at the Chelsea School of Art for three years before World War II took him into the Air Ministry. As an RAF draftsman he drew airplane parts until his

discharge, then resumed his art studies at Chelsea.

His first cartoons, reflecting his political leanings, were published in the left-wing weekly *Tribune* in 1939, and the same magazine took him on in postwar days as an illustrator for the book page. He contributed cartoons of a political nature until 1948, when, at his father's suggestion, he applied for a job on the *Daily Express*. After a trying trial period he made the grade and provided the *Daily* with three cartoons a week, plus one for the *Sunday Express*. He published a book, *These Uproarious Years*, in 1954.

D.G.

CURRIER AND IVES (ca. 1834-1898) The Currier and Ives operations—first under Nathaniel Currier's name and later in partnership with James M. Ives—made many contributions to American culture: popular art was introduced to the masses, lithography was refined under its aegis, the spirit of an age was almost inadvertently but uncompromisingly captured and, certainly not least important, the American appetite for visual humor was given great impetus.

Lithography on stone, a unique medium of Bavarian descent, was new to America when Nathaniel Currier was engaged as an apprentice by one of the pioneering firms in Boston. Currier was only 15 but soon experimented with his own shop—and, later, his own techniques—as his bookkeeper, Ives, handled the business affairs so he could continue to concentrate on themes and art direction.

Of course, Currier and Ives prints were to become synonymous with sentiment, primitive political persuasion and scenes of racetrack, steamboat and railroad Americana, but one of the firm's most successful lines was its humorous portfolios. Much of the humorous

Gib Crockett. © *Washington Star-News.*

work was submitted by Thomas Worth (he never lithographed directly on the stones), but Currier himself had a famous sense of humor and was responsible for many of the concepts and comic prints. Sol Eytinge was another prolific artist. By far the most popular series through the years was Worth's *Darktown* series. Without regular characters, these prints lampooned practically every aspect of black life and were best sellers; they presaged Kemble's *Coontown Sketches* by more than a generation.

Aside from the purely humorous prints, political cartoons were a Currier and Ives stock-in-trade. They flourished, of course, at every presidential election, although most of the activity in this genre occurred during the Civil War and dealt with Abraham Lincoln. It should be noted that as mere "printmakers to the people," Currier and Ives sometimes issued, simultaneously, prints supporting opposing sides of an issue. Many cartoons were crude, and balloons were frequently employed.

Currier and Ives print portfolios ranged in price from twenty cents to four dollars, although cartoons were always at the cheap end of the scale. Virtually none were lithographed in color; rather, a dozen or so German ladies worked in production-line fashion, adding watercolors to bring the prints to life.

The firm sold its last original lithograph in 1898, after the deaths of Currier and Ives (in 1888 and 1895, respectively). Descendants of the founders and employees struggled for several years until the stock and equipment was liquidated in 1907—even the stones

"The Bad Man at the Hour of Death," a Currier and Ives lithograph, ca. 1858.

member of W.C.T.U.

—For a female Anarchist—

For Quaker Girl—

~ Otho Cushing ~

Otho Cushing.

"Cyborg 009." © *Toei Studio.*

were cleaned and auctioned by the pound. The Currier and Ives phenomenon really lost its vitality in the mid-1870s. Several reasons can be suggested, including the fading novelty of colored prints. But certainly a major factor must have been the rise of illustrated journalism and particularly the advent of colored lithographic cartoons in *Puck* and similar weekly magazines.

R.M.

CUSHING, OTHO (1871-1942) American cartoonist born in Fort McHenry, Maryland, in 1871. Otho Cushing, a descendant of Nicholas Cooke, colonial governor of Rhode Island, received art training from the Boston School of Fine Arts and was graduated with honors. He later studied at the Académie Julian in Paris and then became a professor of drawing at the Massachusetts Institute of Technology. After the turn of the century Cushing returned to Paris to become art editor of the European edition of the *Herald-Tribune*. In late 1906 Cushing submitted his first cartoons to *Life* and upon acceptance also received an offer to join the magazine's staff. He made his mark early when a series satirizing President Theodore Roosevelt in a Ulyssean motif—*The Teddyssey*—created a stir in the press because of its cleverness. It was ultimately reprinted in book form.

Cushing's style was heavily mannered and ultra-formal. Perhaps a third of all his cartoons used Greek gods and goddesses as characters (oftentimes attempting social or political comments in a satiric vein); one has the feeling that *all* his characters were Olympian. His society women didn't wear gowns, they seemed to wear togas. High-society jibes, historical mixups and "socio-classical" departures formed nearly his total subject range.

During World War I, Cushing left *Life*. As a captain in the Army Air Corps he was in charge of camouflaging American airfields on the Western Front. His mentor, J.A. Mitchell of *Life*, must have been proud, as France's fight was as dear to his heart as any of the magazine's crusades through the years. After the war Cushing retired to his home in New Rochelle, New York, where he became a successful watercolorist. He died on October 13, 1942.

R.M.

CYBORG 009 (Japan) Japanese cartoonist Shotarō Ishimori created his successful comic strip *Cyborg 009* in 1964; the feature became so popular that it gave rise to a long-running animated series of television cartoons in 1965 and was adapted to theatrical animation a year later. In this feature-length animated film, closely following the original script, Cyborg 009 and his cybernetic companions fought the Black Ghosts, a host of malevolent characters bent on taking over the world. Helped by their inventor, Dr. Gillmore, the cyborgs succeeded in thwarting the devilish schemes of the Black Ghosts and their leader, Beagle. The action was swift and suspenseful, and the animation (directed by Yugo Serikawa) well handled.

The whole enterprise was so successful that it inevitably spawned a sequel, *Cyborg 009—Underground Duel*. In this film the cyborgs and their mentor, Dr. Gillmore, fought the second round of their duel against Beagle and his surviving Black Ghosts. After destroying a monster robot that was wreaking havoc on the high seas, Cyborg 009 and his companions finally destroyed the headquarters of the Black Ghosts, thus putting an end to this international band of evildoers. Again the feature was directed by Serikawa; the script, however, was repetitive, and the animation, though done at the Toei Studio, like that of its predecessor, somehow seemed wooden. There were no more *Cyborg 009* features after this second version (1967).

M.H.

CYNICUS
See Anderson, Martin.

Dd

DAFFY DUCK (U.S.) "That darnfool duck," as he was called before he got his official name, first appeared in Tex Avery's 1937 cartoon "Porky's Duck Hunt" as the elusive target of at least three dozen hunters. He returned—as Daffy Duck—in the 1937 "Daffy Duck and Egghead," also directed by Avery, and proved popular enough to be given his own cartoon series by producer Leon Schlesinger, releasing through Warner Brothers. The personality of the insanely active duck was well established early on: that of the supremely confident, albeit totally incompetent, con man whose nefarious schemes invariably backfired on him. In "Daffy Duck in Hollywood" (1938) he played to the hilt the role of a dictatorial movie director, and in "Plane Daffy" (1940), that of a daredevil aviator. In both he ended up getting the boot.

Never were the fast-talking duck's pretensions so promptly deflated as on the numerous occasions that found him confronting the unflappable Bugs Bunny. In cartoon after inspired cartoon ("Beanstalk Bunny," "A Star Is Bored," "The Abominable Snow Rabbit," etc.) Daffy played his most underhanded tricks on Bugs, only to be outwitted at every turn. The last shot usually showed the duck crawling up to the carrot-munching Bugs and uttering the heartfelt apostrophe "You're despicable!" In "Robin Hood Daffy" (possibly the best of the *Daffy Duck* cartoons), Daffy, posing as Robin Hood, vainly tried to persuade a skeptical Porky Pig (as Friar Tuck) to join his band, and decided to join the order instead ("Friar Tuck, meet Friar Duck!"). One of Daffy's best solo efforts came in "Aqua Duck" when, searching for water in the desert, he only came upon useless gold.

In addition to Avery, notable directors of the *Daffy Duck* cartoons have included Frank Tashlin, Chuck Jones, Bob Clampett, Friz Freleng and Bob McKimson. Like the rest of his Warner Brothers compères, Daffy disappeared from theater screens in 1969 but still appears on television on the *Bugs Bunny and Friends* show. He has also been continuously featured in comic books since 1951.

M.H.

DAGGY, A. SMITH (1858-1942) American cartoonist born in 1858. A.S. Daggy is representative of turn-of-the-century magazine cartoonists who handled all genres well. He also had a secret life as a quite respectable painter. Daggy studied fine arts in Paris and at the Pennsylvania Academy of Fine Arts, where he trained under Thomas Eakins and became his close friend. In the 1880s Daggy's cartoons and back-of-the-book drawings began appearing in *Harper's Monthly*, where only the finer and more genteel magazine cartoonists could cross over. In the 1890s his work was a pillar of *Judge's* cartoon establishment; he had no specialty of themes but rather was a journeyman gagster who vied with the best of his fellows for the apportioned ethnic, rural and household cartoons.

His style ranged gently from the illustrative to the exaggerated (when Sullivant and others introduced big-headed characters to cartooning). One area in which he excelled was visualized puns—the audacity of some is admirable!

Daggy's best friend was the great A.B. Frost, with whom he studied and painted through the years. Daggy's own canvases show a respectable talent for media other than pen and ink. His "straight" artistic activities brought him to the vice-presidency of the Silvermine Guild in Norwalk, Connecticut. He died in Stamford, Connecticut, on June 16, 1942.

R.M.

Daffy Duck in "The Wise Quacking Duck." © *Warner Brothers.*

DALE, ARCHIBALD (1882-1962) Canadian cartoonist born in Dundee, Scotland, on May 31, 1882. Arch Dale began his cartooning career on the Aberdeen *Courier* at age 17. For the next ten years or so he worked on the *Courier*, the Glasgow *News* and finally *Comic Cuts* and *Funny Wonders* in London.

In 1908, Dale left for Canada. He later said that glowing accounts by friends of the rich homesteads in Saskatchewan convinced him to come to Touchwood Hills. After arriving, he came to the conclusion that there are many Scottish settlers on the prairies because Scotsmen like company in their misery and are ready to suppress the truth to get it. After a few months behind the plow, he moved to Winnipeg, Manitoba, and spent two years there, cartooning for the *Free Press* and the *Grain Growers' Guide*. In 1910 a windfall from a real estate boom enabled him to finance a trip back home. He stayed for three years, cartooning for papers in Manchester and London, but returned to Canada in 1913, later stating that he became fed up with the extremes of wealth and poverty in England.

Dale again worked for the *Grain Growers' Guide*, remaining until 1921. During this time, he married Claire Porter (their only child, Julie Dale, was to become head of the Winnipeg *Free Press* art depart-

181

"NOW your seasickness is gone! The cruise is over!"

Gregory d'Alessio. © *d'Alessio.*

ment). In 1921 Dale went to Chicago to work for the Universal Feature and Specialty Company, which syndicated his *Doo Dads*. Here Dale portrayed the humorous experiences of Doc Sawbones, Old Man Grouch and other little people who populated this weekly strip against a surrealistic background. Dale left the United States in 1927, afterwards observing that he had spent most of his time there on streetcars getting to and from work.

Dale's position as a major Canadian political cartoonist dates from his return to the Winnipeg *Free Press* in 1927; he remained there until his retirement in 1954. He began with little knowledge of the political situation in an affluent, inflationary society, but the 1930s provided Dale with many targets for his pen. Prime minister R.B. Bennett, with his top hat, pince-nez and pinstriped suit, embodied the Conservative party image to western farmers hit hard by the Depression. Dale exploited this image and continually pointed out the failings of the Conservatives. Yet Mr. Bennett often wrote to Dale for originals of these cartoons, and once, when an original was lost, Dale drew a copy and sent it to him. Not all of Dale's barbs were reserved for the Conservative party, however. After World War II, the *Free Press* attacked the Liberal party's wheat policy, and Dale drew a cartoon with Minister of Agriculture Gardiner upside down and everyone else right side up. Unfortunately the point was somewhat lost when a printer accidentally put the cartoon in upside down.

Three collections of Dale cartoons were published in Winnipeg: *Five Years with R.B. Bennett* (1935); *$25 a Month, Adventures in Aberhartia* (1938); and *The Left and the Right with Arch Dale of the Winnipeg Free Press* (1945).

Eight years after his retirement, Dale died in a Winnipeg hospital on June 18, 1962.

D.K.

D'ALESSIO, GREGORY (1904-   ) American painter, cartoonist and art teacher born in New York City on September 25, 1904. Gregory d'Alessio worked as an assistant to a commercial artist and as a bank teller on Wall Street prior to the Depression. Fired from his Wall Street job, he began freelancing cartoons, at the same time studying at Pratt Institute and the Art Students League. About 1932 he sold his first cartoon to the *Saturday Evening Post*. This was quickly followed by sales to *Collier's, Esquire,* the *New Yorker* and most of the major cartoon markets of the day. In the 1930s his feature *Twimbly Twins* was published by the *Saturday Evening Post*. After World War II, *Collier's* magazine featured his panel *Welcome Home*, about the arrival home of the American troops and the humorous problems that arose.

In 1940 a daily panel, *These Women*, starring the svelte secretary Miss Jones, was syndicated by Publishers Syndicate. The panel was stylish, and d'Alessio's quick brushwork gave it a light, relaxing quality. His magazine cartoons were also mostly brush and ink plus wash to the exclusion of much pen work. But since his magazine work was directed to specific audiences, d'Alessio could be more sophisticated in his humor and art than with *These Women*. A classic *Esquire* cartoon shows a shapely woman in a fur coat and hat walking past two other sophisticated New York women. One woman says to her companion, "There's a mink, from a rat, on a cat."

During World War II, d'Alessio was chairman of the committee on war cartoons of the American Society of

Jenö Dallos. © *Dallos.*

Magazine Cartoonists. The committee worked closely with different government agencies in determining how cartooning could help the war effort and morale of the people.

Gregory d'Alessio eventually decided to end his distinguished cartoon career in favor of painting. He has long been associated with the Art Students League in New York City, where he teaches drawing and anatomy. His wife, Hilda Terry, whom he married in 1938, is one of the foremost women cartoonists in America.

B.C.

DALLOS, JENÖ (1940-　　) Hungarian cartoonist born near Budapest, Hungary, in 1940. After studying art in various Budapest schools, Jenö Dallos started contributing cartoons to magazines and newspapers around 1965, rapidly becoming one of the top Hungarian cartoonists. Since 1970 he has been on the staff of *Ludas Matyi,* a satirical weekly magazine with a circulation of over five hundred thousand. In addition to a successful career in his home country, Dallos has had many of his cartoons printed abroad in such publications as *Pardon, Interpress Grafik, Das Magazin* in Germany, and *Punch* and *City* in England.

Dallos's main concerns are threats to the environment and the endangered future of mankind; he treats his themes in a sparse, linear style not dissimilar to that of Michel Folon and often develops his usually captionless cartoons in a sequential form close to that of the comic strip.

Dallos has been the recipient of a number of international awards, including the special prize at the 1975 Bordighera Humor Salon and the second prize at the 1969 Moscow Cartoon Exhibition.

M.H.

DALRYMPLE, LOUIS (1861-1905) American cartoonist born in Cambridge, Illinois, on January 19, 1861. Louis Dalrymple, educated in public schools, studied art at the Pennsylvania Academy of Fine Arts, where he was graduated with credit, and at the Art Students League in New York.

In 1886 he submitted drawings to Joseph Keppler, founder and art director of *Puck,* and was engaged as a staff member. The magazine was then in a rebuilding period following the departure of Bernard Gillam and Eugene Zimmerman to *Judge,* and the death of James A. Wales. Nevertheless, Dalrymple's hiring was not out of desperation; although some consider his work crude, he had the flavor of early Opper, Frost and Bush. Dalrymple's work never really transcended the first rough impression it made, but he was prolific and his style was full of native humor. There was much animation in his figures, and he proved a valuable asset to *Puck* for 15 years.

Dalrymple handled lithographic political subjects as well as black-and-white humorous cartoons. In spite of occasional masterpieces, his anatomy could sometimes be awkward and his composition unsure. Just after the turn of the century, when he also dabbled in Sunday comic strips, Dalrymple left *Puck* and drew for its Republican rival, *Judge.* It was a short tenure, however, as he died in 1905.

R.M.

Louis Dalrymple, 1898.

DAME OYAJI (Japan) *Dame Oyaji* (roughly translatable as "No-Good Daddy") is a long-running and hilarious Japanese comic strip that first appeared in the magazine *Shōnen Sunday* in 1970. Created and drawn by Mitsutoshi Furuya, *Dame Oyaji* relies for its humor on role reversals of stereotypes in the Japanese family.

Dame Oyaji, the central figure, has the misfortune to marry Oni Baba ("Demon Hag"). Totally dominated by her, he spends his wretched existence trying to find ways to assert himself and to somehow convince both himself and his two children that he is not completely incompetent. Alas, nobody respects Dame Oyaji; at work he is despised by his superiors and tolerated by his peers, and at home he is a pathetic, persecuted figure. As might be expected, he is tiny in comparison with his wife, who towers over him like a scowling Sherman tank. At the slightest offense Oni Baba is liable to fly into a blind rage and attack her husband with whatever happens to be at hand, be it chair, shovel or meat cleaver. Between moments of pathetic cowering, Dame Oyaji often makes appeals to his children for support, but to his ultimate chagrin they usually remain impartial and impassive bystanders.

In actual Japanese families, the father is usually a rather distant and dominant figure, especially from the viewpoint of children, and as befits a male-oriented society, his word is law (although the women do have their own foolproof methods of getting their own way). *Dame Oyaji*, by successfully parodying this family relationship and the male role in it, has tapped a virtually inexhaustible source of humor for children.

Furuya supposedly derived inspiration for the strip both from his compatriots at work and from his own experience. He was born in Japanese-controlled Manchuria in 1936 and repatriated to Japan after the war; upon graduation from middle school he worked for three years in a clothing store. He has worked as an assistant to Osamu Tezuka and also as a staff member of Fujio Productions, and his drawing style is clearly influenced by Fujio Akatsuka in its use of simple lines with no shading and maximum deformation of facial features. Furuya is well known in Japan for other humorous works such as *Techan* and *Nettarokun*, but *Dame Oyaji* remains his most representative and comical work to date.

F.S.

DARCY, THOMAS (1932-   ) American cartoonist born in Brooklyn, New York, on December 19, 1932. Tom Darcy grew up in Long Island and studied art at the Cartoonists and Illustrators School (later the School of Visual Arts) under Jack Markow and Burne Hogarth. While in art school, he sold his first cartoons—gags to men's magazines—and in 1959 he took a job on the art staff of the Long Island newspaper *Newsday*. Shortly thereafter he worked for the *Phoenix Gazette* for a year, but the liberal attitudes he expressed in his editorial cartoons soon caused difficulties, and he returned to advertising, a field he had worked in briefly after art school.

Starting in 1964, Darcy held a succession of political cartooning jobs that both matured his style and reflected his political drift leftward. The *Houston Post* published him for just under two years, and in 1966 he switched to the *Philadelphia Bulletin*. Two years later he found a comfortable berth on *Newsday* again; in another two years he was the possessor of the Pulitzer Prize for editorial cartooning. In 1977 Darcy abandoned editorial cartooning to do a weekly potpourri page of social comment and reportage, "Tom Darcy on Long Island," for the Sunday *Newsday*. "After Nixon, Vietnam and civil rights, what's left to attack?" Darcy asked. "I had too much of the sixties and seventies."

Darcy's later style is reminiscent of Herblock and Conrad but retains its individuality. His lines are bold, and he uses facial expressions and emotions to advantage in depicting his characters. In his political cartooning career Darcy copped three Overseas Press Club awards and a National Headliners award.

R.M.

DARLING, JAY NORWOOD (1876-1962) American cartoonist, twice a Pulitzer Prize winner, born in Norwood, Michigan, on October 21, 1876. Jay Darling first signed himself "Ding" (a contraction) in a Beloit, Wisconsin, school yearbook lampooning faculty members as chorus girls; he was suspended for a year.

In 1900 Ding was a reporter for the *Sioux City* (Iowa) *Journal*. In tracking down a story, he sketched a lawyer who refused to be photographed, and he became a sketch artist for the paper on the strength of its quality. While honeymooning in the West Indies in 1906, Ding was offered a job by wire with the *Des Moines Register and Leader*. He worked there until offered a position with the *New York Globe* and its syndicate. There he drew editorial cartoons and two comic features, *Alonzo Applegate* and *The Iowa Farmer*. An obvious homesickness for Iowa was further manifested in 1913, when he accepted a position with the *New York Tribune*, one of the most prestigious papers in the country: his terms were to be the *Tribune*'s regular cartoonist while maintaining residence in Iowa. These arrangements were long-standing, with Ding also doubling as the regular cartoonist of the *Des Moines Register and Tribune*. He was syndicated by the Herald-Tribune Syndicate.

Tom Darcy. © Newsday.

Jay Norwood Darling ("Ding"). © Des Moines Register & Tribune.

Ding was as famous for his friendships and causes as for his cartoons. He was close to Theodore Roosevelt and especially close to fellow Iowan Herbert Hoover. For years he was the nation's most famous conservationist and promoted wildlife protection in particular. In 1934 he was named chief of the Biological Survey in the Department of Agriculture but resigned soon thereafter, angry over New Deal red tape and frustrated over FDR's evident lack of sincerity in appointing and charging him. He remained active in conservation work, however, serving on committees and designing a wildlife stamp. He won many awards, including the Distinguished Service Medal from the Theodore Roosevelt Memorial Association for appropriating $20 million and setting aside 4.5 million acres during his brief tenure in office.

Ding's first book was a collection of war cartoons published in 1917; he has been anthologized much through the years. *Ding's Half Century* was published in 1962; *As Ding Saw Hoover* in 1954; and *Calvin Coolidge: Cartoons of His Presidency*, wherein he was the featured artist, in 1973. *Palimpsest*, journal of the Iowa State Historical Society, published a superb issue devoted to Ding in March 1972. He wrote text and drew cartoons for *Ding Goes to Russia* in 1932 and wrote *The Cruise of the Baby Bouncer* (about a trailer trip from Des Moines to Miami) in 1937.

Originals by Ding are extremely large; he drew in slashing brushstrokes that, reduced, looked like stiff pen lines. Ding gloried in the traditional conventions of his craft and never really sought to simplify his art; his cartoons are full of crosshatching and labels, are crammed with visual humor and usually seek a chuckle as well as a message. The spirit of his cluttered masterpieces is as important as any transitory object lesson they may illustrate.

His work was sometimes confused with that of Tom Carlisle, who was for awhile his assistant—one of the few instances of an editorial cartoonist employing help on art (Rube Goldberg was another). When a cartoon was wholly Ding's it would contain an x after the signature. Dan Dowling, a Des Moines man with a similar name who succeeded Ding on the *Herald Tribune*, was also confused with him at times.

In his day the great Ding Darling was one of the most influential and most often reprinted cartoonists in America. He died on February 12, 1962.

R.M.

DARROW, WHITNEY, JR. (1909-) American cartoonist born in Princeton, New Jersey, on August 22, 1909. Whitney Darrow, Jr., was initially more interested in writing than in art. During his sophomore year at Princeton University, however, his doodlings in a notebook inspired someone to suggest that he submit some drawings to the school's humor magazine. He did so, they were accepted, and so began his career.

While attending summer classes at the Art Students League in New York and serving as art editor of the *Princeton Tiger*, Darrow refined his approach in matters of style (though he remains to this day, he says, primarily an idea man). He also changed his major from English and history to art and archaeology. Graduating in the midst of the Depression, he decided to try freelance cartooning and had immediate success with submissions to *Judge*, *Life* and *College Humor* (at fifteen to twenty dollars per sale). As a young cartoonist, Darrow's idol was Peter Arno, and his fondest desire was to have his work represented in the *New Yorker*. He first approached the magazine in 1933, and with his second submission he enjoyed success, selling seven of ten pieces. His first panel appeared in 1934, and he has been one of the most prolific and consistent of the *New Yorker* cartoonists ever since.

Darrow is a keen observer of the world around him and has an infectiously amusing way of conveying his conclusions about what he sees. His humor is of the sort that takes a familiar idea or a cliché and pushes it

"At first we thought, 'Oh, well, puppy love';
but now we find he's asked her here for a week end."

Whitney Darrow. © Collier's.

just beyond the borders of plausibility. The result is seldom without its intended effect—as in the panel where the secretarial-school teacher explicates a demonstration she has arranged for her students: "Notice, class, how Angela circles, always keeping the desk between them." Regarding his brand of humor, Darrow has claimed that the various liberation movements of our time frustrate him in his search for subjects because reality seems to be constantly outstripping fantasy. Most *New Yorker* readers would hardly agree, for Darrow manages to use this predicament to advantage in cartoons like the one of a voluptuously nude female balloon floating above the holiday parade in company with the usual comic and mythic creatures. As it passes by, one onlooker remarks matter-of-factly to another, "I suppose Macy's was bound to fall in line."

The style of Darrow's pencil, charcoal and wash pieces is functional and takes second place to the substance of his work; his ideas are so often self-explanatory that complex or detailed representation is unnecessary. Even so, his renderings are disciplined and pleasing to the eye, and there is a definite if subtle individuality to them. Though his cartoons are less immediately identifiable than those of Arno or Price or newcomers like Koren and Hamilton, one learns to recognize and appreciate the quiet craftsmanship that supports Darrow's comic inventiveness.

Collections of Darrow's work include *You're Sitting on My Eyelashes* (1943), *Please Pass the Hostess* (1949), *Stop, Miss* (1958) and *Give Up* (1966). He has also illustrated a number of books, including Sam Levenson's *Sex and the Single Child* and Jean Kerr's *Penny Candy*.

R.C.

DART, HARRY GRANT (1869-1938) American cartoonist born in Williamsport, Pennsylvania, in 1869. Harry

Grant Dart's first job as an artist was making portraits of deceased personalities for the National Crayon Company; thenceforth he was connected with various periodicals. In the mid-1890s he worked briefly for the *Boston Herald*, and in 1898 the *New York World* sent him to Cuba to cover the Spanish-American War as a sketch artist. After the war he joined the *New York World*, rising to the rank of art editor, a working position in which he covered news events and court trials with his staff. Dart later worked for the *New York Recorder* and the *Denver Times*, but he is best remembered for his freelance magazine work, chiefly for *Life* during the first decades of the century, and for *Judge* and *Life* in the late 1920s.

Dart's work, always vast in scope and large in size, was characterized by enormously complex perspective viewpoints or architectural superstructures. For years he was obsessed with fantastic flying machines and consequently drew many aerial shots. His perspectives were always perfect, his drawing precise, his crosshatching exactly neat, and his figures—there would often be dozens and dozens in a drawing—carefully drawn and funny. Invariably the cartoons took a full page or ran as double spreads.

The cartoonist, a member of the Players and the Society of Illustrators, died in Laconia, New Hampshire, on November 15, 1938. His work deserves rediscovery and republication today.

R.M.

DAUMIER, HONORÉ (1808-1879) French caricaturist, cartoonist and painter born in Marseilles, France, on February 20, 1808. At age seven Honoré Daumier moved to Paris with his family. There he received a middle-class education, but he liked only to draw, and he was apprenticed to the painter Alexandre Lenoir.

We'll all be happy then.

Harry Grant Dart, 1911.

Honoré Daumier, "Two Barristers."

Daumier's first original drawing appeared in 1822, and by 1830 he was already publishing lithographs in *La Silhouette*. In 1831 he served a six-month jail sentence for his cartoon "Gargantua," in which he depicted King Louis-Philippe as a bloated Rabelaisian monster. In 1834 he landed in more trouble after another of his famous political cartoons, "Le Ventre Législatif" ("The Legislative Belly"), in which he castigated the entire legislative branch as one monstrous belly gobbling up the wealth of the nation.

After 1835—the year in which a stern new censorship law was passed in France—Daumier thought it prudent to abandon the more blatant political themes, and he decided to launch a more general attack on the values bred by the capitalist economic system. During that time he produced his most famous series of cartoons—*Les Bons Bourgeois* ("Solid Citizens"), *Les Moeurs Conjugales* ("Matrimonial Mores"), *Philanthropes du Jour* ("Philanthropists of the Day"), *Les Plus Beaux Jours de la Vie* ("The Best Years of Life") and others—in which he mercilessly satirized every aspect and representative of middle-class society: doctors, lawyers, judges, the army, the banks, the stock exchange—the entire structure of bourgeois life.

Daumier's wit found its best expression in two series: *Caricaturana* (1836-38), in which he depicted with obvious relish all types of fakes and charlatans—quack doctors, corrupt politicians, "bought" judges, crooked stock promoters, pandering journalists, phony evangelists and degenerate nobles; and *Robert Macaire* (from a stage character created by actor-playwright Frédérick Lemaître), a series of over one hundred cartoons detailing the imaginative swindles perpetrated by a suave and dexterous con man.

After 1850 Daumier turned more and more to painting (his masterpiece in this field is considered to be *The Third-Class Carriage*), with only occasional forays into cartooning. Toward the end of the Second Empire, he violently attacked the regime of Napoleon III, and in 1871 he ardently supported the Paris Commune. Daumier died in obscurity on February 11, 1879.

Daumier's fame grew slowly after his death. In 1893 Henry James established Daumier's preeminent position in modern art in his famous essay "Daumier, Caricaturist." A general reevaluation followed; from relative obscurity during his lifetime, Daumier now rests on a lofty pedestal as the patron saint of cartooning. Best of all, Daumier's incomparable books of cartoons have been kept in print continuously over the last 70 years, not only in his native France, but in the United States and many other countries as well.

M.H.

DAVENPORT, HOMER CALVIN (1867-1912) American cartoonist born near Silverton, Oregon, on March 8, 1867. Homer Davenport had no art training and precious little general education; he worked in his youth as a jockey, railroad fireman and circus clown. He claimed that admiration for Thomas Nast's cartoons led him to secure a job with the *Portland Oregonian*, where his abysmal artistic performance sent him on his way in short order. He had similar experiences at the *San Francisco Chronicle* and several newspapers in Chicago, but his efforts attracted the attention of William Randolph Hearst, who sensed a special quality in Davenport's crude cartoons hand offered him a position with the *San Francisco Examiner* in 1892.

What Davenport lacked in draftsmanship he made up for with conceptual force, whether the political venom was his own or was supplied by a Hearst staffer. His cartoons attacking political bossism soon drew statewide attention, and when Hearst moved to New York in 1895 to take over the *Journal*, he brought Davenport along as a linchpin in his drive to agitate

Honoré Daumier, caricature of Victor Hugo.

cluding the breeding of the only (at that time) pure white Arabian horses in America, a gift of the sultan of Turkey, who made Davenport the Desert Brother of Akmut Haffez, the Great Bedouin. Davenport was the author of *Cartoons by Homer C. Davenport, The Bell of Silverton and Other Short Stories of Oregon* and *The Dollar or the Man?* He died at his home in Morris Plains, New Jersey, on May 2, 1912.

If Nast was a bit stiff as a draftsman, Davenport was a puzzle: anatomy, composition and rendering were unknown elements in his artistic universe. The figures in his drawings are awkward—arms fall to different lengths, heads fit on necks strangely—and backgrounds scribble off into confusion. But Davenport was never embarrassed. Every cartoon was a devastating statement, an attack that riveted attention so forcibly as to render criticism of the drawing superfluous—a rare feat for a bad artist. In spite of his shortcomings as an artist (in justice, it must be said that some of his cartoons were handsome, or at least adequate), Davenport stands as the best proof that artistic competence is but one component of the political cartoonist, and not necessarily the most important.

R.M.

DAY, CHAUNCEY ADDISON (1907-   ) American cartoonist born in Chatham, New Jersey, on April 6, 1907. Chauncey ("Chon") Day attended Manlius Military School from 1923 to 1926 and then Lehigh Uni-

Wall Street's New Guardian

Homer Davenport, 1898.

the city. Less than a decade later, Davenport drew a series of cartoons unrivaled in savagery and effectiveness since the days of Nast in his prime and *Puck's* Blaine series. Hearst published the cartoons in an extremely large format, and Davenport's work is perhaps the closest a major American cartoonist has come to pure propagandizing and cynical rejection of reasoned advocacy. In 1896 he was paid to bludgeon McKinley; his portrayals of the candidate and his manager, Mark Hanna, as slave-driving murderers competed in irresponsibility with Republican cartoons of William Jennings Bryan as a crazed anarchist—but they did attract attention to the fledgling *Journal*, which was all they were really supposed to do. Hanna's exaggerated corpulence and his suit festooned with dollar signs ("Dollar Mark" was his nickname) were Davenport's contribution to cartoon iconography. Other targets included Republican boss Tom Platt of New York, who tried in vain to pass an anti-cartoon bill (such efforts were not unknown at the turn of the century) because of Davenport's barbs.

Davenport admired Theodore Roosevelt, and in 1904 the cartoonist switched to the Republican *New York Mail*, where he drew his most famous cartoon, "He's Good Enough for Me," Uncle Sam's endorsement of the Rough Rider for reelection. It was widely reprinted as a campaign document. As an advocate, however, Davenport lost his force. He drew less often after 1904, though he returned to the pro-Roosevelt cause during the Bull Moose campaign, just before his death. He turned increasingly to private pursuits, in-

"Well, the curse is starting to work.
My wife is on her way out here."

Chon Day. © *True.*

versity. His father was a lawyer who felt Chon should become a civil engineer, not a cartoonist. At Lehigh he drew humorous spot art for the *Burr*, the university's humor magazine. As his father wouldn't finance art school, Chon Day was on his own and held a variety of jobs. In 1928 he sold cars, such long-extinct makes as the Hudson and the Essex. He was also a dispatcher for Western Union.

He eventually attended the Art Students League in New York City and there studied under Boardman Robinson and George Bridgman. Day felt he learned quite a bit from Bridgman, but he left the school the day Bridgman took a drawing Day had worked on for two weeks, erased it and sketched in how he said it should look. Day promptly erased Bridgman's drawing and walked out of the class. He began publishing cartoons in 1929, with sales to the *New Yorker*, *Film Fun*, *Ballyhoo*, *Slapstick* and *Hooey*.

Chon Day's distinctive style gives a sense of open space to his cartoons, which are drawn in a thin, shaky line. He draws with a variety of fountain pens, and his line style began during World War II, when paper was scarce and he got an excellent buy on some thin charcoal paper with a rough finish. Once his initial supply was gone he found #1025 paper by Bee Paper Company the most compatible with his needs. Editors seemed to love the shaky look, and Day stayed with it and refined it. Most of his cartoons have some benday or wash tone to round out the figures or cast a shadow. He has never felt comfortable with strong, heavily inked black areas in his compositions.

Chon Day's cartoons have been published by nearly every major national magazine, from the *New Yorker*, *Saturday Evening Post* and *Look* to *Playboy*. His most famous cartoon feature, *Brother Sebastian*, was created at the request of Gurney Williams when the renowned cartoon editor left *Collier's* to join *Look*. Williams was taking Larry Reynolds's panel *Butch* with him to *Look* and wanted a companion piece. As *Butch* featured two bumbling robbers, a gentle little monk was the perfect foil.

Chon Day's ability to sell the gag with his simple, ordered and well-designed cartoons and the year-in-year-out consistency of his humor have earned him a spot at the pinnacle of the magazine cartoon field. In 1956, 1962 and 1971 he won the National Cartoonists Society's award for Best Magazine Cartoonist.

B.C.

DAY, CHON
See Day, Chauncey Addison.

DAY, ROBERT JAMES (1900-) American cartoonist born in San Bernardino, California, on September 25, 1900. Robert Day studied at the Otis Art Institute in Los Angeles between 1919 and 1927, when he was also employed in the art department of the *Los Angeles Times*. In 1927 he moved to the *Los Angeles Examiner*, and in 1930 he came east to New York, where he joined the staff of the *Herald-Tribune*. As a cartoonist he has been widely represented since the early 1930s in the *New Yorker*, the *Saturday Evening Post*, *Punch*, *Look*, *Saturday Review*, *This Week* and *Sports Illustrated*, among others. A prolific producer of comic art, he seems less wedded to a particular style than many of his colleagues, using a quick ink line here, a highly detailed wash there. One of his early *New Yorker* pieces—which has become something of a classic because of the gag, Eleanor Roosevelt visiting a coal mine—illustrates Day's mastery. One would be hard put to find a more genuinely gloomy setting—the darkened pit of a mine feebly illuminated by head lamps—applied to the purposes of humor.

At his best Day is a very funny man capable of sharp asides about a world he has seen change a great deal since his entry into it at the turn of the century. On the effects of television, for example: a man changing a flat tire in a driving rainstorm explains to his two small children inside the car, "Don't you

"I'll look it up to be sure,
but I'm positive you're not in our free-delivery area."

Robert Day. © *Collier's.*

understand? This is *life*, this is what is happening. We can't switch to another channel." If he has a flaw, it lies in his very productivity. He is certainly one of the most widely published cartoon artists of the century, and it is not surprising that he should occasionally strike a flat note. For the most part, however, his consistency is admirable. Along with Steig, he was the most frequently reproduced artist in the *New Yorker*'s 50th anniversary album, and his cartoons have been exhibited in shows throughout the United States and Europe.

Books: *All Out for the Sack Race* (1945); *We Shook the Family Tree* (1946); *Fun Fare* (1949); *Lower Prices Are Coming* (1950); *Stories I Like to Tell* (1952) and *Little Willie* (1953) by Arthur Godfrey; *Any Old Place with You* (1958); *Mad World of Bridge* (1960); *Over the Fence Is Out* (1961); *What Every Bachelor Knows* (1961); *I've Only Got Two Hands and I'm Busy Wringing Them* (1966); and *Rome Wasn't Burnt in a Day* (1972).

R.C.

The Lickin'

"The Days of Real Sport." © New York Tribune.

DAYS OF REAL SPORT, THE (U.S.) A nostalgia-packed, sentiment-filled panel, *The Days of Real Sport* was Clare Briggs's recollection of and paean to his own small-town boyhood. It is difficult to ascertain the exact date of the feature's start, but it seems to have originated in the *New York Tribune* in the early 1910s.

The Days of Real Sport consisted of small vignettes with a constantly expanding cast of characters, the most prominent being Skinnay, who was never seen but whose presence was always made known by some of the other kids ("Oh, Skin-nay!"). Thus Briggs lovingly recalled the small joys and vicissitudes of a young boy growing up, from the paternal licking to the first pair of long pants ("Are they your pa's, ha, ha?"). The panel characters (boys were primarily featured) were depicted as high-spirited and prank-loving but never mean or vicious; there was not one juvenile delinquent in the lot. Each panel had a descriptive subtitle ("The Talking Machine," "The Party," "The Giant Cracker," "Fifteen Years Old," etc.) which immediately set the mood of the piece.

The Days of Real Sport was one of Briggs's most celebrated panels and continued to be reprinted in newspa-

pers around the country long after its creator's death in 1930.

M.H.

DEAN, ABNER
See Epstein, Abner.

DEBUCOURT, PHILIBERT-LOUIS (1755-1832) French caricaturist and engraver born in Paris, France, on February 13, 1755. After studying art with the renowned master Joseph-Marie Vien, Philibert Debucourt was admitted to the Academy in 1782. He first practiced oil painting but then, starting in 1785, took up watercoloring and especially etching.

Debucourt was greatly influenced by William Hogarth's engravings, and he was one of the first artists to introduce the tradition of English caricature and cartooning to the Continent. He often depicted the fads and manias of his times, and since he lived through one of the most troubled periods in French history, his drawings and etchings carry a historic importance at least equal to their artistic quality. He spurned Hogarth's more vulgar proclivities, always preferring the velvet glove of irony to the mailed fist of caricature. Emmanuel Bénézit characterized him as "the engraver of French elegance," but he could also be biting and vigorous, as in his depictions of aristocratic decadence (*La Manie de la Danse* and *La Promenade Publique*) and later of bourgeois smugness. Debucourt's position as one of the founding fathers of French cartooning was later reinforced when he made a number of engravings from sketches by his contemporary Carle Vernet. So great was his fame in these years that his color etchings (described as belonging to "the grotesque genre") were usually sold with an English as well as a French text.

Debucourt died at his country home in Belleville (then a village outside Paris, later incorporated into the city) on September 22, 1832.

M.H.

DECAMPS, ALEXANDRE-GABRIEL (1803-1860) French cartoonist and painter born in Paris, France, on March 3, 1803. Alexandre Decamps studied art with Abel de Pujol, and early in life he developed a conviction that art should serve socially useful causes. He started his cartooning career on the Parisian magazines of his time and soon became famous for his biting political caricatures of the leaders of the day. His targets included King Charles X, whom he satirized in two famous and savage cartoons, "Charles X, the Pious Monarch" and "The Year of Grace 1830, Fifth of the Glorious Reign," that depicted the king as a decadent, ridiculous and senile figure soon to be engulfed by the winds of revolution.

In the late 1830s Decamps abandoned cartooning in favor of oil painting. He did a number of Oriental compositions which he based on his two-year stay in Turkey in 1827-28, as well as a number of socially conscious paintings (*The Beggars*, which he completed in 1845, is probably his most significant work in this genre).

Alexandre Decamps died in Fontainebleau, near Paris, on August 22, 1860.

M.H.

Philibert Debucourt, "The Public Promenade," 1792.

DECKER, RICHARD (1907-   ) American cartoonist born in Philadelphia, Pennsylvania, in 1907. Richard Decker studied at the School of Industrial Design in Philadel-

Charles X as "le pieu monarque."
Alexandre Decamps, 1830.

phia. His work first began appearing in the *New Yorker* in the early 1930s, when he was also a frequent contributor to *Collier's, Life* and the *Saturday Evening Post*. Using watercolors, oils and woodblock prints, Decker specialized in humorous art as opposed to caricature. This choice of media and approach places him in the tradition of great political cartoonists like Nast and Daumier and links him with his older *New Yorker* colleague Garrett Price rather than with the modern gagsters. Yet he remained primarily a gag cartoonist, and unlike his contemporaries Constantin Alajalov and Norman Rockwell, he stuck to a format employing art and caption in a mutually reinforcing context. Occasionally he did simple line drawings in ink, but for the most part he was a painter who thought like a cartoonist.

And a rather funny cartoonist, at that. One especially fine example of Decker's work is a church scene featuring two anything but delicate-looking workers and a priest. The picture reveals that one of the workers has just dropped a hammer from his perch up on a ladder and bounced it off his colleague's head. While the priest looks benevolently on, the injured party remonstrates with his fellow in a most unlikely way: "Gee, Jack! That was very careless of you." This sort of symbiosis between art and humor is characteristic of Decker's output and exemplifies his technique.

Decker's work has been exhibited at the New York Illustrators Show, the Philadelphia Art Alliance, the Philadelphia Academy of Fine Arts and the Salon of American Humorists in New York. Decker's cartoons appeared regularly in the *New Yorker* into the mid-1950s, after which his output somewhat declined.

R.C.

DEDINI, ELDON LAWRENCE (1921-   ) American cartoonist born in King City, California, on June 29, 1921. Eldon Dedini grew up in the Salinas Valley region and

Gene Deitch, "Where the Wild Things Are," from Maurice Sendak's story. © Weston Woods.

has lived in California throughout his career, though his submissions have mainly been to magazines with editorial offices in the East. His cartoons have been a most enjoyable feature of national magazines since 1940, when he sold his first to *Esquire*.

Dedini decided to become a cartoonist while in high school. He learned how to submit roughs to magazines and gleaned the names of cartoon editors from a how-to book by Lawrence Lariar. Encouraged by an art teacher at Salinas Junior College, Dedini submitted samples and for experience offered to work for free on the *Salinas Index-Journal* and the *Salinas Morning Post*. With the teacher's help Dedini earned college credits for his editorial cartoons.

In 1942 he won a scholarship to Chouinard Art Institute in Los Angeles, but he deliberately went to school only four days a week so he could continue to freelance magazine cartoons. From 1944 to 1946 he did storyboards for the Disney studio. One day at Disney he received a call from Dave Smart, editor at *Esquire*, who offered to double Dedini's salary if he would work exclusively for *Esquire* as a gag man and featured cartoonist. This arrangement lasted from 1946 to 1950. However, he continued to sell to *Esquire* into the 1960s.

In 1950 he began selling to the *New Yorker*, and in 1960 Hugh Hefner began to publish Dedini cartoons in *Playboy*. The full-page color Dedini cartoon in a wet watercolor style has become a regular *Playboy* feature. Rubenesque nymphs and licentious satyrs, themes Dedini first did for *New Yorker* cartoons, have subsequently blossomed to their full potential in *Playboy*. In addition, he excels in the humorous treatment of historical period pieces. Social and political comment also surfaces in Dedini's work.

Dedini writes almost all of his own gags, and back in his *Esquire* days he wrote many of the gags for other *Esquire* cartoonists such as Paul Webb, Barbara Shermund and E. Simms Campbell. He acknowledges having been influenced in the development of his style by the watercolors of E. Simms Campbell and the work of Peter Arno and Whitney Darrow, Jr.

Dedini's color cartoons are carefully staged. He calls them "productions." However, simplicity of design and gag, usually arrived at through hard work, are hallmarks of his style. The lush, painterly richness of his color work blends perfectly with the ripeness of the female form he draws for his *Playboy* cartoons. With heavy washes running the full range of tone from light gray to black, Dedini keeps this painterly look in his black-and-white cartoons. No matter what his theme, Dedini's work seeks the good strong laugh, not the chuckle. More often than not, he succeeds.

An anthology of his work, *The Dedini Gallery*, was published in 1961. He is also included in many cartoon anthologies published by *Playboy* and others. In 1958, 1961 and 1964 he was voted Magazine Cartoonist of the Year by the National Cartoonists Society.

B.C.

DEITCH, GENE (1924-) American animator and producer born in Chicago, Illinois, on August 8, 1924. Gene Deitch's father was a salesman who often took his family along on his travels around the country. Deitch was educated mainly in southern California, and with the encouragement of a teacher he made his first animated cartoon at the age of 13. After graduation from high school in 1942, he was drafted into the U.S. Air Force.

Upon his return to civilian life Deitch joined with the original founders of UPA in 1946. He worked as a layout assistant and in-betweener for Bob Cannon on the "Flight Safety" series (for the U.S. Navy) and also assisted on some of the *Fox and Crow* cartoons and the first *Mr. Magoo*. In 1949 Deitch left to join the Jam Handy Organization in Detroit, where he directed a number of industrial and promotional cartoons. Returning to UPA in 1951, he subsequently became the creative director of its New York studio. During his four-year tenure, Deitch directed the celebrated Bert and Harry Piels commercials, as well as many other advertising films; he also wrote and directed the delightful entertainment cartoon *Howdy Doody and His Magic Hat* (1952).

After a short hiatus drawing a comic strip, *Terr'ble Thompson,* for United Feature Syndicate (1955-56), Deitch returned to animation. As the supervising director for Terrytoons, which had just been taken over by CBS, he oversaw the production of *Tom Terrific, Flebus, Clint Clobber* and *Gaston Le Crayon,* among other cartoons. He also directed (with Al Kouzel) the much-acclaimed *The Juggler of Our Lady* (1957).

Deitch's life took a decisive turn in 1959, when he left for Czechoslovakia to supervise Rembrandt Film's animation studio in Prague. There he directed *Samson Snap and Delilah, Anatole* and the Oscar-winning *Munro.* He also later directed many cartoons for the *Tom and Jerry* series (1960-61), the *Popeye* series (1961-62) and the *Krazy Kat* series (1962-63). He further produced a series of cartoons of his own, *Nudnik,* which Paramount released in the United States from 1963 to 1967. In recent years Deitch has been producing the ambitious "Animated Picture Book" project, adapting children's books to the animation medium. So far he has brought to the screen the works of such author-illustrators as Tomi Ungerer (*The Beast of Monsieur Racine, The Three Robbers*), Pat Hutchins (*Changes, Changes* and *Rosie's Walk*), Crockett Johnson (*Harold's Fairy Tale, A Picture for Harold's Room*), Gail Haley (*A Story–A Story*) and Maurice Sendak (*Where the Wild Things Are*). His latest entries in the series are *Strega Nonna* and *Smile for Auntie* (both 1978).

Deitch's cartoon work has been much honored over the years. His cartoons have earned one Academy Award and five nominations, the New York Art Directors Club gold medal and many international awards. As a bridge between East and West he is also regarded as a symbol of the universality of the animated cartoon. Gene Deitch's two sons, Kim and Simon, are also cartoonists.

M.H.

DELANNOY, ARISTIDE (1874-1911) French cartoonist born in Béthune, in northern France, in 1874. After studies at the Paris Ecole des Beaux-Arts, Aristide Delannoy started on a career as a socially conscious painter around the turn of the century. His stark, soot-filled landscapes and pictures of begrimed miners were derived from the realistic school of Gustave Courbet. At the same time, his cartoons were published in the leading humor and satire magazines of the day, including *Le Rire, La Guerre Sociale, Les Hommes du Jour* and especially *L'Assiette au Beurre*, where he first appeared in 1901.

Delannoy's cartoons were, like his paintings, strongly tinged with social protest; some of his topics included child labor, police corruption and official malfeasance. In 1908 he was sentenced to one year in prison and a heavy fine for "defamation of the honor of the military." It has been said that Delannoy's imprisonment eventually led to his death in 1911, at the age of 37.

Delannoy drew in a heavy, dark style especially suited to the gloom expressed by his captions; his emaciated, empty-eyed victims and orphans bear a strong similarity to the characters later depicted by Käthe Kollwitz.

M.H.

DEL RÍO, EDUARDO (1934-   ) Mexican cartoonist born in Zamora, Michoacan, on June 20, 1934. Born to a poor family, Eduardo del Río went to work at the age of

"Army service really changes a man; since I'm back, the only thing I care about is cockfights!"

Aristide Delannoy, 1903.

Eduardo Del Río ("Rius"). © Ja-Ja.

15. He worked as an office boy, bookstore employee, door-to-door salesperson and mortician's assistant. In 1965 he made his debut as a professional cartoonist on the humor magazine *Ja-Ja*. Since that time Eduardo del Río (who signs "Ríus") has worked for most of the leading magazines and newspapers in Mexico, including *La Prensa, Novedades, Diario de México, Siempre, Politica, La Nacion* and dozens of others.

Ríus has also edited a number of humor publications, such as *La Gallina, Marca Diablo, El Mitote Illustrado* and *La Garapata*. It has been with his politically committed and socially conscious comic books, however, that Ríus has finally achieved widespread popularity. These include *Los Supermachos* ("The Supermales"), created in 1965, and *Los Agachados* ("The Stooped Ones"), which has earned Ríus fame and fortune since its inception in 1968.

The most famous political cartoonist in his country, Ríus has tackled national and international problems—government repression, guerrilla warfare, world hunger, corruption and inflation—in a straightforward, almost simplistic way. His leftist convictions strongly permeate all his works, even his comic books. He has received many awards, including first prize at the 1968 Montreal Cartoon Show. Ríus has had several collections of his cartoons published in book form, *Cuba para Principantes* ("Cuba for Beginners"), *La Jóven Alemania* ("Young Germany") and *Pequeño Ríus Illustrado* ("Little Ríus Illustrated") being the most notable.

M.H.

DE MARIA, GUIDO (1932-   ) Italian cartoonist and animator born in Lama Mocogno, Italy, on December 20, 1932. After graduation from high school, Guido

Michel Demers. © L'Aurore.

De Maria attended the University of Bologna but soon abandoned his studies to devote himself to cartooning. In the 1950s he became one of the most prolific of Italian cartoonists, and his work appeared in the major Italian newspapers and magazines.

In 1960 De Maria went into advertising and later founded a production studio, Vimderfilm, which brought out a great number of short subjects, in live action as well as in animation. Among his entertainment cartoons was *Salomone, il Pirata Pacioccone* ("Solomon, the Chubby Pirate"), which can still be seen on Italian television. In 1968 he worked on the movie *Flashback*, and in 1969 he left Vimderfilm and moved to Modena, where he worked for a year with Bignardi's studio.

In 1971 he founded a new studio, Playvision, and with Franco Bonvicini ("Bonvi") created *Nick Carter*, a series especially designed for television. In 1972, again for television, he produced the *Gulp, i Fumetti in TV* program and several specials devoted to the comics. From 1972 to 1976 he produced 25 *Nick Carter* shorts, as well as other shorts featuring famous comic characters, among which *Alan Ford e il Gruppo TNT* ("Alan Ford and the TNT Group") was the most successful. Since March 1977, De Maria has been directing *Supergulp, i Fumetti in TV* ("Supergulp, the Comics on TV"), which is an expanded version of his earlier *Gulp*.

L.S.

DEMERS, MICHEL (1949-   ) Canadian cartoonist born in Quebec City, Canada, on April 20, 1949. After studies in Quebec and Montreal, Michel Demers had his first cartoon published in the French-language weekly *Sept-Jours*; since that time he has been contributing one cartoon to the magazine every week.

Michel Demers is now busily engaged in a promising and prolific professional career. His political and gag cartoons have appeared in such publications as *Forum*, *Perspectives* and the daily *Le Jour*. He has also produced several comic strips, the most notable being *Célestin* for *Le Jour*, but none have proved long-lived.

Michel Demers has been influenced, in his graphic style as well as in his choice of themes, by Tomi Ungerer and Jean-Jacques Sempé: his drawings have a dry, sparse look, while his themes lean heavily toward surrealism, social protest and black humor.

M.H.

DEMOCRITO II
See Cao, José María.

DENI
See Denisov, Viktor Nikolayevich.

DENISOV, VIKTOR NIKOLAYEVICH (1893-1946) Soviet cartoonist and poster designer born in Moscow, Russia, on February 24, 1893. After studying art under the noted teacher Nikolay Ulyanov, Viktor Denisov started his cartooning career in 1913 (under the pseudonym "Deni") with contributions to the magazines *Bich, Satirikon, Sontse Rossii*, etc.

After the outbreak of the Russian Revolution in 1917, Deni turned to social and political cartooning. During the ensuing civil war he also devoted his talents to poster painting, first in Kazan and later in Moscow. In 1921 he became the permanent editorial cartoonist for *Pravda*, and he exerted a tremendous influence on the course of Soviet political cartooning. His style, hard-edged and almost realistic, became the official norm for all aspiring cartoonists of the period in the USSR. In addition to his daily cartoons Deni also designed a number of propaganda posters (those he did during World War II are now highly regarded as among the best efforts in the field).

Deni was made an Honorable Art Worker of the Soviet Federated Socialist Republic in 1932. He died in Moscow on August 3, 1946.

M.H.

DEPOND, MOISE (1917-   ) French cartoonist and animated cartoon director born in western France on October 9, 1917. Moise Depond was taking courses at the Ecole des Beaux-Arts of Tours and also earning a living as a schoolteacher when he saw Saul Steinberg's *All in Line* (1945) and decided to embark on a cartooning career in 1946. Under the pen name "Mose" he has worked mainly for *Paris-Match*.

His drawings, which are more like visual gags, show in a clear, direct and unobstructed style the inescapable absurdity of fate: a man drowning in a puddle or a truck driver crushed to death by a falling rock in a barren desert. Not all his cartoons are so cruel; in one, a cop surreptitiously gives a ten-franc note to a hobo—who is totally flabbergasted.

Mose's drawings have appeared in several albums, among them *Manigances* ("Underhanded Machinations," 1953, with Chaval and François), *Noirs Dessins* ("Black Designs," 1956), *Paris Ma Rue* ("Paris Is My Street," 1964, a 24-page continuous strip) and *Mosaïque* (1971). His artwork has also been exhibited in Prague, Casablanca, Paris and Brussels. In addition to book illustrations (e.g., Swift, Twain, language texts) Mose has created more than fifty animated cartoons, from *Bonjour Paris* for Jean Image (1951-52) to the TV series *Romeo* (1965) to *Animoses* (1973).

P.H.

DES

See Asmussen, Andreas.

DESCLOZEAUX, JEAN-PIERRE (1938-) French cartoonist born near Paris, France, in 1938. After finishing his studies, J.-P. Desclozeaux went to work as a commercial artist and industrial designer. In the early 1960s he started sending cartoons to different publications, and he now appears widely in such magazines as *Paris-Match, Le Nouvel Observateur* and *Elle*, as well as in the yearly cartoon exhibitions he has organized since 1966 in Avignon, in southeastern France.

Desclozeaux's cartoons are often cruel and unyielding, and the artist himself is frequently classified as a "black humorist." Yet he can also be dreamlike and even nostalgic, as in his flippant retelling of fairy tales. His satire is pointed, but it aims more at the human condition than at any political or social aspect of society. There are two sides to Desclozeaux's work: the bitterness of his cartoons of a world gone mad (as in his depiction of office workers imprisoned in cabinet drawers), and the lightheartedness of his drawings of circuses, jugglers and clowns. It is no wonder, then, that an essay discussing his work was titled "Tender and Cruel Desclozeaux."

Desclozeaux's cartoons have been anthologized in a number of books, the latest being *L'Oiseau-Moqueur* ("The Mocking-Bird," 1977).

M.H.

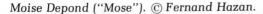

Moise Depond ("Mose"). © Fernand Hazan.

Jean-Pierre Desclozeaux. © Albin Michel.

DESETA, ENRICO (1908-) Italian cartoonist and illustrator born in Catania, Italy, on February 17, 1908. Enrico Deseta's father, a lawyer, moved to Rome with his family when Enrico was still a child. Deseta went to school in Rome, where he developed a talent for drawing; his first drawing was accepted by the satirical weekly *Serenissimo* when he was not yet 15.

In 1930 Deseta joined the staff of *Il Travaso*; in the color pages he drew for this magazine, he already displayed mastery of the humor cartoon with his limpid, wriggly, highly individual line. He reached his height, however, with his collaboration on *Marc' Aurelio*, which began publication in 1938. There he created his famous gallery of neurotic characters, sexually repressed and always on the verge of exploding, drawn with a stylized line that prefigured the work of Johnny Hart or Charles Schulz. Some of these characters have become legendary, such as Bacu the Magician, whose likeness was painted on the fuselages of warplanes, and whose supernatural powers have passed into the Italian language.

In 1937 Deseta formed a small group of Italian cartoonists around the weekly *Argentovivo* in order to compete against the flood of foreign comics. He edited and drew several comic strips for *Argentovivo*, including *Capitan Rosmarino* and *Ludovico*. During the 1940s Deseta contributed short stories to the girls' weekly *La Piccola Italiana*, but his efforts were mainly devoted to the Fascist youth weekly *Il Balilla*, for which he drew cartoons, illustrations and several comic strips; one of these strips, *Re Giorgetto d'Inghilterra* ("King Georgie of England") became famous because of its central character, Ciurcillone (Li'l Churchill), who was a favorite with children. Since this defeated the purpose of making Churchill into a hated symbol, Deseta was reprimanded by his boss.

Deseta pursued his activities regardless of historical circumstances. In 1944, along with Federico Fellini, he founded the Funny Face Shop, where the Allied soldiers who had just liberated Rome could have their caricatures drawn by the two cartoonists against the background of the Colosseum or Saint Peter's Basilica. In recent times Deseta has collaborated on *Clown*, where he drew with particular humor a panel titled *La Ballata del Povero Cittadino* ("The Ballad of the Poor Citizen"). Since the collapse in the 1970s of most of the humor magazines, he has devoted most of his time to designing movie posters.

S.T.

DEVÉRIA, ACHILLE (1800-1857) French cartoonist, book illustrator and lithographer born in Paris, France, on February 6, 1800. In Paris Achille Devéria studied with Girodet and Laffitte. His lithographs (totalling almost 450) of high-society ladies and their coquettish ways and of the most important personalities of the arts express charming wit, good humor and graceful elegance. The most interesting series of women are *Galerie Fashionable*, *Le Goût Nouveau* ("The New Taste") and *Les Heures de la Parisienne* ("The Hours of the Parisian Woman," 1840). His portraits of the high priests of French romanticism (Hugo, Balzac, Liszt, Dumas, Delacroix, etc.) are remarkable for the way they capture the very essence of the artists' characters without the caricatural devices found in Nadar and Gill. Using wood engraving, a technique which had then been repopularized, Devéria also illustrated numerous literary works, among them La Fontaine's *Fables* (1826) and Defoe's *Robinson Crusoe* (1836).

Achille Devéria was assistant curator of the Prints Department of the Imperial Library (now Bibliothèque Nationale) from 1848 to April 1857, when he was promoted to head of the department. He died that same year on December 23.

P.H.

DEVILMAN (Japan) *Devilman* was created by the Japanese comic book artist Gō Nagai at the request of Toei Dōga ("Toei Animation") in 1972. It was unique in that it appeared simultaneously as a comic strip and as an animated television series. It was inspired by the success of a previous work of Nagai's entitled *Maō Dante* ("Dante, Lord of the Devils"), which first appeared in the comic book *Bokura Magazine*. In both formats, *Devilman* was a stunningly exotic work characterized by powerful images and plenty of action. The plot of the comic strip formed the basis for the movie. Akira Fudō, the young hero, learns that the forces of evil as personified by a host of devils are attempting to destroy mankind. The only way he can combat this menace is to become one of them: Akira becomes Devilman and devotes his life to battling hordes of monsters and demons.

The comic strip managed to interweave a bizarre vision of a universe populated by spine-chilling monsters with a fascinating theme of good versus evil. It was graphically violent and at times filled with erotic imagery. The animated version, however, was of necessity aimed at a younger audience, and the plot had to be toned down considerably. At its worst it was a series of endless battles between Devilman, who had seven super-powers, and the innumerable monsters arrayed against him, but the cartoons were in brilliant color (which the comic strip was not), and the images never lost their impact. Nagai relied on illustrated books of flora and fauna as his source of inspiration for the countless monsters he created. Comic relief was provided in the animation by minor characters such as Akira's girl friend's little brother. *Devilman* ran from July 8, 1972, to April 7, 1973, on the NET television network in Japan for 39 episodes. It was produced by Yoshifumi Hatano (who also worked on *Okami Shōnen Ken*, Japan's first animation for television), and the script was written by Masaki Tsuji.

In 1973 Devilman appeared in a full-length animation feature titled *Majinger Z vs. Devilman*, based on a story developed by Nagai and his company, Dynamic Productions. In it Devilman and Majinger Z, another character created by Nagai in his comic strip of the same name (1972), were involved in a series of battles, but the movie lacked the suspense and gripping power of the *Devilman* television series and comic strip. It was produced by Toei Dōga with Junichi Toishi. Koichi Kadota was in charge of animation.

F.S.

DING
See Darling, Jay Norwood.

DINGODOSSIERS, LES (France) In 1965 comic writer René Goscinny and gag cartoonist Marcel Gotlib teamed up to produce a weekly panel series entitled *Les Dingodossiers*, which can be loosely translated as "The Goofy Files." The first installment appeared in the May 27 issue of the comic weekly *Pilote*.

As the title implies, these were freewheeling improvisations on a number of unrelated subjects, sometimes takeoffs on current topics, sometimes mock-serious studies of broad fields of interest, sometimes satires on well-known personalities. The similarities to *MAD* magazine were obvious, even down to the breakdown of the panels and the outrageous, pun-riddled captions. Goscinny and Gotlib attacked with relish such features of modern life as the high school newspaper, transistor radios, television news and Polaroid cameras; they slaughtered with vigor such sacred cows as paid vacations, compulsory education and space exploration; and they demolished with verve a variety of accepted ideas, from the desirability of physical exercise to the culturally enriching qualities of foreign travel (in the last one Goscinny and Gotlib had a field day showing tourists returning home from abroad even more prejudiced and parochial than before they left).

After awhile Goscinny tired of the game, or maybe ran out of ideas, and the series folded on November 30, 1967. Many of the *Dingodossiers* were later collected into two books published by Editions Dargaud in the late 1960s.

M.H.

DINKY DOODLE (U.S.) Dinky Doodle (not to be confused with Terrytoons' later Dinky Duck) arrived on the animation scene in cartoon adventures created by Walter Lantz and produced by the Bray studio from 1924 to 1926.

The *Dinky Doodle* series can be divided into two groups. The first had the title hero, a resourceful little boy, marching bravely into some outlandish adventure or looking for new worlds to conquer ("Dinky Doodle and the Bad Man," "Dinky Doodle in the Army," "Dinky Doodle in the Wild West" and "Dinky Doodle in the Arctic" are good examples of this trend). In the second—and more interesting—group, Dinky confronted some famous personage from legend, folklore or literature. This was the larger category and included such enjoyable little tales as "Pied Piper," "Robinson Crusoe," "Little Red Riding Hood," "The Three Bears" and "Uncle Tom's Cabin." These cartoons proved something of a trend-setter, and the formula was widely imitated in years to come, not only in animated cartoons but in comic strips as well.

All of the *Dinky Doodle* cartoons were written and directed by Walt Lantz, who was then in his twenties, and it can be assumed that the experience thus acquired helped immeasurably when Lantz set up his own animation studio later in the decade.

M.H.

DINOV, TODOR GEORGIEV (1919-   ) Bulgarian animator and filmmaker born in Alexandropolis, Greece, on July 24, 1919. After showing early talent for art and drawing, Todor Dinov attended the Academy of Art in Sofia, Bulgaria, from which he graduated in 1943 with a major in stage design. He became a member of the Bulgarian Communist Party in 1945 and was sent to study animation in the USSR.

After serving his apprenticeship on different phases of animation, Dinov went back to Bulgaria, where he made his first animated film, *Iunak Marko* ("Marko the Hero"), in 1955. He then brought to the screen *The Little Guardian Angel* (1956), from the humor cartoons of Jean Effel, followed by several more pleasantly drawn and competently handled cartoons. Notable among them are *The Fox Outfoxed* and *In Cannibal Country* (both 1958), *Prometheus* and *The Golden Slippers* (both 1959), *Story of a Twig* (1960), *Duo* (1961), the much-praised *The Lightning Rod* (1962), *The Apple* (1963), a rather ponderous fable called *The Daisy* (1965) and the ambitious but disappointing *Exile from Paradise* (1967). In 1970 Dinov tried unsuccessfully to adopt a more modernistic style with the overly trendy *The Artist and the Girl*. Dinov has also co-directed, with Khris Khristov, the feature film *Iconastasis* (1962). He is now involved mainly in live-action films and documentaries, although he directed a cartoon film, *The Drum*, in 1974.

Todor Dinov is without a doubt the best known of Bulgarian animators. He has received a number of prizes and awards and was declared an Honored Artist of the People's Republic of Bulgaria in 1969.

M.H.

DIRKS, GUS (ca. 1879-1903) American cartoonist born in Chicago, Illinois, around 1879. Gus Dirks was the brother of cartoonist Rudolph Dirks, who was two or three years his senior. After moving to New York in 1895 and meeting with success in the cartooning world, Rudy Dirks induced his brother to move east from Chicago. Gus did so—twice, as it turned out, for his first foray yielded few sales to magazine markets. In the late 1890s, however, he hit his stride in the humorous weeklies. In *Judge* particularly he was an instant success; readers could expect at least two Gus Dirks cartoons an issue, many of them half a page, and in color in special and holiday numbers.

In his cartoons, Dirks dealt exclusively with bug and small animal life; he was a leader in that very popular genre of the times. He utilized confident pen strokes and achieved shading effects with short thick-and-thin lines combining for textures and crosshatch patterns.

The ever-alert William Randolph Hearst noted Dirks's immense popularity around the turn of the century and

Snail newsboy: "Extree—Extree! All about Washington crossing the Delaware!"

Gus Dirks, 1901.

Walt Disney. © Walt Disney Productions.

secured the cartoonist's services for his Sunday supplements. For Hearst Dirks drew *Bugville Life*, a collection of panel gags named after a book of drawings published by *Judge*, with verses by R.K. Munkittrick. Tragically, Dirks's life ended in suicide in 1903. The young genius's feature was continued by Paul Bransom, but the charm and inventiveness that could have delighted another generation or two of readers was sadly absent.

R.M.

DISNEY, WALTER ELIAS (1901-1966) American animator, producer and businessman born in Chicago, Illinois, on December 5, 1901. Walt Disney's father kept moving throughout the Midwest, taking his family with him. Young Walt grew up in a variety of places and became accustomed to hard work at an early age. He sought refuge in drawing and at 14 enrolled in an art class at the Kansas City Art Institute. After briefly serving as an ambulance driver in France in World War I, he returned to the United States in 1919.

Disney then sought employment in Kansas City, where he met Ub Iwerks. The two worked together at the Kansas City Film Ad Company and in their spare time produced a series of short animated films for a movie theater, the Newman Laugh-O-Grams. This experience spurred Disney to form his own company to produce animated cartoons. The Laugh-O-Gram Company lasted until 1923, at which time Disney decided to leave for Los Angeles, where more and bigger opportunities abounded. Soon striking a deal with an independent producer, Margaret Winkler, he produced a series called *Alice in Cartoonland*; in the course of producing these cartoons (which ran from 1924 to 1926), he assembled the nucleus of his animation team, including Ub Iwerks, Hugh Harman and Rudolph Ising. In 1927 Disney embarked on a new animated series, *Oswald the Rabbit*, but it was taken away

from him the next year by his scheming distributor, Charles Mintz (who had married Margaret Winkler).

With the help of Iwerks, Disney then created his most famous character, Mickey Mouse, who debuted late in 1928 in the first sound cartoon, "Steamboat Willie." In 1929, following the success of *Mickey Mouse*, Disney released *Skeleton Dance*, the first of his *Silly Symphonies*. In the course of the 1930s more winning characters were added to the Disney menagerie: Goofy, Pluto and the cantankerous Donald Duck. The Disney cartoons enjoyed tremendous popularity, and Walt, with the help of his brother Roy, decided to consolidate his studio's position in the filmmaking world. In addition to his extensive use of song and color, he took the lead in the production of feature-length animated films.

The first feature was *Snow White and the Seven Dwarfs* (1937), and its success encouraged Disney to venture further into feature filmmaking. *Pinocchio* followed in 1940, and *Fantasia* later that year. In the meantime the spreading effects of World War II had drastically reduced the studio's income, and Disney was among the first to produce films for the U.S. government. At the same time he continued to make entertainment cartoons, including the whimsical *Dumbo* (1941), the almost naturalistic *Bambi* (1942) and two package films, *Saludos Amigos* (1943) and *The Three Caballeros* (1945); in a class by itself was *Victory Through Air Power*, a 1943 animated film advocating long-range bombing, based on a book by Major Alexander de Seversky.

After World War II, feature-length animation became the mainstay of Disney's production as shorts were phased out of movie house showings. From 1946 until the time of Disney's death, the studio produced the following cartoon features: *Make Mine Music* (1946), *Song of the South* (part live action, 1946), *Fun and Fancy Free* (package film, 1947), *Melody Time* (part live action, 1948), *Ichabod and Mr. Toad* (1949), *Cinderella* (1950), *Alice in Wonderland* (1951), *Peter Pan* (1953), *Lady and the Tramp* (1955), *Sleeping Beauty* (1959), *101 Dalmatians* (1961) and *The Sword in the Stone* (1963). *The Jungle Book* (1967) was completed after Disney's death.

Starting in the late 1940s Disney diversified into live-action features and documentary films. His *True-Life Adventure* and *People and Places* won a number of Oscars in their category and were widely popular. Among his best feature films, *Treasure Island* (1950), *20,000 Leagues Under the Sea* (1954), *Davy Crockett* (1955), *The Absent Minded Professor* (1961) and *Mary Poppins* (1964) are particularly noteworthy. The studio also produced the popular TV program *Disneyland* (later renamed *Walt Disney Presents*) for ABC, and its successor, *Walt Disney's Wonderful World*, for NBC. These programs have been broadcast every season since 1954. Other Disney TV series include *The Mickey Mouse Club* and *Zorro*. Disney also built the Disneyland amusement park in California in 1955; another park, Disneyworld in Florida, was well on its way to completion when Disney died in St. Joseph's Hospital, directly across from his studio in Burbank, on December 15, 1966. The empire he built endures, as strong as ever.

No man ever dominated his field as Disney dominated animation. His cartoons were the most popular, the most farsighted and the best crafted of any in the 1930s. He monopolized the Academy Award for animated shorts from the creation of the category in 1932 until 1940 (with many more Oscars afterwards). The awards and distinctions bestowed on Disney numbered more than a thousand at the time of his death, and the U.S. Post Office issued a commemorative stamp in his honor. There have been more articles and studies written on Disney than on any other film personality, with the possible exception of Charlie Chaplin. Notable among the full-length books about the man and his career are R.D. Feild's *The Art of Walt Disney* (1942), Richard Schickel's *The Disney Version* (1968) and Christopher Finch's *The Art of Walt Disney* (1975).

M.H.

DISTELI, MARTIN (1802-1844) Swiss cartoonist and illustrator born at Olten, Switzerland, on May 28, 1802. Martin Disteli's father ran a successful cotton-goods factory, and young Martin had the leisure to gather notions of art technique in a dilettantish way while pursuing loftier philosophical studies in various Swiss and German cities. In 1820 he was jailed in Jena for participation in student demonstrations and decorated his cell with clever parodies of ancient Roman legends. Around 1826 he studied art in Munich for awhile, under the guidance of Peter von Cornelius. His world changed in 1829 when his father's business crumbled and the family became part of the dispossessed petty bourgeoisie of their Swiss canton. Disteli's reaction was that of a fighter for human rights.

His artistic skills now became his means of making a living. At first he drew scenes from Swiss history for liberal publishers in Aarau. Fame, but not ease, came from his illustrations of the *Fables* of Abraham Emanuel Fröhlich, etched in a manner influenced by Grandville and other contemporary Frenchmen. In 1836 Disteli became an art instructor at his old secondary school in Solothurn, but his difficult nature led to many conflicts with the authorities, a situation that was echoed in his bumpy career as an army reserve officer. Unhappy in both his marriage and his extramarital affairs, Disteli at times led the life of a true vagrant.

During the 1830s he contributed to various magazines and almanacs. He did political cartoons for J.J. Reithard's *Republikaner-Kalender* in 1834, and between 1831 and 1839 he was regularly represented in the publication *Alpenrosen*. In 1838 he founded the annual with which his name is most closely linked— the *Schweizerischer Bildkalender* (often called *Disteli-Kalender*, a term that was long used as a designation for satirical almanacs in Germany as well as in Switzerland). This liberal organ reviewed the events of the past year from a progressive point of view and aimed at enlightening the common people politically. Disteli's lithographs struck out at local and national authorities, earning him numerous lawsuits and attacks by conservative politicians and churchmen.

In the last five years of his life he worked on illustrations of the Munchausen tales, the Reinecke Fuchs (Roman de Renard) stories and other cycles about humanized insects and beasts. Most of this work was never published because of Disteli's early death (in Solothurn on March 18, 1844), but the highly interesting drawings are preserved in Swiss public collections.

S.A.

DOBBINS, JAMES J. (1924-   ) American political cartoonist born in Woburn, Massachusetts, on August 12, 1924. His education included navy courses at Cornell and a bachelor's degree from the Massachusetts College of Art in 1951. Jim Dobbins's early interest was sports cartooning, and he was influenced by Willard Mullin and Bob Coyne. He began his career on the weekly *Woburn Press* in 1945-46 and then switched to the *Woburn Daily Times* (1947-49). During the presidential campaign of 1952 and into the next year he was engaged by the *Lowell* (Mass.) *Sun*, and he substituted on the *New York Daily News* in 1953 during C.D. Batchelor's vacation. The *Boston Post* had Dobbins from 1954 to 1956, but then he went to the *Traveler* and *Herald-Traveler* until 1972 and to the *Herald-American* until 1977, when he switched to William Loeb's *Manchester* (N.H.) *Union Leader*, one of the nation's prominent right-wing dailies.

Democrat Dobbins is a Boston institution, and his broad, freewheeling cartoons in crayon and brush show much enthusiasm. A collection of his cartoons, *Dobbins's Diary of the New Frontier*, was published after the death of John F. Kennedy. Among a host of awards Dobbins has received are thirteen Freedoms Foundation honor medals (and two grand prizes), three National Safety Council awards and the Christopher Literary Award. He is the father of ten children—five boys and five girls.

R.M.

DOBUZHINSKII, MSTISLAV VALERIANOVICH (1875-1957) Russian cartoonist and graphic artist born in Novgorod, Russia, on August 14, 1875. Mstislav Dobuzhinskii studied art at the St. Petersburg School of Drawing from 1895 to 1897, then in Munich with A. Azbè and S. Hollosy from 1899 to 1901. He started his cartooning career in 1905 with contributions to the antiestablishment magazine *Zhupel* ("The Bogeyman"). His graphic style, heavily influenced by the Jugendstil school, was very distinctive and lent to his cartoons a stark, almost ghostly quality. He also did paintings and designed sets for the theater.

After the Russian Revolution, Dobuzhinskii turned primarily to book illustrations and also taught at the Academy of Art in Petrograd (now Leningrad), starting in 1922. In 1925 he moved to Lithuania and taught at the Kaunas School of Art. At the outbreak of World War II, Dobuzhinskii moved first to London, then emigrated to the United States. He designed sets for numerous Broadway productions and occasionally drew a few cartoons.

Dobuzhinskii died in New York City on November 20, 1957. Despite his self-imposed exile he has not been forgotten in his native land. His works are still being exhibited in several galleries in Leningrad, and a number of articles and monographs on his art and career have recently been published in Moscow.

M.H.

DONAHEY, JAMES HARRISON (1875-1949) American cartoonist born near West Chester, Tuscarawas County, Ohio, on April 8, 1875. J.H. ("Hal") Donahey worked in downstate Ohio as a printer's devil before moving to Cleveland in 1895. He studied drawing and sculpture at the Cleveland School of Art and supported himself by doing little busts of political figures before taking a job as a news sketch artist on the *Cleveland World*. He soon switched to the *Plain Dealer* to do cartoons at $35 a week. His first editorial cartoon appeared in the *Plain Dealer* on January 2, 1900; he subsequently drew a daily cartoon

199

Rocky pushing Romney in N.H.

Jim Dobbins. © Boston American.

until three weeks before his death on June 1, 1949.

Donahey's only major book, *In Egypt*, an illustrated account of his travels to that still-exotic land, was published in 1915. About the same time he did illustrative reporting of the U.S. Senate for *Cartoons* magazine. Donahey's older brother Vic was a U.S. senator and three-time Ohio governor; his younger brother William was a cartoonist on the *Plain Dealer* and the *Chicago Tribune* who created one of the all-time children's classics of text and art, *The Teenie Weenies*.

The bare facts of Donahey's career mask one of the most remarkable bodies of work in cartooning history. J.H. Donahey was one of the greatest—the most talented, prolific and influential—of American native cartoonists. His drawing style, widely copied, was a combination of mature, sophisticated composition and informal, scratchy, homespun lines. He developed a method of tying all the elements in his cartoons together with a handsome crosshatch "cloud" that would float through the drawing. He worked almost exclusively in pen and ink.

Donahey's major contribution to our heritage was not a stylistic one, competent and individual though his drawing was. His genius lay rather in his method of presentation (searingly powerful but never vicious in political cartoons, a mellow nonexaggeration in caricature) and his choice of themes. Only a portion of his output was political. The rest of his panel cartoons were on subjects of home and hearth, farm and suburbia. He caught everyday events and workaday pursuits, seeming to challenge himself by dealing with even the most mundane habits of his Plain Folks characters. But in the end he succeeded in becoming the premier artist-chronicler of American democracy. His glimpses of American life are warm, sympathetic, tender, sometimes gibing, often tinged with pathos. Donahey's portraits of farmers washing up for dinner, middle-class husbands shopping for Christmas presents, little kids crying over the loss of

their dogs, arguably place him ahead of McCutcheon and Briggs in this genre and certainly put him in the front rank of American cartoonists.

Discovering Donahey's lifework is one of the genuine treats awaiting cartoon historians and fans in the future. He never drew outside Cleveland, despite many offers, but his cartoons were reprinted widely; his current obscurity is one of the many ironies of cartooning history. But the body of his work—particularly the homespun material—stands as a textbook example of the genius of the art form of the cartoon: that one man could in such a simple and restricted format completely capture the soul of a people.

R.M.

Donald Duck in "Donald's Dilemma." © Walt Disney Productions.

DONALD DUCK (U.S.) Donald Duck made his debut in a 1934 *Silly Symphony, The Wise Little Hen,* and the first line he uttered was "Who, me? Oh, no! I got a bellyache." His character—cantankerous, ornery and irascible—was established from the first and later developed in such *Mickey Mouse* cartoons as "Orphan's Benefit" and "Mickey's Service Station." The duck's persona owed much to Art Babbit and Dick Huemer, who were responsible for his early incarnation, and to Clarence Nash, who supplied Donald's high-pitched, squawking voice.

Donald came into his own in "The Band Concert" (1935), in which his persistent fife playing constantly disturbs and finally overwhelms Mickey's performance of the *William Tell* Overture. From this point on, Donald was to co-star in most *Mickey Mouse* shorts (often alongside Goofy), contributing much of the slapstick in such classics as "Moose Hunters," "Clock Cleaners" and "Don Donald." The duck's violent and intemperate displays of emotion comically contrasted with Goofy's phlegmatic unconcern and Mickey's stiff-upper-lip determination in these and other cartoons of the period.

By the mid-1930s Donald had risen to unprecedented heights of popularity and was fast eclipsing Mickey as the star of the Walt Disney studios. He made his solo debut in 1937 in "Donald's Ostrich." In 1938 Donald's mischievous nephews, Huey, Dewey and Louie, made their appearance, and many of the subsequent *Donald* shorts revolved around the adversary yet affectionate relationship between the duck and the ducklings. (In addition to the initial "Donald's Nephews," best examples of the trend can be found in "Good Scouts," "Donald's Vacation" and "Fire Chief.")

After the outbreak of World War II Donald, along with other Hollywood stars, was prepared to do his duty for his country, as evidenced by such efforts as "Donald Gets Drafted," "The Vanishing Private" (in which Donald accidentally discovers invisible paint) and, most memorably, "Der Fuehrer's Face," which won a 1942 Academy Award. (Just as notable in this respect is *The Spirit of '43*, a cartoon short made for the Treasury Department and credited with leading millions of Americans to pay their income tax ahead of time.) Donald's most important contribution to U.S. policy came in the "good neighbor" department when the patriotic duck made two well-publicized visits south of the border, first in *Saludos Amigos* (1943), and later in *The Three Caballeros* (1945), where he was teamed with the Brazilian parrot José Carioca and the Mexican rooster Panchito.

After the war Donald retired to a more sedate, middle-class life. In addition to his nephews he found two new adversaries in the persons of the spunky twin chipmunks Chip and Dale ("Chip 'n' Dale," "Trailer Horn," "Up a Tree," etc.). Some of the best cartoons in Donald's later career were directed by Jack Hannah, and their fast pace and inventiveness made them as good as any in the series. Donald was depicted to best advantage in exotic situations, as in "Clown of the Jungle" (where the duck is confronted by the loony araquan bird) and "Frank Duck Brings 'em Back Alive" (in which Donald hunts for wildman Goofy, only to be left stranded in the jungle when Goofy hotfoots it back to civilization in Donald's motorboat).

The *Donald Duck* series came to an end in the late 1950s, only a few short years after *Mickey Mouse.*

"Knock it off, you two . . .
this is no time to settle your differences."

Robert Donovan. © *Leatherneck Magazine.*

Donald can now be seen only in reissues or occasionally on some of the Walt Disney programs on television. During his long career the duck has been featured on every conceivable product, from soap to toy trains. Donald Duck was also portrayed in books, in newspapers (the *Donald Duck* strip started in 1936, first as part of the *Silly Symphonies* feature, then under its own title, and was drawn most memorably by Al Taliaferro), and especially in comic books. Donald's comic book adventures, originated in 1943 under the aegis of Carl Barks, the supreme "duck artist," have contributed in perhaps even greater measure than his screen escapades to the continuing popularity of the silly duck in the silly sailor suit.

M.H.

DONOVAN, ROBERT (1921-   ) American cartoonist born in Buffalo, New York, on August 12, 1921. Bob Donovan, whose father was also a cartoonist, went to St. Monica's Parochial School in Buffalo, where he displayed his early talents lettering and illustrating the school newspaper. After graduation from high school in 1939, he worked in a conservation camp near Binghamton, New York, and later as an assembly worker for General Motors. After the start of World War II, he enlisted in the Marine Corps and served in Guadalcanal, Guam and Okinawa from 1942 to 1945. He later joined the staff of the corps newspaper, *The Leatherneck,* where he met fellow cartoonist Fred Lasswell.

After receiving his discharge, Donovan joined Lasswell as an assistant on the *Barney Google and Snuffy Smith* newspaper strip while freelancing a number of cartoons and panels to various publications. In 1950 he joined the staff of the *Danbury* (Conn.) *News-Times,* where he drew a daily panel called *Felty Fedora* about a meek little hat salesman (1950-54). In 1959 Lasswell encouraged Donovan to create his own strip, and this resulted in *Biddie and Bert,* a feature about a retired couple, which the Hall Syndicate distributed from 1960 into the early 1970s. After the feature was dropped, Donovan returned to freelancing sport and editorial cartoons and assisting on *Snuffy Smith.*

M.H.

DÖRBECK, FRANZ
See Burchard, Franz.

Gustave Doré, "Musical Soirée," 1855.

DORÉ, GUSTAVE (1832-1883) French illustrator, cartoonist and painter born at Strasbourg, France, on January 6, 1832. Gustave Doré came from a wealthy family. At 13 he started to contribute lithographs to newspapers in eastern France. Brought to Charles Philipon's attention, Doré published from 1848 to 1852 a weekly satirical drawing in Philipon's *Le Journal pour Rire*. These drawings, which made gentle fun of French foibles and fashions, were later collected in albums released as *Ces Chinois de Parisiens* ("Those Parisian Characters," 1851), *La Ménagerie Parisienne* ("The Parisian Zoo," 1854) and *Les Différents Publics de Paris* ("The Different Parisian Publics," 1854).

However, it was as a book illustrator that Doré became deservedly famous, starting with *Les Travaux d'Hercule* ("The Labors of Hercules"), which he did when he was 15 years old. Full of verve and irony, the sketches debunk the Hercules myth and already indicate young Gustave's interest in the blacks and whites that became so prevalent in his later works.

In 1854, a turning point in Doré's career and in the history of the comic strip, he published an illustrated version of Rabelais's *Gargantua et Pantagruel* (new edition, 1873) and the *Histoire Pittoresque, Dramatique et Caricaturale de la Sainte Russie*. The first shows the artist's growing delight in the fantastic and menacing world of death and nightmares, probably stemming from his Germanic romantic background; the second is technically a brilliantly executed comic strip that traces the "picturesque, dramatic and caricatural history of Holy Russia," using such devices as white squares of different shapes to reflect uninteresting periods or an enormous black stain to symbolize the reign of Ivan the Terrible.

Of the more than two hundred books he illustrated, the most important and best known are Balzac's *Contes Drolatiques* ("Droll Stories," 1855), Dante's *Inferno* (1861), Cervantes's *Don Quixote* (1863) and the Bible (1866). Most of his illustrations are interpretive and reflect the gloom and horror of his outlook: grotesque and bizarre representations of nature with haunted forests and terrifying storms; an abundance of crows, vultures, wolves, rats and supernatural creatures; dark, gloomy, foreboding medieval towns and streets; men, women and children, tortured, hanged, beheaded.

Gustave Doré died in Paris, a very rich man, on January 23, 1883, leaving behind over ten thousand works.

P.H.

DOSH
See Gardosh, Kariel.

DOTAKON (Japan) *Dotakon* is a humorous work by Hōsuke Fukuchi that began running in the magazine *Manga Sunday* in 1968. It falls into the genre of "salaryman cartoons" because it depicts the everyday life of the typical white-collar worker in Japan. Dotakon, the hero, is the average worker to a tee. He is, in fact, the proverbial cog in the machine, and therein lies the humor of the work. In one classic episode Dotakon, who follows a machinelike pattern in his daily life, arrives at the office at the scheduled time only to discover that the position of his desk has been ever so slightly changed—which, of course, plays havoc with his entire day.

Fukuchi's characters are invariably low-ranking employees who are clumsy, lazy and irresponsible save for their mindless devotion to routine. His drawings depict the frustration and anomie experienced by the mass of employees in a seniority system where there is no danger of being fired, but where there is also little encouragement or recognition of individual achievement. One episode shows workers in an office building exclaiming over the exploits of a young Japanese who sailed solo across the Pacific. In his own little way, Fukuchi's hero tries to match this feat by taking his desk to the top of the office roof and sitting alone.

Hōsuke Fukuchi was born on June 1, 1937, in Gifu Prefecture, Japan. He attended Waseda University, where he was a member of the Waseda Manga Kenkyukai ("Cartoon Study Group") at the same time as Shunji Sonoyama and Sadao Shōji. All three men today do strikingly similar work. Fukuchi's drawings are deceptively simple, to the point of looking as though they could have been drawn by a child. Like Shōji and Sonoyama, he had no formal art training, which contributed to his unique style. His humor at its best is hilarious; at its worst it is banal. He draws in a variety of formats, from single-panel cartoons to five-page comic strips, and his subjects are often both topical and political. In 1970 the best of *Dotakon* was compiled by Chikuma Shōbō into a volume called *Gendai Manga Fukuchi Hōsuke Zenshu* ("Modern Cartoons: The Collected Works of Hōsuke Fukuchi"), which was also released in two single volumes titled *Dotakon* and *Dotakon Koiyatsure* ("Dotakon Lovesick").

F.S.

DOTY, ROY (1922-) American cartoonist born in Chicago, Illinois, on September 10, 1922. Roy Doty was taken by his parents to Columbus, Ohio, where he grew up and went to school. Drafted in 1942, he worked as an artist on different army projects, and following his honorable discharge in 1946, he began freelancing cartoons in New York City. Soon Doty's work was appearing in all the major publications, from the *Saturday Evening Post* to *Look* and *Collier's*. In the 1950s Doty worked on many advertising campaigns and illustrated a number of books and magazine stories.

In 1968 Doty was asked to produce a Sunday newspaper version of the then-popular *Laugh-In* television show. Working feverishly, he designed a graphic counterpart to the TV program that was as funny as anything on the show. His gags for such subfeatures as "Mod Mod World," "Sock It to Me Time" and "Ask Gran Flanders" were hilarious. Unfortunately *Laugh-In* went off the air a few years later, and Doty's panel expired in 1971.

Since the demise of *Laugh-In* Doty has resumed his work for magazines, trade journals and corporations such as Mobil Oil. He is one of the most prolific cartoonists around today, and his style, deceptively simple and easy, commands much respect in the profession.

M.H.

DOVNIKOVIĆ, BORIVOJ (1930-) Yugoslav cartoonist and animator born in Osijek, Yugoslavia, in 1930. After studies in his hometown and in Belgrade, Borivoj Dovniković enrolled at the Art Academy in Zagreb in 1949. The following year he began contributing cartoons to the humor magazine *Kerempuh* and sold a number of comic strips to publications such as *Jez*, *Plavi Vjesnik* and *Glas Slavonije* (for Dovniković's career in the comics see *The World Encyclopedia of Comics*, Chelsea House, 1976).

Dovniković went into animation in the early 1950s as an assistant animator for Duga Film; there he worked notably on *The Big Meeting* (1951), *The Gay Experience* and *The Goal* (both 1952). When Duga Film closed down in 1952, he went back to drawing gag cartoons and comic strips, also continuing to do advertising cartoons. When his unit was absorbed into Zagreb Film, he returned to entertainment animation and was head animator on *The Little Train* (1959) and on a number of *Slucaj. . .* and *Inspektor Masku* series cartoons.

Dovniković made his directorial debut on the *Slucaj. . .* cartoons in 1961. The same year he also directed *Lutkića* ("The Doll"), followed by *Olé Torero!* in 1962. Recognition came to Dovniković with the 1964 *Bez Naslova* ("Without Title"), a witty cartoon in which words spell out the predicament of a meek little Everyman. More inspired cartoons followed: *Ceremony* and

Scientific Interview

Dan Dowling. © New York Herald-Tribune.

The Story of Fashion (both 1965), *Curiosity* (1966), *Krek* (1967), *The Strange Bird* (1969) and *The Flower Lovers* (1970).

Unlike many Zagreb cartoonists whose creativity has faltered in the last decade, Dovniković remains prolific and inventive. The 1971 *Maneuvers* was a little masterpiece of sardonic humor, and the 1973 *Second-Class Passenger* proved that the artist had lost nothing of his keen sense of observation and his sensitivity to the little ironies of life. In 1975 he realized a series of eight television cartoons to teach the Croat language; his latest cartoon, *Walking School*, came out in 1978.

Though he started later than some of his colleagues, Dovniković soon established himself as one of the masters of the "Zagreb school" of animation. His style is more subtle, less flamboyant than, say, that of Vukotić, and he is thus less well known in the West. But as Ronald Holloway observed in his study *Z Is for Zagreb* (1972), Dovniković's "humor is mixed with a fine sense of psychology and keen observation of the human species."

M.H.

DOWLING, DANIEL B. (1906-) American political cartoonist born in O'Neil, Nebraska, on November 16, 1906. Dan Dowling was raised in Iowa, where he daily saw the cartoons of Jay Norwood ("Ding") Darling, who started cartooning the year of Dowling's birth and influenced the style of the younger cartoonist immeasurably. (Carey Orr was another influence, but one that must be called ideological and conceptual.)

Dowling studied at the University of California at Berkeley and at the Chicago Academy of Fine Arts before getting a job as a police reporter for a Chicago newspaper. From 1940 to 1942 he was editorial cartoonist for the *Omaha World-Herald*, a job interrupted by World War II. A brief return to Omaha preceded an

Borivoj Dovniković, "Maneuvers." © Zagreb Film.

offer from the *New York Herald-Tribune*. His work was patently derivative of Darling's, and the paper's editor, Geoffrey Parsons, sought out Dowling precisely because Ding, star of the *Trib*'s stable, was nearing retirement age. Dowling remained with the New York paper—syndicated by the *Tribune* and its successor agency, Publishers-Hall Syndicate—until 1965, when he switched to the *Kansas City Star*. He cartooned there until his retirement in 1973.

Dowling, a Republican, won several awards during the course of his career, the major ones being the 1960 Sigma Delta Chi and Freedoms Foundation citations. He was the first president of the Association of American Editorial Cartoonists. Besides the similarity to Darling (in style and even in name!), Dowling's trademark was the high dose of humor injected in each cartoon; exaggeration figured prominently in his pen-brush-crayon and benday cartoons.

R.M.

DOYLE, RICHARD (1824-1883) British cartoonist born in 1824. Richard Doyle, the cartoonist who created the classic cover of *Punch* which graced that weekly magazine from 1849 to 1956—a world's record run—was the son of artist John Doyle, who drew cartoons under the signature "H.B." John Doyle encouraged artistic expression in his large family—all seven children had to participate in a weekly Sunday-morning "salon." "Dickie's" first published work was a burlesque of the Eglinton Tournament, and its publisher, W. Fores of Piccadilly, commissioned him to execute a series of color designs for envelopes (1840). He illustrated his first book, *The Fortunes of Hector O'Halloran*, in 1842, and the following year, at age 18, he joined *Punch*. In March 1849 the first of his famous series *Ye Manners and Customs of Ye Englyshe* appeared, and this led to his experiments in the serial strip form. *The Pleasure Trips of Brown, Jones and Robinson*, Part One ("The Visit to Epsom") appeared in *Punch* on July 6, 1850, and led to a long series of adventures in which Doyle's heroes took

Richard Doyle, design for the cover of "Punch."

Nedeljko Dragić, "Diary." © Zagreb Film.

the Grand Tour of Europe. Unhappily, his excellent association with *Punch* ended abruptly with an argument arising from that paper's antipapal attitude. Doyle resigned, taking *Brown, Jones and Robinson* with him. He continued to do more book illustration but died of a stroke on December 11, 1883.

Books: *The Eglinton Tournament* (1840); *Jack the Giant Killer* (1842); *The Fairy Ring* (1846); *Rejected Cartoons* (1848); *Fairy Tales from All Nations* (1849); *Book of Ballads* (1849); *Pip's Diary* (1849); *An Overland Journey to the Great Exhibition* (1851); *The Newcomes* (1854); *The Foreign Tour of Brown, Jones and Robinson* (1854); *The Juvenile Calendar* (1855); *Merry Pictures* (1857); *The Scouring of the White House* (1859); *A Bird's Eye View of Society* (1864); *An Old Fairy Tale* (1865); *Fairy Tales* (1868); *The Visiting Justices* (1868); *Puck on Pegasus* (1869); *Christmas Books* (1869); *In Fairyland* (1870); *Piccadilly* (1870); *Snow White and Rosy Red* (1871); *Fortune's Favourite* (1871); *The Enchanted Crow* (1871); *Feast of the Dwarfs* (1871); *Benjamin Disraeli* (1878); *Princess Nobody* (1884); *King of the Golden River* (1884); *A Journal Kept in 1840* (1885); *Comic Histories* (1885); *Scenes from English History* (1886); *Home for the Holidays* (1887); *Early Writings of Thackeray* (1888); *The Fairy Book* (1890); *The Queen and Mr. Punch* (1897); *Sad Story of a Pig* (1901); *Mrs. Caudle's Curtain Lectures* (1902); *The Enchanted Doll* (1903); *Humorous Masterpieces* (1905); and *God's Englishmen* (1948).

D.G.

DRAGIĆ, NEDELJKO (1936-   ) Yugoslav cartoonist born in Paklenića, Yugoslavia, in 1936. Nedeljko Dragić studied law in Zagreb, but his love of drawing led him to abandon his studies and devote himself to cartooning. As early as 1953 he had contributed numerous cartoons to Yugoslav publications and had gained a modest reputation as the creator of several "anti-comic strips." In 1964 a collection of his cartoons, *Alphabet for Illiterates*, was published in Belgrade.

It was, however, as an animator that Dragić made his mark. In 1961 he joined Zagreb Studio as a designer on such productions as *The Dreamer*, *Cupid* and *Rivals*. He was also one of the directors on the *Inspector Mask* series (1962). After a brief hiatus he directed his first independent cartoon, *Elegy* (1965), which he adapted from his newspaper cartoons. There followed the much-awarded *Tamer of Wild Horses*

(1966), with which Dragić gained international recognition. Two more cartoons of the period, the ambiguous *Diogenes Perhaps* (1967) and the lyrical *Passing Days* (1969), definitively established him as one of the most innovative and creative talents in animation. Dragić, through his two short, ironical works *Per Aspera and Astra* and *Striptiz* (both 1969), was also responsible for the trend toward the so-called minicartoons.

In recent years Dragić has again been a prime mover in the animation field, scripting, designing and directing many award-winning films. Two of the more notable are *Tup Tup* (1972), which won the Melbourne Prize in 1973 and was nominated for an Academy Award, and especially *Diary* (1973). An overwhelming stream of images, both figurative and abstract, *Diary* was described by its creator as "an attempt to animate at 24 frames per second the inexplicable in man." Dragić's most impressive effort to date, it won first prize at the 1974 Zagreb Film Festival.

M.H.

DREAMY DUD (U.S.) It is reported that Wallace Carlson, after one full year of dogged and solitary effort, brought out a five-minute animated short that so impressed Essanay Studios that they commissioned him to direct a cartoon series for them. That series became *Dreamy Dud*, and the first entry, "Dreamy Dud Lost in the Jungle," was released in June 1915. The series lasted only a year, and Carlson abandoned *Dreamy Dud* in 1916.

Like J.R. Bray's early creation *Colonel Heezaliar*, Carlson's *Dreamy Dud* was built around the tall tale; as his name implies, however, Carlson's titular hero was not a boastful curmudgeon but rather a daydreaming urchin whose imaginary feats of valor and flights of fancy were born out of boredom and loneliness. "Dreamy Dud in Love" is typical in this respect; it shows the little character projecting himself into all kinds of heroic situations in order to win the affections of the haughty girl who spurns him.

Carlson directed more than a score of *Dreamy Dud* cartoons, sending his hero, along with his loyal dog Wag, into wilder and wilder imaginings as the series rolled on. "He Goes Bear Hunting" is a rather conventional hunting story, but "Dreamy Dud Lost at Sea" and especially "Dreamy Dud in King Koo Koo's Kingdom" are little gems of fantasy, inventiveness and humor that cry out to be rediscovered. "Dreamy Dud Sees Charlie Chaplin" perhaps epitomizes the series as the ragamuffin dreams that he finds a dime so he can watch a Charlie Chaplin movie.

M.H.

DROOPY (U.S.) The dog Droopy, the most popular character created by Tex Avery during his tenure at MGM, made his first appearance in a 1943 cartoon entitled "Dumb-Hounded," in which the unflappable police dog thwarted all attempts at escape by a shaggy wolf.

The pattern was repeated in a number of other cartoons, notably "The Shooting of Dan McGoo" (based on a Robert Service poem), "Northwest Hounded Police" and "Drag-Along Droopy," which pitted the sad-faced little dog against his old adversary, the Wolf (not otherwise named). In the 1949 cartoon "Wags to Riches," Avery introduced a new rival for Droopy, the dumb bulldog Spike, who had first appeared in the

Tom and Jerry cartoons and was later to star in his own series. Spike and Droopy engaged in the most hair-raising competition, from the Canine Olympics ("The Chump Champ") to a circus show ("Dare-Devil Droopy").

After Avery left MGM in 1954, *Droopy* cartoons continued to be produced (often from old drawings stretched to Cinemascope size), but they had become tired and repetitive. When they were discontinued after the studio closed down in 1957, hardly a murmur was heard.

M.H.

DRUCKER, BORIS (1920-) American cartoonist and painter born in Philadelphia, Pennsylvania, on May 22, 1920. Educated in Philadelphia's public schools, Boris Drucker attended the Philadelphia College of Art from 1938 to 1942, graduating with a degree in advertising design. After service in the Army Air Corps (1942-46), he began his career as a freelance artist, selling his first drawing to the *Saturday Evening Post* in 1946. Since that time, his cartoon art has appeared in all the major magazines, including the *New Yorker*, *Punch*, *Ladies' Home Journal*, *Collier's*, *This Week*, *Redbook*, *McCall's*, *Holiday*, *True* and *Playboy*.

As a cartoonist, Drucker works mainly in pen and wash and turns out a variety of drawings, from simple inked outlines of minimal detail to elaborate panels representing more complex ideas. A cartoon in the first category, an ink line sketch, simply shows a man standing before a doctor's desk. Nothing more is necessary to underpin the gag: "You can be glad you're having problems, Harkness. A man without

"Let me know if that falls on you."

Boris Drucker. © *Saturday Evening Post.*

problems is usually dead." In a wash of the second category, the caption—"That's Quiet Quiet Baily, our school librarian"—depends heavily for its humor on the drawing, which shows a small boy addressing his father as the latter turns to regard the devastatingly apparent charms of the young woman he's just walked past. Drucker is also capable of some fine representational art, as with the locker room scene in wash that features a number of battered football players being lectured by a disgruntled coach. Rendered in watercolor, it would make a fine cover for some football-season issue of the New Yorker, so well does it capture the sense of the moment.

In addition to comic art, Drucker has worked widely in advertising art and animation for such accounts as Bell Telephone, Du Pont, the Insurance Company of North America and Atlantic-Richfield. His work has garnered six gold and ten silver medals at the Philadelphia Art Directors' Shows over the years. He was represented in the Philadelphia Art Alliance's 1971 show, Geometric Paintings by American Artists, and was commissioned in 1975 as the muralist for the Finley Playground in Philadelphia. He wrote and illustrated a children's book, Henrietta (1965), and illustrated the volume How to Play with Your Baby (1971). A full record of Drucker's published work is on file at the George Arendts Research Library at Syracuse University.

Drucker is a member of the Cartoonists Guild (board of directors, 1971-78) and has served at various times on the boards of the Philadelphia Art Directors' Club and the Philadelphia College of Art, where he also taught advertising art (1960-65).

R.C.

DRUCKER, MORT (1929-   ) American cartoonist and illustrator born in Brooklyn, New York, on March 29, 1929. A graduate of Erasmus High School in Brooklyn, Mort Drucker was more interested in sports as a young man than in cartooning. Although he did pencil sketches, he was not the high school's cartoonist-in-residence, as so many successful cartoonists have been in their school days.

His first contact with professional cartoonists came shortly after his high school graduation in 1947. Through the help of a family friend, Mort Drucker was hired by Bert Whitman as an assistant to do the backgrounds in Whitman's comic strip Debbie Dean, Career Girl. The strip was begun on January 11, 1942, with Debbie Dean as a rich, beautiful debutante turned cub reporter. Debbie later returned to her hometown of Deansburg to become its, and the comics', first woman mayor. The former mayor, her uncle Gunga Dean, was allowed to make a most painful pun by saying, "She's a better man than I, Gunga Dean." Debbie Dean was syndicated by the New York Post Syndicate. "The style of the strip was similar to the Milton Caniff style," remembers Mort Drucker. "I only worked for Whitman about six months but it was my first contact with cartooning as a career."

In 1948, Drucker joined National Periodicals and was assigned to make slight corrections on the artwork. He remembers it as on-the-job training. His three years at National Periodicals were Drucker's initiation into the business of cartooning. His own artwork improved, and in 1951 he became a freelance cartoonist. He handled many comic book assignments, including war, romance and teenage stories. He drew the Bob Hope comic book.

However, a freelance artist always has to be on the lookout for new work. When Drucker spotted a classified ad seeking two artists for MAD magazine, he applied. MAD needed new artists in 1956 because the departure of Harvey Kurtzman and several MAD cartoonists had created openings on the staff. Although many cartoonists had already been interviewed, the MAD editors liked Drucker's samples, and he got the job.

His first assignment for MAD was a parody of a cigarette ad. Soon Mort Drucker's art became the standard for MAD's movie and television takeoffs. His assignments at MAD were consolidated to mostly movie parodies when his freelance advertising art commitments became more demanding. Of all the parodies he's drawn, Mort Drucker says The Godfather, Parts I and II, is among his favorites.

Drucker tries to capture the physical attitude of the people he caricatures. Emphasis is placed on the slightly-larger-than-true-proportioned heads and hands of his characters. His so-called MAD look presents a page with little white space left. The characters of the parody and details of the background are presented in a finely drawn pen outline with gray wash distinctive to MAD.

Mort Drucker has painted several movie posters, including the one for American Graffiti. He has also illustrated a number of Time magazine covers. However, his most phenomenally successful venture was The JFK Coloring Book that he and MAD magazine writer Paul Laiken created in 1962. Turned down by almost every publisher in New York City until Kanrom Publishers decided to take a chance on it, The JFK Coloring Book appeared on May 8, 1962, and to everyone's surprise quickly climbed onto the New York Times best-seller list, selling about two million copies.

B.C.

DRY BONES (Israel) Dry Bones is Israel's answer to Feiffer. Like its American counterpart, it exhibits a wry, sophisticated, sarcastic and often bitter humor, as well as a disillusioned commentary on the state of the world.

Ya'akov Kirschen, the creator of Dry Bones, is a transplanted New Yorker living in Jerusalem. After a career as a cartoonist in the United States, during which time he had drawings published in Playboy, Esquire and other magazines, Kirschen decided to emigrate to Israel in 1968. He promptly began drawing what he terms "a radical Zionist comic strip" for underground Jewish newspapers. The feature, Dry Bones, was picked up in the early 1970s by the Jerusalem Post, in which it currently appears. (The title is derived from Ezekiel.)

Although it has been called "Israel's first comic strip," Dry Bones is closer to the conventions of the cartoon, and it does in fact often appear as a single panel. In it Kirschen lampoons everything and everybody from Yasir Arafat to Henry Kissinger, from the United Nations to Israel's own bloated bureaucracy. "Jewish humor is traditionally based on grotesquely desperate situations," Kirschen once declared, "and, lucky for me, we have a desperately grotesque situation. . . . "

Dry Bones cartoons have often been reprinted outside Israel. In 1977 Kirschen's sardonic plan to divest the United States of its "occupied lands" and return it to the frontiers of the 13 original colonies drew an amused comment from President Jimmy Carter. A collection of Dry Bones cartoons was published in 1976 by Cherryfield Associates in Tel Aviv.

M.H.

Albert Dubout, detail from "Jour V." © *Dubout.*

DUBOUT, ALBERT (1905-1976) French cartoonist, poster designer, illustrator and animated cartoon director born in Marseilles, France, on May 15, 1905. While a student at the Montpellier Ecole des Beaux-Arts he started to submit cartoons to various newspapers in 1923, in particular to *L'Echo des Etudiants.* These drawings already had many of the themes and characters that would appear later in Dubout's work: the skinny little fellow, henpecked and terrorized by his big-busted and overbearing wife; Sparadra, the mean and muscular hood with the hangdog look and the unshaven face covered by a Band-Aid (*sparadrap* in French); and especially the crowds of thousands who are shown from very weird angles and whose faces, physiques, dress and gestures are depicted in the most grotesque manner.

After being expelled from art school, Dubout went to Paris at the age of 17 and placed his sketches with small newspapers (*Pêle-Mêle, Gens Qui Rient, Paris-Flirt*) and weeklies (*Le Rire, Le Journal Amusant, Candide*). In 1929, he illustrated his first book, Boileau's *Les Embarras de Paris,* a 17th-century satirical poem on the traffic jams of Paris. This was followed by illustrations for almost a hundred books, among them works of Rabelais (1936-37), Rostand's *Cyrano de Bergerac* (1947), Poe's *The Fall of the House of Usher* (1948), Dumas's *The Three Musketeers* (1968), *The Kama Sutra* (1973) and his favorite, Cervantes's *Don Quixote* (1937-38 and 1951). De-

vaux's *La Rue sans Loi* ("The Street Without Law"), for which he did the drawings, was published in *Ici Paris* as a daily comic strip (October 1950-March 1951); it was released in 1951 as a film, and Dubout wrote the scenario and drew the poster.

His own albums include, among others, *Du Bout de la Lorgnette* ("From the Binocular's End," 1937, with a pun on his name), *Dubout . . . en Train* ("Dubout on a Train," 1952), *Corridas* ("Bullfights," 1966) and *Dubout* (1974). In addition to a couple of animated cartoons, *Anatole Fait du Camping* ("Anatole Camps Out") and *Anatole à la Tour de Nesle* ("Anatole in the Tower of Nesle"), which are quite funny but do not have the quality found in American animated shorts, Dubout drew hundreds of publicity posters for restaurants, newspapers, wines, beers and films (e.g., Chaplin's *The Great Dictator*).

Despite his being a shy man, all his drawings show his love for crowds and trains and for "noninvisible mending" jobs: there are overcrowded beaches, free-for-all fights, gigantic assemblies of people (as in the famous VE Day cartoon of 1945, "Jour V"); his trains, especially the one serving the southwestern burgs between Montpellier and Palavas-les-Flots (in 1974, the Palavas city fathers renamed the Rue de la Gare "Rue de la Gare Albert Dubout"), are all antiquated, dilapidated, obsolete, malfunctioning, overcrowded, of course, and literally held together by tape, Band-Aids, knots, patches. Finally, his characters are naturally

Conclusion!

Gaston Duchamp ("Jacques Villon"), 1902.

ugly; the women have warts, chin whiskers, pimples, and men do not fare any better. They have long noses, stupid faces, funny-looking moustaches or long beards which always get caught in something; most of the time, they are proverbial 98-pound weaklings.

This "virtuoso artist" (as the French surrealist poet Philippe Soupault called him), this modern Bruegel or Doré who loved to disguise himself with false moustaches, wigs, pince-nez, beards and baggy pants held up by suspenders, died in Montpellier on June 27, 1976.

P.H.

DUCHAMP, GASTON (1875-1963) French painter, engraver and cartoonist born in Damville, France, on July 31, 1875. Known to posterity as Jacques Villon, Gaston Duchamp was the brother of the well-known painters Suzanne Duchamp and Marcel Duchamp and the sculptor Raymond Duchamp-Villon.

After his high school studies, Villon worked as a clerk in a notary's office in Rouen. Clerking left him unfulfilled, and he went to Paris in 1894. Over the next fifteen years he made his mark as one of the most sought-after cartoonists in the French capital. His work appeared in all the major publications, including *Le Chat Noir, Le Rire, Le Courrier Français, Gil Blas Illustré* and *L'Assiette au Beurre*, where he was featured in the very first issue. So well established was Villon the cartoonist that it is said that the owner of *Le Courrier Français* had his coach and coachman sent to the artist's domicile in order to sign him up for his magazine.

Villon left all this acclaim in 1911 to throw in his lot with the Cubists. He then repudiated his cartooning work as mere "potboiling," but there is no doubt that the discipline he showed in his early drawings, their almost abstract composition and their precise lines, helped form his later artistic idiom. Villon never achieved the celebrity status of other Cubist artists such as Picasso, and he

had to struggle all his life. He died, more or less forgotten, in Puteaux, near Paris, on June 9, 1963.

M.H.

DUFFY, EDMUND (1899-1962) American cartoonist and three-time Pulitzer Prize winner born in Jersey City, New Jersey, in 1899. The son of a policeman, Edmund Duffy studied at the Art Students League from 1914 to 1919 with George Bridgman, John Sloan and Boardman Robinson. His first published work was a page of Armistice Day celebration drawings for the *New York Tribune Sunday Magazine* in 1918; he soon was selling illustrations to the *New York Evening Post* and *Scribner's* magazine. In 1920 he sailed for Europe to study in Paris; he also contributed to the London *Evening News* and mailed back cartoons to the *New York Herald.*

Upon his return to America Duffy drew for *Collier's* and the *Century*; he became a staff cartoonist with the *Brooklyn Eagle* (1922) and then the *New York Leader* (1924), until he was "borrowed" to draw cartoons advocating the presidential candidacy of John W. Davis for the *Baltimore Evening Sun*. He was to remain there for 24 years, gathering three Pulitzers as well as a national reputation for liberal policies and devastating presentations. His themes, he said, were "politics, peace, and the poor taxpayer." While on the *Sunpapers* he dabbled in book reviews and reporting (he filed memorable accounts of Will Rogers's funeral in 1935). In 1948 he yearned for semi-retirement and, having turned more conservative, accepted a post as editorial cartoonist for the *Saturday Evening Post*, his first cartoon appearing on January 15, 1949; he remained until 1957, five years before his death.

The Outstretched Hand

Ed Duffy, Pulitzer Prize-winning cartoon, 1940. © Baltimore Sun.

Stoyan Dukov. © Starchel.

Duffy's drawing style, always arresting, resembled that of his teacher, Boardman Robinson: heavy brushstrokes, deliberate use of dark shading (and scraping with a razor blade to achieve highlights) and a brutally employed sense of the ridiculous. His compositions were handsomely balanced, and his themes never equivocated. Duffy won the George Washington Honor Medal from the Freedoms Foundation in 1956.

R.M.

DUKOV, STOYAN (1931-) Bulgarian cartoonist and animator born in Sofia, Bulgaria, in 1931. Stoyan Dukov graduated from the Higher Institute of Pictorial Arts in Sofia and started his professional career in 1950 with contributions to Bulgarian newspapers and magazines, notably *Starchel*.

Dukov had become an established print cartoonist when he decided to join Todor Dinov at the fledgling Studio of Animation in Sofia in the mid-1950s. There he worked as an animator for several years before co-directing (with Dinov) his first cartoon, *The Apple*, in 1963. In succeeding years Dukov directed more animated films, including *Golden Treasure* (1964), *Adventures* (1965) and *Travels in the Cosmos* (with Troyanov, 1966). All these were intended for children, but in 1967 Dukov came out with the adult film *Fortified Houses*, which was hailed as an imaginative experiment in line and composition. After a relapse into routine animated filmmaking, Dukov redeemed himself with *Sisyphus* (1975), a witty burlesque that contains such hilarious moments as Jove getting entangled in his thunderbolts and the Olympians playing practical jokes on Sisyphus—including getting him to lift a heavy boulder up a steep hill, of course. (This cartoon should not be confused with a Hunga-

Indignant Anglo-Saxon (to Provincial French Innkeeper, who is bowing his thanks for the final settlement of his exorbitant and much-disputed account): "Oh, oui, Mossoo! pour le matière de ça, je PAYE! Mais juste vous regardez ICI, mon Ami! et juste—vous—marquez—mes—MOTS! Je PAYE—MAIS JE METTE LE DANS LA 'TIMES'!"

George Du Maurier, "The Time-Honoured British Threat."

rian short of the same name and year that was nominated for an Academy Award.)

After Dinov, Dukov is the artist most responsible for the remarkable development of Bulgarian animation. He has also maintained his position as a noted gag cartoonist with regular contributions to foreign and Bulgarian publications.

M.H.

DU MAURIER, GEORGE LOUIS PALMELLA BUSSON (1854-1896) British writer and cartoonist born in Paris, France, in 1854. George Du Maurier's youthful years as an art student in Paris's Latin Quarter later provided him with the authentic background for his famous novel *Trilby*, a four-volume romance published in 1894. His first novel, *Peter Ibbetson* (1892), was based on his happy childhood in Paris, but in his last novel, *The Martian* (1897), he wrote about the accident which had lost him the sight of one eye. That tragedy halted his projected career as a portrait painter and resulted in his coming to London as an artist in black and white. His delicate and refined cartoons, virtually illustrations to lengthy captions of high society's conversations, capture the dress and manners of his Victorian age; they were published once a week from 1859 and in *Punch* from 1860.

Du Maurier was elected to the famous Punch Table when the death of John Leech created a vacant chair. His artwork and his jokes, both polite and refined, suited the

tastes of his middle-class readers, and he created a gallery of types: Sir Georgius Midas, the newly rich parvenu; Mrs. Ponsonby Tompkins, the social climber; and, of course, his elegant ladies, gowned goddesses who preceded the American Gibson Girls. He died in 1896.

Books: *English Society at Home* (1880); *Society Pictures* (1891); *Peter Ibbetson* (1892); *Trilby* (1894); *In Bohemia* (1896); *The Martian* (1897); *English Society* (1897); *A Legend of Camelot* (1898); *Social Political Satire* (1898); *Pictures by George Du Maurier* (1911); *Satirist of the Victorians* (1913); *George Du Maurier and Others* (1937); *George Du Maurier, His Life and Work* (1948); *Young George Du Maurier* (1951); and *George Du Maurier* (1969).

D.G.

DUNN, ALAN (1900-1974) American magazine gag cartoonist born in Belmar, New Jersey, on August 11, 1900. Alan Dunn studied at Columbia University in 1918-19 and then spent four years at the National Academy of Design. In 1923-24 he studied at the American Academy in Rome.

The most prolific of all the *New Yorker* magazine's cartoonists, Alan Dunn was published 1,915 times by the magazine between August 7, 1926, and May 6, 1974, including 9 published cover drawings. Several more of his cartoons were published posthumously by the *New Yorker*.

Dunn considered himself a social cartoonist "whose

Alan Dunn. © *Architectural Record Books.*

pen is no sword but a titillating feather that reminds us constantly that we do not act as we speak or think." He felt that this approach, gentler than the sharp satire of political cartooning, was more effective in enlightening his readers about society's foibles. It was his belief that people were a combination of "true virtue" and "pure human cussedness." Using a distinctive realistic style, Dunn commented on a wide range of topical subjects.

The literary quality of Dunn's cartoons was important to him, and he spurned both gag writers and attempts by editors to change his gag lines. Drawing with charcoal and grease pencil on paper with a pebble finish, Dunn successfully used the medium of many political cartoonists to a much subtler and often more memorable end. His drawings were always vigorous. In his later years they gained a lyrical quality.

A man of tremendous personal style, Dunn worked seated at a card table in the small apartment he shared with his wife, *New Yorker* cartoonist Mary Petty. The couple were self-styled recluses. Alan Dunn was referred to as a "hermit around town" by Harold Ross, the *New Yorker's* editor for many years. Thin, dapper, with a tiny moustache and deep-set eyes, Dunn also suffered from many phobias. Fear of fire was a major phobia, and the couple's apartment on East 88th Street in New York City was on the ground floor.

Architecture was Dunn's avocation, and he became a regular contributor to the *Architectural Record* beginning in 1936. The changes of architectural styles in New York City and their relationship to people were constant themes of his cartoons. For example, a man is shown picking himself up from the debris of a caved-in apartment wall and addressing a surprised couple seated having breakfast: "Sorry, neighbors. I just happened to lean against it." In another cartoon a small sports car pulls into the garage of a towering apartment building that looms straight up out of the drawing. The passenger says to the driver, "It's good to be home."

His cartoons were published in innumerable *New Yorker* anthologies and in book form under the titles *Rejections* (1931), *Who's Paying for This Cab?* (1945), *The Last Lath* (1947), *East of Fifth* (1948), *Should It Gurgle?* (1956), *Is There Intelligent Life on Earth?* (1960) and *A Portfolio of Social Cartoons—1957-1968* (1968).

In addition to his cartooning, Dunn was a devotee of chess and woodworking. His manuscripts are at Syracuse University. On May 20, 1974, at the age of 73, Alan Dunn died at his home.

B.C.

DUNN, ROBERT JOSEPH, JR. (1908-) American cartoonist born in Newark, New Jersey, on May 15, 1908. Bob Dunn was educated at St. Benedict's Preparatory School in Newark and St. Anselm's College in Manchester, New Hampshire. He studied at the Art Students League in New York City while selling magazine gags to *Judge* and *Life*. Dunn then went from a job on the art staff of the *Newark Ledger* to a six-month stint with Hearst's

International News Service, where he has remained ever since.

In 1932 Dunn became Milt Gross's assistant on his several features and seven years later was taken on by Jimmy Hatlo, with whose creations—*They'll Do It Every Time* and *Little Iodine*—Dunn was to become permanently associated. His own efforts, however, flourished through the years: he invented the "knock-knock" joke (in a million-selling book); wrote several other books, including *I'm Gonna Be a Father* and *One Day in the Army*; and drew his own Sunday cartoon, *Just the Type*, for nearly two decades. Since Jimmy Hatlo's death in 1963 Dunn has signed the Hatlo features, on which he has been assisted through the years by Moyer S. Thompson, Fred Faber, Al Scaduto and Hy Eisman.

Dunn's style is an amalgam of Gross's and Hatlo's: animated, exaggerated, full of characterization and broad humor. *They'll Do It*, of course, relies on readers' contributions, but Dunn's own *Iodine* scripts display a sure mastery of mayhem and zany anarchy—the title character is a one-girl equivalent of the Katzenjammer Kids.

A past president of the National Cartoonists Society, Bob Dunn is in constant demand as one of America's funniest, most entertaining after-dinner speakers and raconteurs.

R.M.

Relief (coming in): "Couldn't yer wait till yer got out to 'ave yer flamin' wash? Yer know we've got ter sleep in this ruddy water."

Frank Dunne. © *Smith's Weekly.*

DUNNE, LAWRENCE FRANCIS (1898-1937) Australian illustrator and cartoonist born at Boorowa, near Harden, in New South Wales, in 1898. Frank Dunne, who succeeded Cecil Hartt as a portrayer of Digger humor, had been a process engraver before World War I and enlisted in 1915, just after his eighteenth birthday. He served in the Australian Imperial Forces overseas with the First Field Ambulance until 1919. After his war service he progressed from process engraving newspaper blocks into press art and worked on the Sydney *Truth* as an illustrator before joining the staff of *Smith's Weekly*.

Dunne was known to *Smith's* readers as Frank. His strong, vigorous pen drawings, detailed and accurate down to the correct color flashes of the various army units—infantry, Pioneers, and so forth—were, like Cecil Hartt's drawings of Diggers, outstanding for the facial characterization of their subjects. His drawing technique, owing nothing to Phil May, was traditional and realistic, based, like that of Norman Lindsay, on drawing in the round, with light and shadow falling correctly. He blended this technique well with a zesty comic sense that was thoughtfully conceived. With splendid composition and figure placement, Dunne's drawings were almost alive with expressive movement. What could be termed the timing of his humor was faultless; there was never any confusion in his drawings as to who was saying what, nor was the reaction of the listener ever other than fitting. This was a point of subtle concept with Frank Dunne, for these exchanges in comic art are often ignored or more commonly confused.

To many ex-soldiers in the 1930s, Dunne's drawings and humor undoubtedly recalled not the shellfire, suffering and privation, but a nostalgic journey back to a slangy, aitch-dropping world of rum rations, flamin' chats (fleas), affable padres asking silly questions—and getting silly answers—and a certain brazening it out with humor under fire. It was partly this kind of nostalgia that fostered the perpetuation of the Digger spirit; Australians have tended, more than most peoples have, to look back on the "good old days" when soldiers were all mates together. This strain in Australian male life was encouraged not only through the pages of *Smith's Weekly* but also by the soldier organizations.

Frank Dunne, although color-blind to red and green, was a capable landscape painter in oils of the "tonal" school. He had planned an exhibition of his paintings prior to entering a Sydney hospital for elective treatment. But there Dunne's career was sadly ended by his death following a tonsilectomy in 1937.

A collection of Dunne's *Smith's Weekly* cartoons, *Digger Days*, subtitled *Laughing Through the Great War*, was published in 1931. Priced then at two shillings, (twenty cents), this publication is among the very rarest items of "Australiana" of interest to comic collectors.

V.L.

DUNNING, GEORGE (1920-1978) Canadian animator born in Toronto, Canada, in 1920. George Dunning studied at the Ontario College of Art, then became a freelance illustrator. He later settled in England to produce some of the funniest and most revolutionary cartoon films, including the trend-setting feature *The Yellow Submarine*.

In 1943 he was the third cartoonist to be hired by John Grierson for the animation unit at the National Film Board of Canada. Working under the inspired supervision of Norman McLaren, Dunning made his directorial debut with *Auprès de ma Blonde* (1943), a French-Canadian sing-along in the *Chants Populaires* series. A propaganda film, *Grim Pastures* (1944), and an accident prevention cartoon, *Three Blind Mice* (1945), followed before the individuality of Dunning as an artist first emerged in *Cadet Rousselle* (1946). His use of flat, jointed, painted figures was quite new; instead of working with paper cutouts, Dunning made his characters of metal. With Jim McKay, who had helped him on the film, Dunning left the NFB to form a company called Graphic Associates (1949), but he later returned to Canada on a Film Board grant to experiment with an animation technique involving painting on glass.

In 1956 Dunning contracted with the New York animation company United Productions of America to open a production subsidiary in London, England, and make cartoon commercials for the newly established Independent Television. During this period

Dunning directed *The Gerald McBoing Boing Show* for U.S. television. When UPA folded their English outpost, Dunning remained to establish his own company, TV Cartoons. Many successful commercials poured from the company for products ranging from Mother's Pride Bread, Golden Wonder Crisps and Start-Rite Shoes to Mentholatum Deep-Heat Rub. Sponsored documentary cartoons include *The Ever-Changing Motor Car* (1962) for Ford, *The Adventures of Thud and Blunder* (1964) for the National Coal Board, and *Discovery Penicillin* (1964).

Dunning's association with scriptwriter Stan Hayward began with his first theatrical cartoon for public entertainment, a crazy comedy, *The Wardrobe* (1959). His paint-on-glass experiments bore fruit when *The Flying Man* (1962) took the Grand Prix at the International Animation Festival in Annecy. Two television series for America followed, directed by Dunning's partner, Jack Stokes: *Cool McCool* and *The Beatles* (1967). The latter series, cartoon adventures of the internationally acclaimed singing group from Liverpool, led to the production of *The Yellow Submarine* (1968), an influential cinema feature designed by the German Heinz Edelmann, and an epic of animated pop art. Dunning also produced the only triple-screen cartoon, *Canada Is My Piano* (1967).

Other films by Dunning include *Memory* (1969), *Moon Rock 10* (1970), *Horses of Death* (1972), *Plant a Tree* and *The Maggott* (both 1973), *Damon the Mower* (1974) and *Teamwork* (1976).

D.G.

DUPRAS, PIERRE (1937-   ) Canadian cartoonist born in the province of Quebec on June 3, 1937. Showing precocious talent, Pierre Dupras completed his first painting at the age of 12 (he has since exhibited widely). He later drew for his high school paper and for *Quartier Latin*, the publication of the University of Montreal, from which he graduated in 1960.

Pierre Dupras has contributed many cartoons (mostly of a political nature) to such Canadian newspapers as *l'Indépendance*, *Dimanche-Matin* and *Québec-Presse*. He draws in an old-fashioned, straightforward style, well suited to his rather doctrinal political and social views. His humor is also simple and rather one-dimensional. He has, however, achieved a notoriety that extends well beyond the borders of Quebec and Canada, making him a force to be reckoned with on the Canadian cartooning scene.

His cartoons and comic strips have been reprinted in book form: *Vive le Québec Libre* ("Long Live Free Quebec," 1967), *La Drapolice* (1969), *La Bataille des Chefs* ("The Battle of the Chieftains," 1971) and *Recettes pour Grévistes et Chômeurs* ("Recipes for Striking and Unemployed Workers," 1972) are the most notable. Dupras has also drawn *Les Oraliens*, a series of cartoon shorts for Canadian TV.

M.H.

DYER, ANSON (1876-1962) British cartoonist born in Patcham, Brighton, Sussex, on July 18, 1876. "Britain's Answer to Walt Disney" the press called him, and he was—in every way except success. Ernest Anson-Dyer (he dropped the Ernest and the hyphen) studied at the Brighton School of Art, specializing in ecclesiastical design, then began work in the stained glass studio of C.E. Kempe. He remained in this field for many years,

and his windows are said to still decorate many an English church and cathedral.

His bent towards humorous cartooning first showed in his habit of sketching funny animals to amuse his children. On the outbreak of World War I in 1914, Dyer, rejected by the army, tried for an acting job in films. Although turned down because of his excessive height, he met the managing director, and the result was a contract to make his first animated cartoon. *Dicky Dee's Cartoons*, a series of three, were released by the British and Colonial Kinematograph Company through the last three months of 1915. Dyer gave a fascinating account of his early experiences in animation as a lecture to the British Kinematograph Society, published as number 40 in their series under the title *Technique of Film Cartoons* (1936).

Dyer then joined the Cartoon Film Company, and his cartoons alternated with those of Dudley Buxton in the series *John Bull's Animated Sketchbook*. Dyer's first was number 8, and it introduced a caricature of George Robey, the famous music hall comedian. Dyer made eight in the series, then in 1917 joined Kine Komedy Kartoons with Buxton and Ernest H. Mills. His first release for Kine was *The Kaiser's Record* in June, but by October 1918, he had completed ten. With the end of the war, the topical comment cartoon died, and Dyer switched styles to produce his first series of children's cartoons. *Uncle Remus*, based on the Joel Chandler Harris stories, ran for three films through 1919, under the blanket title of *Phillips Philm Phables*.

Dyer then joined the pioneer producer Cecil M. Hepworth at his Walton-on-Thames Studio (having in the interim animated battle scenes for the live-action film *Nelson*), where he produced a series generally called *Cartoon Burlesques*. These were parodies of Shakespeare plays: *The Merchant of Venice*, *Romeo and Juliet* and *'Amlet* were 1919 releases, followed by *Othello* and *The Taming of the Shrew* (1920). A series of three came next for Hepworth, featuring Bobby the Scout (1922), Dyer's first original character for the screen. Unhappily, Hepworth crashed into bankruptcy and Dyer's career went with him, for awhile. Two titles that were made during this dim period were *Little Red Riding Hood* and *The Three Little Pigs* (1922).

In 1927 he made what was announced as the first full-length animated feature film, *The Story of the Flag*, but Archibald Nettlefold, the producer, decided it would stand a better chance if released in single reel parts. Nettlefold later secured financial backing for Dyer's most ambitious project, a color cartoon studio, and in 1935, amid much local publicity, the "New Competitor for Mickey Mouse" was launched. As Anglia Films, with a studio supervised by Sid Griffiths, Dyer swung into intensive production. The Dunning process, a two-color system, was used, and with Stanley Holloway narrating, *Sam and His Musket* was shown in October 1935. The series of six was released through 1937, and in between came *Carmen* (1936), a musical cartoon of Bizet's opera, *The Lion and Albert* (1937) and *Three Ha'pence a Foot* (1937), both adapted from Marriott Edgar-Stanley Holloway monologues.

Also in 1937 Dyer began the production of commercial cartoons for sponsors: *The King with the Terrible Temper* (released as *The King Who Had Terrible Hiccups*), narrator Sutherland Felce, and *All the Fun of the Air*, both for Bush Radio. In 1938 *Red White and Blue* was produced by Publicity Films for Samuel Hanson's "Red White and Blue Coffee Essence," again with Sutherland Felce narrating.

Art holding the Mirror up to Nature.

Will Dyson, "The Royal Academy Opens," 1913.

With World War II (1939), Dyer formed Analysis Films to produce cartoon shorts for the Ministry of Information, the War Office, and the Air Ministry, but the titles have gone unrecorded. After the war (1946), under production manager D.R. Gardiner, he made "Diagram and Technical Films." The J. Arthur Rank renaissance of British cinema provided a new opportunity to produce cartoons for the Saturday matinee programs of the Odeon and Gaumont children's clubs. *Squirrel War* (April 1947) was another first, a cartoon serial. Three episodes were made (11 minutes; 12 minutes; 10 minutes) from the story by Helen Williams, screenplay by Mary Cathcart Borer and designs by A.A. and W.M. Carter. José Norman, who had provided Dyer's cartoon music before the war, came back for the score. *Who Robbed the Robins* (1947) was the last Analysis Film, running 9 minutes in technicolor. *Fowl Play* (1950) was released as an Apex-Halas and Batchelor Production through Grand National and ran 11 minutes (animator, Harold Whittaker).

For a long life devoted to animated cartoons, Anson Dyer received remarkably little acknowledgment, either during his life or after. He died on February 22, 1962.

D.G.

DYSON, WILLIAM HENRY (1880-1938) British caricaturist and political cartoonist born in Ballarat, Australia, in 1880. "The first major cultural figure since Charles Dickens to champion the working man forthrightly and without reserve," wrote historian Vane Lindesay about Will Dyson in his *Inked-In Image*, a history of Australian cartoons and cartoonists. But Dyson's main political work was done in England.

William Henry Dyson was born into a veritable nursery of cartoonists: his elder brother Ambrose (born in 1876) drew cartoons for the famous weekly the Sydney *Bulletin*, and his friends, the brothers Norman and Daryl Lindsay, were cartoonists on the Melbourne *Punch*. Will Dyson taught himself to draw by emulating his elders and began to get his work published in the *Bulletin* and the *Lone Hand* from the age of 17. In 1903 he took over his brother's weekly stint on the Adelaide *Critic*, where his cartoons were printed in color, the first in Australia. He contributed to C.J. Dennis's weekly *Gadfly* (1906), and drew more caricatures in color for the covers of the *Clarion* (1908). In 1906 he illustrated a book written by another brother, Edward Dyson, called *Fact'ry 'Ands*, but he tended to concentrate more on caricatures. An exhibition of these works opened in Melbourne in May 1909, and the following year he set sail for the broader horizons of Fleet Street, London.

The *Weekly Herald* was the official magazine of the Labour party, and Will Dyson found it a perfect platform for his political cartoons. Still a caricaturist at heart, he drew distorted symbolic figures that, executed in brilliantly bold brushwork, brought a new style to British cartoons. The underdog who was the British working man became a new and dominant figure of latent power; the capitalist lost his comical topper-and-spats image for one of a bloated boss and bully.

With the outbreak in 1914 of World War I, Dyson's art took an even more grotesque turn as his bullies changed nationality to become the German enemy. His newspaper series of *Kultur Cartoons* was reprinted in book form with an introduction by H.G. Wells. In 1915 Dyson was appointed an official war artist and was twice wounded while sketching Australian soldiers in action on the Western Front.

After the war his career was blighted by the death of his wife, Ruby (the sister of childhood friend Norman Lindsay). Dyson returned to Australia in 1925 and was appointed staff cartoonist to the Melbourne *Herald*. In 1930, after a trip to America to exhibit his newly adapted technique of drypoint etching, Dyson returned to London. Here he was appointed cartoonist to the new *Daily Herald*, the first Labour newspaper, and his cartoons were often featured on the entire front page. He died, in harness, in January 1938, age 58.

Books: *Fact'ry 'Ands* (1906); *Syndicalism and the Cooperative Commonwealth* (1913); *Cartoons by Will Dyson* (1913); *Cartoons No. 2* (1914); *Kultur Cartoons* (1915); *War Cartoons* (1916); *Australia at War* (1918); *Poems in Memory of a Wife* (1919); *Drawings by Dyson* (1920); and *An Artist Among the Bankers* (1933).

D.G.

Ee

EFFEL, JEAN
See Lejeune, François.

EFIMOV, BORIS EFIMOVICH (1900-   ) Soviet cartoonist born in Kiev, Russia, on September 28, 1900. Boris Efimov, who is largely self-taught, started contributing cartoons to the newspapers *Pravda* and *Izvestia* and to the humor magazine *Krokodil* in 1922. He soon became one of the most popular, as well as one of the most mordant, cartoonists in the USSR. His popularity reached its peak during World War II, when his cartoons helped in no small measure to keep up the morale of the Soviet citizens. He is best noted for his savage depictions of the Nazi leaders, especially Josef Goebbels, whom he never tired of lampooning.

Efimov's style, sparse and to the point, is very close to Western cartooning. His cartoons have been collected in a number of books over the years, including *Political Cartoons from 1924 to 1934* (1935), *Hitler and His Gang* (1943), *International Reporting* (1961) and *Boris Efimov in Izvestia* (1969).

Boris Efimov has been the recipient of many awards and honors, including the State Prize of the USSR in 1950 and 1951, and is a member of the Academy of Arts of the USSR. One of the best internationally known Soviet cartoonists, Efimov has also had a number of his cartoons reproduced in Western European and American publications.

M.H.

EGGELING, VIKING (1880-1925) Swedish animator and artist born in Lund, Sweden, in 1880. Viking Eggeling was fascinated by forms and colors from his earliest age, and in 1897 he went to Paris in order to study art. When World War I broke out, Eggeling went to Switzerland, and he became one of the founders of the Dada movement in Zurich in 1917. In 1919 Eggeling settled in Germany and applied his artistic tenets to the fledgling art of animation.

Working in Berlin, Eggeling explored the relationships between images and time sequences: he carried out his experiments by painting abstract figures or motifs on scrolls or strips of paper, later transferring them to film. It appears that Eggeling made only two independent films before his untimely death at the age of 45: *Horizontal Vertical Orchestra* (1920) and *Diagonal Symphony* (1923). But these films exerted a seminal influence on subsequent avant-garde and abstract animation, inspiring a whole school of German (and later, European and American) animators, starting with Eggeling's friend and collaborator Hans Richter. *Diagonal Symphony* was particularly impressive for its new concepts of rhythm and the movement of images synchronized to sound and music (this years before the first commerical sound cartoon was released).

Viking Eggeling died in Berlin on May 19, 1925; his achievements are now being resurrected.

M.H.

EHRENFRIED, GEORG (1893-1959) German cartoonist and painter born in Berlin, Germany, on July 26, 1893. Georg Ehrenfried, widely known as George Grosz, lost his father when he was seven; his widowed mother cooked for army officers in northeastern Germany. He studied at the Dresden Academy from 1909 to 1912, and by 1910 he was already sending cartoons to the Berlin magazines *Ulk*, *Lustige Blätter* and *Sporthumor*. He continued his art studies in Berlin in 1912. After a year in Paris (1913) came military service in the war. By 1915 Grosz's personal cartoon style had pretty well crystalized: a jagged, unlovely, expressionistic approach consciously based on toilet and fence graffiti. (Was Grosz, who as a boy had reverently studied and copied the famous cartoonists of the time, perhaps influenced by the intentional imitation of children's art practiced by Adolf Oberländer, the celebrated *Fliegende Blätter* artist?)

By 1915 Grosz had already met the liberal writer and publisher Wieland Herzfelde and his artist brother, who went by the name of John Heartfield. In 1916 the Herzfelde brothers established the left-wing

In search of "dangerous thoughts"—
the Statue of Liberty under investigation.

Boris Efimov. © *Krokodil.*

Ouch! "What a washout! The boy turned out to be a real girl!"

Georg Ehrenfried ("George Grosz"), 1926. © *Grosz.*

Malik-Verlag, which was to publish Grosz's most significant work up to 1930. The first two *Grosz Albums* appeared in 1917, followed by such masterworks as *Das Gesicht der Herrschenden Klasse* ("The Face of the Ruling Class," 1921), *Ecce Homo* (1922), *Abrechnung Folgt!* ("The Account Will Be Settled!," 1923), *Die Gezeichneten* ("Marked Men," 1930) and many others. Grosz depicted—with savage relish, unmitigated contempt and a decidedly erotic bias—the militarists, capitalists, profiteers, sensualists, mindless murderers and monsters of his Germany, whom he repeatedly showed alongside exploited workers, handicapped veterans and those wiped out by inflation and hard times. In the eyes of many, these albums make him the greatest of all German cartoonists.

On and off between 1919 and 1924 Grosz worked on the 11 issues of the Herzfeldes' paper *Die Pleite* ("The Bankruptcy"). In the later 1920s he sent a few drawings to *Simplicissimus* and did important innovative stage designs, the most famous being those for Erwin Piscator's production of *The Good Soldier Schweik*.

In 1932 Grosz left Germany for the United States. For a few years he was associated with Maurice Sterne in a private New York art school, but he is better remembered for his 20 years on the staff of the Art Students League (1933-53). *Vanity Fair*, *Esquire* and *Harper's Bazaar* commissioned drawings from him, but these were chiefly to illustrate weird stories; strong political statements and overtly expressionist methods were not wanted. At the same time, Grosz himself seems to have become weary of his early bitterness and turned increasingly to a genre that had interested him as a young man: nature and landscape

studies. These oils and watercolors were generally very finely executed but extremely bland.

In 1959 Grosz returned to West Berlin but died almost at once, on July 6 of that year.

S.A.

ELFINGER, ANTON (1821-1864) Austrian cartoonist born in Vienna, Austria, on January 15, 1821. Like Heinrich Hoffmann, creator of *Struwwelpeter*, Anton Elfinger was a physician by profession, but while the self-taught Hoffmann gained immediate celebrity as a draftsman, the well-trained Elfinger was not generally identified as the cartoonist "Cajetan" until quite recently.

Elfinger, born into an impecunious family of druggists, felt compelled to study medicine (1839-45) rather than devote himself to art, but as a youngster his talent for drawing had been nurtured by instruction from Matthias Ranftl and Leopold Kupelwieser, both of whom had been friends of Moritz von Schwind in the 1820s. Even in his medical work, Elfinger made use of his art training: in the then very progressive dermatological section of the Vienna General Hospital, he did watercolor illustrations of skin diseases that were highly regarded and subsequently published in lithographic portfolios. In 1849 he became official medical illustrator at the hospital and later published several books of anatomical plates.

But while still a medical student, Cajetan (the pseudonym may have been taken from the name of a 17th-century anatomical wax modeler) began contributing humorous drawings to the most widely circulated Viennese magazine, the *Wiener Allgemeine Theater-Zeitung*, which had been edited by the popular playwright Adolf Bäuerle since 1806. Between 1841 and 1853, Elfinger drew over a hundred *satyrische Bilder* (generally social satire), theatrical costume studies and devilishly difficult punning rebuses for the *Theater-Zeitung*. Elfinger was also as-

Anton Elfinger ("Cajetan"), "The Ladies' Rejuvenation Tax,"
1850.

sociated with more politically oriented humor magazines, which were necessarily very short-lived in the repressive atmosphere of Vienna at that time. In 1846 he worked on the 6 issues of Otto Bernhard Friedmann's *Kasperl im Frak* ("Punch in a Frock Coat"), and in 1849, the year of the abortive revolution, he edited the 12 issues of *Blitzstrahlen* ("Flashes of Lightning"). He also designed an extremely popular political tarot deck.

After 1849 political satire was out of the question, but Cajetan continued to work at least into the mid-1850s as an illustrator for books and for various popular almanacs, including some edited by the outstanding Viennese humorist Moritz Gottlieb Saphir. Influenced by Grandville, Gavarni and Cham, Cajetan's humorous art is generally heavily shaded and modeled in a supple version of basically academic manner.

Elfinger, whose parents and elder brother had all died young, was himself carried off by a hemorrhage of the lungs on January 19, 1864, a few days after his 43rd birthday.

S.A.

ELIES I BRACONS, FELIU (1878-1948) Spanish cartoonist born in Barcelona, Spain, in 1878. Feliu Elies (who used the pen name "Apa" throughout his career as a cartoonist) began contributing to satirical magazines when he was still a teenager. His cartoons were published in *L'Esquella de la Torratxa, La Campana de Gracia, Cu-Cut* and *En Patufet.* In 1904 he founded the very popular magazine *Papitu,* which he also directed for the first two years of its existence. Later Elies had his cartoons published in most major humor magazines in the country, including *El Poble Català, Picarol, La Publicitat, Mirador* and *Iberia.*

During World War I Elies savagely attacked German military power and war policies; his cartoons of this period, which originally appeared in the pages of *Iberia,* were later collected in a book titled *Kameraden.* In addition to his work as a cartoonist, Elies painted, wrote, and was a respected and often feared music critic. He is best known, however, for his acute and satirical cartoons. Public performers were often targets of his wrath and could expect to be caricatured along with politicians and other public figures. He also attacked with special harshness the Catalan political party La Lliga Catalana, as well as other conservative or moderate parties of the period. Feliu Elies died in Barcelona in 1948. (His brother, Lluis Elies, was also a cartoonist.)

J.M.

EMETT, ROWLAND (1906-   ) Cartoonist, builder of fantastic working models and sole proprietor and stationmaster of the Far Tottering and Oyster Creek Railway, born in London, England, on October 22, 1906. Rowland Emett was one of the first British eccentrics to express his eccentricity—an obsession for Victoriana—in his drawings. His police flying squad arrive in horse-drawn chariots, a Mississippi paddleboat crosses the stormy Atlantic to entertain the GIs, and, of course, there is always Nellie, the quaint yet sturdy steam-driven "Puffing Billy."

Emett, of the oft-misprinted surname, was born in 1906, just too late for his beloved Victorian age. Educated at Waverley Grammar School, he studied art at

"Of course we are prepared to make
one or two small alterations for suitable tenants."

Rowland Emett. © Punch.

the Birmingham College of Arts and Crafts. His first work was for Siviter Smith, Ltd., a commercial studio in Birmingham where he worked until 1939. During World War II he was a draftsman working on the development of the jet engine.

Emett's first cartoon to be published in *Punch* (1939) was realistic, but he quickly developed his unique brand of fantasy. His technique was seen at its best in the full-color covers and color plates for *Punch* specials and almanacs. His American magazine work includes *Vogue, Life, Harper's Bazaar, Holiday* and *Cosmopolitan.* Much in demand with advertisers, he has designed campaigns for Shell fuel, Abdulla cigarettes and Guinness stout.

In 1951 he designed and built a full-size working version of his cartoon railway for the Festival of Britain Pleasure Gardens at Battersea, London. This led to his equally famous construction, the Guinness clock. His mechanical cartoons have been featured in many window displays and exhibitions in England and abroad, including the British Trade Fair in New York (1960).

Books: *Anthony and Antimacassar* (1943); *Engines, Aunties and Others* (1943); *Sidings and Suchlike* (1946); *Home Rails Preferred* (1947); *Saturday Slow* (1948); *Buffers End* (1949); *Far Tottering* (1949); *High Tea* (1950); *Peacock Pie* (1951); *Festival Railway Cutout Book* (1951); *The Forgotten Tramcar* (1952); *Nellie Come Home* (1952); *New World for Nellie* (1952); and *Hobby Horses* (1958).

D.G.

EMMWOOD
See Musgrave-Wood, John.

EMMY LOU (U.S.) Cartoonist Martha (Marty) Links originally produced her newspaper panel dealing with the antics of a teenage girl for the *San Francisco Chronicle.* Syndicated nationally by Consolidated News Features as a daily panel on November 20, 1944, it was titled *Bobby Sox* but was later rechristened *Emmy Lou* after its heroine (the *San Francisco Chronicle* still retains the former title, perhaps for old times' sake).

Emmy Lou is an awkward, gangling, freckle-faced brunette whose days are mostly spent waiting for the phone to ring or in helpless dependence on her mooching, no-good boyfriend Alvin. Emmy Lou and Alvin have broken up time and time again (to the unconcealed glee of Emmy Lou's harassed parents), only to make up just as often. When she is not busy dreaming about her love life, Emmy Lou is wont to talk about it in endless (and boring) detail to her long-suffering school friend Taffy. The drawing of the feature, adequate if unoriginal, is now mostly done by Links's assistant, Ted Martine, while many of the gags are supplied by Jerry Bundsen.

Emmy Lou (which has been distributed by United Feature Syndicate since 1958) is a pleasant, rather innocuous feature. Its longevity may be due, at least in part, to its unabashed attachment to American types and attitudes that belong to the nostalgic past.

M.H.

The Candidate for Holy Orders
—"Please let me go, Your Reverence. I must get back to the kitchen, or my goose will burn!" —"Don't worry, Josephine. As long as you're with me, your goose is in God's hands!"

Josef Engl, 1900.

ENGL, JOSEF BENEDIKT (1867-1907) Austrian-German cartoonist born at Schallmoos, near Salzburg, Austria, on July 2, 1867. Though he was born in Austria (his father was a railroad technician who was transferred from place to place), Josef Engl's whole life and career were bound up with Munich, where he moved as a child. As a cartoonist he was the typical spokesman—never condescending, never severely critical—of the workingmen and peasants in and around the Bavarian capital.

Showing early signs of artistic talent, Engl was apprenticed to a lithographer for two years and in 1885 was able to enter the Munich School of Applied Art (second only to the Academy in prestige). To earn his tuition he did all sorts of commercial artwork, including the production of souvenir plaster statuettes. By 1888 Engl was contributing cartoons to a Munich magazine specializing in satires on the bicycle craze, *Radfahr-Humor* (for which his future *Simplicissimus* colleagues Eduard Thöny and Ferdinand von Reznicek also drew). In 1894 the venerable and beloved *Fliegende Blätter* opened its pages to Engl, who kept up with his art studies at the Academy in the evenings, working under Franz von Stuck. Unfortunately, before his consecration into *Simplicissimus*, Engl suffered an accident—a severe kick by a horse while in military service—that was eventually to shorten his days.

Virtually the only artist from Munich itself on the early staff of *Simplicissimus*, he was with it from its very beginnings in 1896. Much milder in tone and more easygoing in draftsmanship than most of his colleagues on that hard-hitting magazine, Engl soon found his weekly cartoon pushed into the advertising pages, but he made that niche his very own, with a very faithful readership. He was his own gagman and wrote his own captions, which were usually couched in a savory and authentic Bavarian dialect. His celebration of the common man in everyday situations caused him to be compared with the Berlin artist Zille, but Engl lacked Zille's deeper strain and latent reforming zeal.

An album of Engl's *Simplicissimus* work was published under the title *Münchener Humor*. He died in Munich at only 40 on August 25, 1907.

S.A.

"Just think, Daddy—that phone is still warm from Alvin's voice!"

"Emmy Lou." © *United Feature Syndicate.*

ENGLEHARDT, THOMAS ALEXANDER (1930-) American cartoonist born in St. Louis, Missouri, on December 29, 1930. Tom Englehardt studied at Denver University (1950-51), the Ruskin School of Fine Arts at Oxford University (1954-56) and the School of Visual Arts in New York (1957). He freelanced in New York until 1960, when a staff job in the editorial cartooning department of the Newspaper Enterprise Association opened up; Englehardt drew for the NEA's Cleveland office for nearly two years. In 1962 Bill Mauldin left the *St. Louis Post-Dispatch* for the *Chicago Sun-Times*, and Englehardt was chosen as the successor to Robert Minor, Dan Fitzpatrick and Mauldin. He continues there today, one of the few cartoonists who still uses (with beautiful mastery) the lithographic crayon.

Englehardt has said that Fitzpatrick was his idol, but it is obvious that Mauldin's is the style he has adopted through the years. His cartoons are drawn in vertical format, handsome and tightly rendered, with a sense of reserve rather than exaggeration. He is consistently left-wing in his concepts.

R.M.

ENGSTRÖM, ALBERT (1869-1940) Swedish painter, cartoonist and author born in Småland, Sweden, in 1869. More than any other, Albert Engström has most fully shown the innermost human characteristics and impact of the Swedish people. In a brilliant way his work has succeeded in laying bare the desires of the country, good or bad, and one common trait throughout is his sympathy and respect for the free individual, and for all human freedom.

Engström studied Greek and Latin at the University of Uppsala. There he learned the importance of the classical languages and developed into a brilliant literary stylist. Few of the world's greatest artists have succeeded to the same extent in combining the drawn and the written into a sublime unity. A director of the Painting School Valand in Göteborg saw his talent and encouraged him to go to Stockholm to pursue a career as a cartoonist. There he worked for the humor magazine *Søndags-Nisse* from 1894 to 1896, until his friends helped him start the magazine *Strix* and the foundation for his art and books was laid. Though a bohemian, he worked steadily and hard and obtained a respected position in all the leading circles.

Engström's characters' ease in relating to each other—whether they are drinking pals, aristocrats, intellectuals or financial wizards—is seen through a razor-sharp eye and an attentive ear. Typical is the situation where the family counsel in a lower-nobility family considers securing a mistress for the oldest, unmarried squire. The grandmother, who with age has become somewhat prejudiced, exclaims, "Might it then at least be a *believing* woman!"

Engström's well-developed instinct for language was always perfect, in dialogue as well as in thought. In Scandinavia he is an institution copied by many but

On a joyous occasion, Kolingen meets his childhood friend Pale Phil, who has embellished his otherwise rather disheveled costume with an almost new hat: "Jumping Jehosophat, Phil! Are your lice swarming since you've given them a new hive?"

Albert Engström, © *Søndags-Nisse.*

James Ensor, "My Portrait in 1960," 1888.

never surpassed. He became a professor at the Academy of Art, one of *De Adotons* ("The Eighteen") honorable doctors, and was the recipient of countless honors and titles. He died in 1940.

J.S.

ENSOR, JAMES (1860-1949) Belgian etcher and painter born in Ostend, Belgium, on April 13, 1860. James Ensor studied at the Brussels Academy of Fine Arts (1877-79), where he was influenced by French impressionist and intimist artists. He quickly developed an original style that is closer to Flemish expressionism, as in his *Woman Eating Oysters* (1882). A protégé of Félicien Rops, he founded Les XX in 1884 with other painters and sculptors to fight against the philistine backwardness and incomprehension of academic judges, but even this group refused to exhibit Ensor's *Entrance of Christ into Brussels*, and he became more and more bitter about having his work rejected.

Ensor's social and political etchings bitingly satirize the powerful members of middle-class society: gendarmes (1888), judges and lawyers ("The Good Judges," 1894), doctors ("The Bad Physicians," 1895), etc. His work shows a violent, anarchistic power and an unrestrained anger which finds its best expression in the grotesque world of macabre visions, masks, specters. In the fantastic tradition that runs from Bosch to Flora, and using violent colors, grimacing, stupid faces and repulsive skeletons and allegories, James Ensor presents human comedy as it is really performed on the world's stage. Among his most interesting etchings are *Masks in Front of Death* (1888), *Skeletons Warming Themselves Around the Stove* (1889), *The Intrigue* (1890), *Skeletons in the Studio* (1900), *Pierrot and Skeletons* (1907) and especially the morbid, playful and self-deprecating *My Portrait in 1960* (1888).

In December 1898 the French review *La Plume* devoted a special issue to Ensor in conjunction with an exhibition of his work, and this established him as one of the important artists coming out of Belgium. As early as 1895, however, he had more or less given up painting and etching, only occasionally producing a piece or two a year. Indeed, success came belatedly to Ensor, but he was eventually honored with a barony, membership in the Belgian Academy, exhibitions in France, England and Belgium, artworks hanging in French, German, Belgian, American and other galleries and museums, and a commemorative statue in his hometown, where he died on November 19, 1949.

P.H.

EPSTEIN, ABNER (1910-   ) American cartoonist born in New York City in 1910. Known professionally as Abner

Dean (a derivation from his mother's first name, Deanna), Abner Epstein attended Dartmouth College in Hanover, New Hampshire, from which he received his B.A. in 1931. He then enrolled in the National Academy of Design and continued his art studies. His first work in the field was freelancing, particularly in advertising and industrial illustration. It was probably in this latter capacity that he designed the industrial folding table for which he holds the patent.

One hesitates to call Dean a gag cartoonist, though one often laughs at the absurd but familiar antics of his simple, naked pen-and-ink figures, usually set against stark, almost lunar landscapes. A strong vein of alienation, however sardonic, runs through all his work, and his (not uncritical) debt to Freudian psychology is at times naively apparent. His captions are frequently "attitude" words or the intellectual and social clichés of modernity, and his capricious realization of them is undeniably unique. An example from one of his anthologies, *It's a Long Way to Heaven* (1945): a man hanging by the neck from a single blasted tree in one of Dean's characteristic barren landscapes scribbles away on his "appeal," his face contorted into a ghastly burlesque of a smile; the caption, "Optimism." As is so often the case with a Dean work, it is as depressing as it is amusing. (A clue to the reaction Dean is seeking in this and his other cartoons in *Heaven* can perhaps be found in the brief introduction to the volume, penned by no less an "angry young man" than Philip Wylie.)

Perhaps the best brief, serious appraisal of this controversial artist's work comes from Clifton Fadiman's introduction to Dean's 1947 anthology *What Am I Doing Here*, published by Simon and Schuster. "The urge to call Dean bats," Fadiman writes, "will be strong; but that is only because we have so large a vested interest in being 'normal' that we panic easily when this investment is threatened."

As an artist Dean has been represented in many of the major magazines, including the *New Yorker*, and has published no less than eight anthologies of his work, bearing such provocative titles as *Come As You Are* (1952), *Cave Drawings for the Future* (1954), *Not Far from the Jungle* (1956) and *Abner Dean's Naked People* (1963).

R.C.

EVANS, RAYMOND OSCAR (1887-1954) American cartoonist born in Columbus, Ohio, on July 15, 1887. Ray O. Evans received his B.A. from Ohio State University in 1910 and became an advertising artist in Columbus. He joined the art staff of the *Columbus Dispatch* in 1910, receiving on-the-job training from Billy Ireland, and drew editorial cartoons for the *Dayton News* in 1912 and 1913. In 1913 he transferred to the *Baltimore American*, a Hearst paper, drawing editorial cartoons until 1920 and freelancing for *Puck* in 1915 and 1916. He drew briefly for the combined *Baltimore News and American* before returning to Columbus in 1922 and remaining there until his death on January 18, 1954.

Evans taught cartooning at the Maryland Institute, created school features in cartoon formats and illustrated for *Better Homes and Gardens* ("The Diary of a Plain Dirt Gardener"). He had an uncluttered style and effectively used the brush and crayon. In his political leanings, he was a Democrat. Evans's son, Ray, Jr., was also a cartoonist.

R.M.

EVE (G.B.) *The Adventures of Eve,* subtitled "An Irresponsible Record of Some Incidents in the Career of a Frivolous Little Lady, To Say Nothing of Adam, Aunt Matilda, Uncle Fred and Tou-Tou," appeared weekly in the *Tatler,* a slightly upper-class glossy magazine. During World War I the *Tatler* was advertised as "the brightest, prettiest, most unique weekly paper in the world," and it brought a delightful touch of decorative humor to an unfunny and undecorative era.

Eve, a decidedly society "sweet young thing," did her best to cope with 1914-18 conditions in her own feminine way. She joined the police with her socialite sisters Evelyn and Evelinda, became a hospital nurse in a cute kilt, stayed on the east coast of England with Uncle Fred and survived a zeppelin raid by hiding under the dining room table, did her bit as a postman in cute boots, and was saved from the seaside tide by a handsome submariner. She also made it from the printed page into films, and a set of 12 silent two-reel comedies was produced by Gaumont in 1918. Eileen Molyneux portrayed Eve, with Pat Somerset as boyfriend Adam and Cecil Morton York as Uncle Fred.

Eve was drawn by "Fish" and "written and designed by Fowl." Fish was, in fact, Miss Fish, one of those rare birds, a woman cartoonist. Her artwork, thin line balanced against solid blacks, is still extremely original and stylish. The cartoons departed from the standard strip technique by dispensing with panels and being laid out over full pages and occasional spreads, with an eye to decorative composition rather than to progression. *The Eve Book* was published in 1917.

D.G.

22

23

22. Gabriele Galantara, cartoon for "L'Asino." Along with Guido Podrecca, Galantara founded the satirical weekly "L'Asino" in Rome in the late 1890s. The success of this socialist and anti-clerical publication was due to the incisiveness of Galantara's cartoons, which he signed with the anagram "Rata-Langa."

23. Giulo Gianini, "Ali Baba." ©Gianini/Luzzati. The duo Giulo Gianini and Emanuele Luzzati have made some of the most enchanting cartoons in Italy. They have often dwelt on legends and folktales, as in this example.

24. Theodore Geisel ("Dr. Seuss"), cover illustration for "Judge." ©Judge. Better known for his children's books, Dr Seuss is also a cartoonist of long standing. He started drawing cartoons and covers for "Judge" in the mid-1920s. His depictions of natural history and animal life, accompanied by soberly couched explanations, were totally absurd.

25. Bernard Gillam, cartoon for "Puck." One of the stars of "Puck," Gillam is most remembered for his vicious anti-Blaine cartoons during the American presidential campaign of 1884—of which this is one good example. Gillam's cartoons were technically proficient and carefully detailed; in his time he was regarded as one of the giants of his profession.

HE instituted the ordeal—can he stand it himself?
Uncle Sam: "We have heard from Mr. Cleveland. Now then, Mr. Blaine, YOU made this issue; it is your turn to step up and—TELL THE TRUTH!"

DECEMBER 28, 1918

PRICE 10 CENTS

Judge

Drawn by JOHN B. GRUELLE

Christmas Eve at Yapp's Crossing

27

26. John B. Gruelle, cover for "Judge." ©Judge. Johnny Gruelle's biggest success came with his "Raggedy Ann" stories, illustrated with his own cartoons. Before that, however, he had created the "Yapp's Crossing" series, which ran weekly on the cover of "Judge" magazine; this is a fine example.

27. Seichi Hayashi. ©Hayashi. This Japanese artist's work is almost psychedelic in its evocation of moods. His women characters are unique in that they tend to be frail but erotic women of the world, as in this example.

28. Ub Iwerks, "Aladdin and the Wonderful Lamp." ©Celebrity Productions. After years of working with Walt Disney, Iwerks set up his own studio in the 1930s. There he produced the enchanting "Flip the Frog" cartoons, as well as a number of "Comicolor Cartoons" based on fairy tales and popular stories; "Aladdin" is an example of Iwerks's work in this vein.

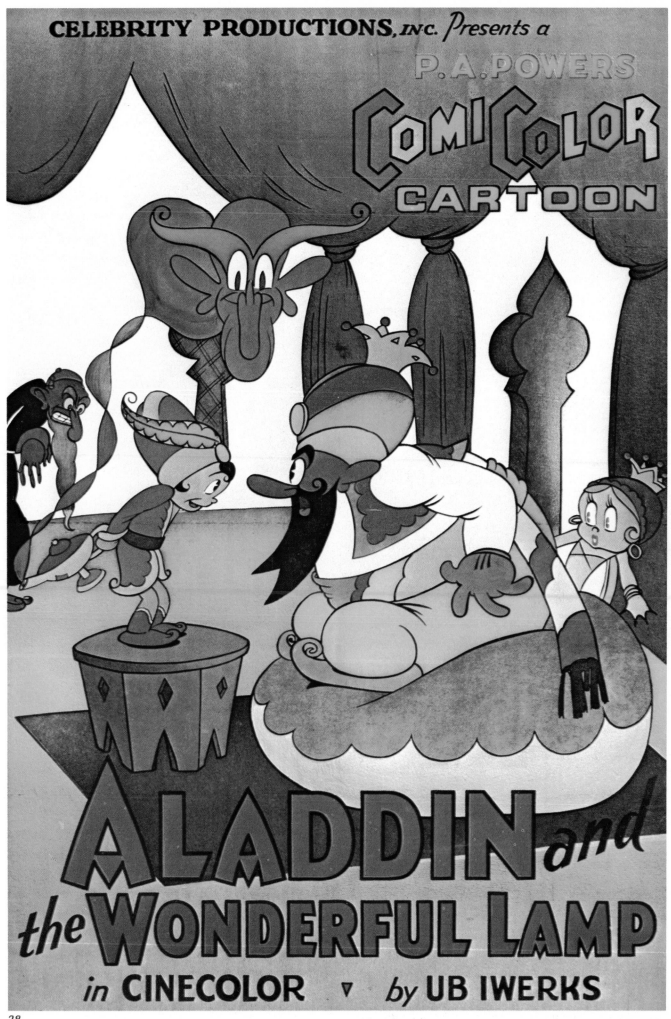

CELEBRITY PRODUCTIONS, INC. Presents a

P. A. POWERS

ComiColor

CARTOON

ALADDIN and
the WONDERFUL LAMP

in CINECOLOR ▽ by UB IWERKS

29

29. "Jungle Tatei." ©Mushi Productions. Japanese cartoonist Osamu Tezuka himself adapted his long-running comic strip, "Jungle Tatei," for animation. "Jungle Tatei" also bears the distinction of having been the first color animated cartoon shown on Japanese TV.

A Harmless Explosion

30. Joseph Keppler, cartoon for "Puck." Keppler, a German born immigrant, founded the famed humor magazine "Puck" in the 1870s in New York. He also contributed many political cartoons to the magazine, often laid out with a heavy hand.

31. "The Kewpie Korner." ©Rose O'Neill. The "kewpies," Rose O'Neill's famed elfin cupids, appeared in a variety of newspapers and magazines from 1905 to 1918. "The Kewpie Korner" was essentially a work of intense visual charm, with little wit or humor.

32. Renzo Kinoshita, "Made in Japan." ©Lotus Productions. Kinoshita is one of the most prolific Japanese animators. His animation short, "Made in Japan," parodies the commercialism of modern Japan. It won the Grand Prix at the 1972 International Animation Festival, held in the United States.

31

眼で見る時局雜誌

漫画

號月二

30セ

ИЗ ПЕТЛИ, ИЗ ЭТОЙ ЕМУ НЕ УЙТИ!

34

33. Hidezo Kondo, *caricature of Franklin Roosevelt.* ©Manga. *Kondo drew his famous (or infamous) color cover portraits of the "evil demons" Churchill, Roosevelt and Stalin during World War II. He often painted their faces green to give them an appropriately ghoulish appearance, and sometimes, as in this example, he added fangs.*

34. Kukryniksy, *"The Big Three Will Tie the Enemy in Knots." Kukryniksy is the collective signature of three Soviet cartoonists: Mikhail Kupryanov, Porfiry Krylov and Nikolay Sokolov. The trio's anti-German posters and cartoons are justly famous for their incisive style and visual impact.*

35. Jan Lenica, *"Ubu-Roi."* ©Lux Film. *The Polish-born Lenica is unquestionably one of the most famous and representative of today's animators. His films are pessimistic explorations of a decadent world, full of foreboding, terror and absurdity, portrayed with a high sense of drama and punctuated with a steady stream of jarring images.*

35

Ye GOOD·OLD·THANKSGIVING·TIME

Ye Good old Cheer From Ye Good Old Folks

Ye Good Old Dinner with Ye Good Old Jokes

Ye Good Old Voices In Ye Good Old Airs

Ye Same Old Quarrels And Ye Same Old Flares

Then With Clearing Skies, Come Ye Fond Good Byes

DRAWN BY
ALBERT LEVERING

37

38

36. Albert Levering, Christmas page for "Puck." Levering was one of the mainstays of "Puck" magazine, to which he contributed large topical drawings around the turn of the century. This multi-panel page is a good example of his draftsmanship.

37. Sandro Lodolo, humorous drawing. ©Lodolo. While best known as an animator (chiefly for Italian television), Lodolo is also a noted cartoonist whose works are often exhibited in galleries.

38. George Luks, political cartoon. Better remembered as a fine artist, Luks also contributed many cartoons to turn-of-the-century humor magazines. His style, at first awkwardly stiff, later became pleasantly free in execution. His cartoons were often reproduced in chromolithography.

39

39. "Mr. Magoo." ©UPA. The nearsighted Mr. Magoo was created by John Hubley in 1949. He was a bald-headed, crotchety old gent who got himself involved in all kinds of misadventures due to his sight impairment. The "Magoo" cartoons proved so popular that the character was starred in a 1959 feature-length film, "1001 Arabian Nights."

Ff

FABLES FOR THE TIMES (U.S.) The creation that first brought widespread attention to T.S. Sullivant, *Fables for the Times*, ran in *Life* beginning with the issue of February 13, 1896, with text by H.W. Philips. It was an up-to-date *Aesop's Fables* rendered in slang, with ironic twists and in a generally sarcastic vein. After the tale (usually with animals, in the Aesopian tradition), an *im*moral rather than a moral would follow.

The cartoons were snappy and made social and political points that obviously delighted the readers of *Life*, but their most striking characteristic was the artwork of freshman T.S. Sullivant; he had just begun to explore the visual delights of his singular exaggeration and composition. His line was still delicate, but his formats were bold—qualities rarely surpassed by others, or in his own later work. In several instances the cartoon ran one narrow strip the height of a page. In this series Sullivant staked a claim as a brilliant cartoonist unbound by conventions of format, perspective or rendering. Henceforth he became one of *Life*'s heralded attractions.

The popular series ended with the issue of July 30, 1896, and was immediately published in book form by R.H. Russell and Son.

R.M.

FABLIO LE MAGICIEN (France/Hungary/Romania/Bulgaria) *Fablio le Magicien* ("Fablio the Magician") may possibly represent the ultimate in the growing internationalism of animated filmmaking. This 85-minute feature was produced by Edic Films in Paris and animated in the studios of Pannonia Film in Budapest, Animafilm in Bucharest and the Sofia Animation Studio; it was released in 1969.

The program was based on six different fables of La Fontaine. Attila Dugay, a Hungarian, directed no fewer than four of the fables: "The Frog That Wanted to Be As Big As the Ox" (a satire on overreaching),

"Your Excellency, pardon . . . we're closing up."

Abel Faivre.

"The Dog and the Wolf" (a backhanded tribute to freedom), "The Lion and the Gnat" (a musical and animal parody on the David and Goliath theme) and "The Tortoise and the Two Ducks" (a twist on the old saw "Curiosity killed the cat"). The program was completed by the Romanian Victor Antonescu's version of the well-known fable "The Grasshopper and the Ant" and the Bulgarian Radka Batcharova's whimsical tale "The Cat and the Old Rat."

The six sketches were linked together by introductory sequences featuring the title character, a little magician who wove elements of poetry, fantasy, and humor into these well-worn tales. Despite some nice pieces of animation (principally by Dugay) and the clever use of color, *Fablio* was not a commercial success, nor was it an unqualified artistic achievement. It is noted here as a noble experiment.

M.H.

FABULOUS WORLD OF JULES VERNE, THE See *Vynález Zkázy.*

FAIVRE, ABEL (1867-1945) French caricaturist, cartoonist, poster designer and painter born in Lyons, France, on March 30, 1867. Abel Faivre attended the school of Fine Arts before studying at the Ecole des Beaux-Arts in Paris (1886-89). He started his caricaturing career by contributing from 1895 on to *Le Rire*, which became *Le Rire Rouge* during World War I; he

"Fablio le Magicien." © EDIC.

223

"Ah! Here it is! 'The Discourse on Method.'"

Jacques Faizant. © Faizant.

also contributed for 37 years to *Le Journal* and for 7 to *Le Figaro*, as well as to other humor magazines, especially *L'Echo de Paris* and *L'Assiette au Beurre*. For *L'Assiette*'s issue of March 22, 1902, Faivre, the son and brother of physicians, drew a biting series of cartoons satirizing doctors. Probably the most famous drawing is the one where a physician dressed in black carries a funeral wreath bearing the inscription "To My Clients" and smilingly declares, "Ils ne l'ont pas volée. . . ." ("They richly deserve it").

His cartoons and caricatures make use of many right-wing themes, from anti-Semitism to anti-German revanchist spirit; his "We'll Get Them" (1917) or the French Victory Loan posters (1918) epitomize this genre. He imputes an unrelieved ugliness to his victims, often presenting them in an angry black humor manner. Some of his war sketches were published in the albums *56 Dessins de Guerre* ("56 War Cartoons," 1915) and *Jours de Guerre 1915-1919* ("War Days," 1921). On the other hand, his paintings and murals have an agreeable, airy, almost lighthearted pleasantness about them, rather reminiscent of the 18th century. Some received prizes and now hang in museums in Paris and Lyons (for instance, his *Woman with the Fan*, in the Louvre).

Abel Faivre died in Nice on August 14, 1945.

P.H.

FAIZANT, JACQUES (1918-   ) French cartoonist born in central France on October 30, 1918. After taking a degree in hotel management at the Ecole Hôtelière of Nice and working for several years in the trade, Jacques Faizant abandoned the hotel business to try his hand at animation (1942-45). When this venture failed, he became a cartoonist (1945) and collaborated on all the important weeklies, especially *Jours de France* and *Paris-Match*. Since 1967 he has also drawn political cartoons for *Le Figaro* and *Le Point*.

His drawings have been published in the highly successful albums *Les Vieilles Dames* ("The Old Ladies"), *Histoires de France* ("Histories of France"), *Les Caprices de Marianne* (1969), *C'est Ouvert* ("It's Open," 1970), *Les Vieilles Dames et les Hommes* ("Men and the Old Ladies," 1972) and *Allons-y à Pied* ("Let's Go There on Foot," 1974). He also illustrated his own novels, *Ni d'Eve ni d'Adam* ("Neither from Eve nor from Adam," 1954), *Les Marins* ("The Sailors," 1964), *Les Gros Soucis* ("Big Worries," 1972) and *Albina et la Bicyclette* (1976).

Faizant has an uncanny knack for showing the contradictions in our character or behavior, as with the man who, having unmethodically emptied his bookcase and thrown the books pell-mell on the floor, joyfully exclaims, "Ah! Here it is! Descartes's *Discourse on Method*!" or the king who brings the phone to one of his guards and says, "It's for you." His most famous series, however, features "the old ladies," all more or less looking alike, with their hanging jowls, their white buns, their long black dresses showing flashes of petticoat white, their knitting. These little old ladies are not necessarily gentle and sweet. As a matter of fact, they are often mischievous, if not somewhat mean, as in the case of one lady blowing up a paper bag at the very moment another old lady is walking by with an armful of dishes. This kind of humor has helped to make Jacques Faizant's books and cartoons well-deserved successes.

P.H.

FALLS, CHARLES BUCKLES (1874-1960) American cartoonist and illustrator born in 1874. Charles Falls was largely responsible for the brighter moments of the last years of *Puck* magazine in the late 1910s. His line drawings graced James Hunecker's "Lively Arts" column and were among the best of Falls's career of

The way the Kansas druggist toiled behind his prescription case seven years ago was a caution to galley slaves.

Charles Falls.

decorative brushwork. C.B. Falls was also known as a designer, muralist and portrait painter, and he taught for years at the Art Students League in New York. His early work in *Puck* was signed with a little black square.

His style was impressionistic and full of contrasts and solid blacks. His lush brushstrokes later gave way to a drybrush technique, and his illustrative work for *Puck*, sometimes running a full page and sometimes with monochromatic shading, was very striking.

Books: *Our Friend the Dog* (1904); *Snow White* (1913); *The ABC Book* (1923), a classic done in woodcuts and still reprinted; *Poems from "Life"* by Oliver Herford (1923); *The Color of a Great City* by Theodore Dreiser (1923); *When Jesus Was Born* (1928); *Two Medieval Tales* by Robert Louis Stevenson (1929, for the Limited Editions Club); and *Reveries of a Bachelor* by Ik. Marvel (1931).

R.M.

FAMILIA SISTACS, LA (Spain) *La Familia Sistacs*, a panel created by the cartoonist Valentí Castanys i Borrás, was first published in the humor magazine *Xut!* prior to the Spanish civil war and was compiled in book form after the war. The panel represented the aspirations of the Spanish middle class trying to ape the manners, mores and rituals of the higher class. At the same time, the Sistacs family embodied many of the wishes, problems and characteristics common to all those who worked hard trying to escape from the cultural limitations of the lower classes.

Castanys showed great interest in customs and traditions springing from regional and subcultural roots. The cultural mix—the melting pot, as it were—that Spain really is under the surface was analyzed with an unjaundiced eye through the Sistacs family. For instance, the language used by Castanys in the feature was half Spanish-Castilian and half Catalan. The cartoonist blended a lively humor into the pathos, however, and *La Familia Sistacs* was one of the most popular features in Spain for over twenty years, until the author's death in 1965.

J.M.

FAMILY CIRCUS, THE (U.S.) The official birthdate of *The Family Circus* is February 19, 1960, the day the Register and Tribune Syndicate started distribution of Bill Keane's popular daily panel. Keane himself feels that the idea for a newspaper panel about family life came to him as early as 1952. The panel's goings-on revolve around an average American family originally made up of Mommy, Daddy, and three children—the eldest son, Billy; his ponytailed sister, Dolly; and Jeffy, the tot of the family. In 1962 a third baby boy, P.J., was added to the household. Barfy the dog rounds out the cast of principals.

Bill Keane draws his daily panel within a circle to accentuate the feeling of closeness and also to symbolize the title by suggesting a circus ring. The Sunday panel is rectangular, but the ring motif is retained around the logo. (A companion panel, *Side Show*, in which the cartoonist illustrates puns submitted by his readers, completes the Sunday feature.) Keane's own wife and family are the models for the panel's family, which may account for the close identification many readers feel with the feature. The happenings are ordinary, everyday incidents only slightly emphasized for humorous effect. "There's a general tendency among people who want to be funny to exaggerate,"

"Why CAN'T you play cards with us, Mommy? Grandma always does."

"The Family Circus." © Register and Tribune Syndicate.

Keane stated in a 1966 interview. "I do just the opposite. I tone down every idea I get. I also keep my drawing style simple, only the lines necessary.... Each cartoon must have life; it should be current and fresh. For instance, the house, the neighborhood, the trappings, the paraphernalia, are kept up-to-date."

Success has amply rewarded Keane's simple cartooning creed. *The Family Circus* is one of today's most popular newspaper panels; it won the National Cartoonists Society Best Syndicated Panel award twice, in 1967 and 1971. Many of the cartoons have been collected into books, the latest being *The Family Circus Treasury*, published by Sheed, Andrews and McMeel in 1977. And in 1978, a TV special, "A Special Valentine with the Family Circus," was aired on NBC.

M.H.

FANTASIA (U.S.) Walt Disney had been planning a musical cartoon film as a vehicle for Mickey Mouse (whose popularity was waning) as far back as 1938. Eventually this project evolved into a full-length feature, considered by most critics as Disney's single most stunning achievement: *Fantasia*, first released at Christmastime 1940.

Intended as a marriage between animation and musical arts, the film was introduced by musicologist Deems Taylor, while the score was conducted by maestro Leopold Stokowski. The program itself consisted of the following pieces: Bach's Toccata and Fugue in G Minor (as adapted for orchestra by Stokowski); excerpts from Tchaikovsky's *Nutcracker* Suite; Paul Dukas's scherzo "The Sorcerer's Apprentice"; Stravinsky's "Rite of Spring"; Beethoven's *Pastoral* Symphony; Ponchielli's "Dance of the Hours" (from his opera *La Gioconda*); and a combination of Moussorgsky's "Night on Bald Mountain" and Gounod's "Ave Maria."

As can be expected from the diversity of the selected pieces, the resulting sequences were of uneven quality, but there were dazzling moments in each of them.

225

The "Dance of the Mushrooms" sequence of "Fantasia." © Walt Disney Productions.

Perhaps the most flawlessly realized sequence, from the point of view of pure animation, was "The Sorcerer's Apprentice," in which Mickey played the title character; but "The Dance of the Hours" (with its hilarious cast of animal ballerinas) was not too far behind. Special mention should go to the abstract treatment of the Toccata and Fugue, clearly inspired by the work of Oskar Fischinger (who was called in to help with the sequence); the dinosaur battle in "Rite of Spring" and the delicate color work on the *Nutcracker* must also be cited.

Fantasia drew mixed reviews upon its first release and proved an unmitigated disaster at the box office. Eventually the work was reappraised, and is now regarded as a forceful and masterly statement of animation art. Thanks to its many reshowings in later years, it also finally managed to turn a profit for Walt Disney Productions.

M.H.

FANTASTIC PLANET

See Planète Sauvage, La.

FARKAS, ANDRÉ (1915-   ) French cartoonist, poster artist, set designer and painter born in Temesoara, Romania, on November 9, 1915. He studied at the Budapest School of Fine Arts before going to France, where he began his cartooning career in 1944 under the name "André François."

François has contributed cartoons to numerous magazines, in particular to *La Tribune des Nations* (1953-60), *Holiday* and *Sports Illustrated*, and designed covers for the *New Yorker*, *Punch*, *Esquire* and *Fortune*. He has also created posters for Kodak, Olivetti, Citroën and Esso, as well as illustrating, among other works, Homer's *Odyssey* and Jarry's *Ubu-Roi* (1958). A collection of his drawings entitled *The Biting Eye* (1960) has been released by Perpetua (Ronald Searle's publishing company). In addition, he has done several animated cartoons for American TV ads, the most interesting being for Jack-in-the-Box drive-in restaurants and the American Gas Association.

Notable among François's own books are: *The Tattoed Sailor*, with an introduction by Walt Kelly (1953); *The Half-Naked Knight* (1958); *Les Larmes de Crocodile* ("Crocodile Tears"), which won the U.S. Best Children's Book Award (1956); and *You Are Ridi-cu-lous* (1970). Finally, François has designed stage sets for Roland Petit's ballet company (1956), Peter Hall's production of *The Merry Wives of Windsor* (1958) and Gene Kelly's *Pas de Dieux* (1960).

All these works present a modern look at a world which is poetic and absurd, where man does the incongruous with normality and aplomb, where the underlying joke is at once cruel, tender and ingenuous: an engineer drawing at his drafting board with flowers growing out of his head, a woman wearing a witch's mask on her face and having her breakfast, a young boy in the Napoleonic pose, holding a watermelon on his head and standing beside his father, who is eating a watermelon slice. Searle's and Steinberg's influence is apparent in the clarity and beauty of the lines, while Grosz and Klee have undoubtedly played a role in his choice of grotesque themes and characters.

Since 1960, André François has devoted himself mainly to painting, and his figurative canvases have been exhibited in New York (1962) and at the

André Farkas ("André François"). © Punch.

Stedelijk Museum in Amsterdam (1967), the Musée des Arts Décoratifs in Paris (1970), the Chicago Arts Club (1975) and the Galerie Delpire in Paris (1965 and 1976).

P.H.

FARMER AL FALFA (U.S.) Paul Terry created his first cartoon series, *Farmer Al Falfa*, in 1916 for the Thomas A. Edison Corporation. The early cartoons were rather crude; they showed an old farmer with white whiskers vainly trying to cope with the various animals around his farm. The 1917 "Farmer Al Falfa's Wayward Pup" is typical in this respect. In 1921 Terry went over to Pathé Exchange, and it was there that the series took its definitive form. Farmer Al Falfa is chiefly remembered today for his epic battles against the hordes of mice that were always invading his property ("Rats in the Garret" is one good example), but he had his troubles with all kinds of animals, as evidenced by such titles as "The Farmer and the Ostrich," "The Farmer and His Cat" and "Farmer Al Falfa's Pet Cat."

After the founding of Terrytoons, *Farmer Al Falfa* became the first series of the fledgling studio, starting in 1932. Under the close supervision of Terry, and with the help of directors Frank Moser, Mannie Davis and George Gordon, the Farmer (as he was simply called) went through a number of entertaining if hardly memorable adventures: "Farmer Al Falfa's Birthday Party," "Farmer Al Falfa's Bedtime Story" (both 1932), "Mice in Council" (1934) and "Farmer Al Falfa's Surprise Package" (1936) are some of the better-known cartoons. In 1936 Terry released "Farmer Al Falfa's Twentieth Anniversary," a compilation of some of the highlights of the series.

The series degenerated rapidly in the 1940s as it became progressively more repetitive and predictable. The title character was later renamed Farmer Gray but appeared only sporadically through the 1950s.

While not a classic by any means, *Farmer Al Falfa* was one of the earliest American cartoon series and one of the longest-running (it was discontinued in the early 1960s). As such, it deserves greater attention than it has hitherto received.

M.H.

FARMER GRAY
See Farmer Al Falfa.

FARRIS, JOSEPH (1924-   ) American cartoonist, painter and sculptor born in Newark, New Jersey, on May 30, 1924. Joseph Farris was raised in the Danbury, Connecticut, area. When he was 14 or 15 he saw an article in the *Danbury News-Times* saying that Richard Taylor, the famous *New Yorker* and *Esquire* cartoonist, would conduct an art class in neighboring Bethel. That same week *Collier's* magazine had profiled Taylor. Suitably impressed, Joseph Farris joined thirty or forty others in Taylor's art classes. "He gave me the very basics in art, and he wasn't particularly trying to make cartoonists of us," remembers Farris. "I was impressed by the quality of his life-style and with his ability to see things freshly." Farris continued his art lessons with Richard Taylor until he graduated from high school and entered the army during World War II.

He served in the military from 1943 to 1946, and some of his cartoons were published in *Stars and Stripes*. At

"You can't raise my property tax anymore. It's yours!"

Joseph Farris, "Farriswheel." © *Chicago Tribune-New York News Syndicate.*

the end of the war he studied in a three-month school for GI's in Biarritz, France, and then as a civilian studied fine arts for four years at the Whitney School of Art in New Haven, Connecticut. After a year of book and magazine illustration, he began his freelance cartoon career in earnest. One of Farris's first magazine cartoon sales was to a Catholic religious publication, *The Victorian*. Not knowing the nature of the magazine, he accidentally sprinkled some risqué cartoons into the ones he submitted for general readership. *The Victorian's* editors forgave him that sin, and his career was launched.

Joseph Farris considers himself a "social cartoonist," and philosophically he is very much a kindred spirit to cartoonist Alan Dunn. His cartoons are pointed comments on man and society, but with a chuckle. They are drawn with pen and ink in a decorative style that rests on the quality of the line. A regular contributor to the *New Yorker* and many other magazines, he has also been published in *Playboy*, his cartoons having a social comment rather than a sexual gag. He is one of the select cartoonists under contract to the *New Yorker*. From 1971 to 1974 the Chicago Tribune-New York News Syndicate distributed his panel *Farriswheel*. The feature was a daily cartoon with social comment.

Joseph Farris's painting and sculpture represent the "fine-arts side of me completely free of commercialism." While his paintings have a humorous flair, his sculpture is mostly abstract. In 1969 a series of cartoons he had sold to various magazines on the topic of unidentified flying objects was published in a collection called *UFO HoHo*.

B.C.

FATHER CHRISTMAS (G.B.) In an iconoclastic age, it is perhaps to be expected that the traditional image of Jolly

Old Santa Claus with his red cloak, white beard and happy "Ho-ho-ho!" would be shattered. But the artist who finally "upped and did it," Raymond Briggs, did it with such unexpected good humor, wit and pleasant drawing that the result is not the destruction of a childhood dream (hence tears), but a humanization of the gentleman of legend (hence chuckling delight). "Happy Blooming Christmas to you, too," grumbles the tired old boy at the end of his busiest day, and as he tucks himself into his lonely cot we sympathize with his aching old bones and wonder, perhaps, if we might not somehow stick a present in his darned old sock.

Raymond Briggs was born in 1934 in Wimbledon, London, and attended the School of Art there from 1949, going on to the Slade School of Fine Art (1955-57). He freelanced as a general illustrator for the BBC, Conde Nast, Oxford University Press, Penguin Books, and many other publishers, specializing in writing and illustrating books for children. His first book, *The Strange House*, was published in 1961, and his *Mother Goose Treasury* (1966), with over eight hundred pictures, was awarded the Kate Greenaway Medal for the best illustrated book of the year.

His first venture into the strip cartoon idiom, *Father Christmas*, a 32-page full-color picture story, was published in 1973. It remains his most successful book, having been translated into 16 languages (including Serbo-Croat). He drew a sequel in 1975, *Father Christmas Goes on Holiday*, and one further adventure of the character for the Christmas 1976 issue of *Ally Sloper* magazine.

D.G.

FAWKES, WALTER ERNEST (1924-   ) British political cartoonist, comic strip artist and musician born in Ontario, Canada, in 1924. "Trog," the familiar pseudonym that hides Wally Fawkes, is short for Troglodyte, the name of a small jazz band specializing in playing in cellars. Fawkes plays clarinet whenever he can find time, which is less often than he would like, since he draws a daily strip as well as his weekly stint of political cartoons.

Fawkes came to England at the age of seven, in 1931, was educated in Sidcup, then studied art at the Camberwell School of Arts and Crafts. During World War II he drew maps and painted camouflage, but when some of his work in an exhibition caught the eye of Leslie Illingworth, political cartoonist of the *Daily Mail*, Illingworth, recognizing talent, got the young artist a job on the art staff of the *Daily Mail*. From 1945 small spot illustrations began to appear over the Trog signature. At that time the *Mail* also had a healthy book department, and Trog drew cartoons and illustrations for the *Daily Mail Children's Annual* every year. In 1949 he was given the chance to draw a new daily strip for children, *Rufus*, which eventually developed into *Flook*. Originally decorative whimsy, the strip advanced into caricatural satire (see *The World Encyclopedia of Comics*, Chelsea House, 1976). At the same time, Trog's technique pared down overdecorative Victorianism to a clean, bold black and white.

Trog began to draw political cartoons for the weekly *Spectator* in 1959, then moved to another political weekly, *New Statesman*, and then to the Sunday national, the *Observer*. When his mentor Illingworth retired from the *Daily Mail*, Trog was thrilled to take over the spot and drew the paper's principal cartoon from 1968 to 1971, when the *Mail* reduced to tabloid

size. Trog then moved to *Punch*, where he draws brilliant full-color covers and the weekly political cartoon.

D.G.

F.C.G.
See Gould, Sir Francis Carruthers.

FELIX THE CAT (U.S.) The exact birthdate of one of animated cartooning's most celebrated characters, Felix the Cat, has long been a matter of speculation. It varies from one historian of the field to the next, falling somewhere between 1914 and 1925. To compound the confusion, Pat Sullivan, Felix's creator, had a very casual attitude toward copyright regulations, and the first *Felix* cartoons were not copyrighted until 1925. Finally, two live-action comedies featuring another hero named Felix (*Felix Gets in Wrong* and *Felix on the Job*) were released in 1916 by Universal.

Felix's complicated genesis resulted from the collaboration between Sullivan and his talented animator Otto Messmer, whom Sullivan hired in 1916. That same year they developed a black feline character for use as the animal hero of a new series of cartoons. The dry run for the series was released in 1917 after Messmer had left to fight with the American Expeditionary Force in Europe; titled *Tail of Thomas Kat*, it can be considered the first Felix cartoon in all but name (already the cat was using his tail as a removable object to get him out of all kinds of predicaments).

With Messmer back from the war in 1919, the series was launched in earnest. The first entry was the 1920 *Feline Follies*, in which the cat was still called Tom. More titles followed, to the tune of two a month; in these cartoons, released by Educational Films throughout the 1920s, the cat finally acquired the name Felix. Messmer directed most of them, assisted by a team of animators that included at one time or another Al Hurter, Hal Walker and Raoul Barré. Sullivan, meanwhile, spent less and less time in the studio and took less and less interest in the further development of his cartoon series. Though his animators had been working on a sound system as early as 1926, for instance, he vetoed the proposal for sound cartoons as too costly and thus lost his preeminent position in the animation field to Walt Disney.

Felix was by then an established figure. The game little black cat with the soulful eyes not only engaged in the outlandish adventures required of a cartoon hero, braving the elements and fighting hordes of enemies in exotic climes (as in "Eats Are West," "Arabiantics," "Felix the Cat Scoots thru Scotland" and countless others) but also embarked on wild flights of fancy through time and space ("Felix the Cat Trifles with Time," "Felix the Cat in Land o' Fancy," "Felix the Cat in Futuritzy," etc.). Messmer constantly experimented with his character, giving him depth and pathos: the cat was seen as an outsider fighting all odds to win the love of the flighty Phyllis ("Felix the Cat as Roameo," "Two-Lip Time"), to stay ahead of the pack ("A Tale of Two Kitties," "Jack from All Trades") or simply to get a square meal ("Felix the Cat on the Farm," "Scrambled Yeggs").

The success of *Felix the Cat* was enhanced by a catchy song played in movie houses showing the shorts: "Felix kept on walking/Kept on walking still." In 1923 a *Felix* newspaper strip came into being (drawn by Messmer); comic books followed. There were also Felix toys, books, games and other artifacts. By 1930, however, the *Felix*

"Felix the Cat." © *Pat Sullivan.*

cartoons had come to a halt; still silent in a movie world agog with sound, they could no longer compete. In 1936 Van Beuren tried a comeback with "Felix the Cat and the Goose That Laid the Golden Eggs," but it proved short-lived. Joe Oriolo acquired the title in the 1940s; he successfully revived Felix for television. By 1961, when production was discontinued, he had turned out 260 shorts.

Felix will be remembered for the extraordinary cartoons directed by Messmer in the 1920s. They not only brought the animated cartoon close to technical perfection; they also sometimes approached art in their inspired exploration of the infinite possibilities of motion (translation, dislocation, gyration, etc.). They represent a high-water mark in the history of silent animation.

M.H.

FELLOWS, LAURENCE (1885-1964) American cartoonist and advertising artist born in Ardmore, Pennsylvania, in 1885. Laurence Fellows studied art at the Pennsylvania Academy of Fine Arts, and in England and France. In 1914 he was drawing regularly for *Judge,* sharing spots with the newly sophisticated F.L. Fithian—their subjects were droll society cartoons. Fellows (at one time he signed his work "Felloes") drew large, decorative-type cartoons that usually ran a full page or most of a page and were often tinted in two tones.

Fellows's style must be described as trendy: it was highly mannered and reminiscent of fashion drawings of the day. Heads were small, and everything that could be—clothes, cars, furnishings—was "correct" and thoroughly modern. Lines were thin, and Fellows achieved a handsome balance of open spaces, highlight areas, and pastel shading. This very smart look inspired a school that followed his style into the early 1920s; Ralph Barton and John Held, Jr., were obvious imitators early in their careers.

Fellows, who also drew for *Vanity Fair, Apparel Arts* and *Esquire,* is most remembered for his weekly advertisements for Kelly-Springfield tires. They ran full pages and were insipid cartoon gags hiding behind a smart illustration betraying great technical competence as well as a flawless design sense. Fellows died in 1964.

R.M.

FENDERSON, MARK (1873-1944) American cartoonist born in Minneapolis, Minnesota, in 1873. The Fenderson family moved to Temple, Maine, but upon his father's death young Mark was sent by his mother to her brother's school in Billerica, Massachusetts. Here Mark's uncle discerned in the boy a talent for drawing and encouraged his artistic instincts.

Later, Fenderson was to study art in France and Italy before he returned to America as a newspaper sketch artist. In the 1890s his work began appearing in *Life* on a regular basis. In 1894, he got credit, with Walt McDougall in the *New York World,* for the first colored comic strip in an American newspaper: *The Unfortunate Fate of a Well-Intentioned Dog.* The drawing style suggests that Fenderson supplied the idea; collaborations were uncommon in those days, and the young cartoonist might not as yet have graduated from the apprentice stage, especially where a veteran like McDougall was concerned.

Fenderson's own style was breezy and casual. In later years he seldom drew large-scale cartoons, often confining himself to little squibs, perhaps one column by one inch. He drew in loose, heavy pen or a handsome gray wash. One of his most popular pieces was done for *Life:* a dejected rooster musing, "What's the use? Yesterday an egg, tomorrow a feather duster!" *Life* made a print of the cartoon, and it was a big seller for years. Fenderson also drew for *Judge* and in the 1910s for *Puck,* but he gradually retired from cartooning and became an accomplished and famous wood-carver. He also taught art at the special Townsend Harris High School in New York from 1918 to 1941. He died on December 6, 1944.

R.M.

FERNANDES, MILLÔR (1924-   ) Brazilian cartoonist and playwright born in Rio de Janeiro, Brazil, on August 24, 1924. In 1937, at age 13, Millôr Fernandes (better known as Millôr) started a 25-year-long collaboration with the magazine *O Cruzeiro* as a cartoonist. Under the pseudonym "Emmanuel Vão Gôgo," he contributed cartoons to *O Pif-Paf* (of which he was the founder) and other publications. He was art director of several magazines, including *A Cigarra* and *O Guri* (1940-44), *Detetive* (1940-42) and *Revista do Brasil* (1944-46).

In addition to *O Pif-Paf,* Millôr founded another short-lived magazine, *Voga,* in 1952. He published a book, *Tempo e Contratempo,* in 1956. He is also a talented playwright and the author, among other works, of *Liberdade, Liberdade* (with Flávio Rangel), *Do Tamanho de um Defunto* ("From the Size of a Dead Man"), *Um Elefante no Caos* ("An Elephant into the Chaos") and *O Homem, do Princípio no Fim* ("Man, from Beginning to End"). Millôr has also translated plays by

Laurence Fellows. © *Judge.*

Aramis and the Ferocious Saladin, two characters from "le figurine Perugina." © Perugina.

Shakespeare, Synge and Molière, and has written several teleplays. Among the many awards he has received as a cartoonist are first prize at the 1960 exposition of the Museum of Caricature in Buenos Aires (jointly with Saul Steinberg) and second prize at the 1963 Montreal Salon of Humor. His works have been exhibited in galleries in Rio and elsewhere.

A.M.

George Finey, caricature of prominent Sydney magistrate. © Smith's Weekly.

FIGURINE PERUGINA, LE (Italy) In 1937 the spaghetti and chocolate manufacturers Perugina-Buitoni hit upon the idea of organizing a competition based upon the collection of a series of one hundred trading cards. Whoever completed one album would receive a prize; whoever completed 150 albums would get a car. The cards were placed in each package of chocolate or spaghetti. To design the cards the company called upon newspaper cartoonist Angelo Bioletto, who dreamed up a humorous gallery of celebrated figures from legend and history: D'Artagnan, Buffalo Bill, Tarzan, Greta Garbo, Shanghai Lil, etc. Bioletto's tongue-in-cheek caricatures proved very popular in their own right. By a strange oversight, however, the card representing "the ferocious Saladin" had only limited circulation and caused despair among millions of Italians who could not complete their collections.

After a legal dispute with Perugina, Bioletto designed another series of trading cards for a competing chocolate manufacturer. In 1939 he came back to Perugina to draw more cards for them. Entitled *Two Years Later*, this second Perugina series gave rise to a book but was not as profitable as the first, since this time there was a more exact card count. Bioletto was then sent to Paris to design a similar series based on French movie stars for the French subsidiary of Perugina. He had drawn only 15 figures when war broke out between France and Italy in June 1940.

Bioletto went back to drawing cartoons for newspapers. In 1942 he designed the characters of one of the most famous Italian animated cartoons, *La Rosa de Bagdad*. He is now a noted book illustrator, but in the eyes of many he is still remembered chiefly for his creation of the *figurine Perugina*.

S.T.

FINEY, GEORGE (1895-   ) Australian caricaturist and political cartoonist born in Parnell, Auckland, New Zealand, in 1895.

No appraisal of the great draftsmen working for the Australian press would be complete, or just, without reference to another New Zealander who in 1919 came to Sydney. He is George Finey. At 14 Finey sold his drawings to local newspapers in Parnell. Later, during World War I, he served as an underage private with the New Zealand Expeditionary Force; there, having served three and one-half years on active service, he was appointed an official war artist. After the war, Finey decided to take a refresher course at the Regent Street Polytechnic Art School in London. In 1921, after traveling to Australia, he approached Alek Sass, the art editor of *Smith's Weekly,* and was instantly engaged at £9 ($18) a week, a small fortune in those days, and a sum that was increased to £2,000 ($4,000) a year. Although he drew comic jokes in Australia, it was not for that work but for portrait caricatures that Finey became one of the most famous of 20th-century artists working in this field.

The art of caricature did not have the continuity or persistence of tradition in Australia that it did in Europe, although there was something of a local school of caricature that had been distinguished, though at widely spaced intervals, by the likes of Phil May, Will Dyson and David Low. In recent times it has been furthered by the geometrically stylish caricatures of the Adelaide artist Lionel Coventry, by the outstanding comic portraiture of Noel Counihan (both onetime contributors to the *Bulletin*) and by the highly finished work of Tony Rafty, who is striving to keep this art alive in Australia.

Universally, the convention for popular caricature was to draw a big head, in left or right profile, on a little body; Finey's emphasis was on portraiture—stark, powerful and tremendously dramatic. With his approach to the human face, Finey's caricature portraits were fantastic—pushing and punching his subjects' features across the paper with grotesque but controlled draftsmanship. Finey drew big: often his caricature portraits were nearly twice life size. And he worked in many media—with pen and ink, with oil paint and in a medium recently revived by designers, known as collage. For Finey the latter was a method of picturemaking achieved by pasting down colored paper torn from the advertising pages of magazines.

George Finey was by temperament a bohemian. His hatless, sockless, collarless appearance around the Sydney streets, his tremendous generosity, his perversity and scorn for diplomacy were backed by an artistic achievement that made him a legend during his heyday in the period between World Wars I and II. During World War II Finey drew political cartoons for the *Daily Telegraph* and later for the *Tribune*, both Sydney newspapers. Now in retirement, Finey paints and produces carvings and ceramics.

V.L.

FISCHER, ANTON OTTO (1882-1962) American cartoonist and painter born in Munich, Bavaria, on February 23, 1882. Anton Fischer was orphaned at age five and sent to the local archepiscopal seminary, where he lived for three years. He ran off to sea at age sixteen and saw quite a bit of adventure on sailing and merchant vessels; memorable to him was sailing around Cape Horn.

Following an interest in art, he enrolled at the Académie Julian in Paris, studying there from 1906 to 1908. Fischer decided to come to the United States after having his money stolen; he was then to settle and ultimately become a citizen upon the entrance of America into World War I. Before entering the cartooning and illustration fields, however, he raced on yachts and taught sailing.

After an initial sale to *Harper's Weekly* and a Jack London illustration assignment for *Everybody's*, he did many cartoons for *Life*. He drew cartoons and covers for years, mostly through the 1910s. The bulk of his cartoon work was in the Angus MacDonnall-Power O'Malley vein—nostalgic and sentimental scenes. As time went on, marine themes dominated his work, and he eventually left cartooning to become a noted marine painter. Even in the 1930s and 1940s, when he frequently illustrated for the *Saturday Evening Post*, much of it was sea-oriented. He did humorous illustrations for the riotous, classic *Glencannon* stories by Guy Kilpatrick and the *Tugboat Annie* stories of Norman Reilly Raine.

During World War II Fischer was active in the Coast Guard as artist laureate, was named a commander in the reserves, and published a book, *Fo'c's'le Days* (1947). He died on March 26, 1962.

R.M.

FISCHETTI, GIOVANNI (1916-   ) American artist born in Brooklyn, New York, on September 27, 1916. John Fischetti lived a childhood of varied experiences, dropping out of Catholic Sunday school to be confirmed as a German Lutheran, and dropping out of high school to travel and seek employment around

"Forward!"

Giovanni Fischetti. © Chicago Daily News.

the country. He took a job for a time operating the elevator in the hotel of Rollin Kirby, his idol, and he spent a year at sea working on a steamer. From 1937 to 1940 Fischetti studied art at the Pratt Institute and then traveled west to seek a job in cartooning. He worked for awhile at the Disney studios until eyestrain forced him to abandon in-betweening. Freelancing in Los Angeles, San Francisco and Chicago followed, including work for *Coronet* and *Esquire*. Just before the war, he became the editorial cartoonist for the *Chicago Sun*.

In Europe, during his military service, Fischetti rose to the rank of sergeant and was a staffer on *Stars and Stripes*, where he formed friendships with future cartoonists Gill Fox, Dick Wingert and Curt Swan. Back in America, with his *Sun* job unavailable, he freelanced in various capacities and cartooned for *Coronet*, *Pageant*, the *Saturday Evening Post* and the *New York Times Magazine*. He also painted color editorial cartoons for *Collier's* and assisted Dick Wingert on *Hubert*. He drew for the *New York Herald-Tribune* before joining the Newspaper Enterprise Association as its editorial cartoonist, succeeding Dorman H. Smith.

The NEA served many hundreds of papers, and during his years there (1951-62) Fischetti was probably the most published editorial cartoonist in America. But editorial strictures and the necessity of keeping everything general enough for an army of editors of various persuasions eventually made him restive. Fischetti accepted an offer to join the *Herald-Tribune* in New York but insisted on his own terms: utter editorial freedom. Having won this much, he went a step further and sought to change the look of his—and hopefully, by example, others'—formats and concept presentation.

Fischetti's style had been solid and somewhat traditional, executed in the vertical format with brush and crayon. He now sought to emulate the European convention of horizontal cartoons and abandon the tired icons of donkeys and Uncle Sams, replacing them with social-commentary themes. Points were scored through wry humor rather than by a cluster of labels, and in this he borrowed the magazine approach. (Indeed, he had been contributing to *Punch* for several years before the thematic inspiration struck.) His cartoons at once became influential and widely reprinted, due as much to the format innovation as to his very real sense of conceptual execution and literate partisanship. And he very clearly paved the way for the "new look" of Oliphant and others several years later.

With the demise of the *Herald-Tribune* in 1966, Fischetti moved to the *Chicago Daily News*, the paper of his syndicate's half-owner, Marshall Field. Within three years he had won a Pulitzer Prize. Other awards include the National Headliners Medal in 1951, the Sigma Delta Chi award in 1956 and 1958 and the National Cartoonists Society editorial award in 1963 and 1964. He was also presented with an honorary doctor of fine arts degree from Colby College. In 1973, the liberal cartoonist penned an autobiography, *Zinga Zinga Za!*, relating his life story, telling tales of many cartoonist friends (by whom he is beloved), and collecting the best cartoons of his career.

R.M.

FISCHINGER, OSKAR (1900-1967) American animator and painter born in Gelnhausen, Germany, in June 1900. Oskar Fischinger, who always had a talent for drawing, had to quit school in order to help support his impoverished family. He worked as an apprentice in a furniture factory and later designed church organs. Finding his surroundings too constricting, Fischinger moved first to Munich in the early 1920s, and then to Berlin in 1927. While in Berlin he became interested in film and devised the special effects photography for Fritz Lang's 1928 science fiction movie, *Die Frau im Mond*.

In 1930 Fischinger started work on a series of startlingly original film cartoons in which he used abstract forms synchronized to music on the soundtrack. Some of his most famous creations include *Studie No. 8*, to the accompaniment of Paul Dukas's "The Sorcerer's Apprentice," *Hungarian Dance* (on Brahms's music), and *Lieberspiel* ("Love Game"). In 1933 he began experimenting with color, and this gave rise to his best-known work, *Komposition in Blau* ("Composition in Blue"), a delightful kaleidoscope of forms, shapes and patterns moving rhythmically to music.

With the coming to power of the Nazis Fischinger's experimentation was increasingly hampered; his works were branded as decadent, and he finally went to the United States on a contract with Paramount Films in 1936. His credits at Paramount include a number of special effects for films, particularly *Allegretto*, his animated introduction to *The Big Broadcast of 1937*. It was Fischinger who first suggested to Leopold Stokowski the idea for a feature-length animated film on music; this eventually led to Walt Disney's *Fantasia*. Fischinger was hired to work on *Fantasia* (the Toccata and Fugue sequence was based entirely on his designs) but quit after nine months. Fischinger's last work of animation was *Motion Painting*, on a grant from the Guggenheim Foundation.

Oskar Fischinger was a pioneer in the use of abstract design and music in animation. He received many awards for his work, notably at the Venice and Brussels festivals. In the 1940s, however, he decided to abandon animation for painting. He exhibited widely in the United States and abroad; his last painting, fittingly titled *Nirvana*, was completed a few weeks before his death in 1967.

Fischinger's widow, Elfriede Fischinger, is currently at work on a biography of the artist.

M.H.

FISHER, DUDLEY (1890-1951) American cartoonist born in Columbus, Ohio, in 1890. Dudley Fisher entered Ohio State University in 1910, attending classes at the Arts College for a little over a year. Dropping out of college, he went to work in the art department of the *Columbus Dispatch* at the end of 1911. During World War I, he was commissioned a second lieutenant and commanded the 45th Photo Section of the army. While flying over enemy-held territory taking pictures, Fisher acquired his individual bird's-eye-view style of drawing scenes from his war experience.

Returning to the *Dispatch* in 1919, Fisher redesigned the photo department and later that year created *Jolly Jingles*, a two-color daily panel of illustrated verse which eventually developed into a Sunday feature. It was while working on an idea for *Jolly Jingles* in 1937 that Fisher came up with the concept of a Sunday page illustrating in a single panel the doings of a farm family being visited by their big-city relatives. He later developed the feature more fully under the title *Right Around Home*, and in January 1938 King Features started syndicating it nationally. The panel proved so successful that King asked Fisher to do a daily spin-off in comic strip form: this was *Myrtle*, started in 1942.

A diligent sort, Fisher continued to work for the *Dispatch*, drawing his daily and Sunday features at the same time. He died of a heart attack on July 10, 1951, while on a vacation trip in Rockport, Massachusetts. *Right Around Home* and *Myrtle* went on, however, for almost two decades longer.

M.H.

FISHER, HARRISON (1877-1934) American cartoonist and illustrator born in Brooklyn, New York, on July 22, 1877. Harrison Fisher's father, Hugh Antoine Fisher, was a landscape painter who began to instruct his son when he was only six. When the family moved to San Francisco, young Harrison entered the Mark Hopkins Institute of Art and by age 16 was already drawing for the *San Francisco Call* (and later the *Examiner*).

Returning to New York in the late 1890s, Fisher submitted two drawings to *Puck* and soon was hired as a staff artist. His pen-and-ink work showed the same spirit as Charles Gibson's—handsome women and virile men—but it has to be judged mostly on its imitative qualities, as aping Gibson was the major goal of the young artist. It was a fault, however, common to a whole generation of new cartoonists, and Fisher soon distinguished himself.

His style attained a maturity without ever losing its boldness. The "Fisher Girl" became another American favorite, and his pretty heads and striking groups soon graced the pages of the *Saturday Evening Post, Ladies' Home Journal, McClure's* and *Cosmopolitan*, among others. Eventually *Cosmopolitan* hired him exclusively for covers, often rendered in pastels, before he retired to paint portraits and etch. Fisher died on January 19, 1934.

R.M.

FITZPATRICK, DANIEL ROBERT (1891-1969) American Pulitzer Prize-winning cartoonist born in Superior, Wisconsin, on March 5, 1891. Dan Fitzpatrick was educated at public schools in Superior and attended art classes at the Chicago Art Institute. In 1911 he accepted a job on the *Chicago Daily News* drawing editorial cartoons and general art assignments. In two years his forceful cartoons, signed "Fitz," attracted the Pulitzer organization; *New York World*-bound Robert Minor's position as chief editorial cartoonist for the *St. Louis*

Post-Dispatch was offered to the 21-year-old cartoonist. It was another fateful match, just as with Rollin Kirby at the *World* later the same year. Fitzpatrick was to become a fixture in St. Louis and nationally for the next 45 years. He was widely reprinted and copied and was the recipient of many awards, including Pulitzers in 1926 and 1955.

Fitzpatrick was Minor's heir in another way—the generous utilization of grease crayon as a shading device. When Fitzpatrick began to use it, most cartoonists still shaded with crosshatching. He was to use it more heavily than most, and his cartoons—built on lush brushstrokes—are dark, brooding, powerful statements. The crayon-on-grain also covered minor deficiencies, such as Fitzpatrick's faulty rendering of anatomy; indeed, many cartoons have absolutely no figures in them or have characters occupying a very small proportion of the space. Mood was essential to the typical Fitzpatrick cartoon.

He was fiercely liberal and influenced the styles of many of the succeeding generation of cartoonists, including Ross Lewis and Tom Little. Fitzpatrick drew for *Collier's* in the 1920s and won many distinctions, including the John Frederick Lewis Prize for caricature at the Pennsylvania Academy of Fine Arts in 1924 and the Distinguished Service Journalism Medal from the University of Missouri in 1958. He retired in 1958 and died on May 18, 1969.

R.M.

FLAGG, JAMES MONTGOMERY (1877-1960) American cartoonist and illustrator born in Pelham Manor, New York, on June 18, 1877. Young James Flagg was raised in Brooklyn and Yorkville and displayed an early interest in drawing. He sold his first cartoon to *St. Nicholas* magazine at age 12—it was a group of illustrated Latin

Wings over Europe

Daniel Fitzpatrick. © St. Louis Post-Dispatch.

James Montgomery Flagg, 1911.

axioms, a humorous device common since pre-Civil War days—for $10.

Although Flagg later claimed to be "firmly established" on the staffs of *Life* and *Judge* at the age of 14, his work did not regularly begin appearing until the mid-1890s. Through association with *St. Nick*, he had entrance to the *Century* offices and gained access to the originals of Frost, Abbey, Pyle, Kemble and others, the better to study their work. His first sale, to *Life* for eight dollars, was followed by almost forty years' association with that magazine as well as with its rival, *Judge*.

Flagg's style grew less cartoony as he joined the multitudes seeking to copy Charles Gibson's style—rather awkwardly at first. But he preserved his cartoon discipline for interior work in the magazines (paintings graced the covers); *Nervy Nat* was a colored comic strip with captions instead of balloons that ran in *Judge* for years and was wildly successful, inspiring even the young W.C. Fields as he fashioned his vaudeville tramp character. Also, illustrated puns were common, pictured limericks danced for years through *Life*'s pages, and ultimately, of course, Gibson-style society drawings by Flagg were spread over double pages.

Flagg's friendships with J.A. Mitchell, founder and art editor of *Life*, and Grant Hamilton, art editor of *Judge*, stood his career in good stead—Flagg's famous force of personality and grand manner were as much responsible for his popularity as was his artwork. In later years he was the toast of Broadway and Hollywood for his famous impromptu portrait sketches of celebrities. These two-minute drawings were among the best works of his career, certainly as mature and accomplished as any pen-and-inks, covers or posters.

It was as a poster artist that Flagg gained his greatest recognition, particularly for "Uncle Sam Wants You!," a recruiting poster from World War I that first appeared as a cover for *Leslie's Weekly*, which was owned by *Judge*. He also did other posters during both World Wars and conservation posters in the 1930s.

Flagg's artistic influence was great; if he never had the elegance of Gibson, he had an overwhelming sincerity and forcefulness in his work. Where Gibson was reserved, Flagg had flair, mirroring his own personality. His men were not only good-looking, but dashing and virile. His women (and *Judge* early touted the "Flagg Girl") were seldom demure but rather handsome and assured.

His social influence was great, too, and many

The Fleischer studio's Ko-Ko the Clown. © *Fleischer.*

anecdotes in and out of art circles survive. He was a founder of the Dutch Treat Club and a prime figure in the Artists' and Writers' Balls. His many portraits, sketches and program covers for the Lambs attest to his conviviality. He was the friend of actors, presidents and other artists. And his themes and delineations of women were so individual that they became a genre bearing his name. Flagg died in New York on May 27, 1960.

Books: *The Diva's Ruby* (1908); *City People* (1909); *Yours Truly* (1910); *Personality Plus* by Edna Ferber (1914); *I Should Say So* (1914); *His Soul Marches On* (1921); *A Lighter of Flames* by William S. Hart (1923); several small books published by *Life* before 1910, including *Tomfoolery, If, or a Guide to Bad Manners* and *Why They Married*; and his autobiography *Roses and Buckshot* (1946).

R.M.

FLEISCHER, DAVID (1894-1979) American animator and producer, younger brother of Max Fleischer, born in New York City on July 14, 1894. Dave Fleischer exhibited a strong penchant for drawing in his early years, but upon leaving high school, the only job he could find was as a theater usher. Soon afterward, however, he found work at an engraving company and in 1912 became a cutter for Pathé Films.

Dave Fleischer's career in animation started in 1915, when he joined his brother Max in the production of the *Out of the Inkwell* cartoons. After a brief stint in the army during World War I, Fleischer went back to animation and in 1919, again with his brother Max, set up Out of the Inkwell Films, later to become Fleischer Studios. From that time on Dave became the titular director of all the Fleischer cartoons (Max being the producer), working on *Betty Boop, Popeye, Gulliver's Travels* and others. His main contribution took the form of the many gags that he was endlessly able to work into the Fleischer cartoons.

In 1942, after a falling out with Paramount (which released the Fleischer films), Dave became the head animator at Columbia Pictures. He produced some of the *Fox and Crow* cartoons, as well as a short-lived *Li'l Abner* series, before leaving in 1944 for Universal. There, among other things, he is reported to have been in on the origin of the *Francis the Talking Mule* series of live-action films. Dave Fleischer retired in 1967 and died in June 1979.

Dave Fleischer's career has been retraced in Leslie Cabarga's *The Fleischer Story* (Nostalgia Press, 1976).

M.H.

FLEISCHER, MAX (1883-1972) American cartoonist and film producer born in Vienna, Austria, on July 19, 1883 (not 1885 or 1888, which have for a long time been the accepted dates). At the age of four Max Fleischer was taken to the United States by his parents, who settled in New York. He attended Evening High School, the Mechanics and Tradesmen's School, the Art Students League (where one of his teachers was George Bridgman) and Cooper Union. Having completed his training, Max Fleischer starting working in 1900 as an errand boy for the *Brooklyn Eagle*, later graduating to the art department. After a few years he left for Boston to take a better-paying job as a retoucher and photoengraver.

Returning to New York in 1914, he became the art editor of *Popular Science Monthly*, where he wrote and illustrated articles on recent inventions. Combining his talent as an artist and his taste for technical innovation, Fleischer developed, in collaboration with his brother, Dave, the "rotoscope," a device for tracing live action into animated footage, thus eliminating many painstaking steps in the animation process. The machine was patented in 1917. (Fleischer's love of science stood him in good stead; in 1923 he produced an animated film called *The Einstein Theory of Relativity*.) With the help of the rotoscope, Max and Dave Fleischer completed their first cartoon, *Out of the Inkwell*. They presented it to J.R. Bray, who commissioned them to do an animated cartoon a month, to be released through Paramount. After the start of World War I, Fleischer also produced a number of technical cartoons for the U.S. Army.

In 1919 Max and Dave Fleischer founded Out of the Inkwell, Inc. They turned out not only *Inkwell* cartoons (which featured the famous Ko-Ko the Clown) but also the celebrated *Screen Songs* series, in which the spectators were urged to "follow the bouncing ball" and sing along. When sound came to film, Fleischer was one of the first to see its possibilities; he produced his *Talkartoons*, introducing Bimbo the Dog and later Betty Boop (1930), who soon became the star of the Fleischer studios. In 1933 Fleischer brought Popeye to the screen, and he soon had two hits on his hands.

A strike by the employees in 1937 briefly threatened the Fleischer studios, leading Max to open his new studio in the more propitious environment of Miami, Florida, in 1938. There he embarked on his most ambitious project, a full-length animated version of *Gulliver's Travels*, completed in 1939. It proved moderately successful, but another feature, *Mr. Bug Goes to Town* (1941) was a dismal flop. This precipitated a conflict between the Fleischer brothers and their distributor, Paramount Pictures, and in 1942 the Fleischers were summarily dismissed by Paramount, which took over their production directly (mainly *Popeye* and *Superman* cartoons).

Max Fleischer remained in animation for some time, producing *Rudolph the Red-Nosed Reindeer* in 1944 and starting his own animation correspondence course in 1951. In 1955 he sued Paramount for title to his old cartoons but lost. In 1958 he went back to the J.R. Bray studio as head of the art department, and in 1961 he produced a new, cheaply done series of *Out of the Inkwell* cartoons. Dispirited and bitter, Max Fleischer retired to the Motion Picture Country Home and Hospital in Woodland, California, where he died, almost completely forgotten, on September 11, 1972.

A full-length study of the Fleischer studios, Leslie Cabarga's *The Fleischer Story*, was published by Nostalgia Press in 1976.

M.H.

FLINTSTONES, THE (U.S.) The Hanna-Barbera studios produced the first animation series ever to be seen on prime-time television. It was called *The Flintstones* and debuted on CBS in the fall of 1960. For this series Hanna and Barbera simply adapted the clichés of 1960s situation comedy to a Stone Age setting, the mythical town of Bedrock.

Reputedly modeled on the tremendously popular *The Honeymooners*, *The Flintstones* featured the loudmouthed, know-it-all Fred Flintstone (in a variation on the Jackie Gleason character) lording it over gaping, gullible Barney Rubble (a takeoff on the Art Carney role). The "boys" were often in competition with their domineering spouses, the acidulous Wilma Flintstone and the sarcastic Betty Rubble, and they had to concoct all kinds of excuses in order to get out to an evening of bowling or a meeting of the Waterbuffaloes lodge. The stories were carried in an adequate but pedestrian style of limited animation, a far cry from Hanna and Barbera's halcyon days at MGM.

"The Flintstones." © *Hanna-Barbera.*

"Flip the Frog." © *Celebrity Pictures.*

The gags were often supplied by the incongruity of modern appliances in prehistoric times: foot-propelled automobiles, pterodactyl-winged planes, dinosaur-powered cranes and so on. After awhile, however, these inventions began to wear thin. The marital fights that fueled the plots of many of the half-hour episodes also became hackneyed and increasingly repetitive. Two infants were introduced to the series in an attempt to bring new life to it: the mischievous Pebbles (daughter of the Flintstones) and the muscular Bamm-Bamm (son of the Rubbles). Their shenanigans failed to save the show, which mercifully ended in 1964. This was not the end of the Flintstones, however, as they went into wide syndication the next year; Fred Flintstone's famous battle cry, "Yabba Dabba Doo," can still be heard on the *Flintstones and Friends* show broadcast over hundreds of stations.

The Flintstones was Hanna and Barbera's most popular and successful creation. It was transposed to the movie screen in the spy-thriller spoof *A Man Called Flintstone* (1965), in which the animation, while expertly handled, still did not amount to much. The Flintstones have enjoyed a long career in newspapers with their own comic strip, drawn by Gene Hazelton and distributed by McNaught Syndicate since 1961; and they also have appeared in comic books without interruption since 1961.

M.H.

FLIP THE FROG (U.S.) After leaving Walt Disney in 1930, Ub Iwerks set up his own animation studio; there, the following year, he created his most celebrated series, *Flip the Frog*. In the beginning the series was more than a little reminiscent of the *Mickey Mouse* shorts (to which Iwerks's contribution had been decisive), but it slowly acquired a style and pace of its own. Iwerks had a great talent for drawing and animation, but he lacked a strong story sense, and his plotting tended to meander.

In all, Iwerks made 36 cartoons for Celebrity Pictures (which at one point intended to rename the title character Tony). All of these are scintillating little gems, the more notable (if a choice has to be made) being "The Cuckoo Murder Case" and "Fiddlesticks" (both 1931), "Africa Squeaks," "Spooks" and "Phoney Express" (all 1932), "Flip's Lunch Room" and "Chinaman's Chance" (both 1933). The last entry in the series was released in 1934.

The *Flip the Frog* cartoons enjoyed only moderate success when they were first released. They are now being rediscovered and shown at animation festivals around the world—a fitting if belated tribute to the brilliant but star-crossed creativity of Ub Iwerks.

M.H.

FLOHRI, EMIL (1869-1938) American cartoonist born in 1869. Emil Flohri joined the staff of *Leslie's Weekly* as an artist at the age of 16 and soon switched to the affiliated *Judge* magazine, where he drew humorous panels in pen and ink before switching to stone. Flohri became an accomplished lithographer, and his political cartoons in color are masterpieces of subtlety. He developed a technique of capturing photographic likenesses and drew many decorative holiday covers for *Judge* as well as specialties like the *Sis Hopkins Joke Book* magazine covers. Around 1910 he took up the brush and executed many of *Judge's* last colored political cartoons.

Flohri remained in New York through the 1910s, drawing pen-and-ink cartoons and illustrating. In 1920 he moved to California and there painted portraits of silent film stars—a carry-over from similar duties on *Film Fun* magazine, a *Judge* publication, in the 1910s. In the late 1920s he went to work for Walt Disney and remained there for nearly a decade. He died in Van Nuys the day before Christmas, 1938.

Flohri had an amazingly agreeable style, at once comic and realistic. His moods were gentle, and his humor never of the slapstick variety. He was a strong Republican, and his cartoons were very influential in every presidential campaign between 1896 and 1908.

R.M.

FLORA, PAUL (1922-   ) Austrian cartoonist and illustrator born in Glorenza, Italy (which is called Glurns by Austrians and lies in the much disputed South Tyrol-Alto Adige area), on June 29, 1922. After schooling in Innsbruck, Paul Flora studied from 1942 to 1944 at the Munich Academy under Olaf Gulbrannson, the master of line drawing and a great contributor to *Simplicissimus*. After military service in 1944 and 1945, Flora set up as a freelance artist in Innsbruck. His varied work is published in Germany and Switzerland as well as in Austria, so that he is one of the key artistic figures of the entire German-speaking territory.

During the 1950s Flora built up an unshakable reputation as an intellectual and witty cartoonist with imaginative subject matter and a quizzical, probing line akin to Steinberg's or Thurber's. Among his highly successful albums of that decade were two that punned on his name—*Flora's Fauna* and *Trauerflora* (without the final *a*, this means "mourning crepe" in German)—as well as *Das Musenross* ("The Steed of the Muses"), *Das Schlachtross* ("The War Horse"), *Menschen und Andere Tiere* ("People and Other Animals") and *Vivat Vamp*. In the same years, he was busy illustrating numerous books, including an edition of Wilde's *Canterville Ghost*, a literary anthology by Erich Kästner, H. Weigel's *O Du Mein Osterreich* ("My Austria") and anthologies of ghost and spy stories.

Meanwhile, in 1957, Flora began a secondary career as a political cartoonist for the Hamburg weekly *Die Zeit*. These drawings are more stumpy, sketchy and simple than the bulk of his work and reveal no profound insight into world affairs, but they are genuinely amusing and likable. A collection of 200 of them was published in 1962 with the punning title *Ach du Liebe Zeit!* ("Oh, What Wonderful Times!").

In the 1960s Flora turned to more pretentious albums in which, without an appreciable growth in technique, he concentrated on ominous scenes of empty houses, assassinations of kings in frightening palaces, the seamy side of cities and the like, indulging in a personal mythology made up of such figures as omnipresent scarecrows. Albums in this series include *Der Zahn der Zeit* ("The Tooth of Time," 1961), *Königsdramen* ("Royal Dramas," 1966) and *Veduten und Figuren* ("Views and Figures," 1968), which boasts an appreciative foreword by the major Swiss dramatist Friedrich Dürrenmatt.

S.A.

FLUFFY RUFFLES (U.S.) Wallace Morgan's *Fluffy Ruffles*, a verse-captioned, multi-panel Sunday color page about a woman so stunningly lovely and superbly dressed that she proved too disconcerting to susceptible males to hold any job, began in the *New York Herald* just after the turn of the century. It was distributed across the country to a multitude of papers printing *Herald* features and proved to be a nationwide hit by the close of the year. *Fluffy Ruffles* was so winningly drawn by Morgan, and her outfits so stylishly representative, that she was accepted from coast to coast as a weekly symbol of what young American womanhood should emulate and young American manhood should admire.

Fluffy's lightly comic attempts to hold one position after another, each failing because of her devastating effect on men, was the weekly theme of the Morgan feature until its close on January 3, 1909. After 14 months of globe-girdling career pursuits, Fluffy's quest climaxed in her conquest of Paris and receipt of the "freedom of the city" on a silver salver. In the meantime, one thousand stores across the nation had featured "Fluffy Ruffles sales" or singled out particularly attractive gowns and dresses as "Fluffy Ruffles specials"; at least one hit song had been published ("My Irish Fluffy Ruffles" by Will A. Heelan and Albert Gumble, in November 1908); a book collection had seen print; and the heroine's name had entered the language for the next few decades as a synonym for any woman dressed in the height of fashion and dashingly lovely as well.

Morgan moved on, the week after *Fluffy Ruffles*'s close, to start a new but similar weekly feature for the *Herald* called *Cynthianna Blythe*, with verses written by Harry Grant Dart, himself a cartoonist of note. *Cynthianna Blythe* ran until February 1910 and was replaced by a new verse-and-picture weekly feature titled *The Widow Wise*, by a different artist and writer. Morgan then returned to the magazine illustration work which had already gained him national fame.

B.B.

FOGELBERG, OLA (1894-1952) Finnish cartoonist born in Oulunkylä, Finland (then part of the Russian empire), on July 7, 1894. During his relatively short life Ola Fogelberg experienced and depicted in his car-

Ola Fogelberg ("Fogeli"), "Finland and Russia."

toons all the great and traumatic changes in recent Finnish history: the czarist repression, independence, revolution and civil war, short-lived monarchy, and two world wars.

In the 1910s, after his school years, Fogelberg (alias "Fogeli") devoted himself to cartooning. He studied art and animated film in Paris, Italy, Leipzig and Berlin. He traveled extensively and published a book based on his experiences (*Harhateillä*, 1920). Fogeli's work seems to have been influenced by the Jugendstil movement. He also mentioned the work of the Swedish satirist Albert Engström as one of the most important influences on him.

In the golden era of the humor magazines of the Finnish workers' movement, Fogeli was the most active political cartoonist in the most important magazine, *Kurikka*. In his cartoons he slashed at political trials, prisons, lawlessness, excessive authority, and the rise of fascism. Earlier he had courageously attacked the czar, Rasputin and Kerensky, and in this connection his character, the young "maiden Finland" (*Suomineito*) became well known. He also drew portraits of the workers' leaders and scenes of the 1918 civil war.

Most of the time Fogeli worked for the large cooperative chain Elanto, where he was first a commercial artist and then, for a long time, the head of the advertising department. Many of his cartoons and books were meant to advance the ideals of the cooperative movement. He did posters, vignettes, and children's books. His cartoons appeared in such publications as *Elanto*, *Kuluttajain Lehti* and *Suomen Kuvalehti*, among others.

Fogeli was an amiable, impulsive and colorful man, and a versatile one—a nationally famous athlete, a family man, an inventor. He was a pioneer of animation in Finland (starting in 1927) as well as a comic strip artist. Fogeli left Elanto in 1944, and during his later years he drew almost exclusively his wonderfully funny comics, notably *Pekka Puupää*, which he had created in 1925. He worked on them even on his deathbed. He died on August 25, 1952, in Helsinki.

J.R.

FOGELI
See Fogelberg, Ola.

FOGHORN LEGHORN (U.S.) During his long tenure at Warner Brothers, Robert McKimson proved himself a skilled and imaginative animation director; yet he contributed only one memorable character to the Warner cartoon menagerie, and that was Foghorn Leghorn, the boisterous rooster who sprang to life in 1946 in a cartoon titled "Walky Talky Hawky."

In this first cartoon, as in many of the later ones, Foghorn was bedeviled by the diminutive Henery Hawk, who kept trying to catch the imposing bird despite their disparity in size ("I'm a chicken hawk and you're a chicken; are you coming with me, or do I have to use force?"). Another thorn in Foghorn's side was the widow Priscilla, who was also forever trying to ensnare the rooster, but for matrimonial purposes. To humor the old hen, Foghorn would take her genius son Egghead on country outings and try to teach him the rudiments of life, only to be shown up by the precocious youngster (in "Crockett Doodle-Doo," for instance, Foghorn tries to teach Egghead the art of building a fire, baiting a trap and catching fish, but he is hopelessly outclassed in every department by his charge).

Foghorn Leghorn is reported to have been inspired by Fred Allen's impersonation of Senator Claghorn. As voiced by Mel Blanc in an irresistible twang, the rooster came through as an overbearing and obnoxious ignoramus who never learns from his mistakes. Never quite as popular as his Warner *compères*, Foghorn Leghorn made his last bow, along with the others, sometime in the 1960s.

M.H.

"Foghorn Leghorn." © *Warner Brothers.*

Peter Foldes, "Daphnis et Chloé." © ORTF.

FOLDES, PETER (1924-1977) Hungarian cartoonist, painter and animator born near Budapest, Hungary, in 1924. Peter Foldes moved to England in 1946 and studied at the Slade School of Art and the Courtauld Institute. In 1951, with a grant from the British Film Institute and in collaboration with his wife, Joan, he realized *Animated Genesis*, a surrealistic work of animation characterized by unpredictable motions and bold patterns (the film was awarded a prize at the 1952 Cannes Festival). *A Short Vision*, on the theme of nuclear devastation, followed in 1954 (it also won a prize, at Venice in 1956). Despite his *succès d'estime*, no work was forthcoming in Britain, and Foldes left for France.

For ten years (1956-66) Foldes devoted himself entirely to painting, moving from abstract to minimal art, and from stabiles to mobiles. His paintings were widely exhibited throughout Europe, in the United States and in South America. Foldes's first love remained animation, however, and he returned to the field in 1966 with *Un Garçon Plein d'Avenir* ("A Lad with a Future"), a fantastic gallery of metamorphoses and transformations. Three more works followed in quick succession: *Un Appétit d'Oiseau* ("Eating Like a Bird"), a ferocious description of the war between the sexes; *Plus Vite* ("Faster"), a fanciful statement about a society gone stark mad; and *Eveil* ("Awakening"), a more sedate short subject.

In the 1970s Foldes's talents blossomed in all directions. He went on painting, tried his hand at a short-lived comic strip, *Lucy* (1974), and directed a number of advertising films. Occasionally he went back to animation: *Daphnis et Chloé, La Faim* ("Hunger," 1974) and *Je, Tu, Elles* ("I, You, They"), which blend animation and live action, are among his most notable later works. At the same time he experimented with computer animation, notably in Canada, and his works became more and more detached from objective reality. He died in Paris in 1977.

Peter Foldes was one of the most fascinating of modern animators. His works have received the highest praise and have been just as vehemently condemned. Lack of consistency always plagued even his best efforts, and his *oeuvre* remains enigmatic and somewhat disappointing.

M.H.

FOLGER, FRANKLIN (1919-   ) American gag cartoonist born in Westboro, Ohio, on January 28, 1919. Franklin Folger, whose popular newspaper-panel gag feature about suburban housewives, *The Girls*, was widely followed in the 1950s and 1960s, sold his first gag cartoon at 15. He studied at the art academy in Cincinnati, Ohio, for three years in the mid-1930s and continued with gag cartoon work while sharing a Manhattan studio with fellow cartoonist Stan Stamaty. Folger was drafted in 1942 but returned to civilian cartoon work four years later. He also did advertising art for awhile before he created *The Girls* for the *Christian Science Monitor* of Boston in 1948.

Moving on to the *Cincinnati Enquirer* in 1952, Folger saw his increasingly popular feature (essentially his interpretation of the Helen Hokinson clubwomen types long featured in the *New Yorker*) syndicated nationally in 1953; it continued to be widely syndicated for the next two decades. *The Girls* is now distributed by Field Newspaper Syndicate and has been collected in several books. Folger still lives near Cincinnati, where he contributes cartoons to various magazines.

B.B.

FOLON, JEAN-MICHEL (1934-   ) Belgian cartoonist, illustrator and lithographer born at Uccle-Brussels, Belgium, on March 1, 1934. J.M. Folon attended the Brussels School of Architecture but soon dropped out to move to Paris in search of a career in graphic art. In the early 1950s he contributed many cartoons to *L'Express* and *Le Nouvel Observateur*, two French newsweeklies. His drawings for *Fortune* and the *New Yorker* in the 1960s spread his fame to the United States. In 1965 an exhibition of his works was held at the School of Visual Arts in New York.

Folon, who is also the author of a number of books, perceives the world as dehumanized and desensitized. "We live in the jungle of the cities, signs grow like trees, in the place of trees," he says. His cartoon universe, in which men are dwarfed by the proliferation of panels,

Jean-Michel Folon, "The Jungle of Cities." © Folon.

signs and symbols, reflects this dark view. It is worthy of note, however, that Folon, himself a successful creator of advertising symbols, is one more contributor to the very alienation he denounces. Folon has largely abandoned cartoons in recent times in favor of lithographs and serigraphs.

One of the most significant graphic artists of our time, Folon is representative of a whole generation of graphic practitioners who hold that multiplicity of clever and imaginative design ideas can make up for paucity of philosophical concepts. It is therefore not surprising that Folon should be most celebrated in New York City, where this view is most prevalent.

M.H.

FOOLISH QUESTIONS (U.S.) Rube Goldberg's earliest separately titled continuing feature to become an individual hit with readers was *Foolish Questions*. This intermittent daily panel was first drawn as a small part of Goldberg's large *New York Evening Mail* sports page cartoon layout in late 1908. Contrived as a mild putdown of the sort of pointless questions anyone can encounter (or ask) about the obvious, *Foolish Questions* had no continuing characters and was essentially patterned on the following format: a goofy-looking person asks another engaged in some visually evident course of action (e.g., smoking a pipe, putting a golf ball, typing) if that is indeed what he is doing ("Hey, are you smoking a pipe . . . putting . . . typing . . . ?"). The second individual, disgusted, makes a sarcastic riposte ("No, I'm frying smelt for dinner . . . kicking a field goal . . . tiptoeing through the tulips. . . ."). The gag was funny the first few times, simply on a self-recognition basis, but Goldberg repeated it hundreds of times over the years. He revived it over and over again in later miscellany gag pages, seemingly to inexhaustible reader approbation, with only minor variants and only a vestige of imaginative relevance in the sarcastic responses to the questions.

A very typical *Foolish Questions* exchange from 1908—the second one, reprinted in Peter C. Marzio's *Rube Goldberg* (1973)—runs flatly as follows: Goofy: "Hello, George. Are you going automobiling?" Driver, dressed in full gear of the period, near his car: "No, I'm going out to play a game of checkers." The panels carried multiple-digit numbers for each question, largely to indicate the endless quantity of such inquiries, so that *Foolish Questions No. 308,792* might be followed the next day by *Foolish Questions No. 997,608*, and so on. Not very memorable or amusing in bulk, *Foolish Questions* ran in one form or another in Goldberg's work through his last potpourri page, *Sideshow*, in the late 1930s.

B.B.

FORAIN, JEAN-LOUIS (1852-1931) French cartoonist, lithographer, etcher and painter born in Rheims, France, on October 23, 1852. After one year of studies at the Ecole des Beaux-Arts of Paris, Jean-Louis Forain earned his living as a cartoonist for various minor newspapers and periodicals, mainly *Le Scapin* and *La Cravache Parisienne*, where his first sketches were published in 1876. Taking Parisian life as his inspiration, he attacked, often in sarcastic fashion, the world of politics, high finance, law and the theater in series such as *Les Affaires* ("Business") or *Dans les Coulisses* ("In the Wings"); starting in 1887, these series appeared in the most important publications of the

"Foolish Questions," 1912.

period: *Le Figaro, La Vie Parisienne, Le Rire, Le Journal Amusant*. Later these more than three thousand drawings were collected and released in albums like *Comédie Parisienne* ("Parisian Comedy," 1892), *Les Temps Difficiles* ("Hard Times," 1893) and *Doux Pays* ("Sweet Country," 1897).

In 1889, Forain launched *Le Fifre* in order "to narrate everyday life, to show the silliness of certain sorrows, the sadness of numerous joys, and to record, sometimes harshly, how hypocritically Vice tends to manifest itself in us. This is my goal." This journal was even more ephemeral than *Psst. . . !* (1898-99), which he founded with his friend and fellow cartoonist Caran d'Ache, and which served as a vehicle for his violent attacks on Dreyfus and his supporters. Forain's cartoons were drawn in a caustic and even cruel style further underlined by biting captions, direct and to the point. It is no wonder, then, that Forain has often been called "the Juvenal of the pencil."

In 1879 and 1880 he exhibited some of his paintings alongside the Impressionists, many of whom admired his work (especially Degas, from whom he borrowed the quick-line technique). During World War I he returned to etchings, paintings and lithographs, mainly of religious themes. Many of his drawings, along with Steinlen's, were exhibited at the Arden Gallery of New York in January 1919.

Rich, famous, the host of Parisian high society in his mansion near the Bois de Boulogne, Forain died on July 11, 1931, at the age of 79.

P.H.

FORATTINI, GIORGIO (1932-) Italian cartoonist born near Rome, Italy, in 1932. Giorgio Forattini never com-

Giorgio Forattini. © La Repubblica.

pleted his college studies; instead he went to work in an oil refinery in the 1950s. He then became a salesman for a record company, rising to the position of sales manager. When a flowering of political cartooning took place in Italy in the wake of the 1960s student revolt, Forattini thrust himself to the forefront of the movement. His first drawings appeared in the late 1960s in the daily *Paese Sera* (where he was then working as a graphic designer) and in the weekly *Panorama*. In the 1970s he went over to the daily *La Repubblica* as their regular editorial cartoonist. At present, he also works in Italian television, contributing political and topical cartoons.

Forattini's favorite targets are the high and mighty in all fields; in recent years he has never lacked for models. An anthology of his cartoons, *Quattro Anni di Storia Italiana* ("Four Years of Italian History"), published by Mondadori, reviews the principal deeds (and misdeeds) of Italian politicians, with a few forays abroad (Nixon and Brezhnev are attacked with particular vehemence). In contrast to many other cartoonists, Forattini prefers to ridicule his targets directly, at times focusing on some physical defect (as in the case of former premier Amintore Fanfani), but never falling into vulgarity. More often he denounces with harshness and irony the faults of the powerful, especially the Christian Democrats.

In a sense, Forattini is the cartoonist who most belongs to the tradition of Scalarini and Galantara; but in contrast to these earlier cartoonists, whose vision of the society they fought against was gloomier and more bitter, Forattini is more cheerful, more flippant, more ironic, breezier. In his cartoons there is always a pinch of optimism and confidence that raises a smile even when reality is darker than the mood of his cartoons.

C.S.

FORBELL, CHARLES H. (1886-1946) American cartoonist born in Brooklyn, New York, in 1886. Charles Forbell received his art training from the Pratt Institute in New York and then secured a position on the art staff of the *New York World*. Around 1910 he began submitting cartoons to *Life* and *Judge*, almost all in wash and written by Arthur Crawford. They dealt with all subjects but

often displayed the technical expertise Forbell had acquired at Pratt. Soon he was to restrict himself to a certain few subjects and exploit them for years.

His series involved individual cartoons, usually full-page, that would have taxed a cartoonist with no technical and mechanical background. They were full-scale perspective drawings, complicated architectural scenes and mazes of balconies, parapets and minarets peopled by scores of animated figures. The major series were *In Ye Goode Old Days* for *Life*, and *In Ancient Times* and *Ancient Sources of Modern Inventions* for *Judge* in the 1920s. They were busy drawings, but Forbell was always in control.

"My profession is psychological," he once said. "The art—the draftsmanship—this one must have, but it is a tool through which the message is presented to the public." Even so, he in no way slighted the visual factor.

Forbell also drew daily cartoons featuring a little lamb as advertisements for a clothing company (Rogers Peet) for almost thirty years and produced popular cartoons for the Aetna Casualty Company and the Central Savings Bank of New York. He died in Bayside, New York, on April 15, 1946.

R.M.

FOUGASSE
See Bird, Cyril Kenneth.

FOURBERIES DE FEMMES (France) The theme of the "cuckolded husband" runs through the entire history of French caricature and cartooning. Gavarni mined this rich vein in a series of drawings published between 1837 and 1840. Entitled *Fourberies de Femmes en Matière de Sentiment* ("Women's Deceptions in Matters of the Heart"), they catalogue a whole array of

"Here he comes! Take off your hat."
"Fourberies de Femmes," 1840.

tricks played by cheating wives on their husbands. In one particularly telling cartoon Gavarni shows a visiting "friend" lounging in an armchair with his fly open and his high hat on; the woman, knitting by the window, spies her husband coming and whispers, "Here he comes! . . . Take off your hat."

There was a note of levity in the hundred-odd lithographs Gavarni dedicated to womanhood unrepentant. The cartoonist rarely sided with the husbands, whom he depicted as gross, overbearing, stupid and blind (the lovers usually fared no better). He marveled at the eternal resourcefulness of women more than he sympathized with the eternal plight of husbands. His women, deceiving though they might be, were clearly the most lovable side of the eternal triangle. (Gavarni was probably the French cartoonist most sympathetic to women; he loved to represent them in his drawings, and whatever their rank or status in life, he never ridiculed or castigated them.)

M.H.

FOX, GILBERT THEODORE (1915-   ) American artist born in Brooklyn, New York, on November 29, 1915. Gill Fox evinced an early interest in art and studied at New York's Textile High School, along with future cartoonists John Stanley and Vincent Alacia. He took life drawing lessons at Washington Irving High School and subscribed to the full Landon Correspondence Course. At Textile, he drew for the school paper, *The Spinning Wheel.*

Fox applied to the Fleischer New York animation studios in 1936 and secured a position as an opaquer working on *Popeye* and *Betty Boop* cartoons. He had risen to the rank of inker by the time of the famous strike that ultimately resulted in the studio's move to Florida—and Fox's loss of a job. For a year he drew movie and sports filler pages for the Chesler comic book studio and freelanced to the Major Nicholson shop; then he joined Busy Arnold's comic book crew (1939-43). *Wun Cloo* was Fox's first sale—it was a two-page strip about a Chinese detective—and he soon graduated from filler pages to the assistant editorship of Quality Comics. Here he drew *Poison Ivy, Cyclone Cupid, Super Snooper,* and *Slap Happy Pappy,* as well as covers for *Plastic Man, Doll Man, Uncle Sam, Black Condor* and other titles.

In 1943 Fox joined the army. For *Blood and Fire,* his stateside divisional paper, he drew a strip called *Bernie Blood* and sports and editorial cartoons. In Europe he worked on maps and codes in a G-2 unit near the Siegfried Line and ultimately was transferred to *Stars and Stripes,* working at various times on four editions of the armed forces newspaper and running the Paris office art staff for two months. Fox rejoined the Arnold crew in 1946 and until 1951 worked on such titles as *Daffy, Torchy* and *Candy.* In 1950, while penciling for Arnold, Fox joined the Johnstone and Cushing advertising agency—the legendary shop that produced comic strip ads for dozens of products. Fox's accounts included Ex-Lax, the Ford Times, Campbell's beans, Smith Brothers, Realemon, and Prestone. At this time he also became associated with *Boys' Life* magazine, ghosting several of their monthly color strips.

Fox's first syndicated feature was *Jeanie,* a comic strip done in collaboration with writer Selma Diamond for the Herald-Tribune Syndicate in 1951 and 1952. Another artist continued the strip for a year

"Fox and Crow." © Columbia Pictures.

while Fox returned to Johnstone and Cushing, although he again created a syndicated feature the following year (*Wilbert,* a one-column panel for General Features, which ran until 1959). *Bumper to Bumper* was a Sunday filler feature for the *New York News* and other papers; approximately twenty-five to thirty ran each year between 1953 and 1963.

On the recommendation of Newspaper Enterprise Association editorial cartoonist John Fischetti, Fox took over the feature *Side Glances* in 1962. He drew a portion of each week's panels, sharing duties with William Galbraith Crawford; he took full charge and began signing the feature with the release of November 12, 1962. Fox remains with *Side Glances,* for which he was twice nominated for the Reuben award; as of this writing, he was planning a Sunday companion page.

For many years Fox has been widely known as the cartoon industry's "man for all styles." He has adapted to any requirement with utter mastery. With *Side Glances,* the oldest continually running and still one of the most popular cartoon panels, Fox has maintained freshness and a unique, slightly bird's-eye view. One of his changes has broadened its appeal: he has expanded topical gags from a couple per month to half of all gags. His fierce Middle America sympathies cause many to identify with the feature and its treatments.

R.M.

FOX AND CROW (U.S.) Following Charles Mintz's death, Frank Tashlin became the head of the animation unit at Columbia in 1940. The following year he brought out "The Fox and the Grapes," a cartoon based on the familiar Aesop fable, introducing the characters Crawford Crow and Fauntleroy Fox, two friendly enemies in the tradition of Tom and Jerry. The cartoon enjoyed enough success to give rise to a *Fox and Crow* series of cartoons, several of which were directed by Tashlin himself before his departure from Columbia in 1943.

In a switch from the original fable, the plots revolved around the unceasing efforts of Crow to separate Fox from whatever food, money or material goods he happened to have in his possession at any given moment. The extraordinary lengths to which Crow was prepared to go in order to cheat Fox (concocting the most outrageous schemes or donning the most unlikely disguises) constituted the basis of the stories.

The *Fox and Crow* cartoons were ably written and well directed by such veterans as Bob Wickersham, Howard Swift and Art Davis. Some of the post-Tashlin entries include "A-Hunting We Will Go" (1943), "Be Patient, Patient" (1944), "Ku-Ku Nuts" (1945), "Foxey Flatfoots" and "Mysto Fox" (both 1946). In 1948 Columbia closed down its animation unit, and *Fox and Crow* was briefly taken over by UPA, only to be abandoned the following year.

Fox and Crow have lasted longer in comic books, where they have enjoyed a long career spanning more than twenty years, from 1945 to 1968.

M.H.

FRADON, DANA (1922-) American cartoonist born in Chicago, Illinois, in 1922. Dana Fradon studied at the Art Institute of Chicago, then moved to New York, there continuing his art education at the prestigious Art Students League. He served in the Army Air Corps from 1942 to 1945, returning after the war to New York to begin work as a freelance illustrator. Besides his work for the *New Yorker*, where he became a regular contributor in the 1950s, he has also appeared in *Look, Saturday Review* and the *Saturday Evening Post*.

As an artist, Fradon does not show the highly individualized style of *New Yorker* colleagues like George Price or Charles Addams. He generally avoids portraying physical-action situations in his sparsely populated panels, preferring instead to concentrate on the delivery of sophisticated gag lines through the medium of clean, simply drawn, strong-featured representational figures. His favorite targets include the IRS, television and television's inseparable mate, Madison Avenue. One particularly clever example of his penchant for twitting the tax man portrays two wealthy Romans over a bowl of wine, one complaining to his obviously understanding guest, "I'd hate to tell you how much I'm going to have to render unto Caesar this year."

Fradon's success as a cartoonist rests on his ability to be topical without becoming easily dated. Thus, much of his work from as far back as the 1950s remains, upon reacquaintance, as fresh now as it was then. His talent shows no sign of flagging in the 1970s, when he can have a shocked and concerned chemist finding traces of tuna fish in his latest shipment of mercury.

Besides his voluminous contributions to the best of the mass circulation periodical press, Fradon has also been published in two separate anthologies, *Breaking the Laugh Barrier* (1961) and *My Son the Medicine Man* (1964). His work is represented in the permanent collection of cartoon art in the Library of Congress.

R.C.

FRANÇOIS, ANDRÉ
See Farkas, André.

FRANK AND ERNEST (U.S.) In 1972 cartoonist Bob Thaves started *Frank and Ernest*, a daily panel that occupies the entire space of a comic strip, for NEA Service. The horizontal format—unusual for a panel feature—allowed Thaves to depict the action in the left side of the picture while the right side was taken up by text or dialogue lettered in large, bold print. The experiment proved successful, and a Sunday *Frank and Ernest* feature was later added.

Frank and Ernest are two zany characters hovering on the fringe of normal society. At first they were only two

among a large cast, but they stood out to such an extent that the feature was almost entirely given over to them after only a few weeks. The shaggy, tall Frank, who does most of the talking, and the short, awestruck Ernest, who does most of the reacting, are placed by Thaves in the most unusual situations and in settings that may vary from day to day. In the tradition of earlier cartoons, the two are bank tellers one day, door-to-door salesmen the next, and so forth, but they remain basically the same in character. The illogical and the outlandish are the main sources for the gags. In one panel, for instance, Frank looks bemusedly at the drooping beam issuing from his flashlight and mutters somewhat self-consciously, "Maybe the battery is getting weak."

Bob Thaves, an industrial psychologist by profession, manages to keep up with his consulting career while working on the *Frank and Ernest* feature, but he admits it is not easy. The success of his panel, however, may induce him to become a full-time cartoonist.

M.H.

FRED
See Aristides, Othon.

FRELENG, ISADORE (1905?-) American animator and producer born in Kansas City, Missouri, around 1905. Isadore ("Friz") Freleng went to work at the Kansas City Film Ad Company in 1924. Like many alumni of this fabled outfit (which at one time employed Walt Disney), he went on to join Disney's Hollywood studio (in 1927). After a short stint working on Charles Mintz's *Krazy Kat* series in 1929, Freleng joined Hugh Harman and Rudolph Ising in 1930 as an animator on the cartoons they produced for Warner Brothers. Except for a brief period at MGM (1938-40), he remained with Warner until the closing of the studio in 1963.

Freleng first assisted Harman and Ising on their *Bosko* cartoons. After the pair left Warner in 1933, he became a director of animation, notably directing *My Green Fedora* (1935), *The Fella with the Fiddle* (1937) and the first *Porky Pig* cartoon, "I Haven't Got a Hat" (1935). He really hit his stride, however, during his second, longer association with Warner Brothers. He directed a number of memorable *Bugs Bunny* cartoons, from his first, "Hiawatha's Rabbit Hunt" (1941), to the Oscar-winning "Knighty Knight Bugs" (1957), not to mention such glittering gems as "Captain Hareblower," "Rabbitson Crusoe," "Hare Lift," "Bugs Bunny Rides Again," "Fresh Hare," "Hare Splitter" and "Hyde and Hare." He also directed two more Oscar-winners, "Tweety Pie" (1947) and his own creation, "Speedy Gonzales" (1955).

In 1963, in association with David DePatie, Freleng formed DePatie-Freleng. The new company created, among other cartoons, *The Pink Panther* series and took over many of the former Warner cartoon characters. In recent years DePatie-Freleng has concentrated on animated film series for network television. The studio's entries in this field include *The Pink Panther, Baggy Pants* (a cartoon version of the Charlie Chaplin silent movie shorts), *The Nitwits* and animated adaptations of Marvel Comics' horde of comic book superheroes.

Friz Freleng was one of the most prolific and gifted of Warner animators, and his work has earned him an impressive number of awards, including four Oscars.

"Frank and Ernest." © NEA.

Yet his cartoons have never received as much attention as those of other Warner animators, probably because Freleng has obdurately chosen to remain a private person and has rarely granted interviews.

M.H.

FREMURA, ALBERTO (1935-) Italian cartoonist born in Leghorn, Italy, in 1935. Alberto Fremura embarked on a cartooning career soon after completing his studies. In the 1960s he started collaborating regularly on *La Nazione* and *Il Resto del Carlino*, two conservative dailies published respectively in Florence and Bologna.

Fremura has virtually never left his native region, Toscania, but his fame has spread beyond its confines, and his talent has put him at the forefront of Italian political cartoonists. He is perhaps Forattini's most forceful antagonist, not so much on the levels of draftsmanship and inventiveness, where the two cartoonists have much in common, but in the political field. While Forattini usually hits at the conservative forces (not forgetting to take a few swipes at the left), Fremura always picks his targets out of left field.

Fremura's polemics are never personal, violent or mean; he is an ironist rather than a satirist and prefers a smile to a grimace. For this reason his cartoons often take the form of a slap on the wrist rather than a whipping on the shoulders (unlike the drawings of Scalarini, for instance). Instead of attacking individuals, Fremura illustrates and denounces emblematic situations in the Italy of the 1970s—as seen, of course, from the vantage point of a conservative. In this respect his cartoons go beyond the urgency of daily concerns; taken together, as in one of the many Fremura cartoon collections from *Pelle e Ossola* ("Skin and Bones") to *Italia Purtroppo* ("Italy Alas"), they provide a bitterly ironic chronicle of modern Italy.

C.S.

FRITZ
See Mota, Anísio Oscar da.

FRITZ THE CAT (U.S.) In 1970 Ralph Bakshi and Steve Krantz, who had just started their own animation company, approached underground comic artist Robert Crumb with a proposal to film his famous creation, Fritz the Cat. Crumb first demurred, then relented and sold the rights to *Fritz* for a flat fee (he later claimed to have been misled by his associates). Crumb's protestations notwithstanding, the pair went to work with alacrity, and with Krantz producing and Bakshi directing, *Fritz the Cat* was released as a theatrical feature in 1972.

Bakshi remained faithful to the original, using many of Crumb's drawings and a number of his compositions; many of the original situations were also utilized to good effect (particularly Fritz's continually interrupted orgy in the bathtub, itself reminiscent of the stateroom scene in *A Night at the Opera*). The story line also followed closely the plot of the original stories. Fritz the Cat, a winsome if slightly unsavory feline, went through a number of obligatory "scenes," including barroom brawls, all-night bull sessions in tacky New York flats and a confrontation with cops portrayed as pigs. Fleeing the police, he then moved west, fell in with a group of rather seedy revolutionaries and got involved in "direct action." The

STUKA IN PICCHIATA
EDIZIONE 1978

Nose-diving Stuka, 1978 Model

Alberto Fremura. © La Nazione.

"Fritz the Cat." © Steve Krantz.

final sequence depicted Fritz in a hospital, blown up and dying of his wounds, only to be revived by the sight of his weeping girl friends and engage in a tumultuous sex orgy on the hospital bed—a fitting fade-out to a bawdy movie.

Fritz the Cat caused an instant sensation upon its release. It was the first animated cartoon to receive an "X" rating, a fact which doubtless attracted many spectators who would not otherwise have gone to see an animated film. The feature proved to be a critical as well as a commercial success; in his 1973 study, The Animated Film, Ralph Stephenson, for instance, enthused, "Scandalous, irreverent, satiric but pulsing with life, Fritz the Cat . . . is a major work."

Despite a few weaknesses and some nonartistic sour notes (such as a lawsuit brought in by the disgruntled Crumb), the feature is well on its way to becoming a classic. Prompted by the success of the original film, an obscure outfit brought out a would-be sequel in 1974, The Nine Lives of Fritz the Cat, which turned out to be a dismal artistic failure as well as a box-office disaster.

M.H.

FROST, ARTHUR BURDETT (1851-1928) American cartoonist and illustrator born in Philadelphia, Pennsylvania in 1851. Self-taught in art, A.B. Frost grew up in the Philadelphia area at a time when it was perhaps the most fertile city in America for artistic growth and innovation; Edwin Abbey and Howard Pyle were active there, and Frost belonged to several of the drawing and print clubs. In the 1870s he first achieved prominence as the front-page cartoonist for the New York Graphic, the nation's first illustrated daily. His first illustrated book, Out of the Hurly-Burly by Max Adeler, appeared in 1879.

From that time on, for half a century, Frost was in a position of near-dominance of American illustration and cartooning. He produced strips (mostly for Harper's Monthly for years), panel cartoons (occasionally for Puck but also for Life in the 1880s and especially in the 1920s), editorial cartoons (for the Graphic and Life) and painted illustrations (for books, Harper's Weekly and Collier's). Among his scores of book credits are collections of his own works (The Bull Calf, Stuff and Nonsense, The Golfer's Alphabet, Sports and Games in the Open and A Book of Drawings) and illustrations for others, most notably the series of Uncle Remus books by Joel Chandler Harris, who acknowledged Frost's contribution by writing, "The book was mine, but you have made it yours."

Very simply, Frost held sway in just about every possible way. Technically, he made the strip a viable format in which cartoonists could express concepts. Thematically, he introduced broad humor, slapstick and animation in treating rural and suburban subjects. Artistically, he was among the first major artists to use exaggeration as a major element, and he had a photographer's eye for arresting action at the point of greatest tension or movement. Among his followers in these respects were the greatest names in the next two generations of American cartooning: Opper, C.J. Taylor, Sullivant, Kemble, Donahey, Ireland.

Frost was an absolute master of anatomy and composition, in total charge of his media—pen and ink for cartoons, a handsome gray wash for illustrations. With the introduction of photoengraving, he became the pathfinder in achieving subtle, almost photographic tones in his reproductions. His magazine work, especially in Collier's after the turn of the century, was not only solid illustration, but a perfect, sympathetic mirror of rural, suburban and sporting America. Frost drew with a scratchy, informal line that perfectly suited his subjects. His favorite targets were animals, farmers, rural painters, golfers, prissy clerics, blacks and dandies. In the 1880s and 1920s, his figures were drawn with enormous heads, hands and feet—the better, it must be assumed, to focus on characterization and action.

A.B. Frost died on June 22, 1928. It is difficult to conceive how American cartooning would have developed without his presence. For his reportorial eye and his intrinsic artistic merit, he deserves major recognition today.

R.M.

FRUEH, ALFRED (1880-1968) American caricaturist and cartoonist born in a house on Main Street, Lima, Ohio, in 1880. Alfred Frueh pronounced his surname "free," and usually shortened his first name to Al. This brisk disyllabic name, pronounced "alfree," was as much an exercise in brevity as was his style of caricature.

Frueh was raised to be a farmer but also worked in a brewery prior to taking a job in the art department of the St. Louis Post-Dispatch. He stayed with the paper from

"Keep dry!! How can I help it?"

A.B. Frost, 1922.

Alfred Frueh, caricature of Winifred Lenihan as Saint Joan.
© Frueh.

1904 to 1908. Fame came to Al Frueh in 1907, when a newspaper caricature of music hall star Fritzi Schneff so enraged her that she canceled a performance in St. Louis.

Frueh traveled to Europe in 1909 and then went to New York City, where he drew for the *New York World* from 1910 to midway through 1912. This was followed by another trip abroad that included his marriage in London in 1913. He returned to caricature for the *New York World* again from 1914 to 1925 and then joined the staff of the fledgling *New Yorker* magazine. The first issue of the *New Yorker* had two Al Frueh cartoons, and he drew the cover of the second issue. It depicted two huge policemen squeezing into a tiny new patrol car. He was 45 years old when the *New Yorker* began, and he was a regular contributor until the advanced age of 82.

He is most famous for his theatrical caricatures covering a period of American theater from 1905 to 1962. Frueh once said that he became interested in caricature while studying in a Lima, Ohio, business school as a young man. He began by turning the Pitman shorthand symbols into caricatures.

Swiftness, economy of line and a sure likeness were hallmarks of Frueh's style. His work relied heavily on first impressions, and he preferred to sit in the eighth row on the side aisle in a theater so he could see the actors at close range when they entered on his side of the stage, but also in differing perspectives when they moved across the stage. He did no drawings at the theater, nor did his subjects pose for him. Instead he would return to his Greenwich Village studio and draw his impressions on scraps of brown paper.

Al Frueh didn't consider himself a critic. He stated,

"My job was just to draw." He was at his best with the fewest lines creating his caricature. Capturing the physical characteristics of a subject was as important to him as facial caricature. One of his most famous drawings was of George M. Cohan. The face is blank. The entire caricature is based on Cohan's body.

His magazine cartoons for the *New Yorker* included a series on suggested designs for buildings. His classic is a skyscraper in the shape of a beautiful woman's leg. It was his design for a Midwest center for the glorification of the American woman to be built by showman Florenz Ziegfeld. He also drew the decorative heading at the top of Frank Sullivan's annual Christmas poem.

Frueh gained a considerable reputation at the *New Yorker* for being an eccentric. He favored an old-fashioned, wide-brimmed brown fedora, and in slushy winter weather he would appear at the *New Yorker's* offices with unbuckled galoshes and his caricature rolled up in an old newspaper to protect it from the weather. He was a tall, rangy, shy man who made a point of not socializing with his theatrical subjects lest it interfere with the accuracy of his caricature. Al Frueh owned a hundred-acre farm in Sharon, Connecticut, where he planted seven thousand pine trees and forty varieties of grapes, and tried unsuccessfully to hybridize a soft-shelled black walnut. Only in his later years and to please his wife did he allow electricity and some central heating in the farmhouse. He died in the hospital in Sharon after a long illness on September 13, 1968. He was then 88 years old and had created one of the longest continuous records of caricature in the annals of American theater.

B.C.

FÜCHSEL, FRANZ (1927-   ) Danish cartoonist born in Skærbæk, Denmark, on September 16, 1927. Füchsel, who also draws under the pen name "Skærbæk," became

"Hansen, 21 Homecastle Street . . . I suppose this is the place."

Franz Füchsel. © Hendes Verden.

245

"Shadowing" Members of Parliament

Harry Furniss.

widely known around 1955 when he was part of a team and shared a drawing office with cartoonists Quist and Holbæk. They created a new type of newspaper cartoon and, though having different styles of artwork, they complemented each other extremely well.

Füchsel, who sells his cartoons throughout Europe and frequently is seen in American media, has a "realistic," only slightly caricatured style. He is a master of all cartooning's special effects, from thin-line to broad brushstrokes—and also does full-page illustrations in watercolors and oil. His several tries as a comic strip artist (*Barbarossa*) were without much success.

His humor is often centered around classic topics—desert islands, problems with in-laws, etc.—but he is most outstanding when he takes four drawings and works with an often trivial, everyday topic to present a brand-new and funny angle. Outside the cartoon columns, his drawings appear as funny illustrations to ads, as eye-catchers in brochures and on book covers.

J.S.

FURNISS, HARRY (1854-1925) Irish cartoonist, caricaturist, illustrator, author, publisher, lecturer, entertainer and star of silent films born in Wexford, Ireland, on March 26, 1854. Harry Furniss's very productivity has tended to lessen his appreciation in sophisticated circles. The son of a Yorkshireman and a Scotswoman, he was educated at Wesleyan College, St. Stephen's Green, Dublin, where he edited and drew his own magazine, *The Schoolboy's Punch*. He also studied art at the RHA Schools, Dublin, and the Life School of the Hibernian Academy, and at 17 he freelanced his first professional cartoons to *Zozimus*, a satirical weekly.

He came to London two years later, drew for *London Society, Illustrated London News, Cornhill, Graphic,* etc., and sent his first joke to *Punch* in October 1880. At first infuriated with the magazine for having his work redrawn by another artist, he settled his differences with the editor and became a regular contributor for 14 years. His weekly feature, *Essence of Parliament,* often portrayed William Gladstone, a character Furniss made his own thanks to his predilection for the winged collar! In his time with *Punch* Furniss drew 2,600 cartoons, from small thumbnails to the largest ever to appear in the paper (Christmas 1890). In 1884 Furniss's cartoon of a tramp writing to the manufacturer of Pears soap ("Two years ago I used your soap since when I have used no other") became the most famous advertisement of its era. From the ridiculous to the sublime, he also created that Victorian-Edwardian lovely known as the "Furniss Girl."

Furniss's paintings were exhibited in London galleries from 1875, and he fought a long and vociferous feud with the Royal Academy: *Harry Furniss's Royal Academy, An Artistic Joke* (1887) and *Royal Academy Antics* (1890). He created a regular cartoon in 1886, *Our Own Juggins,* for the weekly comic *Illustrated Bits,* and in 1894 he launched his own humorous weekly, *Lika Joko.* His book illustration work began in 1879 with William Makepeace Thackeray's *Ballads* and continued through Lewis Carroll's *Sylvie and Bruno* (1889) and G.E. Farrow's *The Wallypug of Why* (1895) to an 18-volume edition of the works of Charles Dickens (1912), for which he produced 500 full-page pictures. His daughter, Dorothy, was also artistic and often collaborated in his illustration work. Furniss went to New York in 1912 to write and star in a series of short comedy films for the Thomas A. Edison Company, and he wrote up his experiences in a book—which of course he illustrated—*My Lady Cinema* (1914). He died in 1925.

Books: *A River Holiday* (1883); *Talk of the Town* (1885); *Romps at the Seaside* (1885); *Parliamentary Views* (1886); *Romps in Town* (1886); *Romps All the Year Round* (1886); *The Comic Blackstone* (1887); *Travels in the Interior* (1887); *The Incompleat Angler* (1887); *Harry Furniss's Royal Academy* (1887); *How He Did It* (1887); *Pictures at Play* (1888); *MPs in Session* (1889); *Royal Academy Antics* (1890); *Diary of the Salisbury Parliament* (1892); *Flying Visits* (1892); *The Grand Old Mystery Unravelled* (1894); *How's That* (1896); *Pen and Pencil in Parliament* (1897); *Australian Sketches* (1899); *Confessions of a Caricaturist* (1901); *Financial Philosophy* (1902); *Our Joe* (1903); *Harry Furniss at Home* (1904); *How to Draw in Pen and Ink* (1905); *Harry Furniss's Christmas Annual* (1905); *Friends Without Faces* (1905); *Poverty Bay* (1905); *My Undiscovered Crimes* (1909); *My Lady Cinema* (1914); *More About How to Draw* (1915); *Byways and Queerways of Boxing* (1919); *My Bohemian Days* (1919); *Years Without Yawns* (1923); *Some Victorian Women* (1923); *Some Victorian Men* (1924); *Paradise in Piccadilly* (1925); and *The Two Pins Club* (1925).

D.G.

Gg

GALAKTIONOV, STEPAN FILIPPOVICH (1779-1854)

Russian cartoonist and graphic artist born in St. Petersburg, Russia, in 1779. Stepan Galaktionov studied at the St. Petersburg Academy of Art from early childhood in 1785 to 1800. He worked mainly in drypoint in combination with etching and later mastered the art of lithography. Primarily a book illustrator and landscape artist, Galaktionov also regularly contributed cartoons on everyday life and St. Petersburg events to several newspapers and almanacs. His familiar scenes of Russian life were depicted with good-natured humor tinged with a touch of pathos. Some of his drawings were later collected in book form.

Galaktionov's drawings of the 1820s are probably among the first genuine Russian cartoons. They are only mildly amusing and rather tame (Galaktionov never touched social or political subjects), but they show a good knowledge of what was happening artistically in France and England at the time. Galaktionov became a professor at his old alma mater in 1817, and he taught there until his death on July 2, 1854.

M.H.

We must go on guillotining because . . . Society must be avenged—by the death of a dumb brute, a madman or an idiot.

Demetrius Galanis, 1907.

GALANIS, DEMETRIUS EMMANUEL (1882-1966)

French cartoonist and painter of Greek origin born in Athens, Greece, on May 22, 1882. Demetrius Galanis published cartoons in Athens newspapers as early as 1897. In 1899 he won a drawing contest sponsored by the Paris daily *Le Journal* and came to Paris to study, first at the Ecole de la Rue Bonaparte, then at the Beaux-Arts. While still a student, he started contributing cartoons to many French publications, such as *Le Rire, Le Sourire, Le Matin, Le Journal du Dimanche* and especially *L'Assiette au Beurre,* where he had several issues devoted entirely to his cartoons.

Galanis went to Germany in 1907 to work for the *Lustige Blätter* but returned to Paris in 1909. At the outbreak of World War I, he joined the French Foreign Legion and became a French citizen while serving in Corfu. After the war Galanis veered away from cartooning and devoted most of his time to painting (mostly portraits) and to book illustration. He received many honors and awards, was named a professor at the Ecole des Beaux-Arts and taught there from 1945 to 1952. He died in 1966 in his native Greece, to which he had returned some years earlier.

Galanis's work as a cartoonist was vibrant and vital. His affinity with the Fauves and the post-Impressionists is clearly evident, although notably absent from his paintings. While he made his name primarily as an academic artist, Galanis will probably be best remembered as a peerless and innovative cartoonist.

M.H.

GALANTARA, GABRIELE (1865-1937)

Italian cartoonist born in the Emilia region of Italy in 1865. After a brief stay in Bologna, where he started his career by contributing cartoons to the magazines *Bononia Ridet* and *La Rana,* Gabriele Galantara moved to Rome in 1890. There, together with Guido Podrecca, he founded the satirical *L'Asino* a few years later. From the first issue, the success of this socialist and anticlerical weekly was due to the incisiveness of Galantara's cartoons (which he signed with the anagram "Rata-Langa"). The political background of these last years of the 19th century—punctuated by scandals, conspiracies, mad colonial adventures and miscellaneous corruption—provided ample grist for Galantara's socialist mill.

In his cartoons (as also in some of his watercolors and oil paintings) Galantara depicted with vigor the growing power of the masses and represented the proletariat smashing the chains forged by the bourgeoisie and the dictatorship and rising to shake the world. Rather than drawing cartoons in the traditional sense, Galantara gave life to the themes of socialist ideology. Unlike Scalarini, he did not limit himself to topical polemics but strove to represent the epochal struggle between the haves and have-nots. Some of his cartoons and caricatures have the impact of Daumier's drawings and remain powerful even today.

Gabriele Galantara ("Rata-Langa"), an ironic comment on the conquest of Tripoli, 1911.

Galantara worked for many publications other than *L'Asino,* including the Italian daily *Avanti!* and foreign magazines like the German *Der Wahre Jacob* or the French *L'Assiette au Beurre,* both close in spirit and ideological content to *L'Asino.* Galantara's activity, like that of Scalarini, came to a virtual end in 1926 when the Fascist laws of exception conclusively stifled freedom. Lawsuits, persecutions and jailings punctuated Galantara's last years, and he died in 1937.

Together with Scalarini, Galantara is indisputably Italy's major editorial cartoonist; in a way the two artists complemented each other. While Scalarini, in his *Avanti!* cartoons, denounced the misdeeds of the capitalist world with a violence that hit immediately, Galantara, mainly in *L'Asino,* depicted the grotesque and horrid images of a world dominated by war, dispossession, misery and hunger.

C.S.

GALLAGHER, GEORGE GATELY (1928-   ) American cartoonist born in Queens Village, New York, in 1928. George Gately (as he signs his work in order to avoid confusion with his older brother, John Gallagher, also a cartoonist) grew up in Bergenfield, New Jersey, where he received his primary and secondary education. After graduating from high school in 1946, Gately attended Pratt Institute and went to work for an advertising agency, where he remained for 11 years. "One day in the spring of 1957," he later recalled, "I decided to give cartooning a try. About three months later I had my first important sale. I've been doing well ever since."

Gately's gag cartoons appeared in the *Saturday Evening Post, Parade, This Week* and other publications. In 1964 he created *Hapless Harry,* a comic strip about a fat little man always thwarted by chance. Distributed by the Chicago Tribune-New York News Syndicate, it had only a brief career and disappeared

in the late 1960s. After *Hapless Harry* folded, Gately went back to freelancing cartoons and also worked briefly for a greeting card company. In 1973 he came up with *Heathcliff,* a panel cartoon about a self-assertive cat; with the success of this feature (distributed by the McNaught Syndicate) Gately began devoting all his time to the exploits of his rascally feline.

A conscientious craftsman, Gately exhibits a pleasant style and a fine sense of humor. There is nothing wildly original about his drawings, but they instantly strike a familiar, almost homey note that puts his readers at ease.

M.H.

GALLEPPINI, AURELIO (1917-   ) Italian cartoonist born in Casal di Pari, Italy, on August 28, 1917. Aurelio Galleppini moved to Sardinia, where he paid his way at the School of Architecture by contributing humor cartoons to the magazine *Candido.* Dropping out of school to devote himself entirely to drawing, Galleppini collaborated from 1937 to 1939 on the Napolitan magazine *Modellina* and also illustrated for them the book *Il Segreto del Motore* ("The Secret of the Motor").

Galleppini is best known, however, for his work in the comics field, which he began in 1939 during his military service. He drew the comics *Pino il Mozzo* ("Pino the Cabin Boy") and *Le Perle del Mare d'Oman* ("The Pearls of the Arabian Sea") for the illustrated weekly *Topolino.* Discharged in 1940, Galleppini moved to Florence, where he wrote and drew a number of comic strips for the Nerbini publications. After a recall to service in 1942, he went back to Sardinia the next year, freelancing cartoons, designing advertising posters and teaching drawing. In 1947 he again drew a number of comic strips for the publishers Del Duca and Nerbini, including a highly controversial version of *Mandrake.* Galleppini's main opportunity came in 1948, when he was asked to draw *Tex Willer* (on a scenario by Gianluigi Bonelli), a western strip that became a phenomenal success in Italy and is still among today's top-ranked comic features.

S.T.

Mrs. Stalin: "Ah, you finally decided to take me to the mountains."

Aurelio Galleppini, 1941. © Galleppini.

Bill Gallo, "Basement Bertha." © *Chicago Tribune-New York News Syndicate.*

GALLO, BILL (1922-) American cartoonist born in New York City on December 28, 1922. Bill Gallo is of Spanish, not Italian, descent, as is often erroneously assumed. He started publishing cartoons while still in high school. In 1942 he joined the Marine Corps and served for more than three years. After an honorable discharge, Gallo attended the Cartoonists and Illustrators School (now the School of Visual Arts) and Columbia University on a GI scholarship. But, as he himself stated, "most of (his) education came from the *New York Daily News*."

Gallo had joined the *News* even before entering the Marine Corps, and he has remained with the paper to this day. After doing various cartooning and art jobs at the *News*, Gallo became its standby sports cartoonist and later its regular sports illustrator, after Willard Mullin's partial retirement in the late 1960s. In addition Gallo also draws an occasional editorial cartoon, and in the early 1970s he created *Basement Bertha*, a Sunday half-page with a sports theme (Basement Bertha was originally Casey Stengel's most loyal and vociferous fan in Gallo's cartoons about the New York Mets).

Bill Gallo has received many cartooning and sports awards, including several Page One awards and National Cartoonists Society Best Sports Cartoonist awards. He was president of the NCS from 1973 to 1977.

M.H.

GANDY GOOSE (U.S.) Terrytoons' web-footed cartoon character made his first appearance in a 1938 short titled, logically enough, "Gandy the Goose." The definite article was subsequently dropped, and he was simply Gandy Goose in later cartoons.

Gandy was a smart-alecky, street-wise and tough-minded creature who got himself involved in all kinds of scrapes, as in "G-Man Jitters" (1939), for instance, where he helped the FBI bag a gang of criminals. With the coming of World War II Gandy applied his talents to fighting the minions of the Axis (if one can picture a goose having it out with goose-stepping storm troopers!). Some of the cartoons of this period bear such titles as "Lights Out," "Camouflage" and "Somewhere in Egypt." After the war Gandy settled for somewhat more sedate pursuits and conventional situations in cartoons like "Mother Goose Nightmare," "Mexican Baseball" and "Gandy Goose and the Chipper Chipmunk."

Most of the *Gandy Goose* cartoons were directed by the trio of Mannie Davis, Connie Rasinski and Eddie Donnelly. Fairly popular in the 1940s, the series petered out in the 1950s. It should be noted that Gandy Goose had a short and checkered career in comic books from 1953 to 1958.

M.H.

GARBANCITO (Spain) In 1947 Arturo Moreno, who had previously enjoyed a successful career in advertising cartoons, brought out an ambitious 72-minute animated film featuring a game little hero named Garbancito (literally, "little chick-pea" in Spanish). *Garbancito de la Mancha* was the title of the feature; like his literary model, Don Quijote de la Mancha, Garbancito was fired up by tales of chivalry and dreamed of becoming a fearless knight. His wish was granted by his fairy godmother, and Garbancito, with the help of the other children and his goat, Pelegrina, valiantly and victoriously defended his village against the depredations of the ogre Caramanca and the schemes of the evil wizard Pelocha. The success of the feature inevitably gave rise to a sequel. Almost as inevitably, the sequel, *Alegres Vacaciones* ("Happy Holidays"), did not measure up to the original, and the characters romped through the plains and mountains of Spain in what amounted to an unending travelogue.

The two *Garbancito* films brought no innovation to the animation medium and were in fact very much in the tradition of the Disney cartoons. Their importance lies in the fact that they were the first feature-length animated films ever produced in Spain and signaled a revival of Spanish interest in animation after a long period of silence and sterility.

M.H.

GARCÍA CABRAL, ERNESTO (1890-1968) Mexican cartoonist born in Huatusco, province of Veracruz, Mexico, in 1890. Ernesto García Cabral went to Mexico City in 1907 to study art at the famed San Carlos Academy, from which he graduated two years later. He embarked on a cartooning career in 1910, contributing cartoons to the humor and political magazines *La Tarántula*, *Multicolor* and *Frivolidades*.

Garcíía Cabral received a grant from the Mexican government in 1912 to pursue his studies in Europe. He graduated first in his class from the Colarossi Academy in Paris and thereupon resumed his cartooning career with contributions to the French humor magazines *Le Rire* and *La Vie Parisienne*. When World War I broke out, he chose to remain in Paris, and he expressed his staunch anti-German feelings in cartoons published in the patriotic magazine *La Baïonnette*. In 1917 he was named cultural attaché at the Mexican embassy in Paris; he later served in Madrid and Buenos Aires.

Ernesto García Cabral, self-caricature.

Returning to Mexico City in 1918, García Cabral soon became one of the most popular and sought-after press cartoonists. He contributed countless gag and editorial cartoons to most major Mexican publications and drew a number of comic strips (*El Fifi*, about a frustrated man-about-town, is probably his best-known creation in this domain). He was also a talented mural painter, decorating the Pavilion of Tourism in the city of Toluca, among other projects. He died in Mexico City on August 8, 1968.

M.H.

GARCÍA-JUNCEDA I SUPERVÍA, JOAN (1881-1948) Spanish cartoonist born in Barcelona, Spain, in 1881. Joan García-Junceda (who signed simply Junceda) began to draw at an early age. His first cartoons appeared in 1902 in the newly created humor magazine *Cu-Cut*. His cartoons were radical and often controversial, and he was very sharply criticized for some that appeared in *Cu-Cut* and *Papitu*, another humor publication, to which he began contributing in 1908. (As a result of one Junceda cartoon in *Papitu*, the political party La Lliga Catalana decided to withdraw its financial support from the magazine.) Junceda also contributed cartoons to *L'Estevet, La Tralla, En Patufet, Paginas Viscudes* and other, lesser-known publications. In view of his radical leanings, his 30-year association with *En Patufet* (1904-38), a magazine closely tied to the conservative party, can only be explained by his close friendship with the manager, Folch i Torres. In the 1930s Junceda illustrated a great number of children's stories and is recognized internationally for his work in children's books.

Junceda's career went into eclipse with the coming to power of Generalissimo Franco, and he died at his country home in Blanes, near Barcelona, in 1948. Because of his radical political positions, evaluations of his cartoon work are often prejudiced, and his long association with *En Patufet* leaves him open to charges of hypocrisy. Objectively, however, his clear and subtly critical drawings mark him as an important cartoonist. Junceda's style was personal and often poetic, very much in the Catalan tradition of Josep Lluis Pellicer and Apel. les Mestres.

J.M.

GARDOSH, KARIEL (1921-   ) Israeli cartoonist born in Budapest, Hungary, in 1921. Kariel Gardosh received his art education first in Budapest and later in Paris, where he started his career as a cartoonist just before the outbreak of World War II. During the war he joined the underground movement, and in 1948 he emigrated to Israel. After contributing a great number of cartoons and illustrations to various Israeli and European publications, Gardosh in 1953 joined the staff of the afternoon newspaper *Ma'ariv*, where his cartoons (signed with his pen name, "Dosh") became instantly popular.

Gardosh created the figure "little Israel," a spunky young boy who soon became the symbol of the country; he used his little character to comment with mordant irony on political, social and economic issues confronting the state of Israel. Gardosh's cartoons have also been published in the English-language *Jerusalem Post* and in the Hungarian-language daily *Lej Kelet*, as well as in many newspapers outside Israel. Gardosh has illustrated books and written short stories and one-act plays, but it is as a cartoonist that he is most famous. His cartoons have been collected several times in book form. *Selihah she-Nizzahnu!* ("So Sorry We Won," 1967) and *Oifla Menazzehim* ("Woe to the Victors," 1969), two volumes dealing with the Six-Day War and its aftermath, are probably the best known. *To Israel with Love* was published in the United States by Sagamore Press in 1960.

M.H.

GAREL, LEO (1917-) American cartoonist and painter born in New York City on October 8, 1917. Leo Garel studied at the Parsons School and at the Art Students League of New York with George Grosz and Vaclav Vytlactil. A serious painter in the abstract expressionist mode, Garel has gained broad critical acceptance with his watercolors and gouaches of northeastern landscapes and seascapes. His paintings have been widely exhibited, and he has had shows at the Zabriskie Gallery in New York (1957), Mills College (1960), the Cober Gallery in New York (1967), the Berkshire (Mass.) Museum (1967), the Pennsylvania Academy of Fine Art at Philadelphia (1969) and the Montclair (N.J.) Art Museum (1975). His work is also represented in the permanent collections of the Norfolk Museum of Arts and Sciences, the Albany Institute of History and Art, the Santa Fe Museum and the Chase Manhattan Bank Collection. In 1961 he took a first prize for his watercolors at the Albany Institute of History and Art.

Cartooning is apparently of secondary interest to Garel; in fact, he makes no mention of his comic art in his *Who's Who in American Art* biography. Yet during the 1940s and 1950s he was a regular contributor of cartoons to the *Saturday Evening Post*, and probably to other magazines as well. His style as a cartoonist was not particularly distinctive, but his panels were always well planned, and important detail work was never neglected. Drawn with the same broad, quick strokes characteristic of his brushwork, Garel's pen-and-ink caricatures are not only quite "readable" but also show a fair talent for the workable gag line. Thus the retirement ceremony portrayed in a 1950 *Saturday Evening Post* panel. It is arranged in an almost formalistic way, with the boss (standing on a chair and taking the office clock off the wall) and the old retiree in the center, flanked by clusters of employees. "Pearson," the boss is saying, "for years I've noticed you admiring this clock, so I thought it only fitting to present it to you on your retirement." Or the panel in which a cheerfully smiling dentist tells his cringing patient just before starting to drill, "Let me know when it gets excruciating."

Garel seems to have stopped cartooning in the 1950s to devote himself full time to painting, apparently with good success, as has been noted. In this he is rare, for most of those who come to the comic field from the fine arts are eventually diverted into some commercial variation like illustration or ad art. Garel has avoided this route, remaining the abstract watercolorist he always wanted to be.

R.C.

GASOLINE REGGIE AND HIS AUTO

See Little Johnny and His Teddy Bears.

GATELY, GEORGE

See Gallagher, George Gately.

GAVARNI, PAUL

See Chevalier, Guillaume-Sulpice.

GAVIOLI, GINO (1923-)

Italian cartoonist and animator born in Milan, Italy, on May 9, 1923. After completing his studies at the Brera Art Institute in Milan, Gino Gavioli began his cartooning career in 1940, drawing comic strips for the Italian publisher Traini in collaboration with Paolo Piffarerio. He was drafted in 1943 and did not resume his artistic activity until 1948, when he drew *Nonno Bigio* ("Gray-Haired Grandpa") for Edizioni Alpe. In 1952, together with his brother Roberto and Paolo Piffarerio, Gavioli founded Gamma Film, an animated cartoon studio. Most of Gavioli's production

Gino Gavioli, "Puttiferio Goes to War." © Gamma Film.

was geared to television commercials, and many of the characters he created became popular, including Il Vigile ("The Watchman") and Babbut, Mammut and Figliut, as well as Gregorio, Capitan Trinchetto, Pallina and more recently Taca Banda and Cimabue.

In 1952 Gavioli also started doing a panel featuring anthropomorphized animals for the magazine *Il Monello*. In 1960 he drew covers and game pages for *Il Corriere dei Piccoli*, and the following year he did cover illustrations and comic features for *Il Giornalino*, a collaboration that continues to this day. He has also written and illustrated several children's books, including *Eroi in Pantofole* ("Heroes in Slippers"), *Mio Nonno Pirata* ("My Pirate Grandfather") and *Le Invenzioni Quasi Tutte* ("Almost All the Inventions"). In the field of theatrical animation Gavioli worked on the 1961 *La Lunga Calza Verde* ("The Long Green Stocking") and directed *Puttiferio Va alla Guerra* ("Puttiferio Goes to War," 1967); he also directed *La Maria d'Oro* (1972) for a German production company.

L.S.

GAY NINETIES, THE (U.S.)

Life, by the 1920s, had become one of the freshest of American magazines after the infusion of such talents as Robert Benchley, Robert E. Sherwood, Dorothy Parker, Heywood Broun, Gluyas Williams and John Held, Jr. It also had the best of an older generation in staffers like T.S. Sullivant, E.W. Kemble, A.B. Frost, E.S. Martin and the magazine's new owner, Charles Dana Gibson. But in its role as the respectable leader of American comic papers, it hit an ambiguous snag in the Roaring Twenties. Although it would never get as raucous as the later *College Humor* and *Ballyhoo*, or even *Judge*, it did have to acknowledge the "new morality" and life-style of the 1920s. The new writers (as well as Held and later Russell Patterson) were to reflect the times, but tradition was still honored.

A manifestation of this dichotomy was a *Life* series of black-and-white half-page cartoons, *The Gay Nineties*, debuting in the issue of April 9, 1925. A less reverent publication would have taken off with a mocking tone, as Perelman was about to do in *Judge* and Held in the *New Yorker* with his woodcuts. But the *Life* series, drawn by Richard V. Culter, seldom ridiculed; it was steeped in nostalgia and fondness. Indeed, when an anachronism was noted, it was usually in order to point out how superior the 1890s were to the frenzied, irreverent 1920s. Sometimes no comment was implied, as in the similarity between the novelty of the phonograph and that of the later radio. Culter's chronicles pointed to the fact that far more than 30 chronological years separated him and his subject; in spite of (or perhaps because of) the different atmosphere of the Jazz Age, the series was an enormous hit.

There were no continuing characters save the spirit of the age, which was widely acknowledged as captured perfectly. Culter proved himself a provident researcher rather than an able memorialist—his work relied heavily on books and personal accounts. The series was approved and admired by Gibson, who nevertheless was somewhat embarrassed at finally proving himself a *bona fide* relic: the Nineties were *his* age inseparably.

The cartoons were executed in crayon and sought photographic likeness. Needless to say, all fashions and decoration were historically accurate. Each cartoon was more an archaeological expedition than a knee-slapping gag, but the series was popular enough to inspire several editions of a reprint book (published first in 1927 by Doubleday Doran with an introduction by Gibson). The cartoons in the book included those in *Life* up to December 23, 1926. *Life* devoted a whole issue to the nostalgia craze generated by the series on October 7, 1926; there was a double-page cartoon by Culter for the occasion.

The Gay Nineties, which gave its name to the decade it dissected, ran weekly at its inception and then with varying frequency until its last appearance on March 22, 1928, when it was discontinued due to the untimely death of the artist. Culter had found a formula—and provided succeeding generations with a truthful and sympathetic portrait of an age. The only cartoonists who did it better were Gaar Williams (in *Among the Folks of History*), who managed an infusion of gags, and Clare Briggs, who was overwhelmingly evocative.

R.M.

GÉBÉ
See Blondeau, Georges.

GEISEL, THEODOR SEUSS (1904-) American cartoonist, author and publisher born in Springfield, Massachusetts, on March 2, 1904. Theodor ("Dr. Seuss") Geisel went to Dartmouth College and graduated in 1925. His cartoons in the campus humor magazine attracted the attention of Norman Anthony of *Judge*, and soon his *Birdsies and Beasties* page of nonsense was a weekly feature. It consisted of various soberly couched explanations of natural history and animal life—all, of course, absolutely absurd—with the wildest concoctions in the cartoons that illustrated the captions. Soon Dr. Seuss's name was appearing on gags and strips inside the magazine and on color covers. After Anthony switched to *Life* magazine, Dr. Seuss's zany humor was sought there as well; his chores were similar, except that his page was retitled *Life's Zoological Charts*. His other work at this time included cartoons for *Vanity Fair* and *Liberty*, as well as advertising campaigns for insecticides ("Quick, Henry, the Flit!" was a classic series).

As the magazines faded during the Depression years, Dr. Seuss began turning out children's books of a variety that delighted adults with their whimsy and enchanted children with colors, rhymes and comical drawings. During World War II he served with the Army Signal Corps and Educational Division and won, among other distinctions, the Legion of Merit for his film work. In the 1940s his versatility led him to conquer ever more fields; he drew political cartoons for the newspaper *PM* in New York and entered the field of animation, winning Academy Awards in 1946 (Best Documentary Short for *Hitler Lives*), 1947 (Best Documentary Feature for *Design for Death*) and 1951 (Best Animated Cartoon for the strikingly innovative *Gerald McBoing Boing*).

As president and publisher of Beginners Books, Dr. Seuss changed the nature of children's books in the 1950s and thereafter with the *Cat in the Hat* series. Once again his charming drawings were combined with clever, amusing, comprehensible phrases and stories—a classic formula for young readers. His work spawned a generation of books, both under his direction and otherwise, featuring large, colorful cartoons, whimsical subjects, simple (often alliterative) phrases and large type. Indeed, he launched a new tradition that later found expression in *Sesame Street* and other modern approaches to children's education.

Lately Dr. Seuss has entered the TV world, animating many of his creations and winning awards thereby (Peabody awards for *How the Grinch Stole Christmas* and *Horton Hears a Who*; Critics' Award at the Zagreb festival for *The Lorax*). Among his other credits are honorary degrees from his alma mater (he also studied at Lincoln College, Oxford, England, in 1925-26) and from American International College. He has continued his educational work as president of the Beginners Book Division of Random House and publisher of Bright and Early Books. He also designed a line of toys for Mattel and furniture for Sears, Roebuck.

Dr. Seuss, for all his activities, remains basically a cartoonist, one of the profession's proudest members. His work is always a special mixture of drawings and thoughts, with a unique sense of humor thrown in. His cartoon style has consistently been one of confident but loose pen lines, with a masterful use of composition and color. His animal creations are classics, supremely logical in an inimitably Seussian way. Most of his books are readily available, but the early cartoon work of this genius—nonsense easily the equal of Perelman's—begs republication for audiences who, without regard to generation or background, could not fail to fall in love with it and be enchanted by its humor.

Books: *And to Think That I Saw It on Mulberry Street; The 500 Hats of Bartholomew Cubbins; The Seven Lady Godivas; The King's Stilts; Horton Hatches the Egg; McElligot's Pool; Thidwick the Big-Hearted Moose; Bartholomew and the Ooblick; The Lorax; Marvin K. Mooney, Will You Please Go Now!; Did I Ever Tell You How Lucky You Are?; The Shape of Me and Other Stuff; There's a Wocket in My Pocket; Great Day for Up; Oh, the Thinks You Can Think!; The Cat's Quizzer; Scrambled Eggs Super; Horton Hears a Who; On Beyond Zebra; If I Ran the Circus; How the Grinch Stole Christmas; The Cat in the Hat; The Cat in the Hat Comes Back; Yertle the Turtle; Happy Birthday; One Fish Two Fish Red Fish Blue Fish; Green Eggs and Ham; The Sneetches and Other Stories; Dr. Seuss' Sleep Book; Hop on Pop; Dr. Seuss' ABC Book; Fox in Socks; I Had Trouble in Getting to Solla Sollew; The Cat in the Hat Songbook; The Foot Book; I Can Lick 30 Tigers Today and Other Stories; My Book About Me; I Can Draw It Myself; Mr. Brown Can Moo, Can You?;* and many others.

R.M.

GEORGE AND JUNIOR (U.S.) *George and Junior* is one of Tex Avery's less-celebrated cartoon creations, but while it is certainly not on a par with the impeccable *Droopy*, it does have merit. The cartoons featured a duo of uncouth bears and started unobtrusively in 1946 with "Henpecked Hoboes." The heroes of the piece were cartoon parodies of John Steinbeck's George and Lenny characters in *Of Mice and Men*; Avery's George was suitably nasty and short-tempered, and Junior exceedingly big and obtuse.

The pair reappeared in two 1947 cartoons, "Hound Hunters" and "Red Hot Rangers." In the first they proved helpless as dogcatchers, and in the latter they displayed the same ineptitude fighting forest fires. The exchanges between them were quite funny, and Avery's sight gags kept coming at a fast and furious pace. Somehow the characters never caught on with the public, and in 1948, following one last effort, "Half-Pint Pygmy," Avery gave up on the series.

"Gerald McBoing Boing." © Columbia Pictures.

George and Junior are still fondly remembered for George's comic double takes and exasperated efforts at communication with Junior, whose feeble attempts at comprehension were sure to bring some untold disaster to both bears. The cartoons themselves (which Avery directed for MGM) were very hip, but the two characters were too ill-defined and not lovable enough to become popular.

M.H.

GERALD MCBOING BOING (U.S.) Gerald McBoing Boing came into the world in 1949 in an animated cartoon of the same name created for UPA by Robert Cannon from a story by Dr. Seuss. The sad-eyed little boy with the booming voice capable of uttering the weirdest sounds (the squeaking of tires, the clanging of a bell, etc.) became an instant hit with moviegoers. The cartoon won the 1950 Academy Award for shorts, and the *Gerald McBoing Boing* series was on its way.

"I just cancelled your vote!"

David Gerard, "Citizen Smith." © Register and Tribune Syndicate.

The cartoons revolved around Gerald's inability to speak human words, and the mishaps and contretemps resulting from his handicap. In "Gerald's Symphony" (1953) the little boy substituted for an entire symphony orchestra when the musicians failed to appear for a radio program; in "How Now, Boing Boing?" (1954) the only way he could converse with his parents was through a scrambler telephone; in "Gerald's Birthday" he caused first panic, then glee among his little companions with his weird sound effects; and in "Gerald McBoing Boing on Planet Moo" he led the inhabitants of an alien planet to believe that all earth people talked like he did.

Most of the *Gerald McBoing Boing* cartoons were directed by Cannon until the late 1950s. DePatie-Freleng, which had bought most of the UPA properties, tried to revive the character in a television series of his own in the mid-1960s, but it lasted only one season. *Gerald McBoing Boing* also had a short comic book run in 1952-53.

M.H.

GERARD, DAVID (1909-) American cartoonist born in Crawfordsville, Indiana, in 1909. Dave Gerard attended Wabash College, where he edited the school magazine. Graduating in 1931, he went to New York the next year to try a career in cartooning. After two years of unsuccessful efforts he returned to Crawfordsville in 1934. From there he freelanced cartoons to a number of national magazines, including the *Saturday Evening Post* and *Collier's*. He signed a contract with the latter publication in the early 1940s for a weekly full-color cartoon.

In 1949 Gerard created a nationally syndicated panel, *Viewpoint*, for the National Newspaper Syndicate. The feature lasted four years; upon its demise the syndicate asked him to draw a kid strip, *Will-Yum*, which ran daily and Sundays from 1953 to 1967. That year Gerard went over to the Des Moines Register and Tribune Syndicate, for which he created *Citizen Smith*, a daily panel that reflects, in Gerard's own words, a "type of current, relevant humor." It also reflects the artist's interest in politics: Dave Gerard has served two terms on the city council and in 1971 was elected mayor of his hometown.

M.H.

GÉRARD, JEAN-IGNACE-ISIDORE (1803-1847) French illustrator and cartoonist born in Nancy, France, on September 15, 1803. The son of a fashionable portrait painter and the grandson of a famous stage actor, Gérard showed talent at an early age in his caricatures of his father's subjects. Moving to Paris at age 20, he took the pseudonym "Grandville," by which he is best known. He soon became one of the contributors to the newly created satirical magazine *Le Charivari*, even before Daumier started drawing for it. Grandville's forte was the depiction of scenes teeming with human characters with animal heads. His 1829 book *Les Métamorphoses du Jour* ("Metamorphoses of the Day"), in which he made systematic use of this device, was a sensation, as was his later *Scènes de la Vie Publique et Privée des Animaux*.

Grandville then took up a whole series of liberal and radical causes, using his pen to mercilessly attack the regime of King Louis-Philippe. At the same time he also illustrated La Fontaine's *Fables*, Swift's *Gulliver's Travels* and Defoe's *Robinson Crusoe*, for which he created a weird menagerie of half-human, half-animal characters.

Ravens as medical students.

Jean-Ignace-Isidore Gérard ("Grandville"), lithograph from "Les Métamorphoses du Jour," 1829.

In the 1840s Grandville suffered a series of personal tragedies—first the death of two young sons, then that of his wife—and these losses embittered him further. He started drawing morbid, nightmarish scenes in such works as *Métamorphoses* and especially in *Un Autre Monde* ("Another World," 1844). When his third son died, it was too much for Grandville to bear, and he himself died a short time later, on March 17, 1847.

Grandville's visionary and hallucinatory art has been much praised by the Surrealists, who claimed him as one of their precursors. In 1857, in a very lucid essay on Gérard and his work, Baudelaire wrote, "There are some superficial minds who are amused by Grandville; as for me I find him terrifying." After a long eclipse, Grandville's artistic reputation is now at its zenith; many of his books have been recently reprinted in France, and a number of his cartoons have appeared regularly in the *New York Review of Books.*

M.H.

GERTIE (U.S.) Winsor McCay's *Gertie, the Trained Dinosaur* may well be the most famous cartoon short in the entire history of animation. Hundreds of articles and glosses have been written on its inception, its technique, its artistry, its influence—yet there is uncertainty as to the date of its first showing. For a long time it was generally accepted that *Gertie* was released as a vaudeville act in 1909; recent research, however, has led some to settle on 1914 as the likeliest date. This conclusion is based on the actual date of copyright and on various newspaper announcements of *Gertie*'s theatrical release. Yet the Museum of Modern Art, in its description of the films in its archives, gives *Gertie*'s date of birth as 1909 and flatly states that the 1914 showing was a reissue. Some doubt, therefore, still persists. (To add to the confusion, there are two sets of *Gertie* prints in existence: one of the original one-reel cartoon, and the other with live-action film of McCay, George McManus and other cartoonists added at the beginning and end.)

Gertie was reportedly the result of a bet made between McCay and McManus (and recorded in the prologue of the extended *Gertie* print); to win his bet McCay single-handedly turned out the more than ten thousand drawings that went into *Gertie*. The artist then took his creation on the vaudeville circuit, where, dressed as a circus lion tamer, he would order his cartoon dinosaur through her paces, even throwing a ball for her to balance on her nose.

Gertie, the Trained Dinosaur created a sensation with the public and elicited unbounded admiration from fellow cartoonists. It is unquestionably the first work of animation art. Dick Huemer, Isidore Klein and others have described the shock *Gertie* created in the ranks of the cartooning profession when it was first released. The cartoon was such a commercial and critical success that McCay was prompted to follow with *Gertie on Tour* (1916), a two-minute sequel not without charm and invention, but decidedly less spontaneous and exuberant than the original.

It should be noted that McCay's son Robert tried to bring his father's creation to the newspaper pages in the 1940s in a comic strip called *Dino*, but this attempt at resurrection met with little success.

M.H.

GETTERMAN, ORLA (1913-   ) Danish cartoonist born in Copenhagen, Denmark, in 1913. Orla Getterman, whose pen name is "Get," started out as a cartoonist on a number of minor dailies and weekly magazines. He made a name for himself with his front cover cartoons in the cartoon magazines that mushroomed during the German occupation of Denmark (1940-45). With his clean and realistic, sometimes quite streamlined style of drawing, he is sure to produce eye-catchers, and his strong point is in the one- or two-column panel.

Getterman's international success is *Naboens Helle,* a daily panel that is syndicated to more than one hundred European dailies (in the United States and South America it is distributed under the name of *Ginger* through United Feature Syndicate). A *Ginger* Sunday

"Gertie, the Trained Dinosaur," 1914. © Winsor McCay.

page was discontinued, however, failing as have many of his attempts at strips (among them *MacMoney*, a daily strip running from 1953 to 1959). In the pantomime drawing, however, his abundant imagination and impact of line always come into their own, as in *Televiews*, a panel syndicated to a substantial number of dailies, now in its 20th year.

Getterman is a frequent supplier to magazine and newspaper humor columns and also an illustrator of crossword puzzles, humorous short stories, etc.

J.S.

Orla Getterman. © *PIB.*

GIANINI, GIULO (1927-   ) Italian cartoonist and animator born in Rome, Italy, in 1927. Giulo Gianini started his career in the 1950s as a movie cameraman. At the same time he indulged his love for drawing by contributing occasional cartoons to Rome newspapers. In the late 1950s this double interest led him into partnership with Emanuele Luzzati to produce animated films. Their collaboration has given birth to a number of quality cartoons, with the better-known Luzzati taking credit as director and Gianini acting as his chief operator and assistant. Starting with *The Paladins of France* in 1960, the films produced by Gianini and Luzzati include *House of Cards* (1962), *The Thieving Magpie* (1964), *The Italian Girl in Algiers* (1968), *Ali Baba* (1970), *Marco Polo* and *Pulcinella* (1973).

Gianini has also worked on his own, and the films he produced have a more somber, less sunshiny look than the ones done in partnership with Luzzati. *Le Message* (1967) and *Swimmy* (1970) are both based on the disturbing drawings of the Belgian cartoonist Michel Folon, while the 1969 *Federico* is a children's tale more terrifying than entertaining.

S.T.

Giulo Gianini (and Emanuele Luzzati), "The Thieving Magpie." © *Gianini-Luzzati.*

GIBSON, CHARLES DANA (1867-1944) American artist born in Roxbury, Massachusetts, on September 14, 1867. With Thomas Nast, Charles Dana Gibson had more impact on American life than any other artist or cartoonist.

Gibson was born into a somewhat prominent family of New England stock and early betrayed artistic talent, producing marvelous cutout silhouettes of realistic human figures and fanciful animals. As a young man he lived in Flushing, Long Island, and aspired to a career in art. His companions, fortunately, provided the contacts and environment for an entry into the cartooning profession: among his friends were Victor and Bernard Gillam, Grant Hamilton and Dan Beard. In Beard's studio Gibson took the entrance examination for the Art Students League, and then entered the school in 1884.

After two years of study, some decidedly poor drawings were rejected by various New York humor magazines, but finally one cartoon—unsigned—was accepted by *Life* and ran in the March 25, 1886, issue. Thereafter Gibson's cartoons appeared with greater frequency (in *Life*, profusely in *Tid-Bits* and *Time* and occasionally in *Puck* into 1887). Seldom does an artist display such a discernible, rapid and qualitative progress in drawing style as Gibson did over those next

Charles Dana Gibson, "The Eternal Question," 1903.

few years. His drawings were transformed from awkward, tight scribblings to breezy, carefully cross-hatched cartoons; for awhile, however, the figures alternated from anatomical curiosities to obvious swipes from classic and academic poses. He drew, in these early days, as many political as social cartoons.

In 1878 he traveled to England (where he paid a call of homage on George Du Maurier) and France and returned to America with a mature, photographic style that immediately made him the illustrator most sought-after by the popular monthlies. His work was gripping and detailed, breathing life. He had mastered (one of his many tangible and intangible improvements) the art of molding and shaping his figures by means of fluid shading lines; every pen stroke indicated depth and texture as well as shadow.

But Gibson reaffirmed his status as a cartoonist, favoring his cartoons in *Life* over "finer" illustrations (indeed, in later years, when the genteel dubbed him a "caricaturist," he rejected the euphemism and proudly called himself a cartoonist). In the early 1890s, when Gibson's society cartoons were attracting widespread notice, *Puck's* Charles Jay Taylor was drawing his *Among the 400* series featuring his beautiful high-bred "Taylor-made Girl"; and Sid Ehrhart's earthy, busty beauties were also appearing in *Puck*. *Life* responded by bestowing the monicker "Gibson Girl" on its prize artist's creations, and this alliterative fortuity combined with Gibson's "voguishness" to produce a national sensation that spawned many imitators and dictated the fashions and mores of a generation. Beards were suddenly out, due to Gibson's depiction of the "ideal beau." And the American woman became a wasp-waisted, somewhat tousled, haughty, athletic beauty.

Gibson's models included the ill-fated but lovely actress Evelyn Nesbit and a close friend, dashing Richard Harding Davis.

As his pen line became firmer, his cartoons became more striking—in characterization if not conception. His cartoons at once reflected and led manners, fashions, morals. They stand today as representations of what Gibson's contemporaries thought, how they acted and reacted and what their very basic social conventions were; many of his themes deal with embarrassing situations and lovers' discussions.

Soon Gibson was one of America's most famous celebrities. The Gibson Girl was merchandised widely, and amid much fanfare her creator signed a $100,000 contract to draw exclusively for *Collier's*, excepting work as he desired for *Life*; Gibson's loyalty to his discoverer was fierce. In 1905, in a shocking move dictated not so much by an aversion to the pen as a desire to conquer new worlds, Gibson announced his retirement as a cartoonist and left America and enormous wealth behind to study and paint in Europe. He returned in 1910 and was persuaded to illustrate a Robert Chambers story; *Life* cartoons resumed a year later. His style now was more sketchy than bold but was softer and dealt with less serious subjects than before, except during the war years when weekly anti-kaiser cartoons by Gibson appeared.

In 1920, after the death of *Life's* founders, Gibson became owner and editor of the magazine that had originally graced him with his first signs of encouragement. Unfortunately he was a better artist than editor, and although in many ways the early 1920s were *Life's* best years, his reign ultimately stultified the magazine. Gibson sold out in the early 1930s after a threatened suit by Norman Anthony, hired from *Judge* to pep up *Life's* circulation and fired because he was succeeding in a jazzy way. Gibson returned to the easel and died in retirement at his estate in Maine in 1944.

Gibson illustrated 20 books, most notably *Gallegher* by Richard Harding Davis. He served several terms as president of the Society of Illustrators, and as head of the Division of Pictorial Publicity during World War I, he waged an impressive propaganda campaign. Among his many honors, he was named doctor of fine arts by Syracuse University in 1931. His popular series included *The Education of Mr. Pipp*, *A Widow and Her Friends* and *Mr. Tagg*. Sixteen collections of his cartoons were published, as well as a larger compilation titled *The Gibson Book* (two volumes, 1906).

Gibson's contribution to American life was enormous, and in the cartoon world his influence can be assessed by the number of imitators in his wake. Some transcended sycophant status (e.g., Flagg, Orson Lowell), but hundreds merely aped Gibson's amazing grasp of his time and his art.

R.M.

GIBSON GIRL, THE (U.S.) The Gibson Girl, never a formal, titled series, was nevertheless one of the most identifiable and avidly followed cartoon creations in history. However, the Girl was not the same character from cartoon to cartoon, except on rare occasions. Rather, Charles Dana Gibson's conception of the ideal American woman was a type. Ultimately the Gibson Girl transcended the comic pages and gave her name to countless real-life imitators.

Gibson's drawings in *Life* in the late 1880s and early 1890s featured handsome men and strong-willed, athletic young women. As Gibson's drawings matured, so did his characterizations and popularity. Soon his cartoons became the arbiter of fashions, coiffures, leisure activities, tonsorial standards and the like. The artist was fortunate to be drawing during the greatest period of ostentation in American high society, but his women were not always members of "the 400." They were to be found in any social position in any cartoon. What made a Gibson Girl was her attitude—a magical blend of authority and winsomeness, the tilt of the hat and arch of an eyebrow. She was liberated but not a suffragist, a post-Victorian phenomenon.

Countless imitators followed in Gibson's path—many aping his style (or trying to), e.g., James Montgomery Flagg, Penrhyn Stanlaws and Howard Chandler Christy. All named their women after themselves and produced series of prints, as Gibson had done; other imitators included R.M. Crosby, Walter Tittle, Rudolph Schabelitz, Orson Lowell and Gordon Grant. Indeed, a whole generation of "pretty girl" magazine cover artists can be traced to Gibson's inspiration.

Not since the *Yellow Kid* blitz had there been such a flurry of cartoon-inspired merchandising and popularization. In 1901, Marguerite Merrington starred in the two-act *Gibson Play*. *The Belle of Mayfair* of the 1906 Broadway season had a song singing the Gibson Girl's praises. The first Ziegfeld Follies (1907) contained the hit song "The Gibson Bathing Girl." The Girl's face and endorsement appeared on all types of ladies' fashions; famous Gibson Girl cartoons were burned into a series of Doulton porcelain plates; next to them on tables were Gibson Girl souvenir spoons. A wallpaper pattern with Gibson Girl heads was a popular seller for bachelor apartments. Pyrography, a popular craft at the turn of the century, appropriated her face for designs on pillows, handkerchiefs, chair backs, etc. And an unending series of prints—often limited and signed—was enormously popular.

R.M.

GIERSZ, WITOLD (1927-   ) Polish animator born in Poraj, Poland, in 1927. Witold Giersz studied economics but later switched to art, graduating in 1950. After working as a painter and newspaper cartoonist in the early 1950s, Giersz joined the animation studio of Bielsko-Biala in 1956, directing *The Secret of the Old Castle* that same year. This was followed by *In the Jungle* (1957), *Musical Adventures* (1958) and *The Gnomes in Spring* (1959), all unpretentious and charming little cartoon fantasies.

In 1960 Giersz organized the Warsaw unit of Bielsko-Biala, which was later to become Miniatur Film Studio. There he produced what is probably his

Witold Giersz, "The Little Western." © Miniatur Film.

"Good evening, Sir Launcelot."

Carl Ronald Giles, 1940. © Reynolds News.

best-known cartoon, *The Little Western* (1960), a clever, good-natured parody entirely painted in watercolors. More cartoons followed: *The Treasure of Black Jack* (1961), a spoof of adventure films; *Dinosaurs* (1962); *Red and Black* (1963), an amused look at bullfighting; *Ladies and Gentlemen* (also 1963), a sharp look at the war between the sexes; and *The File* (1966), a dig at bureaucracy. Giersz abandoned his humorous, lighthearted approach to describe the taming of a wild stallion with dramatic graphic effects (*Portrait of a Horse*, 1967), but he soon reverted to his usual levity with *The Intellectual* (1969). In 1968-69 he worked in Yugoslavia, returning to Poland to direct *The Glorious March* (1970). His output in the 1970s has been mixed, alternating between light and serious subjects. Titles of some of his recent films are: *The Stuntman* (1972), *An Indonesian Family* (1973), *The Old Cowboy* (1974) and *Traces* (1975).

One of the most talented practitioners of the Polish school of animation, Giersz is a dazzling artist of color, spraying bright splashes of paint on celluloid to obtain dramatic effects. He is also an *auteur* of great wit and perception who uses his medium with a deft touch, never descending to preachment or obviousness.

M.H.

GIL
See Lenoir, Carlos.

GILES, CARL RONALD (1916-   ) British cartoonist born in Islington, London, on September 29, 1916. Carl Giles, O.B.E., was the last and perhaps most popular of the great British newspaper cartoonists. His education was of the Council School variety that he has immortalized in his cartoons of Chalky and the kids. His family was from ancient East Anglian stock, and the little black grandma of his cartoons was autobiographical. At 14 he left school to become an office boy in Wardour Street film offices, and with his native ability to draw and fib, he talked himself into a job as an animator with an advertising-short film company. When Roland Davies began to produce his newspaper strip *Come On Steve!* as an animated series from a studio in Ipswich, Giles joined him: Giles was the only experienced animator on the team!

Giles's signature to cartoons and strips first began to appear in the Sunday newspaper *Reynolds' News* during World War II (1940). He drew a weekly topical panel and the pantomime strip *Young Ernie*. He joined the Beaverbrook Newspapers in 1943, alternating with Sidney Strube in the *Daily Express* and weekly in the *Sunday Express*. Here he established his style and regular characters—the Cockney family, the Cockney schoolkids, the wealthy GI's, etc. His sense of humor, present in every drawing, was a new characteristic in the newspaper cartoon and quickly established him at the top of his profession.

Arthur Christiansen, the executive editor of Express Newspapers who "spotted" Giles, wrote in an introduction to one of Giles's annual collections: "Giles does not caricature. He does not fake. He does not invent. He draws real buildings, real pubs, real railway stations. . . . And he draws from the largest and finest selection of models that any artist could wish—the British people." Her Majesty the Queen, awarding Giles the Order of the British Empire in 1959, said: "I might be accused of exaggeration if I said that the Englishman's ability to laugh at himself has won us the British Empire, but I am sure that it has contributed a good deal to keeping it together."

Books: *Sunday and Daily Express Cartoons* (annually from 1943); *Children* (1955); *The Wit of Prince Philip* (1965); and *Nurses* (1974).

D.G.

GILL, ANDRÉ
See Gosset de Guines, Louis.

GILLAM, BERNARD (1856-1896) American cartoonist
and publisher born in Banbury, England, on April 28, 1856. Bernard Gillam moved with his family to the United States in 1866, shortly after the Civil War's end, and settled in New York. He always displayed an inclination toward art, and a perhaps apocryphal story has the famous preacher Henry Ward Beecher encountering the impoverished Gillam in his youth and sponsoring his art training. (If the story is true, Gillam did not respond in kind—or with kindness—as he and fellow cartoonists were later to vilify Beecher mercilessly.) His first job was as a copyist in a lawyer's office, and he studied engraving at the same time.

Gillam sold his first cartoon in 1876 and was soon contributing ideas and cartoons to two of the nation's leading cartoon markets, the Leslie publications and the *New York Graphic*. When James A. Wales left *Puck* magazine to found *Judge* in 1881, Joseph Keppler needed a full-time political cartoonist to balance the social humor in his pages. When he plucked Gillam from *Leslie's* he was following a pattern: Keppler and Opper, another *Puck* mainstay, were alumni of the *Leslie's* shop.

The British-born cartoonist added a new element to the predominantly German *Puck* staff and soon became one of its stars through his powerful cartoons. He is most remembered for his vicious anti-Blaine cartoons in the American presidential campaign of 1884 (such as the Tatooed Man, a concept used by Keppler in similar contexts years before), although Gillam reportedly took little interest in politics (when he did, however, he admitted to Republicanism). He is recorded as actually having voted for Blaine.

In 1886, after Wales made a decided failure of running

Judge and sold it to entrepreneur William J. Arkell, the latter lured Gillam away from *Puck* with a half-interest in the magazine. Eugene Zimmerman also followed Gillam, and it was rumored that the Republican party itself invested heavily in *Judge* to make it a counterpart to *Puck*. Gillam was now able to give his crusades full range, although the fire of the 1884 campaign never returned (as was true with Keppler). *Judge*'s position was somewhat obscured as it straddled the Harrison-Blaine fence, but under Gillam it remained obdurately anti-Cleveland. Gillam died in his prime at Canajoharie, New York, on January 19, 1896.

Bernard Gillam was for a short period the most partisan cartoonist of his day and seemed sure to earn the mantle passed by Nast to Keppler. His fame was great and his cartoons bitingly powerful, but his most famous creations were simple assignments designed in *Puck*'s editorial sessions. His cartoons were technically proficient and carefully detailed, and perhaps it was their stiff, mechanical nature that kept them from achieving Keppler's verve and Opper's native humor.

Lest he be judged too harshly, it should be noted that Gillam is in the league with the early giants because his vision was great and his executions bold. He never shied from difficult subjects, artistically or thematically. His stiff, slashing lines and forthright use of color lent a solidity to the art of the cartoon and accomplished the task of every cartoonist—to command attention.

R.M.

GILLAM, F. VICTOR (1858?-1920) American cartoonist,
brother of Bernard Gillam, presumably his close contemporary. As Bernard Gillam was graduating from the black-and-white *New York Graphic* to the colored *Puck* in 1883, his brother Victor was assuming major cartooning duties on *Puck*'s Republican rival, *Judge*. Until Bernard's death in 1896, the public was largely in ignorance of their family relationship—even when Bernard switched to *Judge* in 1885; for Victor signed his cartoons "F. Victor" until he was the only cartooning Gillam.

Victor Gillam's style was, like his brother's, a bit harsh, with slashing lines instead of the smoother contours of, say, Grant Hamilton or the later Zim. Practically all his work was done on stone in color. As an idea man, in terms of partisanship and biting advocacy, he was easily the equal and perhaps the superior of his brother. He mercilessly attacked Grover Cleveland and even William McKinley in supporting his own favorite Republicans; he was at the cutting edge of the "Full Dinner Pail" campaign of 1896 and accused perennial Democratic presidential candidate William Jennings Bryan of everything from nihilism to vagrancy and lunacy.

Victor Gillam left *Judge* after the turn of the century, in the latter part of the first decade, and was reported to be drawing in Colorado. His later activities included work in the advertising field, where he created and painted the "His Master's Voice" image for Victor records and record players. He died in 1920.

R.M.

GILLIAM, TERRY V. (1940-) American animator, actor
and film director born in Minneapolis, Minnesota, on November 22, 1940. After a college education on the West Coast, Terry Gilliam went to New York and worked as an assistant editor on Harvey Kurtzman's *Help!* (1960), a monthly satire magazine designed as a successor to *MAD*. After the magazine folded, Gilliam

moved to Europe, where he set up as a freelance illustrator and cartoonist. Unable to sustain a steady income, he turned to comedy writing for television and in 1968 sold a couple of short skits to *Do Not Adjust Your Set* (London Weekend). This experimental series attempted to broaden the horizons of juvenile entertainment, and among its team of performers were Eric Idle, Michael Palin and Terry Jones. For Gilliam, it would prove a rendezvous with fate.

An experimental comedy series for adults followed, entitled *We Have Ways of Making You Laugh*. Its scriptwriter, Dick Vosburgh, made a hobby of collecting on tape the inane linking chatter of radio disc jockey Jimmy Young. There seemed to be no way of using this material on television until Gilliam came up with a concept of cutout animation, using clippings of photographs, drawings, lettering and anything visual that came to hand. The resulting sequence was run on the show and proved so hilarious that Gilliam was awarded a regular spot. This led to further animation sequences for the Marty Feldman series *Marty* (1969), which in turn led to a series that proved a watershed in adult television comedy, *Monty Python's Flying Circus*.

Gilliam's reunion on this series with Idle, Palin and Jones, plus John Cleese and Graham Chapman, all as writer-performers, brought a unique, insane, freewheeling humor to television; the stage was set each week by Gilliam's animated title sequence. He also contributed at least one animation sequence per show, always using the technique he had evolved: a combination of cutout ready-made material with original airbrush figure and background art. Not content with supplying the noises and voice-overs, Gilliam began to make bit-part appearances in the body of the show itself: in one famous burlesque he is the bloated figure belching "Beans! Beans!"

Gilliam's animated sequences appeared on the cinema screen for the first time in the Python movie *And Now for Something Completely Different* (1971). He went on to appear in the stage version of *Monty Python*, acted as co-producer on the feature film *Monty Python and the Holy Grail* (1975) and attained a high level of excellence by producing and directing the outrageous live-action fantasy *Jabberwocky* (1976).

D.G.

GINGER NUTT (G.B.) With his cheery cry "Chipetty-chippety!," Ginger Nutt, a red squirrel, scampered out of his treehouse and into *It's a Lovely Day* (1949). He was off on a fishing expedition despite all the pranks played by his pals Corny Crow, Dusty Mole (with the dark glasses on the end of his nose) and Loopy the Mad March Hare. Ginger Nutt (pun-named after a popular biscuit) was the first and only "star" of the *Animaland* series of animated cartoons produced by ex-Disney aide David Hand for the J. Arthur Rank enterprise Gaumont British Animation (GBA). Previous entries in the series (Ginger's debut came in number 8) had all featured on-off characters, and it was felt that greater audience appeal would be found if a cartoon star could be created.

Ginger was given a girl friend in the second of the series, the first to feature his name in the title: *Ginger Nutt's Bee Bother* (1949). She was Hazel Nutt. The third entry, *Ginger Nutt's Christmas Circus* (1949), was very special, as it rounded up all the *Animaland* characters from earlier cartoons for "guest star" appearances. Cooky Cuckoo was the one-man (one-bird) band, Digger

—"We're twelve thousand, eh!"
—"Twelve thousand and twelve, to put your mind at rest!"

Jean-Pierre Girerd. © La Presse.

and Dinkum from *The Platypus* were the jugglers, and Zimmy Lion, Oscar Ostrich and Chester Cat all appeared in supporting roles. The last cartoon, the fourth, was also the last GBA release: *Ginger Nutt's Forest Dragon* (1950).

Director for the series was Bert Felstead, with story supervision by Ralph Wright, screenplays by Pete Griffiths, Reg Parlett and R.A.G. "Nobby" Clark, and music by Henry Reed. Animators included Stan Pearsall, Frank Moysey, John Wilson, Bill Hopper; backgrounds were by Betty Hansford and Kay Pearce. Among the merchandising may be mentioned *The Ginger Nutt Gift Book* (1950), a full-color annual adapted from the films, with illustrations by Reg and George Parlett, among other anonymous artists.

D.G.

GIRERD, JEAN-PIERRE (1931-   ) Canadian cartoonist of French origin born in Algiers, Algeria, on March 6, 1931. Jean-Pierre Girerd attended the Algiers School of Fine Arts from 1952 to 1957 and went to work for the daily *Le Journal d'Alger* at the end of his studies. There he did fashion drawings and courtroom sketches but soon turned to editorial cartooning. In June 1961, toward the end of the Algerian war, Girerd moved to the United States and soon found employment as a cartoonist on the *Minneapolis Star*. In 1964 he decided to settle in Montreal, working as a cartoonist for the newly founded daily *Métro-Express* and freelancing for the weekly publications *Le Petit Journal*, *Dimanche-Matin* and *Le*

Travail. In 1967 he became the editorial cartoonist of the daily *La Presse*, a position he still holds.

Girerd has also done gag cartoons and advertising drawings, illustrated a number of books, and contributed cartoons to the weekly news magazines *MacLean's* and *Perspectives.* He is the author of an album of comic strips, *On A Volé la Coupe Stanley* ("The Stanley Cup Has Been Stolen," 1975), and of a collection of political cartoons, *Chien Chaud. . .et les Aut' Dogues!* ("Hot Dog . . .and Other Dogs!," 1970).

Working with pen gives Girerd's cartoons an impact similar to that of the contemporary French cartoonists. He also uses other techniques, such as charcoal drawing and painting, notably for his caricatures of celebrities. Union bureaucracy, the army and the police are his favorite targets, and his experience of the Algerian war has nurtured in him a profound antimilitaristic sentiment.

S.J.

GITÉ
See Turgeon, Jean.

GLACKENS, LOUIS M. (1866-1933) American cartoonist and animator born in Philadelphia, Pennsylvania, in 1866. Louis Glackens was the brother of Ashcan school painter and illustrator Williams Glackens. Around 1890 his work began appearing in *Puck* magazine, occasionally in the back pages; the special World's Fair *Puck* editions produced in Chicago in 1893 stretched the staff a little thin, and Glackens, still a freelancer, appeared more often. By the late 1890s he was a staffer, producing much of the interior art in the weekly. After the turn of the century, Glackens became *Puck*'s most versatile (and therefore arguably its most important) artist. He drew political cartoons in color as well as all manner of black-and-white art, from decorative pieces to straight gags to continuing strips. Thematically, he ranged from ethnic subjects to depictions of old New York in the New Amsterdam days—a favorite genre of his. Among his

Louis Glackens, 1913.

continuing features was *Hans and His Chums,* a strip about a little German boy and his dachshunds.

Glackens remained with *Puck* almost until it was sold to the Strauss dry-goods concern in 1914; at that time he left to become a pioneer animator. Evidently his many chores on *Puck* taught him speed as well as competence—an animator's natural ally, especially in those early days. Among the studios he worked for was the Barré-Bowers Studio, owned by Bud Fisher, where other magazine alumni turning out *Mutt and Jeff* cartoons each week included Ted Sears and Dick Huemer (*Judge*), Frank Nankivell and Leighton Budd (*Puck*), and Foster M. Follett (*Life*). Glackens also illustrated occasional articles for *Cartoons* magazine during this time. He died in New York in 1933.

Glackens had one of the most agreeable styles in cartooning—understated, not exaggerated, uncluttered, handsomely composed. He used negative space well and in color work let broad patches of pastel shades ease the eye into the cartoon. To add variation, he sometimes gave his work a mannered poster look or used a pseudo-woodcut style, but mostly his figures were drawn half-realistically, half-comically, bigger-than-normal heads being his only concession to comic conventions.

R.M.

GODFREY, ROBERT (1921-   ) British animator born of British parents in West Maitland, New South Wales, Australia, on January 27, 1921. Bob Godfrey, who has been dubbed "the Wild Man of British Animation," was brought to England at the age of six months; he went to school in Ilford and studied art at the Leyton Art School. His first job was with the Unilever organization, where his artistic prowess moved him into the company's advertising agency, Lintas, as a general assistant. After war service in the Royal Marines, he returned to Lintas, then entered animation as a background artist for the Larkins company at Film Producers Guild. He worked on many industrial films, then moved to Talkiestrips, a small company producing filmstrips for industrial sponsors.

Godfrey's first animated cartoon was *The Big Parade* (1952), made with Keith Learner, an associate from Larkins. In 1954 they made *Watch the Birdie,* the first film to reflect the Godfrey sense of humor; with the capers of the camouflage-conscious Uncle Wungle Bird (*Kodachromus panchromaticus*), it echoed the kind of comedy currently popular in the radio *Goon Show.* Made on 16mm film in Godfrey's basement in Tufnell Park at a cost of ten pounds, it won the *Amateur Cine World* Ten Best award. It was the first film of Biographic Cartoons, the company Godfrey formed with Learner and Jeff Hale, and it won them a contract to make commercials for Gillette razor blades. Biographic was enlarged by the enlistment of Nancy Hanna and Vera Linnecar, old colleagues from Larkins, and quickly became the leading independent animation studio.

Continuous production of commercials enabled Godfrey to indulge in an occasional personal production under the imprint of "Biographic 4." His first solo effort, *Polygamous Polonius,* was selected for the Royal Film Performance of 1960. It was the first cartoon to reflect another aspect of Godfrey's humor—a bawdiness linked to the great British tradition of the saucy seaside postcard. He continued to mine this vein after leaving Biographic in 1965; *Henry 9 till 5,*

Robert Godfrey, "Alf, Bill and Fred." © *Biographic Film.*

in which a dull office clerk fantasizes outrageous sexual activities, was produced by his own company, the Bob Godfrey Movie Emporium. The third chapter of what is regarded as the "Godfrey Trilogy" was *Kama Sutra Rides Again*, an animated manual of unlikely sex positions. It was the first Godfrey cartoon to become financially viable and paved the way to *Great*, his 30-minute musical based on the life and exploits of Isambard Kingdom Brunel, Victorian builder. *Great* won the Academy Award as the Best Animated Film of 1975 and in turn paved the way for Godfrey's first feature-length cartoon, presently in production with the working title *Jumbo*.

Godfrey has also produced two successful animated series for television, *Roobarb* (1974) and *Sky-Lark* (1976), featuring Nutty Noah and Nelly, from Grange Calveley scripts. On the side he finds time to teach animation every week at the West Surrey School of Art and Design. He also ran a course on BBC television, *The Do-It-Yourself Animation Show* (1974), and wrote the accompanying book. Other notable animated films by Godfrey include *One-Man Band* (1965); *Rope Trick* (1967); *Two Off the Cuff* (1969); *Ways and Means* (1970); *The Electron's Tale* (1971); *Dear Marjorie Boobs* (1976) and *The Key* (1977).

D.G.

GONZÁLEZ, JOSÉ VICTORIANO (1887-1927) Spanish painter, sculptor and cartoonist born in Madrid, Spain, on March 23, 1887. José Victoriano González—known to posterity as "Juan Gris"—showed a disposition for drawing at the earliest age. His parents enrolled him in the Escuela de Artes y Manufacturas in Madrid in hopes that he would choose an engineering career, but he dropped out of school in 1904 and started contributing cartoons to the Madrid humor magazines *Blanco y Negro* and *Madrid Cómico*. In 1906 Juan Gris moved to Paris (he lived in the same building as Picasso in Montmartre) and resumed his cartooning career with contributions to such magazines as *Le Cri de Paris*, *Le Charivari*, *L'Assiette au Beurre* and *Le Témoin*. His drawing style was straightforward and forceful, and he often chose social themes for his drawings.

Gris met the poet Guillaume Apollinaire, who introduced him to Cubism in 1912. He then completely abandoned cartooning for painting and sculpture. His position in the vanguard of the Cubist and abstract movements is well established and needs no further elaboration here. Gris's health deteriorated after 1923, and he died of uremia in Boulogne, near Paris, on May 11, 1927.

M.H.

GONZÁLEZ CASTRILLO, JOSÉ MARÍA (1930-   ) Spanish cartoonist born in San Sebastian, Spain, in 1930. José María González worked first as a house painter and was then an office clerk for some years. His career as a cartoonist started in 1957, when his work began appearing under the pseudonym "Chumy-Chumez" in *La Codorniz*, the most important satirical magazine of the postwar years. In subsequent years Chumy-Chumez's cartoons were published in all the major Spanish magazines—*Triunfo*, *La Gaceta Ilustrada*, *El Hermano Lobo*, etc.—making him one of the most recognized cartoonists in Spain. Chumy-Chumez has received a number of awards, including one at the International Humor Exhibition in Montreal. He has also published several books; one of these, a fictional autobiography in cartoons, has seen print not only in Spain but also in France, Italy, Greece and the United States.

One of the most creative of Spanish cartoonists, Chumy-Chumez often does collages as well as drawings. His work displays a peculiar humor midway between satire and social criticism, with a lot of crazy inventions thrown in. His cartoons have been called "sub-realistic," and their interpretation is often a matter of vociferous debate. Chumy-Chumez now uses a sun as his trademark, and it has become almost as popular as the cartoons themselves.

J.M.

GOODRICH DIRT (U.S.) In the second decade of the century animation was flourishing in all parts of the United States. Working in Chicago, Wallace Carlson

The supernatural child:
—"You don't have a mommy?"
"No, Papa got me with my aunt."

José Victoriano González ("Juan Gris"), 1908.

José-María González Castrillo ("Chumy-Chumez"), self-portrait. © González Castrillo.

(who had started in animation as early as 1915) produced a number of series which he released first through Essanay and later through Metro. His most notable creation was Goodrich Dirt, a slightly disreputable character in the tradition of the countless tramps and hoboes made popular by Charlie Chaplin and Happy Hooligan. Goodrich was a scraggly, unkempt and unredeemable bum who stopped at nothing in his pursuit of a square meal or a dishonest buck. "Lunch Detective" (1917) is a good example of the early entries in the *Goodrich Dirt* series.

In later cartoons Goodrich was to assume many guises, from railway cop to sheepherder, while remaining true to his unshaven, slovenly self. "Goodrich Dirt, Cowpuncher" (1918), for example, displays the diminutive tramp's underhanded talents in a tale of one-upmanship between rival cowhands. The series unfortunately ended in 1919, when Carlson went on to direct the unsuccessful animated version of *The Gumps*.

The *Goodrich Dirt* series shows that, contrary to commonly accepted belief, silent animation in the United States had achieved a high degree of polish. Carlson's cartoons were excellently drawn, well paced and skillfully animated; even the lack of speech was no hindrance thanks to Carlson's judicious use of word balloons. One of the unsung heroes of early animation, Carlson left the medium in 1923 to devote himself exclusively to comic strip work. (For a complete biography of Wallace A. Carlson, see *The World Encyclopedia of Comics*, Chelsea House, 1976.)

M.H.

GOOFY (U.S.) Goofy developed from a canine character named Dippy Dawg who debuted in the 1932 "Mickey's Revue." Continuing to appear in an increasing number of *Mickey Mouse* cartoons, the character had his name changed to Goofy. Starting in 1935, he went on to co-star alongside Mickey and Donald Duck in some of the funniest shorts produced by the Disney studios in the middle and late 1930s. (The Goof, as he was affectionately called, gave one of his best performances in the 1936 "Moving Day," but he was also featured in "Mickey's Service Station," "Alpine Climbers," "Moose Hunters" and others, many directed by Art Babbitt.)

By 1939 Walt Disney had decided that Goofy had a following of his own, and he starred him in "Goofy and Wilbur." This was followed by more *Goofy* cartoons, including "Goofy's Glider," "Baggage Buster" and "The Olympic Champ." In 1941 Goofy was put into a demonstration spoof called "How to Ride a Horse," and when the short proved popular, he was placed into more incongruous situations, variously illustrating in his own hapless, ingratiating way "The Art of Skiing," "The Art of Self-Defense," "How to Play Baseball," "How to Swim," "How to Dance" and "How to Play Football."

Goofy's unflappable if discombobulated behavior and his unmistakable voice characterization (built up by Disney staffer Pinto Colvig) provided most of the gags. In the late 1940s he was put into more substantial gag situations, especially in the cartoons produced under the able direction of Jack Kinney. "A Knight for a Day," "Two Gun Goofy" and "Motor Mania" are gems of invention, movement and pacing.

Despite its popularity, the *Goofy* series came to an end in the mid-1950s, when it was decided by studio executives that shorts were no longer economically feasible.

Goofy had his own comic book title published by Nedor (later Standard) Comics from 1943 to 1953, at which time the character was picked up by Dell, which published his adventures until 1962.

M.H.

GOOLD, PAUL (1875-1925) American cartoonist born in Casco Bay, Maine, in 1875. Paul Goold began his cartooning career with the *Portland* (Me.) *Sunday Press and Sunday Times* as an illustrator and cartoonist, after graduating from high school. He later studied at the Yale art school.

From 1899 to 1903 Goold was on the art staff of the *New York Times* before modestly entering the magazine field. He drew mostly for *Life* but also for *Judge*. His work appeared frequently in the 1910s and shared formats and a somewhat similar reserved drawing style with fellow cartoonists A.B. Walker, Donald McKee and Paul Reilly. In the 1920s, though, the others loosened somewhat and Goold seemed a little out of place—at least in the raucous pages of *Judge*. His style was tight, uncomplicated and often static. In addition to cartoons on all subjects, he often drew title and decorative pieces. Goold was killed in a four-story fall from his Carnegie Hall studio in New York City on December 6, 1925.

R.M.

GORIAEV, VITALY NIKOLAYEVICH (1910-   ) Soviet cartoonist born in Kurgan, in western Siberia, Russia, on April 14, 1910. Vitaly Goriaev studied at the

Moscow Higher Institute of Art and Technology and the Moscow Polygraphic Institute from 1929 to 1934. He started cartooning soon after graduation, with contributions to *Krokodil* beginning in 1936 and to *Frontovoi Iumor* from 1942. He is one of the most prolific among Soviet cartoonists, having drawn thousands of cartoons on themes ranging from everyday life to international events. Goriaev has also traveled extensively abroad, and his series of cartoons *Americans at Home* (published in 1958) depicts the seamier side of American life.

Goriaev has illustrated a number of books, but his specialty has always been the cartoon, of which he is an acknowledged master. His graphic style, expressive and caricatural, borders on the grotesque. Many of his cartoons have been collected in book form and have earned a number of awards. Goriaev himself was awarded the Order of the Red Star and was made an Honored Art Worker in 1966.

M.H.

GOSSET DE GUINES, LOUIS (1840-1885) French caricaturist, illustrator and painter born in Paris, France, on October 17, 1840. Introduced by Nadar to the publisher Charles Philipon, Louis Gosset de Guines used the pen name "André Gill" for his satirical caricatures for Philipon's *Le Journal Amusant*. His fame spread when, in 1866, he joined the staff of the newly created *La Lune*, subsequently renamed *L'Eclipse*. During his ten-year stay with the magazine, and later for his own *La Lune Rousse* (1876-1879), he contributed a weekly caricature of the most important personalities from the world of arts, letters, politics.

Gill's caricatures of such celebrities as Victor Hugo, Gustave Courbet, Sarah Bernhardt, Richard Wagner and Napoleon III, with their enlarged heads standing

Ray Gotto. © Sporting News.

on undersized bodies in comic poses and costumes, show immediately all the details of facial expression, dress and profession needed to give a very clear idea of who is being represented. Able to magnify the characteristics and idiosyncrasies of his "victims," Gill nevertheless confined himself to mere prickling fun in order not to wound; he lacks the caustic sharpness of a Daumier or a Grandville even in his political cartoons.

In addition to his cartoon work, Gill illustrated several of Zola's novels (*Nana, L'Assommoir, Le Ventre de Paris*) and exhibited his realistic paintings in various salons. At 40 he went mad and died five years later in a Paris insane asylum, on May 2, 1885.

P.H.

GOTTO, RAY (1916-) American cartoonist born in Nashville, Tennessee, on August 10, 1916. Ray Gotto once confessed that he was only interested in football and baseball in high school. Dropping out of school, he toured the country "via freight cars and thumbs," as he puts it, before landing a job as an editorial and sports cartoonist for the *Nashville Banner* in the mid-1930s. During World War II he served in the U.S. Navy as an artist on animated and documentary training films.

Back in civilian life in 1945, Gotto created *Ozark Ike*, a noted sports comic strip, for King Features Syndicate. Despite the success of the feature, he left in 1954 due to a contractual dispute with the syndicate and went on to produce *Cotton Woods*, another sports strip, for General Features later that same year. Unhappily, *Cotton Woods* folded after a few years, and in the late 1950s Gotto went back to his first love, sports cartooning, with occasional forays into advertising and commercial art. He designed

Louis Gosset de Guines ("André Gill"), caricature of Gustave Doré, 1878.

The coalition between Lord Salisbury and Joseph Chamberlain.

Sir Francis Carruthers Gould, 1895.

the New York Mets emblem in 1961, and his cartoons and illustrations for the *Sporting News* have been reprinted many times. (His baseball-uniformed Uncle Sam has by now become part of the sport's popular lore.)

While his comic strip work has been lauded by many (see the entry on *Ozark Ike* in *The World Encyclopedia of Comics*, Chelsea House, 1976), Ray Gotto is best noted as a sports cartoonist. His contributions to the field have been many, and he has earned a number of distinctions from sporting and cartooning organizations throughout the country.

M.H.

GOULD, SIR FRANCIS CARRUTHERS (1844-1925) British cartoonist born in Barnstaple, England, on December 2, 1844. Sir Francis Carruthers Gould, who signed his work with his initials, "F.C.G.," was the first British cartoonist to contribute daily drawings to a newspaper. For more than 20 years he was a member of the London Stock Exchange, and he did not turn to professional cartooning until he was 35. His first published cartoon was printed in the Christmas issue of *Truth* in 1879.

His politically liberal cartoon comments appealed to E.T. Cook, editor of the daily newspaper the *Pall Mall Gazette*, who put Gould on contract in 1888. He began contributing to *Punch* in 1890 and changed newspapers, going to the *Westminster Gazette* in 1893. For this daily he also wrote articles and became the assistant editor. He was knighted in 1906. He was also perhaps the first political cartoonist to develop a "character" out of a living personality: his caricatures of Joseph Chamberlain, complete with distinctive monocle, took on the popular proportions of a fictional creation. Gould reckoned up one hundred different guises in which he had portrayed the prime minister in his cartoons! Outside humorous comment, he is remembered for his landscape drawings of Normandy and Brittany. He died on January 1, 1925.

Books: *ABC of the Stock Exchange* (1880); *Ah Chin Chin* (1880); *Evaluations in the Sit Tee Desert* (1880); *The United Artist* (1880); *Fairy Tales from Brentano* (1885); *New Fairy Tales* (1888); *New Song of Malden* (1889); *Story of the Home Rule Session* (1893); *Cartoons of the Campaign* (1895); *Who Killed Cock Robin* (1896); *Westminster Cartoons* (1896-1900); *Political Struwelpetter* (1899); *Tales Told in the Zoo* (1900); *Struwelpetter Alphabet* (1900); *Snowflakes and Snowdrops* (1900); *The Khaki Campaign* (1900); *Great Men* (1901); *Indian Fables* (1901); *New Fairy Tales from Brentano* (1902); *Froissart's Modern Chronicles* (1902); *The Westminster Alice* (1902); *Book of Country and Garden* (1903); *Peeps at Parliament* (1903); *FCG, Caricaturist* (1903); *Capture of the Schools* (1903); *Political Caricatures* (1903); *Cartoons in Rhyme and Line* (1904); *John Bull's Adventures* (1904); *Later Peeps at Parliament* (1904); *Golden Treasury* (1906); *Wild Nature in Pictures* (1907); *Nature Verses* (1923); and *Nature Caricatures* (1929).

D.G.

GOURSAT, GEORGES (1863-1934) French caricaturist and writer born in Périgueux, France, on November 23, 1863. Georges Goursat is better known under the pen name "Sem." He gave up his grocery store in his provincial hometown and went to Paris at the turn of the century, quickly becoming the most feared and admired caricaturist of the period.

Sem's first album, *Les Sportsmen* ("The Horse Fanciers"), appeared in 1900 and portrayed members of the aristocratic and snobbish Parisian high society. Thereafter, he published annually a new book of sketches with the fashionable people and resorts of *la Belle Epoque* as subjects, and these albums constitute important graphic documentation of one of France's most fascinating eras. All his faces are reduced to one extreme characteristic feature (nose, eyes, hairdo) and are drawn in profile only; the effect is sometimes witty and daring, sometimes monotonous.

Sem also illustrated Courteline's civil-service satire, *Messieurs les Ronds-de-Cuir* ("Government Bureaucrats"), and his own books: *Un Pékin sur le Front* ("A Civilian at the Front," 1917), *Le Grand Monde à l'Envers* ("High Society Inside Out," 1919) and *La Ronde de Nuit* ("Night Watch," 1923). He died in Paris in 1934, a member of the Committee of the Salon of Humorists.

P.H.

GOYA Y LUCIENTES, FRANCISCO DE (1746-1828) Spanish painter born in Fuentetodos, near Zaragoza, Spain, on March 30, 1746. Francisco Goya received a

(Left, Maurice de Rothschild; right, James de Rothschild):
"All the same, he has that English style!"

Georges Goursat ("Sem").

mediocre art education in Zaragoza in his youth, and he traveled to Italy to further his education. In 1775 he was appointed to make carpet designs for the Royal Manufacture of Carpets in Madrid. During the 16 years he worked there, under the reigns of Carlos III and Carlos IV, he had access to the royal art collection. It was at this time that he became familiar with the works of Velázquez and Rembrandt. Throughout his life Goya considered these two artists his masters.

In 1792, as a result of illness, Goya became totally deaf. His deafness and the sadness it brought were strongly reflected in his art. The series of drawings entitled *Los Caprichos*, for instance, was made around this time. In 1808, during the war of independence against Napoleon, Goya painted his most famous subjects, and he also did the renowned and controversial series of engravings *Los Disastros de la Guerra* ("The Disasters of War"). Following the war Goya voluntarily exiled himself to France as the result of difficulties with the new king of Spain, Fernando VII. He died in Bordeaux, France, on April 16, 1828.

Goya was technically and artistically very much ahead of his time; his bitter and satiric tastes and his strong character made him unpopular among his contemporaries. Nobody, however, denied his extraordinary and self-willed competence as a master of the art of painting. Today, of course, Goya is universally regarded as one of the greatest artists who ever lived. *Los Caprichos* establishes Goya as one of the first cartoonists in the world. Indeed, in the 19th century these strong and satiric drawings were highly influential among cartoonists. In *Los Caprichos* "reason becomes dream" and "dream becomes reason," producing strange monsters capable of criticizing cultural regression and political repression in Spain. In the strong Castilian tradition of Quevedo and Góngora, Goya used black humor to express his own political and cultural views.

J.M.

Francisco Goya, plate 53 of "Los Caprichos," 1799.

himself; the little tugboat character has become a classic creation. And, in a full circle of sorts, Disney animated the character in 1946.

Hardie Gramatky died on May 1, 1979.

R.M.

GRAMATKY, HARDIE (1907-1979) American watercolorist, author and cartoonist born in Dallas, Texas, on April 12, 1907. Hardie Gramatky studied at Stanford University (1926-28) and at the Chouinard Art School in Los Angeles (1928-30) while drawing a little weekly strip, *Captain Kidd, Jr.*, for the *Los Angeles Times*. This science fiction/fantasy strip caught the attention of Charlie Plumb, artist on the popular *Ella Cinders*, who engaged Gramatky as penciler and letterer on the strip for $15 a week—while Plumb himself was collecting about $1,800 a week. Shortly after his ghosting stint, Gramatky was contacted by Walt Disney. In June 1932 he wrote six months' continuity for the *Mickey Mouse* strip and was hired by the studio for chores ranging from storyboarding to animation; by 1936, at the end of his four-year hitch, he was chief animator. Gramatky remembers his first sessions, with only a dozen men including Disney; when he left, the department had risen in numbers to about 250.

The major period of Gramatky's career began in 1936, when he moved to New York. He did reporting-painting jobs for *Fortune* magazine, illustrated many articles and books, and became a top-flight watercolorist, winning dozens of awards and prizes. He was a member of the National Academy and director of the American Watercolor Society. He had numerous shows of his watercolors and is represented in many museums and collections. Gramatky is probably best remembered for his series of *Little Toot* children's books, illustrated by

GRANDJOUAN, JULES-FÉLIX (1875-1968) French cartoonist born in Nantes, France, in 1875. Félix Grandjouan started law school in Nantes but then embarked on an artistic career by both writing and illustrating *Nantes la Grise* ("Nantes the Gray City," 1899). He went to Paris a year later and contributed cartoons to the most important satirical (and oftentimes anarchistic) journals of the beginning of this century: *Le Rire, Le Sourire, Le Canard Sauvage, Les Temps Nouveaux, L'Assiette au Beurre*, etc.

Grandjouan's 2,000 drawings deal with every political and social problem from granting Algerian independence to more enlightened labor laws, from foreign spies to the Courrières mine disaster. They have a haunting quality about them that conceals the bitterness of a socially committed artist. Grandjouan was also a fervent admirer of Isadora Duncan, whom he met in Paris in 1901. He drew 25 sketches of the American dancer (1912) in addition to illustrating, along with Bourdelle and Clará, her *Ecrits sur la Danse* (1927).

Félix Grandjouan, who was erroneously reported dead of tuberculosis in 1912, actually died in his bed in 1968 at the ripe age of 93.

P.H.

GRANDVILLE
See Gérard, Jean-Ignace-Isidore.

The lady: "Excuse me, can you tell me—"
The clerk (roaring): "Ask at window 11."

Jules Grandjouan, 1904.

GRAN'POP (G.B.) Gran'pop, an artful and ancient ape, bald of pate with kneecaps to match, ginger-haired with pink patches showing through, was popular with children and adults alike. Indeed, his first appearances were in the very adult magazine *The Sketch*, that glossy weekly which had given birth, in a previous generation, to Bonzo. Lawson Wood, the painter and illustrator who fathered Gran'pop, undoubtedly had G.E. Studdy's popular pup in mind, for Gran'pop followed the trail of success blazed by Bonzo: merchandising via picture postcards, prints, children's books, novelties and, but for the outbreak of World War II, animated cartoons. Wood drew the key drawings for four Gran'pop cartoons and delivered them to the Ub Iwerks Studio in Hollywood, but the films were never made. That they were contracted for is, today, one indication of the worldwide popularity of Wood's cheerful old chimp; since the artist's death, however, the character has virtually disappeared into limbo. All that remains to show for the old ape's years of fame are the battered *Gran'pop's Annuals* and collections of Kensitas cigarette cards (1935) that change hands among nostalgic collectors at ever-increasing prices.

Lawson Wood, one of the finest black-and-white illustrators to excel in watercolor cartoons, was born in Highgate, London, in 1878. His grandfather was L.J. Wood, an architectural artist, and his father was Pinhorn Wood, a landscape painter. Lawson studied art at the Slade School and Heatherley's, with night classes at the Frank Calderon School of Animal Painting. At the age of 18 Wood entered the offices of C. Arthur Pearson, the magazine publisher, swiftly rising to a position of chief artist. The all-round experience as magazine and newspaper illustrator for six years gave him a speed and journalistic sense which, added to his academic training, made his style unique. His main line was poster design, often serious, which he supplemented with humorous cartoon work for weeklies as disparate as the *Graphic* and the colored comic *Puck*. His first "fixation" was on the prehistoric period, and his Stone Age series spanned many years. His first one-man exhibition was held in Sunderland in 1932, where it was remarked: "He is sincere in his work, for he rejoices in making people smile." He died in October 1957.

Books: *The Book of Lawson Wood* (1907); *The Bow Wow Book* (1912); *A Basket of Plums* (1916); *A Box of Crackers* (1916); *Splinters* (1916); *The Art of the Illustrator* (1918); *The Mr. Books* (1916); *The Mr. and Mrs. Books* (1918); *The Mrs. Books* (1920); *Rummy Tales* (1920); *Rummy Tales Painting Book* (1921); *Noo Zoo Tales* (1922); *Lawson Wood's Colour Books* (1925); *Jolly Rhymes* (1926); *The Scot Scotched* (1927); *Lawson Wood's Funny Farm* (1931); *The Old Nursery Rhymes* (1933); *Granpop's Annual* (1935-); *Bedtime Picture Book* (1943); *Granpop's Book of Fun* (1943); *Meddlesome Monkeys* (1946); *Mischief Makers* (1946); and *Popular Granpop* (1946).

D.G.

GRANT, GORDON HOPE (1875-1962) American cartoonist, artist and member of the National Academy born in San Francisco, California, in 1875. Gordon Grant, noted in fine-art circles as a premier marine painter, acquired a love for the sea at an early age. His father, seeking to strengthen racial and ancestral bonds, sent young Gordon to Scotland to attend elementary school; a voyage of almost five months around Cape Horn in a Glasgow sailing vessel seemed to chart the excited Grant's own artistic course.

His art training was received later at the Heatherly and Lambeth school in London. Back in the United States, practical art experience came with jobs as a newspaper artist in San Francisco and New York. These two cities were great cartoon centers, and before long Grant was a regular contributor to humor magazines. Around the turn of the century his work became a fixture in *Puck*, and soon thereafter his illustrations adorned the pages of the second-level popular monthlies.

Grant's work for *Puck* was at first an awkward groping for a Gibson affinity—a foible of too many cartoonists of the period. But Grant was able to rise above the throng and develop quite a handsome and distinctive style of his own: crisp, bold pen lines, judicious shading and empathetic characterizations. His "girls" were heralded, justifiably, as much as other artists' characters who followed the Gibson Girl's successes. Grant worked for *Puck* nearly until its change of ownership in 1914. He had graduated to cover art and seldom dealt with politics in his cartoons.

Gordon Grant's cartoon work is today unfortunately obscured by his other achievements—famous illustrations for Booth Tarkington's *Penrod* stories, his painting of the *Constitution* that became the focal point for the

Gordon Grant, 1912.

restoration of "Old Ironsides," his self-written and self-illustrated books, including *Ships Under Sail* (1941) and *The Secret Voyage* (1943), as well as his representations in many major museums and galleries.

R.M.

GRANT, VERNON (1902-   ) American cartoonist born in Coleridge, Nebraska, on April 26, 1902. Vernon Grant moved with his family to a South Dakota homestead when he was five and to California ten years later. He attended the University of Southern California for two years and received art training at the Otis Art Institute in Los Angeles. Between 1923 and 1928 he also took classes in portraiture at the Chicago Art Institute. It began to dawn on Grant that portraiture was not his calling when teachers and classmates became more excited about the fantasy drawings of gnomes and other creatures that he doodled on the borders of his paintings. He moved back to Los Angeles to do advertising work, with Wrigley, Southern Pacific and Packard autos as accounts. He also taught and had many future Disney staffers in his classes.

In 1932 Grant moved to New York to expand his activities. He immediately became *Judge* magazine's premier cover artist, painted for *Ladies' Home Journal*, *Liberty* and the *American Legion* magazine, and did ad work for Everready, General Motors, Westinghouse, General Electric, Arrow shirts and Junket rennet, among others. In 1933 his first cartoons apeared in Kellogg's Rice Krispies ads, and his characters—Snap, Crackle and Pop—kept Grant busy for 15 years. They are still used today (by other artists) and are among the most famous images in American advertising. King Features Syndicate was the biggest customer of Grant's career; for many years he did one cartoon cover a month for the Hearst Sunday supplement magazine. He wrote and illustrated two books, *Tinker Tim the Toymaker* and *Mixey Dough the Baker*, both for Whitman. Recently Grant has been active in his South Carolina hometown, has executed paintings and cartoons on commission, and has seen the York County Museum dedicate a gallery to him.

Vernon Grant has one of the most unique and agreeable styles in American cartooning. He does very little line work, painting in his broad, flat areas with swatches of color. He characters are cute, big-headed fantasy beings who live in the artist's world of sparse backgrounds and handsome compositions. His special creations rank with the Brownies and the Kewpies in the tradition of fantasy cartoon characters.

R.M.

GRAYSMITH
See Smith, Robert Gray.

GREEN, BERT (1885-1948) American cartoonist and animator born in England in 1885. Bert Green was taken to the United States by his parents when he was a child. After studies in art school he went on to work as a cartoonist on several New York newspapers before being promoted to art department manager on the *Chicago Examiner* in 1914. When Hearst International Film Service was established in 1916, Bert Green became one of its earliest animators and scriptwriters, working notably on *The Katzenjammer Kids*.

After the closing of Hearst's animated film operation in 1918, Green went on to create the comic strip *Kids* for the *Chicago Tribune*, and the feature lasted through the 1920s. He also produced training cartoons for the U.S. Navy through the Vocafilm Corporation during World War I, and he later wrote hundreds of humorous articles and stories for *Liberty*, the *Saturday Evening Post* and others. His satires on Prohibition (illustrated by himself) were later collected in book form under the title *Love Letters of an Interior Decorator*.

During World War II Green served as a member of the U.S. Coast Guard and was assigned to antisubmarine duty. After the war he returned briefly to cartooning. He died after a long illness at the Bronx Veterans Hospital on October 5, 1948. His contributions to the early art of animation deserve recognition.

M.H.

GREEN, WILLIAM ELLIS (1923-) Australian cartoonist born at Essendon, Melbourne, Australia, in 1923.

A visiting cartoonist from England recently remarked in Melbourne how appalled he was at the quantity of work demanded from Australian cartoonists in a week, stating that no cartoonist working in Britain would stand the pace. Among others working in Australian journalism, John Jensen's reference was of course to artists like William Ellis ("Weg") Green of the Melbourne *Herald*. He has been producing, together with other work, 11 joke ideas and drawings every week for 23 years.

Green has a declared disinterest in political cartooning, valuing his independence rather than accepting and expressing the editorial line of a newspaper. He saw one well-known cartoonist destroyed in this way, and that is not for him. His real interest is in social comment: with Weg, humor comes first, but he is adamant about sound drawing.

Weg started with the *Herald* after leaving the army (he served in New Guinea with an army intelligence unit drawing maps and general cartographic work on active service) and after studying drawing at the National Gallery School in Melbourne. Sam Wells, the *Herald*'s political cartoonist, recommended Weg to do the leader

page cartoon while Wells was on holiday. Green's work impressed the staff, and an invitation to join the paper followed during June 1947.

In October 1949, his regular daily feature, *Weg's Day*—a single-column drawing wittily commenting on current news items—appeared on the front page of the *Herald* and has continued to appear daily since that time. Weg was also required to illustrate feature articles, design headings for feature departments and draw caricatures of politicians, sports figures and other personalities.

His popular pocket cartoon had been running for just under four years when, in March 1953, a new feature that made his pen name a household word all over the state of Victoria was introduced into the *Herald* columns. This was the brilliant *Weg's Weekend*, a six-cartoon panel satirizing people and events in the news, at home and abroad, and displayed across the top of a broadsheet page and to a depth of six inches or more. Weg's drawing is broadly comic and wholly original, with only faint echoes of his earlier admiration for the work of William ("Wep") Pidgeon. Drawing with pen, ink and brush, Weg condemns the modern trend of drawing with pentel-type pens, which cannot give sensitivity or quality of line to drawings.

The wonderfully funny drawings by William Green are the work of a thoroughly professional artist, a gently mannered and articulate craftsperson concerned for the future of Australian cartoonists, resenting foreign influences and domination in terms of the threat imposed from syndicated material dumped less expensively upon the market. Although Weg has illustrated several books, no collection of his cartoons has been published.

V.L.

GREENING, HARRY CORNELL (1876-ca. 1930) American cartoonist born in Titusville, Pennsylvania, on May 30, 1876. H.C. Greening was educated in drawing techniques at the Art Students League and in 1896 began selling cartoons regularly to the *New York Herald*, *Life* and *Truth*. He contributed panel cartoons and one-shot strips to Hearst's *American Humorist* Sunday comic section in 1898 and soon was a frequent contributor to *Puck*, *Judge*, *Life*, *Harper's* and *Scribner's*. For *St. Nicholas* he drew the children's series *Prince Red Feather*.

Greening's newspaper work was soon confined to the *New York Herald* again, and there he created such strips as *Percy*, *Fritz von Blitz* and the classic *Prince Errant*. During World War I he served with the American Expeditionary Force as an artist and returned in the 1920s to draw for the McClure Newspaper Syndicate (a kid strip, *Eb and Flo*) and the *Illustrated Daily News* of Los Angeles. He was the inventor of Sporty Sam and Funnyfishes toys and developed the Wishbone Man Game, which was based on his *Eb and Flo* strip, as was a storybook.

At the height of his productive days, between 1900 and 1910, Greening was among the most published of American panel cartoonists. There was a feeling of humor in his work, and he eschewed the obsession with pretty illustrative techniques. His cartoons were nevertheless handsome—boldly composed and carefully shaded. His *Prince Errant*, designed to replace *Little Nemo* in newspapers, was a masterpiece of whimsy and visual delights.

R.M.

COMPLAINTS

"As I was saying when the store closed last night!"

William Ellis Green ("Weg") © Melbourne Herald.

The Labor Question—Both Sides of It

H.C. Greening, ca. 1905.

GRGIĆ, ZLATKO (1931-   ) Yugoslav cartoonist born in Zagreb, Croatia, Yugoslavia, in 1931. Zlatko Grgić studied journalism and law at the University of Zagreb. In 1951 he left his studies to devote himself to cartooning and contributed a number of cartoons to *Kerempuh* and other Yugoslav humor magazines. Turning to animation in 1957, Grgić became an assistant to Nikola Kostelac and worked on *Opening Night* and *Encounter in a Dream*. The following year he was the chief animator on Norbert Neugebauer's *The False Canary* and Dušan Vukotić's *The Great Fear* and *Revenger*.

In 1960 Grgić directed his first animated films for an advertising agency. From 1960 to 1969 he variously assisted and animated for Vukotić, Kristl, Vrbanić, Stalter and Dovniković. Under the supervision of Vukotić, Grgić directed *A Visit from Space* (1964) and *The Devil's Work* (1965), and he co-directed with Stalter two of the most celebrated of Zagreb films, *The Fifth* (1965) and *Scabies* (1969). As an independent director Grgić has realized several entries in the *Inspector Mask* and *Case* series (1961-62), as well as *Little and Big*, the delightful *Inventor of Shoes* (1967) and *Twiddle-Twaddle* (1968). He co-directed with Branko Ranitović *Tolerance* (1967) and *The Suitcase* (1969) and, along with Kolar and Zaninović, produced the popular *Profesor Balthasar* series. In 1970 Grgić also directed the whimsical *Maxi-Cat*.

In recent years Grgić has worked mainly outside of Yugoslavia. One of his more interesting efforts in animation is the 1974 *Who Are We?*, which he directed for the National Film Board of Canada. Zlatko Grgić is one of the most important creators to come out of the famed "Zagreb school"; Ronald Holloway described him as "one of the subtlest poets in the animation business."

M.H.

GRIFFIN, SYDNEY B. (1854-ca. 1910) American cartoonist born on October 15, 1854. Educated in the public schools of Detroit, Michigan, Syd B. Griffin moved to New York in 1888 to become a cartoonist. He took his drawings first to *Puck*, which rejected them, and then to its rival, *Judge*, where he was offered a position on the art staff. Griffin took the trouble to inform *Puck*'s art editor, W.B. Gibson, who replied that Griffin's drawings were refused only because their excellence suggested a lack of

originality; Griffin was then offered, and accepted, a position on *Puck*'s art staff. For that great weekly, he drew—badly—occasional lithographed political cartoons but concentrated mainly on pen-and-ink panels. He remained with *Puck* until the mid-1890s, when he lost control of his drawing hand. Training himself to draw with his left hand (a similar task was to confront H.T. Webster and Tad in later years), he contributed to *Judge*, *Truth* and the early New York newspaper supplements; it was for the *World* that he created *Clarence the Cop* in 1901, later relinquishing it to C.W. Kahles.

In his prime—his "first" career—Griffin had an astonishingly supple line and a style that combined perfectly the animation of A.B. Frost and the sophistication of Charles Dana Gibson. For awhile he threatened to eclipse other *Puck* black-and-whiters like Opper, although his humor was not as evident as Opper's. His themes were largely suburban and rural, and his depictions still come alive on the page, filled with personality and vitality.

R.M.

GRIMAULT, PAUL (1905-   ) French animator born at Neuilly-sur-Seine, a suburb of Paris, France, on March 23, 1905. The son of an archaeologist, Paul Grimault studied art at the Germain-Pilon school, then went to work for the Bon Marché department store. After completion of his military service in 1930, Grimault worked for an advertising agency where he met André Sarrut. In 1936 Grimault and Sarrut founded Les Gémeaux (literally, "The Gemini"), producing animated cartoons for advertisers. In 1939 they released their first theatrical cartoon, *Gô Chez les Oiseaux* ("Gô Among the Birds").

The outbreak of World War II interrupted the collaboration when Grimault was drafted into the army. After demobilization, he went back to animation and in 1942 brought out *Les Passagers de la Grande Ourse* ("The Passengers of the Big Dipper"), again featuring Gô, followed in 1943 by *Le Marchand de Notes* ("The Music-Note Merchant"), in which he created a fantastic character, the Niglo. That same year saw the release of *L'Epouvantail* ("The Scarecrow"), on a script by Jean Aurenche. Grimault's best animated cartoon to date, it related the adventures of a couple of lovebirds pursued by a cruel cat and befriended by a scarecrow that came to life.

The end of the war brought more creations from Les Gémeaux. First there was *Le Voleur de Paratonerres*

Zlatko Grgić, "Who Are We?" © *National Film Board of Canada.*

Paul Grimault, "Le Petit Soldat." © Les Gémeaux.

("The Lightning-Rod Thief," 1945), in which two moustached cops relentlessly pursue but always fail to catch the young thief (the film won first prize at the 1946 Venice Film Festival). Then came La Flûte Magique, on the same story as Mozart's opera (1946), and Le Petit Soldat ("The Little Soldier," 1947), a little masterpiece of poetry, humor and fantasy based on Hans Christian Andersen's tale of the toy soldier who goes to war.

Soon thereafter Les Gémeaux started work on their most ambitious project: a feature-length animated cartoon also based on an Andersen story, La Bergère et le Ramoneur ("The Shepherdess and the Chimney Sweep"). After many vicissitudes, delays, and even a lawsuit, the film was finally released in 1953 in mutilated form.

Having broken with Sarrut in 1951, Grimault founded his own studio, Les Films Paul Grimault, which produced a number of animated films and documentaries such as La Faim du Monde ("World's Hunger," 1958) and La Demoiselle et le Violoncelliste ("The Girl and the Cello Player," 1964), a beautiful cartoon short directed by Jean-François Laguionie. In 1973 Grimault returned briefly to directing with the delightful Le Chien Mélomane ("The Music-Loving Dog").

Paul Grimault is the most widely known French animator, and his work has been hailed in many quarters. In 1956 Philippe Collin and Michel Wyn wrote in their study Le Cinéma d'Animation dans le Monde that Paul Grimault created "a new world in the animated cartoon . . . he is the only cartoonist who can be compared to Renoir in his deep feeling for reality, for humanity, for the joy and sadness of our existence."

M.H.

GRIN AND BEAR IT (U.S.) George ("Lichty") Lichtenstein started his hilarious newspaper panel series, Grin and Bear It, in March 1932, in the pages of the Chicago Times. It has continued to run since that time.

In Grin and Bear It Lichty took a hard, satirical, yet amused look at the ways Americans act, talk and fantasize about themselves. Lichty has seen fit to lampoon all subjects and types in his characteristically scratchy, slapdash style: his politicians are as bombastic as any, his generals as bloodthirsty as they come, and his business tycoons as befuddled as they are ruthless. The "common man" does not come off any better: he is pictured as conniving, lazy, lecherous and gullible. The

institution of marriage has suffered particularly from Lichty's sarcastic pen: the domineering wife and the helpless husband wage unceasing, if hardly equal, warfare upon each other with blind ferocity. Love, death and taxes are also among Lichty's favorite subjects, and it is to his credit that he has made his readers laugh as hard at the latter two as at the first.

In 1934 Grin and Bear It was picked up for syndication by United Feature, which distributed it nationally until 1940. It was then reclaimed by Field Enterprises (which had acquired the Chicago Times and consolidated it into the Sun-Times). It is now being syndicated by Field Newspaper Syndicate.

Lichty retired from the feature in December 1974, and Grin and Bear It is now done by Fred Wagner in a style close to that of Lichty (whose name still appears on the by-line).

M.H.

GRIS, JUAN
See González, José Victoriano.

GROPPER, WILLIAM (1897-1977) American artist and cartoonist born in New York City on December 3, 1897. William Gropper studied art at the National Academy of Design, at the New York School of Fine and Applied Arts and with Robert Henri, George Bellows and Howard Giles. He described his field as "satirical figuration"; his art ranged from biting political cartoons to social-theme murals. Gropper's work first appeared in the New York Tribune in 1919 and then in the pages of radical, Socialist and Communist magazines and liberal newspapers and journals; in 1935 he got Vanity Fair magazine banned in Japan by drawing a vicious attack on the emperor for its pages.

Gropper consistently utilized a free brush and heavy crayon shading, producing the look of a stone lithograph (indeed, many of his works were actually to be drawn on

Another Pact
William Gropper, 1936. © Gropper.

stone). In this regard he was the technical as well as ideological cousin of Boardman Robinson, Robert Minor and Fred Ellis, among others. On various trips to the Soviet Union he produced many cartoons and was honored with a place in the Museum of Western Art in Moscow. Gropper's cartoons were lucid, hard-hitting and very effective—practically propaganda tracts for his viewpoints.

Among Gropper's books of drawings are *Golden Land*, *Gropper*, *The Little Tailor*, *Twelve Etchings* and *The Shtetl*. He also did book illustrations, including those for *Alley Oop* (about acrobats), *Circus Parade* by Jim Tully and *Reminiscences of a Cowboy* by Frank Harris. His work has been collected by several museums, and he won many awards (especially for his lithographic work) and executed murals throughout America. Gropper died on January 8, 1977.

R.M.

GROSS, SAM (1933-   ) American cartoonist born in the Bronx, New York, on August 7, 1933. Sam Gross received his B.A. from the City College of New York, specializing in advertising. According to him, his success in the field of cartoon art has been very gradual, but the process has paid off. Today his work appears with regularity in the *New Yorker*, *Saturday Review*, *Oui*, *Cosmopolitan*, *Ladies' Home Journal*, *Good Housekeeping*, the *New York Times*, *Esquire*, *Audubon* and *TV Guide*. In addition, Gross serves as senior contributing artist on the *National Lampoon*, a position that not only involves him editorially but also indicates the high esteem in which his talent is held at that well-known institution of American humor.

Working in ink (line and washes), Gross creates a manic *comédie humaine* in which certain themes and characters constantly reappear. This recurrence, which seems to be a carefully calculated aspect of Gross's art, can be most fully appreciated in a collection like *I Am Blind and My Dog Is Dead* (Avon, 1978). From page to page, one encounters fairy-tale figures—the gingerbread house witch, the little match girl, the gingerbread man, blind men, frogs (Gross's frogs are marvelously engaging creatures), cornucopias, snakes, nervous old maids, birds, street vendors and other mendicants, and little Soglovian-style kings—at times interacting with one another, as when a bird asks his mother up in the tree if he may eat the gingerbread man who has followed him home.

Such themes impress themselves subtly on the reader, and the sense of hilarity is heightened by increasing familiarity. In the gingerbread-man drawings, for example, each panel is a masterpiece of inspired lunacy, but cumulatively they are even funnier. Thus, by the time one comes upon the drawing of the gingerbread man running out of a pizzeria while two disgruntled bakers look after him, agreeing from now on to stick to pizza, one's laughter is literally uncontrollable. While this happy penchant for thematic consistency makes Gross especially collectible, it takes nothing away from his ability to be brilliantly funny in a solo context. Thus, Goldilocks walks into a cottage and confronts a sign on the wall: "Occupancy by more than three bears is both dangerous and unlawful," signed by the fire commissioner, "Bruin McMirth." Or a single pigeon ignores the man feeding the rest of the flock at one end of a park bench, instead approaching the wino at the other end to announce, "I'm not very hungry, mister, but I sure could use a drink."

The free linear style Gross has evolved to convey his highly individual humor appears to reflect the influences of both Steinberg and Thurber, though the blending is undeniably and effectively personal. Gross's achievement is especially commendable in light of the fact that he has had no formal art training; for it is the self-taught artist who is often the most derivative. Besides the volume mentioned above, the artist is also responsible for *How Gross* (Dell, 1973). Gross originals are represented in many private collections. He is a member of the Illustrators Guild and of the Cartoonists Guild and has served the latter organization as treasurer (1969-71), vice-president (1972-73) and president (1974-75).

R.C.

GROSZ, GEORGE
See Ehrenfried, Georg.

GRUEL, HENRI (1923-   ) French animator and filmmaker born in Mâcon, in the Burgundy region of France, on February 5, 1923. Henri Gruel became interested in animation while in high school, and after a variety of jobs in commercial art, he finally started working in animation with Jean Arcady in 1946, graduating from in-betweener to director in the space of a few years. He first conceived of incorporating children's drawings (as well as some of their idea suggestions) into his cartoons in 1949. His first film using this concept was the charming *Martin et Gaston* (1950). The whimsical *Gitanes et Papillons* ("Gypsy Girls and Butterflies") was also based on children's drawings, but Gruel's treatment was sophisticated and sharply satirical.

In the late 1950s Gruel made a number of cartoons that have since become classics. First came the 1955 *Voyage de Badabou* ("Badabou's Journey"), an utterly enchanting children's film that won the Prix Emile Cohl in 1956, followed in 1958 by the wildly inventive *La Joconde*, a series of Mona Lisa jokes to end all Mona Lisa jokes. That same year Gruel worked with the transplanted Polish animator Jan Lenica on the funny and iconoclastic *Monsieur Tête* (released in 1959). Gruel also made *Un Atome Qui Vous Veut du Bien* ("An Atom Which Means You Well," 1959), about the peaceful uses of atomic energy, and *La Lutte contre le Froid* ("The Fight Against Cold," 1960), two didactic subjects that he treated with unusual wit and humor.

In the 1960s Gruel virtually abandoned the animation medium (with the exception of an occasional advertising film or two) in favor of live action, starting with the 1963 comedy *Le Roi du Village* ("The King of the Village"). He came back to animation, however, as the head of the newly formed Idéfix Studios in 1973.

M.H.

GRUELLE, JOHNNY (1880-1938) American cartoonist and author born in Arcola, Illinois, in 1880. Johnny Gruelle began cartooning in Indianapolis, Indiana, and after the turn of the century drew children's fantasy strips for small syndicates, where he created some of the most wonderful fantasy the comics have ever known. In 1910 he won a $2000 prize offered by the *New York Herald* and had a comic strip, *Mr. Tweedeedle*, accepted; it ran until 1921.

The war: "Have you heard? In order to help the Russians,
Roosevelt has decided to advance the winter."

Giovanni Guareschi, 1942. © Bartoldo.

In 1912 he created the *Yapp's Crossing* series for
Judge. Running weekly, a full page in the front of the
magazine, the series concerned the doings of small-town
folk during celebrations, holidays, events, etc. The
whole town was portrayed from an angled bird's-eye
view. With minor recurring characters, the series
became immensely popular and spawned imitators
(Eugene Zimmerman and Tony Sarg adopted the genre
well); it ran in *Judge* until 1923. Gruelle imitated himself
and ran the *Yahoo Center* series in *Life* and the *Niles
Junction* adventures in *College Humor*.

Gruelle's biggest success was his *Raggedy Ann* series, which included cartoons he illustrated himself.
He had specialized in children's stories in such
magazines as *Women's World*, but his *Raggedy Ann*
stories about dolls and toys that come to life are all-time
classics of children's literature. The very conceptions
are as brilliant as the cartoons, which are often in color.
A whole series of books was produced which continue to
be just as popular today, with much ancillary
merchandising (particularly the Raggedy Ann doll
itself), in the traditions of other children's fantasy
classics like *The Wizard of Oz* and *The Brownies*.

Gruelle's son, Worth, became a cartoonist and
switched assignments with Harry Neigher on the
Bridgeport (Conn.) *Herald* in the 1930s; much of his
work consisted in taking old *Yapp's Crossing* drawings
and writing local captions and labels. Johnny Gruelle
retired from Norwalk, Connecticut, to Miami Springs,
Florida, where he died on January 9, 1938. (His Western
comic strip, *Brutus*, which he had started in 1928, died
with him.)

R.M.

GUARESCHI, GIOVANNI (1908-1968) Italian cartoonist
and writer born in Parma, Italy, on May 1, 1908. The
name of Giovanni Guareschi is indissolubly tied to those
of Don Camillo and Peppone, respectively the priest and
mayor of a fictional Italian village, fighting one another
but ultimately the best of friends. In these two characters
many have seen a prefiguration of the "historic compromise" between the Christian-Democratic and Communist parties in Italy.

Guareschi the writer was preceded, however, by
Guareschi the cartoonist, who started to draw for *Bertoldo* toward the end of the 1920s, and whose cartoons
reflected the honest, ribald qualities of Italian comedy.
His cartoons were so well appreciated, in fact, that he
became the editor in chief of the magazine in 1936,
holding that post until 1943. Right after the end of World
War II, Guareschi founded *Candido*, one of the most
successful of Italian satirical and humorous magazines;
he directed it from 1945 on, first with Giovanni Mosca,
then by himself. During that time he was sentenced to
one year in prison for his attacks on Prime Minister A. De
Gasperi. But if Guareschi did not spare the Christian
Democrats, his favorite targets remained the Communists, whom he represented in his cartoons as ugly,
bullying, ignorant and crude (at the time, Stalin was still
alive, and the cult of personality was very much in
evidence). In 1950 Guareschi wrote the first of the *Don
Camillo* books, and their success led him to do less and
less cartooning. The quality of his cartoons declined
markedly toward the end of his life. He died in July 1968.

C.S.

GUILLAUME, ALBERT (1873-1942) French cartoonist,
painter and poster designer born in Paris, France, on
February 14, 1873. The son of a professor of architec-

Albert Guillaume, "A Bachelor's Life," 1896.

ture at the Paris Ecole des Beaux-Arts, Albert Guillaume studied art there with Gérôme. Starting in the late 1880s, he contributed satirical drawings (sometimes as many as ten a week) to all the important magazines (*Le Rire, Gil Blas, Le Gaulois, Le Musée des Familles, La Revue Illustrée*, etc.). He also decorated the main dining room of L'Auberge du Grand Cerf in Senlis, 30 miles north of Paris.

His cartoons deal mainly with the frivolous life of chic, sophisticated demimonde women and rich, *bon vivant* men forever engaged in eating, drinking and sexual pursuits. They have done much to capture the fashionable turn-of-the-century world of restaurants, seaside resorts and racetracks, and to perpetuate our image of what is commonly referred to as *la Belle Epoque*. These drawings were published in albums, the most important being *Des Bonshommes* ("Goodnatured Men" 1890-92), *Petites Femmes* ("Little Women," 1891), *Y' A des Dames* ("Ladies Present," 1896) and *Frivoles Femmes* ("Frivolous Women," 1902).

Albert Guillaume had the sharpness of a born social observer and an eye for detail which uncovered at a glance not only the erotic connotations of a scene but its vulgar aspects as well. He died in Dordogne on August 12, 1942.

P.H.

GULBRANSSON, OLAF (1873-1958) Norwegian-German cartoonist, illustrator and painter born in Oslo (then Kristiania), Norway, on May 26, 1873. Olaf Gulbransson studied at the Oslo applied-art school from 1885 to 1892 and spent some time at the Académie Colarossi in Paris in 1900. By 1892 he was contributing cartoons to the local publications *Tyrihans, Transvikspost* and *Karikaturen*. By the turn of the century he was Norway's most prominent cartoonist, and his 1901 album of celebrity caricatures, *24 Karikaturer* (including Ibsen, the painter Christian Krohg and many others), was already a masterpiece.

In 1902 Albert Langen, who had founded the Munich satirical magazine *Simplicissimus* in 1896, invited Gulbransson to work for him in Munich. (Langen had long had influential connections with the Scandinavian countries, and such artists as Theodore Kittelsen and Ragnvald Blix also worked for *Simplicissimus*.) Gulbransson accepted, spent a little while in Berlin to learn German and then arrived in Bavaria, which was henceforth to be his physical and spiritual home. He clicked right away as a *Simplicissimus* artist and, with certain interruptions, remained on its staff until its demise in the 1940s, continuing to be one of its two or three most influential and admired associates. His style changed gradually, and not without reverses, from a dark, shaded look to an extremely flexible open contour method of great beauty of line. His celebrity caricatures were always a specialty (as early as 1905 a Munich album, *Berühmte Zeitgenossen*, echoed the successful Oslo album of 1901), but his subject matter was extremely varied and generally on the good-natured side.

Gulbransson also did extensive book illustration, continuing well into the 1950s. He was especially well known for his illustrations of the works of the Bavarian author Ludwig Thoma and for his own hand-lettered autobiography covering his childhood and young manhood, *Es War Einmal* ("Once upon a Time").

In 1924 he started teaching at the Munich Academy, where he became a full professor of drawing and painting in 1929 and could boast over the years of numerous

Olaf Gulbransson, caricature of Isadora Duncan, 1904.

successful students. From 1922 to 1927 he lived in Oslo, working on the magazine *Tidens Tegn* ("Signs of the Times"). He died on September 18, 1958, at his estate, Schererhof, on the Tegernsee in Bavaria.

S.A.

GULLIVER'S TRAVELS (U.S.) Flushed with the roaring success of his *Popeye* cartoons (which a 1938 opinion poll found to be more popular than *Mickey Mouse*), Max Fleischer decided to challenge Walt Disney on his own ground with a full-length animated feature to be produced in the new Fleischer studios in Miami, Florida. Fleischer chose Jonathan Swift's *Gulliver's Travels* as the source for his artistic venture, and after much discussion, it was decided to limit the film to Gulliver's first journey to the kingdom of Lilliput. After much ballyhoo and fanfare, the film finally opened in December 1939.

The Fleischers' *Gulliver* was a mixed bag. Swift's original story had been changed and sugared down to such an extent that only the bare essentials remained. A number of characters were added to the plot, including Prince David and Princess Glory of the feuding kingdoms of Lilliput and Blefuscu, the three comical spies—Sneak, Snoop and Snitch—and Gabby, the cowardly crier of Lilliput who nearly stole the show (Gabby went on to star in his own cartoon series). There were some nice bits of animation (Gulliver being tied up by the tiny Lilliputians, the royal feast in Gulliver's honor, and the slapstick shenanigans of the three spies), but on the whole *Gulliver's Travels* proved something of a disappointment.

Practically the whole studio staff had worked on the picture. Dave Fleischer received his usual credit for direction, but a host of "directors of animation" shared

"Gulliver's Travels." © Paramount Pictures.

the honors, including such stalwarts as Seymour Kneitel, Willard Bowsky, Grim Natwick, Roland Crandall and Orestes Calpini. Ted Husing, "famous CBS announcer," supplied the voice for Gulliver, while the prince and princess spoke and sang through the voices of Lanny Ross and Jessica Dragonette.

M.H.

GURNEY, ERIC (ca. 1920-   ) American cartoonist and author born in Winnipeg, Manitoba, Canada, around 1920. As a boy, Eric Gurney moved with his family to Saskatoon, Saskatchewan, and then to Toronto, where he attended school. After graduating from Central Technical School, he attended night classes at the Ontario College of Art and in 1938 went to California to work at the Disney studios. Over a 10-year period Gurney garnered credits on 20 films, working in various animation departments. In 1948 he moved to the East Coast, where he established himself as a major cartoon-style advertising artist (for such clients as Texaco, Ethyl Gas and Southern Railways) and illustrator (for Collier's, the Saturday Evening Post, Look, Life, Reader's Digest and Outdoor Life, among others).

It was as a book illustrator, however, that Gurney hit his stride. He has a genius for depicting cartoon animals, and his works are consistent best sellers and award winners. Nobody in cartoon history has surpassed his sympathetic portrayals of dogs, cats and birds. His style is one of exacting detail and crosshatching, combined with genuinely funny characterizations and expressions on his subjects. His use of color is handsome, and he steadfastly refuses to "humanize" his animals à la Snoopy or the major animated characters.

His books include How to Live with a Neurotic Dog, How to Live with a Calculating Cat, How to Live with a Pampered Pet, Gilbert, Eric Gurney's Pop-Up Book of Dogs, Eric Gurney's Pop-Up Book of Cats, Impossible Dogs and Troublesome Cats, The King, the Mice and the Cheese and The Return of the Calculating Cat. Several of the books were written by his late wife, Nancy, and the last-named by Nancy Provo. Gurney has illustrated several animal cartoon calendars as well.

R.M.

GUSTAVINO
See Rosso, Gustavo.

Hh

HAAS, LEO (1901-) Czechoslovakian cartoonist and painter born in Opava, Bohemia, in 1901. Leo Haas studied art in Vienna and Berlin; in 1925 he became the manager of a lithographic printing house in his hometown. He became noted for his paintings and for the many cartoons he contributed to the leading Czech magazines of the 1920s and 1930s.

After the Nazi takeover of Czechoslovakia in 1938, Haas was sent to the Theresienstadt (Terezin) concentration camp. There, in a number of drawings that he managed to hide, he made a visual record of the horror surrounding him. Having next survived Auschwitz, he returned to Terezin at the end of World War II; his drawings, published in a book called *The Artists of Terezin*, evoked an immediate worldwide response. Settling in Prague, Haas became one of the leading political cartoonists of his country before leaving for East Germany in 1955.

Leo Haas held a number of exhibits of his cartoons, and his works hang in museums in Prague and East Berlin. (Haas inspired the character of Karl Weiss in Gerald Green's teleplay *Holocaust*.)

M.H.

HADASHI NO GEN (Japan) *Hadashi no Gen* ("Barefoot Gen") is for very special reasons one of the most moving "comics" ever created. It is the semiautobiographical story of the author and artist, Keiji Nakazawa, and his experiences as a child during and after one of history's greatest tragedies—the atom bombing of Hiroshima.

Little Gen Nakaoka, the hero, is in the second grade in 1945. Because of his father's opposition to a war still being bitterly contested, Gen's entire family is subjected to ostracism and persecution. Despite hunger and injustice the Nakaoka's survive—until 8:15 p.m., August 6, 1945. At that instant the world is transformed into a raging inferno the likes of which have never been seen. Gen and his mother survive, but his father, sister and brother are killed (as Nakazawa's were). From that point on, a bitter struggle for existence commences, a struggle against starvation, radiation sickness and social breakdown. In a situation guaranteed to bring out the ugliest aspects of man and society, little Gen serves as an example of compassion, perseverance and the will to live.

Hadashi no Gen was an attempt by Keiji Nakazawa to convey some sense of the horror he experienced to a generation that knows nothing of war, let alone atomic holocaust. It was originally serialized in 1973 in the weekly comic book *Shōnen Jump* (which then had a circulation of one million), but it has since been compiled and published in several four-volume editions, with over six hundred thousand volumes sold. Despite its length (over twelve hundred pages), it won instant popularity and was made into a two-part movie of the same name. Furthermore, *Hadashi no Gen* was the first Japanese comic book of its kind to be translated into English for distribution overseas. In 1977 Project Gen, a volunteer group, was established with the express goal

"Hadashi no Gen." © *Manga.*

of conveying Gen's message to the world, and translation is being done by Dadakai (the Neo Dada group).

F.S.

HAGIO, MOTO (1949-) Japanese cartoonist born in Ōmuta, Fukuoka Prefecture, Japan, in 1949. Moto Hagio is one of the most popular, prolific and talented comic book artists in Japan today. She exhibited a passion for comic books from a very early age, actively drawing them herself. After reading Osamu Tezuka's *Shinsen Gumi*, she became convinced that comics were her future and formed an association with friends of a similar persuasion in her junior year in high school. Upon graduation, Hagio began attending design school. During one winter vacation in Tokyo, she approached a publisher with samples of her work, and this resulted in *Bianca* and *Yuki no Ko* ("Snow Child").

With *Ruru to Mimi* ("Lulu and Mimi"), a humorous work that appeared in a girls' comic in 1969, Hagio began her professional career. Two years later, *Juichigatsu no Gimnajium* ("November Gymnasium"), a tale of two identical twins in a German boarding school for boys, caused her popularity to soar. This was followed by works such as *Juichini Iru!* ("Eleven People Are Here!") and *Pō no Ichizoku* ("Pō's Family"), which won her the 21st Shogakkan cartoon award for 1976. *Juichini Iru!* was a science fiction work that ran in girls' comics to great acclaim. *Pō no Ichizoku*, a humanistic portrayal of a vampire, was influenced by Ryoko Ikeda's classic *Berusaiyu no Bara* ("The Rose of Versailles"), particularly in its dramatic layout. Hagio also crossed over into boys' comics with *Hyaku Oku no Hiru to Sen Oku no Yoru*

("Ten Billion Days and One Hundred Billion Nights").

Moto Hagio is an extraordinarily prolific and successful writer. Seven years after her debut with *Ruru to Mimi* she had turned out sixty-eight works, and a special collection that appeared in *Putchi Komik* in November 1977 was sold out the moment it appeared in the bookstores. Hagio's strength, and the source of her popularity, lies in her draftsmanship and plots. Her drawings tend to be very realistic and almost three-dimensional relative to the fashion-design style so popular in Japanese girls' comics, and her stories are quick to capture and hold the reader with their skillfully unfolding plots and unexpected climaxes. She is, moreover, at home in almost every genre, whether gag strips, science fiction or historical romance. Ironically, nearly all her works feature foreign Caucasian children as subjects, a trend very evident in young girls' comics in Japan, but one she seems to take to an extreme. Nonetheless, her fan mail is enormous, and drawing comics is her true passion.

F.S.

HAHN, ALBERT (1877-1918) Dutch editorial cartoonist born in Groningen, the Netherlands, on March 17, 1877. Like Jan Holswilder a generation earlier, the short-lived Albert Hahn fought ill health (he spent years in the hospital as a boy and suffered from frequent periods of exhaustion) to become a major artistic force of his time. Hahn, a workingman's son turned imaginative and subtle political cartoonist, was said to have created the aesthetic embodiment of the social idealism inherent in the Dutch labor movement during its first period of heroic combat.

From 1890 to 1896 Hahn attended the Academie Minerva in his native Groningen and then continued his studies in the two main art schools of Amsterdam until 1901. After a period as a commercial artist designing bookplates and posters, Hahn joined the staff of the Amsterdam socialist paper *Het Volk* in 1902. For years he was the sole or principal artist of its Sunday supplement. *Het Volk* was only equipped to print black-and-white line art, and Hahn soon became a master of simplification of form and of striking, somewhat ornamental composition, with great originality of visual concepts.

Hahn and *Het Volk* were anticapitalist and anticlerical, so that Dr. Abraham Kuyper, head of the Calvinist political party, was one of their main targets. The titles of a number of the albums in which Hahn's cartoons were collected allude to Kuyper's career: *Van de Dorpspastorie naar het Torentje* ("From the Village Parish to the Tower"), *In Abraham's Schoot* ("In Abraham's Bosom") and *Onder Zwart Regime* ("Under a Black-Clad Regime"). One of Hahn's most famous single cartoons was "The Wooden Sentry," which depicted Kuyper as a toy soldier guarding a safe (the wealth of the country) on top of which the crown and other regalia reposed. Other publications in which Hahn's work appeared besides *Het Volk* were *Der Notenkraker, De Ware Jacob,* and *De Hollandsche Revue.*

Hahn's cartoons during World War I were outspokenly anti-German (Holland was neutral, but it was hard for many Dutch to disregard the unethical invasion of neighboring Belgium). Although his work never became a cause célèbre like Raemakers's, he lashed out against "Hun brutality," the sinking of the *Lusitania* and the defacing of Rheims Cathedral (another of his masterpieces shows the cathedral rebuilt after the war as a montage of bombs and ammunition).

Hahn died in Amsterdam at the age of 41 on August 3, 1918.

S.A.

HAJDU, EMERIC (1911-   ) French animated cartoon director and producer born in Budapest, Hungary, on January 26, 1911. Emeric Hajdu studied at the School of Decorative Art in Budapest and later in Berlin before arriving in Paris in 1932. There he worked as a commercial artist until he went to London for an apprenticeship in animation with John Halas (1936-37).

In 1944, back in Paris and using the name "Jean Image," he directed his first short animated cartoon, *Les Noirs Jouent et Gagnent* ("Black Plays and Wins," 1944). Two years later *Rhapsodie de Saturne* ("Saturn Rhapsody") was produced by his own studios and screened officially at the Cannes Film Festival (1947). Thereafter, there was a series of prize-winning animated cartoons starting with *Jeannot l'Intrépide* ("Johnny the Giant Killer"), his first feature, with the animation done by Boutin, Klein and Breuil. The film, which won the Grand Prize for Children's Film at the Venice Festival in 1951, relates the many adventures of little Johnny in his fight against a mean and frightening ogre. *François S'Evade* ("François Escapes") was awarded a prize at the Mar del Plata Festival in Argentina in 1959. *Aladin et la Lampe Magique* ("Aladdin and the Magic Lamp"), a 1969 feature film, was presented in 1970 at the Mamaia Film Festival in Romania and at children's film festivals in Gijón, Spain, and Tehran, Iran. Although it took him only seven months to direct, *Aladin* is by far his best animated work to date. The script adaptation by Image and his wife is excellent, as is the animation of Boutin, Breuil, Lehideux and Xavier, and the colors and psychedelic backgrounds are absolutely stunning. His latest feature-length venture, *Pluk, Naufragé de l'Espace* ("Pluk in Cosmos"), was released in 1974. It is in the epic tradition of interplanetary travels from Jules Verne to *Star Wars.*

Jean Image, who has been called the French Walt Disney but is probably closer to being the French Hanna-Barbera, has also directed and/or produced five

Emeric Hajdu ("Jean Image"), "Aladdin and the Magic Lamp." © Image.

animated television series: *Les Aventures de Joë* ("Joe's Adventures," 1960-62); *Picolo et Picolette* (1963-64); *Kiri le Clown* (1966-69), actually a puppet series; *Au Clair de Lune* ("In the Moonlight," 1971-72); and *Arago X 001* (1972-73). In addition, he has directed scores of industrial and special events shorts, many of which have won prizes (e.g., *Rhodialine Emballage*, 1957 Cannes Film Festival; *La Petite Reine*, 1958 Cortina d'Ampezzo Film Festival).

P.H.

HAKUJADEN (Japan) *Hakujaden* ("Legend of a White Snake") is a classic of Japanese animation. Produced in 1958 by the newly created animation department of the Toei film company, it was Japan's first technicolor animation feature and also the first film of its kind designed for export.

Hakujaden is a love story based on an ancient Chinese classic. The plot revolves around a young Chinese boy, Kyosen, who has a little pet snake. Scolded by his parents, he reluctantly and tearfully abandons it. After he has grown up, a beautiful girl appears, and she and Kyosen fall in love. The girl is, of course, the spirit of the snake. Many trials and tribulations ensue, threatening to thwart the love of the two young people, and considerable dramatic action results from the confrontation between the snake girl and Hokai, a priest who is opposed to their union. Finally, however, the snake girl becomes a true human on the condition that she renounce her supernatural powers, and she and Kyosen sail off into happiness.

Taiji Yabushita wrote the screenplay and directed the film, and such well-known figures as Yasuji Mori, Akira Kaikuhara and Masao Kumagawa worked on the animation. Overall production took more than a year and required 214,154 drawings. The result was an animated feature film that was acclaimed not only in Japan but abroad and received several awards, including a special mention at the 1959 Venice International Children's Animation Festival. In the years since its release, *Hakujaden* has served as an inspiration to an entire generation of young animators in Japan.

F.S.

HALAS, JOHN (1912-   ) British animator born in Budapest, Hungary, on April 16, 1912.

Animation in Great Britain may never have produced a character to equal Mickey Mouse, but Halas and Batchelor Cartoons is universally acknowledged as the British equivalent of Walt Disney. The company holds a record of continuous production second only to the Disney studio's, dating back over forty years to the chance meeting of John Halas and Joy Batchelor at British Animated Films in 1938.

John Halas freelanced on French magazines in Paris (1930), then returned to Budapest to work for George Pal on the first Hungarian animated cartoons—advertising shorts made in the cutout technique. In 1933 he studied at The Studio, a private graphic design school run by Alexander Bortnyik and László Moholy-Nagy as a split-off from the German Bauhaus. Two years later he established the first Hungarian studio devoted to animation, but it produced only films advertising cigarettes and liquor. However, one of his color cartoons was seen in London, which led to an invitation to come to England and join British Animated Films, a commercial company run by

John Halas, "Animal Farm." © Halas & Batchelor.

photographers Gabriel Denes and Trigg and the financier Weisbach. Here, on the short *Music Man*, Halas met Joy Batchelor.

Halas and Batchelor as a company really got under way in 1942, when the Ministry of Information contracted them to produce entertaining animated propaganda shorts. *Filling the Gap* and *Dustbin Parade*, both in 1942, led the way to a series of four cartoons featuring a regular character, Abu (*Abu's Dungeon*, etc., 1943), but these were not seen by British audiences, as they were made for showing overseas. Special commissions began to flow in, and for the Admiralty they made their first feature-length cartoon, the documentary *Handling Ships* (1945). Another similar feature-length instructional, *Water for Fire Fighting* (1948), was made for the Home Office. A new series character, Charley, was created for the Central Office of Information, and six cartoons were made, beginning with *Charley's New Town* (1947).

After the war, in 1949, came the company's first cartoon for children, an old sea shanty set to animation, *Heave Away My Johnny*. Commercial sponsorship played an increasing role in their output, ranging from *Flu-ing Squad* for Aspro aspirin tablets (1951) to *As Old as the Hills* (1950) and other serious shorts for the Anglo-Iranian Oil Company. For the Festival of Britain in 1951, Halas and Batchelor produced a set of four unusual and artistic shorts, the *Poet and Painter* series, which combined the work of famous artists (Mervyn Peake in *Spring and Winter*, Henry Moore in *The Pythoness*) with that of famous poets (Thomas Nashe's *The Time of Pestilence*), singers (Peter Pears) and speakers (Michael Redgrave, Eric Portman). In 1952 came the first British cartoon in 3-D, *The Owl and the Pussycat*, from Edward Lear's poem.

The year 1953 brought another sponsored feature for the Admiralty, *Coastal Navigation*, with their first "proper" cartoon feature following in 1954. This was *Animal Farm*, an adaptation of the fantasy novel by George Orwell, made for the American producer Louis De Rochemont. The styling of the animals in the currently acceptable Disney mold spoiled for some the satire of the story. Animated sequences for the giant screen of *Cinerama Holiday* (1955) were the next challenge for the little company, and in 1956 came the first of several entertainment shorts for the cinema, *The World of Little Ig*. This was made with television in mind, and shortly the studio embarked on *Habatales* (1959), a series for the new medium, and *Foo-Foo* (1960), an animated series for the international TV market that used no words. Then came *Snip and Snap*, a children's series featuring animated paper sculpture. A live-action feature followed, *The*

Monster of Highgate Ponds (1961), made for the Children's Film Foundation. In 1963 came another experiment, animated sequences made in "living screen" technique for a traveling show, *Is There Intelligent Life on Earth?*

Dodo, the Kid from Outer Space (1965) was the first Halas and Batchelor series for color television, and it led to commissions for *The Lone Ranger* (1967), *Popeye* (1968), *Tomfoolery* (1970), *The Jackson Five* (1971), *The Osmond Brothers* (1972), *The Count of Monte Cristo* (1973), *The Addams Family* (1973) and *The Partridge Family* (1974)—a tremendous output, but one which was, unfortunately for a British studio, geared entirely to the United States. More to English tastes, perhaps, was their second feature-length cartoon, *Ruddigore* (1966), which Joy Batchelor directed from the Gilbert and Sullivan operetta. Unhappily, it was no box-office beater. More successful were their cartoons adapted from the drawings of Gerald Hoffnung, especially *The Hoffnung Symphony Orchestra* (1965). The studio returned to safer, sponsored ground with such efforts as *Cars of the Future* for British Petroleum (1969). Currently, with around one thousand television commercials to their credit, Halas and Batchelor are into both computer animation and entertainment, having completed a television special for Germany based on Wilhelm Busch's immortal comic strip, *Max und Moritz* (1977).

Books by John Halas: *How to Cartoon* (1951); *The Technique of Film Animation* (1959); *Design in Motion* (1961); *Art in Movement* (1970); *Computer Animation* (1974); and *Visual Scripting* (1976).

D.G.

HALL, HELGE (1907-   ) Danish cartoonist whose pen name is Hall, born in Hellerup, Denmark, in 1907. Hall debuted in 1925-26 as a cartoonist in the magazines *Ude og Hjemme, Hjemmet* and the Copenhagen morning paper *Berlingske Tidende*. In 1927, he had his first job as a theater set piece decorator and as a stage drawer in Copenhagen cabarets (Tivoli and Lorry) along with "Storm P." (Robert Petersen) and others. His first strip, *Hilarius Petersens Radio-Oplevelser*, appeared in the daily *Politiken's* radio supplement.

Hall immigrated to the United States in 1928 and tried in vain to sell cartoons to American newspapers. He got a job in a Minnesota music hall, worked at a tile factory and decorated a synagogue in Los Angeles. He returned to Denmark in 1929 as a freelance cartoonist, making panels and features with varied life-spans. In 1947 he originated the biggest Danish success within family strips, *Hans og Grete*, which was syndicated in 1960 by PIB, Copenhagen, to over one hundred client papers. The strip is still going strong and in Scandinavia has a greater readership than, for example, *Blondie*.

Undoubtedly Europe's most industrious cartoonist, Hall has for several decades delivered two daily strips and five to six cartoons *per day*, besides countless book covers and book illustrations. He has been a board member of Danske Bladtegnere (Danish newspaper cartoonists' guild) for many years.

J.S.

HAMILTON, GRANT (1862-ca. 1920) American cartoonist and editor born in Youngstown, Ohio, on August 16, 1862. Grant Hamilton was graduated from Yale in 1880 and resided for awhile thereafter near Flushing, New York, where he and a group of other young cartoonists formed the Nereus Boat Club to race on the Harlem River; among the members were the Gillam brothers, Dan Beard and Charles Dana Gibson. Hamilton began to contribute to *Judge* magazine in 1881, upon its establishment as one of several magazines around the nation in hopeful competition with *Puck*.

Judge soon relied heavily on Hamilton for its political and social cartoons, and when the magazine changed hands in 1886, he was one of the very few staffers retained. He eventually became art editor of *Judge* and, after a merger, of *Leslie's Weekly*. James Montgomery Flagg was one of many cartoonists who had fond memories of the big, genial Hamilton as the man who really held the magazine together, outlasting and outshining text editors who came and went. Hamilton could sense when to give talents like Flagg complete freedom.

Hamilton contributed his own art for years—fortunately for his readers and later cognoscenti—except for the period during the election of 1904 when he drew anti-Republican cartoons for the rival *Puck*. Otherwise, he was a strong Republican throughout his career. His work gradually disappeared from *Judge's* pages in the 1910s.

Hamilton's art is a happily polished style glowing with technical competence and anatomical soundness. His exaggerations were slight, and during his mature years he never fell prey to the overkill school of crosshatching; breezy and rounded pen lines combined with gentle crayon shading in his color work for a comfortable, genial visual feeling. Thematically, he pioneered, no later than Opper, the new cartoon genre of light social comment in the format of casual vignettes and observations. In the late 1880s and early 1890s the back page of *Judge* was his, and he filled it with airy examinations of the fads, fashions and mores of his time. The works of Hamilton and Opper deserve special republication; theirs were superb talents that mirrored their times—a gift peculiarly the cartoonist's in many happy instances. And Hamilton's overall work merits discovery for its substantial contributions to the cartoonist's art.

R.M.

HAMILTON, WILLIAM (1939-) American cartoonist and playwright born in Palo Alto, California, on June 2, 1939. William Hamilton attended Yale University, receiving a B.A. in English in 1962. After a two-year hitch in the army (1963-65), he became a staff cartoonist for the *New Yorker* on the strength of his first submissions—a feat somewhat akin to batting .400 as a rookie.

Hamilton claims no formal training in art, and there is no evidence that he has been influenced by any of the major artists working in the field. An unusually delicate ink line makes his work immediately identifiable. His close-up renderings of features have more the quality of preliminary portrait sketches than of caricature, and various faces clearly recur in his cartoons, suggesting that he works from life, probably using friends or family members as models.

His humor also tends to be of a rather personal stamp—very much New York, corporate and Ivy League in setting, and dedicated to the deflation of intellectual pretension and cliché. It may not be everyone's sort of humor, but those familiar with the rather hermetic environment he satirizes will laugh (or wince) at his thrusts. Especially keen are his frequent variations upon the theme of the cocktail party—surely one of

The Spanish brute adds mutilation to murder.

Grant Hamilton, 1898.

civilization's more persistent forms of self-inflicted torture. The drink is innocuous, the food familiar, and the topics of conversation hopelessly predictable. No wonder the heroine of one panel inquires plaintively of her mate as they emerge from one of these get-togethers, "Why are our new friends always just like our old friends?" Why, indeed?

In addition to his work for the *New Yorker*, Hamilton's cartoons are syndicated to 30 newspapers by the Universal Press Syndicate. Collections of his work include *Anti-Social Register* (1974), *Terribly Nice People* (1975), *Husbands, Wives and Live Togethers* (1976), *Money Should Be Fun* (1976) and *Introducing William Hamilton* (1977). He is also the author of two plays, *Save Grand Central* (1976) and *Plymouth Rock* (1977), and a member of the Dramatists' Guild and the Screenwriters' Guild.

A final and rather surprising note: this consummate New Yorker lives in California.

R.C.

HANCOCK, MALCOLM (1936-) American cartoonist born in Erie, Colorado, on May 20, 1936. After graduating from the University of Denver in 1958, Malcolm Hancock (who signs "Mal") broke into cartooning with features for the George Matthew Adams service, beginning with *Nibbles*, and with initial sales to the *Saturday Evening Post* and *Playboy*. He went on to contribute to most major American publications, including the *New Yorker*, *Saturday Review*, *TV Guide*, the *New York Times*, *National Review*, *Evergreen Review*, *Changing Times* and *Cosmopolitan*. Hancock, a paraplegic who sought diversion in drawing, is also the creator of two newspaper panels, the short-lived *Polly*, about a four-year-old child of nature, and *Fenwick*, about a contemporary Everyman confronted by a mad world. *Fenwick* is currently syndicated by Chronicle Features.

Hancock's style is straightforward, and his line pleasantly simple; his affection for somewhat outlandish situations sometimes results in strained humor, but his cartoons are genuinely droll and warm most of the time. Two collections of Hancock's cartoons have been published: *How Can You Stand It Out There* (1968) and *The Name of the Game* (1969); a third, *Gifford, You're a Very Stupid Elephant*, is scheduled for release in 1979.

M.H.

HANNA, WILLIAM DENBY (1910-) American animator and producer born in Melrose, New Mexico, on July 14, 1910. William Hanna studied to become a structural engineer but had to drop out of college with the onset of the Depression. A talent for drawing led him to join the Harman-Ising animation studio in 1930; there he worked for seven years in the story and layout departments.

When the MGM animation unit was established in 1937, Hanna became one of its first staff members and directed many of the *Captain and the Kids* cartoons in 1938-39, together with William Allen. In 1938 he and Joe Barbera were teamed for the first time on a short titled *Gallopin' Gals*; the association became permanent the next year when the duo directed the first of the *Tom and Jerry* cartoons, "Puss Gets the Boot." Over the next 18 years Hanna and Barbera directed more than 200 *Tom and Jerry* shorts, winning great popularity and a number of Oscars along the way. For a brief period following Fred Quimby's retirement in 1956, they were also in charge of production.

In 1957 Hanna and Barbera struck out on their own and formed Hanna-Barbera Productions with a view to producing cartoon films for television as well as for theatrical release. The success of their early television series, *Huckleberry Hound* and *Yogi Bear*, helped establish them in the field, but their theatrical venture, *Loopy de Loop*, fizzled out. In the early 1960s the phenomenal success of *The Flintstones* boosted the studio to the top of the TV cartoon field; Hanna-Barbera Productions was sold to Taft Communications in 1966 for a reported $26 million, with Hanna and Barbera remaining at the head of the company.

Hanna-Barbera has been churning out animation material at an increasing pace as television has provided a greater and greater market for their product. Among the more than 100 cartoon series and specials produced by Hanna-Barbera in the 20 years of the studio's existence, there are very few that are commendable or even watch-

"Cleared with the state, cleared with the county, cleared with the zoning boys, the building boys, the historical society, the ecology groups, and now the little old lady changes her mind about selling the farm."

William Hamilton. © *Thomas Y. Crowell.*

A married man looking for his rights in the lawbook.

Edmund Harburger, caricature.

able. Some of the series titles are *Atom Ant, Magilla Gorilla, The Perils of Penelope Pitstop, Quickdraw McGraw, Ruff and Ready, Augie Doggie and Doggie Daddy* (an imitation of the earlier *Spike and Tyke* MGM cartoons), *Dastardly and Mutley* and *Birdman;* the specials include *Alice in Wonderland, Jack and the Beanstalk, Cyrano de Bergerac* and *Charlotte's Web.*

Hanna-Barbera has been called "the poor man's Disney," but even that appellation is probably too charitable. There is no artistic reason why Hanna and Barbera, who proved themselves very talented craftsmen during their halcyon days at MGM, could not have used limited animation to better effect than they have in all their days as independent producers. Jay Ward and others have proved that TV animation need not be as dreadful an exercise as Hanna-Barbera made it. On November 24, 1977, CBS aired a special called *The Happy World of Hanna-Barbera,* in which their current production was contrasted with their earlier work at MGM—the worst condemnation that could possibly have been imagined.

M.H.

HANS AND HIS CHUMS (U.S.) *Puck* throughout its history utilized the series concept far less than its rivals for reasons that are not clear; one of the primary functions of a series (as newspapers were to learn in the early days of strips) is to build readership. Suspense, anticipation, character identification—all combine for a more loyal, if not a larger, circle of devotees.

In any event, *Puck* did dabble in the genre occasionally, usually with happy results. One such instance was with *Hans and His Chums,* a long-running series throughout the first decade of the 20th century, by Louis Glackens. The series revolved around a little Dutch boy, three obedient and mannered dachshunds,

and one mischievous dachshund, Dachel. The latter would always involve the rest of the party in some trouble or slapstick misadventure—and of course a rebuke followed in the last panel. The lesson was heeded only until the next week.

Glackens was at that time heralded by *Puck* as its delineator of historical periods; many of his cartoons were set in New Amsterdam or during the American Revolution. For *Hans and His Chums,* the setting was obviously Germany sometime in the past, and this may have been a calculated effort to retain the magazine's German readership (the German-language edition of *Puck,* which predated the English version, was dropped in this period). The series usually ran in color on the back page, though it was occasionally in interior black and white. Verses often accompanied the cartoons. They were drawn in Glackens's marvelously economical cartoon style and colored handsomely in pastel shades.

R.M.

HARBURGER, EDMUND (1846-1906) German cartoonist, illustrator and painter born in Eichstätt, Bavaria, on April 4, 1846. Edmund Harburger grew up in Mainz and, still an adolescent, painted frescoes on a public building there. In 1866 he moved to Munich, where he attended the Technische Hochschule and the Academy. Soon he found work doing book illustrations (some of them were for the publisher J. Scholz in Mainz) and political cartoons for *Die Gartenlaube,* a magazine that is chiefly remembered today as having offered the blandest family fare, but that was somewhat more diversified and adventurous in its early years.

By 1870 Harburger was on the staff of Munich's most important art and humor magazine, Braun and Schneider's *Fliegende Blätter,* where he was to remain for 36 years and produce some 1,500 drawings. Harburger was a masterly delineator of Bavarian types from all classes of the population: professors and students, peasants and proletarians, the arch-conservative beerhall barflies, small householders, musicians, women and children.

Having made a careful study of the 17th-century Netherlandish masters, especially Teniers and Ostade—and having observed all kinds of urban and rural settings during his own travels (including trips to the Tyrol in 1871 and to Venice in 1876-78)—Harburger specialized in placing his humorous figures (themselves very little distorted) in interiors rich in realistic and characteristic details and painterly charm. Indeed, Harburger's constant (and admired) work in oils—genre scenes, still lifes and portraits—had a great effect on his cartoon style; his drawings were done in soft pencil or charcoal and were carefully modeled and shaded. The editors of the *Fliegende Blätter* in this period were happiest when their artists had academic training and made obvious use of it. Harburger apparently suffered very little from the doubts, ambitions and personality clashes that made Wilhelm Busch break away from the *Fliegende Blätter* and made Hermann Schlittgen wish that he had done so when offered the chance.

In the late 1870s, his future certain, Harburger designed his own house in Munich. He worked there successfully up until the time of his death on November 5, 1906.

S.A.

HARDAWAY, JOSEPH BENSON (1891-1957) American cartoonist born near Kansas City, Missouri, in 1891. Joseph Benson (Ben) Hardaway started his career as a cartoonist for the *Kansas City Star* around 1910. During World War I he was the top sergeant in Captain Harry Truman's 129th Field Artillery. After the war Hardaway resumed his cartooning career on various midwestern newspapers, finally deciding to move west and into animation at the end of the 1920s.

In the early 1930s Hardaway was among the first group of artists working on the Merrie Melodies and Looney Tunes produced by Leon Schlesinger; as a scriptwriter he earned the nickname "Bugs" because of the outrageousness of his plot lines. His moment of fame came in 1938 when he co-directed (with Cal Dalton) "Porky's Hare Hunt," in which there appeared for the first time a wisecracking rabbit of whom more was to be heard. In 1940 the rabbit, officially named Bugs Bunny in reference to Hardaway, became the star of the studio—ironically, since 1940 was also the year Hardaway decided to leave Schlesinger for Walter Lantz.

At the Lantz studios Hardaway worked variously as animator, writer and director on many of the *Woody Woodpecker* cartoons. In the early 1950s he left Lantz to write stories for Temple-Toons Productions in Los Angeles. He died at his home in North Hollywood on February 5, 1957.

Bugs Hardaway deserves to be remembered here, if only for his contribution to the Bugs Bunny character.

M.H.

HARDING, NELSON (1877-1944) American Pulitzer Prize-winning cartoonist born in Brooklyn, New York, in 1877. Nelson Harding was educated at the Greenwich Academy in Connecticut and studied art at the Art Students League, the Chase School and the New York School of Design. In 1895 he was apprenticed to an architect but quit in 1898 to serve with the Rough Riders under Theodore Roosevelt at San Juan Hill. He was a lithographer from 1899 to 1907 and then freelanced as an illustrator for a few months before joining the *Brooklyn Eagle* as its staff cartoonist in 1908. He remained with the *Eagle* for 21 years.

Harding's ideas were always well conceived, but his drawings seemed to betray an even more painstaking execution. Indeed, throughout his career Harding's style was stiff, almost awkward. The anatomy was always rudimentary, caricature limited, and attempts at loose shading belabored and mechanical. But Harding's concepts were clever and forceful; his skill and overall excellence were reflected in his two Pulitzers (1927 and 1928) and in the fact that Hearst lured him away in 1929 to draw for the *New York Journal*.

A collection of his cartoons, *The Political Campaign of 1912 in Cartoons*, was published by the *Eagle* in 1912. For years he wrote and illustrated the front-page column "Here and Now" in the *Eagle*. He retired in 1943 and died on December 30, 1944.

R.M.

HARDY, DUDLEY (1866-1922) British cartoonist, oil painter and poster designer born "with a brush in my mouth" in Sheffield, England, in 1866. Son of a marine painter, Dudley Hardy grew up in an artistic atmosphere and was sent to Germany to study art at the age of 15. His studies took him through several European schools, resulting in an almost unique versatility.

His first success came at the age of 22 when his oil painting *Sans Asile* ("Without Home"), a scene of tramps dossing in Trafalgar Square, was exhibited throughout Europe. The "poster boom" in Britain, which came in the last decade of the 19th century and followed the established French school of poster art, found its leading practitioner in Dudley Hardy. His striking design for the first issue of *Today*, a weekly magazine edited by Anglophile and humorist Jerome K. Jerome, had an enormous impact on both the advertising industry and the public. Hardy's image of a contemporary young woman on the move became known as "The Yellow Girl" and was extremely influential in its striking simplicity and use of bold, flat colors.

With cartoonist contemporaries Tom Browne and Phil May, Hardy formed the London Sketch Club, where weekly two-hour drawing sessions were held in an atmosphere of friendly competition. The stimulating experience of these regular get-togethers was seminal in its influence on British commercial art; out of the contact came a regular flow of new styles, techniques and ideas. Hardy's cartoons appeared in all the latest illustrated papers, alongside those of his fellow club members: *The Pictorial World, Black and White*, the *Sketch*, the *Lady's Pictorial* and, of course, *Punch*.

In 1902 Hardy joined the swelling ranks of the postcard artists, painting several series of cartoons for the Davidson Brothers, publishers. These were sets of pictorial puns illustrating "Proverbs" (his first series), "Book Titles," "Song Titles" and cards that formed a set, after the format of a comic strip: "Mr. Smith's Tramp Abroad" and "Little Billy's Love Affair." Other postcards reproduced his posters for the Egyptian Mail Steamship Company, the Royal Naval Tournament and others, including a set of six poster girls, glamorous, healthy young Victorians for which Hardy will always be remembered.

D.G.

HARMAN, HUGH (1903-   ) American animator born in Pagosa Springs, Colorado, in 1903. Hugh Harman studied at Westport High School and at the Art Institute in Kansas City. In the early 1920s he went to work for the Kansas City Film Ad Agency, where his older brother, Fred (the creator of *Red Ryder*) had also worked, and where he was soon joined by his younger brother, Walker. There he met Rudolph Ising, with whom he was to form a lifelong friendship, as well as Ub Iwerks and Walt Disney. He then became a member of the original Disney team that turned out the Laugh-O-Gram cartoons from 1921 to 1923.

In 1926 Harman joined the fledgling Disney studio in Los Angeles. He worked on the last of the *Alice in Cartoonland* cartoons and on the new *Oswald the Rabbit* series. When Charles Mintz, Disney's distributor and the owner of the *Oswald* name, took the series away from Disney in 1928, he hired Harman and Ising to produce it for him. The following year Harman and Ising decided to form a partnership and become independent producers. They produced the first Looney Tunes cartoons in 1930 for Leon Schlesinger, for release through Warner Brothers, followed the next year by the Merrie Melodies. Their most famous cartoon character at that time was Bosko, a little black boy, whom they took with them

281

First swaggie: "Why do yer make it a point
of goin' ter Bourke every couple of years?"
Second swaggie: "Well, I get all me letters addressed there!"

Cecil Hartt. © *Smith's Weekly.*

when they left Schlesinger to become independent producers for MGM in 1933. Their cartoons were called Happy Harmonies and included such memorable shorts as *Hey Hey Fever* (1935) and *The Old Mill Pond* (1936), in addition to the *Bosko* series. In 1938 they produced *Merbabies* for the overworked Disney (he reportedly never even set foot in the Harman-Ising studio). That same year they also joined the newly formed MGM animation studio as producers and went their separate professional ways.

At MGM Harman produced a number of outstanding cartoons, including the antiwar *Peace on Earth* (1939), which was nominated for a Nobel Prize, the haunting *Lonesome Stranger* (1940) and the raucous *Alley Cat* (1941). He also formed Hugh Harman Productions later that year and produced instructional, educational and patriotic cartoons for the U.S. government, including *Gonorrhea* (on the dangers of promiscuity, 1943), *Message to Women* (1945) and *Easy Does It* (1947). In the late 1940s Harman made a few unsuccessful cartoons for TV. Dispirited, he then went into advertising work and soon dropped out of public view. He now lives in retirement near Los Angeles, in close proximity to his old friend Ising.

One of the more interesting of ex-Disney animators, Harman has received a number of awards and honors. He was nominated several times for an Oscar, though he never won. His animation work was simple, direct and handsome and is badly in need of critical rediscovery.

M.H.

HARTT, CECIL LAURENCE (1884-1930) Australian cartoonist and Digger humorist born in Prahran, near Melbourne, Australia, in 1884.

The Australian newspaper the *Bulletin* is rightly credited with the emergence of the first era of Australian graphic humor, when from 1880 up to the period of World War I cartoons and joke drawings began to develop and acquire a distinctive national character. The second development in this field is recognized as the *Smith's Weekly* era—a period that started when this weekly paper was founded in 1919. *Smith's*, which was primarily an illustrated broadsheet newspaper carrying whole pages smothered with joke drawings and political cartoons, quickly established in its pages a department devoted to fostering the Digger (returned soldier) spirit, under the title *Unofficial History of the AIF* (Australian Imperial Forces). Up until it ceased publication in 1950, *Smith's Weekly* continued this page, featuring jokes, anecdotes, cartoon strips and cartoon drawings of army humor—the latter significant and important because they lasted for over a quarter of a century of Australian graphic humor.

Many writers have observed the characteristics of the Australian soldier, but it was the artists of the now defunct *Smith's Weekly* who did most to establish the Digger as a folk type, depicting him as resourceful, casual in speech and attitude, by turns modest and boastful, and rebellious to all forms of military authority and red tape. Two of the artists who gave the Digger page of *Smith's Weekly* its special character and its popularity were Cecil Hartt and Frank Dunne.

Cecil Hartt, himself a soldier, twice wounded at Gallipoli, was the first Digger artist of note. However, very little is known of his early art training, although for a period he did take lessons with Alek Sass, a popular cartoonist for the Melbourne *Punch* who conducted a school in Melbourne before he too joined *Smith's Weekly* in its infancy.

Around 1908, Hartt was freelancing, contributing to *Comments*, a weekly news magazine edited by Grant Hervey, and to Randolph Bedford's *Clarion*. Before Hartt joined the 18th Battalion AIF at the outbreak of World War I, his joke drawings were appearing with some regularity in the *Bulletin*. Like Phil May, Hartt had a fondness and sympathy for the city tramps and down-and-outs, subjects he drew in a fine, finished style of pen drawing.

Cecil Hartt's first Digger humor was drawn in London, where he was invalided in 1916, for publication in his *Humorosities* (1917), a collection of soldier humor and war cartoons. The observations in these drawings are outstanding for their humor and for their character portraits of Australian soldiers. Through his drawings, Hartt revealed a true but kindly record of easygoing, fussless men expressing a sardonic reaction to life in the trenches, on recreational leave, in the training camps and on a spree.

—"Do you like Kipling?"
—"Why, I don't know. How do you kipple?"

Alice Harvey. © *Life.*

After his discharge from the army, Hartt joined *Smith's Weekly* in 1919, where for 11 years he perpetuated the Digger legend with his joke drawings, his city-tramp and occasional "backblocks" themes. He was known as an utterly tolerant and uncritical person, kind and good-hearted; standing just six feet tall, he fit the popular conception of the lean Australian.

The news of his tragic death on May 21, 1930, came to his public and friends as a great shock. He had been found dead, with a wound in the head and a shotgun beside him, on a mountain near Moruya, in New South Wales. In a tribute, the famous Australian cartoonist Stan Cross said: "He was nearest of all his contemporaries to the Australian tradition, as far as humorous art can expound it, and we practitioners, as well as Australian comic art in the abstract, owe him a lot."

Two collections of Cecil Hartt's soldier humor were published: *Humorosities* (London, 1917) and *Digger-ettes* (Sydney, 1919).

V.L.

HARVEY, ALICE (1905?-) American cartoonist born around 1905. Biographical details about Alice Harvey are hard to come by. She began contributing to the *New Yorker* shortly after its foundation in 1925. Of the original trio of major women artists working for the *New Yorker*—the others being Helen Hokinson and Barbara Shermund—Harvey's association with the magazine was the shortest.

For a time Harvey shared a studio (and a famous neighbor, E.L. Masters) with Hokinson back in Chicago's Montgomery Ward Towers, where they worked as fashion illustrators, principally for Marshall Field. In the early 1920s, both left the Windy City for New York, applying upon arrival for jobs in the comic art department of the Hearst-owned *New York Mirror*. Both were hired on the spot by the editor, Arthur Brisbane, at the princely sum of $100 per week. When Hokinson's humor proved too sophisticated for the mass market, she left the *Mirror* and resumed her art studies, eventually catching on in the *New Yorker* as a regular contributor. Soon after (and perhaps by her intervention), Alice Harvey too joined the magazine's regular staff. Harvey worked as an illustrator and occasional cartoonist until, as Dale Kramer reports somewhat vaguely in *Ross and the New Yorker*, marriage and children pushed her art career into the background. In any case, after the mid-1930s, there was no further evidence of her work in the pages of the magazine.

Purely as an illustrator, Harvey was perhaps the most noteworthy of the three contemporaries. Her figures were always clean and rakishly executed (in pen and ink or charcoal), and she had a way of expressing actions and facial expressions that was at times quite striking. The frightened-timid-bewildered face of a young flapper lost in the bustle of her first cruise-ship embarkation (in a December 1930 drawing) is a fine example of this ability. Unfortunately, her eye and ear for amusing situations fell far short of Hokinson's or Shermund's, which probably explains her relatively infrequent appearances as a cartoonist. Still, when it came to rendering the gracefully unfettered femininity of the faintly naughty, style-conscious Jazz Age, there was no other artist, male or female, on the *New Yorker* staff who could carry it off with greater aplomb.

R.C.

HASSALL, JOHN (1868-1948) British cartoonist born in Walmer, Kent, England, on May 21, 1868. "Skegness Is So Bracing": one of the most famous posters in British history. The Jolly Fisherman (as he is known) dancing over the sunny sands of the seaside resort is still seen at railway stations; it is the oldest poster in the business. John Hassall drew it in 1909 and was paid 12 guineas (then 50 dollars) outright.

Hassall was educated at Newton Abbot College, Devon, and at Heidelberg (his father was a paralyzed army lieutenant). Failing his entry into Sandringham Military College, Hassall went to be a farmer in Minnedosa, Canada. From there he mailed a series of sketches to the London *Daily Graphic*, and "A Manitoba Surprise Party" was published on February 26, 1890. Encouraged, he decided to concentrate on art and studied both in Antwerp, Holland, and at the Académie Julian, Paris. Back in London, however, he found himself unable to earn a living as a classical painter, and in 1894 he answered an advertisement of the color printers David Allen and Sons seeking poster designers. Hassall quickly developed a distinctive style inspired by the famous French school of poster design. He used a bold black outline, cartoon fashion, with equally bold flat colors and almost always a sense of humor. Borwicks baking powder ("Let Me Help You to Rise") and Veritas gas mantles ("Dismayed But Not Dismantled") are typical of his work and contrast comically with his dramatic theater posters ("The Only Way," etc.).

Hassall rose speedily to fame, and he was elected to the Royal Institute of Painters in Watercolours in 1901. He shortly opened the John Hassall School and taught many artists of the younger generation, particularly the cartoonists. His first book illustration work was for *A Cockney in Arcadia* (1899). Despite his great output and popularity, by May 1939 he was awarded a civil list pension of £110 per annum, and his bank account stood at four shillings and fourpence. "People don't want my work nowadays. They say I am old-fashioned," he said, yet the government commissioned him for one last poster on air raid precautions. They didn't pay him. But not everyone forgot Hassall; on his death in 1948, the Skegness Corporation sent a wreath in the shape of his "Jolly Fisherman."

Books: *A Cockney in Arcadia* (1899); *Primeval Scenes* (1899); *Two Wellworn Shoe Stories* (1899); *Active Army Alphabet* (1899); *Oh My Darling Clementine* (1900); *By the Way Ballads* (1901); *A Moral Alphabet* (1901); *Six and Twenty Boys* (1902); *Grimm's Fairy Tales* (1902); *Pantomime ABC* (1902); *ABC of Everyday People* (1902); *People* (1903); *Absurd Ditties* (1903); *Round the World ABC* (1904); *The Old Nursery Stories* (1904); *The Twins* (1904); *All the Best Nursery Rhymes* (1905); *The Magic Shop* (1905); *Ruff and Reddy* (1905); *Paris Not to Mention Monte Carlo* (1906); *The Happy Annual* (1907); *Good Queen Bess* (1907); *Sport and Play* (1907); *Through the Wood* (1907); *Book of John Hassall* (1907); *The Princess and the Dragon* (1908); *Little Robin Hood* (1909); *Potted Brains* (1909); *Mother Goose's Nursery Rhymes* (1909); *Miss Manners* (1909); *Tales and Talks* (1909); *The Doll's Diary* (1909); *Friday and Saturday* (1910); *One Hundred Years Hence* (1911); *Tommy Lobb* (1912); *The Sleeping Beauty* (1912); *Love and a Cottage* (1913); *A Day in Tangier* (1913); *Children's Party Book* (1914); *Keep Smiling* (1914); *The Wookey Hole* (1914); *Ye Berlin Tapestrie* (1915); *Peter Pan Paint-*

ing Book (1915); With Love from Daddy (1918); Hassall ABC (1918); Blackie's Popular Fairy Tales (1921); Blackie's Popular Nursery Rhymes (1921); Wembley Leaflets (1925); The Twins (1927); Humours of Bridge (1928); Our Diary (1928); Robinson Crusoe (1930); and Blackie's Popular Nursery Stories (1931).

D.G.

HAUGHTON, WILFRED H. (1893-   ) British cartoonist born in West Norwood, London, England, on December 12, 1893. The first cartoonist to be permitted to draw Mickey Mouse in the United Kingdom was Wilfred Haughton. He was educated at Salters Hill Board School, then Alleyns School, Dulwich. His father was a compositor, but a printers' strike prevented the boy from entering the trade. He became a clerk in commerce and on the outbreak of World War I joined the Kings Royal Rifle Corps. After service in Salonika, he was invalided out and was eventually granted a two-year art course at the Regent Street Polytechnic (1919-20).

He began freelancing cartoons to Passing Show, London Mail and other humor magazines of the period, and in 1921, with a fellow student, set up Meccart Studios. This two-man outfit specialized in creating and designing novelties and paper gimmicks for use in advertising, then marketing them and manufacturing them in conjunction with a small printer, Lydall and Son of Dulwich. The novelties met with immediate success and were mainly purchased by the Amalagamated Press as giveaways and inserts for their children's comic papers. Unfortunately, a bad business partner caused the collapse of the budding studio.

Haughton then met W.H. Cornelius of 23 Paper Street, Clerkenwell, London, a novelty supplier of cheap children's toys to small shops and market stalls. Cornelius signed Haughton as a freelance novelty creator, sending him on periodic trips to Nuremberg, Germany, to supervise the manufacture of his designs. Cornelius had already exploited the cartoon character Felix the Cat to good advantage in silent film days. When Mickey Mouse was opened up for exploitation by Walt Disney's London representative, William Levy, Cornelius obtained the contract through Haughton's ability to draw the new character. Haughton then designed toys, books and novelties, such as color transfers, featuring Mickey, and made trips to Germany to arrange for their manufacture. Dean and Son, publishers of children's books, approached Levy for the rights to produce The Mickey Mouse Annual, and Levy in turn passed the artwork on to Haughton. Haughton drew the entire Annual (128 pages plus color plates) within two months and continued to draw the Annual from 1931 through to the forties. Many of his Annual strips were syndicated abroad, throughout Europe, and appeared as serials in comic papers.

Haughton also drew other Mickey Mouse books, and when Ub Iwerks left Disney to produce his Flip the Frog series, Haughton drew the only edition of Flip the Frog Annual (1932). In 1936 Levy and the Walt Disney-Mickey Mouse Ltd. operation produced the first comic weekly printed in photogravure, Mickey Mouse Weekly, through Odhams Press. Haughton was given the front cover and painted a large tabloid adventure of the Disney characters every week for the first three years. Meanwhile, his connections had pro-vided further opportunities, and for the Sunday newspaper The People, he created and drew the strip Eb and Flo, about two blacks whose "Cheery Coons Club" feature ran from October 30, 1932, to World War II. They also appeared in Eb and Flo Annual (1937?) and in Mickey Mouse Weekly, and in his "spare time," Haughton also drew the daily strip Bobby Bear in the Daily Herald from 1932, plus the colorful Christmas Bobby Bear Annual.

Haughton experimented with animation for films, devising a system of pliable rubber puppets built on wire framework, but unhappily a series of business disasters put an end to his ambitions as an animation producer. For some years he has lived on his old-age pension in South Africa, still actively ambitious to create a successful children's puppet series for television.

D.G.

HAYASHI, SEICHI (1945-   ) Japanese animator, cartoonist, comic book artist, illustrator and film director born in Japanese-controlled Manchuria in March 1945. Soon after the end of the war, Seichi Hayashi's father and older sister died, and he and his mother were repatriated to Japan, where he entered school in the Tokyo area. Hayashi reportedly hated school from the start and spent much of his time drawing cartoons. After graduating from middle school, he watched as many movies as he could for half a year and then found work in the animation department of the Toei film company. At 16 he became an assistant to Sadao Tsukioka, creator of Okami Shōnen Ken ("Ken the Wolf Boy"), Japan's first TV animation. With his talent, and because of the demand for animators that existed at the time, he quickly took on more and more responsibility. At 20 Hayashi quit Toei to help Tsukioka, who was by then doing independent animation, and ever since he has been freelancing actively as a true dilettante in animation, cartoons and illustration.

Hayashi made his debut as a comic book artist in 1966 with Azuma to Musuko to Kuenai Tamashi ("Japan, the Son, and the Inedible Spirit"), which appeared in Garo, the forum for many a new artist in Japan. He was heavily influenced by Yoshiharu Tsuge in the confessional form his work took. He next turned out a series of popular strips, also running in Garo, such as Kyodai na Uo ("Giant Fish"), Aka Tombo ("Red Dragonfly"), Hana no Uta ("Poems of Flowers") and Aka Iro no Ereji ("Red Elegy"). Aka Iro no Ereji appears to be a semiautobiographical work portraying his days at Toei and the dilemma he faced when caught between his job and union activities. Hayashi also did some animation, independently producing a work entitled Kage ("Shadow") in 1968, and the following year doing 10 Gatsu 13 Nichi Satsujin ("October 13 Murder").

Hayashi's work is almost psychedelic in its evocation of moods. His women characters are unique in that they tend to be frail but erotic women of the world rather than the voluptuous middle-class beauties so often depicted by other artists. He concentrates on the development of a lyrical aesthetic in all the mediums he works in, and plot is generally secondary. Today, in addition to comics, cartoons and animation, Hayashi is also an active illustrator of magazines and posters.

F.S.

"If you won't play my way I'll take my ball and go home."

Hugh Haynie. © Courier-Journal.

HAYNIE, HUGH SMITH (1927-) American cartoonist born in Reedville, Virginia, on February 6, 1927. Hugh Haynie was educated at the College of William and Mary, from which he received a B.A. in 1950. He also holds an L.H.D. from the University of Louisville (1968). He began his career on the *Richmond Times-Dispatch* in 1952 as a staff artist and editorial cartoonist. Fired soon thereafter, he secured a similar position with the *Greensboro Daily News* in North Carolina (1953-58), with a six-month stint for the *Atlanta Journal* in the middle (1955-56). Since 1958 Haynie has been the political cartoonist of the *Louisville Courier-Journal*.

Haynie is in the forefront of contemporary American political cartooning on two counts: his ideas—consistently liberal—are cleverly conceived and designed, and his drawing style is one of the most individualistic in the field. It is stylized (some would say too mannered and labored) and rendered carefully in pen and brush with a wide variety of shading media. Shadows and wrinkles are meticulously laid in, and backgrounds often disappear in borderlines to make a stylized whole of the drawing. Haynie's effective cartoons are distributed widely by the Los Angeles Times Syndicate.

R.M.

HAYWARD, STANLEY (1930-) British cartoon scriptwriter born in London, England, on October 30, 1930. The leading and most prolific writer of scripts for animated cartoons in England, Stan Hayward was educated at Dartford Technical College. He joined the merchant navy at 16 and two years later jumped ship in Australia. There he studied chemistry and music, returning to London in 1952 to play electric guitar in the "coffee bar skiffle" boom. Then the navy caught up with him, making him serve another two years, during which he began to try his hand as a writer. In 1956 he contributed gags to the BBC radio *Goon Show* series, and in 1958 he entered the animation industry as a writer for the new TV Cartoons company formed by George Dunning, Dick Williams and Bill Sewell.

Hayward's first solo commercial was for Courage beer. His first entertainment cartoon, *The Wardrobe*, was made by the same company in 1960; it was described as "an exercise in surrealist humor that uses sounds and images forced against the viewer's logical interpretation." It set the style and pace for all subsequent Hayward cartoons; he himself describes this as variations on the theme of "the little man trying to make sense of the world. He knows what he wants, but doesn't know what it is when he gets it." *The Ever-Changing Motor Car* followed; it was a longer film sponsored by Ford, as was *Power Train*, a deliberate departure from the didactic type of film so common at the time (1961).

During 1962, his most successful year, Hayward scripted *The Flying Man*, George Dunning's unique exercise in painted animation; *The Apple*, drawn in black and white but shot in color; *Love Me Love Me Love Me*, in which Richard Williams drew directly onto cels with wax crayons; and *The Rise and Fall of Emily Sprod*, his first association with breezy Bob Godfrey, using a free-style mix of cutouts, live action and animation. A fallow period followed, with Hayward working for awhile as ghost writer on Peter Maddocks's *Daily Express* strip *Hector Cringe*, and *Saints and Sinners*, a strip for the *Glasgow Evening Citizen*. Then Hayward changed direction and became a skin diver. Meanwhile his cartoons were shown at the Annecy Animation Festival, and in consequence the National Film Board of Canada offered him a year's contract. Little came of this on screen, and in 1964 Hayward returned to London, writing *Alf, Bill and Fred* for Godfrey and a number of scripts and loop films for Halas and Batchelor. For this studio he also wrote *Flow Diagrams* and *The Question* (1967), *Topology* and *Linear Programming* (1969) and *What Is a Computer* (1971). He was well able to answer the latter question because he had won his own computer in a contest run by *New Scientist* magazine!

Comedy films continued to spice the line of industrial and educational cartoons: *Whatever Happened to Uncle Fred* and *The Rope Trick* (both Godfrey, 1967), *Two Off the Cuff* (Godfrey, 1968), *The Trendsetter* (Biographic, 1969), *Henry 9 till 5* (Godfrey, 1970), *I Love You, Package Deal* and *Fairy Story* (all Wyatt-Cattaneo, 1970), *I'm Glad You Asked That Question* (Biographic, 1971), *Kama Sutra Rides Again* (Godfrey, 1971), *Way Out* and *When I'm Rich*. The last two cinema cartoons were made in 1975 and 1977 by New Fields Animation, a company Hayward owns with Ted Rockley and Derek Phillips. It represents Hayward's third attempt to go independent. Computer Studio, started in 1970, collapsed, and Video Animation (1973), which made titles for BBC TV shows, was sold to EMI. Hayward's first book, *Scriptwriting for Animation*, was published in 1977.

D.G.

"Hazel." © Saturday Evening Post.

HAZEL (U.S.) The *Saturday Evening Post* added a new star to its list of luminaries in the autumn of 1943: Hazel, the sarcastic, assertive and take-charge maid of the Baxter household. She joined other classic characters like Henry and Little Lulu who had run weekly in the *Post*. Cartoonist Ted Key had been running the maid character in the Sunday supplement *This Week* and in *Collier's* before the *Post* offered a contract and a regular spot in the magazine in return for ownership.

Even during the war Key maintained weekly output, and after the war many movie, Broadway and TV offers were considered. In the 1950s Hazel came to television, played by Shirley Booth, and gathered an accumulated total of 22.5 Nielsen average points and an average 36.4 share of its audience potential. In four years on NBC it was sponsored by Ford Motor; one year on CBS was sponsored by Procter and Gamble. The half-hour comedy episodes are still syndicated. Key also produced several animated Hazel cartoons for commercials.

In 1969 the *Saturday Evening Post* folded, and Hazel lost her familiar back-page berth. But King Features immediately picked up the panel, and it is now one of the most successful of newspaper panels, appearing six days a week; the revived *Post* also runs the feature again. Key has regained rights to his character.

The cast includes Hazel the maid (by circumstances and character the *de facto* head of the household), George and Dorothy Baxter, and their son Harold and adopted daughter Katie. The large dog Smilie and cat Mostly (she's mostly Siamese) round out the regular cast. The kids' friends, who fight a constant battle with the maid for prerogatives, and the Baxters' guests, who never fail to be shocked by some statement or action of Hazel's, provide variety in the lively and unpredictable panel. It is to Key's great credit that what is essentially a single-situation premise in a single-panel format has succeeded so well, and so interestingly, for more than thirty-five years.

The many *Hazel* anthologies include *Hazel, Here's Hazel, If You Like Hazel, Hazel Rides Again, All Hazel, The Hazel Jubilee, Hazel Time, Life With Hazel, Hazel Power, Right On, Hazel and Ms. Hazel.*

R.M.

HEATHCLIFF (U.S.) *Heathcliff* is a newspaper panel created by George Gately (brother of noted cartoonist John Gallagher) for the McNaught Syndicate; it made its debut on September 3, 1973.

Heathcliff is the quintessential fat cat. Smug, self-assured and underhanded, he stops at nothing to get what he regards as his just desserts: a better than square meal, the easiest chair in the house and complete sway over the neighborhood pets. The elderly couple who happen to be Heathcliff's owners do not stand a chance when they try to thwart the schemes of the crafty feline. Always ready to lend a paw when he is least needed, Heathcliff can turn tough on occasion; and even the neighborhood dogs keep a prudent distance when the cocky striped cat ambles down the street.

In a field overrun on all sides by cartoon cats, it is to Gately's credit that he has been able to create a highly individualized, original character. With his sly mien and roguish demeanor, Heathcliff stands out sharply as a worthy successor to such comic strip cats as Felix and Spooky. Gately's drawing style is deceptively easy and pleasingly cartoony, making *Heathcliff* one of the most refreshing gag panels to come along in some time.

M.H.

HECKLE AND JECKLE (U.S.) Heckle and Jeckle burst onto the screen in 1946 in Paul Terry's "The Talking Magpies." They were two identical-looking rascally birds who delighted in playing pranks on all and sundry. Their anarchistic personalities and fast talk carried them to extremes of aggression and outrageousness.

"You'll be glad to know Heathcliff got down off the roof all by himself."

"Heathcliff." © McNaught Syndicate.

"Heckle and Jeckle." © *CBS Films.*

The best *Heckle and Jeckle* cartoons were those produced in the 1940s, when the two birds were at the height of their diabolical inventiveness. In "The Uninvited Pests" they crashed a party and made mincemeat of the hosts and other guests; in "McDougal's Rest Farm" they turned a bucolic oasis of quiet and peace into a madhouse; in "The Stowaways" they wreaked havoc on the crew and passengers of an ocean liner. The two magpies were at their best (or worst) in "In Again, Out Again," during which they repeatedly tried to escape from jail, and in "Magpie Madness," where the animators simply let the birds run amuck without any semblance of rhyme or reason. As the 1950s rolled in, the magpies' mischief became more and more mindless and repetitive. Their personalities were toned down after CBS took over the series, and they simply became filler material on the televised *Mighty Mouse Show*.

Among the directors who worked on the *Heckle and Jeckle* cartoons, mention should be made of such Terrytoons stalwarts as Connie Rasinski, Mannie Davis and Eddie Donnelly. Heckle and Jeckle have been featured in comic books since the late 1940s, and there have also been Heckle and Jeckle toys and puzzles.

M.H.

HEINE, THOMAS THEODOR (1867-1948) German cartoonist, illustrator and painter born in Leipzig, Germany, on February 28, 1867. The son of a chemist and manufacturer of rubber products, T.T. Heine got into trouble with his biting cartoons while still a gymnasium student. After art study at the Düsseldorf Academy, he finally settled in Munich in 1889, painting and submitting cartoons to the *Fliegende Blätter* and, from early 1896, to *Jugend*. He also did posters, commercial art and book illustration, as he was to continue doing through the years.

When the publisher Albert Langen founded the magazine *Simplicissimus*, Heine became one of the charter members and remained on its staff with minor interruptions until 1933, doing about twenty-five hundred drawings for it. He quickly stood out as the most versatile and ingenious artist on the magazine, working brilliantly in either line or color, in either painterly modeling or contour, and parodying anyone else's style with ease. The painter Lovis Corinth said that as an artist Heine could do anything he set his mind to, and the old Berlin master Max Liebermann called him the greatest German draftsman.

All this skill and genius were at the service of an aggressive intelligence that oddly mingled reforming zeal with a penchant for cruelty and sadism. Not well liked personally even by his colleagues, Heine became anathema to the Wilhelmine establishment and even served a jail sentence in 1898.

Though all social folly was his fodder and his means of expression were protean, several visual themes recurred obsessively in his art—especially dogs (he frequently interpreted human society in terms of the interactions of various canine breeds, and he invented a pugnacious bulldog as an emblem for *Simplicissimus*) and a very personal brand of devil, obese and bestial, mingling in all human affairs as a tempter or an avenger.

A rich man of Munich refuses to patronize the arts.

T.T. Heine, 1925. © *Simplicissimus.*

Heine's album publications included *Bilder aus dem Familienleben* ("Scenes from Family Life") and *Torheiten* ("Follies"). He wrote and illustrated a book of cynical modern fairy tales—*Die Märchen* (1935)—and a very thickly veiled autobiographical novel—*Ich Warte auf Wunder* ("I'm Waiting for Miracles," 1945).

In 1933 Heine, who was Jewish, could no longer remain in Germany, and years of wandering lay ahead for the elderly man; he went to Prague, Brno, Oslo and finally, in 1942, to Stockholm. Heine became a Swedish subject and drew for the *Göteborgs Handels-och Sjöfartstidning*. He died in Stockholm on January 26, 1948.

S.A.

HELL (U.S.) Art Young, an atheist by trade, had a lifelong fascination with the infernal region, largely for its possibilities as a comic device and as contemplated last stop for the devils—capitalists, bores, salesmen, quack doctors—who plagued him on this side of the Styx. *Hell* is the generic title for four separate cartoon series appearing over a 47-year period.

Not content to let Homer, Virgil, Dante, Milton and hellfire preachers monopolize speculations about Hell—and Botticelli, Dürer, Bruegel, Callot, Flaxman, Blake and Doré record its physical aspects—the young Young began the chronicle *Hell Up to Date* in 1887. In a book published by Schulte, the Chicago cartoonist averred that the entrance to the region was located in that city. The book, which sold fairly well in the Midwest, carried the subtitle "The reckless journey of R. Palasco Drant, special correspondent, through the infernal regions, as recorded by himself: with illustrations by Art Young." The title of the deluxe edition was softened to *Hades Up to Date*.

Snapshots in Hades was later a long-running feature in *Life*, and Young drew a similar, untitled series concurrently in *Puck*. It featured the fates that awaited the malevolent and greedy. Here the captions and concepts were somewhat more developed than in the published collection. For the fledgling *Cosmopolitan* under John Brisben Walker, Young drew *Hiprah Hunt's Journey Through the Inferno*, about a descendant of New England witch-burners, in May, June, July and August of 1900. Only the first installment carried text, and the series of cartoons was collected in book form in 1901 by C. Zimmerman publishers under the title *Through Hell with Hiprah Hunt*. In this treatment Hell was populated by bad poets and refurnished with modern improvements. "I wanted a democratic Hell," Young wrote, "and modern efficiency."

These series were produced in the years of Art Young's conversion from political orthodoxy to socialism. By 1933 he was a Communist, and the cartoon-and-text series *Art Young's Inferno* was by far his bitterest indictment of life, the system, hypocrisy as he saw it and human nature in general. As a matter of fact, it was probably the most consistently sardonic material of his career, including sustained periods on the *Masses* and the *New Masses*. Here, in line drawings and wash, he excoriated drug and alcohol addicts, radio programs, patriotism, inherited wealth, apathy, subways, Sunday comics, graft, slang, cheerful people, comfort stations, travelogues, country clubs and courage. There was actually little political substance in Young's work, but he injected as much cynicism and vitriol—and basic truth—as Ambrose Bierce at his most caustic. Characteristically, this last visit to Hell (published privately in 1934 by Delphic

Studios) featured the self-caricatured Young as the tourist.

R.M.

HELL UP TO DATE
See Hell.

HENGELER, ADOLF (1863-after 1923) German cartoonist and painter born at Kempten in Allgäu, southern Germany, on February 11, 1863. Adolf Hengeler was one of the foremost contributors to the venerable Munich humor magazine *Fliegende Blätter* in the late 19th century. The son of an estate steward, at the age of 15 he was apprenticed to a lithographer. In 1881 he began attending the Munich Arts and Crafts School, moving on to the Academy in 1885. The year before, he had already begun his association with the famous magazine, which was to publish some 4,000 Hengeler drawings in the next 20 years.

His style was direct and hearty, using a juicy and sinuous line that might or might not be accompanied by washes. His subject matter included witty studies of German life in the earlier half of the century (the cozy and smug Biedermeier period); animal fables, with insects a specialty; travesties of ancient and medieval history; peasant and genre scenes; and a series of intricate machines that prefigured those of Rube Goldberg (one contraption replaces an entire tavern, serving the customer food and drink, playing cards with him and then bouncing him when he grows unruly). These drawings appeared as separate panels or as illustrations for droll verses, or they formed little wordless (or laconic) picture stories in the manner of the Russian-French cartoonist Caran d'Ache. A large number of Hengeler's *Fliegende Blätter* pieces were gathered into a *Hengeler-Album* by the magazine's publishers (the firm of Braun and Schneider) in 1904.

All through his years as a cartoonist Hengeler had been painting secretly for his own satisfaction; about 1899, unfortunately, he decided to share these works with the world, and for at least the next two decades he concentrated on idylls and archaic romantic scenes that were diluted Spitzweg and deluded homage to the Munich academicians. He also painted frescoes on houses in Murnau and in the main chamber of the town hall in Freising.

During World War I, Hengeler kept a pictorial diary containing symbolic representations of "the attack of our (Germany's) enemies on Germany's people and property," as an art critic put it (as late as 1923!). On the occasion of his 60th birthday, in 1923, Hengeler published an album of imaginative colored crayon drawings that combine some of the best elements of his double career as cartoonist and painter. With their real charm and humor, their touch of mystery and their great freedom of execution, these form a very likable close to his oeuvre.

S.A.

HENRY, MAURICE (1907-   ) French cartoonist and animated cartoon director born in northern France on December 29, 1907. After studies at the Paris Law School Maurice Henry became a journalist and art critic for various dailies. One in particular, *Le Petit Journal*, published his first sketch in 1932. Since then,

Henry has drawn close to 30,000 cartoons for over 160 newspapers and magazines, chiefly for *L'Oeuvre*, *Le Canard Enchaîné*, *L'Express* and *Carrefour*.

Much of his artwork has been reedited in albums: *Les Mystères de L'Olympe* ("Olympus Mysteries," 1945), *Les Métamorphoses du Vide* ("Metamorphoses of Emptiness," 1955), *Kopfkissenbuch* ("Pillow Book," 1956), *A Bout Portant* ("Point-Blank," 1958), *Les 32 Positions de l'Androgyne* ("The 32 Positions of Androgynous Man," 1961), *Hors Mesures* ("Beyond Bounds," 1969), etc. In addition, two collections of his *dessins* ("drawings") covering the decades between 1930 and 1970 were published in 1960 and 1970. He was a gagman and adaptor for the movie *Les Aventures des Pieds-Nickelés* and has also done several animated cartoons, the most interesting a short explaining the workings and advantages of the Marshall Plan (1948).

His characters, whether humans or humanized animals, all have big, wide-open eyes that make them look constantly surprised, empty-headed and even deranged. The subjects he treats most often come from mythology, religion (as in the drawing of Christ with the cross, calling for a porter), prison life and especially—in the surrealist tradition Henry belongs to—the oneiric world (as in the cartoon where the husband is sleeping in a parked Venetian gondola

Oliver Herford. © Life.

while his wife, lying in a regular bed, is asking him to "let me climb in your dream").

Maurice Henry is a regular exhibitor at the Salon de Mai and other art galleries.

P.H.

HERBLOCK

See Block, Herbert Lawrence.

HERFORD, OLIVER (1863-1935) American cartoonist, poet and epigrammist born in Sheffield, England, in December 1863. Oliver Herford's father, a minister, was transferred to a parish in Boston when his son was young, and the future cartoonist grew up with a foot in both societies. He was educated at Lancaster College in England and Antioch College in Ohio, and received art training at the Slade School in London and the Académie Julian in Paris.

Herford sold his first cartoon to the *Century* magazine, where only the more respectable cartoonists appeared, and soon became a regular contributor to *Life* and *Punch* in England. At first his cartoons were formal and realistically rendered. By the 1890s he had loosened to a trademark wispiness—breezy and very economical lines always resting on a solid foundation of anatomy and composition. Throughout his life his cartoons were droll, urbane and sophisticated.

The cartoonist himself became as famous as his pen-and-ink (and wash) creations. He was followed slavishly for epigrams and *bons mots*, and with his monocle he was the very essence of an aloof but pointed outlook on life. William Dean Howells called Herford the Charles Lamb of his day. In his sense of presence and wit he was the American Oscar Wilde.

Many notable and classic cartoons (as well as verses for *Life* and the *Century*) were supplemented by a series of books that retain their cleverness today. Most remembered are: *Behind Time* (1886); *Artful Antics* (1888); *Pen and Inklings* (1893); *An Alphabet of Celebrities* (1899); *A Child's Primer of Natural History* (1899); *Overheard in a Garden* (1900); *The Cynic's Calendar* (1902), with many

Maurice Henry. © Henry.

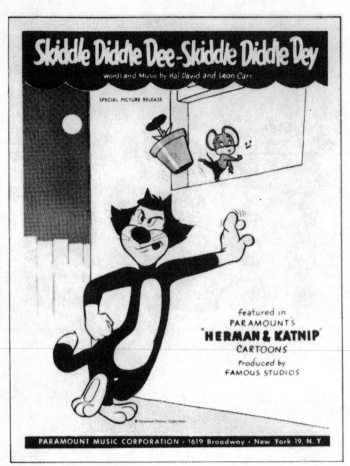

"Herman and Katnip." © Paramount Pictures.

sequels on this theme; *The Rubaiyat of a Persian Kitten* (1904); *Two in a Zoo* (1904); *A Little Book of Bores* (1906); *The Peter Pan Alphabet* (1907); *Confessions of a Caricaturist* (1917); *Poems From "Life"* (1923); and *Excuse It, Please* (1930).

Herford also wrote a column, *Pen and Inklings*, for the *Saturday Evening Post* under Norman Hapgood, and a column for the *March of Events* section of the Hearst newspapers, all the while entertaining an acerbic and quite public aversion for the publisher (Hearst, as always, recognized genius and recruited well). Herford wrote four successful plays: *The Devil, The Florist Shop, The Love Cure* and *Con and Co.* He died, much honored and missed, on July 5, 1935.

R.M.

HERMAN AND KATNIP (U.S.) The success of MGM's *Tom and Jerry* cartoons prompted every other American animation studio to produce its own cat-and-mouse series. Famous Studios/Paramount came up with Katnip, a slow-witted feline perpetually at war with the mischievous mouse Herman. The duo devoted most of their energies to unmotivated pranks, mindless chases and moronic exploits. The *Herman and Katnip* cartoons were like scaled-down versions of *Tom and Jerry*, minus the wit, the pace and the inventiveness.

The series started in 1951 with such entries as "Cat Tamale" and "Cat-Choo"; it plodded along all through the 1950s on such frolicsome titles as "Drinks on the Mouse" (1953), "Bicep Built for Two" (1955), "Cat in the Act" (1957) and "Katnip's Big Day" (1959); and it ended ingloriously in the early 1960s. The *Herman and Katnip* cartoons were of deplorable quality in terms of both story and animation, and it is therefore saddening to find among the names associated with the series those of Seymour Kneitel, I. Sparber and Bill Tytla, all of whom had proved capable of better things.

M.H.

HEROLD, DON (1889-1966) American cartoonist, author and advertiser born in Bloomfield, Indiana, on July 9, 1889. Don Herold graduated from high school in 1907, from the Chicago Art Institute in 1908 and from Indiana University in 1913.

Herold drew newspaper cartoons in Los Angeles for a year before returning to Indianapolis to manage the Hollenbeck Press. From Indiana around 1919 he freelanced stories to *Harper's, Collier's* and the *American* magazine, and articles and cartoons to *Judge*. With the advent of the 1920s his work became popular, appearing in *Life* and the cartoon columns of popular weeklies. His advertising copy and drawings ran frequently, and he established a successful advertising agency in New York. The agency and articles for *Scribner's* occupied the rest of his career, as did a constant stream of books, until his death in 1966.

Herold's style was a totally original and fresh statement of simplicity: flowing, economical lines, characters barely more than stick figures, virtual elimination of backgrounds. In ads his work was in the spirit of Fish and Soglow; Herold was among the first to break the grip of the Gibson school on magazine cartooning. His concepts were fresh and irreverent, and his material is still funny today.

Books: *So Humane!* (1923); *Bigger and Better* (1925); *There Ought to Be a Law* (1926); *Our Companionate Goldfish* (1927); *Strange Bedfellows* (1930); *Doing Europe—and Vice Versa* (1931); *Typographical Handbook* (1946); *Love That Golf* (1952); *Drunks Are Driving Me to Drink* (1953); *The Happy Hypochondrise* (1962); and *Humor in Advertising* (1963).

R.M.

HERR PIEPMEYER (Germany) The year 1848 was one of revolutions throughout Europe. The various German states won numerous civil liberties but not liberty in general; republican movements were defeated and unification of Germany was not achieved, largely

—"Your public will ban your pictures when they hear how you treat me." —"I provide them with recreation; I don't see why they should care how I get mine."

Don Herold. © *Tribune Syndicate.*

Herr Piepmeyer practicing oratory.

"Herr Piepmeyer."

because of the almost total incompetence of the constituent assembly that met for several months in Frankfurt am Main beginning in May 1848, with delegates coming from all over Germany.

Nevertheless, that assembly had one important result: no event in German history since the Reformation had inspired satires and caricatures to such an extent! Many of the delegates themselves wielded the pen for this purpose. One of them, Johann Hermann Detmold of Hanover, wrote the scenario and text of a work that would become a classic of humorous art thanks to the drawings provided by Adolf Schrödter, who had already made a mark as a humorous artist in Berlin and Düsseldorf and who would later be active in Karlsruhe for many years.

Published in six issues in Frankfurt in 1849, the 49 lithographs (each containing several panels) that comprise *Thaten und Meinungen des Herrn Piepmeyer, Abgeordneten zur Constituierenden Nationalversammlung zu Frankfurt a/Main* ("Deeds and Opinions of Mr. Piepmeyer, Delegate to the National Constituent Assembly at Frankfurt am Main") tell a continuous story. Totally ignorant but inordinately ambitious, Piepmeyer (this proper name occurs in *Münchhausen*, a novel by the humorous writer Immermann, and may also have referred to an actual person named Mittermaier) promises everything to his local electors, no matter what their political persuasion, and is unanimously chosen as delegate to Frankfurt. Once there, he changes political sides frequently according to the pressure of events (he is always on the side of the majority) and in pursuance of an unscrupulous journalist's advice. He practices orations and appropriate attitudes in front of his mirror but never gets to make an important speech at the assembly. One bit of advice given by the journalist leads to a lot of fruitless research on Piepmeyer's part: a unified Germany, he is convinced, needs a single national beverage that will combine the attractions of the beer, wine and brandy that are now preferred by various segments of the population.

The self-taught cartoonist A. von Boddien was apparently involved in the creation of *Herr Piepmeyer* at the very outset of the project, but the major credit belongs to Adolf Schrödter.

S.A.

HERZMANOVSKY-ORLANDO, FRITZ VON (1877-1954)

Austrian writer and cartoonist born in Vienna, Austria, in 1877. Although he enjoyed a long life, Fritz von Herzmanovsky's fame, to the extent that it exists, is a matter of the last twenty-odd years since his death. His complete literary works, eccentric humorous stories and plays, have been published, and some of the plays have been produced in Munich and Vienna in their difficult local dialect. His legacy as a draftsman, not much more substantial, has been portrayed by certain Austrian art critics and historians, particularly Werner Hofmann, as a small but inalienable exemplification of true Viennese style.

Apparently a leisured member of a family associated with the highest level of the imperial civil service, Herzmanovsky studied architecture at the Vienna Polytechnic (Technische Hochschule) and traveled extensively. He enjoyed the friendship of two other important eccentrics of the decaying Austro-Hungarian empire: the writer Gustav Meyrink, whose famous stories of the German and Jewish elements of Prague include *Der Golem*, and the superb cartoonist Alfred Kubin, whose stylistic influence on Herzmanovsky the artist was definitive. Other visual influences pointed out by Hofmann are the earliest graphics of Paul Klee, with their uncanny elongated figures; Franz Kafka's drawings; the early cartoon style of Lyonel Feininger; the drawings Jules Pascin did for *Simplicissimus*; and the visionary works of James Ensor.

Herzmanovsky provided 24 illustrations for his own satirical novel *Der Gaulschreck im Rosennetz* ("The Cabhorse-Frightener in the Net of Roses"), about a Viennese civil servant in the Biedermeier period—his only piece of writing published in book form within his lifetime (1928). These spindly line drawings are slightly diluted Kubin; the characters have the same eerie aimlessness, and the settings have the same linear impor-

Fritz von Herzmanovsky-Orlando, "The Neighbors," 1909.

291

Step by step—Where are we going?

Don Hesse.

tance in the overall composition. The novel was greatly appreciated by Hugo von Hofmannsthal. Herzmanovsky also did a number of works in crayon and pastel (satires, odd metamorphoses, personifications of death, etc.) that have been exhibited in Vienna; Hofmann sees strong traces of cabaret and operetta, as well as a preoccupation with court ceremony, in this artistic output.

It remains to be seen whether Herzmanovsky's glory will extend beyond the boundaries of his homeland. At any rate, he is now familiar to a much larger audience than the tiny band of connoisseurs who knew of his work while he was alive. This "Sunday painter of the grotesque," who died at Merano in the Tyrol in 1954, has been called "the last genius of baroque Old Austrian humor."

S.A.

HESS, DAVID (1770-1843) Swiss cartoonist and printmaker born in Zurich, Switzerland, on November 29, 1770. Most of the classic German-speaking political cartoonists through the years have used their art on behalf of liberal and advanced views. The case of the important Swiss artist David Hess reminds us that the gods do not bestow all the talent on one side of the fence. This army officer of aristocratic, *ancien régime* views, who lived during the French Revolution, Napoleonic Wars and the days of the early socialists, was influenced in his opinions by the official British position on these matters, and was influenced in his art by the great British caricaturists Rowlandson and Gillray. Not only did Hess's cartoons reflect the drastic action, oddly shaped bodies and intense play of "physiognomy" characteristic of these Englishmen; he even signed some of his pieces "Gillray, junior."

From 1787 to 1795 Hess was in one of the Swiss regiments that served the traditional government of Holland, but in the latter year French might drove out the stadholder, and a puppet République des Provinces-

Unies, or "Batavian Republic," was established. Hess's regiment was disbanded without pay. This situation inspired his most famous series, *Hollandia Regenerata*, 20 drawings that were etched by none other than James Gillray himself and published in London in the summer of 1796. These drawings heap abuse on the various public agencies set up on the French revolutionary model by the Batavian Republic: the members of the welfare committee are shown gorging themselves while the populace starves, the fraternity committee is engaged in a hostile free-for-all, and so on down the line.

The year 1801 was a fertile one for Hess; among several other successful works, he produced his second most important series, the six plates comprising *Der Scharringelhof, or Die Positionen* (published under the pseudonym Daniel Hildebrandt). In this series two men—the owner of a townhouse and a guest—take leave of each other with endless exaggerated ceremony, an orgy of bowing and scraping; no doubt they are meant to be uppity bourgeois enriched by the wars and foolishly aping their "betters." It is hard not to be reminded of the Alphonse and Gaston of a century later (or, for that matter, of a famous early cartoon by Paul Klee), especially since *Der Scharringelhof* has some of the elements of a comic strip: the leave-taking continues through the series from within the house through different rooms to the exterior; in the next-to-last plate, the viewer can tell that the departing guest, lost to the world in his fatuous courtesy, is almost certainly going to trip over a stone and fall—and in the last plate ("panel") he does so!

Other celebrated Hess items are his satirical drawing on the phrenology fad (1808) and his book about his trip to Baden, the *Badenfahrt* (1818). He also wrote poems, stories, satires and biographies. He died in Zurich on April 11, 1843. His son Ludwig Adolf Hess (1800-1826), who drew landscapes and figures, also did some cartoons.

S.A.

HESSE, DON (1918-) American cartoonist born in Belleville, Illinois, on February 20, 1918. Don Hesse studied at the St. Louis School of Fine Arts at Washington University and joined the *Belleville* (Ill.) *Daily News-Democrat* as an artist-photographer in 1935; he remained until 1940. In 1946 he joined the *St. Louis Globe-Democrat* art staff and has worked there ever since, becoming chief political cartoonist in 1951. He was syndicated for years by the McNaught Syndicate and is now distributed by the Los Angeles Times Syndicate; it is possible that he is the most published political cartoonist in America, as the Hesse cartoon is picked up by hundreds of rural papers as well as by big-city dailies.

Hesse may also be the strongest defender of conservative positions in American cartooning. His cartoons are consistently simple, direct, lucid and attractively presented statements. He draws with a brush and continues to effectively employ grained paper, which he judiciously shades with crayon. He has won many Freedoms Foundation and National Headliners awards.

R.M.

HICKS, WOLFGANG (1909-) German editorial cartoonist born in Hamburg, Germany, in 1909. Wolfgang Hicks attended schools in Hamburg and Hanover but had no special art training beyond the ordinary drawing classes of these institutions. His earliest work was published in the *Hamburger Fremdenblatt* in 1928. It was not until the early 1930s that he entered the field of political cartooning, and then it was for a publication called *Echo der Woche* that abruptly ceased to exist in 1933. For the rest of the 1930s he drew advertising and other nonpolitical cartoons for the *Hamburger Anzeiger*, the *Hamburger Illustrierte*, *Koralle* and the *Berliner Illustrierte*.

During World War II, Hicks served in the navy and did front-line reportage while continuing to draw for magazines. It was in the new West German republic established after the war that he found the place he continued to occupy with such distinction, as senior editorial cartoonist for the two chief Hamburg news periodicals. Hicks joined the staff of *Die Zeit* when the paper was founded in 1946 and stayed there until 1957, when he switched over to *Die Welt*.

There can hardly have been an anthology of German cartoons that has not included a generous sampling of Hicks's ingenious drawings, with their strongly personal style. Thus, for instance, he was amply represented in the two major omnibus volumes chronicling Adenauer's career: *Konrad Sprach die Frau Mama* ("'Konrad,' Said Mother," 1955) and *Konrad Bleibst Du Jetzt zu Haus?* ("Konrad, Are You Going to Stay Home Now?," 1963). But Hicks has also had at least one album completely devoted to his own cartoons for *Die Welt*, the 1966 volume *Das War's* ("That Was It").

Hicks draws in a very fluid and rounded pen style (sometimes with sharper lines over a softer base) characterized by the prominence of certain especially thick lines singling out a principal figure or object. As with most of his colleagues, his viewpoint is independent and liberal.

S.A.

HILDE
See Weber, Hilde.

HILDEBRANDT, DANIEL
See Hess, David.

HILL, DRAPER (1935-   ) American cartoonist and historian born in Boston, Massachusetts, on July 1, 1935. Draper Hill graduated from Harvard magna cum laude in 1957, having written a thesis on Joseph Keppler, the cartoonist who founded *Puck* magazine. Hill decided on a cartooning career, and a visit with the legendary David

Albert Hirschfeld, caricature of Geraldine Fitzgerald. © New York Times.

Low in London cemented his enthusiasm.

Hill's staff work on the *Patriot Ledger* of Quincy, Massachusetts, evolved from obituary assignments to spot illustrating to editorial cartooning. In 1959 he received a Fulbright Fellowship to study political cartooning in London. A matured historian's perspective and several books on Gillray (the most notable being *Gillray the Caricaturist*) resulted. Hill drew political cartoons for the *Worcester* (Mass.) *Telegram* between 1964 and 1971, at which time he switched to Memphis to assume the post of *Commercial Appeal* editorial cartoonist Cal Alley, who had recently died. In 1976 he moved to the *Detroit News*, succeeding Art Poinier.

Draper Hill's drawing style is one of the most singular in American cartooning. Interestingly, though he is a student of 18th- and 19th-century cartoonists, his work bears little resemblance to that of his mentors, Gillray

Draper Hill. © Commercial Appeal.

and Keppler, except in terms of conceptual originality and effectiveness. Hill draws with a wide, loose brush, and his broad strokes are then shaded with doubletones. His caricatures are simple, as are the backgrounds and nonessentials in his handsome, liberal-oriented cartoons.

R.M.

HIPRAH HUNT'S JOURNEY THROUGH THE INFERNO *See Hell.*

HIRSCHFELD, ALBERT (1903-) American caricaturist and writer born in St. Louis, Missouri, on July 21, 1903. Al Hirschfeld studied at the National Academy and the Art Students League in New York City, the County Council in London and the Académie Julian in Paris. He also traveled extensively in France, Italy, Spain and North Africa in the years following World War I.

Hirschfeld contributed his first caricatures to the *New York Times* in 1925. He became theater correspondent for the *New York Herald-Tribune* in Moscow in 1927-28 and the following year became the theater caricaturist of the *New York Times*, a position he holds to this day. A peripatetic soul, Hirschfeld has traveled around the world almost without cease, either on assignment for such publications as *Holiday* and *Life*, or on U.S. government-sponsored tours.

Hirschfeld has been married twice. The name of his daughter by his second marriage, Nina, has become well-known among the artist's many admirers, as he is wont to slip it into every one of his caricatures. In the course of his long career Hirschfeld has depicted the greats and the near-greats of the artistic and political worlds with an uncanny eye and an unflinching pen. His works have been exhibited in galleries throughout the world and have earned him countless awards and distinctions from organizations and governments.

Though best known for his caricatures, Hirschfeld has also authored a number of books: *Manhattan Oases* (with Gordon Kahn, 1932); *Harlem by Hirschfeld* (1941); *Broadway Scrapbook* (with Brooks Atkinson, 1947); *Show Business Is No Business* (1951); *The American Theater* (1961); *Rhythm* (1970); and *The World of Hirschfeld* are the most notable. The artist was the subject of a monograph, Lloyd Goodrich's perceptive analysis in *The World of Hirschfeld*, which provides a lucid comment on the art of the famed caricaturist.

M.H.

HISTORIC AFFINITIES (U.S.) Otho Cushing found an outlet for his individual, classically inspired style in the series *Historic Affinities* for *Life* in 1911. Throughout his career, he frequently cast contemporary political and social notables in Greek or Roman settings, but *Historic Affinities*, wherein the ancients and moderns meet, was his cleverest and most popular series. Purely humorous on the surface, it made telling critical points.

Beginning on February 2, 1911, the following encounters—or misalliances—were portrayed: Dr. Parkhurst and Catherine II; Anthony Comstock and Sappho; Dr. Cook and Queen Isabella; Andrew Carnegie and Queen Boadicea; Mrs. Leslie Carter and Michelangelo; Dante and Lillian Russell; Richelieu and Maude Adams; Uncle Joe Cannon and Mary Stuart; Hetty Green and Lucullus; Catherine de´ Medici and John D. Rockefeller; Launcelot-Drew and Julia-Guinevere-Arthur; Augustus

and Emma Goldman; Sir Galahad and Sarah Bernhardt; Queen Elizabeth and President Taft; J.P. Morgan and Helen of Troy; and Jack London and Madame de Sévigné.

The popularity of *Historic Affinities*, which ran half a page in black and white, led to a contract for Cushing to illustrate auto advertisements with a motif of classical settings for the modern vehicles.

R.M

Dick Hodgins. © New York Daily News.

HODGINS, RICHARD HENRY, JR. (1931-) American cartoonist born in Binghamton, New York, on May 9, 1931. At the age of 12, Dick Hodgins moved with his family to New York City, where he made his first cartooning sale—a dollar for a sports page filler—to the *New York Mirror*. He studied at the Cartoonists and Illustrators School (later the School of Visual Arts), received art instruction from his father, a professional cartoonist, and took the Kuhn correspondence course. Hodgins cartooned and did illustrations for filmstrips before and after army service in Japan (1949). During his hitch he edited the base newspaper and contributed to *Pacific Stars and Stripes*; at this time he also sold gags in America by mail (mostly to Crestwood publications). Upon his discharge, he took on many national advertising accounts.

Between 1956 and 1969 Hodgins was a staff artist with the Associated Press in New York, doing feature art and substituting for editorial cartoonist John Milt Morris. During the last two years of that hitch he also drew occasional editorial cartoons for the *New York News* under the name "Dick Henry." Thereafter Hodgins switched to the *News* and worked under his own name as backup cartoonist for Warren King. He also became a full-time ghost for Hank Ketcham, working on the *Half*

Hitch comic strip for King Features and on its 1975 reincarnation, *Poopsy*, for Field. He now assists Dik Browne with various art chores on *Hägar the Horrible* and its spin-offs and handles numerous national advertising accounts. Hodgins has served the National Cartoonists Society for years in various capacities, most recently as editor of its magazine, and he won the 1979 Silver T-Square award for his services. He also drew for the Smith Service package for weekly newspapers, run by Al Smith.

Hodgins has a versatile style, ranging from the somewhat stiff renderings of his Associated Press days to his contemporary supple look of lush crosshatch shadings and format innovations. His work has always been marked by a feeling for humor and solid composition. His artwork on the *Half Hitch* strip was just about its only redeeming feature, especially on Sunday pages rich with detail and handsome colors.

(Hodgins's father, Dick Hodgins, Sr., was born on July 13, 1905, and was a cartoonist for General Electric publications before drawing editorial cartoons for the *Orlando Sentinel-Star* in Florida; he retired in 1970 after cartooning there for 13 years. He is currently curator of the Cartoon Museum in Orlando.)

R.M.

HOFF, SYD (1912-   ) American cartoonist and author born in New York City on September 4, 1912. Syd Hoff was educated in the public schools of the city but dropped out before finishing high school. He reports that he started drawing at the age of four and planned on becoming a "serious" artist all through his youth. To this end, he spent a term at the National Academy of Design, but at age 16 he sold his first cartoon. Thereafter, he says, his interest in serious art faded. An incredibly prolific artist, Hoff has been a *New Yorker* staff cartoonist since 1939 and has contributed to virtually every major mass-circulation periodical of his time, from *Look* and the *Saturday Evening Post* to *Playboy*.

Hoff works in a variety of media, including watercolors, crayon, washes and ink. His dumpling-shaped, round-nosed, wisecracking characters are

"I've given you a home, clothes, luxury. NOW what do you want?"

Syd Hoff. © Collier's.

E.T.A. Hoffmann, "Fantastic Figures in the Manner of Callot,"
ca. 1810.

often stock types, obviously drawn from the New York City Jewish neighborhoods in which he grew up—the aggressive wife, the mother with the marriageable daughter, the ambitious girl, the *ganef*, the small merchant—but they are universally accessible, even while remaining immediately recognizable as his creations. Of course, no one boasting 61 titles in his *Who's Who* entry is going to hit the mark every time, and in truth, Hoff registers his full share of misses. But he is frequently and insightfully funny, too. Consider the dean of a college looking over the record of a dreamy-eyed new coed and blandly asking, "Is there anyone besides Elvis Presley we can notify in case of emergency?" Or the hippie-radical artist to the model who's just walked into his studio: "In this picture I want to capture the surge of jet power in the second industrial revolution. Take off your clothes."

Besides the many collections of his cartoons—including *Oops, Wrong Party* (1950), *Twixt the Cup and the Lipton* (1962) and *How to Run a Country* (1963)—Hoff has written and illustrated numerous children's books, illustrated books by other authors—Paul Gallico's *How to Name a Boy*, for example—and written or compiled three volumes about cartooning: *It's Fun Learning Cartooning* (1956), *How to Draw Cartoons* (1975) and *Editorial and Political Cartooning* (1976).

In a field boasting so many original and inventive artists, Hoff's sheer good nature and love of what he is doing is perhaps more important than critical evaluation of his work. These qualities are apparent in his drawings—even the most ingenuous of them—and in his writings about cartooning, directed particularly to young people. There can be few professions more deserving of a boost than those concerned with making people smile—and Syd Hoff has certainly done more than his share in this regard.

R.C.

HOFFMANN, ERNST THEODOR AMADEUS (1776-1822) German writer, composer and cartoonist born in Königsberg, East Prussia (now Kaliningrad, USSR), on January 24, 1776. E.T.A. Hoffmann (born Ernst Theodor Wilhelm Hoffmann) was astoundingly versatile, successful in all his artistic fields of endeavor; he is of course best remembered today for his "tales," fanciful stories in which modern critics have discovered realism and social and political awareness. His graphic output, however, even if it is only a small part of his total activity, is at the core of his work. Essentially a visually oriented man who had thought of becoming a professional painter (in Warsaw he did important murals), Hoffmann was continually inspired in his writing by works of art (Callot especially) and used graphic art to establish the scenes and characters of his stories and novels.

Born into a family of jurists, Hoffmann too studied law, and between 1800 and 1806 he practiced as a judge in East Prussian cities that are now part of Poland: Posen (Poznań), Plock and Warsaw. In 1806 the invading French armies caused the collapse of this German realm, and Hoffmann began freelancing: in Berlin in 1807 and 1808; in Bamberg from 1808 to 1813 as music director, composer and stage designer for the local theater (it was here that he wrote his first tales, as well as music criticism that has earned him the title of "founder of modern musical aesthetics"); and in Dresden and Leipzig in 1813. In 1814-15 Prussia was reconstituted, and Hoffmann settled in Berlin, where he wrote the bulk of his stories and also served efficiently and courageously as a court aide. He died in Berlin on June 25, 1822.

Although Hoffmann worked as a cartoonist throughout his career, the following high points can be cited. It was his bold caricatures of his government superiors in Posen that got him fined and transferred to the remote and dreary Plock in 1802. In Berlin in 1808, he drew three caricatures of actors published as *Groteske Gestalten nach Darstellungen auf dem Nationaltheater zu Berlin* ("Grotesque Figures After Performances at the Berlin National Theater"). In Leipzig in 1813 he drew several anti-Napoleonic cartoons for local print publishers (these are pleasant but much more formal and constrained than his private caricatures). Lastly, in Berlin between 1814 and 1822 he constantly drew illustrations and covers for his own stories, as well as street scenes and portraits of himself, of friends and chance acquaintances encountered at his favorite wine shop, Lutter and Wegner's, which he did so much to immortalize.

S.A.

HOFFMANN, HEINRICH (1809-1894) German cartoonist born in Frankfurt am Main, Hesse, on June 13, 1809. Heinrich Hoffmann was the creator of *Struwwelpeter*, perhaps the most influential of all German works of humorous art, and surely the most popular, along with Busch's *Max und Moritz*. Ironically, he was never more than an amateur as a draftsman and versifier. Hoffmann was by profession a practicing physician, a teacher of anatomy and, from 1851 to 1888, Frankfurt's leading doctor for mental diseases. He was an enlightened, if conservative, citizen with many interests; his club life brought him into contact with various intellectuals, and he had turned his hand to writing even before his great comic creation.

In 1842 he published a volume of poetry and in 1843 a clever verse play, *Die Mondzügler* ("The Colonizers of the Moon"), a satire on Hegelian philosophy and on aspects of German society that offended the author. It was at Christmastime in 1844 that, dissatisfied with the dry and pedagogic children's books then available, he wrote and illustrated the original manuscript of *Struwwelpeter* for his three-year-old son. Published by a personal friend in 1845, these cautionary tales of disobe-

Adloph Hoffmeister's famous "V-cartoon." © *Hoffmeister.*

dient and careless children started to sell like hotcakes. As German editions followed one another rapidly and the translations piled up (even into Latin and Esperanto!), Hoffmann found himself the world's most popular children's author (see the entry "Struwwelpeter").

Further children's books by Hoffmann, all with the primitive draftsmanship and often limping verse of *Struwwelpeter* but never equaling that volume's appeal, included: *König Nussknacker und der Arme Reinhold* ("King Nutcracker and Poor Reinhold," 1851), Hoffmann's own favorite, a story with characters based on actual folk toys; *Bastian, der Faulpelz* ("Bastian the Lazybones," 1854); *Im Himmel und auf der Erde* ("In Heaven and on Earth," 1857); and *Prinz Grünewald und Perlenfein mit Ihrem Lieben Eselein* ("Prince Greenwood and Pearlfine with Their Dear Little Donkey," 1871). Similar material he had composed for his family was gathered into a posthumous volume, *Besuch bei Frau Sonne* ("Visit to Mrs. Sun," 1924). Like *Struwwelpeter*, a number of these later books feature the same type of bloodthirsty violence that is found in many folktales and that Hoffmann bequeathed to Busch, Dirks and many others; too wildly exaggerated to be taken seriously by any normal child, this kind of extreme slapstick has often been impugned by hypersensitive 20th-century education teachers.

The revolution year of 1848 and the years immediately following led to some further adult satirical writing by Hoffmann, particularly the very witty, though antirepublican, *Handbüchlein für Wühler oder Kurzgefasste Anleitung in Wenigen Tagen ein Volksmann zu Werden* ("Little Handbook for Agitators, or Brief Guide to Becoming a Man of the People in a Few Days," 1848), which he signed "Peter Struwwel, Demagog" and illustrated with a title vignette.

Hoffmann died in Frankfurt on September 20, 1894. Some time earlier he had added his wife's maiden name, Donner, to the end of his own surname, so that he is now known to pedants and librarians as Heinrich Hoffmann-Donner.

S.A.

HOFFMEISTER, ADOLF (1902-1973) Czech cartoonist, writer and diplomat born in Prague, Bohemia (then part of the Hapsburg empire, now in Czechoslovakia), on August 15, 1902. Adolf Hoffmeister displayed remarkable talents as a writer and artist while still in high school and had his first book published at the age of 17. After he graduated from Charles University in Prague in 1925, he went to work as a writer, editor and cartoonist on several Czech magazines. When Hitler came to power in Germany and started laying claim to the Czech Sudetenland, Hoffmeister ridiculed him in savage cartoons that were reprinted all over Europe.

After the 1938 Munich agreements, Hoffmeister spent several months in solitary confinement. He went into exile in France and worked for the Czech resistance movement there; when the Germans invaded France in 1940, he was put into a concentration camp. He then escaped to Casablanca, was interned by the Vichy regime, and escaped from there to Spain, only to be interned again by the Franco government. In January 1941 he made his final escape, to the United States from Spain via Havana. A book reflecting his experiences, *Animals Are in Cages*, was published in New York at the end of 1941. (Adolf Hoffmeister is reported to have inspired the character played by Paul Henreid in the movie *Casablanca*.) Settling in New York City, Hoffmeister worked as a cartoonist and poster designer and edited the Czech programs of Voice of America.

In 1944, at the behest of President Beneš, Hoffmeister returned to Czechoslovakia. He was appointed delegate to the United Nations in 1945 and from 1948 to 1951 served as ambassador to France, and later to China. Hoffmeister never stopped drawing, however; he was officially declared "national artist" in 1950, and his graphic works were widely exhibited in Prague, Paris, Brussels, Venice, London, New York and other places.

Hoffmeister supported Alexander Dubček in his unsuccessful attempt to bring democracy to Czechoslovakia in the mid-1960s. After Czechoslovakia's occupation by the Russian army in 1968, he went into disgrace. He was allowed neither to publish nor to exhibit, and his cartoons (many of them classics) were expunged from official anthologies. Hoffmeister died in Prague of a heart attack on July 25, 1973.

M.H.

HOFFNUNG, GERARD (1925-1959) British cartoonist, writer, musician, speaker and eccentric, born in Berlin, Germany, on March 22, 1925. To those who saw him and heard him it is impossible to think Gerard Hoffnung has been gone for so long. His rise to fame was meteoric, and his memory continues to delight through reprintings of his books, recordings of his broadcasts and speeches, and restagings of his extraordinary tongue-in-cheek music festivals that rocked London in the 1950s.

Gerard Hoffnung, so superbly British, was a student at the Highgate and Harrow School of Arts and Crafts under J.G. Platt, and then served as art master at Stanford School (1945) and assistant art master at Harrow (1948). In between, in 1947, he worked as a staff artist on the London *Evening News*, contributing funny lit-

Gerard Hoffnung. © Punch.

"I'll never feel as safe again as I did with Mr. Coolidge."

Helen Hokinson. © Collier's.

tle "spot" drawings and column-breakers that livened the tabloid pages of the time. In 1950 he went to New York to draw for the Cowles chain of magazines, returning to England the following year to freelance in art and his main hobby, music. He drew for *Punch,* *Lilliput* and other weeklies, illustrated books for children, and became a regular radio broadcaster for the BBC, delivering superb and lengthy anecdotes in a rich, fruity voice. In 1956 he created the Hoffnung Music Festival, which became a regular and hilarious treat at the Royal Festival Hall, a kind of upper-crust Spike Jones show. It became the Hoffnung Interplanetary Music Festival for 1958 and 1959.

He died quite suddenly in 1959, at the age of 34: everyone thought him a much older man. His cartoons, much collected, are eternally witty, and the John Halas-Joy Batchelor animation studios converted a number of his little books and sequences into a technicolor *Tales from Hoffnung,* which remains among that studio's best work.

Books: *The Right Playmate* (1952); *The Maestro* (1953); *The Hoffnung Symphony Orchestra* (1954); *The Isle of Cats* (1955); *The Hoffnung Music Festival* (1956); *The Hoffnung Companion to Music* (1957); *Hoffnung's Musical Chairs* (1958); *Ho Ho Hoffnung* (1959); *Hoffnung's Acoustics* (1959); *Birds, Bees and Storks* (1960); *O Rare Hoffnung* (1960); *Hoffnung's Little Ones* (1961); *Hoffnung's Constant Readers* (1962); and *The Boy and the Magic* (1964).

D.G.

HOFMAN, EDUARD (1914-   ) Czechoslovakian animator born near Prague, Czechoslovakia, in 1914. Eduard Hofman was trained as an architect but started working in animation as early as 1943. He joined the Barandov studio as an administrator in 1945, but under the influence of Jiří Trnka, he acquired a taste as well as a talent for animation. He refined his newfound skills on educational cartoons before venturing into entertainment animation. Hofman's first theatrical film, *All Aboard,* was released in 1947, followed the next year by *The Angel's Cloak,* a delightful tale of a magic cloak that had the power of changing evil into good.

In the 1950s Hofman became one of the most prolific of Czech animators, with countless shorts to his credit; *ABC* (1950), *The Golden Apples* (1952), *Where Is Misha?* (1954) and *The Fox* (1955) are among the more notable. From 1950 to 1954 Hofman also directed the hilarious *Dog and Cat* series. In 1956 he released his masterwork, *The Creation of the World,* a feature film based on the work of French cartoonist Jean Effel. Other cartoons by Hofman include *Tale of the Dog* (1959), *My Twelve Daddies* (1960), *The Postman's Story* (1961) and *The Ladder* (1964), all of which received awards or nominations. Since the mid-1960s Hofman has devoted his talents to turning out routine cartoons for children and for television, although he did make a second animated feature, *The Tribulations of Adam and Eve* (1974), also inspired by Effel.

M.H.

HOKINSON, HELEN ELNA (1893-1949) American cartoonist born in Mendota, Illinois, in 1893. The daughter of a farm-equipment salesman, Helen Hokinson was of Swedish descent, and until her father's time the family name had been spelled Haakonson. Her first recognition as an artist came when her surreptitious sketches of the teachers at Mendota High School were found by the teachers themselves in a mislaid sketchbook.

Helen Hokinson studied fashion illustration for five years at Chicago's Academy of Fine Arts. She then went to the Parsons School of Design in New York City, where her studies with Howard Gile were based on Hambridge's theory of dynamic symmetry. Her drawings had a natural humorous flavor, and with fellow artist and cartoonist Alice Harvey she sold a comic strip to the *New York Daily Mirror.* This strip, *Sylvia in the Big City,* had a short run.

In 1925, at the encouragement of friends at the Parsons School of Design, she submitted a drawing to the brand-new *New Yorker* magazine. Much to her surprise the *New Yorker* purchased it. The cartoon appeared without caption or signature on page one of the July 4, 1925, issue, in the middle of "The Talk of the Town" column. It was a rear view of a plump woman in floppy hat and sensible shoes who had climbed a railing to wave bon voyage at a pier. Most of her early work for the *New Yorker* was captionless.

Helen Hokinson's most famous cartoon characters were her so-called Hokinson Girls. These amiable but vague clubwomen were duly noted by the *New York Times* as being the inspiration for a cult which avidly followed her cartoons in the *New Yorker* and considered her characters as "the emblem of clubwomen the country over." (The concept of the clubwoman series was created in 1933 by James Reid Parker, a *New Yorker* writer who from 1931 to 1949 was Hokinson's silent partner and gag writer for her cartoons.)

Hokinson's style depended on a simple line drawing painted in gray wash to give it depth and form. She loved to roam New York City with her pocket-sized sketchbook, making drawings in soft pencil. Flower shows and department stores proved especially fruitful in researching real-life Hokinson Girls. They were depicted on incessant shopping sprees, tangling traffic, molesting flowers, cajoling maids and generally indulging themselves to pass the time. Mature women, they were more weighty physically than intellectually. A typical cartoon shows two Hokinson Girls seated in a Schrafft's restaurant for lunch. One says, "Sometimes I think Schrafft's doesn't *care* about calories." Helen Hokinson's aim was to poke fun at these American matrons without wounding. However, in light of the women's movement and general female consciousness-raising of the 1960s, to be a Hokinson Girl today would be considered an insult by most women.

Hokinson herself never married, and as early as 1929 she divided her time between a New York City apartment and a cottage in Wilton, Connecticut. James Reid Parker remembered that her youthful flair for colorful blouses and scarves gave way to more conservative fashions as she aged. Her interests ranged from Shakespeare, backgammon and French Impressionists to Gilbert and Sullivan, wildflowers and Connecticut's back country. One of her last projects was a play about women in which her Hokinson Girls would be funny but would not be ridiculed.

The play was never finished. On November 1, 1949, Helen Hokinson, en route from New York City to Washington, D.C., for a speaking engagement, was killed when a P-38 fighter recently sold to the Bolivian air force split the aircraft in which she was traveling. All 55 people aboard were killed in the worst American civil aircraft disaster up to that time.

Helen Hokinson's cartoons were published in a number of collections, both before and after her death. They are *So You're Going to Buy a Book* (1931), *My Best Girls* (1941), *When Were You Built* (1948), *The Ladies, God Bless 'Em* (1950), *There Are Ladies Present* (1952), and *The Hokinson Festival*, with a memoir by James Reid Parker (1956). She also drew a cartoon panel featuring men, entitled *The Dear Man*, that was published for a time in the *Ladies' Home Journal*. She illustrated three books by Emily Kimbrough and a poetry book entitled *Garden Clubs and Spades* by Laurence McKinney.

B.C.

Poul Holck. © Holck.

HOLCK, POUL (1939-   ) Danish cartoonist born in Copenhagen, Denmark, on September 30, 1939. Holck's specialty is innocent sophistication, and in his drawing style he shows the simple and the wonderful, knowing that there is something ugly in everything beautiful. Since his debut he has worked as a house cartoonist at the daily *Politiken*, where he, at a fixed spot that he shares with two or three others, gives his comments on topical events several times a week. He also illustrates articles and editorials.

Holck often appears on television as an illustrating political commentator. Here, too, the curls and the chins appear, always displayed with kindness and tact. His well-developed sense of motion comes across whether his cartoons are animated or printed on paper. On his way to world fame, he won first prize at the 13th International Salon of Caricature in Montreal in 1976, with participants coming from 57 countries.

J.S.

HOLLAND, BRAD (1944-   ) American cartoonist and illustrator born in Fremont, Ohio, in 1944. Brad Holland is one of the youngest of the prominent artist-illustrators in the modern graphic art tradition of the Push Pin Studio school. He grew up in Fort Sumter, Arkansas, a relatively isolated rural community, and his peculiar artistic development owes much to this environment. Driven by an inner need to express himself in a graphic style, yet cut off from all sources of artistic inspiration save Norman Rockwell magazine covers and Walt Disney comics, Holland developed a very personal approach to expression.

His first attempts at drawing, he recalls, were pornographic cartoons over which he would labor, only to tear them up lest his mother find them. By the age of 13, he was drawing cartoons and sending them to various magazines, without success. Undaunted, Holland left Arkansas at the age of 17, determined upon a career in art, notwithstanding his lack of formal education. He moved to Chicago, where his first job as an "artist" was in a tattoo parlor; this was followed by a job with Hallmark Cards, which Holland recalls as no more "artistic" than the tattoo parlor. There he received a small salary because of his lack of formal training and worked in a separate room in the art department because his stuff was so "weird." In keeping with his reputation, he founded during this period the Asylum Press, through which he and a group of friends printed "eccentric projects."

When he moved to New York City, however, everything began to come together for Brad Holland. With his alien style now fixed, he was able to refine it in the hothouse artistic environment of the city in the 1960s—the lively underground press, the more serious pop and op movements, the downtown gallery scene and finally the museums. With this refinement came some commercial success, notably in the *Playboy* "Ribald Classic" series. But his most striking work haunted the pages of the underground press organs—black-and-white illustrations unequivocally stating his own (and the underground movement's) opposition to the established order. By 1971 the relevance of his work had triumphed over its weirdness, and he was hired as a staff artist by the *New York Times*, where his work has become a staple of the Op-Ed Page.

His work does not readily lend itself to description, though the title of a 1975 Paris exhibition of the work of Holland and his fellow *Times* artists perhaps comes close: "Beyond Illustration." It has a peculiar quality of depth reminiscent of grotesque china figurines—alienated Hummels, perhaps—and an impact that is frequently anything but benign.

In keeping with the visibility the *Times* connection has gained him, Holland's work has become fashionable. Besides appearing in other outlets like *Intellectual Digest*, he has received increasing numbers of commissions to illustrate books. A collection of his work has also been published under the title *Human Scandals*

Brad Holland. © New York Times.

(Crowell, 1977). This book is worth looking at, not only as art but as documentary evidence of the strange and wonderful visions that isolated, eccentric development can sometimes promote and as a testimony to innate human creativity. In this respect, Holland's achievement perhaps provides the best antidote to the bleak view of humanity frequently represented in his work.

R.C.

HOLLAND, DANIEL E. (1918-) American cartoonist born in Guthrie, Kentucky, on February 2, 1918. Daniel ("Ed") Holland was educated at David Lipscomb College (1936-38) and the Chicago Academy of Fine Arts (1938-39). The man who was to become the last of the *Chicago Tribune's* classic-style cartoonists followed his immediate predecessors, Carey Orr and Joe Parrish, from Nashville to Chicago. Holland went from the *Nashville Banner* (1939-41) to the *Chicago Tribune* (1945-50) to the *Washington Times-Herald* (1950 until its merger with the *Post* in 1954) and back to the *Chicago Tribune*. He shared duties until 1972 and was then chief editorial cartoonist until his retirement in 1975.

Stylistically, Holland belonged to the Billy Ireland school of photographic likenesses amidst unexaggerated but simplified cartoon figures. He seldom used crayon shading, relying on handsome crosshatching rendered in a supple line. Many of his cartoons ran in color on the *Trib's* front page. Holland was probably the last major American cartoonist to receive such a regular place of honor, and also the last of a distinguished line of fierce, old-school conservatives. His pleasant style formed an amiable link with the earlier look of American political cartoons. He won many Freedoms Foundation citations and taught for years at the Chicago Academy of Fine Arts.

R.M.

HOLLEY, LEE (1933-   ) American cartoonist born in Phoenix, Arizona, on April 20, 1933. Lee Holley displayed a love of cartooning at an early age, and he started selling his cartoons at the age of 15. He attended Chouinard Art School in Los Angeles, and in 1954 he joined the Warner Brothers animation studio, where for three years he worked on *Bugs Bunny, Road Runner* and *Daffy Duck* cartoons, as well as on a number of *Porky Pig* comic books. In 1957 he became assistant to Hank Ketcham, helping him draw the *Dennis the Menace* Sunday feature.

All the while Lee Holley kept submitting cartoon ideas to syndicates, and in 1960 he finally succeeded in selling a teenage panel to King Features. Called *Ponytail*, it is now running daily and Sundays. Drawn in a seemingly slapdash but effective manner, it tells of the everyday trials and tribulations of the title heroine and her teenage cohorts. While the theme is neither new nor startlingly original, Holley has been able to impart to it an impish charm that redeems its more obvious and hackneyed situations.

M.H.

HOLLREISER, LEN (1923-   ) American cartoonist born in Brooklyn, New York, on September 16, "the year Casey Stengel beat the Yankees twice in the World Series with home runs," which, according to the record books, turns out to be 1923. Soon after graduation from high school in 1941, Len Hollreiser embarked on a fledgling cartooning career that was nipped in the bud by his induction into the army. After demobilization in 1945, he worked briefly for comic books and magazines. In 1947 he met Willard Mullin and on his recommendation was hired as the sports cartoonist for the *New York Herald-Tribune*.

In 1953 Hollreiser created for the Chicago Tribune-New York News Syndicate *Looking Back in Sports*, a cartoon panel of sports history that was followed a few years later by *This Day in Sports*, a daily installment of vignettes retracing some sports event of the past. The panel ran for years, but in 1975, partly due to deteriorating eyesight, Hollreiser was forced to drop it.

Hollreiser was one of the few remaining syndicated sports cartoonists. His style, heavily inspired by Mullin's, is by turns realistic, with heavy shading and accurate body placement, and cartoony, with whimsical figures popping out in odd situations.

M.H.

HOLSWILDER, JAN (1850-1890) Dutch cartoonist, painter and printmaker born in Leiden, the Netherlands, on November 17, 1850. Despite the weak health that shortened his life—only the last 10 of his 40

"What's your second choice for a career if you can't be a bunny?"

Lee Holley, "Ponytail." © *King Features Syndicate.*

years could be devoted to cartoons and caricatures—Jan Holswilder gained the reputation of having freed Dutch humorous drawing from a blight of allegory and amateurism, and of having been the first Dutch political cartoonist to reflect in his work the advanced level that fine art had reached in his time.

In 1878 Holswilder moved permanently to The Hague, and his intimate knowledge of life in the Dutch capital was to be of paramount importance in his production. After art study at the Academy there and a period of ordinary clerical jobs, he worked for some time in a lithographic printshop, where he acquired essential technical know-how. His first important published cartoon work was an 1880 series called *Haagsche Penkrassen* ("Pen Sketches of The Hague"). In 1882 he began drawing for the magazine *Uilenspiegel*. The decisive move in his career occurred in 1885, when he became the chief draftsman for the new semimonthly *De Lantaarn* (named after a lively Dutch paper of the era of the French Revolution).

The new *Lantaarn* was an aggressively liberal and anticlerical publication that had its hands full in the 1880s (as did the *Uilenspiegel*) combatting two powerful parties that seriously threatened the separation between church and state: the Calvinist group led by Kuyper and the Catholic group led by Schaepman. Holswilder's long, careful acquaintance with Hague affairs made him a natural as a chronicler of daily infighting in Parliament; he knew all the deputies, and his was essentially an art based on reality and direct observation. While working for *De Lantaarn*, he changed his basic cartoon technique from his earlier lithographlike charcoal drawing on rough paper to straight pen work in a sketchy, impressionistic man-

The girl he left behind

Ed Holland. © *Chicago Tribune.*

ner. He was also known for his caricatures of the politically prominent, some of which were published in Netscher's book *Uit Ons Parlement* ("From Our Parliament").

Holswilder was also a painter, etcher and lithographer who produced portraits, landscapes and figure studies. He died in The Hague on August 20, 1890.

S.A.

HONDA, KINKICHIRO (1850-1921) Japanese artist and cartoonist born in Edo (now Tokyo), Japan, in 1850. Kinkichiro Honda was one of the typical progressive artists of the Meiji period (1868-1912). In 1863 he traveled to Hiroshima to undergo military training based on British methods of instruction. The exposure to Western-style education stimulated young Honda to take an interest in the English language, and in 1868 he enrolled in the school of Western learning that Fumio Nomura had founded after his return from studies in England. Nomura had taken an interest in the humor magazines he saw during his travels abroad, and it was no doubt his teacher's interest in cartoons that prompted Honda to travel to Tokyo four years later and begin a career as an illustrator and cartoonist.

In March 1877, Fumio Nomura founded the *Marumaru Chinbun*, one of the historic humor magazines of the Meiji era, and Honda joined his former teacher to draw the back cover for every issue. His first illustration showed three *Punch*-style characters with somewhat comic expressions, the *Marumaru Chinbun* logo and a horse and a deer at the top of the page (the words *horse* and *deer* read together in Japanese are pronounced *baka*, a common expression meaning "stupid" or "foolish"). In the years that followed, Honda produced many satirical cartoons on human rights, civil liberties and other political affairs. He was fond of atrocious puns, a characteristic that reveals his classical upbringing; like many of the early cartoonists, Honda was heavily influenced by the light, farcical *haikai* and *haiku* literary traditions. Bad puns were a legacy of these earlier literary forms, and Honda and others transmitted them to the modern cartoon. One such example was a Honda cartoon entitled "Minken Tohai," which could be interpreted as "Colleague of Human Rights" or "Howling Dog of the People." Of course, Honda completed the pun by drawing a huge dog howling over some government officials and thus produced a humorous statement on the growing demand for human rights.

Honda's contributions as an artist are significant not only for their historical value but also for the techniques by which they were produced. Honda worked in a printshop in Tokyo that was owned by a foreign printer, and he used the shop's lead-plate presses to produce copies of much better quality than the wood-block prints that had been common until then. Honda eventually gave up drawing for the *Marumaru Chinbun*, turning his pen over to Kiyochiku Kobayashi. He spent his final years drawing and designing traditional Japanese gardens. He also published several books on the art of garden making. He died in 1921.

J.C.

HONOBONO-KUN (Japan) *Honobono-Kun* was a four-frame cartoon in the traditional Japanese format that first appeared in the *Tokyo Shimbun* ("Tokyo Newspaper") in 1956. It was drawn by Kimihiko Tsukuda. The hero of this piece was a three- or four-year-old little boy called

Honobono (meaning "glimmer" or "hope") who was usually accompanied by his dog. For reasons never really clarified, he had no mother, but this created a format for a warm bond with his round-faced father. The daily chores that they performed together were often a central theme, and part of *Honobono-kun*'s popularity may have stemmed from the fact that most Japanese children feel very distant from their fathers. The thought of a home where a father is not only a "friend" but also performs household chores was both appealing and amusing.

Honobono-kun was very simply drawn, and as a result the overall subtle sentimentality of the work was further increased. Moreover, it tended to concentrate on the little things that happen in ordinary, everyday existence and therefore had a particularly broad appeal. A unique characteristic of *Honobono-kun* was its "silent" or "pantomime" technique (Tsukuda was apparently greatly influenced in this respect by Erich Ohser, a German cartoonist who, among other things, wrote *Vater und Sohn* under the name of E.O. Plauen.) The resulting atmosphere of *Honobono-kun* is one of wistful solitude. Later, *Honobono Ojisan*, a slightly altered version starring the father, ran in *Asahi Shimbun* ("Asahi News"), but it did utilize some words.

Tsukuda, the artist, is also known for his *Aisubekya Tsura* ("Face That Should Be Loved"), *Dorobo Shinshi* ("Gentleman Thief") and *Honobono Kazoku* ("Honobono Family").

F.S.

HOOK, GEOFFREY RAYNOR (1928-   ) Australian political cartoonist born in Hobart, Tasmania, in December 1928.

Since World War II a significant factor in the style of Australian political cartooning has been the filtered influence of the drawing and presentation initiated by William ("Wep") Pidgeon during the 1940s. In theme, the "grand manner" approach, the sort previously drawn with allegorical or symbolic figures labeled "Nationhood" soberly indicating rising suns labeled "Health-Wealth-Prosperity," has completely disappeared. One of the present-day press cartoonists to favor humor above moral posturing is the Melbourne *Sun-News Pictorial*'s Geoffrey ("Jeff") Hook. Jeff has the distinction of being the first political cartoonist to work for the *Sun* since it was founded in 1922.

Hook joined the art staff of this morning paper in April 1964 as a layout artist, and during this period, keen to be a cartoonist, he fed cartoon ideas to the editor, who eventually asked Jeff to produce one finished cartoon a week, then two, then five a week plus a football cartoon for the *Sporting Globe*, another of the *Herald* group weekly newspapers. In this early period of his career he assisted with feature page layouts as well!

Jeff took a night-school commercial art course at the Hobart Technical School while working as a public servant. He secured a job with the Hobart *Mercury* as a press artist in 1959, coming to Melbourne five years later. Politically, Jeff has stated that he prefers no party but remains permanently in opposition to all, believing that this is the way the man in the street is most of the time.

His cartoons, drawn with bold lines, with their first-class portrait caricature of personalities in politics, are compulsively readable and display well on the tabloid page of the *Sun*. And, as in the old *Cole's*

Family of Man!

Jeff Hook. © *Melbourne Sun-News Pictorial.*

Funny Picture Book puzzle-drawings—"Here is the pig, here is the horse, and here is his dog. Where is the farmer?"—or as with the Souter cat or Emile Mercier's gravy cans, Jeff hides away in his cartoons his personal pun, a small fishhook, the discovery of which gives *Sun* readers a feeling of triumphant satisfaction.

None of Jeff's cartoons have been published as a collection, but he has illustrated a number of books displaying in another context his fine comic skill.

V.L.

HOOVER, ELLISON (1890-1955) American cartoonist born in Cleveland, Ohio, in 1890. Ellison Hoover studied art at the Art Students League in New York before landing a staff position with the *New York World*. He later worked for the *New York Evening News* and the *New York Herald-Tribune*.

In the 1910s and 1920s Hoover frequently drew for *Judge* and *Life*; his fat little German-Americans attracted some attention amid the fervid anti-German hysteria preceding and during World War I, and one character, Otto, later starred in a short-lived strip for the *Herald-Tribune*. As depicted by Hoover, however, these characters were so ridiculous as to undermine the intended venom of the drawings. In the 1920s much of his work consisted of full-page drawings on speculative themes such as "Visiting —— City by One Who Has Never Been There," and other series in this genre, which was really handled better by Gluyas Williams, Forbell and Rea Irvin. Hoover also frequently lampooned the art form of the comic strip, viciously accusing it of low humor, monotony and an absence of talent.

Hoover had a chance to set the world straight when he inherited the comic strip *Mr. and Mrs.* upon the death of Clare Briggs. He failed miserably. His work was an insult to Clare Briggs's genius, and for years the strip reflected low humor, monotony and an absence of talent—in spite of the fact that the otherwise clever comic writer Arthur H. Folwell contributed gags. Aside from his poor imitation of Briggs, Hoover's style was sterile and empty. His full pages are curiously unbalanced, and white spaces dominate instead of framing the points of interest. His shading was always done with methodical parallel lines that, if nothing else, indicate dedication.

Hoover died in his New York apartment on March 17, 1955.

R.M.

HOPPIN, AUGUSTUS (1828-1896) American cartoonist, illustrator and lawyer born in Providence, Rhode Island, on April 13, 1828. Augustus Hoppin graduated from Brown University in 1848 and the Harvard Law School in 1850, when he was also admitted to the Rhode Island bar. The growing (or creeping) sophistication of woodcut engraving, however, and the increasing tribe of native American humorists, combined to lure Hoppin away from law and toward drawing. His drawings appeared in many monthly magazines and in a long list of humorous books, including *The Potiphar Papers* (1853), *The Autocrat of the Breakfast Table* (1858), *Hay Fever* (1873), *A Fashionable Sufferer* (1883), *Two Compton Boys* (1885) and *Married for Fun* (1885). He also authored romances anonymously. Whether he contributed to the later humor magazines is doubtful; his work is often mistaken for that of Livingston Hopkins.

But in the very early comic sheets and in the humor columns of the early monthlies his work is omnipresent. As late as 1872 he was producing three daily cartoons for the four-page sheet *Jubilee Days*. To Hoppin must go a large share of the credit for priming the American public for the panel cartoon. He was essentially an illustrator who devoted his career to funny subjects, but as such he paved the way for the new profession of magazine cartooning. He died in Flushing, New York, on April 1, 1896.

R.M.

Scenes from the lives of domestic servants.
Theodor Hosemann.

HORRABIN, JAMES FRANCIS (1884-1962) British strip cartoonist and illustrator born in Sheffield, England, on November 1, 1884. James Francis ("Frank") Horrabin, one of the most prolific strip cartoonists and illustrators of his time, studied historic ornament at the Sheffield School of Art and designed flower show prize cups for his father's silverplate works before joining the art department of the *Sheffield Telegraph* in 1906. On that provincial newspaper he provided a daily topical strip in the format popularized by W.K. Haselden in the *Daily Mirror*. He quickly rose to art editor and went to London in 1911 to take up the same position on the *Daily News*.

It was the time of the Balkan Wars, and Horrabin, a keen geographer, began to supply his paper with maps of the war. Popular, topical cartography would become a major sideline to his cartoon activities, and he map-illustrated the progress of both world wars in newspapers and books and on television. His "serious side" took him into lecturing on geography at the London Labour College, and thence to the editorship of *The Plebs,* the monthly Labour magazine, and finally into Parliament itself: he campaigned for and was elected Labour member of Parliament for Peterborough (1929-31).

Frank Horrabin's first daily strip, *Adventures of the Noah Family Including Japhet,* began as a single panel in the *Daily News* on June 13, 1919. This was later known as *Japhet and Happy,* and still later as *The Arkubs.* It transferred to the *News Chronicle* in 1930 and continued until after the war. Many annual volumes of this popular children's strip were published from 1920 to the 1950s. For the same publisher's evening newspaper, the *Star,* Horrabin created *Dot and Carrie.* This office strip about two typists began on November 18, 1922, and ran to March 1, 1962, when it was ended on Horrabin's death.

Besides running both daily strips, Horrabin drew many book illustrations and was a regular on prewar television, with *Newsmap* shows and "Lightning Cartoon" appearances. Horrabin is largely forgotten today, except by nostalgic collectors of his *Japhet and Happy Annuals,* but a *Dot and Carrie* supplement was reprinted as a pullout to the revived *Ally Sloper* magazine in January 1977.

Books: *Some Adventures of the Noah Family* (1920); *The Noahs on Holiday* (1921); *More About the Noahs* (1922); *Mr. Noah* (1922); *Japhet and Fido* (1922); *Dot and Carrie* (1923); *Economic Geography* (1923); *Outline of Economic Geography* (1923); *The Japhet Book* (1924); *Dot and Carrie and Adolphus* (1924); *Working Class Education* (1924); *Dot and Carrie Not Forgetting Adolphus* (1925); *About Japhet* (1926); *Japhet and Co.* (1927); *The Workers History of Great Britain* (1927); *Japhet and the Arkubs* (1928); *Short History of the British Empire* (1929); *Japhet and the Arkubs at Sea* (1929); *Japhet and Co. on Arkub Island* (1930); *The Japhet and Happy Book* (1931); *Socialism in Pictures and Figures* (1933); *Japhet and Happy Annual* (1933-51?); *Atlas of Great Events* (1934); *Atlas of European History* (1935); *The Japhet Holiday Book* (1936-40); *How Empires Grow* (1935); *The Opening Up of the World* (1936); *Atlas of Europe* (1937); *Plebs Atlas* (1938); *Atlas History of the Second World War* (1940-46); *Geography of the War* (1940); *Outline of Political Geography* (1942); *Youth Service in an English County* (1945); *Atlas of the USSR* (1945); *Land of the Soviets* (1946); *Search for Peace* (1949); *The Japhet and Happy Painting Book* (1949); and *Atlas of Africa* (1960).

D.G.

HOSEMANN, THEODOR (1807-1875) German cartoonist, illustrator, painter and printmaker born in Brandenburg, Prussia (just west of Berlin), on September 24, 1807. The most complete published catalogue of Theodor Hosemann's works included over a hundred oils and watercolors and over five hundred graphics, of which about four hundred are illustrations for books, magazines and almanacs, about seventy-five are individual prints and about a hundred are commercial and occasional works (menus, greeting cards, calendars). Among this large production, humorous drawings are prominent.

Hosemann came from an old family that had furnished Prussia with many pastors and many soldiers. His father was an officer stationed in Brandenburg at the time of Theodor's birth. The boy spent an unsettled childhood because of the Napoleonic Wars. In 1816 the family, now impoverished, made their home in Düsseldorf. At the age of 12 Theodor began working in a lithographic printshop. He worked as a commercial artist from 1822 to 1828 and also studied at the Düsseldorf Academy under such masters as Peter von Cornelius and the younger Schadow. There he met the cartoonist Schrödter, who had followed Schadow down from Berlin. Hosemann maintained relations with the artistic circles of Düsseldorf even after he left that city and later contributed to the important art and humor magazine *Düsseldorfer Monatshefte*.

In 1828 the partners that Hosemann worked for, Arnz and Winckelmann, split up, and Hosemann accepted Winckelmann's offer to come along to Berlin and illustrate a line of children's books—a major innovation for Germany at that time. Once in Berlin, Hosemann also did work for such publishers as Meyer and Hofmann, Julius Springer and G. Reimer. Among the authors whose works he illustrated, aside from the many children's books he did, were Eugène Sue (very famous pictures for *The Mysteries of Paris*), E.T.A. Hoffmann and "Munchausen." A great deal of work was also done for clubs and private festivities.

Last but not least, there was the publishing firm of Gropius, which commissioned numerous witty lithographs about Berlin everday life of the same sort that the elder Schadow and Dörbeck did. It is this aspect of Hosemann's production that is best remembered and most often reproduced today, and that was later of the greatest importance to his pupil Heinrich Zille. Hosemann became known as "the Gavarni of Berlin." Besides the individual prints, his albums and books in this area included *Buntes Berlin* ("Colorful Berlin") and *Berlin Wie Es Ist—und Trinkt* ("Berlin As It Is—and Drinks," with a pun on *isst*, "eats"), with text by the famous humorist Adolf Glassbrenner.

Hosemann began painting about 1840. He continued working until his death in Berlin on October 15, 1875, but his style did not materially develop after 1840. In 1857 he began teaching at the Berlin Academy and became a member in 1860.

S.A.

HOWIE, ROBERT LANGFORD (1933-   ) American cartoonist born in Jackson, Mississippi, on April 8, 1933. Bob Howie was educated in Jackson public schools and attended the University of Southern Mississippi and Tulane University, from which he was graduated in 1955 with a degree in journalism.

While in high school, Howie contributed sports cartoons to the *Jackson Clarion-Ledger,* and in college to the *New Orleans Item.* Since 1955 he has been the sports and editorial cartoonist for the *Jackson Daily News.* His early influences were Karl Hubenthal, L.D. Warren and Willard Mullin; the conservative-Democratic cartoonist has won three Freedoms Foundation awards.

His ideas are strongly Southern and forthright; although he draws a number of general-theme editorial cartoons, his political subjects are biting. His style is a stiff, uncluttered brush rendering with crayon shading.

R.M.

HUARD, CHARLES (1875-1965) French cartoonist, illustrator and etcher born in Paris, France, in 1875. Charles Huard studied at the Ecole des Beaux-Arts in Paris for one year. He contributed drawings satirizing the foibles of Parisian life and the vanities of provincials to many French and foreign humor journals, especially *Le Rire, Le Journal Amusant, La Baïonnette, Scribner's Magazine* and *Punch.* Some of these cartoons were published as albums, the most important and amusing being *Paris, Province, Etranger* ("Paris, Provinces, Abroad," 1906). Huard also traveled extensively in Europe and the United States,

"ꓘOKTOꓤ KISSINGEꓤ, I PꓤƎSUMƎ?"

Solution to Nothing

Karl Hubenthal. © *Los Angeles Examiner.*

bringing back a series of sketches on New York (1906), Berlin (1907), London (1908), etc. In addition, he illustrated many of the important books of the 19th and early 20th centuries: Clemenceau's *Figures de Vendée* ("Vendean Figures," 1903), Flaubert's *Bouvard and Pécuchet* (1904) and Balzac's *The Human Comedy* (1912-40), Huard's best work. Finally, his impressionist etchings, although they do not have the satirical bite of his cartoons, present interesting country street scenes set mainly in Normandy (124 on the small fishing port of Granville alone). They were exhibited in 1915 at the Panama-Pacific International Exposition in San Francisco, California.

Charles Huard was a strong draftsman who very ably used the graphic contrast between slender men all in black and fat women all in white, between well-delineated figures and bare background outlines. He died near Dijon on March 30, 1965, at the age of 90.

P.H.

HUBENTHAL, KARL (1917-   ) American political cartoonist, illustrator and sports cartoonist born in Beemer, Nebraska, on May 1, 1917. Karl Hubenthal was raised in California, graduating from Hollywood High School and Chouinard Art School in Los Angeles. Early in his artistic career Hubenthal worked with George Herriman, Will Gould and Willard Mullin, each of whom influenced his development. His first job was with the art department of the *Los Angeles Herald-Express* from 1935 until his induction

John Hubley, "Of Stars and Men." © Hubley Studio.

into the Marines in 1942. During the war he was on the staff of *Leatherneck* magazine.

In 1945 Hubenthal achieved his art-school goal of being a successful advertising artist and commercial illustrator; he worked in both New York and Los Angeles. But in 1949 William Randolph Hearst, in the twilight of a long career of discovering and developing cartoon talent, recognized some of Hubenthal's commercial work and remembered his cartoons on the old *Herald-Express*. Hubenthal became the sports cartoonist for the *Los Angeles Examiner* until 1955 and has been chief editorial and political cartoonist with the *Examiner*—later the *Herald-Examiner*—since then.

A Republican, Hubenthal has won a roomful of awards, including the National Headliners award, the Helms Foundation medal for sports, 21 Freedoms Foundation awards, 3 National Cartoonists Society Best Editorial Cartoonist awards, one NCS sports cartoon award and others. He was on the board of governors of the NCS and is a past president of both the Society of Illustrators and the Association of American Editorial Cartoonists.

Hubenthal's cartoons display amazing command of composition, anatomy and his media—brush and crayon or toned shading. His work is handsome and easy to look at; Hubenthal can make a hard-hitting point or elicit a chuckle with equal ease. His activities take him beyond the daily political cartoon; he continues to do commercial art and still draws occasional sports cartoons after a ten-year stint for the *St. Louis Sporting News*.

R.M.

HUBLEY, JOHN (1914-1977) American cartoonist and producer born in Marlette, Wisconsin, in 1914. A graduate of the Art Center of Los Angeles, John Hubley started his cartooning career with Walt Disney in 1934. Working his way up from cel painter and in-betweener, he rose to become an art director on *Pinocchio* (1940), the "Rite of Spring" segment of *Fantasia* (1940) and *Bambi* (1941). That same year Hubley's career with Disney came to an end in the aftermath of the celebrated animators' strike.

Hubley worked on several army cartoons during World War II (including the famous *Flathatting* for the U.S. Navy in 1945) and was one of the founders of United Productions of America (UPA) that same year.

As a director at UPA he was responsible for some of the most acclaimed cartoon films of the postwar era, such as *Robin Hoodlum* (1948), *The Magic Fluke* and *Punchy de Leon* (both 1949) and *Rooty Toot Toot* (1952). He also directed some of the more memorable *Mr. Magoo* cartoons, including the first one, "Ragtime Bear," in 1949.

Hubley left UPA in 1953, and in 1955 he founded his own company in collaboration with his wife, Faith, a former film editor and script supervisor; it was called Storyboard, Inc. Working closely with his family (his children have often contributed to story lines and have voiced some of the characters), Hubley produced *Adventures of an Asterisk* in 1956, followed by *The Tender Game, Harlem Wednesday* and *A Date with Dizzy* (all 1958). These were gentle, cheerful works, as were *Seven Lively Arts* (1959) and the Oscar-winning *Moonbird*, as well as *Children of the Sun*, produced for UNICEF. It is, however, with his later, less rosy works that Hubley gained worldwide fame and recognition. Most notable among these are *The Hole*, a story about a nuclear holocaust, and the Oscar-winner of 1962; the military fable *The Hat* (1963); and the 1971 *Eggs*. Hubley occasionally went back to his earlier, gayer mood, as with the delightful *Of Stars and Men* (1963), the swinging *Herb Alpert and the Tijuana Brass* (1966 Academy Award winner), and the whimsical *Windy Day* (1968).

Hubley also directed many commercials. His last completed film was a 1976 television special, *Everybody Rides the Carousel*, based on the works of psychoanalyst Erik H. Erikson. John Hubley died shortly thereafter, on February 21, 1977, during heart surgery at the Yale-New Haven Hospital. At the time of his death he had been working on an animated version of Garry Trudeau's *Doonesbury*; the film was completed by his wife and aired on television in November 1977.

John Hubley stands as one of the greats of cartoon animation. His work is personal, original and highly innovative. Many articles have been written about Hubley and his films, and he was the recipient of countless honors. He was nominated for an Academy Award no fewer than eleven times, and he won on three different occasions.

M.H.

HUDON, NORMAND (1929-   ) French-Canadian cartoonist, painter and television personality born in Montreal, Quebec, on June 5, 1929. After finishing high school in 1947, Normand Hudon attended the Montreal School of Fine Arts. While still in school, he contributed illustrations to several newspapers (*La Presse* as early as 1945, *La Patrie* and *Le Petit Journal* in 1948-49). In 1949 Hudon left for Paris, where he briefly studied art and drawing with Fernand Léger. Back in Montreal in 1951, he succeeded the following year to Robert La Palme's position as editorial cartoonist for *Le Devoir*, at the same time collaborating on the political weekly *L'Autorité du Peuple*. When La Palme, also back from Paris, reclaimed his cartooning job later in 1952, Hudon embarked on a television career that eventually made him famous.

The decade between 1955 and 1965 proved to be highly productive for Hudon. He held a very successful showing of his cartoons in 1955 and in 1958 mounted a one-man show of his paintings that met with critical praise as well as public acclaim. He also did two murals for Expo '67, as well as many posters. During this period

Hudon was omnipresent in the Montreal press, as a political cartoonist upon his return to *Le Devoir* in 1959 and as a social caricaturist. He also published a number of his cartoons in book form: *J'Ai Mauvaise Mine* ("I'm Not Looking Well," gag cartoons, 1954), *La Tête la Première* ("Head First," caricatures, 1958), *A la Potence* ("To the Gallows," political cartoons, 1961), *Un Bill 60 du Tonnerre* ("A Dynamite Bill 60," 1964) and *Parlez-Moi d'Humour* (1965).

Hudon's importance as a political cartoonist is best perceived in *A la Potence*. This collection reproduces all his cartoons for *Le Devoir*, including those that were censored. With drawings of extreme simplicity and fierce partisanship, Hudon attacked Maurice Duplessis, then prime minister of Quebec, whom he pictured either as a ravenous wolf or as a sick old man sunk in an armchair, on the back of which a vulture was perched. Hudon is regarded today, along with René Lévesque—who was then a journalist—as one of the engineers of the "quiet revolution," the political awakening of Quebec that started in 1960. In this respect Hudon's work for *Le Devoir* may be more historically significant than the cartoons he has been publishing regularly in the mass-circulation daily *La Presse* ever since 1961.

S.J.

HUEMER, RICHARD (1898-) American animator born in Brooklyn, New York, on January 2, 1898. Dick Huemer went to school in Brooklyn and the Bronx and developed an early love for drawing. After graduating from high school in 1915, he attended the Art Students League in New York City, studying with George Bridgman for about a year. He also contributed cartoons to *Judge*.

Huemer started in the animation field in 1916 as an animator on the *Mutt and Jeff* cartoons. In the early 1920s he joined Max and Dave Fleischer and soon became their top animator. At the Fleischer studios, Huemer worked on many of the *Out of the Inkwell* and *Ko-Ko the Clown* cartoons and created the character Bimbo the dog.

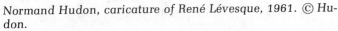
Normand Hudon, caricature of René Lévesque, 1961. © Hudon.

Alberto Huici. © Ja-Ja.

He left the studio in 1928 and briefly drew a newspaper strip, *Good Time Guy*, which was syndicated by the Metropolitan Newspaper Service and lasted for about a year. Like so many other East Coast cartoonists, Huemer then left for California, where he joined the animation staff of Charles Mintz in 1930, directing many of the *Scrappy* and *Toby the Pup* cartoons. In 1933 he moved over to the Disney studio, where he did animation work on a number of *Silly Symphonies* (*Lullaby Land, The Tortoise and the Hare, The Wise Little Hen*, etc.) and *Mickey Mouse* cartoons (most notably "The Band Concert").

Huemer stopped doing actual animation work in 1938 ("I'd really had it," he declared simply in a 1969 interview). After directing a couple of shorts, he found his niche as a story director, working on many of the studio's most ambitious projects (*Fantasia, Dumbo, Saludos Amigos, Make Mine Music, Alice in Wonderland*). During World War II he wrote many of the instruction and propaganda shorts produced by the studio. After a short stint in the early 1950s as an independent producer, Huemer went back to Disney in 1953, working on the Oscar-winning *Toot, Whistle, Plunk and Boom*. He also later collaborated on many of Disney's television programs. He is now retired but occasionally acts as a consultant on animated film productions and animated cartoon retrospectives.

M.H.

HUICI, ALBERTO (1929-) Mexican cartoonist born in Mexico City on March 10, 1929. Alberto Huici exhibited a love of drawing at an early age, and he sold his first cartoon in 1945, while still going to school. From then on he worked as a freelancer, contributing a number of cartoons to various Mexican newspapers and publications.

In 1952 Huici went to Los Angeles and tried to break into the U.S. market. While submitting contributions to various magazines (most of which sent back rejection slips), he worked as gas station attendant, dishwasher and garbage collector in order to support himself. Coming to New York in 1954, Huici again was turned down more often than not, and he went back to Mexico City the following year. With the experience he had acquired in the United States, he soon rose to the top of his profession, having his gag cartoons regularly published in the humor magazine *Ja-Ja*, and his political cartoons distributed by Editorial Excelsior. He also occasionally contributes cartoons to Los Angeles and New York publications.

Huici's style is simple, almost stark, with weird characters cavorting in strange surroundings. His humor is mostly visual, and he uses captions sparingly. His cartoons have earned awards in the United States, Europe, and Central and South America, as well as in his native Mexico.

M.H.

HUMAN COOK BOOK, THE (U.S.) One of James Montgomery Flagg's last magazine cartoon series before he engaged in full-time cover and illustration work, *The Human Cook Book* closely followed in format his earlier series. It featured tableaux of characters with exaggerated heads and had humorous rhymes underneath; this series, which began in *Life* on February 11, 1911, and continued through 28 treatments, proved to be among Flagg's cleverest work.

In the series Flagg poked satirically at the pretensions of individual types and professions. His witty and quite wise observations on human nature and sham were all executed in the form of kitchen recipes, and Chef Flagg served up a consistently engaging fare. Typical of the subjects are two captions: a Sweetheart—"Take a Peach and remove both her parents / Add a suggestion of Dough / Garnish with bon-bons and flowers / And turn the gas rather low"; and the Actor—"To one slice of Ham add assortment of rolls / Steep the head in mash notes till it swells / Garnish with onions, tomatoes and beets / Or with eggs—from afar—in the shells."

Other targets included the Straphanger, the Policeman, the Editor, the Orchestra Leader, the Telephone Operator, the Vaudevillian, the Chauffeur and the Suffragette. The cartoons ran two or three to an issue and were unfortunately not collected in book form as were other series from earlier in the decade.

R.M.

HUMBERT, ALBERT (1835-1886) French cartoonist and illustrator born in eastern France on February 24, 1835. After an unsuccessful attempt at painting, Albert Humbert turned to full-time cartooning and collaborated on the most important satirical papers of the second half of the 19th century: *La Lune, Le Journal Amusant, L'Eclipse*, etc. In 1868, he launched his own humor and satirical journal, the antimilitarist and anticlerical *La Lanterne de Boquillon* (first titled *Le Reverbère de Deux Sous*), which became immediately popular and ran for 18 years (1868-86).

Humbert also wrote and illustrated (sometimes under the pen name "Onésime Boquillon") novels narrating the endless vicissitudes faced by the character he had created, a simple, average Frenchman portrayed in various life situations. The most noteworthy of these are *Le Plébiscite de Boquillon* ("Boquillon's Plebiscite," 1870), *L'Art de Ne Pas Payer Ses Dettes* ("The Art of Not Paying One's Debts," 1874), *Vie et Aventures d'Onésime Boquillon* ("The Life and Adventures of Onésime Boquillon," 1876) and *Lettre du Soldat Onésime Boquillon* ("Letter from Private Onésime Boquillon," 1877). In addition, he was the author of non-Boquillon comic novels and of several comedies (written with his brother).

He died in Paris in 1886.

P.H.

HUMORS OF HISTORY (G.B.) "History," says the learned Herr Niemand, "is the consolidation of doubtful traditions into undoubted facts. Such are the histories of dry-as-dust historians; but Mr. Moreland, in his pictorial past, is on surer ground. All his events are founded on fact, and all his details are stranger than fiction." This excerpt from the preface to one of the many collected editions of *Humors of History* indicates the style of Arthur Moreland's once-famous, long-forgotten series: classic incidents of history brought up to date and given an anachronistic topical twist.

Beginning with the cartoon entitled "Ages, B.C.: Prehistoric London" (depicting dinosaurs snorting on the banks of the Fleet River at Blackfriars "where now L.C.C. Tramcars attempt to arrive and depart") and concluding with "The Present Day" ("remarkable for great activity in financial circles"—a cigar-puffing City gent outside the offices of the Brique d'Or Syndicate), *Humors of History* was perhaps the first regular "series cartoon" in British newspapers. It began in the *Morning Leader* in 1898 and wound up in the *Daily News* some 160 cartoons later. There were many paperback and hardback editions of the series, including one in full color (1905).

Of the artist, Arthur Moreland, little is known save that to judge from his book list, he continued to work as an illustrator into the thirties.

Books: *Humors of History* (1898, 1903, 1905, 1913, 1915, 1918, 1920, 1921, 1923); *Gentle Golfer* (1905); *History of the Hun* (1917); *The Comic History of Sport* (1924); *More Humours of History* (1925); *The Difficulties of Dr. Daguerre* (1927); *Dickens in London* (1928); *Lays from Lancashire* (1930); and *Dickens Landmarks in London* (1931).

D.G.

HUNGERFORD, CYRUS COTTON (ca. 1890-) American cartoonist born in Manilla, Indiana, around 1890. Cy Hungerford began his cartooning career for the *Wheeling* (W. Va.) *Register* in 1907. In 1912 he switched to the *Pittsburgh* (Pa.) *Sun*, where he claims the engraving method was still chalk-plate (he was succeeded on the *Register* by Terry Gilkison).

Between 1915 and 1926, Hungerford drew *Snoodles*, a syndicated comic strip for kids. Warm, sympathetic and zany—akin to Payne's *S'Matter, Pop?*—the strip was a minor classic and a personal favorite of colleague John McCutcheon, who nicknamed his son Shaw (now an editorial cartoonist) after the title character. In 1927

Hungerford switched from the *Sun* to the *Pittsburgh Post-Gazette*, where he drew editorial cartoons for an incredible 50 years, until his retirement in 1977. He traveled abroad as a reporter-cartoonist in 1923, 1937, 1947, 1948 and 1953, and he received a National Headliners award in 1947 and a Freedoms Foundation award in 1953.

Hungerford's style hardly varied at all from the first day of his career to the last. He worked in simple, bold pen and brush lines, never used shading, and relied on streamlined caricature rather than gross exaggeration. A pleasant, uncluttered atmosphere and a genial outlook pervaded every Hungerford cartoon. He was, needless to say, a Pittsburgh institution.

R.M.

HURD, EARL (ca. 1880-ca. 1950) American animator born around 1880. Earl Hurd is one of the most important figures in early animation, and possibly the most shadowy. Very little is known of his background before he burst onto the animation scene in 1913, developing with J.R. Bray the process of drawing on celluloid.

In 1914 Bray and Hurd formalized their partnership and formed the Bray-Hurd Processing Company, which lasted into the 1920s. In 1915 Hurd created his cartoon series *Bobby Bumps*, which was released through Bray. On this series he honed his animation skills to a fine point and brought out some of the best-crafted cartoons up to that time. In 1923 Hurd left Bray and went into independent production, setting up Earl Hurd Productions. Under the overall name Pen and Ink Vaudeville, he made such cartoons as *Artist's Model, Hoboken Nightingale, Boneyard Blues, Two Cats and a Bird* and *He Who Gets Socked*, as well as a few *Bobby Bumps* cartoons; he also seems to have produced several live-action comedy shorts. At any rate, he was not successful, and his studio closed down in 1925.

After an absence of almost ten years, Hurd surfaced again in the mid-1930s at the studio of Charles Mintz before going on, like so many others, to Walt Disney. At Disney he worked on a number of shorts and received credits for story adaptation on *Snow White* and as a character designer on the "Dance of the Hours" segment of *Fantasia*. Hurd left the Disney studio in the late 1940s and is reported to have died on the West Coast in the 1950s.

Earl Hurd was not only a technical innovator (as Dick Huemer put it, he "invented things") but also a master of the art of animation. It is to be hoped that more information will come to light as his achievements are rediscovered.

M.H.

HURD, JUSTIN (1912-   ) American cartoonist and publisher born in Cleveland, Ohio, on November 12, 1912. Justin ("Jud") Hurd showed a love of and talent for drawing at an early age, but he graduated from Western Reserve University in 1934 with a degree in economics. During his college years, however, he was the art editor of the college magazine, *The Red Cat*, to which he contributed numerous cartoons. After a year of classes at the Chicago Academy of Fine Arts, Hurd got his first professional job, as an in-betweener, at the Charles Mintz animation studio (1935-36). For two years (1936-38) Hurd drew a feature about movie celebrities, *Just Hurd in Hollywood*, for the Central Press Association, but he felt homesick in Los Angeles and returned to Cleveland and

Jud Hurd, "Ticker Toons." © United Feature Syndicate.

a job in the Newspaper Enterprise Association's art department drawing weekly political cartoons (Herblock was doing the dailies during that same time).

Hurd spent four years with the Signal Intelligence Section of the U.S. Army in World War II; his duties included the drawing of a daily panel, *Crypto Chris*, about the pitfalls of operating codes and ciphers. Demobilized in 1946, Hurd opened an industrial art studio in Cleveland and ran it until 1959, when he decided to move east. In 1959 he also started *Ticker Toons*, a daily financial panel that he first syndicated himself before United Feature Syndicate picked it up (it ran until 1969). In collaboration with Michael Petti, M.D., he created a medical panel in 1961, *Health Capsules*, also for United Feature.

Jud Hurd is best known, however, for his founding and editing of *Cartoonist Profiles*, a unique professional magazine exclusively devoted to comics and cartoons. Since its first appearance in 1969, the publication has featured innumerable articles, vignettes and reminiscences about all aspects of cartooning, thus providing an invaluable record for scholars and students in the field of graphic art.

M.H.

HURD, NATHANIEL (1730-1777) American cartoonist and silversmith born in Boston, Massachusetts, on February 13, 1730. One of the first American cartoonists and visual propagandists, Nathaniel Hurd was in the Paul Revere school—a metalsmith who dabbled in cartooning and caricaturing. He was trained by his father to engrave on silver and gold; he experimented with engraving on copper—which later became a standard medium—and mainly confined himself to working on bookplates. Among Hurd's most famous drawings was an editoral cartoon produced as a handbill, dealing with the subject of counterfeiters.

Hurd, whose portrait by John Singleton Copley hangs in the Cleveland Museum of Art, died on December 17, 1777.

R.M.

HYDE, WILLIAM HENRY (1858-1943) American cartoonist and painter born in New York City on January 29, 1858. W.H. Hyde graduated from Columbia in 1877 with an A.B. degree and studied painting in Paris with Boulanger, Lefebvre, Doucet and Harrison. His cartoons began appearing in the earliest issues of *Life* in 1883 (he was an exception to the Harvard corps at work there) and continued into the 1890s. His pen-and-ink work was among the smartest to appear in the weekly's pages—especially in the awkward early years—and was marked by supple lines, confident crosshatch shading and a reserved, dignified sense of composition. His subject was almost always society folk.

A member of the National Academy, Hyde died in Albany, New York, on February 7, 1943.

R.M.

Clodhoppers: "Good-for-nothings! On my rye straw!"

Henri-Gabriel Ibels, 1901.

Ii

IBAÑEZ, FRANCISCO (1935-   ) Spanish cartoonist born near Madrid, Spain, in 1935. Francisco Ibañez never finished his high school studies but went to work as a clerk in a Madrid bank in the early 1950s. He is a self-taught artist, and his love of drawing led him to send contributions to the various Spanish magazines of the day. His first cartoons were published in the humor magazine *La Risa* in 1954. Ibañez's work was a sharp contrast to the sorry state of Spanish cartooning during the Franco regime. His drawings were crisp and neat, and his humor was brisk and cheerful, marking him as an obvious disciple of the classic cartoonists of Spain. He was also a keen observer with an eye for the telling line or detail.

In 1957 Ibañez joined the Editorial Brughera publishing house and scored a hit the next year with an original comic strip, *Mortadelo y Filemón*, about a pair of outrageous private eyes; the strip became the most successful Spanish comic feature of the 1960s. The artist has been in such demand since then that he has a tendency to repeat himself, with the same stories and situations cropping up again and again. Ibañez, how-

ever, keeps his cartoons filled with the same crazy dynamism, and it can be said that he is a baroque artist who has been able to keep up with the realities of his time, always at full speed.

J.M.

IBELS, HENRI-GABRIEL (1867-1936) French cartoonist, painter and writer born in Paris, France, on November 30, 1867. Henri-Gabriel Ibels was largely self-taught and studied art mainly from nature. He was noted, from the age of 17, for the freshness and spontaneity of his landscape paintings. He exhibited widely, and in 1893 he coauthored with Toulouse-Lautrec an album of lithographs, *Le Café-Concert.*

Ibels is best remembered today as a political and editorial cartoonist. In 1899 he founded a short-lived magazine, *Le Sifflet*, in which he expressed through his drawings his strong sense of outrage at the injustice meted out to Captain Dreyfus in the course of what has been called "the Dreyfus affair." After his magazine folded, Ibels went to work for various satirical magazines, notably for *L'Assiette au Beurre*, in which his cartoons appeared regularly from the first issue (1901) until 1910. Ibels's drawings, full of verve, often undercut his sometimes bitter captions.

After World War I Ibels devoted himself mainly to painting and lithographing. He taught art in a number of Paris schools and had several of his plays produced on the stage. He was also active in lobbying for artists' rights. Ibels died in February 1936; during his lifetime he had received many honors, including the Legion of Honor, bestowed upon him in 1913.

M.H.

IF THEY SHOULD COME BACK TO EARTH (U.S.) Winsor McCay, who had drawn a series of strong anti-imperialist cartoons for *Life* following the Spanish-American War, returned in 1900 to do a series that, while perhaps not wholly original, was certainly the first strong link in a chain of similar themes explored by such artists as Otho Cushing, Harry Grant Dart, Charles Forbell and R.B. Fuller through the late 1920s.

If They Should Come Back to Earth featured historical figures in modern settings. The series began in the issue of September 20, 1900, and ran through November 8 of the same year. The large single-panel cartoons included Eve shopping for clothes, Ben Franklin besieged by newsboys, Nero watching firemen, Meissonier crowded by photographers, William Penn at a prizefight, Sir Walter Raleigh among tobacco fiends, Shakespeare nosed out by the Theatrical Syndicate and James Watt contemplating a horizon of smokestacks.

The cartoons were all executed in wash and typically were crowded with figures and architectural fancies. An important series that has gone unrecorded by McCay scholars, the cartoons were signed "Winsor Mc," as was most of his work for *Life*. This cartoon series was evidently submitted by mail from Cincinnati, and it preceded by more than two years his seminal newspaper cartoon series *Tales of the Jungle Imps by Felix Fiddle*, drawn for the *Cincinnati Commercial Tribune* beginning on January 18, 1903.

R.M.

ILLE, EDUARD (1823-1900) German cartoonist, illustrator, painter and writer born in Munich, Bavaria, on May 17, 1823. In 1842, Eduard Ille entered the Munich Academy, where he studied under the major painters Schnorr von Carolsfeld and Moritz von Schwind (himself a humorous artist on occasion). It became clear that Ille would never be a master of the grandiose religious painting style then so much in demand, and he turned to illustration in the 1850s. Among the magazines to which he contributed were *Punsch* (edited by M. Schleich) and the *Illustrirte Zeitung* (edited by J.J. Weber). He also did drawings for fairy-tale writer Ludwig Bechstein's 1853 volume *Deutsches Sagenbuch* ("Book of German Legends").

Eventually Ille was drawn into the orbit of Munich's principal publishers of humorous and popular art, Braun and Schneider. First he worked for their *Hauschronik*, then for their *Münchener Bilderbogen* (with a total contribution of some sixty items) and at last for their flagship publication, the celebrated *Fliegende Blätter*. In 1863 Ille became one of the editors, playing a big part in the magazine's continuing success and remaining with it until his death.

Largely because of his thorough academic training, Ille was a master of historical styles; it was he who illustrated the *Fliegende Blätter* poems (by L. Eichrodt) that gave the period of German cultural history from about 1815 to 1848 its lasting designation, "Biedermeier." With uncanny skill (and, no doubt, great personal satisfaction) he parodied the style of various 19th-century academic painters—not only his own teachers, Schnorr and Schwind, but also Peter von Cornelius, Kaulbach, Overbeck and Piloty. In another genre, Ille produced drawings of humanized animals that recalled those of the French artist Grandville.

Among Ille's separately published volumes were several children's books (illustrations of Grimm tales and of his own stories, books with movable figures and so on). He also continued to illustrate serious works and wrote poems, poetic dramas and opera librettos. Other artistic activities included puppet designs and two projects for the eccentric king Ludwig II of Bavaria: a watercolor cycle on German legend and history, and in the 1870s, wall paintings (on cloth)—about the lives of the poets Walther von der Vogelweide and Hans Sachs—for the king's dressing room in the castle of Neuschwanstein.

Ille died in Munich on December 17, 1900.

S.A.

ILLINGWORTH, LESLIE GILBERT (1902-   ) British newspaper cartoonist, humorous artist and book illustrator born in Barry, South Wales, in 1902. Leslie Illingworth had a Yorkshire father and a Scottish

"I'm the Guy." © Rube Goldberg.

mother: this perhaps explains why his artwork is so "typically" British! He left school in Cardiff with a scholarship to the Royal College of Art but gave up his studies after six months to become a cartoonist for the provincial daily the *Western Mail* in 1920. Illingworth was 18 years old, and his weekly wage was £6. In 1926, his first humorous drawing was published in *Punch*, and in 1927, after touring the United States, he returned home to become a freelance cartoonist.

His drawings, including excellent full-color, full-page cartoons in *Punch Almanac* and the "summer specials," soon established him as a top cartoonist, although he supplemented his humor work by illustrating magazine stories, articles and books. In 1939, he won the coveted position of *Daily Mail* cartoonist after the retirement of Percy ("Poy") Fearon, and he held this exacting job through the reigns of no fewer than nine editors! He retired from the *Mail* in 1968 but has been busy ever since. Currently he is drawing a weekly cartoon for the Sunday paper *News of the World*.

When Illingworth (as he always signs his drawings) was asked to describe his work, he replied that it gave people "symbols to think with." In fact, Illingworth broke away from the old-style symbolic cartoons. Although he physically inherited the symbol technique when substituting for, then taking over from, Sir Bernard Partridge in *Punch* (1945), his sheer excellence of drawing and draftsmanship enabled him to do without the labels and symbols beloved by the earlier cartoonists.

D.G.

IMAGE, JEAN
See Hajdu, Emeric.

IMPRESSIONS BY ONE WHO HAS NEVER BEEN THERE (U.S.) In the late 1910s and early 1920s Ellison Hoover became a favorite cartoonist of *Life's* editors, and presumably of its readers. He was a cartoonist who constantly mocked newspaper comics, yet he was destined to draw *Mr. and Mrs.* after Clare Briggs's death; he strove to emulate the compositions of Rea Irvin and Gluyas Williams but was for the most part doomed to produce empty, unbalanced full-page line drawings. His *Intimate Glimpses of American Generals of Industry*, for instance, was not original; neither was Gluyas Williams's *Industrial Crises*, which was contemporaneous but far superior. If Hoover was a deficient wit, he was nevertheless respected as an advocate—Benchley was one who lauded him as a satirist.

In *Impressions by One Who Has Never Been There*, Hoover transcended his limitations and his frequent editorializing and produced a very funny series of double-page black-and-white cartoons for *Life*. Here was a travelogue by reputation, a Cook's tour of stereotypes. Hoover collected every chestnut and mistaken impression about famous cities and drew bird's-eye views of them, exercising a consistent disregard for geography, history and logic. Hence, New York had Cohan giving his regards to Broadway, a tiger inside Tammany Hall and a flat bush in Brooklyn; Dublin was full of Blarney stones, begobs and begorras and signs indicating a long way to Tipperary.

It was great fun and is still fresh reading today. Held worked a similar theme with his woodcut-style

maps, but not as well, which demonstrates that Hoover could indeed originate a successful format. Some of the cartoons in this series were collected in *Cartoons from Life* by Hoover, published by Simon and Schuster in 1925.

R.M.

I'M THE GUY (U.S.) One of Rube Goldberg's many intermittent continuing panel gag features, published daily in the 1910s as part of his nationally distributed *New York Evening Mail* sports page potpourri, *I'm the Guy* was a particularly memorable hit with Goldberg readers when it was introduced early in 1911. It ran for many months thereafter and appeared across the country in lapel-button reproductions by the tens of thousands. With no continuing feature characters, *I'm the Guy* was basically a one-line gag panel in which individuals of wildly differing appearance proclaimed to other startled individuals, at the rate of one per panel, that each was the guy who had made some fundamental contribution to a general term, as in the following examples (all considered hilarious at the time): "I'm the guy that put the germ in Germans"; "I'm the guy that put the saint in St. Louis"; "I'm the guy that put the gum in gumption"; "I'm the guy that put the ham in Hamburg"; "I'm the guy that put the wish in wishbone"; and so on.

The little feature caught on so much that a songwriter named Berg Grant wrote the lyrics to a 1912 song called "I'm the Guy" that was popular for over a year and was an early phonograph record hit. (Oddly, however, Grant's lyrics paid no attention to the structure of Goldberg's gag line and went their own way on the same theme—without any more wit or point, however.) Eventually dropped by Goldberg after a few years, *I'm the Guy* continued in word-of-mouth use for some time afterward on the same low-brow level as "twenty-three skidoo" and similar catchphrases of the imitative and unimaginative.

B.B.

INDEPENDENT NEW PARTY
See Tattooed Man, The.

INDOOR/OUTDOOR SPORTS (U.S.) As a diversion from his coverage of sports events in the *New York Journal*, Thomas Aloysius Dorgan ("Tad") conceived his *Indoor Sports* panel around 1910 and began discoursing with unmitigated glee on such unathletic pursuits as poker, crap shooting and betting on football scores. Later Tad added *Outdoor Sports* to his lineup of newspaper features, alternating the new panel with *Indoor Sports*. In the 1920s the two became almost indistinguishable in theme, as Tad had by that time moved away from sports into the field of social and psychological observation. Only the setting justified the use of either the "indoor" or "outdoor" label.

Tad's slice-of-life cartoons were quite amusing and often insightful. He joyously deflated the pretensions of small-town hucksters, would-be financiers and self-appointed experts. He had as fine an ear for language as he had an eye for observation, and the dialogue he put in the mouths of his bums, mountebanks and social climbers was accurate and excruciatingly funny. Tad also started the trend of having various matchstick figures cavort in a corner of the panel and comment (sometimes in song) on the action.

"Indoor Sports." © King Features Syndicate.

Tad died in 1929, but his *Indoor/Outdoor Sports* panel survived him for a long time in countless reprintings in the *Journal* and in newspapers across the country.

M.H.

INOUE, YŌSUKE (1931-) Japanese cartoonist and illustrator born in Akasaka, Tokyo, Japan, on March 7, 1931. After graduating from the Western art department of the Musashino Art University, Yōsuke Inoue joined the Dokuritsu Mangaha ("Independent Cartoonists Faction") in 1952 and actively contributed cartoons to its magazine, *Gamma*. When *Gamma* folded and the Dokuritsu Mangaha dissolved, Inoue sought other outlets and joined the now famous and influential Manga Shudan ("Cartoonists Group") in 1964. The same year, he began holding exhibitions of his paintings and cartoons, as he continues to do today. Exhibition titles include Eroticism (1966), Yōsuke Inoue (1969) and Nonsense (1974). In 1965 his *Kaiki Nonsense Manga Sakuhin* ("Strange Nonsense Cartoons") won the eleventh Bunshun award for cartoons, and in 1970 he received the fourth Tokyo Illustrators Club prize.

Yōsuke Inoue is often referred to as an avant-garde cartoonist, and the subjects he chooses indeed lend themselves to this description. Often they are nonsensical, Kafkaesque sketches like "Ippon Michi" ("One-way Street"), which appeared in the magazine *Bunshun Manga Dokuhon* in April 1967. It depicted two bored and tired-looking little men approaching each other from opposite directions on a narrow bridge and then actually walking through each other, much to their mutual surprise. Inoue is comfortable in nearly all media, working skillfully in oils, prints, or pen and ink, with terse, single-panel cartoons or multi-panel cartoons covering several pages. His simple, wiggly line sketches are often accompanied by a humorous narrative as surreal as the subject they treat, and they frequently have erotic overtones.

Among the books written by Inoue, *Sado no Tamago* ("Sado's Egg," 1963), *Hakorui Zukan* ("The Picture Book of Boxes," 1964) and *Inoue Yōsuke Tanpen Gekigashū* ("Yōsuke Inoue's Collection of Short Comics") are representative. He is also active as an illustrator of picture books such as *Dare ga Pai o Tabeni Kita* ("Who Came to Eat the Pie?"), and he formerly taught cartooning at the Tokyo Design College.

F.S.

INSPEKTOR MASKU (Yugoslavia) In 1959 Vatroslav Mimica wrote and directed, and Aleksandar Marks

"The Inspector Returns Home," from the "Inspektor Masku" series. © Zagreb Film.

PROFESSOR BUTTS TRIES TO FIX A LEAK IN THE BOILER AND WHEN HE IS RESCUED FROM DROWNING HE COUGHS UP AN IDEA FOR AN OUTBOARD MOTOR THAT REQUIRES NO FUEL. AS YOU REACH FOR ANCHOR, BUTTON (A) SNAPS LOOSE AND HITS SPIGOT (B) CAUSING BEER TO RUN INTO PAIL (C). WEIGHT PULLS CORD (D) FIRING SHOT GUN (E). REPORT FRIGHTENS SEA GULL (F) WHICH FLIES AWAY AND CAUSES ICE (G) TO LOWER IN FRONT OF FALSE TEETH (H). AS TEETH CHATTER FROM COLD THEY BITE CORD (I) IN HALF ALLOWING POINTED TOOL (J) TO DROP AND RIP BAG OF CORN (K). CORN FALLS INTO NET (L). WEIGHT CAUSES IT TO SNAP LATCH OPENING FLOOR OF CAGE (M) AND DROPPING DUCK INTO SHAFTS (N). AS DUCK (O) TRIES TO REACH CORN IT SWIMS AND CAUSES CANOE TO MOVE AHEAD. IF THE FALSE TEETH KEEP ON CHATTERING YOU CAN LET THEM CHEW YOUR GUM TO GIVE YOUR OWN JAWS A REST.

"The Inventions of Professor Lucifer G. Butts." © Rube Goldberg.

designed, a witty confection blending object and cartoon animation, *Inspektor Se Vratio Kući* ("The Inspector Comes Home"). Produced by the famed Zagreb Film studio, the cartoon, which depicted a day in the life of an inept police inspector, won first prize at Oberhausen. It proved so popular that it gave birth to *Inspektor Masku* ("Inspector Mask"), a series named for the hero, which started production in 1962.

In the series the inspector appeared in the guise of various objects in order to track down a clever band of crooks. There were chases, fights and various kinds of violence, but the attempt at emulating the fast pace and breathless action of American cartoons was not successful. *Inspektor Masku* was discontinued in 1963, after 13 entries in the series had been completed.

Virtually every hand at Zagreb Film worked on the series. Most notable were Boris Kolar ("Citizen IM-5"), Nikola Kostelać ("The Rape of Miss Universe") and Ivo Urbanić ("El Cactusito").

M.H.

INVENTIONS OF PROFESSOR LUCIFER G. BUTTS, THE (U.S.)
Rube Goldberg started drawing crazy and impractical "inventions" for the delight of his readers soon after he went to work as a cartoonist for the *New York Evening Mail* in 1907. These developed some time later into a regular feature whose complete title, *The Inventions of Professor Lucifer G. Butts*, was as ludicrous as the crackpot contraptions purportedly invented by Goldberg's alter ego, Professor Lucifer Gorgonzola Butts, A.K.

Professor Butts perfected such ingenious devices as a painless tooth-extractor, an automatic typewriter eraser, and a moth exterminator, all with a generous helping of pulleys, electric fans, bellows and sundry household items arrayed in the most bewildering system imaginable. In later years Goldberg averred that the inspiration for Professor Butts and his inventions had come to him during his college days at the University of California, but it is more likely that he was influenced, at least in part, by Clare Dwiggins's panel *School Days*.

The Inventions (which were later syndicated through King Features) ran for decades, until Goldberg finally tired of the feature in the mid-1930s. He revived it, however, in 1939 for the Register and Tribune Syndicate, which distributed it until 1948.

Of all Goldberg's creations, *The Inventions* is the one that most contributed to his fame. Even after he had abandoned drawing them on a regular basis, he continued to throw in an "invention" or two, usually on some burning issue of the time, for a magazine or on a TV program. The "inventions" also earned him an entry in the dictionary as an adjective (a "Rube Goldberg" contraption is synonymous with an implausibly complicated device).

M.H.

IRELAND, WILLIAM A. (1880-1935)
American cartoonist born in Chillicothe, Ohio, on January 8, 1880. Educated in public schools, Billy Ireland secured his first cartooning job with the *Chicago Daily News* in 1897. The next year he switched to the *Chicago News-Advertiser* and in 1899 returned to Columbus, Ohio, near his birthplace, to draw for the *Columbus Evening Dispatch*.

Ireland's style was highly cartoony in its appearance but technically very competent. He had a sure sense of composition and anatomy and drew with a self-confident hand. His shading was never overdone; economy of line was a watchword but not a fetish. Almost all of his political cartoons were partisan (he was a Democrat) but exceedingly good-natured. His neat, bold cartoons gave rise to a whole school, beginning with Carey Orr in Tennessee. When Orr moved to Chicago, the style lived on in him and his successors on the *Tribune*, Parrish and Holland.

Except perhaps for Joe Donahey of the *Cleveland Plain Dealer*, Ireland was the most democratic of American cartoonists. He stayed close to home up to the time of his death in 1935 and had no pretensions to greatness or fame. It is said that the *New York Herald-Tribune* offered him a blank check to draw in New York; he refused, saying, "My object isn't to break into New York—it is to break back to Chillicothe." The *Trib* settled for Ding Darling.

Ireland seldom left his part of Ohio; he was reprinted widely but not syndicated. His weekly full-page color collection of observations, *The Passing Show*, is remembered by many as a minor masterpiece. And one of his great contributions was the kindly advice and guidance he gave to local youngsters interested in cartooning, two of whom

Bill Ireland, "The Passing Show," 1932. © Columbia Journal-Dispatch.

were Noel Sickles and Milton Caniff, who revere Ireland's memory today. Generally, he is all but forgotten, and he deserves to be reprinted in a major collection.

R.M.

IRONIMUS
See Peichl, Gustav.

IRVIN, REA (1881-1972) American cartoonist and editor born in San Francisco, California, on August 26, 1881. Rea Irvin was educated at the Mark Hopkins Institute of Art and worked on the art staffs of several newspapers, including the *Honolulu Advertiser*, before becoming an actor in 1903. This career was short-lived, however, and Irvin moved to New York and began contributing to *Life* magazine. He soon became a major fixture there, doing covers and many interior cartoons, and his influence was widespread. It was a coup for Harold Ross in 1925 to lure Irvin to the fledgling *New Yorker*, where he served as art editor. In 1951, after the death of Ross, Irvin quarreled with the founder's successors and left the publication. He continued to paint and draw cartoons for his own outlets, attended functions of the Players and the Dutch Treat Club, and finally moved to the Virgin Islands, where he died at the age of 90 on May 28, 1972.

It is hard to fully appreciate Irvin's enormous impact on American cartooning. His simplified, posterlike drawings were almost revolutionary and inspired a generation of imitators. His composition was flawlessly attractive, and his figures, for all their animation and exaggeration, were anatomically sound. He used broad brushstrokes and flat shaded areas. For *Life* and *Collier's* he illustrated Wallace Irwin's *Letters of a Japanese Schoolboy*. He drew many series of full-pagers for *Life*, illustrated many books, created the cover design for the *New Yorker*, and helped shape that magazine's formidable approach to cartooning, certainly one of the major forces in American graphic arts.

R.M.

ISING, RUDOLPH (1903-) American animator born in Kansas City, Missouri, in 1903. Rudolph (or Rudolf) Ising went to work at the Kansas City Film Ad Company soon after graduating from high school. From 1921 to 1923 he helped Walt Disney in the production of his Laugh-O-Grams cartoons and joined Disney in Los Angeles in 1926. Ising was one of the first members of the Disney staff and worked on *Alice in Cartoonland* and later on *Oswald the Rabbit*. In 1928, in collaboration with Hugh Harman, he produced the *Oswald* cartoons for Charles Mintz, Disney's former distributor.

In 1929 Ising and Harman formed a partnership

"Sure, if it's dramin' I am, I'll niver touch anither drop, but if it's the real ting, I'd loike a big drink right now!"

Rea Irvin. © *Life.*

It's Against the Law

"It's Against the Law." © The Reader's Digest Association.

(Harman-Ising); they first produced cartoons for Leon Schlesinger for release through Warner Brothers, then became independent producers for MGM in 1933. The partners' best-known creation was *Bosko*, a series that continued throughout the 1930s. They also produced the Happy Harmonies cartoons for MGM. Their collaboration came to an end in 1938, when Harman and Ising became producers on the newly formed MGM animation unit (their friendship remained unaffected). Ising produced the 1940 *Milky Way*, the first animated short ever to break the Disney monopoly on Oscars. He also created the *Barney Bear* series, starting with "The Bear That Couldn't Sleep" (1939), and directed a number of entries in the series between 1939 and 1942.

Ising left MGM in 1942 (his last cartoon, *Bah Wilderness*, was released the following year) to join the Hal Roach studio, where he was in charge of animation and training films for the U.S. Air Force. After World War II Ising drifted out of the animation field and variously worked in advertising and industrial promotion. He now lives in retirement in the Los Angeles area, near his longtime associate Hugh Harman.

Ising's name is indissolubly tied to that of Harman; they made many memorable cartoons together. Like Harman, Ising was a remarkable animator and skilled designer. In addition to his Oscar, he received several other honors, including an exhibitors' award.

M.H.

IT'S AGAINST THE LAW (U.S.) Humorist Dick Hyman reportedly got his idea of collecting some of the ludicrous laws still on the books from an Alabama judge. Be that as it may, Hyman's first compilation of silly statutes appeared in the *New York Mirror* in 1933. A few months later it was picked up by Hearst's *American Magazine*, which ran it as a monthly cartoon panel drawn by Otto Soglow starting in 1934.

The feature was exactly what its title implied—a depiction of some of the more harebrained prohibitions spelled out by states and municipalities across the United States. "A Colorado law forbids the serv-

ing of food in a room used for any other purpose," one caption read, while Soglow's cartoon depicted a hotel servant lugging breakfast to a moustached gentleman taking a leisurely bath in his tub; "Gloversville, New York, prohibits women wrestlers appearing in the city," said another, under a cartoon of a brawny female about to throw her opponent over the ropes as two cops show up at ringside. The feature was funny not so much because of the captions, which became monotonous after awhile, as for the loony Soglow cartoons depicting befuddled humans and mixed-up animals in an endless and hilarious gallery of incongruities.

The feature folded along with the *American Magazine* in 1956. Some of the texts were later run as filler material (minus the cartoons) in the *Reader's Digest*. The Reader's Digest Association published an *It's Against the Law* booklet (this time adding some of Soglow's cartoons) in 1971, with great success.

M.H.

IVANOV, ALEKSANDR VASILYEVICH (1899-1959) Soviet animator and filmmaker born in eastern Russia on June 5, 1899. Aleksandr Ivanov studied at the Tambov Teachers Institute and then went on to attend the Tambov Art Studios. Upon graduation in 1921, he became a cartoonist for such satirical publications as *Gudak* and *Rabochaya Moskva*. In 1924, in collaboration with A. Bushkin, he produced the first Soviet animated cartoon, *Soviet Toys*, under the supervision of Dziga Vertov.

From the mid-1920s on, Ivanov became one of the Soviet Union's most distinguished animators. In 1927, in collaboration with H. Voinov, he made *The Cockroach*, a frightening allegory about a giant cockroach conquering the world. This was followed by a number of delightful films, mostly for children: *Vor* ("The Thief," 1935), *The Popular Favorite* (1937), *The Magic Flute* (an enchanting retelling of the Mozart opera, 1938) and *Okhotnik Fyodor* ("Fyodor the Hunter," 1939) are the most notable among his pre-World War II production. After turning out propaganda films during the war, Ivanov returned to entertainment animation with his 1947 fable *The Fox and the Thrush*. In 1948 he released two impressive works, *Kvartet* ("Quartet," a musical cartoon) and the sometimes bitter *Champion*. More films followed, usually on nature themes, and with an often somber outlook: *Zay i Chik*

Aleksandr Ivanov, "The Cockroach."

("Zay and Chick," 1952), *In the Depths of the Forest* (1954), *The Forest Story* (1956) and *The Sorceress* (1957).

Concurrently with his animation career, Ivanov was also a political cartoonist and poster designer of some repute. He received a number of awards for his films, including first prize at the 1958 Moscow Film Festival. Aleksandr Ivanov died in Moscow on March 13, 1959.

M.H.

Ivan Ivanov-Vano, "Tales of Czar Duranda."

IVANOV-VANO, IVAN PETROVICH (1900-   ) Soviet animator and filmmaker born in Moscow, Russia, on February 8, 1900. Ivan Ivanov-Vano graduated from the State Higher Art and Technical School in 1923, and he started his long and prolific career in animation the next year as an assistant director. In 1927 he directed his first film, *Senka the African*, the dream adventures of a little boy, followed by *Katok* ("The Skating Rink," 1929), an enchanting exercise in white line on black background in a manner reminiscent of Emile Cohl, *Black and White* (1932), *Tales of Czar Duranda* (1934) and *The Three Musketeers* (1938), to cite only his most notable achievements.

World War II interrupted Ivanov-Vano's career when, along with other Soviet moviemakers, he was called upon to produce propaganda films. In 1945 he went back to animation with the much-awarded *A Winter's Tale*. Since that time Ivanov-Vano has been turning out animated cartoons by the score, most of them screen versions of Russian classics and folktales, notably *The Little Hunchbacked Horse* (1948), *Wild Geese* (1950), *The Snow Maiden* (1952) and *Seasons of the Year* (1969). Of somewhat greater interest are his puppet film, *The Mechanical Flea* (1964), and especially a medium-length cartoon film, *The Battle of Kerzhenets* (1971), which received first prize at the 1972 Zagreb Festival.

In addition to his career as a filmmaker, Ivanov-Vano has taught since 1939 at the All-Union State Institute of Cinematography (as a full professor since 1952) and has written a number of books on the subject of animation. Ivanov-Vano was named a People's Artist in 1969 and has received a host of honors in Russia, including the coveted State Prize in 1970.

M.H.

IVEY, JAMES BURNETT (1925-   ) American editorial cartoonist born in Chattanooga, Tennessee, on April 19, 1925. Jim Ivey received his formal education at George Washington University and the University of Louisville, and his art training at the National Art School in Washington, D.C. (1948-50), as well as from the Landon Correspondence School.

Ivey started his cartooning career on the *Washington Star* (1950-53), moving from there to the *St. Petersburg (Fla.) Times* (1953-59) and the *San Francisco Examiner* (1959-66). After a short interlude as a freelance cartoonist, he joined the staff of the *Orlando Sentinel* in 1970, contributing many political and editorial cartoons, as well as a great number of topical graphic comments on local issues. In 1977 he went back to freelancing again. Ivey is also the author of a syndicated panel, *Thoughts of Man*, in which he illustrates in a woodcut style quotes from some of the famous men in history.

Jim Ivey's strong points are a humorous approach, a good sense of caricature, variety in the physical shapes of his cartoons (often in keeping with the particular theme) and a loose, modernistic line. In 1964 the *National Observer*, commenting on Ivey's work, said, "He's imaginative, always prowling for a fresh approach. His cartoons often appear without a caption, reflecting his belief that 'cartooning is a graphic and not a verbal art.'"

Jim Ivey is also a noted scholar of the cartoon field. In 1959 he was granted a Reid Fellowship to observe political cartooning in Europe: his conclusion that

Ignorance is less remote from the truth than prejudice.
—Denis Diderot

Jim Ivey. © Chicago Tribune-New York News Syndicate.

Ub Iwerks, "Summertime." © Celebrity Pictures.

European cartoonists were, in style and approach, far ahead of their colleagues in the United States was met with controversy but paved the way for radical changes in American cartooning. Ivey has written many articles for cartoon and comic art magazines, has been the editor of his own fanzine, *Cartoon*, and is now the coeditor of *Cartoonews*. He is also the founder and curator of the Cartoon Museum in Orlando.

M.H.

IWERKS, UBBE (1901-1971) American cartoonist and animator born in Kansas City on March 24, 1901. Ubbe ("Ub") Iwerks displayed an early talent for drawing and caricature. He dropped out of school to work at various odd jobs in commercial art shops in and around Kansas City; it was in one of these shops that he first met Walt Disney in 1920. An informal partnership developed between the two young men: they worked together again at the Kansas City Film Ad Company and, for a brief period, as independent producers in Kansas City. Later, after Disney had become established in Los Angeles, he sent for Ub Iwerks, and Iwerks joined his studio in 1926.

Iwerks's greatest contribution to the art of animation came the following year when he designed and developed the character of Mickey Mouse (his work on "Plane Crazy" was especially decisive). He also defined (and refined) the concept of the early *Silly Symphonies*. In 1930 a contractual dispute led Iwerks to leave Disney and strike out on his own. Setting up his own studio, he produced the enchanting *Flip the Frog* cartoons for Celebrity Pictures, which released them through MGM. These enjoyed moderate success, as did Iwerks's companion series, *Willie Whopper*, and a number of so-called "Comicolor Cartoons" based on popular stories (*Don Quixote, Aladdin and His Magic Lamp*, etc.).

In the mid and late 1930s Iwerks worked as an independent producer, turning out *Porky Pig* cartoons for Warner Brothers, *Color Rhapsodies* for Columbia, and a number of commercial cartoons. In 1940 Iwerks returned to the Disney studios and worked mostly in the technical and development departments. (His perfecting of the multiplane camera was his most notable achievement in this field.)

For over 25 years Iwerks thus lived in obscurity until he was suddenly "discovered" at the Montreal International Animation Festival in 1967 and found himself acclaimed as "the creator of Mickey Mouse." Many international awards and distinctions followed—a fitting, if belated, tribute to a man and an artist whose unique contributions to the art of animation put him on a par with the giants of the field.

Ub Iwerks died on July 8, 1971.

M.H.

Jj

JACKSON, RAYMOND (1927-   ) British cartoonist born in London, England, in 1927.

"Homo-electrical-sapiens Britannicus 1970" was the caption to a cartoon that almost closed the London *Evening Standard* for good. The picture was of a boneheaded British "bolshy" trade unionist, and the signature was "Jak." The cartoonist behind the pen name is Raymond Jackson, the son of a tailor. Jackson attended Clipstone Road School during World War II, then studied at Willesden School of Art before being called into the army. At first a driver, he transferred to the Education Corps, where he taught conscripts to paint. On demobilization he joined a publishing house art staff, where one of his jobs was retouching the pubic hairs on photographs for a naturist magazine called *Health and Strength*. Discharged when the magazine collapsed, he worked for awhile in an advertising agency, freelancing gag cartoons to *Lilliput* and *Punch*.

He applied to the London *Evening Standard* when they advertised for a visualizer and won the job of spot illustrator instead. He supplied thumbnail sketches to illustrate the television page. Then came a chance to draw a large cartoon for the Saturday edition, and finally, one year after the death of "Vicky" (Victor Weisz), the *Standard*'s famous cartoonist, he inherited the vacant space on the Diary Page. Jak has supplied a cartoon a day since, in a style not dissimilar to that of Carl Giles of the *Daily Express*: bold art, amusing characters, humorous ideas. In 1972, he signed a 20-year contract with the newspaper and is perhaps the highest paid cartoonist in Fleet Street. His motto: "Never explain, never complain." A collection, *Jak*, has appeared annually since 1968.

D.G.

JACOVITTI, BENITO (1923-   ) Italian cartoonist born in Termoli, in the Abruzze region of Italy, on March 19, 1923. When he was 16, Benito Jacovitti started drawing stories for *Il Vittorioso*, a Catholic children's weekly magazine. From that time until 1967, when *Il Vittorioso* closed down, he gave life to hundreds of different characters in scores of comic strips (for Jacovitti's career in the comics, see *The World Encyclopedia of Comics*, Chelsea House, 1976). His burlesque and parodistic talents found their best expression, however, in the single-panel cartoons and color pages he drew during the same period. In these outsized cartoons (some as big as an entire newspaper page), Jacovitti gave free rein to his volcanic fantasy: surrealistic, crazy vignettes and pointed satires, gigantic wives and diminutive husbands, black humor and ingenuous irony, all colliding, intertwining and becoming lost in an immense caricatural panorama of demented proportions.

Jacovitti also drew cartoons for a number of humor magazines (such as *Il Travaso*) and for daily newspapers (such as *Il Giornale d'Italia*, for which he has recently been commenting on the day's major events); but he has

"Your money or your life . . . um . . . um . . . I mean . . . tarinlalle-tarinlalla. . . . "

Benito Jacovitti. © *Jac.*

not been able to give to his editorial cartoons the biting and sometimes mean tone of other cartoonists. His best efforts in the cartooning field (although in a somewhat looser key) remain his large panels, particularly those he drew in the course of the 1960s.

C.S.

JAGUARIBE, SERGIO DE MAGALHÃES GOMES (1932-   ) Brazilian cartoonist born in Rio de Janeiro, Brazil, on February 29, 1932. Largely self-taught as an artist, Jaguar (as he is best known) saw his first cartoon published in *Manchete* in 1957. His career took off dramatically the next year, when he started contributing cartoons to the magazines *Pif-Paf*, *Revista da Semana*, *Senhor* and *Revista Civilização Brasileira*, as well as to the daily newspapers *Ultima Hora* and *Tribuna da Imprensa*. In the 1960s he started working for *Correio da Manhã* and *Pasquim*. Jaguar also collaborates regularly on the Swiss magazine *Graphis*.

Jaguar has received several awards, notably at the Bordighera and Montreal cartoon festivals. His cartoon anthology, *Atila, Você é Bárbaro* ("Attila, to Yell Is Barbaric"), was published in 1968. In 1960 he opened (along with the designers Glauco Rodrigues and Beatriz Feitler) an internationally renowned studio of commercial art, Studio G in Rio. He has a very striking graphic style, very modern in approach, with bold strokes and ambiguous lines. He also often utilizes collages and montages in his cartoons.

A.M.

JAK
See Jackson, Raymond.

"János Vitez." © Pannonia Film.

JÁNOS VITEZ (Hungary) In recent years every country, it seems, has tried to come up with at least one feature-length animated cartoon. *János Vitez* ("John the Hero") is Hungary's most notable entry in this category.

Based on Sandor Petöfi's epic tale, *Childe John*, the film was directed by Marcell Jankovics, produced by Pannonia Film in Budapest, and released in 1973 in commemoration of the 150th anniversary of Petöfi's birth. It tells of the tribulations of Jancsi, the orphan shepherd boy, and his sweetheart, Ileska, victimized by her vicious foster mother. Jancsi sets out to conquer the world, coming back as Childe John, the boy hero; fighting dragons and witches, he finally arrives on the Isle of the Fairies, where he is reunited with Ileska.

The story was handled with great fidelity to the original tale, without losing its dynamic thrust. The battle scenes were particularly well rendered by a team of animators that included József Nepp, Bela Ternovsky and Jankovics himself. The result was a pleasant, entertaining cartoon, well crafted and without stylistic surprises.

M.H.

JEFF
See Hook, Geoffrey Raynor.

JERRY THE TROUBLESOME TYKE (G.B.) "Jerry the Cardiff Film Star," the *South Wales Echo* proudly announced him in May 1925, and two months later, in July, *Jerry the Troublesome Tyke* made his cinematic debut. He appeared as the tail-end item in *Pathé Pictorial* number 382, in the position previously occupied by Felix the Cat. This British magazine film had lost the rights to the American animated animal after a dispute with Pat Sullivan, who wanted his films released as separate cartoons, not as serialized items in a compilation. The cartoon item had for years been a popular part of the *Pathé Pictorial*, and the Wardour Street company was delighted when a Welsh cinema projectionist sent them a reel of his homemade cartoons.

Sid Griffiths, a Cardiff man, was sent for and promptly commissioned to produce a regular series for the *Pictorial*. A dog was selected as hero, to contrast with the dispossessed cat, and the series ran for two years, with one adventure every other week. Typical titles were: *In and Out of Wembley* (a topical trip to the annual exhibition), *Treasure Island Travel*, *One Exciting Nightmare* and *Ten Little Jerry Boys*.

Griffiths was aided with the series by Brian White, ex-animator on the *Bonzo* series. After Jerry was discontinued, Griffiths and White remained in partnership, making cartoon filmlets for Superads (1929), including a sequence for use in a stage production starring Jack Hylton and his band, called *Tiptoe Through the Tulips* (1930). With the coming of sound, Griffiths and White formed the Comedy Cartoon Sound Films Company and made *Topical Breezes* (1930), starring "Hite and Mite." In 1933 they produced *Colonel Capers* and *Down on the Farm*, two cartoons based on the artwork of H.M. Bateman (see *The World Encyclopedia of Comics*, Chelsea House, 1976). These were made in the Raycol Color Process, a system doomed to failure by the necessity for special apparatus affixed to the cinema projector. In 1935 Griffiths joined Anson Dyer to work on the ambitious *Sam* series, while White became a successful strip cartoonist with his *Nipper*. Griffiths died on November 11, 1967, forgotten except by his former colleagues.

D.G.

JETSONS, THE (U.S.) Encouraged by the success of their animated series *The Flintstones*, Hanna-Barbera developed *The Jetsons*, which debuted on ABC in 1962. While the Flintstones were a typical suburban family that happened to live in the Stone Age, the Jetsons were a typical suburban family of the future. The formula was otherwise the same and never varied from the time-honored clichés of television situation comedy: George and Jane Jetson, their children Judy and Elroy, and the family dog Astro found themselves week after week in some kind of trouble or predicament, such as the family rocketship being stolen or the children wrecking the astro-set. The drawings were undistinguished, and the limited animation was especially disappointing in view of the almost unlimited opportunities provided by the futuristic setting.

"The Jetsons." © Hanna-Barbera Productions.

322

Despite these drawbacks *The Jetsons* was fairly successful. After its run on ABC, it was picked up for syndication by CBS, and in 1971 NBC in turn programmed the series on its Saturday morning schedule. *The Jetsons* was also adapted into comic books from 1963 to 1973.

M.H.

JOB

See Onfroy de Bréville, Jacques.

Two of John Citizen's "colleagues," Dilly and Dally, the procrastinating bureaucrats.

JOHN CITIZEN (G.B.) The first national hero to win the approval of the British public, John Citizen differed significantly from his predecessor, John Bull. The contrast would in itself provide sufficient material for a book. Where the big, bold, bluff Bull, human counterpart of "The Roast Beef of Old England," was the personification of Olde England (he was created in 1712 by John Arbuthnot, pamphleteer), the bespectacled, wing-collared, umbrellaed Citizen represented the new backbone of the nation, 20th-century style: meek, mild and middle-class. The long-suffering, tax-paying John C. made a typical appearance on a dark day during World War I. His mouth was spread into a false grin by a glove-stretcher, and the caption was "Smile, Damn You, Smile!"

John Citizen was created by a cartoonist named Percy Fearon, who signed himself "Poy," and was one of many cartoon symbols he originated. These characters, who came and went regularly in newspaper cartoons, included Dilly and Dally, the procrastinating bureaucrats, Dux and Drakes, the cheerful dispensers of public funds, Cuthbert the Whitehall Rabbit, and Dora, the dreary old biddy who personified DORA, the dreaded Defense of the Realm Act (1914).

Percy Arthur ("Poy") Fearon was born in Shanghai, China, in 1874. He studied art in New York, where the locals pronounced his name as "Poicy"—hence the pseudonym. He began drawing daily political cartoons for British newspapers in 1905 and produced 10,000 during the ensuing 34 years. His main work was for the *London Evening News* (1913-35) and *Daily Mail* (1935-38). He died in November 1948, leaving behind an immortal gallery of pleasantly drawn characters.

Books: *Poy's War Cartoons* (1915); *Dilly and Dally* (1919); *100 Poy Cartoons* (1920); and *How to Draw Newspaper Cartoons* (1930).

D.G.

JOHNSON, HERBERT (1878-1946) American artist born in Sutton, Nebraska, on October 30, 1878. Herbert Johnson studied at the University of Nebraska and at Columbia University. Around 1903 he created several comic strips for boiler-plate syndicates and shortly thereafter became a frequent contributor to *Life*, specializing in equestrian cartoons.

Johnson held editorial and cartooning positions on the *Denver Republican* (1896) and the *Kansas City Journal* (1897-99) before freelancing in New York (1903-05) and accepting a position with the *Philadelphia North American* during the years of political insurgency. He was head of the Sunday art department (1906-09) and was also a cartoonist (1908-12). Van Valkenburg's *North American* was a Progressive paper, and Johnson was to retain the Theodore Roosevelt creed throughout his life.

By 1912 Johnson's cartoons had attracted the attention of his Philadelphia neighbors, the Curtis family and George Horace Lorimer of the *Saturday Evening Post*. He was offered a job as regular cartoonist and art editor of the prestigious weekly; he accepted (though relinquishing the latter post in 1915) and drew editorial cartoons, often several per issue, until 1941.

He continually upheld Republicanism and was most effective in fighting the New Deal. Indeed, Johnson graphically portrayed some of the most telling arguments against FDR's brand of government controls and finance capitalism. After his initial devotion to the pen-and-ink style of drawing—at which he excelled—he adopted for the *Post* a very breezy, casual brush-and-wash look that lent an air of informality to his work. His cartoons were mostly in a horizontal format and were full of animation, action and cartoon conventions, including his version of the Common People used by Opper and Shoemaker.

The bulk of Herbert Johnson's work deserves to be resurrected as a fine portrayal of his times. One collection was published in his lifetime, *Cartoons by Herbert Johnson* (1936). He died in 1946.

R.M.

JOHNSTON, DAVID CLAYPOOL (1799-1865) American cartoonist and actor born in Philadelphia, Pennsylvania, in March 1799. From the first, like later cartoonists Joseph Keppler and Bill Mauldin, Johnston divided his attention between acting and drawing. In 1815 he was apprenticed to Philadelphia engraver Francis Kearny, but six years later he made his acting debut as Henry in the play *Speed the Plow*; he was to act full time in Boston and Philadelphia from 1821 to 1826.

He worked in both lithography and woodcuts with simplicity of style and economy of labels. As an artist he was enterprising: he painted (exhibiting at the Bos-

PLAIN SEWING DONE HERE

Symptoms of a Locked Jaw

D.C. Johnston, ca. 1834.

ton Atheneum and the National Academy of Design), made prints and illustrated books, including *Fanny Kemble's Journal* (1835) and Joseph C. Neal's *Charcoal Sketches* (1838). As a cartoonist he was widely circulated in broadsides and handbills—his attacks on Jackson were famous—and published annual collections of his works as *Scraps* for years. He also wrote and illustrated in cartoons *The House That Jeff Built* (1863), a satire on Jefferson Davis.

Johnston died in Dorchester, Massachusetts, on November 8, 1865.

R.M.

JOLLIFFE, ERIC (1907-   ) Australian cartoonist born in Portsmouth, England, in January 1907. Eric Jolliffe, one of a family of 12 who came to Australia in 1914, went outback to work when he was 15. Returning to the city at age 21, he enrolled in an art course at Sydney Technical College. For years he freelanced cartoons while window-cleaning for a living. Eventually, in the late 1930s, he became a regular contributor to the *Bulletin* and launched his outback farmer character, Saltbush Bill, in the weekly magazine *Pix*. This feature, together with his *Witchetty's Tribe* (outback humor about an aborigine tribe) and his comic strip *Sandy Blight* (starring a typical struggling farmer), was later drawn for the Sydney *Sun* and the weekend *Sun-Herald*. Jolliffe's cartoons, drawn with watercolor washes in monotone, are renowned for their authentic "bush furniture" and background details: a broken wagon wheel, an old weathered barn, a pig trough fashioned from a large log, rabbit traps—anything that

appeals is interesting.

Jolliffe's annual outback wanderings, which he spends sketching, photographing and collecting bush paraphernalia, last from three to four months. It is on these trips that he paints his wash studies, which are fine tonal exercises of outback farm buildings and portraits of aborigines. Nearly one hundred books of Jolliffe's cartoons have been published, and they have sold more than six million copies.

V.L.

JONES, CHARLES (1912-   ) American animator and producer born in Spokane, Washington, on September 21, 1912. Chuck Jones grew up in Los Angeles, where he received his art education at the Chouinard Institute. In the early 1930s he joined the Leon Schlesinger studios as an animator, working for such directors as Friz Freleng, Bob Clampett and Tex Avery. He graduated to director status in the late 1930s (one of the first cartoons he directed was the 1938 "Presto-Change-O," featuring Bugs Bunny in one of his early incarnations).

Chuck Jones's talents came to full fruition in the 1940s and 1950s, when he contributed some of the most imaginative cartoons ever produced by the Schlesinger/Warner Brothers studios. "What's Opera, Doc?," "Mississippi Hare," "Frigid Hare" in the *Bugs Bunny* series; "Duck Amok," "Duck Dodgers in the 24½ Century," "Robin Hood Daffy" among the *Daffy Duck* cartoons; and the *Tweety and Sylvester* entry "Birds Anonymous"—these are but a few of his classics. In collaboration with Michael Maltese he created the characters of Pépé le Pew, the romantically inclined skunk, and of Wile E. Coyote and his nemesis, the Road Runner. During World War II Jones directed the campaign film *Hell-Bent for Election* for Stephen Bosustow and helped create the *Private Snafu* series of cartoons for the U.S. Army.

In 1966 Jones joined the MGM studio as head of its animation department. While there, he briefly took over the *Tom and Jerry* series after Hanna and Barbera had left and Gene Deitch had failed. In 1970 he was appointed vice-president in charge of children's programming for ABC-TV and created the Saturday morning program *The Curiosity Shop*. He then founded his own company, Chuck Jones Enterprises, and in recent years he has been directing and producing a number of memorable TV specials, including *Rikki-Tikki-Tavi* (adapted from Rudyard Kipling), *Horton Hears a Who*, *The Grinch Who Stole Christmas* (both from Dr. Seuss stories) and *The Pogo Special Birthday Special* (based on the Walt Kelly comic strip). Jones has also gone back occasionally to his old Warner characters—Bugs Bunny, Daffy Duck, *et al.*—featuring them in such TV specials as the Saint-Saens-inspired *The Carnival of Animals* (1976) and the Twain-derived *A Connecticut Rabbit in King Arthur's Court* (1978). In addition he has produced a full-length animated cartoon, *The Phantom Tollbooth* (1969). Chuck Jones's latest venture, a kid strip called *Crawford*, started syndication in 1978.

Once called by scriptwriter Heck Allen "an intellectual in a non-intellectual business," Jones nonetheless managed to win four Oscars; he was also executive producer on a fifth Oscar winner, *A Christmas Carol* (1972). One of the most respected names in the animation field, Jones has lectured extensively on university campuses in the United States and abroad.

M.H.

"Are you kids comin' out f'r y'r bath or do I send these ferrets in after y'r?"

Eric Jolliffe. © *Sydney Sun.*

Chuck Jones. © *Warner Brothers.*

JONSSON, JOE (1890-1963) Australian cartoonist born in Halmstad, Sweden, in 1890. In the distinctiveness of its technique and in its extremely deceptive drawing style, the work of *Smith's Weekly* cartoonist Joe Jonsson was truly unique. Compared with the subtle draftsmanship of Norman Lindsay or the elegant, mannered drawing of George Molnar, Jonsson's drawings looked as if they had been drawn with a toothbrush instead of with a pen. Yet his brilliant pen drawings were outstanding for their distinction, skill and humor: they were drawn with tremendous dash and zest.

Jonsson, "a bletty Swede," as he termed himself, left his family's farm for the sea at age 18, sailing before the mast for nine years and arriving in Australia in 1917. Before he became a professional comic artist with *Smith's Weekly* in 1924, Jonsson worked at a variety of jobs: timber cutter in Queensland and high rigger on Sydney's wheat silos at White Bay. Then when he decided to become an artist, he studied at the Watkin Art School, where he was so successful he became an art instructor within a year. Then followed a period as a commercial artist prior to his joining *Smith's Weekly*, where he remained until it ceased publication in 1950. In that year, Jonsson was engaged by Sir Keith Murdoch of the Melbourne *Herald* and produced weekly, until his death, his popular, nationally syndicated comic strip *Uncle Joe's Horse, Radish*, featuring an outlandish racehorse that was the answer to the punter's dream.

Joe Jonsson's humor fitted *Smith's Weekly* perfectly. It was tough, sometimes cynical and always uninhibited. Older readers of *Smith's* will recall his wonder-

Missus: "What made you buy a whole barrel of beer?"
Husband: "There are rumors that we're going out on strike."

Joe Jonsson. © *Smith's Weekly.*

ful comic strip *Oigle*, with a small boy prankster and Gran'pa, a fatefully incompatible pair. His drawings and rollicking humor about burglars, cardsharps, turf punters, jockeys and "blottos" (drunks) were a continuation in theme of the work of the early *Bulletin* artists Alf Vincent and Ambrose Dyson. No comic artist in Australia has drawn as many jokes around the theme of drunks and drinking as Jonsson. His many comic drawings on this social activity in Australia have continued since the time of the Rum Corps through the era of the gold field sly-grog shanties to the present. (In 1961 Australia occupied second place on the list of the world's top beer-drinking nations, leaving Australians with a rather frothy tradition.) Appropriately, a large, fellow-brush wake was held in Sydney to pay tribute to "the gentle Swede" following his funeral in March 1963.

V.L.

JUCH, ERNST (1838-1909) Austrian cartoonist, painter and sculptor (of German birth) born in Gotha, then capital of Saxe-Coburg-Gotha, on April 25, 1838. At the turn of the century the eminent historian of humorous art Eduard Fuchs considered Ernst Juch far and away the best cartoonist in Austria. Nor was Juch merely a brilliant comet: he was on the staff of the Vienna *Figaro* from 1869 (not long after it was founded) almost until his death in Vienna on October 5, 1909.

Juch's father, a painter, died when the boy was very young. Ernst was then slated to become a designer of porcelain statuettes and was apprenticed to a local sculptor. As a journeyman he wandered to Passau, and from there to Vienna, where he settled in 1859. He did some sculpture and designs for metal objects, but his drawings soon brought him more fame and money. His first published cartoons appeared in the

weekly *Der G'rade Michel* in 1864. Then, five years later, came the *Figaro*.

When Juch became an artist for that publication (at first alongside Leopold Müller, who was soon invited to teach at the Academy, leaving Juch in sole possession of the field), the *Figaro* was edited by the outstanding author of Austrian folk plays Ludwig Anzengruber, with whom the artist formed a close friendship. Not only did Juch illustrate Anzengruber's almanac *Der Wiener Bote* with storytelling pictures, but he did numerous private drawings for "Die Anzengrube," the club to which both men belonged. Juch was also known for the ingenious watercolor postcards he sent his friends. Among the books he illustrated were the *Krebsbüchlein des Figaro* ("The Figaro's Crab—or Remaindered—Book," 1881) and J. Bendel's *Allerlei Weisen und Märlein* ("All Sorts of Tunes and Tales," 1892).

The special feature of Juch's cartoon style was its intentionally distorted anatomy, with certain parts of the body strongly emphasized to the detriment of others. His people's faces were small but very clearly drawn and recognizable. He was famed as an unsentimental but also good-natured observer of Viennese life.

Shortly before his death, Juch transferred from the *Figaro* to its rival, *Kikeriki*. After he died, it was learned that he had indulged in meritorious private experiments in painting that he had withheld from public view.

S.A.

The politician Thuns trampling on the Austrian constitution.

Ernst Juch, 1898.

"Judge Rummy," 1921. © King Features Syndicate.

JUDGE RUMMY (U.S.) A funny animal character created by Tad Dorgan for his daily Hearst sports page space in 1910, Judge Rummy was a dog of no apparent breed whom Dorgan usually portrayed in judicial black presiding over his courtroom. Originally drawn for the *New York Evening Journal* at Dorgan's sports department desk, the often unnamed *Judge Rummy* strip was published nationwide in a number of Hearst afternoon dailies and ran intermittently as a Dorgan feature until the cartoonist's death more than twenty years later. Although it was never printed or designed as a Sunday color page, it often appeared in Hearst Sunday sports sections in its weekday format.

Initially an occasional three-, four- or six-panel gag strip (in which Judge Rummy was floored by a riposte from one of the culprits brought before him or capped a felon's gag with one of his own), few of which had anything whatever to do with sports, the all-dog character feature developed considerable continuity when the Judge became a principal figure in Dorgan's long-running and popular narrative of the 1910s, *Silk Hat Harry's Divorce Suit.* During its run *Judge Rummy* was seldom seen as a separate title. Revived after the explosive climax of the *Suit* strip, *Judge Rummy* continued as an irregular gag feature between panels of Dorgan's *Indoor Sports* and *Outdoor Sports* features until a few weeks after Dorgan's death on May 2, 1929.

Judge Rummy was one of the Dorgan animal characters involved in a curious experiment by the cartoonist late in the 1910s. Dorgan arranged an onstage metamorphosis of his dog figures, such as Rummy, Silk Hat Harry, Curlock Holmes and others, into human equivalents. This was apparently met with widespread protests, for Dorgan hurriedly returned his characters to their original canine state.

Basically a rather simple hit-or-miss gag strip, very simply drawn, *Judge Rummy* was nevertheless an enormously popular strip with Hearst metropolitan readers; it was reprinted for years, with other Dorgan material, in Hearst papers after Dorgan's death.

B.B.

JUMP, EDWARD (ca.1838-1883) American cartoonist born in France, probably in 1838. E. Jump traveled the world with his sketchbook and lived in various parts of Europe and in Australia before arriving in the United States. It is reported that he first settled in San Francisco as a commercial artist designing whiskey labels before moving to Washington, D.C., as a portrait specialist demanding high commissions.

He was active in New York, Montreal, Cincinnati, St. Louis and Chicago as a freelance artist. It was in New York that he executed most of his work—or rather, New York was his base once he became the leading staff artist on *Leslie's Weekly* in the 1870s. In 1867 he had illustrated the book *Beyond the Mississippi* by A.D. Richardson and thereby established a reputation for western subjects. One notable *Leslie's* series was a Jump sketchbook report of activities in Leadville, Colorado, published between February and June, 1879.

As an important *Leslie's* staffer, Jump also contributed to the Leslie humor publications; there, along with Frank Beard, he was one of Opper's teachers, and he also came to know the elder Bellew and Keppler. Jump was an able caricaturist and also freely contributed to *Wild Oats*, the *Graphic* and minor imitations of *Puck*, into 1882.

E. Jump died a suicide in Chicago on April 21, 1883.

R.M.

327

JUNCEDA
See García-Junceda i Supervía, Joan.

"Jungle Tatei." © Mushi Productions.

JUNGLE TATEI (Japan) *Jungle Tatei* ("Jungle Emperor") was Japan's first color animation series for television and was produced by Osamu Tezuka's Mushi Productions in 1965. It was based on the comic strip of the same name, also by Tezuka, which ran for years in the magazine *Manga Shōnen* from 1950 on and was briefly revived again in 1964 by Kodansha in a magazine called *Disneyland*. When *Jungle Tatei* finished its television run in September 1966, it was followed by *Shin Jungle Tatei: Susume Leo!* ("New Jungle Emperor: Go Ahead Leo!"), which ran from October 1966 to March 1967.

The animated versions of *Jungle Tatei* closely followed the original comic in depicting the life of Leo the white lion and his efforts to reconcile the animals in Africa with the men who encroached upon their domain. Leo was no ordinary lion; he could talk to humans when the need arose, and he devoted himself to attempting to organize the animal kingdom into a civilization that could withstand the human threat. He was brilliant, strong and fast, but at the same time he was gentle and had a sense of humor.

In the first series Leo's age was equivalent to that of a third-grade child, but viewers had a chance to watch him gradually mature, and in *Susume Leo!* he assumed his final form, complete with throaty roar and flowing mane. Supporting characters also changed. In the first series Leo's father, Panja, and his mother, Raga, both appeared, but Panja died battling humans and Raga was captured. As Leo matured, he too took a wife named Raiya, and they produced two cubs. Numerous other animals also appeared, such as Bubu, an evil lion who competed with Leo for spheres of influence; Koko, a parrot; Tommy, a Thomson's gazelle; and Mandy the Mandrill. Bubu was assisted by a variety of villains, including two comical hyenas.

The animated versions of *Jungle Tatei*, like the comic strip, were a spectacular success—full of brilliant color and action, and incorporating Tezuka's favorite themes of idealism, perseverance and the vitality of life. Humor, tragedy, love and drama were skillfully woven into the main theme and its subplots. The first series, which ran in 52 episodes of 23 minutes each, won a host of awards, including one from the 1967 International Children's Film Festival in Venice. Some of the best talents in animation in Japan were used on both, with Masaki Tsuji writing most of the scripts, and people like Shinji Nagashima and Sadao Tsukioka directing some of the episodes. Eichi Yamamoto served as chief director and producer, and brilliant music was composed by Tomita.

In the United States the first series ran on NBC television in 1965 under the title *Kimba the White Lion*; it was produced by Fred Ladd. The second series, in which Leo appeared as a grown lion, ran on Canadian television in French with the title *Le Roi Leo*.

F.S.

JÜRGENSEN, FRITZ (1818-1863) Danish cartoonist born in Copenhagen, Denmark, in 1818. Considered to be Denmark's first real cartoonist, Fritz Jürgensen was also a watchmaker. His father was watchmaker to the royal court and "General Inspector for the Public Measuring of Time," and he encouraged his son to enter the profession. But in 1835, before Jürgensen started as an apprentice, he made a trip to Italy, and then another extensive trip to Switzerland on behalf of the watchmaker profession. There he blossomed as a letter and diary writer, two occupations that, together with his drawings, were to become main parts of his life.

In 1842, 24 years old, he married his cousin and childhood sweetheart, Lise, and succeeded his father as court watchmaker. His first 48 drawings, *Gysse-bogen*, are from this period and are dedicated to his nephew, who was called Gysse. A year later his wife died in childbirth, and Jürgensen sold his watchmaker business, led somewhat of an idler's life, practiced music and was a treasured party guest, not least because of the many drawings he left with the families he visited.

Jürgensen's gallery of characters is the Copenhagen citizenry, their narrow-mindedness, human weaknesses and vanity. It has often been said that his drawings are dilettantish and competently amateurish in style. On the other hand, the naiveté—as it was later in James Thurber's drawings—is a charming addition to his witty captions. For example, an office clerk who practices his speech in front of an empty chair says: "You know too much about the business, sir, not to be aware how much our work load has increased. But to ask for a raise for all the employees would be too forward. I *only* wish it for myself." But he was no merry soul, which his diaries and drawings also show. He was a student of Søren Kierkegaard and talked about "the state of things in Denmark: mediocracy, dullness, philistinism. Ideals are lost, forgotten, and mediocracy has complacently moved up to take the seat of honor." The fact that Jürgensen's production first and foremost was a historical picture of society does not eliminate the possibility that later times and other countries can identify similar traits. His humor was ironic and bitter, though filled with empathy.

His melancholy was interrupted by momentary bouts of merriment, and a contemporary painter appropriately likened him to the cuckoo in the clock, coming out to call and right away withdrawing in silence. On an artistically lower level he is related to Honoré Daumier and has to a great degree inspired succeeding generations of Scandinavian cartoonists. In 1854 he had a violent hemorrhage, and in the following years he suffered from fevers, coughs and headaches. He drank heavily, and in the spring of 1863 he died from tuberculosis.

J.S.

JÜSP
See Spahr, Jürg.

Kk

KAMLER PIOTR (1936-) Polish animator born in Warsaw, Poland, in 1936. After completing his art studies in Warsaw, Piotr Kamler went to France in the late 1950s. He started animation work in 1960 for the research department of the French television system. His first films were abstract compositions such as the 1960 *Etude* and *Conte* ("Tale"), *Composition* and *Structures* (both 1961) and *Lignes et Points* ("Lines and Dots," 1963). He then moved to less abstract if equally cryptic themes with the 1964 *Meurtre* ("Murder") and the 1965 *Prière Enfance* ("Prayer Childhood"). The same year he also directed *La Planète Verte* ("The Green Planet"), a science fiction tale entirely drawn on a green background, with extraordinary visual effects reinforced by a narrative written by Jacques Sternberg. In 1968 he came out with the no less extraordinary *L'Araignéléphant* (which can be translated "The Spiderlephant"), about a monstrous creature on the loose. The 1970 *Délicieuse Catastrophe*, which seems to be a parable of the mating ritual, reinforced Kamler's position as one of the most intriguing of contemporary animators.

Kamler's production in recent years has somewhat declined in quantity, but its quality remains high. *Coeur de Secours* ("Spare Heart," 1972) is an ironic mirroring of the modern quest for fulfillment, and *Les Pas* ("Steps," 1975) is an outstanding abstract film that appears to recapitulate the whole of Kamler's discourse. A recipient of many awards and prizes (at Annecy, Zagreb and elsewhere), Kamler has been the subject of a number of studies in France and abroad.

M.H.

KAMOGAWA, TSUBAME (1956-) Japanese cartoonist born in Fukuoka Prefecture, Japan, in 1956. Tsubame Kamogawa, one of the youngest and most eccentric Japanese cartoonists, began drawing cartoons soon after learning how to hold a pencil and thereupon resolved to make it his career. In what was a dramatic act of courage given Japan's highly competitive school system, Kamogawa reportedly submitted a completely blank test paper during his high school entrance examination (compulsory education extends only to the ninth grade in Japan). The reverse side was filled with cartoons. In 1974, at age 17, he dropped out of high school and began working as an assistant to Yoshimoto Baron, the creator of numerous popular comic strips, but supposedly was told that his drawings resembled those of a first grader. This served only to strengthen his resolve to make it on his own, and after ten rebellious, grueling months he quit.

After an initial period of hardship, Kamogawa began having his works accepted by various magazines, and in 1977 he came out with *Macaroni Hōrenso* (roughly, "Macaroni-Spinach Apartment") in the weekly magazine *Shōnen Champion*. *Macaroni Hōrenso* became an immediate success and represented a type of humor totally different from that of Fujio Akatsuka

Piotr Kamler, "L'Araignéléphant." © *Cinéastes Associés.*

(creator of *Tensai Bakabon*) or Tatsuhiko Yamagami (creator of *Gakki Dekka*), two prominent gag strip artists who had been pioneers in their own right. The stars of *Macaroni Hōrenso* are 41-year-old Kindo, 25-year-old Hisakata and 16-year-old Soji, an unlikely trio all in their first year of high school. Their antics can only be described as bizarre, for there is almost no plot whatsoever, the humor deriving from endless outrageous situations and the intersplicing of multiple levels of reality.

Kamogawa refers to his style as "rock-beat"; as other artists have been influenced by jazz or classical music, he draws his inspiration from rock 'n' roll, which he plays constantly as he works. The result is an unprecedented sense of speed in all of his cartoons and comics—as in *Purupuru Propellor* and *Dora Neko Rokku* (also presently running in *Shōnen Champion*)—and frame transitions that border on the surreal. Kamogawa's drawing style is simple to the point of appearing amateurish, and it remains to be seen whether he will have the staying power and flexibility required to survive in Japan's quickly changing market. At present, however, he is riding on a crest of popularity. Tsubame Kamogawa constantly wears a baseball cap and, of all comics and cartoons, claims to enjoy his own the most.

F.S.

KANEVSKII, AMINADAV MOISEEVICH (1898-) Soviet cartoonist and illustrator born in Elizavetgrad (now Kirovgrad) in the Ukraine on March 29, 1898. From 1924 to 1930 Aminadav Kanevskii attended the State Higher Art and Technical Studios and the Higher Art and Technical Institute, where he studied under P. Pavlinov, N. Kupreianov and D.S. Moor, among other leading Soviet graphic artists of the time.

Kanevskii started on his professional career with illustrations for children's books, mostly of a humorous nature. His illustrations for A.L. and P.N. Barto's *The Crybaby* (1934) and Saltykov-Shchedrin's *The Pompadour and the Lady Pompadours* (1935) were particularly well received. At the same time, Kanevskii also did cartoons. In 1936 he became one of the regu-

"Kapten Grogg." © Victor Bergdahl.

lar contributors to *Krokodil*, for which he drew over the years a number of memorable cartoons, some of a political nature, but most on comical situations derived from everyday Soviet life. In addition to his cartooning career Kanevskii developed his interest in caricature with illustrations for Vladimir Mayakovsky's *Satirical Poems* (1964) and for a number of Nikolai Gogol's novels and stories.

Kanevskii has been the recipient of many Soviet distinctions for his work, including the Order of the Red Banner of Labor. He became a corresponding member of the Academy of Science of the USSR in 1962 and was named People's Artist of the USSR in 1973. A book-length study of Kanevskii's work was published by Iuri Khalamenski in Moscow in 1961.

M.H.

KAPTEN GROGG (Sweden) The first two decades of this century were a period of intense research and experimentation in the field of animated cartooning all over the world. One of the early pioneers was the Swede Gustav Victor Bergdahl, who created a character called Kapten Grogg in 1915. (The character was apparently inspired by C.W. Kahles's panel *The Yarns of Captain Fibb*, then published in Sweden). Bergdahl was a newspaper cartoonist who had been greatly impressed by the work of Winsor McCay (contrary to what has been asserted by some historians, he never actually worked for McCay but only decided to follow in his footsteps).

Kapten Grogg (whose name can be loosely translated as "Captain Brandy") was a cheerful, harddrinking sea dog whose adventures took place all around the globe. He first appeared in "Grogg's Underbara Resa" ("Grogg's Wonderful Voyage"). This proved successful enough to allow Bergdahl to launch a full-fledged *Kapten Grogg* cartoon series. The irrepressible old salt next went around the world in an airship ("Kapten Grogg's Balloon Trip," 1917); later he got married to a nagging harridan ("Kapten Grogg's Wedding," 1918). Other notable entries in the series include the 1917 "Kapten Grogg at the North Pole," the 1920 "Kapten Grogg at Sea" and the 1922 "Kapten Grogg Puts on Weight." This last put an end to the *Kapten Grogg* series, which seems to have disappeared in the early 1920s, after a run of 13 cartoons.

Kapten Grogg was a remarkable achievement and is one of the few animated cartoon series originating in Europe during the silent era that can bear comparison with the best of the American production of the period.

M.H.

KARI
See Suomalainen, Kari Yrjänä.

KATZENJAMMER KIDS, THE (U.S.) At the time that W.R. Hearst founded International Film Service in 1916 with the express purpose of bringing to the screen the comics that were syndicated in his newspapers, no comic strip had been so enduring and successful as *The Katzenjammer Kids*, created by Rudolph Dirks in 1897. It was therefore fitting that the two terrible twins be the heroes of the first series of cartoon films produced by the service. (*Happy Hooligan*, *Silk Hat Harry*, *Jiggs and Maggie*, *Krazy Kat*, and others were to follow.)

In 1916 Dirks had already left Hearst and gone on to create a new version of the strip (first called *Hans and Fritz*, it was later rechristened *The Captain and the Kids*), but he was still credited, along with Bert Green, for the story lines. The animation—rather crude and primitive but lovable in its simplicity—was done by John Foster and Walter Lantz, under the direction of Gregory La Cava. Due to the rise in anti-German feelings, the series was discontinued in 1918, and the studio closed soon afterward. (Later, Bray Studios revived the *Katzenjammer* cartoons for a few years.)

Hans and Fritz, der Captain, die Mama and the other protagonists came to life again in a series of animated cartoons released by MGM under the title *The Captain and the Kids*. Based on Dirks's revived strip, 14 cartoons were produced in 1938 and 1939, from "Blue Monday" to "The Winning Ticket," under the direction of Robert Allen and William Hanna (of later Hanna-Barbera fame).

The Katzenjammers again appeared in an undistinguished series of animated shorts produced for television by King Features Syndicate in the 1960s. The Katzies are currently featured in a number of amusing TV commercials.

M.H.

KAULBACH, WILHELM VON (1805-1874) German painter, illustrator and cartoonist born at Arolsen, not far from Kassel, in Hesse, on October 15, 1805. Though contemporary and even later writers condemned certain satirical works by Wilhelm von Kaulbach as sordid betrayals of his serious artistic principles, a careful analysis of his career points to a deepseated dichotomy between his urge to storm Mount Olympus and an equally strong need to hurl down abuse from his lofty peak. His childhood and youth were impoverished, nomadic and unhappy. As an adolescent he studied with his father, a noted goldsmith. When he entered the Düsseldorf Academy in 1822, the historical painter and influential teacher Peter von Cornelius became his protector. It was clear that Kaulbach could paint the kind of allegorical frescoes and grandiose religious pictures so much in demand at the time.

He lived and worked in Munich from 1826 on, not counting a couple of long trips to Italy, the first in 1835, the year of his famous realistic print *Das Nar-*

renhaus ("The Madhouse")—which throughout the 19th century was generally considered one of his humorous works! By 1837 Kaulbach had become a Bavarian court painter. By the early 1840s his graphic wit was already widely appreciated, and the Stuttgart publisher Cotta commissioned what was to be Kaulbach's most famous set of satirical illustrations, those for Goethe's *Reineke Fuchs*, a retelling of the medieval animal epic. In drawing these humanized animals, Kaulbach was directly influenced by the work of the French illustrator Grandville, but he achieved a notable personal creation all the same. *Reineke Fuchs* was published in 1846 with copper-engraved illustrations, and in 1857 with wood-engraved versions.

In the years of revolutionary troubles, 1848 and 1849, Kaulbach drew some political cartoons (one shows a royal snowman melting); he has been tentatively credited with salacious depictions of Lola Montez, the royal mistress who caused the abdication of Bavarian king Ludwig I. The greatest scandal in Kaulbach's career occurred in 1850. Having already executed numerous frescoes, and having been named director of the Munich Academy in 1849, Kaulbach nevertheless could not resist poking fun at old colleagues and masters in his frescoes in the Neue Pinakothek depicting the furtherance of art and culture in the reign of Ludwig I.

Other humorous works include the *Kinderfibel* ("Children's Primer"), delightful drawings he made for his own children in 1852; a lengthy series of *Dance of Death* sketches dating from the 1850s to about 1870, including both generalized victims (as in traditional series in this genre) and specific historical characters; and witty drawings found in sketchbooks of his last years, the early 1870s. He is also said to have done lewd versions of his own successful coffee-table books portraying characters and scenes in

works by Goethe, Schiller and Shakespeare.

Other artists in Kaulbach's immediate family included his brother Karl, his son Hermann and especially his nephew Friedrich August von Kaulbach, also a cartoonist. Wilhelm von Kaulbach died in Munich on April 7, 1874.

S.A.

KAWAMOTO, KIHACHIRO (1924-) Japanese cartoonist and puppet animator born in Shibuya, Tokyo, on January 11, 1924. After graduating from Yokohama University with a degree in architecture, Kihachiro Kawamoto began working as an assistant art designer for Toho Motion Picture Company but quit in 1949 to begin freelancing. Kawamoto quickly established himself as an expert puppet maker, and in 1953 he made two one-minute black-and-white commercial animated puppet films with Tadahito Mochinaga, a former graphic animator and one of the founding fathers of Japanese puppet animation. In 1956 Kawamoto again worked with Mochinaga to create an 11-minute color puppet animation film called *Beer Mukashi Mukashi* ("A History of Beer") for a beer company. By this time Kawamoto was in charge of both puppet making and animation.

In 1959, having gained considerable experience and training with Mochinaga, Kawamoto established Shiba Productions with Tadasu Iizawa, a director and playwright who had also worked with Mochinaga. Shiba Productions specialized primarily in animated commercial films for television, and Kawamoto's abiding interest in puppets led him to quit, leave Japan in 1962 and study for two years in Czechoslovakia under the world-famous puppet animator Jiří Trnka. Returning to Japan in 1964, Kawamoto soon began refining his skills, and in 1968 his *Hana Ori* ("Breaking Branches Is Forbidden"), a 14-minute color puppet animation film, won him the silver prize at the Mamaia International Animated Film Festival in Romania. Since 1968 Kawamoto's independently produced films have regularly won awards internationally and in Japan. Notable among them are *Oni* ("The Demon," 1972), which employed beautiful backgrounds modeled after Japanese lacquerwork and won both the coveted Ofuji award in Japan and a special mention at the Annecy International Animated Film Festival; *Shijin no Shogai* ("A Poet's Life," 1974), a cutout animation film based on a story by the novelist Kobo Abe; and *Dojoji* ("Dojo Temple," 1967), which garnered awards not only in Japan but also at animated film festivals in Annecy and Melbourne.

Most recently, Kawamoto has been working on a 20-minute puppet animation film titled *Kataku* ("House of Flames"), but he also creates puppets for television programs and commercial advertising. Moreover, he regularly works with his colleague Tadanari Okamoto, also an animated filmmaker, to produce highly popular puppet shows (that include animation) annually in Japan.

F.S.

Wilhelm von Kaulbach, illustration for Goethe's "Reineke Fuchs," 1857.

KEANE, WILLIAM (1922-) American cartoonist born near Philadelphia, Pennsylvania, in 1922. Bill Keane, like many other future cartoonists, showed an early talent for drawing, and his inclination was encouraged by his parents. While attending Northeast Catholic High School in Philadelphia, he contributed cartoons to the school newspaper. After graduation from high school in 1940, he became an errand boy for the *Philadelphia Bulletin*.

Drafted into the army in 1941, Keane worked on *Yank* magazine, then was sent to Australia (where he met his future wife) and later drew cartoons for U.S. savings bonds and GI insurance. When the war ended, Keane was a staff member of the army newspaper *Stars and Stripes*, where his first panel series, *At Ease with the Japanese*, appeared.

Discharged in 1946, Keane rejoined the *Bulletin* as staff artist while continuing to freelance cartoons to such publications as the *Saturday Evening Post* and *This Week*. In addition to spot cartoons for the *Bulletin*, Keane also drew *Silly Philly*, a gag panel with a homegrown flavor, and in 1954 he launched his successful *Channel Chuckles* cartoon series. This amused look at television was later picked up by the Register and Tribune Syndicate for national distribution. Keane followed up in 1960 with his best-known creation, *The Family Circus*, an endearing domestic panel, also syndicated by the Register and Tribune.

In 1959 the Keane family moved from Philadelphia to Arizona, where, Bill Keane claims, "I draw *The Family Circus* and *Channel Chuckles* between tennis games."

M.H.

"Now let out the clutch and step on the gas!"

William Keane. © This Week.

KEENE, CHARLES (1823-1891) British comic artist born in Hornsey, London, in 1823. Considered by David Low to be "the greatest of the British comic artists" (he made a distinction between caricaturists, cartoonists and comic artists), Charles Keene was "supreme in catching Nature in her humorous moments." Low also considered Keene an artist's artist, ap-

preciated by his peers rather than his public, which was more amused by the often extensive captions beneath the cartoons. These gags were usually supplied to the cartoonist rather than created by him, but his pictures were all his own. Although working in a period when woodblocks were the style, Keene managed a certain fluidity and lightness about his line work. He drew on scraps of paper with slivers of pointed wood dipped into homemade inks of various colors, which made the task of his translators into wood a difficult one.

Keene was educated at a local London boarding school, then at Ipswich Grammar. He was apprenticed to an architect in 1840 and five years later began to contribute topical sketches to the *Illustrated London News*. His humorous drawings began to appear in *Punch* from 1851 and continued in that weekly to 1890. He died in 1891.

Books: *Voyage of the Constance* (1860); *Ewan Harrington* (1860); *Sea Kings and Naval Heroes* (1861); *Eyebright* (1862); *Cambridge Grisette* (1862); *Tracks for Tourists* (1864); *Legends of Number Nip* (1864); *Mrs. Caudle's Curtain Lectures* (1866); *Our People* (1881); *Robert, Diary of a Waiter* (1885); *Life and Letters* (1892); *Work of Charles Keene* (1897); *21 Etchings* (1903); *Pictures by Charles Keene* (1909); *Charles Keene, The Artist's Artist* (1934); *Charles Keene* (1935); *Charles Keene* (1947); and *Drawings by Charles Keene* (1952).

D.G.

KEMBLE, EDWARD WINSOR (1861-1933) American cartoonist and illustrator born in Sacramento, California, on January 18, 1861. E.W. Kemble's father was the founder and publisher of the *Alta Californian* newspaper but moved to New York when his son was young to take a job as an inspector with the Bureau of Indian Affairs. In 1875 young Kemble was enrolled at a boarding school in Philadelphia, then a hotbed of artistic activity (the likes of A.B. Frost, E.A. Abbey and Howard Pyle had made their first connections there). Kemble returned to New York infused with a yearning to draw and took a job with Western Union, peddling sketches on the side.

In 1880 four of Kemble's sketches were bought by Charles Parsons of the Harper's organization, and *Harper's Bazaar* ran Kemble's first cartoons in September and October of that year. Soon his career was in full swing. He became the major (front-page) political cartoonist for the *New York Graphic* while receiving his only formal artistic training at the Art Students League, taking classes alongside Frederick Remington. In 1883 *Life* magazine was founded, and Kemble was a frequent contributor to early issues of this black-and-white weekly. (Kemble, by the way, was to draw more cartoons for *Life* than for any other publication throughout his career.) His lively cartoons, some of the magazine's most mature work, attracted the attention of Mark Twain, who engaged Kemble to illustrate *Huckleberry Finn*. The marriage, of course, was a happy one; the cartoonist's line and the writer's prose were perfectly suited and led to further collaborations.

Kemble was a staff political cartoonist for *Collier's Weekly* (1903-07) and *Harper's Weekly* (1907-12) before returning to *Collier's, Leslie's Weekly* and *Judge* in the late 1910s. In his capacity as political analyst he accompanied Colonel George Harvey to Princeton, New Jersey, on the fateful visit that cemented Harvey's support of the somewhat obscure college president Woodrow Wilson

A soft answer, &c. Stout lady passenger (wincing—
he had trod on her best corn): "Phew!—Clumsy—"
Polite old gent: "Very sorry, my dear Madam, but if you had
a foot large enough to be seen such an accident couldn't occur!"

Charles Keene, ca. 1880.

for the U.S. presidency. Kemble also drew for *Puck* and the Hearst papers over the years. In the decade between 1896 and 1905 he drew various Sunday strips and colored panels and was an active advertising artist and book illustrator. In the early and mid-1920s, the last years of his professional life, he returned almost exclusively to the pages of *Life*. Kemble died on September 19, 1933.

For all his fine illustrative and political work, E.W. Kemble is best remembered—and justifiably so—for his specialty, cartoons of the Negro. He is perhaps cartooning's supreme delineator of the Afro-American, and his characterizations were often sympathetic. While his treatments were usually comic, Kemble took care to study the real urban and rural environs and living conditions of blacks. His caricatures were never absurdly exaggerated, although every convention—wild dress, chicken stealing, etc.—was thematically exploited to the fullest. Kemble produced many sensitive, almost photographic portraits of blacks.

It is practically impossible to overestimate the influence and popularity of E.W. Kemble. Like A.B. Frost, his technical cousin, he brought a stunning vitality to cartooning and illustration, and his stylistic imitators—at least those who inherited the freedom and animation of his drawings—were many. Kemble drew with a scratchy, loose pen line that in later years gave way to an economical use of thick emphasis lines. Almost every figure he drew was alive with emotion, tension, anticipation, surprise. Kemble had a photographic gift for arresting action and motion, again like Frost; his cartoons featured characters in midair, writhing, dancing, jumping, running, laughing uproariously. In his illustrations, often

sophisticated reportorial assignments on social themes, Kemble employed a classical, attractive crosshatch. Like his talented compatriots Frost, Bush and Taylor, Kemble the cartoonist is woefully neglected today and deserves to be rediscovered as an accomplished observer and penman.

Among the books Kemble illustrated are: *Huckleberry Finn, Pudd'nhead Wilson* and *The Library of Humor* by Mark Twain; *Uncle Tom's Cabin; Knickerbocker's History of New York; On the Plantation; Uncle Remus; Col. Carter of Cartersville; Samantha on the Race Question;* and *Phoenixiana.* His own books include the *Thompson Street Poker Club* anthology for *Life; Blackberries; Kemble's Coons; Rosemary; Virginia Creeper; Billy-Goat and Other Comicalities; Comical Coons; A Coon Alphabet; Coon Calendar; Kemble's Sketchbook; Coontown's 400; A Pickaninny Calendar; The Gold Dust Twins;* and others.

R.M.

KENDRICK, CHARLES (1841-1914) American artist born in London, England, in 1841. Charles Kendrick first achieved prominence as a principal artist on the *Illustrated London News*. Around 1870, when the journal sought to establish a Canadian edition, Kendrick went to Montreal.

In 1871 Kendrick moved to Brooklyn and attached himself to the Leslie publications. His facile pen work appeared occasionally in *Puck* after 1877 and frequently in the heavily illustrated *New York Graphic*. He was a major factor in the early respectability and success of *Life*, to which he contributed regularly for several years, beginning with the second issue (January 11, 1883).

In the 1870s Kendrick's theatrical caricatures were popular, and he continued personality themes in the *Graphic*, *Chic* (a *Puck* imitation) and *Life*, where he was its first major (and exclusively) political cartoonist. For *Life* throughout 1883 he illustrated the

"If I can only manage to skin out and go home without fussing with those other brats, I'll be thankful."

E.W. Kemble.

333

weekly *Biographettes*. He contributed to the *New York Herald* and to the major monthlies and for years taught at his Manhattan studio.

Kendrick was an important and polished pen-and-ink artist when photoengraving was introduced. His style was the illustrator's, but he seldom left the realm of political cartooning or humorous sketching. Realism and a dimensional and evocative method of shading were his trademarks; he influenced many cartoonists and illustrators, among them True Williams, an obvious follower. Kendrick died at his home in Brooklyn after an illness of three months on June 16, 1914.

R.M.

KEPPLER, JOSEPH (1837-1894) American artist and publisher born in Kieligenstadt, Austria, on February 1, 1837. Joseph Keppler's father, probably a descendant of astronomer Johannes Kepler, was a participant in the 1848 political upheavals and was obliged to flee to the United States, settling in Missouri. His family remained in Austria, and young Joseph enrolled in the K.K. Akademie der Bildern Kunste to study art. When a hoped-for scholarship to study in Italy failed to materialize, the impulsive and romantic Keppler joined a theatrical troupe departing for that country.

Keppler became a moderately successful stage performer and, resettling in Vienna, divided his time between acting and drawing (for such papers as *Kikeriki*). Within a year and a half he joined his father in America and pursued the same activities, with the same success. On August 28, 1869, Keppler launched his first publishing venture, a weekly satirical sheet in German called *Die Vehme*, of which he was the principal cartoonist. The magazine was short-lived (ceasing publication on August 20, 1870) but has the distinction of being the first American humorous journal with lithographic cartoons.

The following March Keppler introduced *Puck* magazine, a German-language weekly that aimed for national circulation. Though his cartoon-and-light-text journal lasted only a year and a half, it brought Keppler's work to the attention of publishing entrepreneur Frank Leslie, who invited Keppler to join the staff of his magazines in New York. Keppler excelled at *Leslie's*, produced some outstanding cartoons, made a large circle of acquaintances and nurtured his dream of running his own cartoon magazine.

In September 1876, the New York *Puck* debuted; it was a quarto in German containing front-, back-, and center-page cartoons by Keppler, and it was run by Keppler and Adolph Schwarzmann, late the business manager of the Leslie publications. The new company was persuaded to issue an English-language edition, introduced on March 14, 1877. Color was soon added to the lithographed cartoons (the interior cartoons were reproduced by photoengraving), and slowly *Puck* became a newsstand eye-catcher, a political force and a breeding ground for cartoonists and humorous writers.

In every presidential election thereafter until his death, the brilliant Keppler contributed at least one symbol, one cartoon icon, to political history. He is variously credited with creating the Tattooed Man, Uncle Sam's Whiskers (during his *Leslie's* days), the figure of the Independent New Party and the Grandfather's Hat of Benjamin Harrison. His powerful support for Grover Cleveland gained Keppler additional respect and, incidentally, a lifelong friendship with the new president.

Except during two trips to Europe, Keppler was very active in assuming art assignments and the management of his magazine, which had become one of the most influential of all American journals. He had surpassed Nast as the premier American cartoonist. Shortly after overseeing an impressive display—the erection of the *Puck* Pavilion at the Chicago World's Fair and the issuance of the *World's Fair Puck*—Keppler died, on February 19, 1894.

The influence of Joseph Keppler on American cartooning can hardly be overstated. Granted that he was indebted to Nast and that they were both potent forces in national politics, Keppler's directing a national magazine gave him additional influence, while Nast was often at odds with his own management. Moreover, Keppler tutored a generation of cartoonists and inspired more imitators than Nast ever did. The point would be academic and slightly irrelevant but for the fact that Keppler should be given more credit; his work deserves major republication.

Keppler worked nearly exclusively on stone. His art always retained a German flavor: a reliance on allegory and the avoidance of extreme exaggeration. He frequently alluded to Shakespeare and Wagner, and was content to depict his subjects in a style approximating portraiture, relying on the concept for the ridicule or satirical point. Keppler's fine arts background served him well in composing and executing cartoons, the backgrounds and incidental props of which were flawlessly drawn.

He was a devastating partisan—after 1884 consistently Democratic—and filled his dramatic work with invective, liberal advocacies and succinct political sermons. After 1881, when he was bolstered by enough other cartoonists on *Puck*, he virtually abandoned social satire to concentrate on political subjects. His favorite causes were civil service reform, women's suffrage and Grover Cleveland; among his dislikes were the tariff, radical labor unions, the Catholic church, Prohibition and politicians like Grant, Robeson, Blaine, Logan, Hill and the high-tariff and Tammany Democrats.

R.M.

KEPPLER, UDO J. (1872-1956) American cartoonist, publisher and Indian rights activist born in St. Louis, Missouri, on April 4, 1872. Udo Keppler, who signed his cartoons "Joseph Keppler, Jr." after the death of his father, was educated at the Gymnasium of Heilbronn, Germany, the Columbia Institute of New York and the Academy of Arts in Munich. He began drawing for his father's weekly cartoon magazine, *Puck*, in 1891, signing his little illustrations and black-and-white panel cartoons "U.J.K." Soon, however, he was drawing full spreads in color, and he assumed leadership of the art staff after his father's death in 1894.

For *Puck* he drew some notable cartoons—his talent would have found him a berth on any art staff—but after 1908 his interest seemed to diminish. The cartoons became less detailed and less frequent. In 1914, as majority stockholder in *Puck*, he sold the magazine to the Nathan Strauss interests. "Kep" continued to draw intermittently into the late 1910s, even doing full-page cartoons for *Leslie's* and *Judge*—once his magazine's hated rivals. Much of the reason for his waning interest

Udo J. Keppler, 1908.

lay in his awareness of American Indian problems, and he, like cartoonist Will Crawford devoted much time to Indian history, lore and welfare. (For his concern and informed efforts, Theodore Roosevelt had once offered Keppler the commissionership of the Bureau of Indian Affairs.) Udo Keppler died in 1956.

Keppler the younger composed in broad strokes and with bold concepts. He was as strong an idea man as his father but simplified his own work to a radical degree, for the most part eschewing labels and allegories. He used massive, powerful muscular, almost classical figures when he could, but he generally let the concept carry the cartoon. He was a strong Democrat, although he refused to support William Jennings Bryan.

R.M.

KEWPIE KORNER, THE (U.S.) An undated daily package panel feature, Rose O'Neill's *Kewpie Korner* was introduced into most subscribing newspapers in December, 1917, on varying dates, at the same time that her companion Sunday page was introduced. The Sunday page, with no regular running title, featured continuity adventures involving the famed elfin cupids that O'Neill had nicknamed "Kewpies" in their first magazine appearance in 1905. On the other hand, the daily feature was initially a one-column, single-panel drawing in which one or sometimes two Kewpies would make a short statement of witty philosophy that was printed beneath the panel. In early 1918, the daily panel was increased to a two-column width and proportionate height, and the Kewpie figures became involved in more elaborate action, although the lower gag line was retained.

Essentially a work of intense visual charm—the

Kewpie image was extraordinarily popular as limned by O'Neill and was featured in hundreds of toys, games and other artifacts—*The Kewpie Korner* had no intrinsic merit beyond its cheerful presence on the newspaper page during a grim war, and its captions had no great wit or humor of their own. Now ferociously collected by hundreds of elderly Kewpie addicts around the country (when they can find copies), *The Kewpie Korner* was folded by a bored and war-distracted O'Neill little more than a year after its highly popular introduction, leaving most papers in late December 1918.

B.B.

KEY, THEODORE (1912-   ) American artist and writer born in Fresno, California, on August 25, 1912. Ted Key graduated in 1933 with a degree in art from the University of California at Berkeley, where he was editorial cartoonist and art editor of the *Daily Californian* and associate editor of the campus humor magazine, *The Pelican*. While in college he sold a gag cartoon to *Life*, and upon graduation he moved to New York; in his first week there he sold cartoons to *Judge*, the *New Yorker* and *Collier's*. In the late 1930s, when he was associate editor of *Judge*, he sold to all major markets and was possibly the most published gag cartoonist in America for several years.

Key scored a hit with a strong-willed maid character who appeared in his gags for *Collier's*, *This Week* and the *Saturday Evening Post* in 1943; by autumn of that year the *Post* had contracted for sole rights. Two and a half years as a master sergeant in the Army Signal Corps did not interrupt Key's new success; he submitted roughs and did one finish a week of *Hazel* throughout World War II. After the war Key was offered a position with the J. Walter Thompson Advertising Agency, where he had done some writing previously, but he decided to cartoon full time instead. *Hazel* became a bigger success, leading to a flock of reprint books and movie, radio and stage offers before a five-year TV series was produced, with Shirley Booth in the title role. When the *Post* folded in 1969, Key turned the panel into a daily feature for King Features.

"I repeat—DO YOU . . ."

Theodore Key. © This Week.

Fyodor Khitruk, "Film Film Film."

Key has been active in other media. For ten years he did the *Diz and Liz* double-page feature for *Jack and Jill* magazine. He also draws a series of widely used industrial posters and has illustrated books for other authors. He wrote a radio play (*The Clinic*, on NBC, which was collected in *Best Broadcasts of 1939-40*) and three screenplays for Disney (*Million Dollar Duck*, starring Dean Jones and Sandy Duncan; *Gus*, starring Ed Asner, Don Knotts, Tim Conway, Tom Bosley and the L.A. Rams; *The Cat from Outer Space*, starring McLean Stevenson, Sandy Duncan, Ken Berry, Hans Conried and Henry Morgan). *Million Dollar Duck* and *Gus* were adapted into serialized comic strips in King Features' *Disney Treasury of Family Classics*. In addition to 11 *Hazel* anthologies, the amazingly prolific Key has produced *Phyllis* (a classic among children's books), *So'm I, Fasten Your Seat Belts, The Biggest Dog in the World* (a movie version of which has appeared in Britain), *Diz and Liz* and *Squirrels in the Feeding Station*.

Key's productivity speaks for itself. Recently his gag production has received an assist from his son Peter, who also writes for other cartoonists. His drawing style reveals a breezy brushstroke, with details expertly reduced to the minimum. Characterization and facial attitudes are the strongest elements of his work. His books and some magazine work reveal an attractive use of color. Key's brother-in-law, incidentally, is cartoonist Fritz Wilkinson.

R.M.

KHITRUK, FYODOR (1917-   ) Soviet animator born in Moscow on May 1, 1917. Fyodor Khitruk joined Soyuzmult'film, the giant Soviet animation studio, in 1938 as an animator. After being drafted into the Soviet army during World War II, he returned to animation in 1947. For some fifteen years Khitruk was content merely to work as an animator on other directors' films (notably Lev Atamanov's and Ivanov-Vano's). In 1962 he finally came out with a work of his own, *Story of a Crime*, an acidulous fable with undertones of social criticism that went unnoticed in the Soviet Union. This was followed by the mischievous *Toptychka* ("Teddy Bear," 1964) and the enchanting *The Lion's Holiday* (1965). Khitruk scored again with *Othello 67* (1967) and especially with *Film, Film, Film* (1968), a very amusing satire on filmmakers and filmmaking.

In 1970 Khitruk went to East Germany to direct, in collaboration with Katia and Klaus Georgi, a German-Russian co-production. Titled *A Young Man Named Engels*, it was a 20-minute cartoon based on the drawings of Marxist theoretician (and would-be cartoonist) Friedrich Engels. In recent years Khitruk seems to have abandoned his earlier, more optimistic attitude in favor of a somber, almost despairing outlook, as evidenced in *The Island* (1973), which concludes on a note of utter alienation.

Khitruk is unquestionably the most exciting of the contemporary Soviet animators. His works have been widely shown and honored around the world, notably at the Zagreb and Mamaia festivals.

M.H.

KHODATAEV, NIKOLAY (1892-197-?) Soviet painter and animator born in Russia on May 9, 1892. Nikolay Khodataev graduated from the Moscow Institute of Painting in 1917. After working in posters and oils, he joined the first Soviet studio of animation in 1924. His best-known film cartoon, *Mezhplanetnaia Revolutsiia* ("Interplanetary Revolution"), was produced the next year. A spoof of Yakov Protazanov's 1924 science fiction film *Aelita*, it was also an incredible feat of animation, depicting all kinds of space vehicles and futuristic weapons years ahead of *Buck Rogers*. Khodataev effectively directed the film, though the credits list him only as an animator, along with Yuri Merkulov and Zenon Komissarenko. In 1925 he also made *China in Flames*.

In the late 1920s Khodataev worked mainly with his sister Olga (*The Ten Rules of Cooperation* and *The Embezzlement*, both done in 1928) and with the Brumbergs (notably on *The Young Samoyed* in 1928). He also experimented with mixing live action and animation in such works as *The Terrible Vavila* and *Auntie Trova*. His solo efforts include *The Happy North* and *Eureka* (both 1930), *The Crocodile in Geneva* (a satire on the League of Nations, 1932), *The Music Box* (a satire on czarist militarism, 1933), *The Career of Fyalkin* and *Organchik* (both 1935). In 1935 Khodataev left animation for painting, although he is reported by Western sources to have made one more cartoon, the 1938 *Little Muck*. He died in the 1970s.

Khodataev's sister, Olga Khodataeva (1894-1968), was also a distinguished animator. In addition to the films she made with her brother, her directorial credits include *Happy Life* (1932, with the Brumbergs),

Nikolay Khodataev, "Mezhplanetnaia Revolutssia."

Return of the Sun (1937), The Boy with the Stick (1938), The Clouded Sun (1943, with Ivanov-Vano), A Song about Chapaev (1944, with Pyotr Nosov), Tale of the Old Bludgeon (1949), The Miracle Mill (1950), Tale of the Taiga (1951), and two cartoons co-directed by Leonid Aristov, The Brave Little Deer (1957), which received an award at the Edinburgh Festival, and The Little Golden Feathers (1960).

M.H.

KIJOWICZ, MIROSLAW (1929-   ) Polish animator born in Leningrad, the Soviet Union, in 1929. Miroslaw Kijowicz graduated from Warsaw University in 1955 and from the Warsaw Academy of Fine Arts in 1961. After making several amateur and experimental films, he joined the Bielsko-Biala animation studio in 1960, directing his first short, Arlekin, that same year. Then, in rapid succession, came The Story of a Dragon (1962), The Town (1963), Cabaret and Portraits (1964), The Smile and The Flag (1965); the last is regarded as one of Kijowicz's best works.

In 1966 Kijowicz took a job with the newly formed Miniatur Film Studios; Rondo and Cages were the first cartoons he produced there. In 1967 he followed with Laterna Magica ("The Magic Lantern"), an utterly charming little fable poking gentle fun at universal human weaknesses. Miniatures and The Blue Ball, both made in 1968, were further explorations of the familiar and commonplace. Kijowicz later became more ambitious with such projects as Panopticum (1969), Science Fiction and Variations (both 1970) and Pandora (1973), but he occasionally returned to his earlier, lighter style, as in the 1969 version of Arlekin and the 1972 Magnolia. His recent efforts have been a mixed bag that includes such works as Welder, The Hand, Manhattan and The Inspection.

Kijowicz has won a number of awards in Poland and elsewhere. His most familiar trademark is the lighthearted satire that has characterized his more successful films. He himself has described his cartoons as "short aphoristic films addressed to mental activity."

M.H.

KILVERT, B.S. CORY (1879-1946) American cartoonist and illustrator born in Hamilton, Ontario, Canada, on April 14, 1879. The son of Francis Edwin Kilvert, member of Parliament, B. Cory Kilvert moved to New York in 1900 to study at the Art Students League. He soon became a regular contributor to Life, where he drew one of the most popular cartoons in that magazine's history—"Hers," a depiction of a young country boy pining over a pair of little girl's panties hanging on a washline. It originally appeared as a cover and was reissued for many years afterwards as a print. Kilvert continued to draw for Life into the 1920s, was a staff artist for the New York World and illustrated many children's books. He died on March 29, 1946.

Although Kilvert often drew with a scratchy, busy pen line, it was exactly the opposite style—flat, heavily outlined, open-spaced—that made his career. It produced a striking posterlike result with broad areas of pastel color and could be described as the technique of Edward Penfield translated to cartoons. In Kilvert's hands, it was employed to good effect.

R.M.

"Has anybody seen an elephant?"

Rollin Kirby, 1930. © New York World.

KINOSHITA, RENZO (1936-   ) Japanese animator born in Osaka, Japan, on September 3, 1936. As a young boy in the early postwar period, Renzo Kinoshita was an avid fan of the comic books then popular, such as those created by Osamu Tezuka and Fukujiro Yokoi. Graduating from high school in 1956 (after majoring in electronics), Kinoshita became increasingly interested in animation and was particularly impressed by Walt Disney's Fantasia. In 1958 he joined a commercial film production company called Ikko, in Osaka, and became a protégé of Tsunoyama Kimura, himself a former disciple of the famous Kenzo Masaoka. Kimura's influence was a determining factor in Kinoshita's decision to pursue a career in animation.

Kinoshita today works on the front line of animation in Japan; one of his strengths is the experience he has gained by working both independently and for a broad range of production companies. He first began working independently in 1963 as Puppe Productions, primarily subcontracting for television commercials. At the request of Tokyo Movie he worked on such TV hits as Obake no Q Taro, and in 1966, on invitation from Osamu Tezuka's Mushi Productions, he moved to Tokyo, where he participated in the creation of such classics as Tetsuwan Atom ("Astro Boy"). In 1968 Kinoshita finally left Mushi Productions and two years later created his own company, Lotus Studio, which is now supported mainly by the production of television commercials but also collaborates on animated television series and produces independent shorts. Kinoshita's wife, Sayoko, whom he met while working at Mushi Productions, is an artist in her own right and assists in productions.

Kinoshita is extremely prolific and has garnered many awards in Japan and internationally for his animated television commercials, animated series and independent works. Among his most outstanding achievements in animation for television are Subarashi Sekai Ryoko ("Wonderful World Journey") for NTV in 1967; Geba Geba 90 Pun, a 90-minute comedy with animation spliced into live-action shots; and Curricula Machine, a 1976 Japanese version of Sesame Street. It is with his independent, experimental productions, however, that Kinoshita and Lotus Studio have made a lasting name for themselves internationally. Made in Japan, a short parodying the commercialism of Japan, won the Grand Prix award in the 1972 USA International Animation Festival, and in 1977 *Japonese*, another film satirizing modern Japan, won the honorary prize at the international film festival in Leipzig, East Germany. Most recently, Kinoshita completed *Pika Don* (1979), perhaps the first attempt to deal with the sensitive subject of Hiroshima in a medium such as animation. *Pika Don* is a nine-minute color short that Kinoshita conceived after viewing paintings drawn by survivors of the explosion in Hiroshima. The experience moved Kinoshita to create a film that would not only appeal to the world but could also be used as an educational tool to further the cause of peace.

Through his versatility and breadth of perspective, Renzo Kinoshita has established himself as one of the more talented animators in Japan today. However, as is often the case, his most imaginative creations have at times received more acclaim internationally than at home. The challenge confronting Kinoshita, as well as other artists, is to achieve international appeal without alienating the Japanese audience.

F.S.

KIRBY, ROLLIN (1875-1952) American cartoonist and three-time recipient of the Pulitzer Prize, born in Galva, Illinois, on September 4, 1875. Around the turn of the century Rollin Kirby traveled to Philadelphia and New York to work as a freelance illustrator. During the next ten years his work appeared frequently in the pages of *Collier's*, *McClure's*, *Harper's* and the *American Magazine*; cartoons ran in *Life* starting around 1909. In this early period his style closely resembled those of his very good friend John Sloan and other nascent Ashcan artists like Everett Shinn and William Glackens. Other lifelong friendships formed by Kirby in New York at that time were with humorists Don Marquis and Franklin P. Adams.

In 1911 Kirby secured a job as editorial cartoonist through Adams with the latter's paper, the *New York Mail*. In 1913 he switched to the *New York Sun*, only to be fired in a dispute a couple of weeks later. But another newspaper dispute across Park Row—as Charles Macauley left the *New York World*—provided an opening for Kirby.

It was with the *World* that Kirby was to become one of the most influential and republished of American editorial cartoonists. He adopted a gentle crayon style that contrasted with his devastating and withering advocacies and attacks. His background as an illustrator served his style well, as its refined appearance never tilted toward caricature but relied on virtual portraiture—his concepts did all the ridiculing. Anatomy was correct in all his work. Kirby used a pencil rather than brush or pen for his outlining, and the careful engraving that was standard for his day captured all the details in reproduction. It is doubtful that today's offset mills could do his originals justice.

Kirby's most famous contribution to cartoon iconography was Mr. Dry, a figure representing Prohibition (and, generously, all the other "anti" crusades of the 1920s) which bore an almost exact resemblance to a figure employed for the same function by Joseph Keppler in *Puck* a generation earlier. The character was clad in a dour frock coat and tall, black hat. He reminded one of a mortician, and some other cartoonists who borrowed the figure strapped a black armband on him.

The cartoonist's glory days were on the *New York World* in the 1920s; he won three Pulitzer Prizes in the decade and his policies happily coincided with those of the liberal journal. What many newspapermen have called the greatest staff in American journalism was jolted by the sale of the *World* in 1931; Kirby remained, unhappy and uneasy, with the new *World-Telegram and Sun* until a dispute with Scripps-Howard in 1939 caused him to switch over to the *New York Post*, a liberal bastion. In 1942 he semi-retired to do occasional work for the *New York Times Magazine* and for *Look* magazine.

Kirby published two anthologies of his works, *Highlights: A Cartoon History of the 1920s* (1931) and *Political Cartoons: 1930-1942* (1942). He frequently wrote and published verse and magazine articles and penned a pair of one-act comedies, *Spin of the Wheel* (1937) and *As the Limb Is Bent* (1938). Kirby, a scholar of his craft, wrote the entry on cartoons for the 14th edition of the *Encyclopedia Britannica*. He died on May 10, 1952.

R.M.

KITTELSEN, THEODOR (1857-1914) Norwegian artist born in Oslo, Norway, on April 23, 1857. Theodor Kittelsen was an artist whose drawings of trolls are legendary in Scandinavia. As an illustrator of Norwegian folktales, he found a style completely his own. His trolls, living in the woods and rambling in the rocky Norwegian mountains, almost seemed to resemble the richly varied gods from mythology. In his animal illustrations (especially in the series *Do Animals Have a Soul?*) he seemed to be a forerunner of Walt Disney; his insects and frogs seemed to become everyday people one could meet on street corners, in buses and shops. One almost looked for their antennae or webbed feet.

Another of Kittelsen's specialties was satirical drawing for dailies that weren't afraid to express an opinion. In his childlike way he made these drawings into great human poems where the grotesque was natural. Many consider him to be Norway's greatest graphic artist.

J.S.

KLEIN, ISIDORE (1897-) American cartoonist and animator born in Newark, New Jersey, on October 12, 1897. Isidore Klein got interested in art during his high school days in Newark and later attended the National Academy of Design in New York. He started his animation career in 1918, working at Hearst's International Film Service on such series as *The Katzenjammer Kids* and *Krazy Kat*. When IFS closed down a few months later, Klein joined the Mutt and Jeff Studio, writing and animating a number of *Mutt and Jeff* shorts.

In 1925 Klein strayed from the animation field and freelanced cartoons to all major American publications, including the *Saturday Evening Post*, *Collier's*, *Judge* and the fledgling *New Yorker*. When animated cartoons began to talk, Klein decided it was time to return to the fold, and in 1934 he went to work with Amédée Van Beuren. Moving to Hollywood the following year, he joined Charles Mintz and worked on the *Scrappy* and *Barney Google* series. In 1936, like so many other animators, he went over to the Disney studio, where he animated and wrote stories for such

Isidore Klein, "Tick Tock." © Klein.

short subjects as *Wynken, Blynken and Nod* and *Woodland Café*. Klein came back to New York in 1939 and joined Terrytoons, working on *Farmer Al Falfa* and later *Mighty Mouse*. From there he went to Famous Studios/Paramount in the late 1940s, and his handiwork can be seen in a number of *Casper* and *Little Lulu* cartoons.

In the 1960s Klein resumed his freelance activities, doing animation for television, producing commercials and directing animated shorts (one of these, *Tick Tock*, won a special citation at the 1967 Montreal Exposition). He is retired now and occasionally writes about animation, sharing his reminiscences of the field's pioneer days with the readers of specialized magazines.

M.H.

KLEY, HEINRICH (1863-1945) German cartoonist and painter born in Karlsruhe, Baden, on April 15, 1863. Possessor of a dazzling pen technique and unbounded visual imagination, Heinrich Kley was perhaps the most successful of the many draftsmen who have humanized animals or created animal-human hybrids. His purely human figure studies, with their strongly erotic emphasis, are also breathtaking. Moreover, none of this is harmless fun, but biting social satire. And when some of his cartoons, such as those done for *Simplicissimus* from 1908 to 1919, are viewed in the light of contemporary events, they prove to be scathing political statements as well.

Much has been made of the dichotomy in Kley's output; his style as a painter was quite different. He studied at the Karlsruhe Academy from 1880 to 1885,

and for a brief time in Munich. In the late 1880s, back in Karlsruhe, he did some illustration but soon became a painter of genre scenes, interiors, portraits and still lifes. In 1893 he completed a series of murals in the Baden-Baden post office. Around the turn of the century he began to specialize in paintings of industrial subjects and was hailed for his canvas *Crucible Smelting at the Krupp Steelworks*. He also did architectural views. It was his move to Munich in 1908 that seems to have released the cartoonist within him, for he was soon supplying the two great local magazines, *Simplicissimus* and *Jugend*, with his remarkable pen drawings, which were gradually anthologized in the albums *Skizzenbuch I* (1909), *Skizzenbuch II* (1910), *Leut' und Viecher* ("People and Animals," 1912) and *Sammel-Album* ("Omnibus Album," 1923).

Yet an interesting catalogue of an exhibition at a Viennese art gallery in March 1912 (preserved in the New York Public Library) demonstrates that there was no definitive break in Kley's production, and that the painter-cartoonist split was not schizophrenic, since that exhibition (shared with two other artists) included a large number of landscapes and scenic watercolors alongside a generous helping of his satirical pen works.

Kley also illustrated several books by authors both ancient and modern. The date of his death in Munich has been called into doubt but is generally given as February 8, 1945.

S.A.

KLIXTO
See Cordeiro, Calisto.

Heinrich Kley, "Tango," 1914.

KNIGHT, BENJAMIN THACKSTON (1895-1977) American cartoonist born in Dillsboro, North Carolina, on April 4, 1895. Benjamin ("Tack") Knight's first cartoon was published in the local *Waynesville Enterprise* when he was 14. In 1913 he moved to San Francisco and studied art at the Mark Hopkins Institute; the next year he became sports cartoonist for the *Oakland Tribune*, an activity interrupted by service in the navy during World War I. After the war Knight began his intermittent lifelong career as a teacher of cartooning (as newcomers to the field often did in the 1910s and 1920s). He published *Tack's Cartoon Tips* in 1923, and for years he operated a correspondence school. He also ghosted for Gene Byrnes on the *Reg'lar Fellers* comic strip (his style was virtually indistinguishable from Byrnes's) before relinquishing those duties to G. Burr Inwood and creating his own strips.

Knight drew *My Big Brudder* and *Peaches* for the very earliest Dell comic book formats in the early 1930s, and *Little Folks* with top-strip *Baby Sister* for the Chicago Tribune Syndicate shortly thereafter. He introduced two kid strips at the same time, and after a poll of readers Knight's strips were retained at the expense of Tom McNamara's *Teddy, Jack and Mary*. Knight also dabbled in animation at the Disney story department in 1935 and at Fleischer in 1939-40. In 1974 he won the Silver T-Square award from the National Cartoonists Society and the Good Guy award from the Northern California Cartoon and Humor Association, on whose advisory board he served. Tack Knight died in San Francisco in 1977.

Knight's style, as noted, was a virtual carbon copy of Gene Byrnes's. He likewise specialized in the kid cartoon and had a flair for capturing the happiness, playfulness, innocent scheming and inquiring confusion of children. His drawings, like object lessons from his cartooning course, were always lively and full of animation.

R.M.

KNOTT, JOHN FRANCIS (1878-1963) American cartoonist born in Austria on December 7, 1878. John Knott studied at the Holmes School of Illustration in Chicago and at the Royal Academy of Art in Munich. In 1905 he secured a position with the *Dallas* (Tex.) *News* as editorial cartoonist. His cartoons were simple, uncluttered affairs with spotted shading areas, some rendered in crayon, others in brush. In 1936 he received an honorary mention from the Pulitzer Prize committee and in 1939 the National Headliners Club award. He died on February 16, 1963, in Dallas.

John Knott is often confused by researchers with Jean Knott, Hearst cartoonist of the 1920s who drew the panel *Penny Ante* in the style of Thomas Aloysius Dorgan ("Tad").

R.M.

KÖHLER, HANNS ERICH (1905-   ) German cartoonist and printmaker born in Tetschen, Sudetenland (now Děčín, Czechoslovakia), on April 17, 1905. Hanns Köhler studied at the Applied Art schools in Dresden and Vienna and at the Vienna Graphische Lehr- und Versuchsanstalt. He began drawing political cartoons in 1935, and from 1942 to 1945 he directed the professional class in illustration and commercial art at the then-existing German school of fine arts in Prague. Since the end of World War II, his excellent political (and social) cartoons have appeared in a host of German newspapers and magazines: the *Deutsche Zeitung* in Cologne and Stuttgart, the *Nürnberger Nachrichten* in Nuremberg, the *Kölner Stadt-Anzeiger* in Cologne, the *Frankfurter Allgemeine Zeitung*, *Die Zeit* in Hamburg and the reincarnation of *Simplicissimus* in Munich.

Köhler's work has been reprinted in numerous anthologies of German political cartoons, such as the two anti-Adenauer omnibus volumes *Konrad Sprach die Frau Mama* ("'Konrad,' Said Mother," 1955) and *Konrad Bleibst du Jetzt zu Haus?* ("Konrad, Are You Going to Stay Home Now?," 1963, cover drawing by Köhler). He has also been represented by albums of his own. The 1959 volume *Wer Hätte Das von Uns Gedacht?* ("Who Would Have Thought That of Us?"), published on the occasion of the tenth anniversary of the German Federal Republic, contained a large selection from the two thousand drawings Köhler had done during that ten-year period. The 1969 book *Nun Lacht Mal Schön* ("Smile, Please") covered the first twenty years of the Bundesrepublik Deutschland and included a number of items that had already appeared in the 1959 volume.

In his work Köhler has cried out against militarism and rearmament, the division of Germany, the opportunistic nature of German political leadership (in his interpretation), the weakness of the UN as a peacekeeping force, the emergence of neo-Nazis in Germany and the vulgarity of everyday life and thought at home and abroad.

Köhler has also done book illustration: for example, an edition of *Don Quixote* in 1952. His home is in Herrsching, on the Ammersee in Bavaria.

S.A.

KOLAR, BORIS (1933-   ) Yugoslav cartoonist and animator born in Zagreb, Croatia, Yugoslavia, in 1933. Boris Kolar exhibited a fondness for caricature from his earliest years. After his high school studies he became a cartoonist for the humor magazine *Kerempuh*. His first encounter with animation came in 1955, when he started working for advertising film cartoons. From 1956 to 1960 he worked variously as an animator, background designer and chief designer for Vukotić, Kostelac and Ranitović (among the cartoons he animated, mention should be made of the celebrated *Concerto for Submachine Gun*).

Kolar's work as a director has included *The Boy and the Ball* (1960), *Boomerang* (1962), *Woof-Woof*

Boris Kolar, "The Monster and You." © *Zagreb Film.*

(1964), *Discoverer* (1967) and *Dialogue* (1968). Kolar has also directed several cartoons in the *Inspector Mask* and *Profesor Balthasar* series. For the National Film Board of Canada he produced *Specialists* (1969), and in 1964 he made *The Monster and You* for the World Health Organization. Kolar's most notable effort in recent years, *Utopia* (1974), is the story of a meek little man slowly being crowded out and crushed by the material objects surrounding him—a brilliant parable of modern life and paranoia.

A typical representative of the "Zagreb school," Boris Kolar is noted for his wit and invention. His cartoons have been awarded prizes in festivals around the world.

M.H.

KONDO, HIDEZO (1908-   ) Japanese political cartoonist born in Nagano Prefecture, Japan, on February 15, 1908. Hidezo Kondo is one of the elder statesmen of Japanese cartooning, and his career parallels the various transitions and developments in the field. He has a reputation as one of the foremost political cartoonists in Japan, particularly in the field of caricature.

Kondo began as a cartoonist with the *Third Tokyo Puck*, a humor and cartoon magazine edited by Kenichiro Shimada. Shimada was a high-spirited social critic whose outspokenness no doubt had great influence on Kondo's growth as a political cartoonist. In the late 1920s, Kondo actively produced a number of single-panel political cartoons, many in the proletarian genre, that criticized the Japanese government's treatment of labor unions. Later, Kondo became involved in another form of Japanese cartoon art called *nansensu manga* ("nonsense cartoons"), which had grown out of the "new art movement" inspired by Dadaism and the artistic and political experimentation of the early 1920s. Kondo joined the production staff of *Manga Man* ("Cartoon Man") in September 1929 and produced a number of artistic cartoons in the *ero* ("erotic") and *guro* ("grotesque") styles of the nonsense genre. This innovative publication introduced some American cartoons and comics and also included pages done in full color. The magazine was short-lived, however, because the government closed it down for political reasons in 1931.

In an attempt to fight the pervasive conservatism of the cartoon world in Japan and gain exposure for lesser-known cartoonists, Kondo, along with 17 other young artists, formed the Shin Mangaha Shudan ("New Cartoonists' Group") in 1932. They had some success in placing new cartoons in newspapers and magazines that had formerly printed only "ready-made" cartoons of the most conservative kinds, but the growth of militarism and the resultant censorship dashed any hope of maintaining an artistically free cartoon organization.

In 1938 Kondo made his first concession to the demands of the military government and began producing propaganda cartoons for the publication *Manga Jōhō* ("Cartoon Report"). In 1939, the Shin Mangaha Shudan became the Shin Nippon Mangaka Kyokai ("New Japan Cartoonists' Association") and began producing *Manga* ("Cartoon"), a wartime propaganda magazine. In it, Kondo drew his most memorable political cartoons, most famous among them the color cover portraits of the "evil demons" Churchill, Roosevelt and Stalin. At times, Kondo painted their faces green to give them an appropriately ghoulish appearance, and a particularly effective touch was the addition of fangs to the portraits of these Allied leaders. Kondo was eventually sent to Borneo, where he spent the rest of the war as a military correspondent and drew more propaganda cartoons for distribution on the battlefront.

After the end of the war, Kondo drew political cartoons for *Van* (1946) and created many one-panel cartoons depicting the severity of postwar life in the black markets and bombed-out cities. In 1948 he revived *Manga* and did the cover drawings for each issue; as during the war, these were portraits of political leaders—minus the fangs this time. In 1951 Kondo covered the San Francisco Peace Conference for the *Yomiuri News*, and he is still a political artist for the Yomiuri firm.

J.C.

KOREN, EDWARD B. (1935-   ) American cartoonist born in New York City on December 13, 1935. Ed Koren received his B.A. from Columbia College in 1957 and went on to study art under S.W. Hayter at Atelier 17 in Paris. Upon his return to New York, he enrolled at the Pratt Institute, receiving a master's degree in 1964. Since entering the highly competitive field of illustration and cartooning, he has developed a graphic style that has earned him serious consideration as an artist of wit and originality. Reviewing the *New Yorker*'s 50th anniversary cartoon album in 1975, *New York Times* art critic Hilton Kramer found in Koren's work a quality that promises to rank him, alone among the newer contributors, with Steinberg and Thurber.

Like the most inventive of his fellow cartoonists, Koren must be considered from the point of view not only of style but also of substance; he has forged a highly personalized mode of representation that he uses to convey his special brand of humor. His pen-and-ink drawings are almost stubborn in their unwillingness to display a fine, unbroken line. (Calvin Trillin, in fact, quotes a *New Yorker* colleague as likening Koren's work to a barbershop floor just before closing time.) The vaguely or overtly reptilian cast of his woolly characters may be inexplicable but somehow does not strike one as inappropriate. Koren has obviously seen something in his fellow man that most of us only sense and incorporated that perception into his work.

Koren's humor finds inspiration along a broad spectrum, from the topical (dropouts, Spock-saturated parents, hip intellectuals) to the lunatic (smooth-talking bulls, pistol-packing carrots and indeterminate crocodilian creatures). Those familiar with the Upper West Side academic scene in New York in the 1960s will find his renderings of it especially amusing (hip critics speaking of graffiti-spattered busses in highly technical "art-ese" and pronouncing them masterworks, or a cocktail party guest announcing, "I used to be a management consultant but now I'm into making up songs and poems"). But alongside this socially acute cartoonist is also a Koren who can send all the animals boarding the ark through a metal detector or have a pet-store owner go out of business by simply throwing open the door of his shop and standing aside, smiling as the liberated birds and beasts stream happily into the street.

In the light of his relative youth, the extent of Ko-

"Krazy Kat." © International Film Service.

ren's recognition as a force in the world of graphic art is impressive. His work can be found in the permanent collections of the Fogg Art Museum in Cambridge, the Rhode Island School of Design, Princeton University Museum, the U.S. Information Agency and the Swann Collection of Cartoons and Caricatures. Exhibitions of his art have been mounted for the Exposition Dessins d'Humeur at Avignon, France (1973), the Biennial Illustration Exposition at Bratislava, Czechoslovakia (1973), the Art from the *New York Times* show organized by the New York Society of Illustrators (1975) and the Terry Dinfass Gallery (1975-77). Koren received a Guggenheim Fellowship in 1970-71, a third prize at the Bratislava competition, designation by the *New York Times* as one of the ten best children's book illustrators of 1973 and the Prix d'Humeur at the Avignon Exposition. He is a member of the Authors' Guild, the Society of American Graphic Artists and the Cartoonists' Guild. He has published collections of his work under the titles *The People Maybe* (1974), *Do You Want to Talk About It?* (1977) and *Dragons Hate to Be Discrete* (1978).

R.C.

KRAZY KAT (U.S.) George Herriman's immortal creation has been a perennial of the animated film, appearing in no fewer than five separate series from the 1910s to the 1960s.

The first series was initiated by Hearst's International Film Service in 1916. Gregory La Cava was in charge of production, and Herriman himself supervised the proceedings. Despite all this attention, Krazy Kat, Ignatz Mouse and the other denizens of Coconino County failed to achieve popular success, and the series (which consisted of one-minute shorts usually running at the end of Hearst's weekly newsreels) was discontinued in 1917.

The J.R. Bray studios then took over the title and produced a series of cartoon films that rank as the best and the most faithful to the style and spirit of Herriman's *Krazy Kat*. Begun in 1919, they lasted into the early 1920s.

Bill Nolan, who along with Bert Green, Frank Moser and Leon Searl had directed the first *Krazy Kat*, now produced a fresh batch of *Krazy Kat* cartoons from 1926 to 1928 for the Winkler Picture Corporation. Nolan's Kat

bore no resemblance to its comic strip counterpart, except in name.

In the 1930s *Krazy Kat* was again adapted to animation, this time by Charles Mintz for Columbia (1936-39). Bill Nolan was one of the directors, but it was an exercise in mediocrity.

King Features Syndicate directly produced a new series of cartoons featuring Krazy Kat in 1963, this time for television. While the title character again looked like the newspaper strip Krazy, the series lacked Herriman's wit and poetry, and it lasted only one season.

M.H.

KRISTL, VLADIMIR (1923-   ) Yugoslav painter, animator and film director born in Zagreb, Yugoslavia, in 1923. Vlado Kristl graduated from the School of Fine Arts in Zagreb and started painting in the mid-1940s. He became one of the first cartoonists on the staff of the humor magazine *Kerempuh* and also dabbled in animation for Duga Film in the early 1950s. Kristl went into self-imposed exile in 1953, working in Europe and South America. He returned to Zagreb in 1959 and joined Zagreb Film that same year. In 1960, along with Ivo Urbanić he directed his first animated film, the brilliant, black-humored *La Peau de Chagrin*, about a gambler who sells his soul to the devil (the script was adapted from a Balzac story).

In 1961 Kristl produced single-handedly the much-praised and much-awarded *Don Quixote*, a fascinating adaptation of Cervantes's tale. After the success of this cartoon, however, disputes arose between the artist and the studio, and Kristl departed again, later that year, for West Germany. Since then he has chiefly directed live-action features such as the hermetic *The Dam* (1964), only occasionally venturing into animation, as with *Prometheus* (1964) and *Das Land des Uberflusses* ("The Land of Plenty," 1967).

M.H.

KRYLOV, PORFIRY
See Kukryniksy.

KUBIN, ALFRED (1877-1959) Austrian graphic artist and cartoonist born in what was then Leitmeritz, Bohemia, in the Hapsburg empire (now Litoměřice, Czechoslovakia), on April 10, 1877. For a man whose

Vladimir Kristl, "La Peau de Chagrin." © Zagreb Film.

artistic capital lay in the realm of the uncanny and the namelessly terrifying, Alfred Kubin had auspicious beginnings: the early death of his mother, the hostility of his father (an ex-army officer turned civil servant), a suicide attempt, a nervous breakdown while in military service, the sudden death of his fiancée. By 1906 he had purchased Schloss Zwickledt, a remote country house in Upper Austria that was to be his home until he died there on August 20, 1959.

His art studies were equally choppy. As a boy he was apprenticed to an uncle who practiced landscape photography; he spent some time at a commercial art school in Salzburg; in Munich, where he arrived in 1898, he attended the Academy and a private art school. His style seems to have been chiefly derived from close observation (sometimes amounting to psychic "inspiration") of such great masters of the fantastic and macabre as Goya, Klinger, Rops, Redon, Ensor and Munch.

Kubin's weird drawings were soon appreciated by the public. The pivotal year in his development, the year in which he wrote and illustrated the unique autobiographical novel *Die Andere Seite* ("The Other Side"), was 1908-09. From 1912 through the 1920s he contributed numerous drawings to the Munich satirical magazine *Simplicissimus* (some of these come as close to being garden-variety "cartoons" as Kubin's work ever got) and a few to *Jugend*. The thousands of drawings in his total production included illustrations for a host of books by himself and by authors such as Poe, Nerval, Dostoevsky, E.T.A. Hoffmann, Hans Christian Andersen and Strindberg. Kubin worked tirelessly into the 1950s.

His mature drawing style is nervous and scratchy, the sheets often being covered with a compulsive network of lines. Every linear element of his landscapes and interiors contributes to the obsessive or hallucinatory quality of the whole configuration. His dramatis personae include murderers, misfits, eccentrics, outcasts, charlatans and animated skeletons; the farms and buildings he draws are often ramshackle; death, pain and shame are always just around the corner. But a fine-honed wit and subtle irony constantly restore balance to Kubin's view of the world, reminding us that there is also humor, grim though it may be.

Kubin, of course, is one of the most highly esteemed 20th-century graphic artists. There is a Kubin-Archiv in Hamburg and a Kubin-Kabinett in Linz.

S.A.

Bureaucrats
Alfred Kubin, 1926. © Simplicissimus.

Later in 1893 Kubota paid his own way to the Columbian Exposition in Chicago, where he made sketches of what he saw and sent them back to Japan to be published in the *Kokumin Shimbun*. The outbreak of the Sino-Japanese war found Kubota back in Japan, and in May 1894 he traveled to what is now Korea as an army artist. There he made sketches of battle scenes and life at the front. Though many of these glorify the courageous Japanese soldier, they also capture accurately the stench, suffering and death found on the battlefield. Many of his works from *Beisen Jugungahō* ("Army Illustrator Beisen's Drawings") powerfully convey the tribulations of the native populace during the conflict.

Kubota's style owes more to the brush than to the pen. His lines are thick and full, and the message of his cartoons is direct and immediate. Dying horses, poverty and despair are frequent themes in his work. His vitality waned toward the turn of the century, and he produced little after the Sino-Japanese war. He died an unknown in 1906, leaving a son who, like his father, worked as an illustrator of the military conflicts before and after the turn of the century.

J.C.

KUBOTA, BEISEN (1852-1906) Japanese cartoonist born in Kyoto, Japan, in 1852. Beisen Kubota's real name was Mitsuhiro Kubota, but he preferred to draw under his pen name, which translates "rice hermit." He studied art in Kyoto and pursued a career as a traditional artist until 1893, when he made his way to Tokyo and contributed cartoons to the *Kokumin Shimbun* ("People's News"). His cartoons, appearing in a section of the newspaper called "Saiankoku no Tokyo" ("Blackest Tokyo"), captured the lives of the lower classes of Japan's largest city. They were stark, literal statements of the sufferings of those who worked in the ditches, cheap kitchens and bars of Tokyo. The most popular of these drawings have been frequently republished and are considered valuable exposés of Japanese society before the Sino-Japanese war of 1894-95.

KUEKES, EDWARD D. (1901-   ) American Pulitzer-Prize winning cartoonist born in Pittsburgh, Pennsylvania, on February 2, 1901. Displaying an early interest in cartoons, especially in the work of Gaar Williams, Ding Darling and Billy Ireland, Ed Kuekes attended, after Baldwin-Wallace College, the Chicago Academy of Fine Arts and the Cleveland School of Art for his artistic training.

His first job was as an artist for the Art Engraving and Color Type Company of Cleveland, and in January 1922 he joined the art department of the *Cleveland Plain Dealer*. He remained in the art department and was the regular cartoonist for the following 17 years.

In 1953, he won the Pulitzer Prize for a comment ("Aftermath") on a Korean War casualty old enough to die but too young to vote. Other honors include three

WONDER IF HE VOTED?

NO, HE WASN'T OLD ENOUGH.

Aftermath

Edward Kuekes, 1953 Pulitzer Prize-winning cartoon. © *Cleveland Plain Dealer.*

Freedoms Foundation medals (one presented by General Eisenhower in 1949) and an honorary doctor of humane letters degree from his alma mater, Baldwin-Wallace College.

Kuekes drew in a lush pen and brush style and occasionally used crayon instead of crosshatches for shading. During his career he also worked on two syndicated features, *Alice in Wonderland* and *Do You Believe,* collected in comic book form by the United Feature group.

R.M.

KUHN, CHARLES HARRIS (1892-   ) American cartoonist born in Prairie City, Illinois, on March 20, 1892. Charles ("Doc") Kuhn was raised in Bushnell, Illinois, and subscribed by mail to the Landon Cartooning Course, which he failed to complete (as did, curiously, many otherwise avid aspirants).

In 1910 Kuhn's first cartoon appeared in the *Message,* a socialist magazine published in Girard, Kansas. Other sales followed: to *Hope* magazine (for 50 cents!), to the *Addressographer,* a house organ, and to the *Galesburg Mail* in Illinois. In 1913, seeking further training, Kuhn enrolled in the Chicago Academy of Fine Arts cartoon school, then in its infancy. At the time, Carl N. Werntz was director, and among his teachers were the local cartoonist Frank King and an unknown, though talented, Will DeBeck.

Around 1915 a chance inquiry at the *Chicago Journal* led to a position as cartoonist alongside J. Campbell Cory, who became Kuhn's mentor. They were later to collaborate on a few cartoons, and Kuhn recalls constantly correcting Cory's misspelling. With America's entry into World War I, Kuhn served in

the navy, and during the postwar depression he took a job in a plow factory. Through Cory, Kuhn then secured a job in Denver as cartoonist for the *Rocky Mountain News,* where he remained for more than two years.

On January 3, 1922, Kuhn received a letter from Gaar Williams of the *Indianapolis News* stating his intention to switch to the *Chicago Tribune* and to recommend Kuhn for his job. This was high honor indeed, as Williams was one of the most respected American political and editorial cartoonists, and one of the most imitated—not least by Kuhn himself. Kuhn was to draw the daily editorial cartoon for the *News* for the next 25 years. Though he followed Williams's style, his work was individual and competent. He seldom used crayon, and he showed a seasoned mastery of the pen and the crosshatch technique. There was much native humor in his work; he deliberately eschewed the savage comment.

During World War II Kuhn conceived the idea of gift boxes or family "CARE packages" for servicemen and profited greatly until cardboard supplies became scarce; then others adopted the idea. He also published several cartoon courses which are remembered today by many professional cartoonists as their starting points.

In 1947, for the Richardson Feature Service of Indianapolis (which had recently flopped with a revived *Little Nemo*), Kuhn created several comic features, including one about a tomboyish, mischievous old lady who was a friend to the neighborhood boys. Duke Richardson syndicated *Grandma* for a year and a half before King Features picked up the strip and enlarged its client list. *Grandma* enjoyed a genteel and popular run until 1969; it was a friendly, old-fashioned strip in the Kuhn style and introduced the innovation of a black-and-white Sunday panel for children to color.

R.M.

PREDICTED FOOD SHORTAGE FOR 1943

U.S.A.

The Stranger at Our Gate

Charles Kuhn, 1942.

Low life high up. Weary Warbler: "I just asked the lady up in the house for a hand-out, and she gave me a worm that wasn't fit to eat."
Walt Kuhn, 1903.

KUHN, WALT (1877-1949) American cartoonist and painter born in New York City on October 27, 1877. Walt Kuhn was educated in private schools and received art training in Germany, France, Holland, Italy and Spain. His first job was as a cartoonist for a San Francisco newspaper at five dollars a week. Freelance sales of cartoons to the *New York Sun* brought him back to New York.

There, just after the turn of the century, he frequently contributed to *Life*. His specialty was little bird cartoons, and his small drawings seemed to fill the spot left by Gus Dirks, who had taken his Bugville cartoons to Hearst at that time. Kuhn's cartoons were small and often served a second function as fillers between blocks of text or ad copy. They were immensely popular, and *Life* printed a collection in a book entitled *A Little Bird Told Me*. The art was crisp, clean and jovial.

It should be noted, too, that although Kuhn gradually left the ranks of cartooning after 1910, his style was continued for another decade. Little bird character cartoons continued to appear, signed "Lang" (Louis Lansing Campbell); they were very close to Kuhn's work. Campbell was later to become a major illustrator of the Howard Garis *Uncle Wiggly* stories.

Kuhn sold his first serious painting in 1907, when he was 30. But in five years he was well on his way to becoming one of the great American painters, the career for which he is, of course, most noted. He was secretary of the 1913 Armory Show, fronting for a group of artists whose work was too modern for the National Academy. Fellow cartoonists John Sloan, Gus Mager and Rudolph Dirks (whom he taught to paint) also exhibited in this landmark show.

Although he was later to aver that "art can't be taught," Kuhn was a respected teacher for years, beginning at the New York School of Art in 1908 and 1909 and running through courses at the Art Students League in 1926 and 1927. His work now hangs in many galleries and museums. He wrote, designed and produced stage plays in pantomime and satirical ballets; his activities even led him to paint railroad club car murals. Kuhn, with other cartoonists and painters, was also active in the artists' community in Ogunquit, Maine. He died on July 13, 1949.

R.M.

KUKRYNIKSY (USSR) Kukryniksy is the collective signature of a team of three Soviet cartoonists: Mikhail Kupryanov (born in 1903 in Teyuschi), Porfiry Krylov (born in 1902 in Tula) and Nikolay Sokolov (born in 1903 in Moscow). The three met while attending the Moscow Institute of Higher Arts and Techniques, and they started working together on cartoons for the students' wall newspaper in 1924.

Deciding to stay together after graduation, they adopted their soon-to-be famous pen name (made up of the first syllables of their names). The first professional cartoons they signed were for the youth magazine *Komsomolskaya*; in 1933 they started to contribute cartoons to *Pravda* on a regular basis. Kukryniksy drew a number of anti-Franco cartoons and posters during the Spanish civil war, and the anti-German posters and drawings they produced during World War II are justly famous for their incisive style and visual impact. They are best remembered for their series of savage cartoons lampooning Goebbels and Hitler.

Kukryniksy is the best-known signature in the history of Soviet cartooning. The team has had a great number of exhibits throughout the Soviet Union, and their cartoons have been reproduced in countless books. They received the Stalin Prize no less than five times (in 1942, 1947, 1949, 1950 and 1951) and were awarded the coveted Lenin Prize in 1955; they are also full members of the Soviet Academy of Arts.

M.H.

The Fascist Lie-Gun
Kukryniksy, 1942.

KUPKA, FRANTIŠEK (1871-1957) Czechoslovakian cartoonist and painter born in Opočno, Bohemia, on September 22, 1871. František Kupka studied art in Prague and Vienna before settling in Paris in 1894. There he started his career with fashion drawings for department

The Foundations of the European Balance of Power

František Kupka, 1904.

stores and various magazines. In 1899 he exhibited his first humorous drawings.

Kupka had his art studio in Montmartre and designed several posters for Montmartre cabarets. His first cartoons were published in the humor magazines *La Plume* and *Cocorico* in 1900. He also contributed to most humor and satirical magazines of the time, including *Le Rire, Le Canard Sauvage* and *La Vie en Rose*, as well as to the anarchistic publications *Les Temps Nouveaux* and *Le Cri de Paris*. His most notable cartoons, however, were done for *L'Assiette au Beurre*, starting with the first issue of the magazine in 1901 and continuing until 1906. His drawings and captions were so savage that they had to be toned down even for such an outspoken publication as *L'Assiette!*

In 1907 Kupka began phasing out his cartoon work, and in 1910 he devoted himself almost exclusively to painting, doing occasional book illustrations. He started the Abstract-Creation group and is now regarded as one of the founding figures of the nonrepresentational school. He died in Puteaux, near Paris, on June 21, 1957.

M.H.

KUPRIANOV, MIKHAIL
See Kukryniksy.

KURI, YŌJI (1928-) Japanese cartoonist, animator and filmmaker born in Fukui Prefecture, Japan, on April 9, 1928. Yōji Kuri first started working in the prefectural tax office, but in 1956 he changed direction and entered the art department of Bunka Gakuin. When he graduated, his cartoons were already appearing in *Chisei*, the supplement to the *Nihon Shimbun Times*. After independently publishing the *Kuri Yōji Mangashū* ("Collected Cartoons of Yōji Kuri"), he won the Bungei Shunju cartoon award for 1958.

In animation Kuri attracted worldwide attention when his three-minute-long *Ningen Dobutsuen* ("Human Zoo") received an award at the 1963 Venice Film Festival. This was followed by a string of international awards for his experimental animation in films such as *Love* (1963), *Za Botan* ("The Button," 1964), *Samurai* (1965) and *AOS* (1967), which all garnered prizes in film festivals in Italy and Germany. *Ningen to Sekai* ("Man and the World") was awarded a silver medal at the Montreal World Exposition Film Festival of 1967. More recently, Kuri made *Froito no Ki* ("The Freudian Tree," 1973), *Jinko Bakuhatsu* ("Population Explosion," 1975), *Shinka* ("Evolution," 1976) and the cartoon short *Shometsu* (1977).

Ironically, because of the lack of Japanese theaters showing experimental or avant-garde films, Kuri has in many respects been more widely recognized outside Japan. His works range from pure animation to montages of photographs and animation to films with no animation at all. Two of his recurrent themes are atomic explosions and weak men being chased by strong women. The former is used to good effect in his *Za Botan*, where a couple visiting a horrendously developed industrial complex press the doorbell, only to have everything transformed into ashes. In *Atchi wa Kotchi* ("There Is Here"), an excellent experimental film made in 1962, Kuri combines animation and photography with an avant-garde seriocomic theme of strange devolution occurring after a missile is fired. Kuri is a prolific animator and cartoonist and has solidly established himself as a master of surreal comedy. He holds exhibitions of his work regularly.

F.S.

Yōji Kuri, "The Human Zoo." © Kuri.

Ll

LA CAVA, GREGORY (1892-1949)

LA CAVA, GREGORY (1892-1949) American cartoonist and filmmaker born in Towanda, Pennsylvania, in 1892. Gregory La Cava started his career as a newspaper cartoonist for W.R. Hearst, then in 1916 joined the newly created International Film Service devoted to the animation of Hearst-syndicated comic strips. La Cava was the titular head of the studio, producing the *Krazy Kat, Happy Hooligan, Maggie and Jiggs, Silk Hat Harry* and *Katzenjammer Kids* cartoon series. What later came to be called "the La Cava touch" was already in evidence in these animated films, which abounded in witty gags. One has only to compare the La Cava-produced *Krazy Kat* cartoons with the later, sorry bunch of cartoons of the same title to see the difference in style and humor.

These gifts of slapstick and humor were to serve La Cava well when he moved into live-action films in the early 1920s. La Cava directed several W.C. Fields comedies, including the memorable *Running Wild* (1927). Later he turned out some of the most enjoyable movie comedies of the sound era: *She Married Her Boss* (1935), *My Man Godfrey* (1936), *Stage Door* (1937) and *Unfinished Business* (1941), to name but a few.

Gregory La Cava died in Los Angeles on March 1, 1949.

M.H.

LADD, FRED
See Laderman, Fred.

LADERMAN, FRED (1927-   )
LADERMAN, FRED (1927-   ) American animator and producer born in Toledo, Ohio, in 1927. Fred Laderman went to Scott High School in Toledo, later attending the School of Radio Production at Ohio State University, from which he graduated with honors in 1949. In 1950 he went to work at WFDR, a leading radio station in the New York area, moving in the mid-1950s to the position of vice-president and general manager of Radio and TV Packages, a production company. While there, he was responsible for bringing to television such programs as *The Greatest Fights of the Century* and the noted animal life series *Jungle;* he also produced over four hundred one-minute animated cartoons, *Cartoon Classics.*

Attracted by the medium of animation, Laderman began in 1960 to bring to American TV, in collaboration with Universal Pictures, such noted animation series as *Astro-Boy, The Big World of Little Adam, Kimba the White Lion* and *Gigantor,* as well as the feature-length *Pinocchio in Outer Space.* In addition to being the producer in charge, Laderman also doubled as writer-director on these films (under his own name as well as under the pen name "Fred Ladd").

Laderman was the co-producer as well as the writer-director of the animated film *Journey Back to Oz* (1972), which was shown on ABC-TV and in the-

Giuseppe Laganà, "L'Om Salbadgh." © Corona Films.

aters abroad. This production featured the voices of such acting luminaries as Liza Minelli, Milton Berle, Danny Thomas and Mickey Rooney. Laderman is currently the writer-director of *The Children's Film Festival* shown on CBS-TV and of *The Greatest Tales,* an animation series based on fairy tales, legends and fables from the entire world.

M.H.

LAGANÀ, GIUSEPPE (1944-   )
LAGANÀ, GIUSEPPE (1944-   ) Italian cartoonist and animator born in Milan, Italy, on July 28, 1944. After finishing his high school studies, Giuseppe Laganà attended the Brera Art Academy. Graduating in the mid-1960s, he worked as a cartoonist for magazines and started his animation career directing commercial shorts along with Paolo Piffarerio and Gino Gavioli for Gamma Film in Milan.

Laganà worked on two of Bruno Bozzetto's full-length animated films, *West and Soda* (1965) and *VIP, Mio Fratello Superuomo* (1968), and was the art director on two sequences of Bozzetto's animated musical, *Allegro Non Troppo* (1976). He directed independently two animated films, *Preghiera nella Notte* ("Prayer in the Night," 1972) and *L'Om Salbadgh* (a 1975 film about a lost child raised in the wild), which were well received in various international festivals. Laganà has also pursued a career as a children's book illustrator and as a cartoonist for a number of magazines, including *Playboy.* From 1970 to 1972 he drew a comic strip, *Orlando,* for the cartoon magazine *Eureka.*

L.S.

LAGATTA, JOHN (1894-   )
LAGATTA, JOHN (1894-   ) American artist born in Naples, Italy, in 1894. John LaGatta grew up in America, studying art at the New York School of Fine and Applied Art under Kenneth Hayes Miller and Frank Alvah Parsons. His early advertising work showed the influence of the French illustrator Drian, but it was under the artistic

René Laloux, "Les Temps Morts." © Laloux.

influence of Coles Phillips that LaGatta hit his stride. Although he eventually liberated himself from this stylistic sycophancy, it was while drawing and painting "fadeaway" cartoons that LaGatta made his first major sales. He executed pieces for *Life* in the early 1910s, mostly covers with gag captions. It was a major market to break, but the young cartoonist showed a real flair for design, composition and color.

In the 1930s and 1940s LaGatta became a major fiction and advertising illustrator. With Jon Whitcomb, Gilbert Bundy and Bradshaw Crandall, he was hailed as the era's chronicler of the American Girl. In his later years LaGatta taught at the Art Center School in Los Angeles, California.

R.M.

LALOUX, RENÉ (1929-   ) French painter and cartoonist born in Paris, France, in July 1929. At the age of 13 René Laloux learned to draw at school, but he was largely self-taught. After World War II, while doing many odd jobs in order to support himself, he studied painting. From 1955 to 1959 he directed an art studio and also produced several shows with the inmates of a mental home at Cour-Cheverny. In 1960, he produced his first animated cartoon, *Les Dents du Singe* ("The Monkey's Teeth"), also with the help of patients. The story of a wicked wizard and of the monkeys who outwit him, *Les Dents du Singe* was awarded the Prix Emile Cohl for animation.

A few years later Laloux met fellow cartoonist Roland Topor, and together they realized *Les Temps Morts* ("Dead Times," 1964), followed the next year by *Les Escargots* ("The Snails"), a weird and disturbing tale of a mad gardener who grows giant lettuce and of the giant snails that destroy everything in their path in order to eat them. After a short interlude devoted to painting (with shows in Paris and Brussels), Laloux, again in collaboration with Topor, started in 1969 on his most ambitious project to date, a feature-length cartoon based on a science fiction novel by Stefan Wul, *La Planète Sauvage* ("The Wild Planet"). It was awarded a special prize at the 1973 film festival in Cannes.

A man of many talents (he is also a screen and song writer), René Laloux is probably the most gifted artist of the new French school of animation. He has received many awards for his work in animation at festivals throughout Europe.

M.H.

LANCASTER, SIR OSBERT (1908-   ) British cartoonist born in London, England, on August 4, 1908.

"You will notice that the line with which he draws his shrewdly observed people is almost juvenile in its deliberation and simplicity. But the artlessness of the style only serves to add pungency to the wit of a very grown-up mind." Thus wrote cartoonist and critic Percy V. Bradshaw in his chapter on Osbert Lancaster in *Lines of Laughter* (1946).

Lancaster's line is still artless, his wit still pungent, almost forty years since the day he invented the "pocket cartoon." Inspired by the French habit of single-column cartoons in newspapers, Lancaster persuaded the editor of the prewar *Daily Express* to allow him to institute the form in England. At first his column-breakers were an added attraction to the William Hickey page, a gossip column written pseudonymously by Tom Driberg, M.P. With the contracting newspapers of the war years, Lancaster's single-column cartoons became instantly more practicable and found their way onto the front page. They were also imitated by every other newspaper, and the small one-off daily cartoon remains a permanent feature of the British press. Only Lancaster's continues the title, *Pocket Cartoon*, and only Lancaster established a permanent cast of recurring characters, the leader of which is the redoubtable Lady Maudie Littlehampton.

Osbert Lancaster was educated at Charterhouse and Lincoln College, Oxford (1926-30); he took an honors degree in English literature and sat several law examinations. He studied art at the Byam Shaw School (1925-26) and at the Slade School of Art (1931-32), where he took stage design under Victor Polunin. He went to work for *Architectural Review* and was encouraged to write and illustrate a series of articles that treated the topic humorously. In his first book, *Progress at Pelvis Bay* (1936), he further explored this vein, giving a solemn account of "this well-known plague spot and eyesore" in a style of tongue-in-cheek humor he would make his own. Meanwhile, he did posters for London Transport, book jackets and a large mural in a hotel in Blandford.

January 1, 1939, saw the first of his *Daily Express* cartoons, which continued with but one break from 1944 to 1946, when he was first secretary with the British embassy at Athens, Greece. On his return to England he joined the editorial board of the *Architectural Review*, designed sets and costumes for the ballet *Pineapple Poll* (the first of many such stage de-

Roman Drayneflete

Osbert Lancaster, from "There'll Always Be a Drayneflete." © *Lancaster.*

signs for the Royal Ballet) and did similar work for the Glyndebourne Opera. He was made Commander of the British Empire in 1953 and knighted in 1975.

Books: *Progress at Pelvis Bay* (1936); *Our Sovereigns* (1936); *Pillar to Post* (1938); *Homes Sweet Homes* (1939); *Pocket Cartoons* (1940); *New Pocket Cartoons* (1941); *Further Pocket Cartoons* (1942); *25 Caricatures* (1943); *More Pocket Cartoons* (1943); *Assorted Sizes* (1944); *Osbert Lancaster Cartoons* (1945); *Clerical Landscape with Figures* (1947); *More and More Productions* (1948); *Saracen's Head* (1948); *A Pocketful of Cartoons* (1949); *Draynefleet Revealed* (1949); *Facades and Faces* (1950); *Lady Littlehampton and Friends* (1952); *All Done from Memory* (1953); *Studies from Life* (1954); *Tableaux Vivants* (1955); *Private Views* (1956); *The Year of the Comedy* (1957); *Etudes* (1958); *Here of All Places* (1959); *Signs of the Times* (1961); *Studies from Life* (1961); *In Laws and Outlaws* (1962); *The Water Beetle* (1962); *All's Well That Ends Well* (1963); *Mixed Notices* (1963); *The Penguin Osbert Lancaster* (1964); *Graffiti* (1964); *The Law and the Profits* (1965); *Parkinson's Law* (1965); *A Few Quick Tricks* (1965); *With an Eye to the Future* (1967); *Temporary Diversions* (1968); *Sailing to Byzantium* (1969); *Fasten Your Safety Belts* (1970); *Signs of the Times* (1971); *Meaningful Confrontations* (1971); *Theatre in the Flat* (1972); and *The Littlehampton Bequest* (1973).

D.G.

LANE, JOHN RICHARD (1932-   ) American editorial and political cartoonist born in Jefferson City, Missouri, on August 12, 1932. John Lane's father, Ralph Lane, was a backbone of the Newspaper Enterprise Association (NEA) art staff for years; he was a gag cartoonist in the twenties and thirties, assisted Roy Crane on *Buz Sawyer* and created his own strip, *Vic Flint*, for NEA. Ironically, when *Vic Flint* folded (under the title *The Good Guys*) it was John Lane who was then its artist. The younger Lane received all his cartoon training and most of his art training from his father, except for two years at the Cleveland Institute of Art.

While yet in his early twenties, John Lane joined NEA as art director, assuming a wide range of duties. Among these were graphics and editorial cartoons. When NEA's chief political cartoonist, Bill Crawford, went into semi-retirement in 1974, Lane filled the void and assumed full duties three years later. His style is trendy and illustrative, a handsome holdover from his graphics days. He uses only pen and ink, with no crayon shading but some very effective crosshatching and linework.

As a political cartoonist serving a presold client list of hundreds of papers, the NEA artist has traditionally trod the middle of the political road—a complaint of John Fischetti during his tenure. Lane, however, seems to have moved slightly to the left.

R.M.

LANG, ERNST MARIA (1916-   ) German architect and editorial cartoonist born in Oberammergau, Germany, on December 8, 1916. Ernst Lang is from the celebrated family of folk artists (potters and sculptors) whose members have so often played major roles (including Christ) in the recurring Passion plays of their Bavarian village. Like Peichl ("Ironimus") in Vienna, Lang in Munich combines the career of leading architect—he is an expert in modern town planning—with that of political cartoonist. He has

John Lane. © NEA.

also been head of an applied-art and architecture school in Munich.

Lang studied architecture in the Bavarian capital, served as an army engineer in World War II, and set up as a freelance architect in 1949. In 1947 his skill as a cartoonist was discovered by the Munich *Süddeutsche Zeitung*, to which he contributed for many years. From 1954 on, he also appeared on Bavarian television.

Lang's first album, *Politische Drehbühne* ("Political Revolving Stage"), consisted of cartoons he had done for the *Süddeutsche Zeitung* between 1947 and 1949. These still lacked the imagination and freedom of pen work that were to come. Fortunately, the heavy, unrelieved black backgrounds and the excessive reliance on standard national and allegorical symbols merely marked a passing phase.

Lang's political verses done for television (each poem illustrated with several small pictures) were the basis of his 1959 album *Die Zwerge Gehn in Volle Deckung* ("The Dwarfs Take Cover"). The title is the same as that of one of the poems inside, about the spirit of the dead Stalin suddenly reawakening during the Hungarian events of 1956 while his puny successors scurry to safety. But the cover illustration shows Adenauer as a giant among his fellow German politicians, so that the title applies to local politics as well. Adenauer would continue to be one of Lang's main targets.

Korsaren und Korsette ("Corsairs and Corsets," 1960), a review of recent European politics, is largely anti-Adenauer, although De Gaulle and others come in for their share of abuse. By this time, Lang's contours were much freer, and his cartoon style thoroughly pliable and capable of clever parodies.

Deutschland, Ich Muss Dich Lassen ("Germany, I Must Leave You," 1963) is completely devoted to Adenauer. Not only is the chancellor's entire political career reviewed sarcastically, but Adenauer-like fig-

Walter Lantz, "Andy Panda." © Walt Lantz Productions.

ures are traced through all of world history in an un-flattering attempt to analyze the old man's character. Lang is generally referred to as a calm South German "laughing observer" of the world scene, but in books like this one, his bite can be pretty savage.

S.A.

LANTZ, WALTER (1900-   ) American animator born in New Rochelle, New York, on April 27, 1900. Walter Lantz started his animation career in 1916 at Hearst's International Film Service, under the supervision of Gregory La Cava. There he animated and later directed a number of *Katzenjammer Kids*, *Krazy Kat* and *Happy Hooligan* cartoons. After the closing of International Film Service in 1918, Lantz joined the studio of John Randolph Bray, who had acquired the animation rights to many of the Hearst characters. At Bray, Lantz worked notably on *Colonel Heezaliar* and *Dinky Doodle*, but his talents for management led him to various production positions.

In the late 1920s Lantz set up his own studio, re-leasing through Universal; one of his first assignments, starting in 1929, was to continue the *Oswald the Rabbit* cartoon series, which Universal had just acquired from Charles Mintz. Oswald became the standard-bearer of the Lantz studio and was later joined by Winchester the Tortoise, Li'l Eight-Ball (a black boy) and Andy Panda. Lantz finally got his first solid success with Woody Woodpecker, who made his appearance in 1941. The *Woody Woodpecker* cartoons were to remain Lantz's only popular series, despite his attempts at producing various other characters, such as Homer Pigeon, Inspector Willoughby and Chilly Willy, the penguin created by Tex Avery. Lantz's studio was one of the last to close its doors (in

1973); Lantz still produces the *Woody Woodpecker Show* as well as occasional specials for television.

It cannot be said that Walter Lantz ever set high standards of excellence for his staff (Tex Avery once characterized the studio's animation work as "crappy"), but he was resilient and resourceful, and his studio outlasted most of the more artistic units. Among the directors who worked on the Lantz cartoons, mention should be made of Bill Nolan, Dick Lundy, Shamus Culhane, Sid Marcus, Paul J. Smith, Jack Hannah and of course Tex Avery.

M.H.

LA PALME, ROBERT (1908-   ) Canadian cartoonist born in Montreal, Canada, on April 14, 1908. In 1918 young Robert La Palme followed his family to Alberta, where his father became a farmer. Returning with his family to Montreal in 1925, he applied to the Ecole des Beaux-Arts but was turned down.

In spite of his lack of formal art training, La Palme has enjoyed a long and fruitful career in cartooning. In 1930 he incorporated elements of cubism into his cartoons, thus becoming one of the forerunners of modern art in Canada. In 1934 he became editorial cartoonist of the intellectual daily newspaper *L'Ordre*, while contributing drawings to such publications as the *Philadelphia Ledger*, *The Nation*, and *Stage* magazine. After a short stint at the Ottawa daily *Le Droit*, La Palme settled in Quebec City in 1937 as the editorial cartoonist of *Le Journal*. Back in Montreal in 1943, he successively worked for *Le Canada* (1943-50), *Le Devoir* (1950-59) and *La Presse*.

In addition to his work as a cartoonist, La Palme has been a librarian at the Quebec Beaux-Arts School and has taught at Laval University in Quebec City. His murals entitled *The History of War* have earned him many awards. He has been active in Canadian television and has worked for the stage as a set designer. In 1968 in Montreal he organized the International Pavilion of Humor, of which he is currently the curator.

Robert La Palme has received many awards, including the Order of Canada for his contributions to Canadian art and a gold medal at the 1967 International Poster Exhibition in Tokyo.

M.H.

LÉANDRE, CHARLES (1862-1934) French caricaturist, cartoonist, lithographer and poster designer born in Normandy, France, on July 23, 1862. Charles Léandre studied with Bin and Cabanel at the Ecole des Beaux-Arts in Paris (1878-84). He later joined the ranks of cartoonists at *Le Chat Noir*, contributing as well to *Le Gaulois*, *Le Rire*, *Le Journal Amusant* and *L'Assiette au Beurre*. While his caricatures of personalities in politics, arts and literature have a satirical bite (especially the ferocious caricatures of an enormous Queen Victoria sitting on poor, "weak" Kruger, or a curly-bearded Edouard Drumont, the vitriolic anti-Semitic politician and writer, shown devouring Jewish heads), most of his cartoons deal with various social problems, from backroom abortions to prostitution. Some of these drawings, reminiscent of André Gill's style, were released as albums: *Paris et la Province* (1898) and *Le Musée des Souverains* ("The Museum of Sovereigns," 1900).

In addition to posters for various singers and actors (Xavier Privas, 1899; Cécile Sorel, 1901; Yvette Guilbert, 1902), lithographs attacking "war idiocies," and book illustrations (especially for Rostand's *Cyrano de Bergerac*, 1902), he also published his delicate yet powerful sketches dealing with life in and around La Nouvelle Athènes, a Montmartre bistro, under the title *Nocturnes* (1896).

A member of the so-called Montmartre school, Charles Léandre died in Paris in 1934.

P.H.

LEAR, EDWARD (1812-1888) British humorist, natural history artist and illustrator born in Highgate Village, London, England, on May 12, 1812.

The Jumblies (who went to sea in a sieve), the Pobble (who has no toes), the Dong (with the luminous nose), the Owl and the Pussy Cat (who went to sea in a beautiful pea-green boat), the Quangle-Wangle, Mr. and Mrs. Discobbulus . . . the list is almost as eternal as the characters themselves, who live on and on, rediscovered by generation after generation of children who respond instantly to the ageless insanity of Edward Lear, the man who "invented Nonsense." Their latest incarnation was in *Tomfoolery*, perhaps the most original television cartoon series ever, produced by Rankin-Bass in 1971—although purists would undoubtedly prefer the very Victorian but still appealing original images of the author's own illustrated text.

Edward Lear was one of 21 children of a bankrupted stockbroker. A sickly child, he was educated mainly by his older sister. At 15 he began to earn a living drawing and coloring for medical research. In 1831 he was commissioned by the London Zoological Society to make colored drawings of the parrots in the Regents Park Zoo, a job that took a year and was published as the first colored book on birds in England. Lear's reputation as a natural history artist was made, and for some years his career was soberly pictorial.

Inspired by the form of the limerick, he created many of his own and eventually published them as *The Book of Nonsense* (1846), illustrating each verse.

Charles Léandre, caricature of the notorious anti-Semite M.E. Drumont, ca. 1890.

| PHATTFACIA STUPENDA | MANYPEEPLIA UPSIDOWNIA | NASTICREECHIA KRORLUPPIA |

Edward Lear, from "Nonsense Botany."

It was a great success, and nonsense verses and pictures became a popular second string to his career as a serious painter—a life which not only took him to foreign parts but raised him to the position of art master to Queen Victoria. The last years of his life saw a return of the ill health that had beset his childhood; he lived in Italy, where he died at San Remo on January 29, 1888, and was mourned by his constant companion, Foss (a cat).

Books: *Illustrations of the Family of Psittacidae* (1832); *Views in Rome* (1841); *A Book of Nonsense by Derry Down Derry* (1846); *Illustrated Excursions in Italy* (1846); *Gleanings from the Menagerie at Knowsley Hall* (1846); *Journal of a Landscape Painter in Albania* (1851); *. . . in Southern Calabria* (1852); *. . . in Corsica* (1870); *Nonsense Songs* (1871); *More Nonsense* (1872); *Edward Lear's London Journal* (1873); *Laughable Lyrics* (1877); *Nonsense Songs and Stories* (1888); *Nonsense Botany* (1889); *Nonsense Drolleries* (1889); *Nonsense Birthday Book* (1894); *Queery Leary Nonsense* (1911); *Edward Lear Coloured Bird Book* (1912); *Nonsense Poetry Book* (1924); *Edward Lear* (1927); *Lear Omnibus* (1938); *Picture Tales for Little Folk* (1938); *Lear in Sicily* (1938); *The Book of Lear* (1939); *Edward Lear's Nonsense Omnibus* (1943); *Complete Nonsense of Edward Lear* (1947); *Teapots and Quails* (1953); *Lear's Corfu* (1965); *Penned and Illustrated by Edward Lear* (1965).

D.G.

LEASON, PERCIVAL ALEXANDER (1889-1959) Australian painter, illustrator and cartoonist born in Kaniva, Victoria, Australia, in 1889. Not every artist distinguishes himself by becoming a household name on a national scale. Percy Leason, though, is known throughout Australia for his wonderfully funny drawings of events disturbing the placid life in the fictitious country town of Wiregrass.

Percival Alexander Leason was born and brought up on a wheat farm at Kaniva in Victoria's Wimmera district. From boyhood he practiced drawing the animals, birds, trees and other subjects he found around the farm. "Then something happened," he once wrote, "that nearly put an end to my interest in art. I went to an art school." Twice a week he traveled on the steam engine of the local train to the nearby town of Nhill for these lessons. "And the town's name represents what I learned there," he added.

On an impulse, Leason came to Melbourne armed with some published clippings of work he had submitted to a children's column of a Melbourne newspaper. This led to his being apprenticed for five years

Hard Luck: —"Is it true that you have races here to-morrow?"
—"Yeh; but you're too late to enter him—entries closed yesterday."

Percy Leason, 1923. © The Bulletin.

as a lithographer with a big city printer. After taking some Melbourne Art Gallery night classes, he freelanced, then moved to Sydney in 1917, still working as a commercial artist, this time with the well-known studio of Smith and Julius. Two years later, as a *Bulletin* artist, he was drawing his nationally popular studies of country people reacting to civilization's progress.

Leason's draftsmanship was faultless; he always drew with a pen, using very fine nibs with etching-like precision. Notable for its accuracy of detail, his draftsmanship showed, like that of Norman Lindsay and David Low, a profound respect for the traditional grammar of drawing. Leason's pen illustrations to the *Selected Poems of Henry Lawson* (1918) are examples of the astonishing technical skill he always brought to his comic art. It was not only Leason's tremendous draftsmanship that was outstanding but also the composition and figure grouping of his comic drawings. For example, in his *Bulletin* drawing "The Finish of the Old Buffers' Race," he drew over ninety people in beautifully arranged groups, plus three old cars, two buggies, two hitched horses, a couple of bicycles, sundry trees—and a dog. It is a typical Leason drawing, one that is, in terms of journalism, breathtaking for its concept, painstaking execution and sheer drawing skill. His drawings, like those of Norman Lindsay, are sure and precise, with no alterations or "chinese-white" corrections.

Leason was lured to Melbourne *Punch* from the *Bulletin* in 1924, and plans were also in hand to attract Will Dyson back to Australia to work for this weekly magazine. With Leason as chief cartoonist, many of Australia's finest black-and-white artists contributed to Melbourne *Punch* in its one year of ownership by the Melbourne *Herald* and *Weekly Times* group. These artists included Will Dyson, Jim Bancks, Hugh McCrae, D.H. Souter, Emile Mercier, Unk White and Mick Armstrong, who was later to earn a strong reputation with his political cartoons for the Melbourne *Argus*. It was no fault of the *Punch* artists that this 69-year-old publication foundered. In December 1925, Melbourne *Punch* was "incorporated" in *Table Talk*, a society gossip magazine also published by the *Herald* group in Melbourne. Percy Leason and Will Dyson, as staff artists, worked out their contracts on

Table Talk, which in turn ceased publication in 1937. Dyson returned to London in 1930, while Leason renewed his association with the *Bulletin*.

For many years, Leason had been passionately interested in the tonal painting theories of Max Meldrum. After a short holiday in America in 1937, he settled there with his family in 1939 and eventually became successful as an illustrator for *Collier's* magazine, the *Saturday Evening Post* and other periodicals, and as an art director and teacher of painting. He surprised the scientific world with his original research and theories on the Cro-Magnon cave artists, believing that they were the first artists to go directly to nature and suggesting that the seeming action and movement in their cave paintings was achieved by their study of dead, not living, animals.

Percy Leason died in New York at age 70 in September 1959.

V.L.

LEBEDEV, ALEKSANDR IGNATEVICH (1830-1898)
Russian illustrator and cartoonist born in St. Petersburg, Russia (now Leningrad, USSR), in 1830. Aleksandr Lebedev studied at the St. Petersburg Academy of Arts under the reputed teacher P.V. Basin from 1849 to 1857.

Lebedev became one of Russia's first and finest cartoonists in the late 1850s with contributions to the humor magazine *Vesel'chak* ("Merry Man") and *Iskra* ("The Spark," not to be confused with the later Marxist newspaper of the same title, of which Lenin was an editor). Lebedev pursued his cartooning career into the 1890s with his lusty depictions of St. Petersburg life and society. He also authored several albums of lithographs, of which the gently satirical *Fallen but Dear Creatures* (1862) is probably the best known, and he illustrated works by Nikolai Nekrasov and Saltykov-Shchedrin, among others.

Lebedev can be said to have been a forerunner of the Soviet school of social cartooning in many of his more iconoclastic cartoons; but he was first and foremost an entertainer whose politically pointed drawings (for which he is much praised today in Soviet publications) do not seem to have bothered the czarist authorities. He died peacefully in St. Petersburg on April 16, 1898.

M.H.

Youth: "You needn't be afraid Ma'am. Stand behind me!"

John Leech, 1860.

Fernand Léger, "Ballet Mécanique." © Léger.

LEECH, JOHN (1817-1864) British illustrator and cartoonist born in London, England, on August 29, 1817.

"The world's first cartoonist" is a title that may well belong to John Leech: he drew the first graphic satire ever to be called a cartoon. In 1843 an exhibition of cartoons proper (the rough designs for frescoes) was held in London: a competition for proposed designs for the walls of the Houses of Parliament. *Punch*, the illustrated satirical weekly, declared it would hold its own exhibition within its pages, "to be called *Punch's Cartoons*." This announcement appeared on July 1, 1843, and then on July 15 "Cartoon No. 1: Substance and Shadow," drawn by John Leech, was introduced. It was a convenient term and quickly caught on for the weekly full-page topical or political drawing which *Punch* and its contemporaries regularly featured.

John Leech was born at the London Coffee House, Ludgate Hill, where his father was a vintner. At age 7 he attended Charterhouse, where the drawing master was Mr. Burgess. At 16 he went to study medicine at St. Bartholomew's, where he executed excellent anatomical drawings. At 18 he drew his first humorous sketches for *Bell's Life in London*. "Etchings and Sketchings by A. Pen" (1835) was his first publication—four quarto sheets sold at two shillings plain, three shillings colored. He became a full-time illustrator from 1838, and his first popular success was a burlesque of Rowland Hill's Penny Post design. He took over the illustration of Charles Dickens's *The Pickwick Papers* upon the sudden death of Robert Seymour. His first *Punch* drawing appeared in the fourth issue (August 7, 1841) and in the next 23 years he executed over four thousand cartoons and illustrations for the periodicals *Illustrated London News*, Jerrold's *Illustrated Magazine*, *Once a Week*, *Bentley's Miscellany*, *The Month* and *The Field*, and for books by Charles Dickens (*A Christmas Carol*, *The Chimes*, *Cricket on the Hearth*) and R.S. Surtees (the *Jorrocks* series).

Leech was also one of the first British cartoonists to work in the comic strip format: his *Mr. Briggs* began in *Punch* on February 24, 1849. Leech more than fulfilled the prophecy made by the sculptor Flaxman when Leech was seven years old: "Let his genius follow his own bent and he will astonish the world." Leech died quite young, at age 47, on October 29, 1864.

Books: *Etchings and Sketchings* (1835); *Comic English Grammar* (1840); *Comic Latin Grammar* (1840); *Fiddle Faddle Fashion Book* (1840); *Colin Clink* (1841); *Portraits of Children of the Mobility* (1841); *Written Caricatures* (1841); *Hector O'Halloran* (1842); *Jack the Giant Killer* (1843); *Whimsicalities* (1844); *Follies of the Year* (1844); *Comic Nursery Tales* (1844); *Punch's Snapdragons* (1845); *Comic History of England* (1847); *Struggles of Christopher Tadpole* (1848); *Mr. Sponge's Sporting Tour* (1848); *Rising Generation* (1848); *Book of Ballads* (1849); *Young Troublesome* (1850); *Comic History of Rome* (1851); *Handley Cross* (1854); *Pictures from Life and Character* (1854); *The Militiaman at Home and Abroad* (1857); *Encyclopedia of Rural Sports* (1858); *Ask Mamma* (1858); *Little Town in Ireland* (1859); *Paul Prendergast* (1859); *Mr. Briggs and His Doings* (1860); *Punch on Pegasus* (1861); *Early Pencillings for Punch* (1864); *Later Pencillings for Punch* (1865); *Carols of Cockaygne* (1869); *The Right Hon. John Bright* (1878); *Disraeli Cartoons* (1878); *Right Hon. William Gladstone Cartoons* (1878); *Fun for Everybody* (1879); *John Leech Artist and Humorist* (1883); *Adventures of Mr. Ledbury* (1886); *John Leech: His Life and Work* (1891); *Plain or Ringlets* (1892); *Mrs. Caudle* (1902); and *Pleasures of Mr. Briggs* (1906).

D.G.

LÉGER, FERNAND (1881-1955) French painter born in Argentan, France, on February 4, 1881. After an apprenticeship as an architect's assistant (1897-99), Fernand Léger came to Paris in 1900. He studied at the Ecole des Beaux-Arts and the Académie Julian. Striking up friendships with André Salmon, Max Jacob and Guillaume Apollinaire, he became one of the most important pioneers and leaders in the modern art movement; along with Juan Gris and Pablo Picasso, he is now regarded as one of the founders of the Cubist movement. From 1918 until the time of his death at his summer home near Paris on August 15, 1955, Léger went on painting oils, watercolors, stage sets, posters and murals. Exhibitions of his works were held throughout the world, and he received countless honors, awards and distinctions during his lifetime.

Fernand Léger belongs to the history of cartoons because of one work, *Ballet Mécanique*, an animated cartoon of extraordinary style and versatility that has been called the "ultimate poem of motion." Léger worked on it all through 1923, and it was released the following year. Painted directly on celluloid, the film presents disjointed figures (including that of Charlie Chaplin) in balletic movement, drawing apart, getting together, whirling, jumping, multiplying, in an ever-changing pattern of forms and compositions. This seminal work has exerted tremendous influence on contemporary animators such as Hans Richter, Viking Eggeling and Alexandre Alexeieff; its impact on the history of experimental animation was enormous and continues to be felt.

M.H.

LEGER, PETER (1924-) German editorial cartoonist born in Brno, Czechoslovakia, on May 4, 1924. Peter Leger is descended from a long line of sculptors and stonecutters. His father was a painter, teacher and museum director in Brno. The German invasion of Czechoslovakia and World War II destroyed young Leger's chances of a normal art education. After the war he felt compelled to

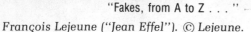
"Fakes, from A to Z . . ."

François Lejeune ("Jean Effel"). © Lejeune.

place his art in the service of a political commitment. He edited a magazine and slowly developed his cartoon style. Since 1947 he has been a freelance political cartoonist.

In the early 1950s his work appeared in the *Hannoversche Presse* (he lives near Hanover and has been connected with several local publications). Since at least as early as 1954, he has published frequently in the organ of the Social Democratic party, *Vorwärts* (located successively during those years in Hanover, Cologne and Bonn). Other newspapers and magazines that run his drawings are the *Süddeutsche Zeitung* (Munich), the *Hannoversche Allgemeine Zeitung*, the *EG-Magazin* (Bonn), the *Wirtschafts-Kurier* (Munich) and the central house organs of several labor unions: metalworking; chemicals, paper and ceramics; public services, transport and commerce; and printing and paper. His work has also appeared in several anthologies of political cartoons lampooning Adenauer, Erhard and Brandt, and in numerous textbooks, where they are valued for their usefulness in making history come alive.

Leger's style is basically ruggedly linear, with skillful use of strong black areas on occasion. It is a true cartoon idiom with no overtones of the academy. Without acknowledging any specific artistic influence, Leger gratefully points to Daumier and Thomas Theodor Heine as political thinkers in the field of art who have inspired him.

His artistic aim is to bring a touch of humanity to the area of political commentary. As a humorist, he recognizes the pitiful smallness of every human being, no matter how highly placed, and tries to restore the proper sense of proportion to epoch-making current events. Prizing his independence, he never accepts directives from the publications he works for.

Leger has also written and illustrated articles on politics, has lectured, and for a long time played a leading role in a journalists' labor union.

S.A.

LEJEUNE, FRANÇOIS (1908-) French cartoonist, poster designer and illustrator born in Paris, France, on February 12, 1908. François Lejeune (better known as "Jean Effel") started his cartooning career in 1933 contributing leftist political drawings to various newspapers and magazines, especially to *France-Soir, L'Express, Le Rire* and *Le Canard Enchaîné*. Most of these have been published in albums, notably *Colonel de la Roque* (1936), *Jours sans Alboches* ("Days Without Dirty Krauts," 1945), *Toujours Occupés* ("Always Occupied, 1947-55," 1955), *De la Mollarchie à l'Empire Mongaulle* ("From Molletgarchy to the Mongaullian Empire," 1959) and *De la Debré à la Pompidour* (1964). He has also illustrated several books, the most beautiful being La Fontaine's *Fables*.

It was in 1943 that Effel hit upon the idea of using little angels as the supporting cast in *Turelune le Cornepipeux* ("Turelune the Bagpipe Player"), the story of a friendly hobo gone to heaven to look for his little bird. From *Turelune* he developed in 1945 the likable characters of the Good Lord, Adam and Eve in Eden, the cherubs and the animals, who became an instant and worldwide success in *La Création du Monde* ("The Creation of the World," 1951), translated into 16 languages. It explains how God, bored with looking into the void, created the world, and how the Devil was always meddling in and sabotaging his work. Other series in this lighthearted look at the Old Testament include *Le Diable et Son Train* ("The Devil and His Train," 1951), *La Vie Naïve d'Adam et Eve,* ("The Naive Life of Adam and Eve," 1956), *Le Roman d'Adam et Eve* ("The Romance of Adam and Eve," 1956-60), *La Genèse Ingénue* ("In the Beginning," 1966) and *Il Créa l'Homme et la Femme* ("He Made Man and Woman," 1967).

Effel's poetic and gentle world full of angels, flowers, birds, the zest and clarity of his line and the very optimism of his irony appealed to animated cartoon directors. Alain Resnais did a TV short based on his drawings (1948), and the Czech Eduard Hofman directed *The Creation of the World* (1956) with the right mix of tenderness and humor.

Jean Effel, who has drawn close to fifteen thousand pieces and published more than a hundred books (including the amusing novel *Plog*, 1970), has exhibited his art all over Europe and received numerous awards. He is a life member of the Academy of Humor.

P.H.

LE LOUARN, YVAN (1915-1968) French cartoonist, engraver, illustrator and animated cartoon director born in Bordeaux, France, on February 10, 1915. After studies at the Bordeaux Ecole des Beaux-Arts, Yvan Le Louarn settled in Paris, where he began a cartooning career under the pen name "Chaval." His drawings have appeared in many magazines (e. g., *Punch, Paris-Match, Le Rire*) and since 1946 especially in *Le Figaro* and *Le Figaro Littéraire*.

Most of his cartoons have been published in albums: *99 Dessins sans Paroles* ("99 Drawings Without Words," 1955), *C'est la Vie: The Best Cartoons of Chaval* (1957), *Les Gros Chiens* ("Big Dogs," 1962), *L'Homme* ("Man," 1970), etc. In addition, Chaval has illustrated numerous books, including Nietzsche's *Beyond Good and Evil* (1955), Swift's *Directions to Servants* and Flaubert's *Dictionary of Accepted Ideas* (1958), and directed several animated cartoons, one of which, *Les Oiseaux Sont des Cons* ("Birds Are Assholes"), won the Emile Cohl Prize in 1965.

Chaval's drawings reveal a certain influence from some of the early 20th-century French cartoonists and from the American Peter Arno, but his style and themes are all his own. Master of the pun and the aphorism, Chaval shows us a world that is both strange and ambiguous, halfway between fear and comedy, as in his series *A Chacun Son Jouet* ("To Each His Toy"), where we see a bullfighter pulling a toy bull on wheels, an African explorer with a globe, a Russian officer with an ICBM on which a dog is relieving himself. His figures all have rather stupid, cowlike faces and a perplexed look, as if they were not sure who and what they are. They are drawn in very thick and very black charcoal lines, as though to stress the ineradicableness both of their blank stupidity and of the sheer absurdity of the world.

No longer able to bear life's petty demands and disillusionments, Chaval committed suicide on January 22, 1968.

P.H.

LEMAY, ARTHUR (1900-1944) French-Canadian cartoonist born in Nicolet, Quebec, on June 5, 1900. Like Russell Patterson before him, Arthur Lemay was given his start by the Montreal daily *La Patrie*. In 1920 Lemay began his cartooning career with the paper with a series of sports panels. He was then asked to take over *Les Aventures de Timothée*, a Sunday strip created by Albéric Bourgeois, which Lemay guided for five years (1920-25), turning it into a burlesque comedy.

In 1922 Lemay went to Paris, studying at the Académie Julian and the Ecole des Beaux-Arts. He financed his studies and his rambles through Europe with the money he received for *Timothée*, which he continued by mail from Europe. Returning to Montreal in 1924, he abandoned *Timothée* the next year (the strip being continued by Maurice Gagnon) to devote himself almost exclusively to political cartooning. This new career was punctuated by Lemay's publication in 1929 of his album *Les Mille Têtes* ("The Thousand Heads"), a series of portraits of Canadian politicians. His graphic style, a little heavy at times, was a hybrid of realism, comic strip techniques and a penchant for lengthy commentary that he had inherited from cartoonists of the 19th century such as Hector Berthelot.

During the 1930s Lemay contributed illustrations to magazines like *La Revue Moderne* and in 1933 published two books: *Trois-Pistoles*, in which he illustrated the landscapes of the St. Lawrence River, and *Noir et Blanc* ("Black and White"), a series of political portraits. He also worked for *L'Illustration* (1930-41), drawing the faces of generations of prizefighters and hockey players. At the outbreak of World War II, Lemay offered his services to the Information Bureau in Time of War

Yvan Le Louarn ("Chaval"). © Paris-Match.

Union worker, which do you prefer?
Freedom? . . .   . . . Slavery?

Arthur Lemay, World War II propaganda cartoon. © Canadian Information Office.

located at Ottawa. He also continued to draw two pages of editorial cartoons a week for *La Patrie*, *Le Monde Comme Il Va* ("As the World Goes") and *La Semaine Illustrée* ("The Week in Illustration"). The tense atmosphere of the times is reflected in Lemay's cartoons as well as in his two cartoon books published by the Information Service, *Album de Guerre* ("War Album") and *Que Préfères-Tu?* ("What Do You Prefer?"). These are typical war propaganda in which the expressionistic imagery competes with the Manicheanism of the captions.

In 1940-41 Lemay stayed in Quebec, where he painted a mural for the planned 1942 New York Universal Exposition. He also contributed cartoons to the *New York News* around the same time. On January 20, 1944, Lemay suddenly died. A retrospective of his work was organized by the International Pavilion of Humor of Montreal in 1976.

S.J.

LEMMI, LEMMO (1884-1926) Brazilian cartoonist of Italian origin born in São Paulo, Brazil, in 1884. The son of the Italian sculptor Ernesto Lemmi, Lemmo Lemmi studied art at the University of Pisa in Italy. Coming back to São Paulo after his studies, he started his cartooning career in 1908 with contributions to the Rio publication *O Malho*, under the pseudonym "Voltolino." Starting in 1911, he collaborated on the São Paulo publications *O Pirralho* (from the inception of the magazine), *Pasquim Coloniale* and *O Saci*. He is best known, however, for his cartoon depictions of the exuberant São Paulo life in *D. Quixote* (from 1919) and for his satires on Brazilian society in *O Parafuso*, under the pseudonym "Cam." He also illustrated children's books and newspaper articles.

Lemmi was one of the most original Brazilian cartoonists, with a zestful style, an eccentric line and an eye for color. His brilliant career was cut short when he died in a car accident in 1926, at age 42.

A.M.

LENICA, JAN (1928-) Polish animator born in Poznań, Poland, on January 4, 1928. Jan Lenica studied music and architecture in college but later turned to art. In 1950 he became one of the founders of the Polish school of poster design with his famous movie posters. He also wrote and illustrated children's books and worked as an exhibition designer.

Jan Lenica, "Ubu-Roi." © Lux Film.

Lenica's involvement with the animation medium began in 1957, when he produced the experimental *Once upon a Time* in collaboration with Walerian Borowczyk. Two more collaborative efforts followed: *Love Requited* (1957) and the sinister, allegorical *Dom* ("House," 1958). Later that year Lenica left for France, where he directed the slyly subversive *Monsieur Tête* ("Mister Head") in collaboration with Henri Gruel. Lenica continued his pessimistic exploration of a decadent world with *Janko the Musician*, the claustrophobic and surreal *Labyrinth* (1962), the despairing *Rhinoceros* (inspired by Ionesco's play) and the unsettling *A* (1964).

In 1963 Lenica moved to West Germany, where he brought to fruition his most ambitious project, *Adam II*, a feature-length film completed in 1969. A nightmarish, frightening, but also strangely affecting work, it projects the disturbing image of a controlled, computerized universe in which man is but one of many cogs. *Adam II* remains Lenica's most eloquent statement and is his masterpiece to date. In 1976 Lenica brought out his long-awaited *Ubu-Roi*, an animated version of Alfred Jarry's black comedy; although it had its moments, it proved a disappointment to Lenica's many admirers because of its many overlong stretches and stilted dialogue.

M.H.

LENOIR, CARLOS (1878-1906) Brazilian cartoonist and caricaturist of French origin born in 1878. Little information on Carlos Lenoir's early years exists, but it seems that he was born in southern Brazil, to which his parents had emigrated in the 1870s. He worked in the Rio de Janeiro central post office at the turn of the century. In 1903 his first cartoon was published in the magazine *A Avenida*; he used the pseudonym "Gil Vaz," which he later shortened simply to "Gil." After this first success, Gil left his post office job and embarked on a prolific cartooning career; his works appeared in most Rio publications, such as *O Malho, O Teatro, Figuras e Figurões, A Comédia, Gazeta de Notícias* and especially *O Tico-Tico*, of which he was one of the founders in 1905.

Gil was one of the most popular caricaturists of the time, and his elegant line was particularly well suited to the depiction (only slightly exaggerated) of theater actors and theater scenes. His cartoons in *O Tico-Tico* were among the most beloved features of the magazine. In the midst of all the acclaim, Gil's life was tragically cut short by illness, and he died in 1906, at age 28.

A.M.

LE POITEVIN, EUGÈNE (1806-1870) French painter, cartoonist, lithographer and illustrator born in Paris, France, on July 31, 1806. After studying with Le Prince at the Paris Ecole des Beaux-Arts, Eugène Le Poitevin started contributing light and naughty cartoons to *La Revue des Peintres* and *La Caricature*. It is, however, for the very amusing series of devils represented in all kinds of postures and situations (some actually obscene) that Le Poitevin is rightly famous. His *Charges et Décharges Diaboliques* ("Diabolical Charges and Discharges") and especially his *Diableries* ("Deviltries")—like those of Grandville but less wittily—poke fun at would-be poets, virginal maidens and middle-class housewives who are all quite literally bedeviled.

In addition to painting battle scenes and seascapes, Le Poitevin illustrated several books, among which are Boccaccio's *Decameron* (1845) and Rousseau's *The New Héloïse* (1846). Rediscovered by the Surrealists, he died in Paris on August 6, 1870.

P.H.

David Levine, caricature of Lyndon Johnson. © New York Review of Books.

"Vandalism, maybe? . . . On the other hand
it could be a wedding anniversary!"

George Lichtenstein ("Lichty"), "Grin and Bear It." © *Field Enterprises, Inc.*

LEVERING, ALBERT (1869-1929) American cartoonist born in Hope, Indiana, in 1869. Albert Levering studied architecture with his father and art in Munich, Germany. After his training, he became an architect, working for eight years before transforming his architect's table into a cartoonist's drawing board.

Levering displayed great talent and real native humor; he worked successively for the *Minneapolis Times,* the *Chicago Tribune* and the *New York American.* In New York, he became a mainstay of *Puck's* art staff just after the turn of the century and formed his happiest association with John Kendrick Bangs during the latter's editorship. Levering illustrated a long-running Bangs *Alice in Wonderland* spoof and contributed large topical drawings; at the same time he drew for *Life* and *Harper's Weekly.* For a time Levering was also engaged on the staff of the *Sunday Tribune* in New York.

His drawing style, perhaps due to his architectural background, had a remarkable fullness and solidity of line. Often he would draw involved scenes and cross-hatch quite precisely, although there never was a stifling rigidity to his work. Figures were animated and very competently drawn; overall, his drawings (Levering worked almost exclusively in pen and ink) commanded respect.

Albert Levering died on April 14, 1929.

R.M.

LEVINE, DAVID (1926-   ) American cartoonist and caricaturist born in Brooklyn, New York, on December 12, 1926. In his discipline, he was the most influential artist of the post-Hirschfeld era.

David Levine was educated at P.S. 241, Junior High 210 in Brooklyn, Erasmus High School, Tyler School of Fine Arts at Temple University and the Hans Hoffman Eighth Street School of Painting in Manhattan. His influences include cartoonists in the 19th-century English and French satirical traditions, 19th-century paintings and Japanese prints.

The field of caricature (and much of illustration) was revolutionized when Levine's spots and caricatures began appearing in the *New York Review of Books* in the early 1960s. They were devastatingly accurate and incisive—which alone would have assured Levine a niche in cartooning history—but in addition, his medium was the pen, his technique the old-fashioned crosshatch style full of shadings, nuances, blemishes and loose hairs. He reveled in fine pen lines and orchestrated his elaborate shadings to give an interpretation capturing the essence of the subject.

When Levine had established himself, the army of imitators—these, even the talented ones, comprise the bulk of a "school" in any field of cartooning and all the arts—switched from aping Hirschfeld to copying Levine's techniques, just as, contemporaneously, political cartooning was switching from the "Herblock school" to the "Oliphant school."

Levine, whose work has been collected several times, and who is a contributing editor both to *Esquire* and *New York* magazines, is a member of the National Academy and was a Guggenheim Fellow. He has received the Tiffany Award for his paintings and was the recipient of Long Island University's George Polk Award, among others. He is an active member of the Association of American Editorial Cartoonists. In 1978 an exhaustive collection of his works, *The Arts of David Levine,* was published by Knopf in New York.

R.M.

LEWIS, ROSS A. (1902-   ) American Pulitzer Prize-winning political cartoonist born in Metamora, Michigan, on November 9, 1902. R.A. Lewis was educated at the University of Wisconsin at Milwaukee, the Layton School of Art, and the Art Students League in New York. He cites the two greatest influences on his work as two instructors at the League: Boardman Robinson and Thomas Hart Benton.

Lewis joined the *Milwaukee Journal* in 1925 as an illustrator and staff artist, after teaching two years at his alma mater, the Layton School. He began to draw editorial cartoons in 1932 after Ding Darling, whom the paper bought as a syndicated cartoonist, declared for Hoover, an advocacy the *Journal* was reluctant to join. Lewis remained the chief political cartoonist, and in 1935, his third year in this position, he was awarded the Pulitzer Prize for his editorial cartoon on industrial strikes and violence. He retired in 1967 after 35 years with the *Journal.*

The style of Lewis's art is reminiscent of Daniel Fitzpatrick and similar to that of Tom Little and other disciples of the crayon. What appears to be a breezy, quick crayon rendering is actually a stylized, careful blend of crayon, brush, thin pen lines and straight lead pencil. It is a style wonderfully suited to newspaper reproduction.

R.M.

LICHTENSTEIN, GEORGE MAURICE (1905-   ) American cartoonist born in Chicago, Illinois, in 1905. George Lichtenstein showed an early talent for drawing and sold his first cartoon to *Judge* at the age of 16. After enrolling at the Chicago Art Institute, Lichtenstein reputedly got dismissed in 1924 for drawing moustaches on some of the portraits hanging in the school's gallery. The following year he entered the University of Michigan, from which he graduated in

"He's been doing the same thing for 40 years but now he calls it 'Golden Age.'"

"*Life's Like That.*" © Bell-McClure Syndicate.

1929. During his college years he edited the *Michigan Gargoyle* and won first prize in the 1928 *College Humor* contest.

In 1929 the *Chicago Times* came into existence, and "Lichty" (as the artist was now known) joined its staff from the beginning, mainly drawing sport cartoons and spot illustrations. In 1930 he created the short-lived *Sammy Squirt*, a gag strip about a soda jerk. Lichty was to prove more successful in 1932 with his panel *Grin and Bear It*, which won immediate recognition and national syndication two years later. In addition to *Grin and Bear It* (which he drew for over forty years, relinquishing it in 1974 to Fred Wagner), Lichty has contributed innumerable cartoons to virtually every magazine in the United States. He was also the author of a satirical anti-Soviet panel, *Is Party Line, Comrade*, which ran during the 1950s and 1960s.

Lichty's style is a winning amalgam of loose penmanship, slapdash composition and broad humor. He works hard and fast ("I can finish a week's work within two days," he once asserted) with almost no wasted motion or redundance of line. Lichtenstein has received countless honors for his work and is a four-time winner of the National Cartoonists Society's Best Newspaper Panel award.

M.H.

LICHTY

See Lichtenstein, George Maurice.

LIFE'S LIKE THAT (U.S.) Fred Neher's daily gag panel, *Life's Like That*, made its debut on October 1, 1934, followed by a Sunday version on October 7. Both were distributed by Bell Syndicate.

Although the panel does contain the usual family—Ollie and Mollie, the middle-aged parents, teenage

daughter Shelley Ann and prankster son Will-Yum, not to mention the family dog Pardner and the goldfish Golde—it is not, strictly speaking, a domestic feature. The goings-on center around the neighborhood and touch on topical subjects, although there is no scarcity of family situations. Just as J.R. Williams did before him, Neher liked to run sub-features such as "Will-Yum," "Us Moderns," "Hi-Teens," "Mrs. Pip's Diary" (so named for the neighborhood gossip) and "Some Punkins" (which refers to the neighborhood siren). The artist kept his gags simple and unaffected, with a view to not offending any of his readers. "I think people have enough grief in their lives without getting more of it on the comic pages," he once asserted. "They come there to be entertained and lifted, not depressed."

Life's Like That was taken over by United Feature Syndicate when Bell-McClure (successor of Bell Syndicate) went out of business in 1970. It was discontinued on August 20, 1977, upon Fred Neher's retirement.

M.H.

LIMA, VASCO MACHADO DE AZEVEDO (1886?-1973) Brazilian cartoonist born in Porto, Portugal, on September 6, 1886 (some sources say 1883). Vasco Lima emigrated to Rio de Janeiro around the turn of the century and studied drawing with João Batista da Costa. His first cartoons were published in the Rio daily *Gazeta de Notícias* in 1903. Starting in 1905, he contributed innumerable cartoons and caricatures to such publications as *A Tribuna* (until 1912), *O Malho*, *A Avenida*, *O Tico-Tico*, *Fon-Fon!*, *Figuras e Figurões* and *A Noite*.

Lima was called in to direct the children's weekly *O Fafàzinho* in 1907. In 1911 he started publishing his monthly (later weekly) *Album de Caricaturas*, which lasted until 1913; he drew all the cartoons of every issue under the pen name "Hugo Lea." Lima's fame as a cartoonist was probably unequaled during his lifetime, and it led to his editorship of *A Noite Ilustrada*, *Carioca* and *Vamos Ler* in the 1930s and 1940s. Toward the end of his long career Lima abandoned cartooning in favor of watercolors, which he

"I guess we both belong to the same group hospitalization plan."

Manfred Limmroth. © *Neue Illustrierte.*

exhibited in a number of group shows in Brazilian galleries. He died on August 7, 1973.

Lima's style was precise, direct and much imitated. His draftsmanship was superb, but his humor sometimes veered toward the macabre. The comic strips he drew in the 1910s and 1920s are now regarded as classics by Brazilian historians.

A.M.

LIMMROTH, MANFRED (ca. 1935-   ) German cartoonist and author born around 1935. Perhaps the most ingenious satirist of his generation, Manfred Limmroth is the master of a superb pen line (his heavily detailed pure contour drawings are very rarely shaded with various benday screens). He is also a clever collagist whose love-hate relationship with the mass-produced wood-engraved illustrations of the late 19th century recalls that of Max Ernst and other great exponents of collage.

Limmroth studied art at the Kassel Academy and in Zurich in the early to mid-1950s, and later worked for *Die Welt* and *Kristall* (both in Hamburg). He illustrated books, did industrial ads (good preparation for his later parodies!) and worked on stage sets and costumes. His best work appeared in his albums of the late 1950s and the 1960s, published in Hanover.

In 1961 he published *Führer durch Deutschland und Umgebung* ("Guide to Germany and Vicinity"), based on a series that had run in *Kristall* that year. These incisive pen drawings touch devastatingly on many social and moral ills of the times: fancy cars that don't work, the destruction of the countryside in the course of army maneuvers, the leveling influence of modern curtain-wall architecture on all large German cities, the pollution of the water supply, etc. The 1963 album *Als Oma Noch ein Backfisch War* ("When Grandma Was Still a Teenager") is an anthology of representative late 19th-century magazine articles and illustrations.

Träum Schön! ("Sweet Dreams!," 1964) consists chiefly of fake ads for incredible products and services (plastic dandruff, roof polish, vicarious book reading, and so on) that appeared alongside real ads in a monthly magazine and fooled many readers with their specific instructions involving real places and mailing addresses. Here again, Limmroth's attack is on the false values of contemporary bourgeois society. His principal artistic vehicle is the wickedly misleading collage.

Other noteworthy Limmroth albums include *Das Güldene Schatzkästlein* ("Ye Golden Treasure Chest"), a handbook of old and new kitsch; *Rathgeber in Allen Lebenslagen* ("Counselor in All Life Situations"), which also uses old wood engravings; and *Liebe am Samstag* ("Love on Saturday"), a five-act play with prologue told in pictures.

S.A.

LINDSAY, NORMAN ALFRED WILLIAMS (1879-1969) Australian cartoonist born in Creswick, Victoria, in 1879.

In the three decades preceding 1900, black-and-white art was seriously regarded as one of the most difficult of all media, and admirable work was produced on the Continent and in England and America. In this medium, the finest penman Australia ever produced was Norman Lindsay.

Lindsay first came into national prominence in 1901, at the age of 21, when at the invitation of its editor, J.F. Archibald, he joined the *Bulletin* staff as an artist. The offer came as a result of an outstanding

Equipped. —Bung: "Hey, Dave! ye've left yer whip behind."
—Dave (too lazy to walk back): "That's all right, Bill. I'll call f'r't comin' back. I got me langwidge."

Norman Lindsay, 1907.

series of pen drawings illustrating the *Decameron* of Boccaccio, which were exhibited in Sydney and reviewed by A.G. Stevens on the famous Red Page of the *Bulletin*. What was remarkable for an artist so young, and self-taught at that, was that these pen drawings were recognized as the finest of their kind yet produced in Australia. (Pen drawing was an art peculiar to the 19th century and came about through the replacement of wood, steel and copper engraving by the new photoengraving techniques of reproduction.)

Norman Lindsay started his career in journalism when he was 16 years of age. From Creswick, a little township near Ballarat in Victoria, he joined his brother, Lionel, to share a studio in Melbourne. He was engaged on his first press work for the *Hawklett*, a Melbourne publication devoted to illustrating crime and the doubtful and seamy side of life. Later, at 19, he worked on lithographic posters. Then followed a period as art editor for the short-lived magazine the *Rambler*. After his appointment to the *Bulletin* staff Lindsay moved on to Sydney to become within a few years an internationally known pen draftsman. Before he had served 12 months, he was given the distinction of drawing a full-page cartoon every week, although before his association with the *Bulletin*, Lindsay had never had any drawings published in that journal and only one in the now extinct Melbourne *Punch*.

As much of the immediate past and present of Australia at that time was rural, much of Norman Lindsay's black-and-white humor dealt with bush types and rural situations. His early joke drawings did much to establish what is today in Australia a legendary outback pattern that originated with the graphic humorists, including Lindsay, George Lambert, Alf Vincent, Frank Mahony, Fred Leist, Benjamin Minns and Ambrose Dyson. Indeed, the whiskers, the waistcoats and the bowyangs of present-day Australian rural comic strips and joke drawings are direct legacies from artists like Lindsay.

But Lindsay's emphasis was not entirely on "backblocks" humor. Lindsay, like Phil May and other artists before him, also drew inspiration from the city. His characters—the larrikins, city tramps, the rabbit-ohs, slum urchins, his "Saturdee" boys and Jiggerty Janes—were all subjects for his superb observation and good-natured ridicule.

Even with journalism's pressures, Lindsay's skill was such that his drawings were never altered or corrected with process-white paint or paste-on patches, expedient devices found repeatedly in the drawings of many artists working under deadlines. Unlike most artists, he never inked in black masses on his drawings. Dark areas were built up with individual strokes and lines to a state perfect in tonal balance—truly a form of pen painting.

Norman Lindsay has produced many thousands of items for the press, but of all his published work—strip jokes, humorous illustrations, joke drawings, political and war cartoons—it is his frolicsome animals that have brought him the most admiration, praise and fame. These drawings of native bears, wombats and bandicoots—and, of course, the animal characters of *The Magic Pudding* (1918), a fantasy Lindsay wrote and illustrated—have, because of the many reprints since 1918, made his name a household word in Australia for the last 50 years.

V.L.

LITTLE, THOMAS (1898-1972) American artist born in Snatch, Tennessee, in 1898. Tom Little was raised in Nashville and followed his artistic inclinations by studying art at that city's Watkins Institute (1912-15) and at the

"Little Audrey." © *Paramount Pictures.*

Bloody Boot

Tom Little. © *Nashville Tennessean.*

Montgomery Bell Academy (1917-18). After much doodling and freelance drawing for merchants' windows, Little landed a newspaper job at age 18—but as a reporter, not a cartoonist.

On the *Nashville Tennessean*, as reporter and police reporter, he developed his interest in cartooning through informal tutoring by Carey Orr, who was about to leave the *Tennessean* for the *Chicago Tribune*. (Little's stylistic mentor, however, was to be Dan Fitzpatrick, who had just left Chicago for the *Post-Dispatch* in St. Louis, replacing Bob Minor.) Wartime service in the army (the marines rejected the five-foot-two volunteer as underweight) interrupted his service for the Nashville paper, as did a year in New York (1923-24), where he drew comic strips and was a reporter for the *Herald-Tribune* and its syndicate.

Because of his mother's illness, however, he returned to Nashville. Back at his old desk, he advanced to city editor and in 1934 began drawing editorial cartoons. (After a dispute with the publisher in 1937, he was relieved of desk duties and drew exclusively.) Immediately Little became one of the nation's most influential and republished cartoonists. A fierce liberal Democrat, he produced cartoons of an artistic style and venom closely resembling Fitzpatrick's work. He was a master of composition, and his concepts were no less forceful than their renderings.

In 1934 Little also began *Sunflower Street*, a syndicated cartoon panel as homely and gentle as his political cartoons were powerful. Originally scripted by Tom Sims, this King Features oversize panel chronicled the doings of rural blacks—not their stereotyped predicaments, but their everyday concerns. The comfortable pen-and-ink feature was killed in 1949 due to fear of racially inspired criticism.

Little's editorial work was rendered in brush and crayon on a grained but not patterned paper. In 1948 he won the National Headliners Club award, and in 1957 the Pulitzer Prize. He died on June 20, 1972.

R.M.

LITTLE AUDREY (U.S.) Inspired by the success of their *Little Lulu* cartoons, Famous Studios/Paramount cast around for yet another comic book girl to bring to the animation screen and came up with Little Audrey. The red-haired, freckle-faced moppet was first seen in the 1949 "The Lost Dream" (written by Isidore Klein and Bill Turner), which proved a fair success with its intended juvenile audience. A number of additional *Little Audrey* cartoons, each more forgettable than the last, came out in the 1950s: "Audrey the Rainmaker" (1951) and "Little Audrey Riding Hood" (1955) are typical of the series as a whole in their cloying cuteness.

Little Audrey and her young companions were put through their paces in conventional situations involving homegrown villains and unthreatening menaces. The cartoons were rather professionally directed (by the likes of Dave Tendlar, Ralph Bakshi and John Gentiella) but hurriedly animated, and they were always a waste of otherwise creditable talent. They deserve to be mentioned here as a glaring example of the pitiful state into which American animation had fallen in the 1950s. (It must be noted, however, that Little Audrey, who started in comic books in 1948, successfully continues her career in that medium to this day.)

M.H.

LITTLE BIRD TOLD ME, A
See Kuhn, Walt.

LITTLE JOHNNY AND HIS TEDDY BEARS (U.S.) The versatile John Randolph Bray conquered one more world—the magazines—with several cartoon series for *Judge* just after the turn of the century. Among these was *Little Johnny and His Teddy Bears*, which obviously capitalized on the great popular affection for President Theodore Roosevelt and on the new rage among children, the "Teddy bear." (Another cartoon series, *The Roosevelt Bears*, by Seymour Eaton and R.K. Culver, ran through many books and cards and is avidly collected even today.)

Bray's series concerned itself with the pranks and pratfalls of Johnny, a little boy in a Buster Brown suit, and his friends, six stuffed, animated bears. Episodes ran to six panels, usually in color on the back page, with the tale often told in verse. Bray's artwork was funny and uncluttered, and it showed a great instinct for narration and sequence—which served him well in his later endeavors. (Bray's series did not confine themselves to children's subjects; in 1910, for instance, he lampooned the automobile craze in *Gasoline Reggie and His Auto*.)

Little Johnny was enormously popular, running with great frequency between 1903 and 1907. In 1907 it was collected in a color reprint book published by *Judge*.

R.M.

LITTLE KING, THE (U.S.) *The Little King* is the best known of all the cartoon series produced by the Van Beuren studio in New York. Based on Otto Soglow's famous *New Yorker* character, it started its short run (all the Van Beuren series had a short run) in 1933. The first director on the series was Jim Tyer, and some of the cartoons he released the first year include "Pals," "The Fatal Note" and "Marching Along." In 1934 Tyer, while remaining chief animator on the series, was replaced as director by George Stallings. Notable among Stallings's efforts are "Cactus King," "Art for Art's Sake" (a funny satire on abstract art), "Jolly Good Felons," "Sultan Pepper" (in which the king matched wits with a visiting potentate) and "A Royal Good Time," perhaps the best cartoon in the series, a wild flight of fancy into the world of clowns and carnivals.

The Little King was quite successful, commercially as well as artistically. Audiences seemed ready to accept the antics of the always silent monarch, while the purely visual humor of the cartoons (there was little dialogue) had an almost surrealistic tinge. The series was discontinued at the end of 1934, reportedly because of a contractual dispute with King Features Syndicate, which had acquired the rights to Soglow's creation earlier that year. In 1936 Max Fleischer tried to bring back the character in a *Betty Boop* cartoon titled, logically enough, "Betty Boop and the Little King," but the effort was not successful, and no further cartoons were attempted.

M.H.

"Little Lulu." © *Harveytoons.*

LITTLE LULU (U.S.) Based on the popular series of cartoons done by Marjorie ("Marge") Henderson for the *Saturday Evening Post*, the *Little Lulu* animated shorts started production in 1944, under the aegis of Famous Studios/Paramount. "Lulu at the Zoo," "Lulu in Hollywood" and "Lulu Gets the Birdie" are some of the early titles. Unlike their magazine (and later comic book) counterparts, the *Little Lulu* cartoons did not contain any attempt at adult humor or symbolism but remained strictly at a child's level. The protagonists, the wise little girl Lulu, her boy companion Tubby and the other kids, went through a series of quite innocuous escapades. The drawing and direction were just as literal, and the series was aimed at a very juvenile audience; its quality steadily declined, and it disappeared from theaters in the 1960s, although it continues to be seen on television.

The *Little Lulu* cartoons of the 1940s are the only ones that are still bearable today, notably "Musicalulu" (1946), "Loose in the Caboose" and "Super Lulu" (1947), and "Dog Show Off" (1948). Isadore Sparber, Seymour Kneitel and Vladimir Tytla were among the directors on the series; many of the stories were written by Otto Messmer.

M.H.

LITTLE ROQUEFORT (U.S.) In the wake of the phenomenal success enjoyed by Tom and Jerry at MGM, Terrytoons (which could already boast Mighty Mouse) came up with yet another rodent, Little Roquefort. Unlike Mighty, however, Little Roquefort used his wits in order to defeat Percy, the villainous feline who was forever lying in wait for him. The fun and games started in 1950 with "Cat Happy" and continued through such forgettable entries as "Flop Secret," "Good Mousekeeping," "Mouse Menace" and "No Sleep for Percy." The *Little Roquefort* cartoons never enjoyed the popularity of the MGM cat-and-mouse adventures, and they disappeared from the screen in the late 1950s.

Paul Terry's able, if unimaginative, stable of directors and animators worked in turns on *Little Roquefort*, with Eddie Donnelly, Connie Rasinski and Mannie Davis the most prominently featured.

M.H.

LODOLO, SANDRO (1929-) Italian cartoonist and animator born in Udine, Italy, in 1929. After finishing high school, Sandro Lodolo moved to Rome in 1950 and attended the Italian Center for Film Training; there he studied (and later taught) the art of animation. After a short stint drawing comics, Lodolo secured a job as a graphic artist for the Italian television network in 1957. Three years of drawing weather maps and diagrams of soccer games prompted him to open his own advertising studio. In 1965 Lodolo renewed his contacts with Italian TV (which in the meantime had discovered animation) and subsequently did more than three hundred animated credits for a number of televised programs. In 1966-67 he animated the titles of three feature films, and since 1968 he has also done a number of animated commercials.

In the early 1970s, at the request of Luciano Pinelli, producer of the TV program *Gli Eroe di Cartone* ("The Cartoon Heroes"), Lodolo decided to experiment with the still animation of comic strips. The film treatment of *Krazy Kat* and *Little Nemo* (with disappearance of the balloons, dissolves, zooms, etc.) proved successful and paved the way for the *Gulp, Fumetti in TV* ("Gulp, Comics in TV") series. The Lodolo studio is currently working on an ambitious project: the television reading of Alex Raymond's *Flash Gordon*.

S.T.

LÖFVING, HJALMAR EDVARD (1896-1968) Finnish cartoonist born on January 26, 1896. After five years of high school, Hjalmar Löfving studied for three more years at the Helsinki University of Arts; he began his long career in the 1910s, at the same time as did other "golden era" cartoonists like Ola Fogelberg and Toivo Vikstedt. His famous cartoon characters ridiculed right-wing fanatics and idealized left-wing youths, but he was also able to satirize the Communists when the need arose.

Known principally as a political cartoonist—and during this period he was probably at his best—Löfving later became a typical children's artist. His works could be seen in publications like *Kurikka, Piiska, Suomen Sosiaaldemokraatti, Elanto, Lipas* and *Koitto* (a temperance movement publication that was read in all the schools in Finland). He published several children's books (such as the educative *Oletko Nähnyt?* in 1938) and, beginning in 1916, had his cartoons exhibited at various shows.

Löfving's strong, hard-edged style is very easy to recognize; it sometimes resembles the art of Chester Gould in its economy of line and exaggeration of facial features. Perhaps the most amazing aspect of Löfving's career was his ability to change his views effortlessly according to the wishes of his employers: he drew for socialist as well as for nonsocialist magazines. He never had a permanent job but remained a freelancer throughout his life.

In the 1960s Löfving was a regular guest on television's *Niksulan TV*, where he told and drew fairy tales as "Uncle Pim-Pom." His comic strips were also very popular, and the innumerable riddles, puzzles and "hidden pictures" which he designed and drew made him the indisputable master of the genre. A short animated cartoon he made in 1927 may have been the first ever produced in Finland.

Hjalmar Löfving died on January 29, 1968, in Helsinki.

J.R.

LONDON LAUGHS (G.B.) *London Laughs*, a daily cartoon gag about London and Londoners featured in the London *Evening News* for 32 years, was not, in fact, drawn by a Londoner! Joe Lee, who depicted the familiar sights of the city (both in its landscape and its population), was a Yorkshireman.

The first *London Laughs* was published in the *Evening News* on May 14, 1934, submitted from a slum tenement in Battersea. The artist, who signed it simply "Lee," was given a month's trial—and continued the panel to its final appearance in July 1966! During World War II the title was changed to *Smiling Through*, and although the theme of the jokes became more topical, the spirit remained the same: the Londoner who laughed whatever the world (or Hitler) might throw at him.

The characters in *London Laughs* (the title was restored after the war) ranged through many familiar types without ever developing into regular "heroes." There were the cheeky Cockney urchins with their ready retorts, the cheery Cockney bus conductors with their equally ready cracks, the Cockney charwomen, the middle-class mums, the upper-class ladies and toppered gents, crusty colonels, wide-boy "spivs," bobbies, taxi drivers, Billingsgate fish porters and, of course, during the war, the Yankee GI's. All were drawn with Lee's flowing line and eye for detail. A book, *London Laughs, 1934-1951*, was published in 1951.

Joe Lee, who simultaneously provided the northern newspapers of the Allied Group with a parallel daily cartoon, was retired on pension in 1966. However, he soon found himself unable to remain idle and began freelancing political cartoons to the *Eastern Daily Press*. Then he took up comic strips. In 1933 he had drawn *Pin Money Myrtle* for the *Daily Mail*, but this time he turned to children's comic weeklies. He took over a number of established characters in *Wham*, including *The Spooks of St. Luke's*, and then drew

Leo Longanesi. © Longanesi.

Angel Face and Dare Devil in *Whizzer and Chips* (1969). He died in 1974.

D.G.

LONGANESI, LEO (1905-1957) Italian cartoonist, journalist and writer born in Bagnacavallo, Romagna, Italy, in 1905. Leo Longanesi's cartoon work, while significant, was only one aspect of his career. He was a talented man who published many books of cartoons and was at the same time a serious, perceptive essayist. His cartoons constitute a lucid running commentary on the events and personages of Italy in the Fascist and Christian Democratic periods.

While he was solidly conservative, Longanesi never espoused the cause of Fascism and conformity. His cartoons and drawings for a myriad of books and publications large and small were often ruthless depictions of the poverty and narrow-mindedness afflicting a world that pretended to renovate itself through rhetoric. Lacking the raw, disruptive force of, say, Grosz's cartoons, Longanesi's drawings did their work more quietly—like pebbles thrown into a stagnant pond. The resultant waves have spread slowly, as has his fame as the premier Italian cartoonist of the period immediately before and after World War II (in which, significantly enough, he did not take part). No postwar Italian cartoonist has been left untouched by his spirit of humor and satire, whether in drawings or captions. Longanesi died in Milan in 1957.

C.S.

LOOPY DE LOOP (U.S.) Although Hanna-Barbera Productions is best known for television animation, it also made a number of theatrical shorts, chief among them the *Loopy de Loop* series, which premiered in December 1959 with "Wolf Hounded." Loopy's character was established early on as that of an uncommonly peaceful wolf whose good intentions, sadly misunderstood by the humans with whom he came into contact, led him into all kinds of trouble. The cartoons stuck closely to this pattern in such entries as "Life with Loopy," "Tale of a Wolf," "Do-Good Wolf" (all 1960) and "Happy Go Loopy" (1961).

Realizing that their series rested on one joke endlessly repeated from cartoon to cartoon, Hanna and Barbera tried to conjure up a fitting *compère* for their ill-starred wolf in the form of a bumbling, befuddled bear. The duo endured countless rounds of catastrophe and mayhem in such forgettable cartoons as "Bearly Able" (1962), "Bear Up," "Bear Hug," "Trouble Bruin" (all 1963)) and "Bear Knuckles" (1964). In spite of all these efforts *Loopy de Loop* failed to catch on, and in 1965 Columbia Pictures, which released the cartoons, persuaded Hanna and Barbera to discontinue the series.

M.H.

"*Loopy de Loop.*" © *Hanna-Barbera Productions.*

David Low. © *London Evening Standard.*

Rendezvous

LORENZ, LEE S. (1933-) American cartoonist, editor and cornet player born in Hackensack, New Jersey, on October 17, 1933. Lee Lorenz attended the Carnegie Institute of Technology in Pittsburgh in 1950-51 but transferred to the Pratt Institute in Brooklyn, receiving his B.F.A. in 1954. He then freelanced as a commercial artist, animator and cartoonist until 1958, when he became a staff cartoonist for the *New Yorker*. In 1973 he was appointed art editor, and in this capacity he has introduced *New Yorker* readers to the work of such fresh talents as Sam Gross, Lou Myers, Bill Woodman and Jack Ziegler.

As a cartoonist, Lorenz is an excellent stylist who works mainly in what appears to be pen and wash. His panels are identifiable by a firm, broad, unbroken line that suggests Peter Arno without being imitative. The wit that infuses his drawings is in the sophisticated *New Yorker* tradition, singling out for particular attention the corporate world, political philosophies and social clichés, all spiced with liberal dashes of lunacy. A good example is the panel featuring a parade of animals, each with a picket sign bearing a popular cliché. Thus a flirtatious duck holds a placard reading "Lord love a duck," while a stubborn-looking horse follows with "You can lead a horse to water, but you can't make him drink." Bringing up the rear is a tiny beetle whose sign is left to the reader's imagination.

Separately published collections of Lorenz's work include *Here It Comes* (1968), *The Upside Down King* (1970) and *Now Look What You've Done* (1977). He is also the illustrator of a volume entitled *The Teddy*

Bear Habit (1966). He has served as president of the Cartoonists' Guild and as a member of the board of directors of the Museum of Cartoon Art. Besides his artwork, Lorenz claims to blow a pretty mean cornet—something he has been doing professionally since 1955.

R.C.

LOW, SIR DAVID (1891-1963) British cartoonist born in Dunedin, New Zealand, on April 7, 1891. "Low," as he signed all his cartoons, was probably the most important, popular and influential cartoonist working in British newspapers in the first half of the 20th century. His swift-seeming, bold brushwork, individual and unmistakable, concealed fine draftsmanship and instantly conveyed the artist's strong opinions.

David Alexander Cecil Low was educated at the Boys' High School, Christchurch. Inspired to draw by imported British comics, he copied Tom Browne and other early masters of simplified black-and-white cartooning and had his first sketch published in the *Christchurch Spectator* in 1902, at age 11. He contributed cartoons to the *Canterbury Times* and by age 20 was cartoonist for the *Sydney Bulletin* (1911).

After World War I he emigrated to England, arriving in London in 1919. He quickly found a regular spot in the evening newspaper the *Star* and drew for that paper from 1919 to 1927. He moved to the *Evening Standard* on a unique contract with its quirky proprietor, the Canadian Lord Beaverbrook. Low was allowed carte blanche to draw whatever he wished, despite the politics and opinions of its owner! He stayed with the *Standard* for 23 years, moving in 1950 to the Labour newspaper the *Daily Herald*. In 1953 he moved again, this time to the *Manchester Guardian*, where he stayed for a decade. Low was made an honorary doctor of law by the universities of New Brunswick and Frederickstown, Canada (1958), and the University of Leicester (1961). He was knighted in 1962 and died on September 19, 1963.

Low created many characters, perhaps none so famous or memorable as Colonel Blimp, who became part of the language. Others include the T.U.C. Horse and the characters of the strip *Hit and Muss on Their Axis*. Winston Churchill said of Low, "He is the greatest of our modern cartoonists because of the vividness of his political conceptions and because he possesses what few cartoonists have, a grand technique of draughtsmanship."

Books: *Low's Annual* (1908); *Caricatures* (1915); *The Billy Book* (1918); *Old Seed on New Ground* (1920); *Man* (1921); *Lloyd George and Co.* (1922); *Low and I* (1923); *Low and I Holiday Book* (1925); *Lions and Lambs* (1928); *The Best of Low* (1930); *Low's Russian Sketchbook* (1932); *Portfolio of Caricatures* (1933); *The New Rake's Progress* (1934); *Low and Terry* (1934); *Ye Madde Designer* (1935); *Political Parade* (1936); *Low Again* (1938); *Cartoon History of Our Times* (1939); *Europe Since Versailles* (1939); *Europe at War* (1940); *The Flying Visit* (1940); *Low on the War* (1941); *Low's War Cartoons* (1941); *British Cartoonists* (1942); *The World at War* (1942); *C'est la Guerre* (1943); *The Years of Wrath* (1949); *Low Company* (1952); *Low Visibility* (1953); *Low's Autobiography* (1956); and *The Fearful Fifties* (1960).

D.G.

LOWELL, ORSON BYRON (1871-1956) American illustrator and cartoonist born in Wyoming, Iowa, on December 22, 1871. Orson Lowell was educated in the Chicago public schools and attended the Chicago Art Institute between 1887 and 1893, after which he went to New York to pursue a career in cartooning and illustration.

His first jobs, reversing a typical pattern, were in illustration work rather than cartooning. His early work was very handsome, if derivative, and was rendered in thin pen lines and careful shading; he seemed to like the interplay of shadows and light and composed well.

"Lucky Luke." © *Belvision/Dargaud Films.*

When he cracked the cartoon market, his style was bolder but, once again, derivative. Lowell's early inspiration seems to have been penman Pyle, whereas his later cartoon work was obviously garnered from Charles Dana Gibson. Lowell was a little less awkward than the horde of other imitators, but he must still be classed an imitator. J.M. Flagg was too, achieving about the same independence: drawings "in the Gibson style" and with Gibson's themes. But Lowell kept his striking sense of composition and managed to gain a name for himself.

From 1907 to 1915 he was under exclusive contract to *Life*—no mean feat—and was lured away by *Judge* with an exclusive contract from 1915 until that magazine shed its classy pretensions in 1923; Lowell's grandiose society drawings were suddenly out of place. They were out of place in almost all cartoon markets, sadly, but Lowell worked successively (and successfully) for the Ericson Advertising Agency (1921-29), *American Girl* magazine (1935-45), the George Matthews Adams Service (1937-38) and the *Churchman* (1943-46).

Lowell died on February 9, 1956.

R.M.

LUCKY LUKE (Belgium/France) In 1946 Morris (Maurice de Bevère) created the parodic western strip *Lucky Luke*; when he became burdened with work, he asked René Goscinny to help him out as a scriptwriter. *Lucky Luke* soon became very popular, and it was inevitable that it would be adapted into a full-length animated feature.

In 1971 Belvision, in association with Dargaud-Films, released *Lucky Luke* as a theatrical feature. Goscinny was listed as the director of the film, but it had in fact been supervised by Henri Gruel. The adaptation and dialogue were signed by Morris, Goscinny and Pierre Tchernia. The action, hewing close to the original conception, centered around Lucky Luke, "a poor, lonesome cowboy" mounted on his faithful stallion, Jolly Jumper. In the course of the film the hero rid the little settlement known as Daisy Town of the dreaded menace of the brothers Dalton. The action was fast, and the animation, while spotty at times, adequate and high-spirited.

The success of *Lucky Luke* led to a sequel produced by the newly created Studios Idéfix under the direction of Gruel. A number of mishaps (including Goscinny's death in 1977) slowed down the filming, and the feature, titled *La Ballade des Dalton* ("The Ballad of the Daltons"), was only released in 1978. It again pitted the protagonist against the four comic-opera outlaws, the Daltons. In some ways (its handling of color, its dream sequences) it was superior to the original, and it was fairly successful.

M.H.

LUKS, GEORGE BENJAMIN (1867-1933) American cartoonist and painter born in Williamsport, Pennsylvania, on August 13, 1867. George Luks was educated in art at the Pennsylvania Academy of Fine Arts, at the Düsseldorf Academy in Germany, and in salons of Paris and London. In 1895 and 1896 he served as a war correspondent and artist in Cuba for the *Philadelphia Bulletin*. He then switched to the *New York World*, where he succeeded R.F. Outcault on *The Yellow Kid* comic strip, approximating the latter's style and perpetuating the emerging journalistic war between the proprietors of the *World* and *Journal*.

Luks was one of the organizers of the 1913 Armory Show that provoked so much turmoil in the art world, and his role in American arts as a member of the Ashcan school is well documented. He won many prizes for his

"Lunatics I Have Met." © Rube Goldberg.

Enzo Lunari, "Fra Salmastro." © Lunari.

After working as a salesman for a chinaware company, he decided to try his hand at cartooning; his first cartoons were accepted by the monthly *Linus* in 1965.

Lunari's career falls into three periods, each devoted to a cycle or a character but connected to the others by an overall theme. The first phase began in 1965 with *Girighiz*, a comic strip with cavemen as protagonists along the lines of Johnny Hart's *B.C.* Lunari's aim, however, was political and satirical; he attacked bad government, conformism and the opportunism of the people in power. He followed suit with *Fra' Salmastro da Venegono*, in which the adventures of an imaginary 13th-century friar provided the vehi-

canvases, including the Temple Gold Medal of the Pennsylvania Academy of Fine Arts, the Logan Medal of the Chicago Art Institute, the Hudnut Water Color Prize, the Corcoran Gallery of Art prize and the gold medal of the Philadelphia Locust Club.

Luks's cartooning work in the weekly humor magazines led to his famous stint on *The Yellow Kid* and established the reputation that led to a career in oils. In this sense he joined his fellows John Sloan, Reginald Marsh and Walt Kuhn, who also began as cartoonists and became painters. Luks's chief contributions were to the weekly magazine *Truth*, which had the format of *Puck*, eschewed politics, often colored its cartoons in chromolithography and was decidedly racy in its appeal. Luks was a major fixture and frequently contributed humorous strip-format cartoons for the back page. His style—before he copied Outcault—was at first awkwardly stiff and later pleasantly free in execution. Luks died in New York City in 1933 as a result of a barroom brawl.

R.M.

LUNARI, ENZO (1937-   ) Italian cartoonist born in Milan, Italy, on January 2, 1937. Enzo Lunari graduated from the School of Political Sciences of the University of Pavia in 1961 but could not find a job in his field.

Via Dolorosa

Ranan Lurie, "Lurie's Opinion." © United Feature Syndicate.

cle for a lively satire on the mores of contemporary society. Finally Lunari invented Sodomate, a land of fantasy not unlike the Italy of the 1970s. Here the clever Berlinguà (a transparent allusion to Italian Communist party chief Enrico Berlinguer) tries with every means at his disposal to join (or perhaps to replace) the wretched leaders of the country.

Lunari has drawn these and other comic strips, as well as political cartoons, for publications such as *Tempo* and *Mondo Domani*.

C.S.

LUNATICS I HAVE MET (U.S.) *Lunatics That I Have Met* (the *That* was soon dropped) was among the first of Rube Goldberg's famous newspaper panels. It started on the sports page of the *New York Evening Mail* in 1907. Goldberg would caricature a type—"the physical culture maniac," "the gasoline nut," "the golf nut," "the show fiend"—in a series of panels that depicted those "lunatics" in the most ludicrous situations imaginable. (One showing a "balloonatic" suspended precariously over Manhattan rooftops and exclaiming, "That must be Australia in the near distance," is a classic; it might have inspired the title and the general feeling of Buster Keaton's 1923 film *Balloonatics*.)

Goldberg even ran short signed articles to accompany the graphic descriptions of his "loons," with titles such as "Is Ballooning a Mania?" or "Golf Bug Harmless." He soon grew tired of this endless enumeration of human lunacies, however, and he dropped the feature only a few years after its inception.

M.H.

LURIE, RANAN (1932-) Israeli cartoonist born in 1932 to a sixth-generation Israeli family whose members were among the first settlers in the country. Ranan Lurie studied fine arts in Jerusalem and Paris. He drew political cartoons for the Israeli press as early as 1948 and established his reputation quickly. By the time he was 30, he was regarded as Israel's national cartoonist, reflecting the views of the majority of his fellow citizens.

In 1968 Lurie was contracted by *Life* magazine to draw a weekly editorial cartoon, and he moved to the United States, settling in New York City. In addition to his cartoons for *Life* (which he drew until the magazine folded in 1973), he has contributed to *Paris-Match*, the *Wall Street Journal* and the *New York Times*, among others. His daily political cartoon panel, *Lurie's Opinion*, was syndicated for a long time by United Feature Syndicate and is now distributed by King Features. Lurie has illustrated books and stories, and two collections of his cartoons have been published by Quadrangle Books: *Nixon Rated Cartoons* (1973) and *Pardon Me, Mr. President* (1975).

Lurie is a veteran of two Middle East wars (1948 and 1967), and his U.S. residency has not dampened his patriotism. His style, caricatural and even outré, and his captions, direct and unabashedly partisan, have won him as many detractors as admirers. He is an influence to be reckoned with, however, in the fiercely competitive world of political cartooning.

M.H

LUZZATI, EMANUELE (1921-) Italian cartoonist, painter and designer born in Genoa, Italy, in 1921.

Emanuele Luzzati (and Giulio Gianini), "I Paladini di Francia." © Gianini/Luzzati Production.

Emanuele Luzzati graduated from art school during World War II and tried to support himself by cartooning after the war. He then went into designing theater sets, becoming one of the most respected names in the profession.

In the late 1950s Luzzati struck up a partnership with Giulio Gianini that resulted in the production of a number of highly regarded film cartoons. The first was the 1960 *I Paladini of Francia* ("Paladins of France"), a medieval ballad featuring cutout characters on a background of violent and contrasting colors. The style of the cartoon, coarse and childlike, suggested a Georges Rouault painting; it became the hallmark of their subsequent efforts, from *Castello di Carte* ("House of Cards," 1962) to *La Gazza Ladra* ("The Thieving Magpie," 1964), in which Rossini's crescendos add a vivifying touch to the graphic universe. *L'Italiana in Algeri* ("The Italian Girl in Algiers," 1968), which again makes use of Rossini's music, blends rhythm, invention and feeling in a joyous burst of movement. In the 1970 *Ali Baba*, Luzzati further accentuated the innocent look of his world through the use of "cheap" materials such as silver and gold foil and crayons.

Luzzati and Gianini animated the fabulous travels of Marco Polo for Italian television in 1972 and then made *Pulcinella* (1973), which can be seen as a summing up of Luzzati's work. It is a fervent homage to the theater but also a fusion of all the elements dear to the artist: fable, naive painting, classical music. The poetic tales imagined by Luzzati and Gianini are peopled by kings and sultans, harem girls and dragons, knights, battles and love scenes, as seen through the eyes of a child, but with the irony of a cultured adult.

Luzzati is also a talented painter and has recently taken up book illustration as well, with felicitous results.

S.T.

LYE, LEN (1901-) New Zealand animator and filmmaker born in Christchurch, New Zealand, in 1901. Len Lye studied at Wellington Technical College and at the Canterbury College of Fine Arts. Disappointed with traditional art, he set out for Samoa to study Polynesian art. He made his first recorded animated film, *Tusalava*, in 1928. In the 1930s he worked for the General Post Office organization in Great Britain, collaborating with John

A LETTER ASKING A PARENT FOR MONEY HAS TO BE GOOD THESE DAYS --- THAT'S WHERE A COLLEGE EDUCATION HELPS.

WITH BEST WISHES FROM J. NORMAN LYND.

THE CITIZEN WHO TRYS TO EXPRESS HIMSELF ABOUT THE OTHER POLITICAL PARTY — AND HAS TO TONE IT DOWN TO GET IT THROUGH THE MAILS. 12-8

J. Norman Lynd, "Vignettes of Life." © Ledger Syndicate.

Grierson on a number of films, such as *North or Northwest*.

In 1935 Lye made his major contribution to animation art with *The Colour Box*. The images were painted directly on the film, thereby avoiding the photographic process—a technique Lye pioneered, although he did not invent it. (There are several claimants to this innovation, including Hans Richter, Man Ray and Marcel Duchamp.) Lye followed with two works that combined animation and live action: *Rainbow Dance* (1936) and *Trade Tattoo* (1937). In the meantime he had also produced a puppet film, *Birth of a Robot* (1935).

During World War II Lye made only one cartoon, *Musical Poster* (1941). He worked mainly on documentaries such as *Kill or Be Killed*, a cold-blooded account of the techniques of street fighting, and the much more entertaining *Swinging the Lambeth Walk*. After the war Lye moved to the United States, where he collaborated with Ian Hugo on the 1952 *Bells of Atlantis*. Since then Lye has increasingly turned to abstraction; his later works of animation include *Colour Cry* (1955), *Free Radicals* (1957), *Rotational Harmonic* (1961) and *Steel Fountain* (1963). Len Lye is currently working in computer animation and does sculptures that make their own music.

M.H.

LYND, J. NORMAN (1878-1943) American cartoonist born in Northwood, Logan County, Ohio, in 1878. J. Norman Lynd, the son of a Presbyterian minister, spent most of his youth in London and North Ireland, where he was educated. Shortly after his return to New York in 1907, he secured a job on the art staff of the *New York Herald*. There he became primarily a news artist and sports cartoonist, working with cub

reporter John Wheeler and drawing in the style of the *Herald*'s soon-to-depart star, Winsor McCay. He remained with the *Herald* until it merged with the *Tribune* in 1924. In the meantime Lynd established himself as one of the most versatile illustrators and cartoonists in magazines; he illustrated humorous fiction for the second-string monthlies and graced the pages of *Puck* and *Life* with his captioned gags.

Beginning on November 20, 1927, Lynd drew the Sunday feature *Vignettes of Life* for the Ledger Syndicate in the style of C.D. Mitchell (his predecessor, whose feature had been called *Follies of the Passing Show*) and Frank Godwin; it contained approximately half a dozen gags on a central theme. The concept was not new (*Puck* had done the trick in the 1880s, and W.E. Hill and Joe McGurk, among others, had worked it for newspapers), but Lynd brought a special look and flavor to the genre. In 1938 Lynd was lured away by Hearst and drew an identical page called *Family Portraits* for King Features. When he died at his home in Lynbrook, Long Island, on November 8, 1943, *Family Portraits* died with him. The *Ledger*, however, had continued *Vignettes of Life* with W. Kemp Starrett, whose style approximated Lynd's.

J. Norman Lynd had one of the most handsome pen lines in cartooning. In his mature work he managed to retain the disciplined crosshatch technique of the early years while infusing an arresting verve both to characters and compositions. His style zeroed in on personality so well that readers were able to recognize character types—a prerequisite for the type of feature Lynd drew. A collection of his work, *Vignettes of Life*, was published by Reilly and Lee in 1930, with a foreword by Charles Dana Gibson.

R.M.

Mm

MACAULEY, CHARLES (1871-1934) American Pulitzer Prize-winning cartoonist born in Canton, Ohio, on March 29, 1871. In 1891 the young Macauley won a $50 cartoon prize from the *Cleveland Press* and on the strength of this secured a position on the art staff of the *Canton Repository* the following year. Through the 1890s he was to draw for the *World, Plain Dealer* and *Leader* (all Cleveland newspapers), *Puck, Life* and *Judge* (freelance) and the *New York Herald* for a short stint. In 1899 he joined the staff of the *Philadelphia Inquirer* as editorial cartoonist; he remained there two years.

From 1901 to 1904 he produced his *Fantasmaland* books and was then hired to succeed the retiring Charles Green Bush on the old *New York World.* There he achieved great fame and was transformed into a fierce partisan. During his career on the Democratic *World,* he contributed heavily to cartoon iconography: Roosevelt's Big Stick, the Camel as the symbol for the Prohibitionists, the Hippo for the wets and the Gold Dust Twins (Taft and Roosevelt) for the campaign of 1912.

In the reform tide that swept John Puroy Mitchell into the mayoralty of New York City, Macauley was active and publicly visible as his campaign finance manager. Pulitzer frowned on such activity, and Macauley was fired—later to sue for his uncollected salary and win. When he finally left the *World* in 1914, he freelanced, comfortably finding temporary berths in Philadelphia and with the *New York Globe* doing war cartoons. He also tried his hand at playwriting; he wrote *The Optimistic Spectator* and several photoplays.

In 1927 Macauley was afflicted with tuberculosis of the spine and endured painful operations, but he bounced back to succeed Nelson Harding on the *Brooklyn Eagle* in 1929. Within five weeks of assuming that position, he drew the cartoon that was to win him the Pulitzer Prize. Two years later he left to draw for the *New York Mirror.*

Macauley's style was bold and occasionally awkward in the way that Davenport's was; like Davenport, he drew with both pen and bludgeon. He stayed loyal to the pen-and-crosshatch technique and was one of its prime exponents; in substance he was primarily a political cartoonist, never dabbling (in his newspaper work) in subjects of the home, hearth or seasons as his fellows often did. In his later years he became a Republican, although he supported Smith in 1928. He died on November 24, 1934.

His published fiction includes *The Red Tavern, Whom the Gods Would Destroy, Keeping the Faith* and *The Man Across the Street.* Macauley was a president of the New York Press Club and a member of the Author's Club.

R.M.

MACAYA, LUIS FERNANDO (1888-1953) Argentine cartoonist and painter born in Barcelona, Spain, on April 22, 1888. Luis Macaya started his artistic career in 1905 at the Workers' Atheneum and Free Workshop of the Artistic Group, founded in Barcelona by Picasso and Gallardo. In 1908 he traveled to France, Belgium and Germany to further his art studies, settling in Argentina in 1911.

Macaya's first job as a cartoonist was for the newly founded magazine *Crítica* (for which he designed the masthead, among other things). Soon he found himself in great demand, and in subsequent years he worked for most major publications in Argentina. His cartoons, elegant and sharply drawn, appeared in *Caras y Caretas* (1912-32), *Fray Mocho* (1912-20), *Plus Ultra* (1912-29), *La Nación* (1928-32), *El Hogar* (1932-53), *Leoplán* (1938), and *Argentina* (1949-50), among others. Macaya was also a noted landscape painter and held many exhibitions throughout Argentina. In 1925 he was awarded first prize at the Salon Nacional.

Luis Fernando Macaya died in Buenos Aires on January 25, 1953. His son, Luis Macaya (born in 1913), is also a cartoonist.

A.M.

Charles Macaulay, ca. 1910. © New York World.

MACCARI, MINO (1898-) Italian cartoonist, engraver and teacher born in Siena, Italy, on November 24, 1898. Mino Maccari attended the University of Siena, graduating in 1919 with a doctorate in law. As

Mino Maccari. © *Il Mondo.*

an artist he was self-taught, and he started drawing cartoons soon after his graduation.

Maccari was closely associated with *Il Selvaggio*, the magazine that best reflected Italian life between the two world wars. Like Leo Longanesi—whom he resembles in his style of drawing—Maccari expressed his fundamental anti-Fascism principally in his cartoons, which convey a sense of revolt not so much against the regime itself as against its bad taste, fake underpinnings and the grotesqueness it promoted in the field of culture. His cartoons were in part inspired by Grosz's work but had a particularly Italian slant; while the German artist's drawings were black and dramatic, Maccari's were simply ironic and bizarre. (The regime felt so little threatened by his cartoons that he was named a professor at the Rome Academy of Fine Arts in 1938.)

In the post-World War II period Maccari collaborated on a number of cultural and political publications (*L'Espresso, Il Mondo*, etc.), producing cartoons and comments that sometimes earned him virulent attacks fom one political party or another. Cartooning is only one of Maccari's talents—he has also done many engravings and lithographs—but it is the one by which he will be best remembered. He is one of the most important cartoonists of contemporary Italy.

C.S.

McCARTHY, FRED (1918-   ) American cartoonist born in Boston, Massachusetts, on September 5, 1918. Fred McCarthy was educated at Boston College and took the vows of the Franciscan order, becoming Father McCarthy, and drawing all the while. He was art editor of school papers (drawing sports and spot cartoons) and of the *Friar* magazine (1953-57). In 1953 he created *Brother Juniper*, a panel about a Franciscan, and by 1957 it had been collected in book form. The next year it was syndicated as a newspaper panel.

McCarthy received permission from Rome to leave the order and has since continued *Brother Juniper* as a layman. He has lectured on the subject of humor and cartoons at more than fifty colleges, including Yale, MIT, Georgia and Georgia Tech, and he even taught a course on Jewish humor at the University of Miami in Florida! McCarthy's style is charming and deceptively simple (it should be noted that because of time pressures, Len Reno ghosted the art for years). His concepts, like Juniper's personality, exude Franciscan warmth.

R.M.

McCAY, WINSOR (1869-1934) American cartoonist, animator and graphic artist born in Spring Lake, Michigan, on September 26, 1869 (some sources say 1871, but 1869 seems more probable in light of McCay's early career and his own comments on the matter). Largely self-taught, Winsor McCay established himself as one of the masters of the emerging medium of the comic strip, principally with his celebrated *Little Nemo* (for full information on McCay's career in the comics, see *The World Encyclopedia of Comics*, Chelsea House, 1976).

McCay was already a successful newspaper comic strip artist when he decided around 1907 to go into animation. In 1909 he completed the drawings for his first cartoon film, *Little Nemo*, which was then photographed by Walter Austin under the direction of J.S. Blackton. Blackton's company, Vitagraph, released it in 1911. The cartoon was based closely on McCay's strip and included all its familiar characters: Little Nemo himself, the Princess, the mischief-maker Flip, Impy the cannibal and others. The success of *Little Nemo* prompted McCay to make a second cartoon, *The Story of a Mosquito* (also known as *How a Mosquito Operates*), released in 1912. In the meantime he had started work on *Gertie, the Trained Dinosaur*, which was first released theatrically in 1914 (although it may have been shown on the vaudeville circuit earlier). Arguably the most famous animated cartoon ever made, and certainly one of the most influential, *Gertie* can be said to have established the animated cartoon as an original art form.

McCay then went to work on his most ambitious project, an animated version of the sinking by a German submarine of the British liner *Lusitania*. *The Sinking of the Lusitania*, a nine-minute featurette, was released in 1918 (it was later expanded to twenty minutes by the addition of live and stock footage). This longest of McCay's cartoons had been preceded by less ambitious efforts, usually two or three minutes in duration, such as

Fred McCarthy ("Fr. Mac"), "Brother Juniper." © *Publishers Syndicate.*

Winsor McCay, editorial cartoon, ca. 1920. © New York Journal.

The Centaurs and *Gertie on Tour* (both 1916), *Flip's Circus* and *The Pet* (1917-18). McCay later made *Bug Vaudeville*, and in 1920 *The Flying House* (which is credited by some to his son, Robert McCay). The last three cartoons were released as a package in 1921 under the title *The Adventures of a Rarebit Eater*.

McCay abandoned animation in the early 1920s, dissatisfied, it is said, with the direction the medium was taking and its increasing commercialism. In addition to his comic strips and early magazine cartoons, he also did editorial cartoons of a conservative bent for the Hearst newspapers. They are much admired today for their draftsmanship and composition, but as means of persuasion they are rather flat and unmoving; while they would have been a credit to a lesser artist, they are dwarfed by McCay's towering achievements in animation and the comics.

Winsor McCay died on July 26, 1934. His fame, already great during his lifetime, has now grown to mythic proportions. As a master of three different cartoon idioms, he deserves the title *primus inter pares*, the first among his peers in the history of American cartoons.

M.H.

McCUTCHEON, JOHN TINNEY (1870-1949) American cartoonist, writer and war correspondent born near South Raub, Indiana, on May 6, 1870. A graduate of Purdue in 1889, McCutcheon published his first cartoons in Chicago, where he had been brought by fellow Hoosier George Ade, for the *Chicago Morning News* (later *Record* and *Record-Herald*). In 1903 he

transferred to the *Chicago Tribune*, from which he retired, ill, in 1946.

McCutcheon's first political cartoon was published in 1896; he had previously done newspaper fillers and illustrations. In 1897 he left on the first of many memorable trips around the world with typewriter and drawing board. This particular trip was on the revenue cutter *McCulloch*, which was to join Admiral Dewey at Manila Bay. He soon was a war correspondent on other battlefields in the Spanish-American War, the Filipino insurrection, the Boer War, the abortive Vera Cruz raids, and World War I, where he was with the Belgian and German armies, was arrested as a spy and was the first newspaperman to fly over the trenches. He witnessed battles in France, Salonica and the Balkans. On a trip to Africa in 1910, he joined up with an expedition of his good friend Theodore Roosevelt. He was the first newsman to cross the Gobi Desert in an automobile. (His party, finding themselves stranded, rigged up a sail to propel themselves to civilization!) In 1906 the *Tribune* sent him on a trip to the Crimea, the Caucasus, Persia, Russia, Chinese Turkestan and Siberia.

Matching the glamour he attracted with these exploits was McCutcheon's skill and fame as an editorial cartoonist. From his early cartooning days he was referred to as "the dean of American editorial cartooning," and he was certainly the primary exponent (rivaled only by Ireland and Donahey) of the Midwest school: utter mastery of technique and media, gentle political gibes and a strong dose of homey and sentimental subjects. His early fame, in fact, was based on

Trying to "square it" with the peerless leader.

John Tinney McCutcheon, 1912. © Chicago Tribune.

Remarkable view for a city tenement.

Angus MacDonall, 1924. © *Judge.*

the nation's acceptance of his *Bird Center* cartoons, doings of rural folk that led the thematic way for Dwig, Briggs, Webster and an army of later cartoonists. One of his best series was *A Boy in Springtime* (and . . . *Summertime*), each presenting heavily evocative and nostalgic statements. His political cartoons, however, were strong and partisan. A lifelong admirer of Theodore Roosevelt, he was at home on the *Chicago Tribune*, one of America's most Progressive newspapers. He was the major American cartoonist to support the Bull Moose candidacy in 1912 and was honest enough to admit a change of heart in the 1930s, after initially supporting the New Deal.

Among his famous cartoons is the classic "Injun Summer," which he drew in 1907 and the *Tribune* has printed annually since 1912 (in color since 1934). It is marked by sentiment, the wisdom of age and the wonderment of childhood. His Pulitzer Prize cartoon for 1932 is typical McCutcheon; it is untouched by severe partisanship or personal attack. He was a truly sage commentator as well as a consummate cartoonist.

McCutcheon was the brother of novelist George Barr McCutcheon, and two of his sons have followed in his footsteps: Shaw is a political cartoonist and John, Jr., is editorial page editor of the *Chicago Tribune*. Two honorary degrees were awarded the revered McCutcheon, an L.H.D. from Purdue in 1926 and an LL.D. from Notre Dame in 1931. He died at his home near Chicago on June 10, 1949.

Books: *Stories of Filipino Warfare* (1900); *The Cartoons That Made Prince Henry Famous* (1902); *TR in Cartoons* (1903); *Cartoons by McCutcheon* (1903); *Bird Center Cartoons* (1904); *The Mysterious Stranger and Other Cartoons* (1905); *Congressman Pumphrey*

(1907); *In Africa* (1910); *Dawson III, Fortune Hunter* (1912); *The Restless Age* (1919); *An Heir at Large* (1922); *Crossed Wires* (1925); *Master of the World* (1928); and his 1950 autobiography, *Drawn from Memory*.

R.M.

MacDONALL, ANGUS (1876-1927) American cartoonist and illustrator born in St. Louis, Missouri, in 1876. Angus MacDonall moved east and was one of the first illustrators to settle in Westport, Connecticut, and establish it as an artists' community. His work began appearing regularly in the popular weeklies and monthlies in the early 1900s.

The bulk of his work was cartooning and light illustration; he readily became a fixture in *Life* magazine. At first a penman in the inevitable (for the time) Gibson style, MacDonall hit his stride when he discovered the pencil as his medium for finished work. Soon he was regularly appearing in all the humor magazines and kept busy doing mood illustrations for magazine fiction. Upon his untimely death at the age of 51, his work was an advertised main attraction in *Judge* magazine.

MacDonall's work was characterized by two things: the subtle and beautiful use of pencil shadings, and the consistent use of haunting, sentimental and nostalgic themes. Occasionally he touched on social issues—even then to evoke compassion rather than to incite anger—and he seldom aimed for the funny bone. His special world was that of memories, wistful love and and shared dreams; the handsome and impressive body of his work deserves reprinting.

R.M.

373

"Gosh, men are changeable!
Only last week I was crazy about Freddie."

Jefferson Machamer. © Collier's.

McGILL, DONALD FRASER GOULD (1875-1962) British
comic postcard cartoonist born at Blackheath, London,
England, on January 28, 1875. "King of the Seaside
Postcard," Donald McGill was the seventh of nine
children. This descendant of an ancient Scottish family was educated at Blackheath Proprietary School,
where he lost a foot after an accident during a rugby
match at the age of 17. He entered the drawing office
of a naval architect and began to contribute painted
postcard cartoons to publisher Joseph Asher in 1905.

"The Pictorial Postcard Company have discovered a
promising young humour-artist, Donald McGill by
name, in the confident expectation that comic cards of
his designing will soon become widely popular." This
was the announcement in the *Picture Postcard
Magazine* in December 1905. The confident expectation was realized: his most famous card, showing a
small child at prayers, "Please Lord, excuse me while
I kick Fido!," sold two million copies. McGill was
paid six shillings (then worth a little over a dollar) for
each card he produced, which included the full
copyright. Working full time, he continued to create
cards at the rate of ten a week.

When Asher was interned as an alien during World
War I, McGill transferred to Hudson Brothers (1914)
and then to the Inter-Art Company of Red Lion Square
(*Comique Series*) from 1920 to 1932. Asher returned
to postcard production in 1932 under the name of D.
Custance (an office employee), and McGill returned to
him to produce *The New Donald McGill Comics*. This
series ran from 1932 to 1962, the year of McGill's
death. He retired officially in 1939 and on the death
of Asher joined the board of the company as director
in charge of postcard design.

An article by George Orwell, the left-wing essayist,
entitled "The Art of Donald McGill," in *Horizon* (February 1941), was the first critical attention paid to
McGill's work. While casting doubts on McGill's existence ("He is apparently a trade name"), Orwell
wrote, "McGill is a clever draughtsman with a real
caricaturist's touch in the drawing of faces, but the

special value of his postcards is that they are so completely typical. They represent, as it were, the norm of
the comic postcard." McGill's gallery of grotesques—
bloated women in skin-tight swimming costumes,
equally balloonlike men ("I can't see my little Willie"), drunks, henpecks, courting couples, soldiers
("How long is your furlough?"), Scotsmen in kilts ("I
thought it was a cat and I stroked his sporran")—is
immortal, a permanent part of the British seaside way
of life.

McGill died on October 13, 1962, at age 87. His
postcards, perhaps 500 a year for 50 years, sold millions: he left exactly £735. A book, *Wish You Were Here*,
was published in 1966.

D.G.

MACHAMER, THOMAS JEFFERSON (1899-1961)
American cartoonist born in Holdredge, Nebraska, in
1899. Jefferson Machamer graduated from Nebraska
University and got his first job on the art staff of the
Kansas City Star. Sales of spot gag cartoons to *Cartoons Magazine* in the late 1910s whetted his appetite
for Big Apple markets, and he moved to New York.
After a stint with the *Tribune* he joined the staff of
Judge around 1924 and became one of that weekly's
major contributors. For *Judge* he did countless boy-
girl cartoons, color covers and *Laughs from the Shows*
(illustrated lines from Broadway hits), and drew the
spots for the *High Hat* feature, a gossipy review of
New York's speakeasies. When Norman Anthony left
for *Life* in the late 1920s, Machamer began writing
High Hat in addition. He later contributed to *College
Humor*.

As the magazine market declined, Machamer scored
variously with newspaper strips and panels: *Petting
Patty* for Hearst; *Gags and Gals*, also for Hearst, beginning in 1937; and *The Baffles* (about a small-town family
in Hollywood) for the *Los Angeles Times* in the early
1940s. He was the author of several revues and conducted a correspondence school in cartooning from
his home in Santa Monica, California until his death
on August 15, 1961.

Machamer had an individualistic drawing style that
varied little from the 1920s to the 1960s. His lack of

"How does it feel to be the first pedestrian I ever hit?"

Dorothy McKay. © Collier's.

art training was obvious, but he never shied from any subject or depiction. He drew in slashing, harsh brushstrokes and stereotyped his characters: men were wistful, bewildered and henpecked; women were assertive, dominant and racy (and in fact trod a thin line between the sexy and the grotesque).

R.M.

McKAY, DOROTHY (1904-1974) American cartoonist and illustrator born in San Francisco, California, in 1904. Dorothy McKay studied art at both the California School of Art and the Art Students League in New York City. The former Dorothy Jones, she was the wife of artist and illustrator Donald W. McKay. The couple lived in Greenwich Village, New York City.

Her cartoons, covers and illustrations appeared regularly in *Life, College Humor,* the *New Yorker, Ballyhoo* and *Forum* magazines. Then, as she said, "Esquire began to corral my time—from the second issue on." It might seem strange that a woman was a popular and regular contributing cartoonist to a magazine such as *Esquire,* which was noted for its risqué gags. However, Dorothy McKay was not unique. Barbara Shermund, another alumna of the *New Yorker's* pages, had a career with many parallels.

Dorothy McKay worked in a fluid style that at times resembled the wash work of cartoonist Eldon Dedini. However, she also enjoyed crowding her cartoons with many characters and objects. The result was a look of controlled clutter that was right for her type of sophisticated humor. One *Esquire* cartoon showed a flock of rich and portly stage-door Johnnies waiting for a bubble dancer to emerge. The figures are packed into the space of the cartoon. On second look, one of the Johns emerges as a court official holding a subpoena for the dancer.

President Franklin D. Roosevelt was so enamored of one Dorothy McKay cartoon that he hung the original in the White House. It showed a little boy in front of a well-to-do suburban home, writing in chalk on the sidewalk while his sister looks at him with disapproval. The caption read, "Johnny just wrote a bad word." The word on the sidewalk was "Roosevelt."

Dorothy McKay died in New York City on June 3, 1974. She is best remembered for her witty *Esquire* cartoons.

B.C.

McLAREN, NORMAN (1914-) British animator born in Stirling, Scotland, on April 11, 1914. One of the true artists in animation, Norman McLaren took the drawing-direct-on-film technique originated by Len Lye and, by refining and continually experimenting, made it all his own. The son of a house painter, he was fascinated from the age of nine by the inventiveness of American animated cartoons. He later founded a film society at the Glasgow School of Art, where he was studying interior design. He scraped the emulsion from a 300-foot reel of old film and, using clear inks, painted a changing design onto the celluloid. The result, McLaren's first animated abstract, was unfortunately lost to posterity when the art school projector chewed it to shreds. Undeterred, he went on to make *Camera Makes Whoopee* (1935), blending cartoons with animated models and objects. Shown at the Amateur Film Festival in Glasgow, the film impressed John Grierson, who invited the student to join his General Post Office film unit in London. Before he did so, McLaren joined an antiwar movement and made *Hell Unlimited* (1936), an impressionistic documentary, with sculptor Helen Biggar. He also visited Spain and filmed some of the events of the civil war with Ivor Montagu (*Peace and Plenty,* 1936).

Joining the GPO film unit, McLaren was trained by Alberto Cavalcanti and Evelyn Spice, makers of documentary films. He made four short films, including *Book Bargain* (1937), a documentary on the telephone directory, and *Love on the Wing* (1938), a plug for the new airmail service which he drew directly onto film. After a short spell with Film Centre, an outfit making sponsored documentaries (here he made *The Obedient Flame*), McLaren went to New York at the outbreak of World War II. On commission from the Guggenheim Museum he drew the film *Stars and Stripes* (1939), this time doing his own soundtrack as well. A few advertising films for Caravelle followed; then came a second invitation from John Grierson, the so-called father of the documentary. Grierson had been made Canadian film commissioner, and he wanted McLaren to start an animation unit at the newly formed National Film Board of Canada. McLaren's first films for the NFB followed his British pattern: *Mail Early for Christmas* (1941), etc. Then he supervised a series of song cartoons, *Chants Populaires* (1944), which used several animation techniques to illustrate favorite French-Canadian songs. *Begone Dull Care* (1949) introduced a new style of hand-drawn film: McLaren ignored the frame lines and used the celluloid strip itself as a continuous canvas.

For the 1951 Festival of Britain McLaren made two short stereoscopic cartoons in three-dimensional sound, *Around Is Around* and *Now Is the Time,* which proved that the 3-D technique is ideal for animation. Unfortu-

Norman McLaren, seven successive frames of visual material, based on sound track images. © *National Film Board of Canada.*

nately McLaren's experiments were not studied by the film industry, whose few stereoscopic shorts in the 1950s lacked both inspiration and impact. McLaren continued to experiment and in 1952 made *Neighbors*, the first effective use of the pixillation technique (the use of live actors as animated objects). After setting up animation schools in China (1949) and India (1953) for UNESCO, McLaren experimented further with his attempt to visualize music. *Rhythmetic* (1956) was a sophisticated use of cutout animation, *Canon* (1964) a complex mix of almost every known animation technique, and *Pas de Deux* (1967) a stroboscopic short of overlapping images. Now far removed from the commercial entertainment field, McLaren has taken animation into the realm of pure personal art.

Among McLaren's other films, mention should be made of the following: *Dollar Dance* (1943), *Alouette* (1944), *Hoppity Pop* (1946), *A Phantasy* (1952), *Serenal* (1959), *Mosaic* (1965), *Spheres* (1969), *Synchromy* (1971) and *Ballet Adagio* (1972).

D.G.

MacNELLY, JEFFREY KENNETH (1947-   ) American artist born in New York on September 17, 1947. Jeff MacNelly came from an artistic family and had his first cartoon published in *Lawrence Life*, the yearbook of Lawrence School in Hewlett, Long Island. Later scholastic markets included the *Mirror* literary magazine at Phillips Academy and the *Daily Tar Heel*, campus newspaper at the University of North Carolina. During his last two years of college he contributed to the *Chapel Hill Weekly*.

On December 1, 1970, MacNelly began drawing political cartoons for the *Richmond* (Va.) *News Leader* and won a Pulitzer Prize for his work during his first full year behind the drawing board. Since then he has won other awards and begun drawing cartoon features. *We Hold These Truths* is a realistically illustrated panel dealing with American history; it is written by his close friend and editor Ross Mackenzie and distributed by United Feature. *Shoe*, a zany comic strip about a colony of birds with all-too-human neuroses, is packaged and edited by Neal Freeman and syndicated by Tribune-News, which also handles his editorial cartoons.

MacNelly is clearly the premier American editorial cartoonist of his generation. He began working in the vein of Oliphant but soon transcended any influences and developed a distinctly individual style. His level of achievement—salient points presented in arresting compositions—is consistently excellent. A cartoonist of

Moolah Be Praised
Duncan Macpherson. © Toronto Star.

conservative political leanings, MacNelly is reprinted widely and has eschewed offers to join larger newspaper staffs across the nation; he prefers to remain in Richmond. His first anthology—*MacNelly*, published by Westover in 1972—clearly demonstrated his technique of couching a devastating political observation in an invariably hilarious format. More recent books include *The Best of MacNelly* and *Shoe*.

R.M.

MACPHERSON, DUNCAN IAN (1924-   ) Canadian editorial cartoonist born in Toronto, Ontario, on September 20, 1924. Duncan Macpherson began sketching as a youth. While in the Royal Canadian Air Force in England during World War II, he started art training. On release from service in 1946, he enrolled at Boston Museum School of Art, and on graduation in 1948 he took a two-year course at Ontario College of Art. Macpherson then freelanced for about ten years. His work appeared in a variety of publications ranging from the *Christian Science Monitor* to Eaton's mail order catalogues. He illustrated several series in the Montreal *Standard* and *Maclean's*.

In 1958 Macpherson joined the Toronto *Star* on the urging of editor Pierre Berton. From there his cartoons have been printed in numerous other Canadian papers and over a hundred different newspapers around the world. Since 1959 he has won the National Newspaper Award six times. His work has also been honored with a 1966 Royal Canadian Academy Medal for distinguished work in the visual arts and the 1971 Molson Prize from the Canada Council for contributing to the arts in Canada. Yearly collections of his editorial cartoons have been published since 1961. He has illustrated several books, including one of his own titled *Macpherson's Canada*.

Macpherson is almost universally recognized as the foremost editorial cartoonist in Canada. His illustrative skills are given a large space at the top of the *Star's* editorial page. In preparation for drawing, Macpherson makes extensive research use of the library and fills his cartoons with props and costumes when needed. Many times his knowledge of magic tricks and circuses has been put to use in his cartoons. His detailed drawings have been exhibited in various places, from art galleries to university campuses. Edmund Wilson, writing in the

Jeff MacNelly. © New York Daily News.

New Yorker, compared Macpherson to James Gillray and stated that his cartoons "may be fascinating quite independently of our interest or knowledge of the happenings they commemorate. Macpherson is a Gillray reduced in scale, a more scaring and grotesque Lewis Carroll."

With his artwork, Macpherson provides a remarkable commentary on events and individuals. His cartoons reveal weakness and flaws in ways almost everyone can understand and appreciate. His typical Canadian is a tattered, chinless fellow who is usually in some pathetic and humorous situation. John Diefenbaker, prime minister when Macpherson started at the *Star*, said, "He is a great cartoonist with an infinite capacity to get to the heart of things. I like a cartoon that is devastating without wounding."

Macpherson isn't known deeply by many of his colleagues. He has been seen both as a rough character and as compassionate beyond measure. He is about six feet two and weighs about two hundred thirty pounds. One friend characterizes him as a combination of Mary Poppins, Mark Twain and Attila the Hun.

D.K.

MADDOCKS, PETER (1929-   ) British writer, cartoonist, animator and one-man syndicate, born in Birmingham on April 1, 1929 ("All Fools' Day," as he is pleased to point out). Peter Maddocks attended the Moseley School of Art from age 11, until he ran away to sea with the merchant marine at 15. Five years later he returned to dry land and set up a small business as a poster writer and designer for a small chain of cinemas, his first professional artwork. He wrote a trial strip, *Shame of the West*, which was drawn by a friend, cartoonist Terry ("Larry") Parkes, and together they tried their luck with the London newspapers. Nobody was interested, however, so Maddocks began to write strip scripts for the Amalgamated Press *Cowboy Comics* ("Kit Carson") and *Thriller Comics* ("The Saint," from the books by Leslie Charteris). He began to contribute cartoon gags to the "Cartoon Sketch" page in the *Daily Sketch*. Editor Julian Phipps liked his style, which was then close to that of "Trog," and gave him a 12-month contract for a daily gag cartoon.

Much attracted by the strip format, Maddocks then adapted the radio series *The Goon Show* as a daily, but this failed to interest editors. A strip in the same style of humor but with an original character did catch the interest of the *Daily Express*, however, and *Four D Jones*, signed for ten weeks, ran for ten years! The central character was a cowboy who used a time hoop to travel through 4-D (the fourth dimension) to sundry adventures in various worlds. This strip was followed by *Horatio Cringe*, about a dimwitted detective, which appeared in the Glasgow *Evening Citizen*. In 1966, Maddocks became sports cartoonist on the London *Evening Standard* and founded the British Cartoonists' Association. Other of his strips include *A Leg at Each Corner* (*Sunday Telegraph*, 1968) and the political strip *No. 10* (*Sunday Express*, 1971), which changes central characters with every general election!

Maddocks's style has become extremely simple, perhaps out of necessity, because he is extremely prolific. He is currently drawing *Slightly Maddocks* daily in the *Evening News* (since 1971), *Useless Eustace* in the *Daily Mirror* (since 1974 when he took the character over from Jack Greenall) and *The Zanies*, a three-

gags-a-day strip that he himself has syndicated since 1970. In addition he draws a full-color three-page folio of permissive gags for *Mayfair* each month and designs and storyboards cartoon commercials for German television, for Credo (a deodorant), Neocid (a fly spray) and Jumbo (a washing powder), to name but a few. His children's comic work includes *The Bouncers* in *Swift* (1959), *Slowcoach* in *Whizzer and Chips* (1970) and *Penny Crayon* in *Lindy* (1975). His books are *The British Elephant Book* (1967) and *No. 10* (1973).

D.G.

MAL
See Hancock, Malcolm.

MANCA, GIOVANNI (1895?-   ) Italian cartoonist born in Milan, Italy, around 1895. Giovanni Manca started his cartooning career in 1914 in the magazine *Numero*, for which he drew political cartoons. After World War I, he devoted his talents to drawing cartoons and stories for boys' magazines.

In 1930, in the comic weekly *Il Corriere dei Piccoli*, Manca created one of the most famous of Italian comic strips, *Pier Cloruro de' Lambicchi*, featuring a bald scientist always full of inventions and optimism in a period that did not lend itself to optimism. The protagonist has been engaging in his slightly hare-brained adventures ever since. After World War II Manca produced two more humor strips, *Macarietto* and the more unusual *Tamarindo*, in which a breezy confidence man went around the world in the company of such strange associates as the Earl and Sister Cipolla.

Manca has continued to draw gag cartoons over the years and has also illustrated a number of books, including a *Pinocchio* in which his caricatural sense of humor was given free rein. Now more than eighty years old, he still lives in Milan and is as active as ever.

C.S.

MANFREDI, MANFREDO (1934-   ) Italian animator and filmmaker born in Palermo, Italy, in 1934. After studying art (he is a painter of great luminosity), Manfredo Manfredi settled in Rome. Starting in 1960, he produced the animated credits for a number of TV programs and also made animated commercials. In 1965, in collaboration with Guido Gomas, Manfredi produced two entertainment shorts: *L'Albero* ("The Tree"), which deals with ecological issues, and *Ballata per un Pezzo da Novanta* ("Ballad for a Heavyweight"), which uses the rhythms of a vibrant popular ballad for

Giovanni Manca. © Il Travaso.

Manfredo Manfredi, "Terun." © *Manfredi.*

an ironical investigation into the world of meat markets infiltrated by the Mafia. Manfredi's *Terun* (1967) is a tale of an immigrant from the Italian south and the prejudices he encounters. In 1969 *K.O.,* an exposé of boxing, was enthusiastically received by the critics. In *Rotocalco* ("Rotogravure," 1970) Manfredi projects the fears, illusions and oppressions of modern man as layouts for a rotogravure press.

In recent times Manfredi has leaned heavily towards the fantastic. In this genre he made *Il Muro* ("The Wall"), *Ritorno nel Futuro* ("Return to the Future," in collaboration with the Romanian Sabin Bălaşa) and *The Cat* (in collaboration with the Yugoslav Zlatko Bourek), all released in 1971 and 1972. Manfredi also directed the 1973 *Sotteranea* ("Underground"), which depicts the terrifying journey of a subway traveler, and the recent *Dedalo* ("Daedalus"), which was nominated for an Academy Award. In a different vein, he was the chief animator on the poetic *Il Giro del Mondo degli Inamorati di Peynet* ("Around the World with Peynet's Lovers," 1974). Manfredi's wife, Maria Grazia Hay, has also directed a number of animated cartoons, such as *Homo Sapiens* and *La Costola d'Adamo* ("Adam's Rib").

S.T.

MANNING, REGINALD (1905-) American cartoonist born in Kansas City, Missouri, on April 5, 1905. Reg Manning moved to Phoenix, Arizona, in 1919 and studied art in high school. Three days after graduation he secured a position with the Arizona *Republic,* starting work on May 1, 1926. He was to hang his hat at that office for the next 50 years.

Manning began as a photographer and spot artist. Soon he was drawing both a weekly full-page review of the news (in the Billy Ireland format) called *The Big Parade* and daily editorial cartoons. The *Parade* was given up in 1948 so Manning could devote more time to his editorial cartoons, and three years later he won a Pulitzer for "Hats," one of the most strikingly simple cartoons ever chosen by that committee.

A Phoenix institution, Manning is famed for his good humor, his many speaking engagements and a series of books produced through the years. Titles include *A Cartoon Guide to Arizona* (1938), *What Kinda Cactus Issat?* (1941), *From Tee to Cup* (1954) and *What Is Arizona Really Like?* (1968). The Republic and Gazette Syndicate distributed Manning's work until 1945, when

McNaught assumed syndication. Manning retired in 1976—Bill Mauldin was the principal guest at the retirement dinner—and now sculpts with as much success as he enjoyed at the drawing board.

Reg Manning was for years one of American cartooning's most prominent conservative voices and won numerous awards. His cartoons were drawn with pen, brush and heavy grease crayon in a somewhat stiff style and signed with his name and a cactus "mascot" whose face registered Manning's own opinions about the subject dealt with—not that the reader really needed assistance!

R.M.

MARANHÃO, PERICLES (1924-1961) Brazilian cartoonist born in the state of Pernambuco, Brazil, in 1924. Pericles Maranhão studied art in Recife and moved to Rio de Janeiro in 1943. He started his career in cartooning later the same year with *As Aventuras de Oliveira Trapalhão,* a strip he created for the comic book publishers Diários Associados and signed with his first name only. Pericles joined the humor magazine *A Cigara* in 1944 as a staff artist, a position he retained for the next eight years. In 1952 he created the popular panel *O Amigo da Onça* ("The Two-Bit Friend") for the daily newspaper *O Cruzeiro.*

Pericles was a gifted and funny artist who endowed his characters with much humor and humanity. Despite the sunny disposition he displayed in his cartoons, his outlook on life was dark, and he finally committed suicide in 1961. *O Amigo da Onça* was taken over by Carlos Estevão de Souza and remains as a reminder of Pericles's talent.

A.M.

MARCUS, JERRY (1924-) American cartoonist born in Brooklyn, New York, on June 27, 1924. Jerry Marcus

Don't look so glum.

Reg Manning. © *Phoenix Republic and Gazette Syndicate.*

grew up in Brooklyn and attended Samuel J. Tilden High School. A skinny kid, he was turned down by the U.S. Navy for being underweight when he tried to enlist in 1943. He joined the merchant marine instead. In 1943 he completed three or four trips to England across North Atlantic convoy routes. During these trips he served aboard tankers loaded with high-octane gasoline. In 1944 Marcus was able to enlist in the U.S. Navy and serve the rest of World War II as a Seabee in the Philippines. While stationed on the island of Calicoan off the tip of Samar, he started a makeshift military newspaper called the *Coral Zephyr.*

Once again a civilian, Jerry Marcus used the GI bill to attend the Cartoonists and Illustrators School in New York City, now known as the School of Visual Arts. He began submitting magazine cartoons and in 1947 made his first professional sale to *Argosy.* A year later he sold to the *Saturday Evening Post, Collier's* and *American* magazines. During the 1950s and early 1960s cartoons by Jerry Marcus were standards in most of the national general readership magazines. He was one of the cartoonists on contract to the *Saturday Evening Post.* The contract assured him of four sales a month to the *Post.* Many of his sports cartoons appeared in *Sports Illustrated.*

Marcus draws everything from kids to pets to suburbia to the classic man-stranded-on-a-desert-island. His drawing style is loose but not sketchy. Sometimes editors would decide they liked his roughs and publish them instead of requesting that more finished drawings be done. Numerous Jerry Marcus cartoons have been published in cartoon anthologies, and presidents Eisenhower and Kennedy both asked for, and received, original Marcus cartoons.

In the early 1960s, he set becoming a cartoonist for the *New Yorker* as a goal. However, after he'd been published five times in the *New Yorker,* the demands of his then-new syndicated comic strip *Trudy* kept him from submitting cartoons regularly. *Trudy* began in March 1963. A daily panel and Sunday page syndicated by King Features Syndicate, *Trudy* stars the young suburban housewife personified.

Recently, Marcus has begun to freelance magazine cartoons as well as doing his *Trudy* strip. *Good Housekeeping, Ladies' Home Journal* and the gag-a-day panels syndicated by King Features and McNaught syndicates have proven ready markets for his cartoons.

A member of the Screen Actors Guild, Jerry Marcus has been an extra in a number of films and acted in television In 1963 a book of his magazine cartoons entitled *Just Married* was published. A collection of *Trudy* cartoons entitled *Hang in There Trudy* was published in 1975.

B.C.

MARGUERITA
See Bornstein, Marguerita.

MARKOW, JACK (1905-   ) American cartoonist born in London, England, on January 23, 1905. Jack Markow moved to New York at the age of two and later studied at the Art Students League under Boardman Robinson and Walter Jack Duncan (1922-29). There have been very few cartoon markets in which Markow's work has not appeared between the 1920s and the 1970s. His gags are almost always based on simple premises, and he draws with a loose, free brush line, usually using crayon shading. His style is one of deceptive simplicity; technical

"You may already be a winner!"

Jerry Marcus. © *Good Housekeeping.*

accuracy and flawless composition are hallmarks of his work.

It is possible that Markow will be remembered more for his instructional work in the cartooning field than for his output on paper. He taught for years at the School of Visual Arts, training a generation of magazine cartoonists. He was cartoon editor of *Argosy* between 1951 and 1953, and for many years he wrote a column on cartooning for *Writer's Digest,* providing invaluable tips and advice. He frequently contributes pointers and reminiscences to *Cartoonist PROfiles* magazine.

Markow's books include *Drawing and Selling Cartoons, Drawing Funny Pictures, Drawing Comic Strips* and *The Cartoonist's and Gag Writer's Handbook,* which many professionals still turn to for masterful instruction on their craft. Markow is also a noted painter and lithographer, with works in the collections of the Metropolitan Museum, the Library of Congress, the Brooklyn Museum, the Corcoran Gallery and the Whitney Museum of Modern Art.

R.M.

MARKS, ALEKSANDAR (1922-   ) Yugoslav cartoonist and animator born in Cazma, Yugoslavia, in 1922. After graduation from the Zagreb Academy of Art, Aleksandar Marks worked as a cartoonist for *Kerempuh* and also did book illustration. He joined Duga Film as an animator in 1951 and later made advertising films. In 1955 he designed Yugoslavia's first color cartoon, *Little Red Riding Hood.*

Marks joined Zagreb Film immediately upon its formation in 1956. Until 1960 he served merely as a designer on others' cartoons (*Cowboy Jimmy, On a Meadow, At the Photographer's* and *Typhus* are some of the films on which he worked). In 1960, in collaboration with Vladimir Jutriša, he started directing as well as designing. The most important Marks-Jutriša films include: *The White Avenger,* a sequel to *Cowboy Jimmy* (1962); *Metamorphosis* (1964); *The Kind-Hearted Ant* (1965); *The Fly,* a much-awarded cartoon about a fly growing to gigantic proportions (1966); *Sisyphus* (1967—either by coincidence or design there have been two other cartoons on the theme of Sisyphus, one by the

Aleksandar Marks, "The Fly." © *Zagreb Film.*

Hungarian Marcell Jankovics, the other by the Bulgarian Stoyan Dukov); and *In the Spider's Web* (1970). Marks has also collaborated on the multiphased *Man the Polluter* (1975), and he independently directed the charming little cartoon fable *Cowhand Marko* in 1976.

Marks stands apart from other Zagreb animators in his insistence on aesthetic and literary elements and in his affinity to the Surrealists, the Bauhaus and other modern art movements. His cartoons have received many awards and much acclaim over the years.

M.H.

MARLETTE, DOUGLAS N. (1949-   ) American political cartoonist born in Greensboro, North Carolina, on December 12, 1949. Doug Marlette is an alumnus of Florida State University, class of 1971, where he majored in philosophy and minored in art. He also took the Famous Cartoonists correspondence course. Shortly after graduation, in January 1972, Marlette started work as the chief editorial cartoonist of the *Charlotte* (N.C.) *Observer.* The liberal cartoonist garnered instant recognition, winning an Overseas Press Club citation, having his cartoons reprinted widely and being syndicated by King Features Syndicate.

Marlette draws in the contemporary mode—

Douglas Marlette. © *King Features Syndicate.*

horizontal format and single-tone shading—but easily manages to distinguish himself and his style. His compositions are surpassed only by those of MacNelly and Oliphant, among his contemporaries. They are masterpieces of planning, crowded but never busy. He has a distinctive wavy-line approach to the art and a consistently devastating delivery of ideas. In short, Marlette is one of the foremost American cartoonists of his time, keeping the great tradition of clever jibes and indictments alive in the political cartooning format.

R.M.

MARTIN, CHARLES EDWARD (1910-   ) American cartoonist and painter born in Chelsea, Massachusetts, on January 12, 1910. C.E. Martin was apparently a self-taught artist (available biographical information offers nothing on his educational background). His first reported success was as a painting supervisor in the teaching division of the Work Projects Administration between 1933 and 1937. In 1937 he was hired as a staff artist by the *New Yorker* and has continued in that capacity ever since. Besides cartoons, he has painted over one hundred fifty covers for the magazine under the signature "CEM." Between 1939 and 1941, he was also a staff cartoonist for the magazine *PM*. Over the years he has contributed cartoons, illustrations and cover art to such publications as the *New York Times, Saturday Review, Time, Saturday Evening Post, Life, Look* and *Playboy*.

An accomplished painter, as his wonderful *New Yorker* covers prove, Martin usually works in watercolors, oils or acrylics. His cartoons for the *New Yorker* are generally more elaborate than the line drawings or washes normally associated with cartoon art, and he seems to have become Peter Arno's successor as the magazine's main contributor of full-page comic paintings. If a rule of thumb for most cartoonists is "Gag first and representation second," with Martin it is more often the reverse. His gags do not usually depend upon visual shorthand but upon full, detailed and vibrant panoramas—renderings in which no element, from focal point to background, fails to receive the painter's careful attention. He likes to set his cartoons and cover art in colorful landscapes, and even when he works in ink lines, his concern with minute detail is an identifying trait.

Martin has had numerous exhibitions of his work, including one-man shows at the Rockland Foundation (1951), the Ruth White Gallery in New York City (1955-60), the Brooklyn Museum (1954-65) and the Graham Gallery (1973); he is represented in the permanent collections of the Metropolitan Museum in New York, the Museum of the City of New York, the Library of Congress and Syracuse University. He has taught watercolors as a member of the faculty at the Brooklyn Museum School of Art (1963-65) and is a member of the Cartoonists' Guild (past president) and the Society of Magazine Cartoonists.

R.C.

MARTIN, DON (1931-   ) American cartoonist born in Paterson, New Jersey, in 1931. Don Martin went to the Industrial Art School in Newark, New Jersey, and later to the Pennsylvania Academy of Fine Arts in Philadelphia. In 1953 he moved to New York City and started doing illustrations for magazines and greeting cards.

In 1954 Martin contributed his first drawings to *MAD*

magazine, joining its regular staff the next year. Since that time he has become one of the most popular of the magazine's cartoonists, billed as "*MAD*'s maddest artist." Martin's humor is often of the ghoulish variety, and he delights in depicting men squashed by falling safes, split open by buzz saws or literally having their brains blown out. His characters are usually unredeemable louts or ugly harridans. Most of Martin's cartoons (often in comic strip form) have been reprinted either in *MAD* anthologies or as paperbacks. Martin also draws occasionally for other national magazines, and he has designed a few television cartoons.

M.H.

C.E. Martin ("CEM"). © This Week.

MARTIN, HENRY (1925-) American cartoonist born in Louisville, Kentucky, on July 15, 1925. Henry Martin was educated at Princeton University and received his bachelor's degree in 1948. Two years of training at the American Academy of Art followed. Besides regular appearances in the *New Yorker*, he has also contributed to *Punch, Ladies' Home Journal, Saturday Review, Good Housekeeping, Gourmet* and *Audubon*. In addition, he has created a syndicated daily panel feature for the Chicago Tribune-New York News Syndicate entitled *Good News/Bad News*. Separately published collections of his work include *Good News/Bad News* (Scribner's), *Yak! Yak! Blah! Blah!* (Scribner's) and *All Those in Favor* (American Management Association).

Martin's specialty as a cartoonist is the world of business. He has apparently studied it well or been part of it and so is frequently encountered peeking into offices and boardrooms or following the executive home after a busy day's work. Working in India ink and wash, Martin renders his ideas with a sharp, unbroken line. His is a bold technique, but it is in substance rather than style that Martin makes his most individualistic statements. He has an ear for the cliché and an eye for the absurd in his gentle satires on the mores of the corporate and advertising communities—which is not to say that he cannot find a fresh twist on an idea as overworked as the desert island or advert with great charm to the days of our Neanderthal ancestors. He also, as befits a Princeton man, has a way with "old grad" humor.

Many examples of Martin's "funny business" have appeared in the *New Yorker*. In one cartoon, he shares with us the contentment of the vacationing businessman who discovers a newsstand advertising the *New York Times* minus the financial section. In another, two executives learn, as a fellow sails toward them from the floor below, that "kicked upstairs" is not after all an empty figure of speech. Finally, in an age when one finds the strangest things advertised on television, we see the shock of a viewer who beholds on his screen "the old bum you often see panhandling on the corner of 43rd Street and Sixth Avenue. As we approach the Christmas Season, I hope you won't forget me. Just mail your dollars today to 'Bum-Christmas' in care of this station."

Martin belongs to the National Cartoonists Society and holds a Deuxième Prix from the Salon International de la Caricature, Montreal. His work is represented in the Swann, David E. Lilienthal and IBM collections, all housed in the Princeton library.

R.C.

MASAOKA, KENZO (1898-) Japanese animator, artist, musician and composer born in Osaka, Japan, in 1898. After receiving an education in art, Kenzo Masaoka joined Makino Eiga ("Makino Films") in 1925 and was ostensibly involved in art direction. In reality he functioned as a jack-of-all-trades, doing everything from creating props to acting. He appeared as an actor in the 1928 film *Hitojichi* ("Hostage").

In 1927 he independently made a children's film entitled *Umi no Gyūden* ("Sea Palace"), utilizing his broad experience to write the script and do the filming and virtually everything else. This work achieved quick recognition and was purchased by Nikkatsu Films for distribution. Two years later Masaoka became the superintendent of the technical section of Nikkatsu's educational film department. When this folded in 1930 he began creating his own animation, first producing a two-reel silent film entitled *Nansensu Monogatari–Saru ga Shima* ("Shipwreck Story—Monkey Island," with the word *nansensu*, also meaning "nonsense," being a double entendre). It tells the story of a baby shipwrecked on an island inhabited by monkeys. He is raised by them until his superior intelligence causes them to drive him away, in a new twist on Kipling. The film used clever paper cutouts on celluloid to create animation.

By 1932 Masaoka had not only made a sequel but had also created his own animation studio in Kyoto. At the same time, he wrote *Manga Eiga no Shōrai* ("The Future of Animated Films"). He was particularly impressed with Mickey Mouse and intrigued by the possibilities of music and animation, interests that led to *Chikara to Onna to Yo no Naka* ("Strength, Women, and the Ways of the World"). The first talkie animation in Japan, it was produced in 1933 for Shochiku Urata. Its story revolved around humorous fighting among a husband, his typist and his wife. Following this success, Masaoka made *Gyangu to Odoriko* ("The Gang and the Dancer," 1934), concentrating in particular on music and timing. Then he produced works such as *Kaitei Ryoko* ("Traveling at the Bottom of the Ocean," 1935), *Mori no Yosei* ("Forest Fairies," 1935) and *Benkei tai Ushikawa* ("Benkei vs. Ushikawa," 1939). The last was unique in that it was created and drawn around prerecorded music.

In the interim Masaoko had created his own institute for the study of animation, which was incorporated into the animation department of Shochiku Films in 1941. Two years later Masaoka produced what remains his most representative work: *Kumo to Chūrippu* ("Spider and Tulip"), based on a story by Michiko Yokoyama about a spider, a tulip and a ladybug. It is a balletlike visualization of music using excellent black-and-white contrast and is regarded today as a classic of Japanese animation.

Kenzo Masaoka left an indelible mark on Japanese animation as a pioneer in the use of sound and especially music. In the postwar period he has continued to do animation-related work, even after suffering a stroke.

F.S.

MATSUSHITA, KIKUO (1917-   ) Japanese cartoonist born in Tokyo, Japan, on September 11, 1917. Kikuo Matsushita is best known in Japan as the illustrator of the series *Tokyo Mukashi Mukashi* ("Once upon a Time in Tokyo") and for his numerous appearances on television as an amateur carpenter. Matsushita, while considering everything he does to be part of his career as a cartoonist, is one of Japan's true dilettantes.

Matsushita began his art career after graduating from the Taiheiyo Gajuku (an art school), but at the start of World War II he was drafted into the press corps of the Imperial Japanese Navy and sent to Java, Indonesia. During this time he produced a piece of cartoon reportage titled *Senzen no Kangofu-san* ("Front-Line Nurse"). With the end of hostilities, Matsushita returned to Japan, destitute like everyone else. In order to make a living he hit upon the idea of drawing cartoon portraits of U.S. soldiers as they arrived in the port of Yokohama. In exchange he received chewing gum, chocolate and cigarettes, which he then sold on the black market or bartered. This turned out to be so lucrative an enterprise that he turned it into a business with other cartoonist friends.

As conditions improved in Japan, Matsushita began drawing cartoons regularly for a variety of magazines and eventually formed the YY Club with fellow cartoonists such as Koichi Yoshizaki and Naruo Morita. The YY Club was established to promote the sale of cartoonists' work, but musicians and other artists were also entitled to join. By 1955, Matsushita's cartoons were running regularly in magazines such as *Manga Times* and *Manga Dokuhon* (an example of his work during that period, *Nishiki Hebi*, depicted a boa constrictor run over by a car, his back having been squished into a brocade pattern). It was not until Matsushita illustrated *Tokyo Mukashi Mukashi* in the *Asahi Shinbun* that he gained much of a following, however, and his popularity further increased with several cartoon/narrative series he did for a variety of women's magazines.

Kikuo Matsushita holds strong views on what it means to be a cartoonist and is critical of the *gekiga* ("graphic story comics") boom presently sweeping Japan. Nonetheless, he believes in diversity, and whether he is on television hosting a show on amateur carpentry (he is director of the amateur carpenters' association of Japan) or building models for an amusement park, he views his activities as "cartooning."

F.S.

MATSUYAMA, FUMIO (1902-   ) Japanese political cartoonist born in Nagana Prefecture, Japan, on May 18, 1902. Fumio Matsuyama's career has been distinguished by the consistency of his political viewpoint during periods of change in which other cartoonists have done radical turnabouts. He is an inheritor of the tradition of the late Masamu Yanase, Japan's foremost proletarian cartoonist, and like him has devoted his talents to the support of leftist and antiestablishment causes. Matsuyama was an early member of Nihon Mangaka Renmei ("Japan Cartoonists Federation") and in 1926 became an assistant first to Sako Shishido, then to Masamu Yanase, successive editors of the federation's short-lived publication, *Humor*. His orientation was determined when he participated in the proletarian art movement and drew cartoons for such magazines as *Rōdō Manga* ("Labor Cartoons") and *Nōmin Manga* ("Peasant Cartoons"), both highly critical of the government of the time.

As the 1930s dawned in Japan, the increasingly rightist government became more and more wary of its critics and made moves to silence them, but Matsuyama was unable to compromise as others quickly did. As a member of the Communist party he was a conspicuous target, and in 1932 he was arrested along with his mentor, Yanase, and spent over three years in prison. In spite of repression, however, Matsuyama continued his opposition to the government. Save when he was actually in jail, he drew cartoons attacking the militarists in magazines that would still consent to publish them, such as *Tokyo Puck* and later *Karikare*; but he was often forced to use a pseudonym. In 1936 an exhibition of his work was confiscated by the police, and as war actually erupted and Japan became united behind the fascist cause, Matsuyama effectively found himself with no outlet for his work. With the end of the war, however, Japan entered a new era of freedom of expression, and in 1945 Matsuyama began working for the revived Communist newspaper, *Akahata* ("Red Flag"). Two years later he helped found *Kumanbachi*, a leftist magazine dedicated to carrying on the tradition of Masamu Yanase, and began drawing cartoons ever more critical of the U.S. occupation.

Fumio Matsuyama has consistently been the gadfly of Japan's establishment. Whether it has been the militarists, the U.S. occupation authorities or the present conservative government, he has satirized them all in countless cartoons that are usually heavily ideological. Among his numerous published works are *Chōjūgiga*, a collection of 30 color political cartoons published over the years (1963), and *Manga de Miru Sengoshi* ("A Postwar History in Cartoons," 1967). Today he still works for the *Akahata*.

F.S.

MAULDIN, WILLIAM HENRY (1921-   ) American author and Pulitzer Prize-winning cartoonist born in Mountain Park, New Mexico, on October 29, 1921. Bill Mauldin grew up on a ranch near Phoenix. He showed an interest in drawing at the age of 3, executed rodeo posters at the age of 12, and made his first sale ($10) while taking a correspondence course from the Chicago Art Institute.

In September 1940 Mauldin moved from the Arizona National Guard to the 45th Division. He saw early combat in Sicily and then through Italy, France and Germany. On the *Mediterranean Stars and Stripes* he was to create out of the spot drawings, cartoons and illustrations produced on the field two classic figures of American cartooning, Willie and Joe. They became the images of the quintessential soldiers—much to the consternation of spit-and-polishers like General George S.

"Just gimme a coupla asprin. I already got a Purple Heart."

Bill Mauldin. © *Mauldin.*

Patton—and personified doggedness, a resigned heroism and cynicism. Willie and Joe were classic partners, with vivid if low-key personalities and complementary roles.

Mauldin's cartoons were popular enough to be syndicated stateside—one won the Pulitzer Prize for 1944—and were continued after the war as a syndicated panel, less and less featuring the civilian Willie and Joe, and increasingly becoming political cartoons. His viewpoint was well to the left, and escalating political pressure was among the reasons he left cartooning around 1947.

For the next decade Mauldin engaged in an incredible variety of pursuits: running for Congress, acting in motion pictures, flying his private plane around the country, covering the Korean War for *Collier's*, writing many articles. In 1958 his plane was grounded near St. Louis, and while visiting the legendary Daniel Fitzpatrick, Mauldin learned of the latter's wish to retire. (Mauldin had recently substituted for vacationing Herblock, and the ink was again starting to flow in his veins.) He soon assumed duties at the *Post-Dispatch* and within a year had another Pulitzer to his credit. In 1962 he switched to the *Chicago Sun-Times*, where he remains, appearing through syndication in about three hundred other papers.

Mauldin frequently uses a humorous panel as the format for his editorial punch. He can be devastatingly direct and has always displayed a masterful talent for succinctness. His drawing suggests a man totally in command of his subject and media; his caricatures are never wild exaggerations, and sound anatomy underlies his figures. In recent years some of his cartoons have been reduced to the barest minimums, with benday shading instead of crayon. This development is simply a function of his working arrangement; the fact that he lives in his native New Mexico and sends his cartoons to Chicago via wire dictates the severest economies of detail.

Mauldin has won many honors besides his Pulitzers: the Sigma Delta Chi award in 1964, several National Cartoonists Society category awards and one Reuben; and honorary degrees from Connecticut Wesleyan (M.A., 1946), Albion College (LL.D., 1970), and Lincoln College (L.H.D., 1970). In 1977 Field Newspaper Syndicate arranged to syndicate thrice-weekly columns of Mauldin's observations and drawings.

In addition to articles in *Life*, the *Saturday Evening Post*, *Sports Illustrated*, the *Atlantic Monthly*, the *New Republic* and other magazines, Mauldin has many books to his credit: *Sicily Sketch Book* (1943); *Mud, Mules and Mountains* (1944); *This Damn Tree Leaks* (1945); *Up Front* (1945); *Star Spangled Banter* (1946); *Back Home* (1947); *A Sort of Saga* (1949); *Bill Mauldin's Army* (1951); *Bill Mauldin in Korea* (1952); *What's Got Your Back Up?* (1961); *I've Decided I Want My Seat Back* (1965); and *The Brass Ring* (1971). *Up Front* and *A Sort of Saga* have been reissued.

R.M.

MAY, OLE (1873-ca. 1920) American cartoonist born in Pleasanton, Iowa, on June 24, 1873. Ole May began his cartooning career in the early 1890s for newspapers in Los Angeles and Houston; later he drew human interest and editorial cartoons for the *Washington Post* and also pursued a lifelong interest by playing in the Marine Corps band. May followed Charlie Payne into Pittsburgh to draw editorial cartoons for the *Gazette-Times* (preceding Billy DeBeck on the staff) before he joined the *Cleveland Leader*.

Cleveland in the 1910s was blessed with a flock of talented cartoonists, among them two of the nation's best: May and Joe Donahey. The two were alike in style and treatment. Both relied on a masterful, feathery use of the crosshatch, which gave their drawings balance and an ethereal air when needed. Figures were soundly but comically drawn. Most important, both artists showed a strong preference for sentimental themes. Boyhood, courtship, family holidays—all were handled warmly and evocatively. While Donahey had the greater fame and dwelt more on home themes, May was the more effective partisan (Republican). His ideas were clear and free of labels, making him one of the first political cartoonists to so liberate himself. His artwork was crisp, animated and arresting.

Ole May, influential during his career, gave life to the symbol of Cleveland, Uncle Mose. He was forced to retire in late 1916 because of his health and died shortly thereafter in Long Branch, New Jersey.

R.M.

MAY, PHILIP WILLIAM (1864-1903) British cartoonist born in New Wortley, Leeds, on April 22, 1864. The creator of the modern, simplified school of cartooning, and the most influential cartoonist of his period, Phil May was the seventh of the eight children of the former Sarah Jane McCarthy of Dublin, Ireland, and Philip May, who worked in the drawing office of George Stephenson. His father died when Phil was nine, but the boy clearly inherited his talent.

Educated at St. George's School (1872-75), then at Oxford Place School (1876) and Park Lane Board School (1877), May learned to draw by copying car-

Lumpenproletariat

Phil May, illustration from "Guttersnipes," 1896.

toons from the humorous magazines *Fun* and *Puck*, and won first prize in a drawing competition, for which he received a T-square and a drawing board. His first job was in a solicitor's office, then for an estate agent, then as the timekeeper in an iron foundry. Fascinated by show business, he helped Fred Fox mix his paints for the scenery at the Grand Theatre, Leeds, and in the evenings sketched portraits of the traveling actors for a shilling a time. For six years he worked behind and in front of the scenes, meanwhile contributing his first professional sketches to the local comic papers the *Yorkshire Gossip* and the *Busy Bee*. In 1884, he began to contribute theatrical caricatures to *Society* and drew 178 for the special Christmas number, *Seven Ages of Society*. The following year found his drawings appearing in *St. Stephen's Review*, and when that weekly turned into an illustrated paper, he joined the staff at £8 a week.

His caricatures in the *Penny Illustrated Paper* (1885) caught the eye of W.H. Traill, who offered him a three-year contract as staff cartoonist of the *Sydney Bulletin*. May accepted and journeyed to Australia, arriving November 11, 1885, and returning to London in 1888, having earned the then-astounding salary of £1,000 per annum. He returned with a brand-new style, for England. The *Bulletin* was printed by the new photo-process engraving method that gave its cartoonists a new freedom of line impossible in England, where the line block system still ruled. May continued to contribute to the *Bulletin* until 1894, and his influence on succeeding Australian artists was as immense as it quickly became back home in London.

May joined the *Daily Graphic*, the first illustrated national newspaper, on November 12, 1890, and in 1893 was sent on a world tour for that paper. He also drew for the weekly *Graphic*, which appeared in color at Christmas. By now he was a master of rapid caricature, and his cartoons captured the common life of the London streets and gutters to perfection, appearing in almost every weekly magazine: *Pick-Me-Up* (1891), *Pall Mall, Black and White*, the *Sketch* (all 1892), and the *English Illustrated* (1893). His first *Punch* cartoon appeared on October 14, 1893. May died somewhat suddenly and sadly on August 5, 1903, of tuberculosis and cirrhosis of the liver, at age 39. But his artistic legacy was enormous.

Books: *The Parson and the Painter* (1891); *Phil May's Winter Annual* (1892, 13 editions); *Phil May's Summer Annual* (1892, 3 editions); *Fun, Frolic and Fancy* (1894); *Phil May's Sketchbook* (1895); The

Comet Crash (1895); *Guttersnipes* (1896); *Isn't It Wonderful* (1896); *Mayville* (1896); *Graphic Pictures* (1897); *Phil May's ABC* (1897); *Zig Zag Guide* (1897); *Songs and the Singers* (1897); *Book of the Bazaar* (1898); *50 Hitherto Unpublished Pen and Ink Sketches* (1899); *Phil May's Album* (1899); *East London* (1901); *Sketches from Punch* (1903); *A Phil May Picture Book* (1903); *A Phil May Medley* (1903); *Littledown Castle* (1903); *Phil May in Australia* (1904); *Phil May Folio* (1904); *Humorous Masterpieces* (1907); *Pictures by Phil May* (1907); *Humorists of the Pencil* (1908); *Phil May* (1932); and *Phil May* (1948).

D.G.

MAYER, HENRY (1868-1954) American cartoonist born in Worms am Rhein, Germany, in 1868. Hy Mayer moved to America when he was 18 but carried the germ of the free-spirited German cartooning fecundity that flowered there 20 years later. He was versatile, prolific and a jovial leader, at the turn of the century, of the rebellion in American cartooning against tight, disciplined, crosshatched illustration-type cartoons; with him were A.Z. Baker ("Baker-Baker"), Gustave Verbeck, Leighton Budd and Art Young.

His first major work appeared in *Life* in the mid-1890s. It was loose, unorthodox and slightly distorted and bespoke a gay spirit. Soon his work was also running in *Puck* and *Judge* and in the minor humor journals. At the same time he was contributing to foreign humor magazines, including *Fliegende Blätter* of Munich, *Punch, Pall Mall, Black and White* and *Pick-Me-Up* in England, and *Le Rire* and *Figaro Illustré* in France. His first book, *The Autobiography of a Monkey* (1896), was followed by many others for children and adults. He joined many other strip and magazine cartoonists (like McCay and Louis Glackens) in the animation field and produced more than fifty *Travelaughs*.

When *Puck* magazine was sold to the Nathan Strauss family in 1914, Mayer, long a fixture, became editor, and his own cosmopolitan flair began that

When the ship rolls and your berth becomes uncomfortable, take your pillow and sleep on the wall.

Hy Mayer, ca. 1910.

weekly's shift towards a more international, sophisticated appeal. From 1904 to 1914, moreover, he drew the weekly *Impressions of the Passing Show*—light commentary—for the *New York Times*. (These were the joyful days when the *Times* did not eschew cartoons; besides Mayer, through the years Ed Marcus and the great Oscar Cesare drew for its pages.) In all, Mayer was a popular cartoonist, writer and versifier, influential in spirit if not style among his colleagues. He was a public figure conspicuous at benefits and shows.

Hy Mayer's style stands up well under scrutiny many years later. His slapdash approach was engaging, and he playfully teased the readers' perceptions with pixieish alterations of perspective. He was fully competent enough to constantly experiment with formats, borders and colors, and he stands as one of the few American cartoonists before World War I to test the waters of the unconventional, as was being done in his native land so splendidly in the pages of *Jugend* and *Simplicissimus*.

R.M.

MECHAM, WILLIAM (1853-1902) British cartoonist, caricaturist and "chalk talker" on the music hall stage, born in 1853. Mecham, whose pen name was Tom Merry, was also the first British cartoonist to appear in a film. More, he was the first professional performer of any kind to be filmed in Britain.

"Tom Merry" was a familiar signature to readers of the many Victorian humor weeklies to which he contributed his social cartoons and contemporary caricatures. Merry was fond of the stage, and his caricatures of popular comedians and other theatrical notables may have led to his appearance at the music halls as a "lightning cartoonist." It was as a stage performer that he appeared in his films, four of which were photographed by the pioneer producer-director Birt Acres toward the end of 1895. In one brief fragment preserved by the National Film Archive in London, the moustachioed Merry may be seen to dash in front of the camera and swiftly flick off a quick caricature of the German emperor Wilhelm. The other personalities he chose to caricature in his series were Lord Salisbury, William Gladstone and Prince Bismarck. They were evidently well-rehearsed regulars from his stage presentation, as their likenesses had to be completed within 40 feet of film (40 seconds running time), which was all the primitive motion picture cameras would permit. The films formed part of the program projected by R.W. Paul at his initial theatrograph performance at the Alhambra Theatre in London on March 25, 1896. Several of the newspaper reviewers mentioned Merry's cartoons, but he made no more appearances before the cinematograph camera.

His final work was to illustrate *The History of Canvey Island*, a small book by Augustus A. Daly. Inside, a dedication reads: "In memoriam of William Mecham, artist, cartoonist, and caricaturist, better known to the British public by his professional sobriquet, Tom Merry, who died suddenly at Benfleet Station (adjoining Canvey Island), Essex, on Thursday, August 21st, 1902, aged 49 years."

D.G.

MEGGENDORFER, LOTHAR (1847-1925) German cartoonist, illustrator and author born in Munich, Bavaria, on November 6, 1847. Though he never rose to great

Lothar Meggendorfer, caricature of Napoleon retreating from Russia, 1813.

artistic heights, Lothar Meggendorfer served the German public long and well in a variety of ways. Since he was a native of Munich, where the humor magazine *Fliegende Blätter* was published, it was natural that he should be a steady contributor for many years. His specialty was a proto-comic-strip genre: a humorous incident or contretemps depicted in a series of several small drawings with no or very little text. These picture stories of Meggendorfer's were very similar to those of Caran d'Ache in France, but much less incisive and inventive. He also contributed over sixty drawings to the *Münchener Bilderbogen*.

In the late 1880s Meggendorfer began editing a weekly humor magazine of his own; its title varied somewhat over the years, but it is generally referred to as the *Meggendorfer Blätter*. It had a comfortable existence, finding and holding on to its own level of relatively undemanding readership. Only in 1928, three years after its founder's death, was it swallowed up by the *Fliegende Blätter*, which was then more than eighty years old. Printed partly in color and partly in black and white, the *Meggendorfer Blätter* had a steady cadre of mildly skillful and mildly enjoyable cartoonists, none offering a serious challenge to Meggendorfer himself, who, far from hogging the magazine, usually appeared discreetly on black-and-white inner or back pages.

In 1906 Meggendorfer was one of a few German (or German-based) cartoonists whose services were sought by the *Chicago Tribune* in an effort to raise the level of its Sunday comic pages at a period of strong competition. The real prize garnered by the *Tribune*, however, was not Meggendorfer but the American-born Lyonel Feininger, who contributed his pioneering strips *The Kin-der Kids* and *Wee Willie Winkie's World* for several months.

Perhaps the most exciting aspect of Meggendorfer's production was the vast number of children's books he wrote and illustrated. In turn, by far the most interesting of these were many kinds of toy books—books with movable figures, three-part segmented transformation pictures, pop-ups and ingenious variations on wheels, wires and slats. These books, which sold over a million copies, were done for two publishers: Braun and Schneider of Munich, who published the *Fliegende Blätter* and the *Münchener Bilderbogen*, and J. F. Schreiber of Esslingen (near Stuttgart), who published the *Meggendorfer Blätter*. The Braun and Schneider archive of Meggendorfiana was destroyed in World War II, but Schreiber's survived, and in New York in 1975 a dealer offered for sale, as a single lot, hundreds of preparatory

Nante becomes a minister.

Adolph von Menzel, illustration for the title page of a Berlin magazine.

drawings, hand-colored guides to the printers and the production files on over sixty titles.

S.A.

MENZEL, ADOLPH VON (1815-1905)

German painter and graphic artist born in Breslau, Prussia (now Wroclaw, Poland), on December 8, 1815. Like Chodowiecki, whose role as universal delineator of life in Germany (especially Berlin) he continued through the 19th century and into the early 20th, Adolph von Menzel had a basic fund of humor that repeatedly surfaced in his works although he was not a professional humorist.

Menzel's father had been head of a girls' school but then became a lithographic printer, and young Menzel was his aide. They moved to Berlin in 1830. When the older man died in 1832, Adolph, mainly self-taught, continued to do commercial art for printers and art dealers, especially Sachse. It was in this decade that most of Menzel's specifically humorous items were done—both original and reproductive (after Adolf Schrödter, for instance). These include several witty Berlin (and Leipzig) scenes of the sort Dörbeck, Schadow, Hosemann and Schrödter had done, New Year's greetings adapted to members of various professions and social classes, music covers illustrated with everyday scenes, party souvenirs, pictures for children and the like. (Even much later in life Menzel was officially called upon to create elaborately illustrated and calligraphed testimonial certificates and diplomas.)

Having proved his merit in "higher" things with illustrations of Luther's life (1833) and a lithographic series based on a Goethe poem about the misfortunes of artists (1834), Menzel quickly became the foremost German illustrator, as well as a major painter and printmaker. The outstanding masterpiece of his earlier life—and his best-remembered work—was his group of 400 illustrations engraved on wood for Kugler's life of Frederick the Great (completed in 1842). This led to a long preoccupation with Frederick's period and with military iconography. Among the Frederick the Great spinoffs were the illustrations for that monarch's own writings (completed in 1849); Menzel's ingenious work in connection with the king's satirical pieces forms another major facet of the artist's humorous production.

As time went on, Menzel was drawn more and more into the highest official circles of the German capital and was knighted in 1898. In addition, he occupied himself

with brilliant technical experiments in printmaking and did important paintings in an impressionist vein as early as the 1840s and 1850s (in 1875 his canvas depicting an iron foundry was a pioneering subject). Still, Menzel never stopped producing fresh, carefully observed drawings—thousands of them—of everything about him. Many of these, such as his picture of people arising stiffly after an uncomfortable night on a train (1877), reveal the wit that never deserted the grand old man. Menzel died in Berlin at the age of 90 on February 9, 1905.

S.A.

MERCIER, EMILE ALFRED (1901-   )

Australian humorist and cartoonist born in Noumea, New Caledonia, in 1901.

It was the graphic humorists of Sydney who were first to set a postwar Australian trend in humor satirically critical of social attitudes. The artists who took the lead in this direction were Emile Mercier of the Sydney *Sun* and George Molnar of the Sydney *Morning Herald*, both of whom must be acknowledged as the two major black-and-white humorists to work in Australia in recent times. Although in approach and drawing style Molnar and Mercier appear to be light-years apart, they nevertheless represent both sides of the social coin, with Molnar satirizing the urban tastes and attitudes of the opulent "gracious living" section of society and Mercier "having a go" not only at high life, as in the past, but at low life, too—and with an approach that is not just humorous. The significant difference lies in a break from the traditional "we're a lot of dags," style that characterized to some extent the humor of an earlier generation and that still typifies much humorous writing and minor works on Australian slang today.

Emile Mercier's view of humor is wide, with a graphic style in the broad historical comic tradition. But Mercier's comment does not contain much that is international in appeal; like that of the early *Bulletin* artists it is specifically a humor that reflects national

"No, I'm not in the mood to swear yet —just wait until I get real mad!"

Emile Mercier. © *Sydney Sun.*

life, with all the indigenous characteristics unique to Australia.

The best humor has always been expressed from a definite point of view; Emile Mercier's is quite clear. It emerges, for example, in a background detail such as a poster on a wall with the wording "Drink Flor de Florita—the Gravy of the Grape! A Symphony in Every Sip!" From his standpoint Emile Mercier presents the typical face of Australian cities—the fly-spotted cafés, noisy pub bars and crowded public transport, the racecourses, back alleys, and people of the city—tired waitresses, rough-and-ready taxi drivers, policemen, barmaids, disc jockeys and tax officials. His comment is unique in Australian graphic satire for its range of social documentation and a wit that is discriminating, responsible and perceptive.

Mercier contributed his joke drawings to the *Bulletin*, *Smith's Weekly* and Melbourne *Punch* in the 1920s. Recognition eventually came, and with it popularity, resulting in full-time work as a comic artist. When the humorous writer Lennie Lower rejoined *Smith's Weekly* in 1940, Emile Mercier was one of the artists selected to illustrate his pieces for the paper. Joe Jonsson took over the illustration of this feature when, during World War II, Mercier was engaged by *Truth* as a political cartoonist. Then, during the war, followed a period drawing political cartoons for the Sydney *Daily Mirror*. From that period until 1967, when he retired, Mercier's brilliance delighted not only the readers of the Sydney *Sun* but his fellow graphic humorists all over Australia.

Emile Mercier's pen drawings are often crammed with fun and rollicking detail—something of a triumph considering that his original drawings were never larger than 7½ by 5½ inches, a size regrettably conditioned by their rather miserable editorial reduction. It is also a triumph for Mercier that during his 40 years or so of drawing he has survived editorial buffeting and resisted the ephemeral fads and fashions of comic art and humor, preserving a sanity in his draftsmanship and satire, and revealing, without preaching, what sort of people Australians are.

V.L.

MERRY, TOM
See Mecham, William.

MESSMER, OTTO (1894-   ) American cartoonist and animator born in Union City, New Jersey, in 1894. The son of a machinist, Otto Messmer studied at the Thomas School of Art. His first published cartoons were gags in the *Fun* supplement of the *New York World* and in *Life* magazine (1914). Around this time, fascinated by the nascent animation field, Messmer made a one-minute test cartoon for Universal called *Motor Matt and His Fliv*. At the studios he met Hy Mayer, who was then doing newsreel cartoons, and the two collaborated on *The Travels of Teddy*. After doing advertising for Auerbach's chocolates, Messmer joined the Pat Sullivan Studios in 1916.

Pat Sullivan had learned animation with Gregory La Cava at the Barré studio. He was a former newspaper strip cartoonist who had inherited his friend Billy Marriner's features and also animated some of them. As a studio head, he encouraged the greatest possible creative and personal freedom in his staff. Thus, he would often let his artists do practically anything they chose, and if the film sold, the studio would get half the proceeds.

Otto Messmer, "Felix the Cat." © King Features Syndicate.

Under this system, before serving in World War I, Messmer created *Fearless Freddy* and *20,000 Laughs Under the Sea*, for which he drew every frame. In France the prolific Messmer, a member of the Signal Corps, won an award for his designs in the Victory Carnival.

Back in America, Messmer drew Charlie Chaplin cartoons and worked with Earl Hurd, Frank Moser and John Terry on *Silly Hoots* (a pun on "silhouettes") for the Paramount Screen Magazine. When Paramount fell behind schedule, they subcontracted the work to Sullivan, who ultimately let Messmer handle it freelance. From there, Messmer's own ideas, the running series *Feline Follies* (or *Frolics*) and probably some other obscure antecedents led to the official birth of Felix the Cat in 1920. Messmer has recalled his formula for success—a sharp, solid, defined black area, a premise with the logic of a child's dreams and fancies, and the exploitation of animation's potential for absurd visual gags—but what really established Felix as an instant classic was Messmer's incredible creativity and childlike imagination. The cat was a huge success and must be recognized not only as a great personal achievement for Messmer but as the prototype for hundreds of other children's fantasy creations, including Disney's.

In 1923 Messmer began drawing a *Felix* Sunday page (which he never signed until the 1940s); earlier a daily strip had begun in the *London Illustrated News* (of all papers), which had asked King Features to arrange with Sullivan for a newspaper version of Felix. (King later assumed the copyright and now owns Messmer's creation.) When Paramount left the picture, the *Felix* cartoons were first syndicated by Margaret Winkler, then by Sullivan's lawyer with the backing of Educational Films; soon the studio was producing one short every ten days. Working with Messmer were Bill Nolan, George Stallings, Bert Gillette and Raoul Barré. Sullivan, who resisted the transition to sound, died in 1933, and so, for awhile, did the animated Felix.

Messmer declined offers to work for other studios. Instead he continued on the strip (until 1954), also working with Douglas Leigh on the development of animated electric signs (1939-40), on the *Felix* comic book for Toby Press and on storyboards for *Popeye*, *Little Lulu*, *Snuffy Smith* and other animated cartoons (1944-45). After failing to interest Sam Buckwalt of Famous Studios/Paramount in reviving *Felix*, Messmer went back into advertising. He retired at the age of 80. In 1967, with a festival in Montreal, he began to receive the recognition he had seldom had previously. Since then, museum shows, retrospectives, interviews, articles and awards have made up for lost time.

Messmer is one of the most remarkable men in cartooning. Though others reaped the financial rewards and, until recently, the credit for his creation, modesty has prevented him from regretting the virtual anonymity in which he worked. He could develop sophisticated story lines with impressive speed; he could draw almost as fast and for years did prodigious amounts of animation and strip work simultaneously; and most importantly, he never lost the child's touch so precious to anyone in the business of creating fantasy. His perspective was a manifestation of genius, the genius that overwhelms by sheer simplicity. "Nowadays, kids don't dream about the moon—they know," he has said. "Then, all was magic. All we had was a pencil and paper. We didn't want to duplicate life; a photo would've done that. Felix was always a cat, but with a boy's wonder about the world. That, and visual tricks, and we had it."

R.M.

MESTRES I OÑO, APEL.LES (1854-1936) Spanish cartoonist born in Barcelona, Spain, in 1854. Apel.les Mestres had his first cartoons published in 1880 in the weekly satirical magazines *L'Esquella de la Torratxa* and *La Campana de Gracia*. Later his works appeared in magazines like *Pel i Ploma*, *La Publicidad*, *El Liberal*, *L'Avenc* and *La Mainada*, to name but a few of the Catalan and national publications to which he contributed.

Throughout his life Mestres participated in a wide variety of artistic endeavors: literature, newspaper writing (notably in *La Campana de Gracia*), children's stories, theater, painting, poetry and music. His involvement with music grew after 1912, when he lost vision in one eye; after 1920, when he became totally blind, he devoted himself exclusively to music. He was a close friend of the famous Spanish composer Enrique Granados.

Apel.les Mestres produced more than forty thousand cartoons in his lifetime. He frequently expressed his political views in cartoons, sometimes using children as a means of ridiculing the "infantile" behavior of adults and politicians. His cartoons kept in close touch with the sentiments of the common people. Every day the entire country enjoyed Mestres's drawings, his earthy humor and witty criticisms. Because he sought to impart moral values through his cartoons, Mestres often sounds a bit didactic, albeit never pompous. He achieved an impact through the use of naturalistic techniques reflecting the true character of the Spanish people. Mestres died on July 19, 1936, the day following the start of the Spanish civil war.

J.M.

MICKEY MOUSE (U.S.) Legend has it that Walt Disney created his most famous character during a 1927 train ride back to Hollywood from New York, where he had just lost his *Oswald the Rabbit* series to Charles Mintz. He wanted to name the little creature Mortimer but was talked out of it either by his wife or by one of his distributors (according to which source one is willing to listen to). Thus was *Mickey Mouse* born.

Setting out to work with his usual alacrity, Disney laid down his concept of "The Mouse." "He had to be simple," Disney later declared, adding, "His head was a circle with an oblong circle for a snout. The ears were also circles so they could be drawn the same, no matter how he turned his head. His body was like a pear and he had a long tail. His legs were pipestems

Mickey Mouse in "Steamboat Willie." © *Walt Disney Productions.*

and we stuck them in big shoes to give him the look of a kid wearing his father's shoes."

Retaining overall direction, Disney turned over the actual drawing to his talented assistant, Ub Iwerks. Soon one Mickey short, "Plane Crazy," was completed; another, "Gallopin' Gaucho," was on the boards when the success of *The Jazz Singer* and other early talkies convinced Disney that the future was with sound. Temporarily leaving the first two Mickey cartoons aside, Disney and Iwerks busied themselves with a third short, "Steamboat Willie," which Disney took to New York. There, with the help of a pickup band, a crudely devised score of his own invention and a couple of sound effects men, he recorded the synchronized sound track (doing the Mickey Mouse voice himself, as he did for over twenty years). On September 19, 1928, "Steamboat Willie" opened at the Colony Theater in New York, and it was an instant success.

The sound versions of "Plane Crazy" and "Gallopin' Gaucho" followed the next year, along with "Karnival Kid," "The Jazz Fool!" (a spoof of *The Jazz Singer*) and "The Opry House." Mickey was now an established star, and scores of Mickey Mouse cartoons poured out of the Disney studio. It would be impossible to list them all, but among the most popular or noteworthy are: "Mickey's Follies," "The Chain Gang," "Mickey's Choo-Choo" (in which Disney indulged his love of trains), "Mickey's Birthday Party," "Mickey's Nightmare" (which the Disney organization later withdrew from circulation as being too gruesome), "Mickey's Revue," "Mickey's Gala Premiere" (in which Mickey, fittingly enough, played host to other Hollywood stars), "Gulliver Mickey," "Orphans' Benefit" and "The Band Concert" (probably Mickey's most beloved adventure and the first one in Technicolor). All were released from 1930 to 1935.

In these cartoons Mickey assumed any role (alpine climber, explorer, cowboy, etc.) and traveled everywhere (to Arabia, the Sahara, the South Seas, by plane, boat and on horseback). His popularity was extraordinary; George Bernard Shaw praised him to the skies, and Soviet filmmaker S.M. Eisenstein proclaimed him "America's most original contribution to culture." British novelist E.M. Forster wrote what was to become the ultimate Mickey Mouse tribute in *Arbinger Harvest*: "Mickey's great moments are moments of heroism, and when he carries Minnie out of the harem as a pot-plant or rescues her as she falls in foam, herself its fairest flower, he reaches heights impossible for the *entrepreneur.*"

Minnie Mouse had been in the cartoons from the first, as had her villainous pursuer, Pegleg Pete. Clarabelle Cow and Horace Horsecollar were two other early stalwarts. Pluto appeared in 1930 and Goofy only came on the scene in 1932. The last two characters became very popular in their own right, but their success was nothing compared to that of the cantankerous Donald Duck, who edged out Mickey himself in popularity soon after his birth in 1934.

By the late 1930s Mickey was largely confined to the role of master of ceremonies. Disney tried to revive his popularity by casting him as the Sorcerer's Apprentice in *Fantasia* (1940) and giving him a role in another of his package features, *Fun and Fancy Free* (1947), to no avail. The Mouse's later appearances became rare, and he practically disappeared in the mid-1950s when the Disney studio stopped making theater shorts.

In the meantime, however, Mickey had assumed mythical proportions. He was adapted to comic strip form in 1930, and to comic books a little later. His likeness appeared on toys, watches, school tablets, soap and every conceivable product—not to mention the heads of countless enthusiastic "Mousketeers" who faithfully donned their Mickey ears and followed his career on TV. His name assured the success of scores of children's newspapers (*Topolino* in Italy, *Le Journal de Mickey* in France, *Mickey Mouse Weekly*

in England, to name a few). It is only fair to say that Mickey must be regarded not as a cartoon character (as successful as he may have been in this respect), but as a genuine cultural phenomenon of the first magnitude.

M.H.

MICKWITZ, CAMILLA (1937-) Finnish animator and cartoonist born in Helsinki, Finland, on September 22, 1937. Aside from another woman—Tove Jansson—Camilla Mickwitz is probably the Finnish cartoonist best known internationally. She studied from 1955 to 1958 at the Helsinki University of Arts and worked in advertising before becoming a freelance artist in 1966. She now works on films, books and illustrations for the large newspaper *Helsingin Sanomat*.

A mother of three, Mickwitz often touches on human relations, and by depicting authentic family and social life, she obviously aims to provide models for children and adults alike. Her figures are simple and cuddly, and the spirit and colors in her works are warm and vibrant. Critics regard her as an important counterweight to commercial mass culture.

Mickwitz has created an animated cartoon series for TV, *Ollaan Yhdessä* ("Let's Be Together"), as well as 13 other animated cartoons, many of which she also wrote herself, and most of which were produced by the Finnish Broadcasting Company. Her books include *Pikku Kanin Hassu Päivä* ("The Crazy Day of the Little Rabbit," 1972, in collaboration), *Jason* (1975), *Jasonin Kesä* ("Jason's Summer," 1976) and *Jason ja Vihainen Viivi* ("Jason and Angry Vivian," 1977). Her film *Jasonin Kesä* won the prize for best children's animation at the 1975 Hollywood Festival of World Television. *Ollaan Yhdessä* received a government award and the first Peace Culture prize given by the Finnish Peace Committee in 1976. Her books have been honored in Finland and abroad for both their content and their artwork, and her illustrations have been exhibited throughout the world.

J.R.

Mighty Mouse. © *Paul Terry.*

MIGHTY MOUSE (U.S.) The first cartoon in the *Mighty Mouse* series, "The Mouse of Tomorrow," was released in 1942. Conceived and created by Isidore Klein for Paul Terry's Terrytoons studios, it was a parody of Superman, "the man of tomorrow," and the principal character was called Supermouse in the first three cartoons (which included the witty "Supermouse in Pandora's Box"). The hero was later rechristened Mighty Mouse (despite objections from Walt Disney) and gained fame under this new name.

The early cartoons were fast-paced and unpredictable, gently spoofing the contemporary *Superman* animated shorts. "Faster than a bullet, stronger than a bull," the announcer would intone at the beginning of each cartoon, "it's Supermouse!" One of the best entries was "Down with Cats" (1942), in which Mighty Mouse defeated horde upon horde of murderous felines. *Mighty Mouse* soon turned into Terrytoons' most profitable series, and the studio ground out scores of films that continued to be well received by a juvenile public despite tedious repetition.

In 1955 Paul Terry sold all his properties to the Columbia Broadcasting System; CBS promptly turned out a *Mighty Mouse* television program which met with astounding success. The producers shrewdly mixed old *Mighty Mouse* films with newly minted cartoons. If anything, the new production was wittier and more entertaining than most of the old series. Very often Mighty Mouse was involved in continuing adventures pitting him against the top-hatted villain, Oil-Can Harry the cat; the object of their rival ardor was the pert Pearl Pureheart. A narrator would imperturbably detail the proceedings while fights, duels, forest fires, floods and every imaginable peril took place on the screen. This spoofing of film serials was often sung by the principals, mock-opera style, with a love duo ("You are my sweetheart," "You are my love") by Mighty Mouse and Pearl at the close.

The *Mighty Mouse* TV program came to an end in the early 1960s, but it can still be seen in syndication. Among the directors who worked on *Mighty Mouse*, mention should be made of Conrad (Connie) Rasinski, Art Bartsch, Dave Tendlar and Eddie Donnelly. A *Mighty Mouse* comic book was also released with varying success from 1946 to 1962.

M.H.

Vatroslav Mimica, "Typhus." © *Zagreb Film.*

MILLÔR
See Fernandes, Millôr.

MILER, ZDENĚK (1921-) Czech animator born in Kladno, Bohemia, Czechoslovakia, on February 21, 1921. Zdeněk Miler first attended the School of Design, then studied at the School of Industrial Arts, both in Prague. In 1941 he started as an animator at the Zlín (now Gottwaldov) studios. At the end of World War II he moved to Prague, where he became one of Eduard Hofman's scriptwriters.

Miler directed his first cartoons, *The Millionaire Who Stole the Sun* and *Red Riding Hood*, in 1948. *The Millionaire* is a tale of greed and cruelty, with the protagonist coming to grief at the end. Miler, however, decided to travel in the direction of his other cartoon, a retelling of the familiar fairy tale; and, with the exception of *The Red Stain* (an allegory of evil made in 1963), all of his work has been aimed at children. *Brigáda* (1950), *Who's Strongest?* (1952) and *The Poppy Pie* (1953) are nice, rather conventional fables. Miler has also created a winsome animal character, the Mole, who has appeared in a series of lively and unpretentious little cartoons ("How the Mole Got His Trousers," "The Mole and the Motorcar," etc.).

In 1958 the Czechoslovakian government awarded Miler a silver medal for his work, which remains largely unseen outside Czechoslovakia.

M.H.

MILLER, FRANK (1925-) American cartoonist born in Kansas City, Missouri, in 1925. Frank Miller is the son of a longtime staff artist of the *Kansas City Star*, the spawning ground of many artists, from C.D. Batchelor to Edward McGeehan. But it was *Star* political cartoonist S.J. Ray whose style influenced the younger Miller most. He studied drawing and painting at the University of Kansas and then continued his art training at the Kansas City Art Institute. His first job was with the *Star*, and he switched to the *Des Moines Register* in 1954, inheriting Ding Darling's mantle. In 1963 Miller's cartoons brought the Pulitzer Prize to Iowa once again.

Miller renders his cartoons in a supple, almost old-fashioned pen line, often with handsome and elaborate crosshatching. He spots his blacks well and lays them in with a wet brush.

R.M.

MIMICA, VATROSLAV (1923-) Yugoslav animator and filmmaker born in Omiš, Yugoslavia, on June 25, 1923. Vatroslav Mimica fought the Nazis as a partisan during World War II. After the war he became a literary critic before going into film. He started his animation career in 1957 as a scriptwriter for Zagreb Film, notably writing the scenario of *Cowboy Jimmy*. Although not a draftsman himself, he directed many of the most celebrated Zagreb cartoons, often with Aleksandar Marks as his designer. These include *At the Photographer's* and the mixed animation short *The Inspector Comes Home* (both 1959); *Spring Tunes* and *Low Midnight* (1960), which he only scripted; the almost despairing *Perpetuum and Mobile, Ltd.* (1961); and the equally somber *Everyday Chronicle* (1962). The 1963 *Typhus*, a haunting evocation of partisan warfare told through the medium of animated linocuts, marked the last collaboration between Mimica and Marks.

Mimica then returned to live-action filmmaking and became one of the more celebrated of the new wave of Yugoslav movie directors (*Prometheus from the Island of Viševica*, *Monday or Tuesday* and *Kaya, I'll Kill You* are some of his best-known feature films). He occasionally returned to animation, writing the scripts for *The Fly* and *Tamer of Wild Horses*. Mimica is justly regarded as one of the founders of the Zagreb school, and his cartoons have earned many awards in such places as Bergamo, Venice, Oberhausen, Cork and Edinburgh.

M.H.

MINGO, NORMAN (1896-) American cartoonist and illustrator born in Chicago, Illinois, on January 25, 1896. Norman Mingo is best known for his cover paintings of Alfred E. Neuman for *MAD* magazine and *MAD* paperback books.

Always interested in art, Mingo won a children's art contest and received art materials and a course from the Scranton Correspondence School. During high school he worked for Hart, Schaffner and Marx, manufacturers of men's clothing, drawing model cards. He was so successful with his art that he dropped out of high school and worked full time for a year before returning to complete his diploma requirements. World War I interrupted his career, and he served three years in the U.S. Navy. Following World War I, Norman Mingo studied art at the Academy of Fine Arts and Art Institute in Chicago. Other art training came at the Cleveland School of Art and the Art Students League in New York.

The 1920s were the great years of advertising art. Mingo organized and was president of the art studio Mingo, Brink and Jipson, Inc. The firm had its headquarters in the Wrigley Building in Chicago and had offices in Detroit, Michigan, and Cleveland and Toledo, Ohio. "I'll never forget our first month's gross billing was $35,000 for artwork produced," said Norman Mingo. The firm lasted from 1923 to 1931, when it fell victim to the Depression. Its clients included Studebaker Corporation and Packard Motors. It was responsible for hundreds of full-page and double-page illustrations in the *Saturday Evening Post*. Work from the studio can be easily identified by a distinctive pine tree logo used to sign the art.

Norman Mingo was one of the lucky ones in the Depression. After his studio folded he moved to New York City and made the rounds with his portfolio. Based on his previous work, he quickly was selected by Lucky Strike cigarettes to illustrate testimonials about its product by famous people of the day. While in New York City, he organized the Guild Artists Bureau, Inc., which existed from 1939 to 1941 as a sales outlet for the Artists Guild of New York.

"I was married, with kids, and too old for World War II, but I was able to serve with the U.S. Coast Guard Auxiliary and participate in the USO Hospital program, where I would do portraits of wounded servicemen," said Mingo.

In 1953, after years of successfully freelancing advertising art, Norman Mingo opened his own silk screening studio. Financially the studio proved a disaster. "I answered two ads from the classified section of the *New York Times*," he remembered. "This was in 1956. First I went to Dancer, Fitzgerald, Sample, Inc., a Madison Avenue ad agency, where I was hired as an illustrator and titular head of the bullpen. Then the same day I visited Bill Gaines at *MAD*, also on Madison Avenue."

Bill Gaines, *MAD*'s publisher, had been searching for an artist to paint Alfred E. Neuman, the magazine's mascot. At the time all *MAD*'s artists were pen-and-ink men not skilled in painting. In 1956, at the age of 60, Norman Mingo painted the first full-color portrait of Alfred E. Neuman. It was published

on the cover of *MAD*, number 30, December 1956. After awhile the work load of the ad agency and *MAD* became too great, and Norman Mingo left *MAD*, to be replaced by Kelly Freas as cover artist. However, in 1963 he was contacted by John Putnam, *MAD*'s art director, and has been with the publication since then.

Norman Mingo doesn't take credit for any cover ideas. His ability was "to bring Alfred to life." An experienced master of illustration, he devotes his attention to composition, color relationships and technique. "I'm essentially concerned with mass and am not a line man," he has stated. Now in semiretirement, Norman Mingo was the most prolific *MAD* cover artist until the mid-1970s.

B.C.

MINI-CARTOONS (Yugoslavia)

In 1969 the artists at Zagreb Film decided to produce a number of oneminute animated cartoons to serve as introductions to their work and as a showcase for new talent. These mini-cartoons (as they promptly came to be called) proved tremendously popular and have been a staple of Zagreb Film production ever since.

Among the most popular—or most gifted—of the mini-cartoon practitioners have been Zvonimir Lončarić (*Dialogue, C'Est la Vie*), Ante Zaninović (*Ab Ovo*), Dušan Vukotić (*Time*, one of the most successful "minis" ever produced) and Zlatko Pavlinić (*Conditio Sine Qua Non, Miserere, Happy End, The Goal*). But the most prolific of all was Milan Blažeković, who has created more than fifty of these films; among the wittiest or most memorable are two "gorilla joke" cartoons, *Maternity Hospital* and *Flight 54321*, as well as the unpredictable *Icarus I, The Apple* and *A Chair*.

Some of the mini-cartoons centering around the same theme were later released as a series within a series. The most popular of these compilations has been *Largo*, built upon the theme of a man stranded on a desert island. The mini-cartoons, singly or *en bloc*, are still going strong, and they are a special favorite of public-television program directors with a minute or two of time to fill.

M.H.

MINOR, ROBERT (1884-1952)

American cartoonist and political organizer born in San Antonio, Texas, on July 15, 1884. The son of a judge, Robert Minor attended public schools and became a sign painter in 1898. He was later employed as a carpenter and then as a cartoonist. He drew for the *San Antonio Gazette*, the *St. Louis Post-Dispatch*, the *New York World* and the *New York Call*. In 1915 he was a European war correspondent for the Newspaper Enterprise Association and, returning to the United States, became a lecturer on antiwar subjects.

In 1919 Minor was one of the founders of the U.S. Communist party and remained a tireless worker in its organization; he ran for governor of New York (1932) and for the Senate (1936) on its ticket, was for awhile acting secretary-general of the party and constantly drew for its organ, the *Daily Worker*. Minor died at his home in Croton-on-Hudson, New York, on November 26, 1952.

Minor's employment record serves to trace the change and extent of his convictions. He left the most influential daily in New York to draw for its puny Socialist rival and later shunned all establishment

"Largo," a mini-cartoon. © Zagreb Film.

Army Medical Examiner: "At last a perfect soldier!"

Robert Minor, 1916. © The Masses.

journals (unlike his fellow traveler Art Young) to draw only for Communist organs. Throughout his career his cartoons were marked by stunningly forthright presentations—though many may find his politics offensive, this cannot diminish the acknowledgment Minor's work deserves.

As important as his presentation of ideas was, his artwork is equally deserving of recognition. He drew at first in a rounded, pleasant style that foreshadowed a stark simplicity. He pioneered the use of the crayon and, in philosophical and representational terms, inspired a generation of outstanding political cartoonists—perhaps the most important school and certainly the one most neglected by historians—including Fitzpatrick, Burck, Fred Ellis, Ross Lewis, Tom Little, Edmund Duffy, Boardman Robinson and others.

R.M.

MR. MAGOO (U.S.) John Hubley created the nearsighted Mr. Magoo, in collaboration with Robert Cannon, for UPA in 1949; the first *Mr. Magoo* cartoon was "Ragtime Bear," directed by Hubley himself.

Mr. Quincy Magoo, a bald-headed, crotchety old gent, got himself involved in all kinds of harebrained misadventures due to his sight impediment, which he steadfastly refused to acknowledge. Mistaking dynamite sticks for candles, grizzly bears for visiting matrons and opium dens for his club lounge, he blissfully wandered from one hair-raising situation to the next without ever losing his composure. Piles of merchandise would go up in smoke behind him, passenger boats would sink in his wake, and entire buildings would collapse after his passage, but Magoo would imperturbably continue on his path of destruction, only muttering to himself in self-congratulatory tones, "Aha, Magoo, m'boy, you've done it again!" (Magoo's ripe, gravelly voice characterization was done by Jim Backus). Unlike most other cartoons of the period, *Mr.*

Magoo's humor rested not on the expression but on the expectation of violence. In the end nothing untoward ever happened to the fussing, cantankerous, but essentially lovable Magoo, and even his unintended victims got away relatively unscathed.

Many UPA directors worked on the *Mr. Magoo* series. John Hubley did "Fuddy Duddy Buddy" the same year as "Ragtime Bear"; Peter Burness, the most prolific of them all, directed "Bungled Bungalow" and "Trouble Indemnity" (both 1950), "Captains Outrageous" (1952), "Magoo Goes West" (1953), "Destination Magoo" (1954), "Stage Door Magoo" (1955) and the Academy Award-winning (in 1954 and 1956, respectively) "When Magoo Flew" and "Magoo's Puddle Jumper." Bob Cannon and Rudy Larriva also worked on the series.

Mr. Magoo proved popular enough to be starred in a feature-length film, *1001 Arabian Nights* (1959), which proved a failure at the box office. In the mid-1960s UPA produced a *Mr. Magoo* TV series as well as several specials which were a long way below their former standards. The character was then sold to DePatie-Freleng, which released a made-for-television version starting in 1977. Saperstein Productions packaged a *Mr. Magoo* comic strip (Chicago Tribune Syndicate) in the late 1960s.

M.H.

MR. MEN, THE (G.B.) "Today looks very much like a tickling day!" said Mr. Tickle, and off he went to town to see who he might tickle with his Extraordinary Long Arms. He tickled a teacher who was trying to control his class, he tickled a policeman who was on traffic duty, and he tickled thousands of little children and their parents who had bought the colorful, pocket-sized book for twenty pence. *Mr. Tickle* was the funniest, and most funnily drawn, children's book in a long time, and before 1971 had closed, he had been joined by *Mr. Greedy, Mr. Happy, Mr. Nosey, Mr. Sneeze* and *Mr. Bump*. The Mr.-book series was immediately recognizable: square, white, with a big cartoon character drawn in bold black, filled in with a bright color. And each Mr. Man, although basically no more than a simple circle with dot eyes, arms, legs and an occasional nose, had a different and instantly obvious characteristic, made clear by his name. The year 1972 brought a new battalion or Mr. Men, each as funny as the last: *Mr. Messy, Mr. Topsy-Turvy, Mr. Silly, Mr. Uppity, Mr. Small, Mr. Daydream* and *Mr.*

Mr. Magoo in "Magoo Beats the Heat." © UPA.

Snow. There would be more, many more.

The Mr. Men were created by Roger Hargreaves (born in 1935), an advertising copywriter with very limited drawing ability. He was drawing them (and still does) with a felt-tip pen to amuse his four children long before the publisher Fabbri took them on. With his advertising background, Hargreaves was able to bring promotional techniques to his brainchildren, and through an outfit called Copyright Promotions, the most successful merchandizing campaign in British cartoon book publishing was launched. The Mr. Men began to appear in every conceivable shape and form, from cereal packet stickers to sticking plasters, duvet covers and toiletries—and, of course, toys. The Mr. Men moved into television via an animated cartoon series of five-minute films, narrated by the popular character actor Arthur Lowe. They moved into children's comics as a full-page color strip, and from December 1, 1976, they have appeared daily in a newspaper strip in the *Daily Mirror*, replacing Bert Felstead's *Little Joe.*

The TV series is syndicated through 22 countries, the books translated into dozens of languages (over 6 million copies sold), and there are currently 26 *Mr. Men*, apart from such specials as *The Mr. Men on Holiday* (1976) and *The Mr. Men Gift Book* (1975). Hargreaves has had less success with his other series, *John Mouse* (1973) and *Hippo Potto and Mouse* (1976).

R.M. D.G.

MR. PIPP (U.S.) Accurately described by Fairfax Downey as the most popular of the Gibson creations after the Gibson Girl herself, Mr. Pipp utterly dispelled whatever doubt may have lingered in 1890s America that Charles Dana Gibson was the premier American social cartoonist and illustrator of his day.

In *The Education of Mr. Pipp,* the title character, a wispy little henpecked paterfamilias with white sideburns, embarks on a European trip, complete with baggage and wife and daughters, to acquire a "liberal education." In upper-class America of the day (the series began in the issue of *Life* for September 8, 1898), "doing the Continent" on an extended vacation was obligatory. The series, intended only for a half-dozen glimpses but extended to 37 weeks by public enthusiasm, chronicled Pipp's seasick voyage, his attempts to steer his two pretty daughters away from foreign mashers, his wife's shopping sprees, breaking the bank at Monte Carlo, the ultimate double wedding of his daughters to two handsome Gibson men—and a glimpse into grandfatherhood.

The series of double-page cartoons was enormously popular. A book published by R.H. Russell appeared immediately after the magazine run, and deluxe editions cost $25. In 1905, six years after the series' end, the character was still so popular as to inspire a play which ran for one season in New York and another on the road, and was eventually transformed into a motion picture. When *Life* in the 1920s sought revitalization, *Mr. Pipp* was resurrected in a newly drawn series pointing up the contrasts between an older generation and the Jazz Age, but the novelty and flavor were gone; Pipp was a sorry shade of his former self.

The first *Pipp* series was drawn with slashing and confident strokes and bold composition. It ushered in the finest few years of Gibson's first pen-and-ink period and was as consistently humorous as anything Gibson was ever able to achieve.

R.M.

MITCHELL, JOHN AMES (1845-1918) American cartoonist and publisher born in New York City on January 17, 1845. J.A. Mitchell graduated from the Phillips Academy and studied architecture at the Laurence Scientific School at Harvard from 1867 to 1870. Interrupted by a short period of work in Boston, Mitchell studied in France, principally at l'Ecole des Beaux-Arts in Paris. Although he studied painting, his primary interest was in black-and-white line work; before he returned to America in 1880, his etchings appeared in *L'Art.*

It was while illustrating *The Summer School of Philosophy at Mount Desert* (1882) that Mitchell conceived the idea of founding a national humor and cartoon magazine, not along the lines of *Puck* (which was then all the rage and had spawned an army of imitators), but modeled after the *Harvard Lampoon*. Assisted by old *Lampoon* staffers and founders, the magazine, *Life*, debuted on January 4, 1883. It was smaller in size than *Puck*, was only black and white, and aimed at a sophisticated audience.

In the early months Mitchell was *Life's* chief cartoonist, but with succeeding issues editorial duties took more of his time; he was to remain the art editor until his death. *Life* was a success, and its pages served as a platform for many of Mitchell's pet crusades: Sunday museum openings, antivivisection, a fresh-air farm for underprivileged urban children. When World War I loomed, he and editor E.S. Martin made *Life* a powerful friend of the Allies. He died on June 29, 1918, before his final desire—the American rescue of France—was accomplished.

Mitchell's cartooning style was competent and assured. He designed the *Life* logo of a cupid dispelling gloom that was used into the 1920s and became a cartoon symbol similar to and as familiar as Puck. His stylistic and thematic preoccupations are vitally important to his role as a cartoonist. As a devotee of line work at a time when photoengraving was being perfected and everyone was trying to duplicate *Puck's* lithography, he ushered in, through *Life's* standards, the great era of pen and ink in cartooning and illustration. Moreover, Mitchell's own cartoons dealt nearly exclusively with society subjects, establishing a heretofore unexplored area for American cartoonists—and lending sophistication to American cartoon magazines. Mitchell was also responsible for the discovery and tutoring of many cartoonists, not the least of whom was Charles Dana Gibson. He was called "the General" by his staff, two generations of which appreciated his kindly advice and counsel.

Mitchell was a prolific writer of fiction who usually concerned himself with either sentimental or socially conscious themes; he was an armchair socialist. He drew title page cartoons or decorations for some of his books, which include *Amos Judd* (1895), *The Pines of Lory* (1901) and *The Silent War* (1906), his three most notable successes; and *A Romance of the Moon* (1889), *The Last American* (1889), *Life's Fairy Tales* (1892), *That First Affair* (1896), *Gloria Victis* (1897) and *Pandora's Box* (1911).

R.M.

MITELBERG, LOUIS (1919-) French caricaturist, cartoonist and illustrator born near Warsaw, Poland, on

Louis Mitelberg ("Tim"). © Paris-Match.

January 29, 1919. Louis ("Tim") Mitelberg studied architecture at the Paris Ecole des Beaux-Arts in 1938 and at the outbreak of World War II joined De Gaulle's Free French forces in London, working as an anti-Nazi caricaturist.

After the war, Tim drew first for *L'Action* (1945-52), then for *L'Humanité* (1952-57) and since 1957 for *L'Express*. His political sketches have also appeared in *Newsweek*, *Time* and *Le Monde*, and occasionally on the Op-Ed page of the *New York Times*, to which he has contributed caricatures of Thieu, Kissinger, Brezhnev, Qaddafi, etc., and a funny depiction of Fisher and Spassky as toddlers in diapers using chess pieces for building blocks. Tim is also rightly famous for taking great paintings and updating them, as in Cézanne's *The Card Players*, featuring De Gaulle and Khrushchev, or Rembrandt's *Night Watch* guards being assisted by giant computers.

Many of his sketches have been released as albums: *Dessins* ("Drawings," 1953), *Pouvoir Civil* ("Civil Power," 1961), *L'Autocaricature* (1974), plus a fine book on De Gaulle, *Une Certaine Idée de la France, 1958-1969* ("A Certain Idea of France," 1969). In addition, he drew a weekly strip for the Zurich *Weltwoche*, *Leben mit Bengo* ("Life with Bengo"), which came out in book form in 1967 as *Junger Hund, Was Nun?* ("Young Dog, What Now?").

As might be expected, Tim has received several prizes, among them the coveted award of the International Caricature Show in Montreal (1967).

P.H.

MITSUHASHI, CHIKAKO (1941-) Japanese cartoonist born in Ibaraki Prefecture, Japan, in 1941. Chikako Mitsuhashi was fascinated by cartoons as an elementary student, and from the third grade on she regularly amused her classmates by drawing cartoons in notebooks on virtually any subject—even while sitting in the front row of the class under the teacher's watchful gaze. From the start she was heavily influenced by Machiko Hasegawa, the creator of *Sazae-san*.

In high school her cartooning aspirations began to gel. Upon graduation she held a variety of jobs, including work as an animator and an apprenticeship to a designer; the noted cartoon critic Ippei Ito was apparently her mentor. Based on her nostalgic memories of high school, she created a work entitled *Chisana Koi no Monogatari* ("A Little Love Story"), hoping that it would fill the gap between children's comics

and those meant for adults. Convinced that it would find a readership, she took the work to a magazine called *Utsukushii Jūdai* ("Beautiful Teenage") and was nonetheless surprised when it was accepted. Since first appearing in 1962, *Chisana Koi no Monogatari* has been a phenomenal success, with over twelve collections subsequently appearing and sales numbering in the millions. It follows the traditional Japanese cartoon format of four frames, in which the shy love of a high school girl for Sari, her boyfriend, is depicted with sweet reserve. The drawings are extremely simple, and the low-key theme has vast appeal among schoolgirls in Japan.

Other works by Mitsuhashi include *Keiko to Matchin* ("Keiko and Matchin"), *Tonari no Ken* ("Neighbor Ken"), *Kata Omoi Kara no Shuppatsu* ("Starting from a One-Sided Love") and *Hatsukoi no Ririan* ("First Love Lillian"), appearing in magazines such as *Koitchi Kōsu* ("Freshman Course"). In addition to her work as a cartoonist, Chikako Mitsuhashi is married and is the mother of two boys.

F.S.

MIYAO, SHIGEO (1902-) Japanese cartoonist born in Tokyo, Japan, on July 24, 1902. After studying under the famous cartoonist Ippei Okamoto, Shigeo Miyao began working as a regular for the newspaper *Tokyo Maiyū Shimbun*, where he drew political and social commentary cartoons. Since most other cartoonists were doing the same thing, however, he decided to try something new. In 1922, after clearing the idea with his newspaper, Miyao began drawing *Manga Taro*, a work for children. This six-panel piece took the form of pictures with a narrative, and it ran for over two hundred episodes. It appealed to children but also found an adult following and helped boost the overall sales of the paper. Later, *Manga Taro* was compiled into a book, most copies of which were destroyed in the 1923 earthquake that demolished Tokyo.

In 1924, undaunted, Miyao created *Dango Kushisuke Manyūki*, the story of a super-samurai boy who travels throughout Japan battling rogues, monsters and assorted villains. The characters all had amusing names, usually puns on names of food, and this contributed to their popularity. With this further success, Miyao firmly established himself as a pioneer in children's cartoons and comic strips. He then began drawing comics for the magazine *Shōnen Kurabu*, starting with *Hanao Bokosuke* (similar to *Dango Kushisuke Manyūki*) and the classic *Songoku*. *Songoku* appeared in 14 episodes, and when it was published in book form it utilized word balloons rather than a straight narrative. It was an amusing, easy-to-understand rendition of the Chinese classic *Saiyuki*, which has often been a theme in Japanese literature (Osamu Tezuka and Toei Doga each made an animated version). Songoku, the hero, is a semi-supernatural monkey who journeys to India from China to obtain sacred Buddhist scriptures.

Following *Songoku*, Shigeo Miyao created a string of other children's comics for *Shōnen Kurabu*, such as *Issun Taro* ("One-Inch Taro"), *Manga no Matsuri* ("Cartoon Festival") and *Karutobi Karusuke* (a pun on the name of a ninja character in Japanese literature, Saru Tobi Sasuke). Miyao's characters were generally very independent, in keeping with the prevailing mood of Japan in the late 1920s, a period in which democracy and individualism flourished. In 1934 Miyao formed a children's cartoonists' association known as Dōshin Manga-dan. During the war he saw action on the southern front while serving in the Imperial Navy. He continued to draw literary cartoons for magazines in the postwar period but also pursued an active interest in *Edo Kobanashi*, or humorous stories from the Edo period of Japan (1600-1867), publishing several books on the subject.

F.S.

MODELL, FRANK B. (1917-) American cartoonist born in Philadelphia, Pennsylvania, on September 6, 1917. Frank Modell studied at the Philadelphia College af Art. His first success as a cartoonist came with the old *Saturday Evening Post*. He became a *New Yorker* regular in the 1940s and remains so to this day. He is also a frequent contributor to *Playboy*, and his work has been published in a volume entitled *Stop Trying to Cheer Me Up* (Dodd, Mead).

As an artist, Modell will use "anything that makes a mark," and his technique varies accordingly. In the course of his long career, his early unbroken-line formalism gradually gave way to the freer quick-study techniques that are more characteristic of his current work—a shift mirrored in the alteration of his signature from "F.B. Modell" to today's simply scrawled "Modell." Given his lack of snobbery about media, it is tempting to speculate that the felt-tip in part explains his stylistic evolution, being more adaptable to sketch techniques than the formal ink-line and wash methods of most other artists of his generation. But this is not to underestimate Modell's capacity for adaptation in general, as anyone surveying the range of his humor will attest. It is in his breadth of imagination that his individual character is most pronounced.

Modell is the quintessential gag cartoonist. In his best work one can clearly see the connection between everyday life and its humorous exaggeration—and marvel that one had never seen it before. This, of course, is the genius of the cartoon humorist. Thus, one of Modell's early *New Yorker* pieces shows a man opening a jam-packed medicine cabinet to test the net installed beneath it for the purpose of catching falling items.

Modell ranges far and wide to find material for his studies. Unlike many of his colleagues, he seems to have no favorite themes and can have as much fun with alienated Cadillac owners as with Bowery bums. His Puritan confined to stocks and fending off an importunate insurance salesman is just as amusing as the cranky waitress in a greasy spoon demanding whether a certain customer intends to eat his entire breakfast with his nose in a newspaper. In almost every case, Modell touches a responsive chord, awakening that laughter which comes as much from sympathetic recognition as from an appreciation of absurdity for its own sake.

Modell is a member of the Cartoonists' Guild and the holder of, as he puts it, "some minor award" for animated storyboards done for *Sesame Street*.

R.C.

MODEST MAIDENS (U.S.) In 1930 cartoonist Don Flowers created a daily panel called *Modest Maidens* for Associated Press. Although some of his gags were quite amusing, what is best remembered about *Modest Maidens* is the loving way in which Flowers handled his female characters. They were long-legged, sophisticated, almost unattainable creatures, in the spirit of the time. Whether they were office workers or socialites, they exuded optimism, *joie de vivre* and charm, and even

"Now, let's see—did you tell me to keep my eyes shut and my mouth open, or my eyes open and my mouth shut?"

"Modest Maidens." © *King Features Syndicate.*

their more scatterbrained moments did not detract from their lovable character. Coulton Waugh commented in his study *The Comics*, "The Flowers girls have a real rhythm running through them," and it was indeed a sense of graceful rhythm that gave *Modest Maidens* its peculiar vivacity.

When Associated Press decided in the early 1940s to produce a color section, *Modest Maidens* became one of its chief attractions. Flowers, however, did not stay with AP much longer, leaving in 1945 to create *Glamor Girls* for King Features Syndicate. *Modest Maidens* passed into the hands of Jay Alan, who did a creditable job of continuation. Without Flowers's flourishes, however, the feature steadily lost readership, and it was dropped in the late 1950s.

M.H.

MOGENSEN, JØRGEN (1922-) Danish cartoonist, lithographic artist and sculptor born in Hillerød, Denmark, in 1922. Jørgen Mogensen, married to cartoonist Gerda Nystad, is one of Europe's most intelligent cartoonists, although his specialty today is the comic strip.

He made his debut, as did so many other cartoonists of his generation, in the monthly humor magazine *Hudibras* and was an editor and a contributor of several hundred gag cartoons from 1946. *The Magic Artist* (1947) was his original and surprising renewal of the comic strip tradition, a surrealistic play with concepts. He made a name for himself with the internationally syndicated comic strip *Poeten og Lillemor* (1948), on which three films were based, and with the pantomime strip *Alfredo*, on which he collaborates with Siegfried Cornelius under the joint signature "Moco." Especially well known is his daily panel *Esmeralda* (also called *Lullabelle*), one-column cartoons about a lovely, not-so-dumb blonde, syndicated through PIB, Copenhagen, to about fifty newspapers and magazines.

Jørgen Mogensen. © *PIB.*

Mogensen has also done some sculpting and has had numerous exhibitions, as well as doing some writing. But his forceful, elegant drawing style and at times completely unsurpassed sense of humor have secured him a leading position among European humorists.

J.S.

MOHASSESS, ARDESHIR (1938-   ) Iranian cartoonist born at Rasht, in the province of Guilan, north of Tehran, Iran, on September 9, 1938. Ardeshir Mohassess displayed an early talent for drawing and caricature but instead chose political science as his major at the University of Tehran, from which he graduated in 1952. Soon afterward he began drawing for Iranian newspapers and magazines, then went on to contribute to such international publications as *Jeune Afrique* and the *New York Times*, where his work has often appeared on the Op-Ed page. He now lives in New York City.

Mohassess's drawings are often disturbing and sometimes even horrifying. He is obsessed with death, inhumanity and violence. His drawing style is stark and somber, in keeping with his subjects. His most frequent themes are some of the more intractable problems of the world: famine, oppression, torture, the dehumanization of modern society and the despair of the disenfranchised of the earth.

Ardeshir Mohassess has been the recipient of a number of international awards; some of his drawings and collages have been collected in book form, and he has had many showings of his work, including one at the Graham Gallery in New York City in 1975.

A collection of Mohassess's cartoons, *Puppets*, was published in 1977 by Carolyn Bean Associates of San Francisco.

M.H.

MOLDREM, STUART (1925-   ) American cartoonist born in Centralia, Washington, in 1925. Stu Moldrem started drawing while in grade school in Bellingham, Washington, and by his own admission hasn't stopped since. He received his formal art education at the Los Angeles Art Center School, at the Lukits Academy of Fine Arts in Los Angeles and later at the Derbyshire School of Fine Arts in Seattle.

After serving two years in the army at the end of World War II (during which time he was sports artist for the Pacific edition of *Stars and Stripes* in Tokyo), Moldrem went back to Seattle and did cartoons for various newspapers. In 1949 he started *Sportrait*, a sports feature

for the *Seattle Post-Intelligencer* that still runs regularly. Moldrem's depiction of sports personalities and his dynamic drawing of athletes in action have earned him a respected position among sports cartoonists and sports enthusiasts across the country.

M.H.

MOLINÉ I MUNS, MANUEL (1833-1901) Spanish cartoonist born in Barcelona, Spain, in 1833. Manuel Moliné studied art with a view to becoming a painter. He soon turned to drawing, however, and his first cartoons appeared in 1859 in the newly founded magazine *El Cañon Rayado.*

Moliné was an extremely able and extraordinarily popular cartoonist whose success can be attributed to the fact that his cartoons were straightforward and could be

مراسم افتتاح شبکهٔ لوله‌کشی آب مشروب بخش

Ceremonies to inaugurate a district drinking-water system in Iran.

Ardeshir Mohassess. © *Mohassess.*

easily understood by everyone. They appeared in most major publications of the day, such as *Un Tros de Paper, La Flaca* and *La Mosca Roja*, but his most important work appeared in the magazines *La Campana de Gracia* and *L'Esquella de la Torratxa.* To commemorate the 20th anniversary of continuous collaboration between the publication and Moliné, *L'Esquella de la Torratxa*

Stu Moldrem, "Sportrait." © *Seattle Post-Intelligencer.*

Manuel Moliné, satire on the military and the clergy, 1882.

dedicated its entire May 3, 1901, issue to him.

In all his works Moliné bitterly satirized the privileges of the Spanish upper classes and attacked, often with passion, the aristocracy, the clergy and the military. He died in Barcelona late in 1901.

J.M.

MOLNAR, GEORGE (1910-   ) Australian cartoonist born in Nagyvarad, Hungary, in April 1910.

International appeal (if not international demand) is a trend in present-day Australian comic art. Much of the comic art produced in Australia today has no indigenous character, idiom or flavor; a large proportion of it would be at home in the *New Yorker* or, with suitably translated captions, in *Paris Soir*. In short, it is a humor with no national identity.

What distinguishes the work of George Molnar as socially significant is its documentary value. Character revelation is the core of Molnar's humor, although his satirical comment usually is aimed at a specific social level (as was that of America's Gluyas Williams), introducing a world of academics, professional and business executives, high society and those occupying the "rooms at the top." Nevertheless, it is humor that spurns all suggestion of syndication-circuit gags of the sort popularized by the *Saturday Evening Post*, which for decades has set an international editorial standard for jokes, not about character, but about men as business creatures, car buyers or meek underlings to overbearing bosses or wives. The London *Times* has said of Molnar: "Mr. Molnar is far and away the best cartoonist—in a country where the tradition of black-and-white illustration is very strong." Molnar has added to the Australian achievement in this field an outlook that is fresh, sophisticated, refined in content and aesthetic in form.

Although born in Hungary, Molnar came to Australia in 1939 and, as an associate professor, has been

lecturing in architecture at Sydney University since 1945, the year he commenced drawing political cartoons for the Sydney *Daily Telegraph*. Molnar's self-taught cartooning style was developed over the six years he was with that paper, but in 1952, he joined the Sydney *Morning Herald*, where his *Insubstantial Pageant* became a unique feature of sharp, penetrating satire, preeminent in postwar Australian journalism.

From the 1950s onward, Australians have witnessed a period of national prosperity and expansion in both domestic and foreign matters. This is evidenced in urban growth, which in turn has reflected international tastes and trends in art and entertainment, new conventions like the bistro, the vanities of dress and fashion and styles of civic and domestic architecture. Molnar examines such social conformities and their effects on the opulent Australian. He is a masterful interpreter of the contemporary environment and those who live in it. His wit, intelligence and flair for social satire are complemented by a graphic style that is tranquil and orderly, drawn with fine lines linking carefully balanced black areas in a manner aesthetic yet free of gimmicks and mystique.

Since his first collection, *Statues*, was published twenty years ago, he has had five other books produced: *Insubstantial Pageant*; *Postcards*; *Molnar At Large*; *Molnar, 1970-76*; and a fine collection of his recent work, *Moral Tales*.

V.L.

"Nothing interesting to say . . . let's join the ladies."

George Molnar, "Insubstantial Pageant." © *Sydney Morning Herald.*

MONNIER, HENRI BONAVENTURE (1805-1877) French cartoonist and satirist born in Paris, France, on June 8, 1805. Henri Monnier, the son of a government employee, dropped out of high school at the age of 16 and went to work in a notary's office, which he left a short while later to become a clerk in the Ministry of Justice. But a desk job was not to Monnier's liking, and he started studying art, first with Anne-Louis

397

Henri Monnier, project of a monument to Monsieur Prudhomme (etching by Champfleury).

Girodet, then with the noted academic painter Antoine-Jean, Baron Gros. There his inordinate penchant for practical jokes soon got him into trouble.

After a try at doing a few sketches and lithographs in 1827, Monnier started his career in earnest the next year, illustrating La Fontaine's *Fables* and especially Béranger's *Chansons*, for which his irreverent style was perfectly suited. Monnier revealed his true talent for satire in a series of ferocious drawings in which he pitilessly lampooned the bourgeoisie and its way of life: *Les Grisettes* ("The Working Girls"), *Moeurs Administratives* ("Administrative Mores") and others asserted his formidable powers of observation and irony in the early 1830s. At the same time he took up writing, collaborating with Emile Augier and Henri Leroux on a couple of farces, *Les Compatriotes* ("Fellow Countrymen") and *Les Mendiants* ("The Beggars").

From the late 1830s on, Monnier became obsessed with the mediocrity, pettiness and servility of middle-class life, which he castigated through his most famous creation, Joseph Prudhomme, the prototype of the hateful bourgeois and everything he stood for. In countless cartoons, comedies and novels he mercilessly attacked the pretensions, follies and stupidities of his age, with Prudhomme as his spokesman; Monnier identified with his creation to such an extent that he played the part on stage, and he even dressed like Prudhomme in private life. The

most significant works in which Joseph Prudhomme appears are *Grandeur et Décadence de Joseph Prudhomme* ("Greatness and Decadence of Joseph Prudhomme," 1853), *Mémoires de Joseph Prudhomme* (1857) and *Joseph Prudhomme, Chef de Brigands* ("Joseph Prudhomme, Brigand Chief").

Henri Monnier died in Paris on January 3, 1877.

M.H.

MOOR, D.S.
See Orlov, Dimitry Stakhiyevich.

MOORES, RICHARD ARNOLD (1909-   ) American cartoonist born in Lincoln, Nebraska, on December 12, 1909. Dick Moores was educated in the public schools of Lincoln, Omaha (where his family moved when he was nine) and Fort Wayne, Indiana, where he moved in 1926. He attended the Fort Wayne Art School and held various local jobs, working as a sign painter, a clerk in a Piggly Wiggly store and an usher (later manager) at the Emboyd vaudeville theater.

In 1930 Moores attended the Chicago Academy of Fine Arts, seeking instruction in illustration. Further study at the Chouinard School in Los Angeles preceded service as Chester Gould's second assistant on the young *Dick Tracy* strip; Moores contributed balanced layouts and handsome, textured shading that later emerged in his own derivative strip, *Jim Hardy*, launched in June 1936. This detective strip became a western, *Windy and Paddles*, and ended in October 1942.

Moores then went to work for the Disney studios and assisted Floyd Gottfredson and Frank Reilly on various strips. He inked *Mickey Mouse* dailies and drew the *Uncle Remus* page, occasionally worked on the *Classic Tales* syndicated feature, contributed to Western comic book titles (1942-56) and did much of the artwork for Disney merchandising during his tenure. In 1956, on the suggestion of Bill Perry, Moores became Frank King's assistant on *Gasoline Alley*, assuming the duties of story blocking and then more of the artwork until he became a full ghost. In 1963 he received credit and on King's death in 1969 took full control of the strip.

Seldom in the cartooning world has an inheritor sparkled on an old property as Moores has done on *Gasoline Alley*. In a certain sense it is a different

"Mopsy." © *Associated Newspapers.*

strip—the story lines are more humorous and rely on eccentric personalities—but the strong characterizations remain, as does the family saga aspect. Moores's main contribution is the stunning visual effect he achieves; he eschews panel borders, mixes up textures and tones (almost all drawn by hand, not mechanically) and depicts the most unusual angles in the comics. Most views are from the ground level up (it is strange that a man more than six feet tall, as Moores is, can see the world from under tabletops and carriage bottoms). In all, it is an exciting strip to behold.

Moores was awarded the National Cartoonists Society's Reuben in 1975. Among his many other credits is his pioneering work with animation and comics on television. In the early 1950s *Telecomics*, coordinated by Moores, ran for a season on the NBC network flagshipped by KLAS. This series translated strips to video primarily via panning and tracking. The first strip, appropriately, was *Jim Hardy*.

R.M.

MOPSY (U.S.) Fresh from her success with *Flapper Fanny*, Gladys Parker created *Mopsy* as a daily panel for King Features Syndicate in 1936, later adding a Sunday page. Mopsy, a pert, tousle-haired brunette modeled after Parker herself, liked to play dumb for the countless solicitous males who were always around her, but she displayed a fine sense of realism and practicality on many an occasion. In her efforts to cope with suitors, female rivals and the myriad aggravations of daily living, she was sometimes exasperated, sometimes dejected, but always smiling through at the end. Though perpetuating many stereotypes of women (the ritual visits to the beauty shop, the backbiting, the fussing with physical appearances that was so large a part of Mopsy's life), Parker also used her feature to deflate male pretensions.

Mopsy prospered mightily through the 1940s, so much so that *Newsweek* ran a piece on the panel and its creator in March 1949. Its popularity declined after the 1950s, however, and it did not long survive Parker's death in 1966. A fresh, funny, ingratiating feature, *Mopsy* is recalled with affection by its many former readers. A *Mopsy* comic book was issued by St. John from 1948 to 1953.

M.H.

MORDILLO, GUILLERMO (1932-   ) Argentine cartoonist born in Buenos Aires, Argentina, on August 4, 1932. Guillermo Mordillo displayed an early flair for cartooning and drawing. He embarked on an artistic career as soon as he got out of high school in 1950, doing illustrations of fairy tales for an Argentine publisher. Between 1952 and 1955 he also tried his hand at animation and comic strip drawing, without much success. Leaving Argentina for Peru in 1955, Mordillo worked at the McCann-Erickson advertising agency in Lima for the next five years; during that time he also illustrated books of fables and fairy tales. He moved to New York in 1960 and first worked for a greeting card company, then for Famous Studios/Paramount, where he animated sequences of *Popeye* and *Little Lulu* cartoons.

Mordillo made his final (and, as it turned out, successful) move in 1963. He went to Paris and, after a few years with another greeting card company, managed to get his cartoons published in the mass-circulation magazines *Paris-Match* and *Lui*. Soon Mordillo established himself as one of the major talents in cartooning, winning acclaim and international recognition. His cartoons have

Guillermo Mordillo. © Mordillo.

been published in major periodicals in France, Germany, Italy, Japan, the United States and other countries. He has also produced several animated cartoons for French and German television and has written a number of original humor books (*Le Galion, Crazy Cowboy*, etc.). Mordillo has won an impressive number of awards around the world, and in 1977 he was voted Cartoonist of the Year at the Montreal International Salon of Cartoons. His cartoons have been collected in a number of books, among them *The Collected Cartoons of Mordillo, Cartoons Opus I* and *Crazy Crazy*.

Mordillo's humor rests heavily on the unusual, the incongruous and the unexpected; his cartoons, usually captionless, are incredibly busy and detailed. As Serge Jongué of the Pavilion of Humor in Montreal has noted: "If we had to describe Mordillo we would say that he is clear to excess. In the themes he deals with, the situations, characters or epic happenings all are ultra-familiar cultural stereotypes." It is this clarity and familiarity that give Mordillo's humor such universal appeal.

M.H.

MOREL-RETZ, LOUIS-PIERRE (1825-1899) French painter and cartoonist born at Dijon, France, on June 3, 1825. Louis Morel-Retz pursued a career as a painter, exhibiting his canvases in various art shows. At the same time, using the pen name "Stop," he also contributed cartoons on the political and social life of the Second Empire, from the Crimean and Franco-Prussian wars to the many scandals prevalent during the Third Republic. Most of his drawings originally appeared in *Le Charivari, L'Illustration* and *Le Journal Amusant* and were released in albums, among which are *Bêtes et Gens* ("Animals and People," 1876), *Ces Messieurs* ("These Gentlemen," 1877) and *Nos Excellences* ("Our Excellencies," 1878). They present an unashamedly nationalistic view of France and her military might. He also wrote light comedies that were very successful.

Morel-Retz died in his birthplace on September 5, 1899.

P.H.

MORGAN, MATTHEW (1839-1890) American and British cartoonist born in London, England, on April 27, 1839. Matt Morgan covered the Austro-Italian war in 1859 as a war correspondent and sketch artist for the *Illustrated London News*. For the magazine *Fun* (1862-67) he cartooned and lampooned many subjects, paying particular attention to the American Civil War. In 1867 he founded, and was chief cartoonist for, *Tomahawk*, and in 1870 he emigrated to the United States.

Soon after Morgan's arrival in New York, he was engaged by Frank Leslie to serve Leslie's papers as an answer to *Harper's Weekly*'s Thomas Nast. For *Leslie's Weekly* Morgan savagely attacked U.S. Grant—one of Nast's idols—and generally upheld a Democratic political point of view in his cartoons, many of which ran over two large pages.

In 1880, having left *Leslie's* (and with his counterpart's influence on the wane), Morgan founded several of his own enterprises, including the Morgan Art Pottery Company; he also managed the Strobridge Lithographic Company of Cincinnati. Drawn back to the publishing world, Morgan became art editor of *Collier's* in 1888, serving until his death in New York City on June 2, 1890, with only a brief respite in 1889 to paint backdrops for Buffalo Bill's Wild West Show.

Morgan was an effective partisan whose style was cleaner and more solid than Nast's. He had a firmer grasp of anatomy and executed his shadings in a handsome fashion, but he lacked Nast's native talent for concept and visualization—no derogation, since hardly any cartoonist since has matched Nast in those departments. Morgan must be considered the last great woodcut-era cartoonist.

R.M.

MORGAN, WALLACE (1873-1948) American cartoonist and illustrator born in New York City on July 11, 1873. Wallace Morgan was graduated from the Albany, New York, high school and spent six years at the Academy of Design Art in New York City. He joined the staff of the *New York Herald* and *Telegram*, where he was to spend ten years as a sketch artist. There he created *Fluffy Ruffles*, a weekly color comic about pretty women; Fluffy was the first such in the comics, and the feature was newspapers' answer to the Gibson Girl. Morgan's other duties included news and courtroom sketches and a stint ghosting *Buster Brown* after Outcault left for the *Journal*.

At age 40 Morgan abandoned "pretty girl" art; the field was indeed glutted, although he excelled. He concentrated on magazine illustrations and shone with Julian Street's *Abroad at Home* series in *Collier's*. Soon thereafter World War I broke out, and Morgan was commissioned an American Expeditionary Force captain and an official artist; his visual records of Chateau Thierry and Belleau Wood are outstanding. After the war he again immersed himself in illustration and did his best work

for comic stories such as the *Jeeves* series by P.G. Wodehouse. He contributed frequently to *Life* in the early 1920s, as well.

Morgan's style was quick and sketchy—a legacy from his sketch-artist days (fellow newspaper artists William Glackens and Everett Shinn acquired similar styles). His tool was the brush, and the quick staccato lines gave the appearance of pen work. Later he used washes and crayon shadings to good advantage. It is said that he never used models and threw away a drawing rather than make corrections.

Morgan was a member of many clubs and an intimate of the great personalities of his day. He was an honorary president of the Society of Illustrators for the two years preceding his death and was president from 1929 to 1936, a long term. He was also an honorary member of the Art Students League, a rare tribute. The year before his death he was named to the National Academy and was honored by the National Institute of Arts and Letters. Morgan was active until his death on April 24, 1948; he was contributing regularly to the *New Yorker, Collier's* and the *New York Times Magazine*.

R.M.

MORI, YASUJI (1925-   ) Japanese animator and director born in Taiwan, then a Japanese colony, on January 28, 1925. After returning to Japan at age 18, Yasuji Mori saw his first animated film, *Kumo to Chūrippu* ("Spider and Tulip"), a classic in Japanese animation created by Kenzo Masaoka. It moved him deeply. Several years later, after graduating from the Department of Architecture at the Tokyo University of Arts, Mori himself resolved to become an animator and went to the Nihon Dōga company, where Masaoka was working on *Torachan to Hanayome* ("Little Tora and the Bride"). He was hired after being cautioned about the hard life of the profession, and thereupon began his training at age 24. In addition to learning from Masaoka, he was also taught by Nihon Dōga's top animator, Masao Kumagawa.

In 1956 Mori created his first animated cartoon, *Kuroi Kikori to Shiroi Kikori* ("The Black and White Woodcutters"), with Taiji Yabushita in charge of direction. The same year Nihon Dōga was incorporated as the animation department of the Toei company, where Mori continued to work until March 1973. One of Toei's first productions was Mori's *Koneko no Rakugaki* ("Kitten's Doodlings," 1957). The next year, Mori was one of the front-line animators whose talents were used by Toei for its first feature-length cartoon designed for export, *Hakujaden* ("Legend of a White Snake").

Mori later turned increasingly to directing, and in this capacity he worked on such films as *Nagagutsu o Haita Neko* ("Puss in Boots," 1969) and *Nagagutsu Sanjushi* ("Three Braves in Boots," 1972). In 1973 Mori finally left Toei and began working as animation director for Nihon Animation on cartoons aimed at television audiences, such as *Yamanezumi Rocky-Chack* ("Rocky-Chack the Mountain Mouse," 1973) and *Kuma no Ko Jakki* ("Jack the Bear Cub," 1977). He has also written several children's books. Mori is at his finest, however, when gently depicting subjects of beauty. To this day, *Koneko no Rakugaki* remains one of his best and most representative works.

F.S.

MORRIS, WILLIAM CHARLES (1874-1940) American cartoonist born in Salt Lake City, Utah, on March 6, 1874. William Morris attended public schools and received no art training; he worked as a gold miner, clerk, teamster and sign painter before landing a job as sketch artist and cartoonist for the *Spokane* (Wash.) *Spokesman-Review* in 1904. There he remained until 1913, when he moved to New York and freelanced; Morris worked for *Puck, Harper's Weekly,* the *Independent,* the *Evening Mail* (each of which he saw in their dying days), the *Tribune* and the George Matthew Adams Service, which syndicated his cartoons widely. He was hired by the Republican National Committee in 1936 to draw propaganda cartoons for use by any papers wishing to print them. Morris died on April 5, 1940.

Morris had an easy, cartoony style that was pleasing to the eye and generally precluded any fierce partisanship, since it could not be presented believably. He seems to have been a gun for hire, as his political convictions changed as often and as simply as he changed employers over the years. His books include *Spokesman-Review Cartoons* (1908), *The Spokane Book* (1913) and *One Hundred Men of Rockland County* (1929).

R.M.

MOSCA, GIOVANNI (1908-   ) Italian cartoonist born in Rome, Italy, in 1908. Giovanni Mosca studied art in Rome and started on a cartooning career in the early 1930s. His humor, then somewhat surreal and a bit light-headed, was best represented in *Bertoldo,* a breeding ground for Italian cartoonists of the time. In its pages, practically impersonating himself with the little man in

Frank Moser, "Happy Hooligan – Doing His Bit." © International Film Service.

top hat and tails who appeared in almost all his cartoons, he subtly sniped at Mussolini's regime. After World War II Mosca spent many years with *Il Corriere d'Informazione* of Milan, to which he contributed a daily editorial cartoon. He is now the regular political and editorial cartoonist of the conservative Rome daily *Il Tempo.* His draftsmanship is faultless and his captions precise, although his humor is often old-fashioned and founded on puns.

One of the reasons for Mosca's popularity is his consistency. In the 1930s he reflected middle-class distaste for the Fascist regime, and since then, without changing his position at all, he has come to represent a nostalgic and conservative viewpoint. His cartoons of recent years express regret and longing for a past that some still regard as a happier time; he draws the present with one eye always on the past.

C.S.

MOSE
See Depond, Moise.

MOSER, FRANK (1886-1964) American cartoonist and animator born in Oketo, Kansas, in 1886. Frank Moser studied at the Art Students League and the Academy of Design in New York. He got his first cartooning job on the *Des Moines Register and Leader* in 1909 and later worked for several Hearst newspapers. Moving to Hastings-on-Hudson, New York, in 1916, Moser became one of the chief animators of the newly created International Film Service (he is listed as co-director, with George Herriman, of the *Krazy Kat* cartoons, but he directed many of the other series as well). In 1929 Frank Moser and Paul Terry established Moser and Terry, which produced the Terrytoon cartoons. Moser worked on the *Farmer Al Falfa* series, among others. In 1936 he sold his interest to Terry, who later suppressed any mention of his former partner.

In his later years Moser painted landscapes and exhibited in galleries in New York City and Westchester. He was the first treasurer of the Hudson Valley Art Association and later became its historian. Moser died in Dobbs Ferry Hospital on October 1, 1964. His contribution to animated cartoons, which appears as considerable as it is neglected, is now being evaluated in a new light.

M.H.

The conservation of the plants and flower beds is entrusted to the education of the citizens.
"It breaks me up, sir, we are so short of manure that we have to substitute civic education for it."

Giovanni Mosca. © Mosca.

MOSHER, CHRISTOPHER TERRY (1942-   ) Canadian caricaturist and illustrator born in Ottawa, Ontario, on November 11, 1942. Christopher Mosher grew up in Toronto, Ontario. He attended several schools, including the Ontario College of Art in Toronto and the Ecole des Beaux-Arts in Quebec City. Serious painting was his goal, and when he drew caricatures of tourists he signed himself "Aislin" (Gaelic for "dream"), preserving his own name for his serious work. After graduation in 1966, when he began to be paid for his caricatures, they became his serious work.

Mosher's work began appearing in various types of publications, such as underground newspapers, university papers and the Montreal *Star*, where he was staff artist from 1969 to 1971. Winning a Canada Council grant in 1971 enabled him to take a sabbatical and study cartooning in Europe. Afterward he joined the staff of the Montreal *Gazette*. His work has appeared on the covers of *Time–Canada* and *Maclean's* and in *Harper's*, the *New York Times*, *Punch* and many other publications. Mosher is also a founding member of an editorial cooperative that publishes the *Last Post*. He has received several awards, including one from the International Salon of Caricature in 1970 and the National Newspaper Award in 1977.

Several collections of Mosher's caricatures have been published, and he has also done some book illustration work. In 1975 he produced *The Hecklers*, a 60-minute television documentary on Canadian political cartooning. He is currently co-authoring a book on the same subject scheduled for 1979 release.

Mosher has been described as "bracingly cruel" and "evenhandedly malicious." He calls himself a caricaturist rather than a cartoonist, and his work "an attack on a person, a public figure, a celebrity. A caricaturist creates images that aren't there." His victims are of all philosophies, races, creeds and colors. "I really don't believe in anything," Mosher says. His personal life has been stormy in the past, and Mosher once said that he figured he'd be "burned out" in ten years. As he wrote in a foreword to one of his books, "I would like to extend my gratitude to a Quebec City plainclothesman who worked me over somewhat back in 1963. Without his help I'm quite sure that I would be selling shirts in Eaton's today . . . and liking it." While this earlier image of Mosher may change, much of his work remains quite unconventional.

D.K.

MOTA, ANÍSIO OSCAR DA (1891-1969) Brazilian cartoonist and sculptor born in Rio de Janeiro, Brazil, in 1891. Working under the pseudonym "Fritz," Oscar da Mota had his first cartoon published in the humor magazine *O Malho* in 1910. In 1913 he became the regular caricaturist on the satirical publication *Figuras e Figurões*. As a cartoonist, he was most prolific between 1915 and 1940, when he contributed to many Brazilian publications (*Jornal do Brasil, D. Quixote, A Manhã, Para Todos, A Notícia, Diário da Noite, O Globo* and others); he also collaborated on the Buenos Aires daily *La Prensa*. In 1925 Fritz created the famous character Pirolito for the humor magazine *O Tico-Tico*, and he drew *Pirolito* as a weekly feature until 1930.

Mota also did a number of monumental sculptures, such as the bronze statue dedicated to "The Little Newsboy" (1933) and two groups for the National Library in Rio de Janeiro. He died in Rio on February 3, 1969, and his passing drew affectionate notices and heartfelt tributes from newspapers throughout Brazil.

A.M.

MOUNTAIN BOYS, THE (U.S.) A classic American cartoon feature of the hillbilly genre, *The Mountain Boys* was created by Paul Webb in 1934. That same year, on August 20, another hillbilly clan, Al Capp's Yokums of *Li'l Abner* fame, also gained national prominence. However, Paul Webb's characters were published twice in the *Saturday Evening Post* prior to the appearance of *Li'l Abner*.

The Mountain Boys was most closely associated with *Esquire* magazine. It was published as a regular monthly full-page color cartoon feature. Webb's "utterly shiftless" hillbillies first appeared in the October 1934 *Esquire* at a time when the magazine was a quarterly. *The Mountain Boys* appeared in *Esquire* until the early 1960s, when the editorial direction of the magazine changed. Luke, Jake, Willie, Maw and Paw, and the rest of the clan still appear annually in a *Mountain Boys* calendar that has been published by Brown and Bigelow Company in St. Paul, Minnesota, since about 1940. The calendars have always contained 12 previously unpublished *Mountain Boys* cartoons.

The feature came to *Esquire* by a fluke. Webb had initially hoped to sell *The Mountain Boys* as a series to the *Saturday Evening Post*. However, the *Post* rejected the idea. Then, unexpectedly, Webb received

"Ears ain't big enuf to be one of ourn—Must belong to Lem Hawkins. I heerd him say he was short one t'other day."

"The Mountain Boys." © Esquire.

word from Richard McCallister, a gag writer and *New Yorker* cartoonist, that he was associate cartoon editor at *Esquire*, then brand-new. McCallister requested that Webb, for whom he had done gag writing, submit some cartoons. As soon as it began publication, *The Mountain Boys* soared in popularity.

Initially the cartoon was published in black and white, but soon *Esquire* began to publish *The Mountain Boys* in color. Webb's style was loose both in black and white and in color. He used everything from charcoal to watercolors and gouache on the feature. The cartoons have a distinctly primitive spontaneity. Colors were not laid in meticulously but with an ease and casualness that is in keeping with the mood of the characters.

The Boys themselves were tall, scraggly, unwashed and usually in a state of activity verging on torpor. They were not just lazy: they were the laziest, most no-account hillbillies in America. They were the epitome of cracker-barrel humor. In their most typical pose, they slouched against a cabin, rifle and jug of moonshine whiskey at the ready. In one cartoon a clan patriarch looks at a bedraggled youngster and says, "Ef yew be one o' Lem Hopkins' kids, git on home—ef yer one o' mine get on into th' house." *The Mountain Boys* sometimes went for the belly laugh, but just as often it created a humorous acknowledgment that, as Paul Webb says, "There's some lazier than I—and more worthless."

B.C.

MOUSE AND HIS CHILD, THE (U.S.) Animator Fred Wolf, who in collaboration with Teru Murakami produced a number of intriguing shorts, directed his first full-length animation feature with a new associate, Chuck Swenson. The result of their efforts, *The Mouse and His Child*, was released in 1978. Adapted by Carol MonPere from Russell Hoban's novel, the film recounts the adventures of a pair of wind-up toys, a mouse and his son linked arm in arm. In their wanderings through the outside world, they encounter all kinds of weird creatures, from Euterpe the stage-struck bird to a white-gloved frog (voiced respectively by Cloris Leachman and Andy Devine). They also run afoul of Manny the Rat (whose voice is superbly modulated by Peter Ustinov) and flee the gloom-drenched tenements and mean streets of the city before finally finding peace with the world in acceptance of their condition.

The Mouse and His Child is a witty and at times thoughtful film. The fact that its heroes are mice further accentuates its stylistic and thematic departures from the animation standards of Disney or Hanna-Barbera (whose mice, whether Mickeys or Jerrys, were never so grimly depicted). While not always successful, the feature signals a possible rejuvenation of the American theatrical cartoon scene.

M.H.

MRÓZ, DANIEL (1917-) Polish cartoonist, illustrator and poster designer born in Kraków, Poland, on February 3, 1917. Daniel Mróz, the son of a respected Polish journalist and newspaper editor, attended the Kraków School of Arts and Crafts, but his education was interrupted by the outbreak of World War II in 1939. During the German occupation (1939-45) he took a variety of odd jobs. Mróz resumed his studies in 1947 at the Kraków Academy of Arts, graduating in 1952.

Mróz started his career as a cartoonist in 1951, when he became a regular contributor to the illustrated weekly *Przekrój*; he also drew for other Polish publications and soon became one of the best-known Polish cartoonists. His drawings, full of eerie humor and strange happenings, often dispense with captions. In 1953 Mróz began illustrating books and has since done more than fifty by Polish and foreign authors. In recent times he has become one of the leading poster designers in Poland, and his work in this field has been widely exhibited at home and abroad.

Mróz has been the recipient of a number of honors for his work in the fields of cartooning, illustration and poster design. In 1959 a monograph on the artist written by Jan Kwiatkowski appeared in Warsaw. His cartoons have frequently been reprinted in the West.

M.H.

MUKUCHI BOSHI (Japan) *Mukuchi Boshi* (which can be translated both as "Silent Mr. Bo" and "Silent Hat") was a collection of fantasy cartoons for children created by Takashi Yanase and published in 1977. It was compiled from a series, *Boshi*, that first appeared in the weekly magazine *Shūkan Asahi* in 1967 and was immensely popular.

Boshi, or "Mr. Bo," was an amusingly drawn little fellow who always wore his hat so far down on his head that his face was invisible—hence the title. He lived in a fantasy world: he could fly, dive into the ocean and swing from the clouds without ever having to worry about his hat coming off. He often traveled in a bigger hat that served as something like a flying saucer. Although Boshi had what amounted to superpowers in his fantasy, he was nonetheless subject to the unexpected. On trying to capture a dragonfly, for example, he might suddenly be swept away by one bigger than himself; when fishing in a pond, he might have his line cut by a mermaid in hiding with a pair of scissors. *Mukuchi Boshi* was a completely silent work, but Boshi, the star, was expressive enough to convey everything the artist attempted. It was a gentle work that appealed to the entire family, and therein lay its broad popularity.

Mukuchi Boshi had its origins in a 1967 contest sponsored by the magazine *Shūkan Asahi*, which offered a prize of nearly $30,000 for the best cartoon submitted. Takashi Yanase, already a professional, entered and won hands down. Yanase was born in Kōchi Prefecture on February 6, 1919. He is extremely versatile and prolific, functioning not only as a cartoonist but also as a poet, animator and song lyricist. Most of his work is for small children, and he is particularly well known for animated films such as *Yasashii Raion* ("The Gentle Lion") and *Chisana Jumbo* ("Little Jumbo"). Most of his written works are published by SANRIO, a Japanese company that specializes in mass marketing books and toys for small children.

F.S.

MULLIN, WILLARD HARLAN (1902-1978) American cartoonist born on a farm near Columbus, Ohio, in 1902. Willard Mullin grew up in Los Angeles, where he worked as a letterer in a sign shop after finishing high school in 1920. In 1923 he went to work for the *Los Angeles Herald*, first doing spot illustrations and later turning to sports cartooning.

After a short stint on papers in San Antonio and Fort Worth, Texas, Mullin went to New York in 1934; the next year he replaced Pete Llanuza as sports cartoonist for the

Willard Mullin. © *United Feature Syndicate.*

World-Telegram. Some time later he created the immortal "Bums," who soon became the trademark of the Brooklyn Dodgers. When the Dodgers moved to Los Angeles in 1958, Mullin put sport shirts, berets and sunglasses on his bums but kept them as seedy and contentious as before. In 1966 the *World-Telegram* closed, and Mullin went on to freelance cartoons for a variety of publications. In addition to his cartoon work, Mullin drew illustrations for magazines (*Look, Life,* the *Saturday Evening Post, Time* and *Newsweek,* among others) and books (the most notable being the 1944 edition of *Menke's Encyclopedia of Sports*).

Mullin's love of his craft and of his subjects shone through in all his cartoons: under the surface roughness lurked a strong undercurrent of affection and optimism. "I'm not an artist," he once said with typical modesty, "I'm a cartoonist." Mullin received many awards during his career; when he retired in 1971, he was hailed as "the sports cartoonist of the century" and a retrospective exhibition of his works was organized in New York City. On December 21, 1978, he died of cancer in Corpus Christi, Texas.

M.H.

MUNTANYOLA I PUIG, JOAQUIM (1914-) Spanish cartoonist born in Barcelona, Spain, in 1914. Joaquim Muntanyola has been one of the most popular cartoonists in Spain since 1931, when he began his career at the age of 17. Throughout the 1930s he worked for three magazines, each very different in nature: *En Patufet,* a middle-class Catalan publication with a strong didactic character; *TBO,* a children's comic magazine with a broad-based audience throughout Spain; and *Bé Negre,* a politically radical magazine. Since the end of the Spanish civil war (1939) Muntanyola has been involved in a variety of activities. His cartoons appear regularly in most of the major newspapers and magazines in Spain, and he continues to contribute to *TBO.* Aside from his cartoons, he has written extensively, often under assumed names; his writings include books, newspaper articles and reviews. He has also illustrated 15 books.

Muntanyola is first and foremost a cartoonist, and his cartoons, filled with unpredictable humor, have a broad following. Their themes draw not only on topical occurrences but also on the traditions established by earlier Spanish cartoonists. Muntanyola's most important creations are the comic strips *Don Felipe, Don Cristobal y Angelina* and *Josechu. Don Felipe* began shortly after the civil war and later became popular in South America. *Josechu* still appears after more than twenty-five years of weekly installments in *TBO.* All three comics reflect in humorous form the anxieties and yearnings of the Spanish middle class.

J.M.

MUSGRAVE-WOOD, JOHN (1915-) British cartoonist and caricaturist born in Leeds, England, in 1915. John Musgrave-Wood (who works under the nationally recognized signature "Emmwood") served in the merchant marine and then with the Chindits in Burma and took his art training at the Goldsmiths' College of Art with a view to becoming a portrait painter. Humor, however, reared its smiling head, and his special ability as a caricaturist combined with a love for show business and won him a post as the theatrical cartoonist for the glossy weekly the *Tatler.*

While playing a round of golf with a friend, he was interrupted by a telephone call from the acting editor of the *Sunday Express:* would he come to their Fleet Street office immediately and execute an urgent caricature for the next edition's show business page? He went (in golf gear) and stayed two years as the newspaper's show-biz cartoonist (1953). In 1955 he was lured to the Beaverbrook Press's London daily, the *Evening Standard,* to produce a regular political caricature for the Diary Page. Then, in 1957, he changed publishers, going to the *Daily Mail,* becoming the principal staff cartoonist and allowing "Trog" (Wally Fawkes) more time with his daily *Flook* strip. When the *Mail* went to tabloid size in 1971, Emmwood began to alternate his cartoons with newcomer Stan ("Mac") McMurtry.

He retired in 1975, after an 18-year run with the *Mail,* leaving that newspaper the emptier for want of his excellent, bold and critical line work.

D.G.

MUSICAL PAINTBOX (G.B.) "*Musical Paintbox* Colour Cartoons created by David Hand. A revolution in animation technique—a screen Sketch Book Fantasy introducing the British countryside in music and picture." These were the words that introduced Great Britain's new animated cartoon series to the film trade in the two-page color advertisement in the *Daily Film Renter,* December 13, 1948.

Musical Paintbox was the second-string series to *Animaland,* which had been created to challenge the power of the Walt Disney cartoons and those from other American studios that had hitherto dominated the "Full Supporting Programme" segment of British cinema programming. With all the wealth of millionaire flour and movie maker J. Arthur Rank behind him, David Hand was hired away from Disney to set up an animation studio in England. Gaumont British Animation, operating from Moor Hall, Cookham in Berkshire, began production in 1947 with short commercials for theatrical release and sing-song shorts for the Saturday morning children's clubs.

The first *Musical Paintbox* cartoon was called *The Thames* (1948), and it set the pattern for the series: a wander through a selected area of the English countryside using several techniques, from a blending of still paintings and drawings to short sequences of somewhat limited animation, accompanied by narration in dialect and snatches of music and song. The whole was, frankly, a device to produce a rapid sequence of releases which would alternate with the more complicated productions of *Animaland*.

Director for the entire series was C. Henry Stringer, with Ralph Wright as story supervisor. The second release was *Wales* (1949), followed by *Somerset* (1949) and, with slightly more appealing titling, *A Fantasy on Ireland*, *A Yorkshire Ditty*, *Sketches of Scotland*, *Cornwall*, *Canterbury Road*, *Devon Whey* and the final entry, *A Fantasy on London Life* (all released in 1949). Scripts were by Nicholas Spargo, Graeme Phillips and R.A.G. Clarke; artists (not always animators) included Norman Abbey, Deryck Foster, Peter Jay, Brian Ward, Alan Gray, Brian O'Hanlon, John Woodward and John Worsley; music throughout was by Henry Reed. Narrators and singers included John Laurie, Bernard Miles and Ian Wallace.

D.G.

MUSSINO, ATTILIO (1878-1954) Italian cartoonist and illustrator born in Turin, Italy, in 1878. While still a high school student, Attilio Mussino had his first cartoons published in satirical magazines such as *La Luna* and *Il Fischietto*. Inspired in equal parts by Giuseppe Scala-

rini's heavy line and by Winsor McCay's oneiric compositions, Mussino (who signed himself "Attilio") developed a style of clarity, grace and "D'Annunzio-like aestheticism," as Antonio Faeti once defined it.

Mussino collaborated from the very first issue (1909) on *Il Corriere dei Piccoli*, for which he created a number of comic strips. The most famous, *Bilbolbul*, was about a little black boy who took figures of speech literally (sprouting wings on his feet, being all at sixes and sevens, etc.), with humorous but slightly sinister results. Other Mussino comic strips include *Schizzo*, *Dorotea e Salmone* and *La Torre del Mago 2000*.

Mussino's masterpiece, however, remains his illustration of Carlo Collodi's *Pinocchio*, which received the Gold Medal at the 1913 International Exposition. A triumph of the zincography process, the drawings prefigure the *Pinocchio* animated by Disney. Mussino later illustrated several *Pinocchio* sequels, as well as innumerable children's classics, including *Tom Sawyer*, *Huckleberry Finn*, *Gulliver's Travels*, and Grimm and Andersen fables. After World War II Mussino devoted himself exclusively to books. The hundreds of books he illustrated have enriched the lives of generations of readers, but Mussino died in utter poverty in 1954.

S.T.

MUTT AND JEFF (U.S.) In 1916 pioneer cartoonist Raoul Barré and promoter Tom Bowers set up an animation unit under the name Barré-Bowers to produce *Mutt and Jeff* cartoons for Bud Fisher (who was the actual owner of the studio). In the weekly cartoons they turned out, the tall, smart-alecky Mutt and the put-upon shrimp Jeff had all kinds of adventures, being brush salesmen one week, African explorers the next (early titles include "In the Submarine," "Jeff's Toothache" and "House Painters"). It is said that during the filming of one of these cartoons a studio animator accidentally hit upon the repeal of the law of gravity as a source of gags. Soon the characters were swimming in mid-air, walking on ceilings and falling skyward, much to the amazement of their audiences. Most of the early cartoons in the series were scripted by Bowers and directed by Barré.

The advent of World War I brought a sense of purpose to the cartoons, which became increasingly bellicose. In "William Hohenzollern, Sausage-Maker," for instance, Mutt and Jeff captured the kaiser single-handedly. It is reported that one of the cartoons—depicting the duo as *poilus* playing jokes on their superior officers—was banned by the French censorship authorities.

In the meantime the relationship between the two partners had steadily deteriorated, coming to a head in 1918 when Barré accused Bowers of swindling; the break became final in 1919. For this and other reasons, Fisher decided to take personal charge of the operation, renaming it simply Mutt and Jeff Studio. *Mutt and Jeff* continued to come out well into the mid-1920s, produced by the studio and by outside contractors (including Paul Terry and Bowers himself). Some of the later entries include "Adventure Shop," "A Trip to Mars" and "Three Raisins and a Cake of Yeast." All these *Mutt and Jeff* cartoons had a tentative air about them, as if waiting for the coming of sound. Withal they were quite entertaining and enjoyed a fair success in the 1920s, second only to *Felix the Cat*. In the early 1930s Walter Lantz tried to revive the series, but by then the characters were no longer in tune with the times, and the attempt lasted little over a year.

The *Mutt and Jeff* cartoons were a proving ground for a

Attilio Mussino, illustration for "Pinocchio." © Mussino.

host of animators. In addition to Barré and Bowers, the cartoonists who worked on the series at one time or another include Dick Friel (who was the top animator at the studio), Burt Gillett, Al Hurter, Dick Huemer, Isidore Klein, Ted Sears, Frank Sherman, Mannie Davis, George Stallings and Ben Harrison.

M.H.

"*Mutt and Jeff.*" © Aedita de Beaumont.

MY GOD (G.B.) The little man, benign and bearded, sits on a cloud. Another cloud floats by bearing the placard God Is Love. "That's one of my favourite advertisements," he muses with a small smile. Mel Calman's God is a very personal (and personable) creation—so personal, in fact, that He might be a mirror image. Benign and bearded (beaming, too), Calman turns out cartoons that are simple in style,

chucklesome in content, yet deep enough under the dashed-down scratches to conceal much thought.

My God appeared as a weekly panel cartoon, column size, in the *Sunday Times* through 1969 and was collected into a paperback reprint in 1970. This comparatively short run of cartoons represents Calman's best work, although others may prefer his experimental comic strip *Couples*, which succeeded *My God* in the *Sunday Times* and ran for a year. This double-barreled strip about love, life and strife in marriage attempted to show both the surface and the subconscious at the same time.

Mel Calman was born in Hackney, London, in 1931, the son of a timber merchant from Odessa. Educated at Perse School, Cambridge, he attended St. Martin's School of Art and studied illustration at the Goldsmiths' College of Art. At the age of 13 he picked up a book by James Thurber, whose simplicity of style immediately intrigued him. From that moment on he wanted to become a cartoonist.

Calman worked in advertising agencies and publishing houses and first drew his thumbnail style of cartoon for the *Daily Express*. He switched to Sunday publication with the *Sunday Telegraph*, *Observer* and *Sunday Times*. In 1972, Calman opened a gallery for the exhibition and sale of original cartoons: The Workshop, 83 Lambs Conduit Street, London. He has appeared on television in *Quick on the Draw* and made the animated cartoon *Arrows*.

Books: *Bed-Sit* (1963); *Boxes* (1964); *Calman and Women* (1967); *The Penguin Mel Calman* (1968); *Through the Telephone Directory* (1969); *My God* (1970); *Couples* (1972); and *This Pestered Isle* (1973).

D.G.

MYRTLE
See Right Around Home.

Nn

NADAR

See Tournachon, Gaspard-Félix.

NAGAHARA, SHISUI (1864-1930) Japanese cartoonist and artist born in Gifu Prefecture in 1864. Son of a samurai family, Shisui Nagahara first made his name as a student of the famous Western oil painter Shōtarō Koyama, but in the mid-1890s he turned to pen and ink to create many cartoons of stinging social and political satire. In 1893 he produced the cartoon magazine *Tobae*. There he introduced such works as *Fūfu* ("The Married Couple"), an earthy cartoon which symbolized the suffering of the lower classes: a man and woman struggle on a muddy road to push a cart carrying their possessions. Typical of Nagahara's early works, this cartoon showed the artist's sympathy for the common people.

In January 1896, Nagahara began to draw the back cover illustrations for the literary magazine *Mezamashigusa* ("Awakening Grass"), published by the famous novelist Ogai Mori. Nagahara continued to do the artwork for this publication until 1902, a span of approximately five years. *Mezamashigusa* provided Nagahara with a highly prestigious intellectual outlet for his political and satirical cartoons, but his drawings remained straightforward, unaffected attacks on the ridiculousness that could be found in a society trying too hard to modernize too fast.

One of Nagahara's most famous techniques was the "split frame," in which he contrasted two pictures or situations to produce a comic result. One such cartoon shows a woman washing rice in a river, and in the accompanying frame, a stack of chamber pots that have obviously just been washed a little farther upstream. Another famous example is Nagahara's drawing of people watching monkeys and monkeys watching people. Nagahara's cartoons were always simple, and his satire clear and to the point. The qualities most obvious in his work were wit, humor, charm and an unending sympathy with the human plight.

Nagahara himself lived a very quiet life. In the 1890s he became an employee of the Tokyo Imperial University's science department, where he drew illustrations for reference books on plants. In 1898 he became an instructor of Western art at Tokyo Bijutsu Gakko (now Geijutsu Daigaku, or Tokyo University of Art), where he taught until his death in 1930.

J.C.

NAKAMURA, FUSETSU (1868-1943) Japanese artist, cartoonist and calligrapher born in Nagano Prefecture in 1868. Fusetsu Nakamura was born into a wealthy family under the name Kintaro Nakamura. He studied art under Shōtarō Koyama and Kakoto Asai before starting his career as an illustrator and drawer of *sagashi-e* ("puzzle pictures," or pictures which have other pictures cleverly concealed within them). In 1893, along with another famous contemporary, Beisen Kubota, Nakamura drew cartoons of the lower classes for the "Saiankoku no Tokyo" ("Blackest Tokyo") section of the socialist newspaper *Kokumin Shimbun* ("People's News"). His works reflected the concern for the masses of the socialist movement of the late 1880s. Typical cartoons included "A View of the Caverns of Poor People," "Steel Workers" and "Farmers." His drawings also appeared in such literary magazines of the time as *Taiyo* ("The Sun"), published in 1895, and *Hototogisu* ("Nightingale"), published in 1897.

Nakamura called his cartoons *haiga*, an allusion to the literary arts of *haiku* and *haikai*. In using this term to describe his work, he attempted to dissociate it from the cartoons found in the *Punch*-style humor magazines that had grown so popular since the start of the Meiji period (1868-1912). Whether his style actually differed from that of the popular cartoons of the period is difficult to tell, but Nakamura was nevertheless a bridge between the arts of premodern Japan and the turbulent era of self-expression that followed Japan's entry into the modern world. Indeed, Nakamura was representative of the early cartoonists who patterned their work after the light, flippant verses of the *haikai* poets of the Edo period. A collection of his art, *Fusetsu Haiga* ("Drawings of Fusetsu"), even included famous words of the Chinese philosophers Lao-tse and Confucius, quoted in such a way that they seemed to be praising Nakamura's cartoons. Such frivolity was certainly not part of the modern tradition, but Nakamura also traveled to France, where he studied Western painting, and he is credited with having established an association for the appreciation of Western art, the Taiheiyō Gakai. He became a staff cartoonist for the *Nihon Shimbun* ("Japan Newspaper") in 1898, evidence that he was concerned with contemporary events as well as traditional literary pastimes.

Nakamura's cartoons reflect his classical upbringing. His brushstrokes closely resemble the simple doodlings the early 19th century poets drew next to their poems (a style frequently encountered in the early Meiji period). Nakamura's significance lies in his transitional role during the early development of the Japanese political cartoon. His simple brush drawings became important visual statements about the socialist movement and the tensions of modernization. Nakamura, however, eventually turned to calligraphy. He built a museum dedicated to the art of Japanese and Chinese writing and spent his later years perfecting his skills as a calligrapher. He died in 1943.

J.C.

NANBU, SHŌTARO (1918-1976) Japanese cartoonist born in Osaka, Japan, on November 23, 1918. As a cartoonist Shōtaro Nanbu was unique in that he never left his home city to move to Tokyo, the capital, as virtually all Japanese artists do. After graduating from a technical school in Osaka, he began working for an architectural

New Year, 1905: "Cleaning House."

Frank Nankivell. © *Puck.*

firm as a draftsman, but he lost his job when World War II ended. Unemployed and at a loss for what to do, Nanbu turned to cartooning and produced a little piece apparently based on his life at that time. He approached the editor of the newspaper *Osaka Shimbun* without much confidence and was surprised when his work was actually accepted.

This break resulted in *Yaneura 3chan*, a strip depicting the humorous life of 3chan, or Sanchan (*san* in Japanese means "three"), which began running in the *Osaka Shimbun* in January 1946. *Yaneura 3chan* was one of the first newspaper cartoons to appear after the end of the war, and it gained instant popularity with its humorous depiction of the problems most people were then experiencing. Living in a room above a barbershop (hence the title of the piece), 3chan was unemployed and disheveled but tried to conduct himself with as much class as possible. Japan in 1946, however, was a land of charred ruins, innumerable thieves, food rationing and constant power blackouts. When 3chan went to the public baths all his clothes were stolen; he bought books in braille so he could read during the blackouts; and he never lost a chance to eat a morsel of food or make a few yen.

As Japan gradually rose from the ashes of defeat, *Yaneura 3chan* declined in popularity, and in 1950 it finally stopped appearing. Nanbu apparently had a nervous breakdown around this time, claiming that he could no longer draw a straight line (although his works were characterized by their humorous wriggly lines). Then, in September 1966, *Yaneura 3chan* was revived in the evening edition of the *Asahi Shimbun*, but it disappeared suddenly after a month, to be replaced by Susumu Nemoto's *Kurichan*. Shōtaro Nanbu virtually vanished from the public eye after 1966. He continued to draw cartoons locally in Osaka but never turned out anything that ranked with *Yaneura 3chan*. On November 5, 1976, he finally died, and his funeral was

widely attended by Osaka cartoonists, who saw in him a local example of a greatness all of them hoped to attain.

F.S.

NANKIVELL, FRANK ARTHUR (1869-1959) American artist born in Maldon, Victoria, Australia, in 1869. Frank Nankivell studied art at Wesley College, Melbourne, and intended to study further in Paris. He sailed for France at age 21 but ran out of funds in Japan. There he cartooned for a living; from 1891 to 1894 he was on the staff of the English-language *Box of Curios*. He made the acquaintance of young Rakuten Kitazawa, taught him editorial cartooning and brought him on the staff as its only Oriental. Kitazawa later became the father of Japanese comic art and the founder of *Tokyo Puck* (presumably named after the New York *Puck*, of which Nankivell was by then staff member), whose title became the generic term for "cartoon magazine" in Japanese. Nankivell left Japan in 1894 to study art in San Francisco; there he published *Chic*, a *Puck* imitation, and drew for the *Call*, the *Examiner* and the *Chronicle*. In 1896 he moved to New York and joined the staff of *Puck*, where he remained until 1909 (except for some intermittent work for Hearst). It is reported that during the Depression Nankivell worked in the Graphic Arts Division of the Federal Arts Project.

If Nankivell was influenced by his stay in the Orient, he seldom manifested it in his later work. A cartoonist whose style reflected the latest art trends, he was among the organizers of the 1913 Armory Show. Nankivell never shied from his subject, and this integrity of purpose in concepts and execution was devoted mainly to social subjects or to state and local political issues. He died on July 4, 1959.

R.M.

NAST, THOMAS (1840-1902) American cartoonist born in Landau, Bavaria, on September 27, 1840. Thomas Nast came to America with his family in 1846, entered the Academy of Design and immediately sought employment as an artist with *Frank Leslie's Illustrated Newspaper*. The lad of 15 was hired and began drawing news sketches and cartoons on wood. In 1859 he switched to the *New York Illustrated News*, which sent him abroad; while drawing for that paper (and for the *Illustrated London News*), he became a very biased artist-reporter, traveling with his hero Garibaldi in Italian campaigns.

Shortly after his return to America in 1861, Nast was engaged by *Harper's Weekly*. His bold signature soon became as distinctive as his themes and presentations; Nast was an instant institution. Politically he was a reformer. During the Civil War he was so effective as a Northern partisan that Lincoln called him "our best recruiting sergeant." In the realm of social subjects, he depicted family life and introduced the now-accepted image of Santa Claus through hundreds of sympathetic cartoons.

Nast's reputation spread after the Civil War. He was a Republican and vigorously defended his friend Ulysses S. Grant; otherwise he was generally a liberal. His greatest influence—indeed, the greatest influence ever achieved by any American political cartoonist—came during the crusade against the corrupt New York political machine known as the Tweed Ring. It culminated in an 1871 series of cartoons that have seldom been equalled in savagery and effectiveness. Almost every member of Tammany Hall was voted out of office,

Thomas Nast, political cartoon of the 1880s.

hounded by the law or, like William Marcy Tweed himself, forced to flee the country. It would be presumptuous—even redundant, since every high school civics class studies Nast's campaign—to attempt to fully chronicle the great Tweed cartoons. Among the most famous, however, are "The Tammany Tiger Let Loose—What Are You Going to Do About It?," "'Twas Him" and "Let Us Prey; A Group of Vultures Waiting for the Storm to Pass Over."

Nast did not temper his venom after the Ring's dissolution. In 1872 President Grant was challenged by Horace Greeley, the Democratic and Liberal Republican presidential candidate. The cartoonist ripped into the eccentric reformer with such vitriol that Greeley's death just after the campaign was attributed as much to Nast as to Greeley's loss of the election and the death of his wife a month before. The first of Nast's several books, *The Fight in Dame Europa's School*, appeared about this time, as did a succession of annual *Nast's Almanacs*.

Nast, at the time the most powerful influence on public opinion in all of journalism, worked smoothly with Fletcher Harper and George William Curtis of *Harper's*.

In the early 1880s, however, the paper became more Mugwump, and Nast more conservative. In addition, friction of a purely personal nature arose. Perhaps inevitably, Nast's cartoons grew a bit stale, and the public seemed to tire of them. Also, *Puck* was leading the field of political cartooning with weekly masterpieces in full color, stealing some of Nast's glamour and novelty appeal. All these factors made for increasing strain between Nast and *Harper's*.

In 1886 he severed his connection with *Harper's*—an action that led to a decline in influence for both Nast and the paper—and formed an association with the struggling *New York Graphic*, flagship paper in a syndicate of Democrat-financed organs. In the pages of the *Graphic*, Nast used his pen on Grover Cleveland's behalf during the campaign of 1888. Thereafter his powers as an artist and partisan—and with them his influence—waned. The rest of his career was a sad succession of short stints on minor papers, erratic chalk-talk lectures and soured business investments. It wasn't just that the public had tired of him; his talents had deteriorated markedly, and his material was embarrassingly bad—an all the more tragic state of affairs for a man still under 50 years of age.

After the *Graphic*, Nast drew for *Time*, *America*, *Once-A-Week*, the *Illustrated American*, the *Chicago Inter-Ocean*, the *New York Gazette* and others. His own paper, *Nast's Weekly*, was a dream come true, but it prospered only while it was a fully subsidized organ of the Republican party. Nast's career ended with a charity appointment by Theodore Roosevelt, another of his heroes, as consul to Guayaquil, Ecuador, where he died on November 7, 1902.

The twilight years of his cartooning service cannot detract from the incalculable importance of Nast in his prime. Very simply, he defined the form of the political cartoon for future generations and set the boundaries of taste, judgment and fairness. That he recognized very few boundaries makes his work and legacy all the more significant. Nast made the political cartoonist in America a force to be reckoned with and removed the cloak of anonymity from his profession. He was the first to fully utilize cartoon icons and himself invented many such symbols, like the Republican elephant. Every political cartoonist since the 1870s has been in Nast's debt, consciously or otherwise; in format, themes, symbols, invective and many other ways the traditions are largely his.

Nast's drawing skills, strangely enough, were not outstanding. Although he could and did produce some stunning graphic masterpieces, most of what he drew was stylistically and artistically unimpressive. In his prime, of course, Nast never drew more than sketches that were transferred by another hand to the wood block for engraving; it is probable that more talented artists improved his work. Little matter, really, for it was his concepts and compositions that were most important, not their execution. And his compositions were devastatingly powerful. Technically, his cartoons were loaded with crosshatch shading and sometimes dozens of labels. Even in decline he was a pioneer—his *Inter-Ocean* cartoons (1892-93) were among the first in newspaper color anywhere.

It is a rare and fascinating thing in any of the arts when a pioneer not only defines a form but also, in the estimation of succeeding generations, remains its foremost exponent. In the field of political cartoons, many have occasionally matched the brilliance of Thomas Nast, but none have surpassed him.

R.M.

NASU, RYŌSUKE (1913-   ) Japanese political cartoonist born in Kumamoto City on the island of Kyushu, Japan, on April 16, 1913. Ryōsuke Nasu is well known in Japan today as the political cartoonist for the *Mainichi* newspaper. His style is characterized by a very direct approach that emphasizes the intrinsic ugliness of politics.

Nasu graduated from Taihei Bijutsu Gakko (the Pacific Art School) but did not attract much attention until he began drawing cartoons for the magazine *Manga* around 1939. At the time, *Manga* was the publication of a cartoonists' group that supported the national policy of militarism, and Hidezo Kondo was its main driving force. With the start of the war with the United States, Nasu's cartoons, as well as those of other *Manga* artists, began to fiercely attack the Allies. Nasu was also hired by the propaganda section of the military general staff to create cartoons that would demoralize enemy troops. These generally relied on portraying the Allies as aggressors and appealing to a Pan-Asian sense of solidarity among the native peoples of Southeast Asia.

After the end of World War II, Nasu continued writing for *Manga* (which was revived, but not necessarily in support of the government this time) and began drawing for the *Mainichi* newspaper, where he remains today. He also submitted cartoons regularly to *Manga Dokuhon* and to *Report*, an exposé magazine that was popular after the war. His work, however, is not confined to caricatures of politicians and policies, for around 1954 he also created a children's work, *Shaboten Mura no Abareuma*, which appeared in *Gekkan Kodomo Manga*.

In 1959 Nasu published a collection of his political cartoons from the *Mainichi* titled *Yoshida kara Kishi e:Seiji Manga Jyūnen* ("Ten Years of Political Cartoons: From Yoshida to Kishi"). It consisted primarily of works critical of the ruling Liberal Democratic party from the time of Prime Minister Yoshida to that of Kishi. On the other side of the political spectrum, however, Nasu also contributed to Hidezo Kondo's *Anpo ga Wakaru* ("I Understand the Security Treaty," 1969). This collection of cartoons supporting the then highly controversial U.S.-Japan Security Treaty was a major boost in the arm to the ruling but beleaguered Liberal Democratic party (which eventually bought a majority of the books). Nasu's cartoons characterized the Soviet Union as a huge bear gazing hungrily at Japan's northern territories, depicted as a little fish.

F.S.

NAUDIN, BERNARD (1876-1946) French cartoonist and etcher born in Châteauroux, France on November 11, 1876. Bernard Naudin received art lessons first from his father, who was an amateur draftsman and sculptor, then from Bonnat at the Paris Ecole des Beaux-Arts. He gave music lessons until he started contributing to *Le Cri de Paris*, whose success stemmed largely from his drawings. He then worked for *L'Assiette au Beurre* (1904-09), where cartoons such as those attacking the penal system or life in the Foreign Legion announced many of the themes later to be found in *La Vierge au Galvaudeux* ("The Virgin with the Tramp," 1917) and *Les Affligés* ("The Afflicted"), moving etchings of the downtrodden masses. Naudin is also famous for his depictions of military scenes witnessed on World War I battlefronts, especially *Dessins pour le Bulletin des Armées de la République* ("Drawings for the Bulletin of the Armies of the Republic," 1916), *Croquis de Campagne* ("Campaign Sketches," 1915) and *La Guerre, Madame* ("The War,

Those who are not killed in battle: At the attack on Port Arthur, a Japanese colonel whose regiment was decimated gave the order to retreat. The next day he was shot by a firing squad.

Bernard Naudin, 1904.

characters are never involved in the action of the cartoon but are simply observers of the robust humor that has been consistently excellent year after year—the more admirable because Australian cartoonists have to create their own jokes and do not employ gag writers to feed them comic ideas. Most of the fun in the cartoon takes place inside, outside or near the "Ettamogah" pub. And, in a sense echoing Percy Leason's "Wiregrass" drawings of the 1930s, Maynard crams his Ettamogah landscape with random groups of figures and incidental but fitting detail.

Since the start of the panel in January 1959, a strange cockatoo-parrot has been flying around the skies of Maynard's cartoons, shod in large lace-up farm boots. The artist has made this curious creature his personal trademark, prompting the inevitable question from many readers: "Why the boots?" To this question the shy, soft-spoken Maynard invariably answers: "Because the tin roofs of the outback houses are too hot to land on barefoot!"

Ken Maynard was born at Albury on the Murray River in June 1928. At the age of 21 he raced with the Albury-Wodonga Cycle Club and won a 50-mile senior state championship. For 20 years Maynard was a uniformed traffic policeman in Melbourne, but bad health forced his retirement from the force. He is a self-taught cartoonist, and his pen-and-ink drawings, which take from eight to ten hours to complete, have been published in trade magazines, in the newspapers the *Argus* and *Truth*, on T-shirts and in a book of his Ettamogah cartoons published a few years ago.

V.L.

Madam," 1918).

In addition to etching portraits of Beethoven and Chopin, publishing a collection of his work (1916-20) and illustrating his own novels, he illustrated Poe's "The Gold Bug" (1929), Villon's "Testaments" and Diderot's *Rameau's Nephew* (1922), among others. All these show most noticeably the influence of Rembrandt and Goya. Bernard Naudin died in a Paris suburb on March 7, 1946.

P.H.

NAVARRO, OSVALDO (1893-1965) Brazilian cartoonist born in Andrade Pinto, in the state of Rio de Janeiro, Brazil, in 1893. When Osvaldo Navarro was a child, his family moved to the town of Barbacena, Minas Geraēs, and it was there that he completed his art studies. From Barbacena he sent his first cartoon to the Rio publication *Carêta* in 1913, thus initiating a long and fruitful collaboration with this magazine.

In 1917 Navarro moved to Rio. Signing simply "Osvaldo," he contributed to such publications as *Rio-Jornal, D. Quixote, Razão* and *A Rajada.* For the pages of *A Rajada* he drew the famous character Jeca Tatu, on texts supplied by the writer José Monteiro Lobato. He also did caricatures for *Alterosa*, a magazine published in Belo Horizonte. He returned to Barbacena in 1928 and died there in 1965.

A.M.

NED AND HIS NEDDY (Australia) Without question the most liked cartoon of its kind, Ken Maynard's *Ned and His Neddy* occupies almost a full page in the *Australasian Post.* Ned is a bush horseman, and "neddy" is old-time slang for a horse. The two title

NEHREBECKI, WLADYSLAW (1923-) Polish animator born in Boryslaw, Poland, in 1923. Wladyslaw Nehrebecki began his career as an illustrator after World War II, soon switching to cartooning. He became one of Poland's first postwar animators, starting at the animated film studio of Bielsko-Biala in the early 1950s. He made his directorial debut in 1952 with an unpretentious little fable, *The Woodpecker Told the Owl.* Later films include: *The Adventures of Gucio the Penguin*, a 1953 exercise that predates Tex Avery's *Chilly Willy; The Gossipy Duck* (1954); and two cartoons featuring a mild-mannered savant, *Professor Filutek in the Park* and *The Strange Dream of Professor Filutek* (1955-56).

In 1958 Nehrebecki produced his much-awarded *Myszka i Kotek* ("Cat and Mouse"), in which he used a simple line drawn on film to depict the adventures of his title characters; the technique was to set a trend in animated filmmaking. He then made a series of cutout and puppet films, the most notable being the 1959 *Tournament.* Between 1960 and 1963, he went back to cartoon animation, producing such films as *The Little Chimney Sweep, The Helicopter, The Crossbow* and *Beyond the Forest, Beyond the Woods.*

In 1963 Nehrebecki directed *The Two Knights.* The success of these cartoon adventures of a mischievous pair of boys, Lolek and Bolek, led to a television series that began in 1964. From then on Nehrebecki devoted most of his efforts to TV animation, working not only on *Bolek i Lolek* but on other series as well (*The Adventures of the Little Blue Knight, Our Grandpa, The Kidnapping of Baltazar Sabka* and others). He occasionally directed an independent cartoon, such as the 1966 *Vendetta*, but since 1973 he has been busy turning out the unprecedentedly popular *Bolek i Lolek* cartoons (including a full-length compilation feature, *Bolek and Lolek Around*

"The boy stood on the burning deck."

Charles Nelan, 1898.

the World, released in 1975).

One of the most prolific of Polish animators, Nehrebecki has yielded to the common temptations of glibness and repetitiveness. Though his *Bolek i Lolek* and other TV cartoons are fresh and often entertaining, Nehrebecki will be remembered for his earlier, more innovative films. In this connection it is interesting to note that the artist's many awards (at Cork, Oberhausen, Bergamo and other places) were received for his pre-1970 works.

M.H.

NELAN, CHARLES (1854-1904) American artist born in Akron, Ohio, on April 10, 1854. Talent and ambition led the young Charles Nelan to parlay his grocery clerkship into a perpetual life class; he retained the job long enough to save money for a trip to New York, where his art samples proved sufficient to gain him entry to the National Academy School. After a year, he earned the Elliot medal there. But money to sustain his art studies ran out, and Nelan returned to Akron and grocery clerking for six years. In 1888 he secured a position as cartoonist for the *Cleveland Press* and was soon picked up by the other papers of the Scripps-McRae League, thus becoming probably the first syndicated newspaper editorial cartoonist. At this time, he was famous largely in the Midwest.

In 1897 he was lured to the *New York Herald* to replace the great Charles Green Bush, who was switching to the *World* after scoring some outstanding hits with his cartoons. The Spanish-American War broke out shortly after Nelan's arrival in New York, and he gained greater fame because of a series of clever and sage comments on the war and America's "Manifest Destiny." In 1899 he was offered a huge contract by the *Philadelphia North American* to be its daily cartoonist. He accepted the post and remained there until his death at Clay Springs, Georgia, on December 7, 1904.

Charles Nelan paved the way for the daily editorial cartoonists in America and proved that partisanship was a salable commodity. His drawing style was a bit stiff (it was asserted after his death that his wife always had to rescue him from a bugaboo by drawing

female figures herself) but was always forceful, not unlike that of Homer Davenport. And like Davenport, Bernard Gillam, Robert Carter and others, Nelan proved that a hired penman could shift his own preferences yet remain an amazingly effective advocate. Nelan published one anthology, *Cartoons of Our War with Spain* (Stokes, 1898).

R.M.

NELL BRINKLEY NARRATIVE PAGES (U.S.) A series of continued full-color graphic narratives, drawn and captioned weekly by Nell Brinkley for the front cover of the Hearst *American Weekly* newspaper magazine-supplement over some twenty years, the "Nell Brinkley Narrative Pages" (they had no formal continuing title in themselves) ran an average of ten weeks per story. They typically consisted of one full-page drawing each week (although there were sometimes subsidiary drawings on the page) and emphasized the sprightlier sides of young romance, superbly limned in Brinkley's intricate webs of line work.

The first narrative was titled *"Golden-Eyes" and Her Hero, "Bill"* and ran from March 31, 1918, to May 5, 1918, for six episodes. It dealt lightly with an American enlistee in World War I, his betrothed and her pet collie, Uncle Sam. A sequel picture-story called *"Golden-Eyes" and Her Hero, "Bill," Over There* ran from September 15, 1918, to February 23, 1919, for 15 episodes (it didn't appear every week, but ran irregularly) and was much wilder and woolier than the first story, involving battle and bloodshed on the Western Front for all characters (Golden-Eyes was a nurse, Uncle Sam a war dog, etc.).

This war-inspired series was popular with *American Weekly* readers, and on November 7, 1920, a third narrative began. *Kathleen and the Great Secret* continued weekly for 18 episodes until March 13, 1921, and again involved two young lovers in worldwide adventures, from camel's back to cockpit. It was followed by Brinkley's best-liked serial, *Betty and Billy–and Their Love Through the Ages*, which began on December 18, 1921, and continued for 23 episodes to June 4, 1922. It told of the reincarnation of the hero and heroine against successive, colorful historical

A Nell Brinkley page, 1925. © International Feature Service.

backgrounds, from caveman culture to the 1920s.

Other serials appeared at greater intervals as Brinkley's daily newspaper and magazine work for Hearst increased. Eventually, in the late 1920s, they moved onto the cover of the Saturday magazine section of the Hearst newspapers, the *Home* magazine, where her last narrative pages appeared, named for such starry-eyed flappers as "Dimples," "Pretty Polly" and "Sunny Sue."

Intensely followed, collected and often even framed by her devoted and largely female readers from 1900 through the 1930s, Brinkley's color narrative pages are still visually striking and fascinating when encountered in the pages of old bound volumes of the Hearst papers. They have considerable value as period prints.

B.B.

NEPP JÓZSEF (1934-) Hungarian animator born in Budapest, Hungary, on June 23, 1934. József Nepp graduated from the Budapest Academy of Fine Arts in 1957 and immediately went to work in animation, introducing the popular *Gustavus* series of cartoons in the late 1950s. Nepp then concentrated on more adult subjects, which he treated with great economy of line, sense of humor and timing. *Passion* (1961) is a winking look at a *ménage-à-trois*, and *Wish Whatever You Want* (1962) is a lighthearted fantasy, as is *From Tomorrow On* (1963). The 1966 *Five Minutes of Murder* is a black comedy that shows Nepp at his most imaginative, depicting with deadpan earnestness the ingenious lengths to which his characters will go to dispatch one another.

Jószef Nepp, "Evolu." © Pannonia Film.

Nepp's output has somewhat diminished recently. He directed *Don't Imitate the Mouse* in 1967 and scripted *Modern Sports Coaching*, a satire on the teeth-grinding techniques of contemporary athletic training, in 1972. With the exception of the winsome but slight *Portrait* (1974), little has been heard from Nepp in the last few years.

M.H.

NERVY NAT (U.S.) Nearly forgotten today, *Nervy Nat* was the cartoon series that firmly established James Montgomery Flagg as a major figure in American graphic humor. Further, it contributed greatly to the emergence of the comic strip and the tramp as hero—a development that, ironically, was otherwise taking place in newspapers, the media arch-rivals of magazines such as *Judge*, where *Nervy Nat* held sway between 1903 and 1907.

"Nervy Nat." © Judge.

Flagg depicted a ne'er-do-well tramp—not as innocent as Happy Hooligan or even Chaplin—in various escapades with railroad police, rich bankers, flirting nurses and the like. It has been reported that W.C. Fields modeled his Tramp Juggler outfit and character after Nat, and their bulbous noses, if nothing else, tend to confirm this. Nat also used hopelessly flowery language. The drawing style was loose and cartoony; Flagg had not yet fallen prey to the slavish attempt to appropriate Gibson's line techniques, a failing that characterized his pen-and-ink illustrations throughout much of his career. *Nervy Nat* appeared in both color and black and white in either 6 or 12 panels per episode, with text under each. The series was numbered, was enormously popular and was reprinted in book form by *Judge*.

In 1907 Flagg left *Judge* to join *Life* exclusively as cartoonist (although he expanded his illustration assignments). *Judge* continued *Nervy Nat* in a second series, drawn with remarkable approximation to the Flagg style by Arthur Lewis; Nat was a bit taller and thinner, but all the trappings of Flagg's delightful cartooning remained. Flagg's work on the series merits republication and fresh appreciation; it is a classic of comic characterization, deflated sham and freewheeling inventiveness.

Nervy Nat was adapted to animation in 1916 by Pat Sullivan.

R.M.

NEWELL, PETER (1862-1924) American cartoonist and children's novelty author born Sheaf Hersey in McDonough County, Illinois, on March 5, 1862. Peter

Newell was raised on the family farm in Bushnell, Illinois, and left home at about 17 years of age. Determined to draw, he entered the Art Students League in New York. His drawings appeared in the mid-1890s in children's magazines and the comic weeklies, particularly *Judge*. His first sale was to *Harper's Bazaar*, the first magazine in which he had seen cartoons. He sent a drawing and inquired whether it indicated talent; the editor replied that he discerned no talent, but he sent a check in payment for the accepted cartoon.

For *Judge* Newell specialized in novelty drawings and visual tricks—upside-down cartoons, etc. This was his forte in books, too, and he was more of a success in the field of humorous illustrated children's books (with huge adult readerships). They employed novel devices like die cuts, slanted pages, camouflaged objects, etc. Notable among them were: *Topsys and Turveys* (1893); *Topsys and Turveys No. 2* (1894); *A Shadow Show* (1896); *Peter Newell's Pictures and Rhymes* (1898); *Alice in Wonderland* (1901); *The Hole Book* (1908); *Jungle Jangle* (1909); *The Slant Book* (1910); and *The Rocket Book* (1912). Several of his books have recently been reprinted by Dover.

Most of Newell's creative period was spent in the artists' colony at Leonia, New Jersey. He was always active with his cartoons, books, and magazine illustrations and even drew a handsome fantasy comic strip, *Polly Sleepyhead*, about 1905. His work stands as a monument to a dazzling imagination and creative fecundity. Newell died at his home in Little Neck, New York, on January 15, 1924.

R.M.

NOBLE, JOE (1894-   ) British animator, writer and director born in Manchester, England, on Christmas Day, 1894. Joe (born Charles) Noble was the son of a notable equine artist, Charles Noble. Joe won a scholarship from a "sixpence-a-week" school and studied art at All Saints School of Art, Manchester. He went to work as his father's assistant in the studio of David Allan and Sons, the leading poster designers and printers of the theatrical profession, where his father was chief artist. Joe designed his first solo poster in 1910, advertising *Ragtime*, a show starring Maud Tiffany. He then came down to London to join E.P. Kinsella, a top poster man of the period, but found himself fascinated by the animated cartoons from America that were becoming the rage: *The Animated Grouch Chasers* by Raoul Barré and *Colonel Heezaliar*. After he served his time in the army, 1919 found him working for the *Daily Cinema News*, designing the "art titles" for the newsreel series. He graduated to title designing for J. Stuart Blackton, the Vitagraph producer (and ex-cartoonist) who was making a picture in London called *The Gypsy Cavalier*, starring Georges Carpentier.

Noble's first brush with animation came in 1920, when he joined Kine Komedy Kartoons at 66 Shaftesbury Avenue (upstairs from the *Daily Cinema News* office). There he assisted Dudley Buxton and the visiting American animator Vet Anderson, learning the rudiments of the trade. Then he moved to Brentford to work for Broda-Jenkins, animating key sketches by two newspaper cartoonists, Tom Titt and W.D. Ford. Tom Aitken, an American war correspondent working for the theatrical agency of Edelstein and Burns, promoted an animated cartoon of Tom Webster's Tishy, the racehorse that crossed her legs! Noble took over

the animation from Ford and worked with Margie Hutchinson (ex-Kine Komedy Kartoons) as a tracer to complete the film by Tuesday, December 12, 1922—the night of a royal performance for King George V and Queen Mary at the London Hippodrome.

In 1923 Noble became production manager for Visual Education, Ltd., animating diagram films on a variety of subjects, and in 1924 he rejoined Dudley Buxton for a series called *Bongo*, which failed to materialize. Tom Webster reentered the animation stakes in 1925, and Noble worked with the ace American animator Dick Friel on the *Alf and Steve* series (a horse and his jockey). Then Noble and Webster produced animation sequences for a unique musical revue at the Criterion Theatre, Piccadilly, entitled *Cartoons*.

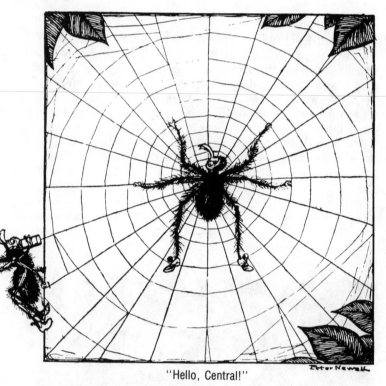

"Hello, Central!"

Peter Newell, 1903.

Sammy and Sausage, Noble's first solo series (with Brian White assisting), was made for regular inclusion in the *Pathé Pictorial* and *Eve's Film Review*, both "magazine film" series issued by Pathé Pictures during 1926-27. In 1928 he began production on the first British sound cartoon, *Orace the Armonious Ound*, using a lip-synchronizing system of his own devising. Produced at the Wembley Studio of British Sound Films, the short was shown in January 1929. Also at Wembley, Noble made the first British animated commercial with sound, *Mr. York of York, Yorks*, for Rowntree's chocolate. Live-action sequences were directed by Bertram Phillips, and the character of Mr. York was created by cartoonist Alfred Leete. In 1933 he joined Brian White and Sid Griffiths on their Raycol color cartoons, based on H.M. Bateman drawings. But most of Noble's work was done for Pathé, for whom he not only supplied animation inserts as required for stories in their *Pathé Pictorial* series but also wrote and directed innumerable live-action sequences and stories. He left Pathé in 1945 to work on naval training films for the Directorate of Naval Training. Apart from a number of animated advertisements, his last important work was animating the fantasy sequences on the British Federation Pictures feature *Mr. H.C. Andersen* (1950).

D.G.

NOÉ, AMÉDÉE DE (1819-1879) French caricaturist born in Paris, France, on January 26, 1819. Having failed his entrance exam to the Ecole Polytechnique, Count de Noé went to work for a short time at the Finance Ministry. He then embarked on his cartooning career (1839), taking the name of Noah's son Cham (Noé is Noah in French).

Cham's most important albums are *La Bourse Illustrée* ("The Illustrated Stock Exchange"), *Nouvelles Leçons de Puérilité Civile* ("New Lessons for Children's Behavior"), *Histoire Comique de l'Assemblée Nationale* ("Comic History of the National Assembly") and *Promenades à l'Exposition* ("Walking Through the Exhibition Halls"). In these and in his 30-year contributions to *Le Charivari*, Cham chronicled with comic verve and exaggeration French pomposity and foibles, especially during the Second Empire. However, even in his jingoistic and unflattering portrayals of the invading Prussian soldiers, he was never biting or cruel; he was indeed a caricaturist for whom wit, not meanness, was the basis of both his art and his captions.

In the 1850s and 1860s Cham also wrote many year-end theatrical reviews that are full of unbridled, madcap silliness and fun. Although forgotten today, he died at his Paris home on September 6, 1879, a very famous man.

P.H.

NOGGIN THE NOG (G.B.) "In the lands of the North, where the black rocks stand guard against the cold sea, in the dark night that is very long, the Men of the Northlands sit by their great log fires and they tell a tale. They tell of a Prince and how he built a long ship and sailed beyond the black ice at the Edge of the World to bring home his bride from the Land of the Midnight Sun."

Thus begins *The Saga of Noggin the Nog*, son of Knut, king of the Nogs, and Queen Grunhilda. His epic journey takes him to the Land of the Nooks to woo and wed Princess Nooka before his kingdom falls prey to his wicked uncle, Nogbad the Bad. Guided by the great bird Graculus, aided by Arup, king of the Walruses, and beset by many an adventure, Noggin's mission was accomplished to the delight of his people and the joy of millions of children who watched the oft-repeated series on BBC television.

The Saga of Noggin the Nog was created, written and narrated by Oliver Postgate, while the drawings, so vital to the success of the series, were by Peter Firmin. Produced by their own Smallfilms Company for BBC, with music by Vernon Elliott, the series was made in 1968 and is the only children's series filmed in black and white that is still regularly shown during school holidays. A number of books and strips were "spun off," and the saga is currently available in a series of ten colored paperbacks published by Kaye and Ward, beginning with *King of the Nogs*.

D.G.

NOGUÉS I CASES, XAVIER (1873-1941) Spanish cartoonist and illustrator born in Barcelona, Spain, in 1873. Xavier Nogués's first cartoons appeared in 1908 in the weekly *Papitu*, under the pen name "Babel" (the use of biblical pseudonyms was typical of the magazine). In 1912 Nogués was named director of the humor magazine

The cravat is just as irksome to women as the crinoline is to men.

Améedée de Noé ("Cham").

Picarol, and in 1914 he joined the staff of the literary *Revista Nova*. Later he contributed cartoons and illustrations to most major Spanish publications. Nogués was a respected illustrator as well as a popular cartoonist. He illustrated some very successful children's books and a number of humorous books. In addition, he was a painter of some repute and produced artworks in wood and glass. He died in Barcelona in 1941.

Nogués is now regarded as one of the most important of Spanish cartoonists. His drawings are extraordinary for their ability to evoke the Spain of the first decades of this century. In them, day-to-day Spanish life seems to unfold before our eyes. Nogués seldom allowed any social or political event to escape his keen critical eye and his elegant but biting pen.

J.M.

NORRIS, LEONARD MATHESON (1913-   ) Canadian editorial cartoonist born in London, England, on December 1, 1913. Len Norris was educated in England, in Port Arthur, Ontario, and at the Ontario College of Art in Toronto. From 1938 to 1940 he was employed as an advertising agency art director. During World War II he served as a captain in the Royal Canadian Electrical and Mechanical Engineers and as editor-writer-illustrator for the Canadian army technical magazine *Cam*. From 1945 to 1950 he was an art director for the Maclean-Hunter Publishing Company, then joining the staff of the Vancouver Sun in January 1950; he remains with that newspaper at present.

Norris reintroduced to the Western Hemisphere one of the dominant cartooning genres of England and the Continent: the nonpolitical, illustrative, news interpretation cartoon. In England its prime exponent was Carl Giles, and in the United States John Fischetti was later to utilize, and Oliphant to appropriate, the format. Norris carried the form to heights never surpassed. His sarcastic, incisive comments are drawn (usually horizontally and sometimes on his paper's front page) in a wildly funny brush and shading manner. A typical cartoon might contain a dozen visual diversions—adjuncts to the cartoon's telling comment rather than distractions.

Norris is one of the most influential cartoonists in

"Our careful check of the records reveals that the job of prime minister is currently filled."
Len Norris. © The Vancouver Sun.

the world, both within his profession and with the public at large. His annual reprint books have sold over a quarter-million copies a year for the last 25 years. Norris has freelanced extensively in a style vaguely reminiscent of Searle's, working on magazine illustration and even children's books.

He was awarded the military M.B.E. in 1945 and has received the National Newspaper Award for cartooning as well as several Art Directors' Club awards. He was granted an honorary doctor of laws degree by Windsor University in 1973 and was elected to the Royal Canadian Academy of Arts in 1974.

His goal, he once stated, is to "interpret the news as it affects ordinary people like me." With his lunatic shots at reality and devastating humor, he is more consistently on the mark than many who strive for weighty analysis.

R.M.

NOVELLI, ENRICO (1876-1943) Italian cartoonist, writer and illustrator born in Pisa, Italy, on June 5, 1876. Enrico Novelli, son of the famous actor Ermete Novelli, wrote his first novel, *Viaggio Sottoterra* ("Journey Underground") at age 14. In 1894 he moved to Milan, working as a newspaperman on *La Sera*. Toward the end of the century he transferred to Rome, where he founded (with others) the satirical publications *Pupazzetto* and *Il Travaso*. Novelli covered World War I as war correspondent; he later worked in the cinema and in 1919 started a puppet theater that toured all of Europe. From 1927 to 1942 he was the director of the daily *Il Nuovo Giornale*, and he died in Florence in December 1943.

Novelli is probably better known under the pseudonym "Yambo" as a writer and illustrator of children's stories. He created hundreds of stories and comic strips, from *Ciufettino* to *Capitan Fanfara*, thoroughly traversing the "archipelago of fantasy"—the title of one of his books but also an apt characterization of his artistic activity. In a style that bears comparison with Albert Robida's, Yambo presented a grotesque and deformed vision of our mechanized world. Instead of demystifying his subjects, however, he preferred giving free rein to his fantasy, thereby mocking the seriousness and high pretensions of scientists and engineers.

C.S.

NOVELLO, GIUSEPPE (1897-) Italian cartoonist, painter and illustrator born in Codogno, Italy, on July 7, 1897.

Giuseppe Novello's law studies at the University of Pavia were interrupted by World War I, and he did not receive his doctorate until 1920. Like other multitalented personalities such as Leo Longanesi and Mino Maccari, Novello is best known for his cartoons, a career he took up in 1923, after three years of study at the Milan School of Fine Arts.

Novello freelanced cartoons and illustrations for a great many publications in the period between the two world wars; his most notable work was done for the *Gazzetta del Popolo* in Turin (1932-38). Many of his cartoons, especially those of the 1920s and 1930s, were reprinted in book form. Titles include: *La Guerra E Bella ma Scomoda* ("War Is Beautiful but Inconvenient"), an illustrated chronicle of his experiences during World War I, drawn on texts by Paolo Monelli; *Il Signore di Buona Famiglia* ("The Well-Born Gentleman," 1934), a kind of humorous epic, grotesque and somewhat bitter, of a middle-class Italian hiding under a cloak of conformity and resignation; *Che Cosa Dirà la Gente?* ("What Will People Say?," 1937); and *Dunque Dicevamo...* ("As I Was Saying...," 1950), in which he resumed the discourse on the middle class that had been interrupted by World War II.

After World War II Novello became a regular contributor to *La Stampa* of Turin with cartoons and illustrations commenting on people and events in the news. He also worked in 1955-56 for the Swiss magazine *Nebelspalter*. Notable among the books of cartoons he published during this period are *Sempre Più Difficile* ("Harder and Harder") and *Resti fra Noi* ("Stay Among Us").

The "tri-carr" driven madly by James.

Enrico Novelli ("Yambo"), illustration for "King of the Worlds." © Novelli.

Novello is a talented painter who has exhibited widely and received many awards, but it is as a cartoonist that he will be best remembered. His cartoons are devoid of poison and of rage; they reflect, in the words of Paolo Monelli, "the poetry of lowliness, of misfortune, of lack of money, the awkward joys and squalid duties of the meek." But there is a kind of humane and affectionate complicity between the artist and the world he satirizes, because in the last analysis Novello belongs to bourgeois society, in which he proposes no radical changes and with which he wants no definitive break.

C.S.

"Nudnik" model sheet. © Rembrandt Films.

NUDNIK (U.S./Czechoslovakia) *Nudnik* is probably the only original cartoon series written and directed by an American producer in an Eastern European studio for distribution in the United States. Working in Prague, Gene Deitch brought out these delightful shorts, which Paramount released theatrically from 1963 to 1967.

Nudnik was an impish, unpredictable little boy whose attempts at exploring the world around him often led to trouble, if not disaster. The cartoons were animated in a winsome and economical style that made full use of the technique of limited drawing. The stories were full of charm, and though they did not display the frantic pace of American animation, they never flagged. In addition to the first cartoon, which was nominated for an Oscar in 1964, some of the most notable entries were "Nudnik on the Roof," "Home Sweet Nudnik," "Good Night, Sweet Nudnik" and the anthology cartoon "I Remember Nudnik."

Deitch once confided that Nudnik was his favorite and most personal character. The series might have matured and achieved success had it been given a chance (only 13 cartoons were made), but it came at a time when theatrical cartoons were being drastically curtailed, and it did not survive.

M.H.

NURIA, POMPEIA (1931-) Spanish cartoonist born in Barcelona, Spain, in 1931. The daughter and granddaughter of distinguished Catalan artists, Pompeia Nuria studied at the Massana School of Art. After graduation she embarked on a career that was interrupted by marriage and the birth of five children. Her first cartoons finally appeared in 1967, in a book called *Maternasis* published by Pierre Tisné in Paris; it was signed simply "9" and dealt with pregnancy and labor. In 1970 she

published *Y Fueron Felices Comiendo Perdices* ("And They Lived Happily Ever After"), a book about the feminine condition, followed by *Pels Segles dels Segles* ("Forever and Ever," 1971), with text in Catalan, about the parallelism between religion and drugs. In 1972 came *La Educación de Palmira* on a text by Manuel Vazquez Montalban, and in 1975 *Mujercitas* ("Little Women").

Nuria started working for magazines with her successful *Metamorfosis* series of cartoons, which appeared in *Triunfo* in 1968 and was later reprinted in several foreign magazines. She has also worked for many other publications, including *Sabado Gráfico, Cuadernos para el Diálogo* and *Cuadernos de Pedagogía,* and for the daily newspapers *El Correo Catalán, Avui* and the now defunct *Diario Femenino.* Her work now appears in the magazine *Por Favor,* where she draws a full page of cartoons, *Nosotros las Mujeres Objeto/ras* ("We the Women Object/ors"), and in the new feminist magazine *Opción.*

Nuria's professional leitmotif is the struggle for the intellectual, physical and social emancipation of women. The subtlety of her cartoons is her trademark; there is no trace of anger or resentment in her work. This perhaps explains why Pompeia Nuria is not only the best known of all Spanish women and feminist cartoonists, but the most popular as well.

J.M.

Gerda Nystad. © Nystad.

NYSTAD, GERDA (1926?-) Denmark's leading female cartoonist, born in Copenhagen, Gerda Nystad made her debut in 1948 with socially satirical cartoons in the daily paper *Social Demokraten.* Later magazine illustrations and cartoons were published in *Bilen Bab, Prik,* etc.

With her sensitive drawing style and bubbling imagination, she actually seems to make roses spring out of women's dresses. Her biting captions, which seem to be in strong contrast to her poetic drawings, add to the general impression of high artistic quality. *Eva's*

Diary, which for more than ten years has been published in the biweekly magazine *Eva*, contains social comments on the changing whims of the times. Married to cartoonist Jørgen Mogensen, Nystad has illustrated several book covers and books (among them, *The Arabian Nights*). She also does a weekly four-column cartoon on the editorial page of the *Berlingske Tidende Week-end*.

J.S.

Oo

O.A.
See Andersson, Oskar.

OBAKE NO Q TARO (Japan) *Obake no Q Taro* ("Q Taro the Ghost") was both a comic strip and an animated television series created by Fujio Fujiko. The main character, Q Taro, became a media star of unprecedented popularity in Japan, spawning not only a host of imitators but also an endless array of children's toys, songs and fashions. Q Taro was a genial and lovable ghost somewhat reminiscent of his American cousin, Casper the Friendly Ghost. Unlike Casper, however, he lived in the house of a human family with two children named Shōta and Shinji, and this format provided for a variety of comical situations and was ultimately responsible for his popularity. Q Taro was certainly a ghost, but he was also very human in his emotions and overall character. He functioned almost as a mischievous pet of the family's children.

Q Taro made his debut in February 1964 in the weekly comic book *Shōnen Sunday*, but it took several months before his character and final form emerged. By 1965, however, he had become a true star, appearing widely in such Shogakkan-affiliated children's publications as *Mebae, Yoiko* and *Yōchien*. Although *Shōnen Sunday* ceased to carry the strip after the end of 1966, Q Taro had in the interim materialized in the more powerful medium of television, where he amused Japanese children from 1965 to 1976. The animated version of Q Taro was produced by Toei and Studio Zero and directed by Daisaku Shirakawa, with the voice of Machiko Soga used to great effect in the title role.

Obake no Q Taro's greatest asset was the lovable character of Q Taro and the excellent differentiation and development of supporting figures such as Shōta and his friends. In the late 1960s Q Taro was in fact the darling of the children of Japan, and his picture was everywhere. Ironically, when the comic book version first appeared in 1964, it was at one point cancelled for three months due to what appeared to be lack of interest. After an overwhelming protest from Q Taro's fans, however, it was promptly reinstated.

Obake no Q Taro's creator, Fujio Fujiko, is really two persons, Moto Abiko and Hiroshi Fujimoto, who work as a duo à la Ellery Queen. They were born in 1934 and 1933, respectively, and have worked together professionally since 1954, when they created *Tenshi no Tamachan* ("Tama the Little Angel"). Their teamwork has contributed to their great versatility and resulted in such classics as *Parman* (1967), *Doraemon* (1971) and *Suzume Roboketto*, which won them the 1963 Shogakkan award for comics. They are active in all genres, from cartoons to comic strips to montage strips combining photographs and drawings, such as *Parman no Hibi* ("The Days of Parman"), currently running in *Big Comic*.

F.S.

O'GALOP
See Rossillon, Marius.

OGAWA, SHIMPEI (1887-1924) Japanese cartoonist born in Hiki, Saitama, Japan, in 1887. Shimpei Ogawa was adopted by his uncle, a judge, at an early age, but what might have been a very comfortable life came to an end when his foster father died. Forced to eke out a living on their own, Ogawa and his mother took up residence in a temple, and Ogawa began working as a clerk in the Nihonbashi district of Tokyo. It was during this time that he made his first attempt at cartooning; adopting the pen name "Hyōe," he began drawing pen-and-ink caricatures of the Tokyo populace.

Ogawa eventually responded to an advertisement for aspiring cartoonists and joined Rakuten Kitazawa, one of the major figures in the early development of Japanese cartoons. His first assignment was to draw for the popular humor magazine *Tokyo Puck*. Later, Ogawa became a cartoonist for the *Yamato* newspaper, where he remained for ten years. During that time, he produced such works as *Engei Gahō* ("Sketches of Plays") and did cover panels for magazines like *Onna no Sekai* ("The World of Women").

Ogawa's cartoons are filled with soft, delicate lines, and they give his drawings a suppleness that belies their sharp humor and sarcasm. Much of his work has been praised for its human qualities; even the most cutting cartoons Ogawa produced seem to retain a mellowness that suggests that the artist is not as tough a social critic as he would have his audience believe.

Later in his career Ogawa again teamed up with Kitazawa to produce the *Jiji Manga*, a Sunday cartoon paper for the *Jiji Shinpō* ("Times Newspaper"). Kitazawa did most of the artwork, and Ogawa acted as editor. Ogawa eventually developed the cartoon section into an eight-page color spread. He also used the paper to advertise for new talent and thus opened the door for young cartoonists to enter the industry in the same manner he had.

In the spring of 1924 Ogawa collaborated with Kitazawa on a special issue of the *Jiji Manga* called the *Jisesō* ("Times"). This publication was perhaps the most significant work of Ogawa's career, since it combined his editorial and cartooning talents and contained material which was not only humorous and satirical but also literary and political. However, on April 10 of the same year, at age 37, Ogawa died from a lung ailment. The 208th issue of the *Jiji Manga* reported that Ogawa's last words were an admonition to his young co-workers to produce more and better cartoons.

J.C.

OGAWA, USEN (1868-1938) Japanese cartoonist born in Ibaraki Prefecture, Japan, in 1868. Usen Ogawa's real name was Shigeyoshi Ogawa, but he later changed it to demonstrate his concern for the masses (*usen* translates "potato money," an aptly proletarian-sounding alias). Ogawa was born in the year that marks Japan's entry into the modern world, and his art reflects the powerful changes that accompanied his nation's attempts at rapid modernization.

Ogawa became one of the major cartoonists on the staff of the *Heimin Shimbun* ("Common People's News"), a socialist newspaper founded in November 1903. He was heavily influenced by the wave of socialist ideology that had begun to sweep over Japan at the end of the 19th century and used this publication to display his anti-war, socialist-inspired attitudes. The Russo-Japanese War (1904-05) was being hotly debated when Ogawa became popular, and he expressed his opposition to it by producing cartoons that are now considered classics of proletarian art. They include drawings of itinerant workers, bean sellers, coal workers—the poor working-class people of Japan who supplied the labor for Japan's modernization. The *Heimin Shimbun* was forced to close down its operations on January 29, 1905, after publishing only 34 issues, but it had remained long enough for Ogawa to become a major spokesman for socialist causes. His drawing of battlefields littered with dead horses and skulls of fallen soldiers no doubt made as great an impact on the masses as it did on the government officials who suppressed the publication.

After the closing of the *Heimin Shimbun*, Ogawa moved to its successor, the bi-monthly *Chokugen* ("Plain Talk"), which began in September 1905. He also contributed proletarian cartoons to other socialist publications, such as *Himuchi* ("The Whip of Fire") and *Hikari* ("Light"). The government soon closed all of these papers, but Ogawa never lacked an outlet for his cartoons. On January 15, 1907, the *Heimin Shimbun* was brought back to life under the name *Nikkan Heimin Shimbun* ("Daily Common People's News"), and again Ogawa produced cartoons depicting the plight of the poor and oppressed. Many of his cartoons from this period show a more sarcastic and satirical tone.

In 1908 Ogawa collected 150 of his drawings and published an anthology called *Kusashiru Manga* ("The Grass Sap Cartoons"). This anthology reveals another side of Ogawa: the literary man with a classical heritage. Many of the selections had appeared in such literary magazines as *Hototogisu* ("Nightingale") and *Ibaraki*, both of which were forums for the most famous Japanese novelists of the period. Ogawa also revealed his classical leanings by organizing the short essays and poems he included in the collection into sections corresponding to the four seasons—an ancient practice in Japanese literature. In fact, even some of his proletarian cartoons bore ancient Chinese proverbs as captions. One such cartoon, which denounced the evils of materialism, proclaimed in classical Japanese, "Possessions eventually become nothing more than stolen property."

After 1910, as the political climate became more tense and arrests, killings and imprisonment of socialist sympathizers more common, Ogawa withdrew from politics and spent his remaining years writing poetry and drawing water nymphs. He died in 1938.

J.C.

OGIHARA, KENJI (1921-) Japanese cartoonist born in Yokohama, Japan, on October 10, 1921. Raised in a neighborhood of professional artisans, Kenji Ogihara too seems to have developed a craftsman's pride in his work. After graduating from elementary school, he attended a technical school at night, and since he loved to draw, he also found time to study art. Shortly thereafter Ogihara began contributing cartoons to magazines such as *Oru Yomimono* and *Modern Nippon*. In 1939, at the urging of Tamotsu Nagai (also a cartoonist), he joined a cartoonists' association then known as the Manga Tot-

"This year it's a judo boom."

Kenji Ogihara. © *Manga Sunday.*

sugekitai ("Cartoon Attack Squad") and began his career as a professional. He was 18 years old.

In 1942 Ogihara was drafted into the Imperial Japanese Army press corps and sent to the front, first in Burma and later in China. Surviving the war, he joined the Manga Shūdan ("Cartoonists' Group") and was soon attracting attention with his *Nihon Igai Shi* ("The Real History of Japan," 1948). This work represented not only his postwar debut but also a pioneering effort at demystifying Japanese history through gentle parody. In humorously reminding people that even the emperor was human, and in making fun of old taboos, *Nihon Igai Shi* helped the Japanese people reformulate their self-image in the wake of the psychological devastation of defeat. Other works followed, such as *Hana Sakeru Bushidō* (1953), *Kurarisan* (1957) and *Ninjutsu Bushidō* (1959).

With the possible exception of *Kurari-san*, Ogihara's works tend to be a humorous mix of past and present. One of his favorite techniques is to put samurai and historical personages in a modern environment replete with telephones and bars. He most frequently works with a one-page, eight-panel layout, but he is also expert at single-panel cartoons. In *Oo! Wa ga Shison* ("Oh! Our Descendants"), which ran in the magazine *Manga Dokuhon* in 1969, Ogihara skillfully employed the "then and now" technique, an excellent example being the two-panel page entitled "Rakujo Mae no Bushō to sono Shison" ("The General Before the Fall of His Castle, and His Descendants"). The top panel shows a samurai general calmly playing a flute before dying, his castle having been captured and enemy arrows having turned the ground around him into a veritable pincushion. The bottom panel illustrates the 20th-century version of a similar situation: a man sits smoking a cigarette in his little house in the midst of Tokyo while a freeway construction crew waits to demolish it. A sign by his door proclaims, "No Relocation!"

Kenji Ogihara received the sixth Bunshun award for cartoons in 1960. Other representative works by him include *Ada Uchi Document* ("Document for Revenge") and *Ogihara no Shakai Gihyō* ("Ogihara's Comical Commentary on Society").

F.S.

OKAMOTO, TADANARI (1932-) Japanese cartoon and puppet animator and director born in Osaka, Japan, on January 11, 1932. After graduating from the University of Osaka with a degree in law in 1955, Tadanari Okamoto made a dramatic change in direction. A growing interest in film, and animation in particular, led him to enter the film department of Nihon University, from which he then graduated in 1961. In the spring of the same year, Okamoto joined MOM productions, headed by Tadahito Mochinaga, and worked primarily in puppet animation on order from U.S. companies. Mochinaga, one of the pioneers of puppet animation in Japan, provided Okamoto with the valuable experience and training he needed, and when Okamoto left MOM to establish his own company, ECHO, he began producing unique works that were immediately well received. His debut piece, *Fushigi na Kusuri* ("Strange Medicine," 1965), won him the Ofuji award and set a level of quality that he has consistently maintained.

Notable among his many award-winning creations are *Home My Home* (1970), a four-minute short that won another Ofuji award; *Hana to Mogura* ("The Flower and the Mole," 1970), which won a silver medal at the Venice International Children's Film Festival; and *Namu Ichi Byosokusai* ("The Happy Weakling"), which won an award at the Tehran International Film Festival in 1973. Okamoto works successfully in a variety of media, using puppets, folded paper, reliefs and cartoons. His originality in using new techniques has helped expand the concept of puppet animation in Japan so that it is now regarded not simply as a vehicle for education but as a broader art form. He often deals with Japanese folktales and frequently makes excellent use of traditional Japanese music, as in *Mochi Mochi no Ki* (1971).

In addition to his many independent productions, Okamoto also creates puppet animation and cartoon animation for television programs and commercials. Since 1972, moreover, he has been actively doing a popular annual show with his colleague Kihachiro Kawamoto in which new and old works are presented along with a live puppet show.

F.S.

OLD BILL (G.B.) "If you knows of a better 'ole, go to it!" was the most famous phrase of World War I, the caption of its most famous cartoon. It was growled by one walrus-whiskered Tommy to another as shells shattered around them, and it was drawn by Captain Bruce Bairnsfather, a soldier who captured the truth about war in ink, wash and wit. His first effort, a sandbagged trench exploding atop a pale-faced group of soldiers ("Where did that one go?"), was actually scribbled in a trench in 1915 during the second battle of Ypres. It was redrawn in a nearby farmhouse and posted off at a brother subaltern's suggestion to the *Bystander*, a slightly upper-class weekly published in London, merely because the size of the sketch suited that magazine's page!

Wounded, Bairnsfather awoke in a Boulogne hospital to see his cartoon in print. Evacuated to the army hospital in Denmark Hill, London, he spent his convalescence sketching more of the same, all of which ran in the *Bystander* as *Fragments from France*. Gradually the characters of Old Bill, his pals Alf and Bert, and his wife Maggie were developed, and Bairnsfather found his cartoons a national craze. They were republished as a part work, published again in book form; he did them as a play, as a silent film and as a talkie. There were short stories, novels, comic strips in the *Daily Graphic* (1921) and *Passing Show*'s comic section (*Old Bill and Bert*, 1934), a film called *Old Bill and Son* for World War II (starring Morland Graham and John Mills) and a new strip, *Young Bill*, in *Illustrated* (1940). The bandwagon seemed never-ending. But end it did, for the humor of World War II was of a different kind, and Old Bill found

"Well if you knows a better 'ole, go to it."

"Old Bill." © The Bellman.

himself out of date. Bairnsfather, born in 1888, died on September 29, 1959.

Books: *Fragments from France* (1916); *Bairnsfather* (1916); *Back to Blighty* (1917); *Bullets and Billets* (1917); *For France* (1917); *Somme Battle Stories* (1917); *From Mud to Mirth* (1919); *The Bairnsfather Case* (1920); *The Better 'Ole* (1924); *Carry On Sergeant* (1927); *Collected Drawings* (1931); *Laughing Through the Orient* (1933); *Wide Canvas* (1939); *Old Bill Stands By* (1939); *Old Bill Does It Again* (1940); and *Old Bill and Son* (1940).

D.G.

OLIPHANT, PATRICK (1935-   ) American cartoonist born in South Australia on July 24, 1935. At the age of 18 Pat Oliphant became a copy boy on the *Adelaide Advertiser* and then rose to staff artist and chief editorial cartoonist; he was deemed to have such promise that his employers sent him on a round-the-world four-month study trip in 1959. Five years later, in the midst of the 1964 presidential campaign, the perspicacious editors at the *Denver Post*, having just lost Paul Conrad to the *Los Angeles Times*, invited Oliphant to America to cartoon for their pages. In 1976 he switched to the *Washington Star*. His cartoons during all those years were syndicated by the Los Angeles Times Syndicate.

In the interim, beginning immediately upon his arrival in the United States, Oliphant became the most influential American political cartoonist of his generation. In three areas he was slavishly imitated: his approach (the use of gag-cartoon formats and the virtual elimination of labels and icons save for Uncle Sam); his media (brush and chemically sensitive shaded paper); and his format (always the horizontal cartoon, and sometimes a multipanel gag situation). His influence in each area was as pervasive and revolutionary as was the use of crayon, stark themes and vertical formats in the 1910s.

"One thing I've found out about oil . . . . it's intoxicating."

Pat Oliphant. © Los Angeles Times Syndicate.

Oliphant has granted many importunate interviews in which he seems to claim credit for complete originality. Students, however, can easily see that Fischetti, in America, pioneered his forms and approach years before, and that there are strong elements of Searle, Giles, Norris and many others in his cartoons; even his mascot—novel in the late 20th century—was a universal convention years ago for editorial cartoonists. The point is that Oliphant is genius enough to have synthesized several great traditions in his unique way. And a claim to total originality would be justified in reference not to his craftsmanship but to each day's individual cartoon—unfailingly brilliant and incisive. He is among the world's—and cartoon history's—preeminent editorial cartoonists.

His drawings almost always convey a sense of mood, whether of a zany bureaucratic orgy or of a desperate scene of starving Third World natives caught in big-nation power struggles. He is generally left of center and in one respect is definitely *not* a conservative: he is liberal with his concepts, sometimes embodying several in one cartoon. Indeed, many readers seek the comments of his mascot penguin before looking at the main cartoon. Oliphant won the Pulitzer Prize and the Sigma Delta Chi award in 1967 and has twice won the National Cartoonists Society Reuben.

R.M.

O'MALLEY, M. POWER (1880-ca. 1930) American cartoonist born in Waterford, Ireland, in 1880. Power O'Malley immigrated to America with his family at the age of six. He studied at the Artisan Institute in New York and continued his painting studies at the National Academy of Design, where he won the Cannon Prize for drawing, the Baldwin Prize for etching, and other distinctions. After the turn of the century O'Malley began submitting pen-and-ink drawings to the popular monthlies and humorous weeklies. *Life* soon became his primary outlet, and since the magazine was just beginning to utilize halftone painted cartoons in a major way, O'Malley's training with the brush stood him in good stead. Into the 1920s his cartoons in *Life* (and illustrations in lesser fiction magazines) graced full pages, center spreads and covers.

O'Malley worked in gray washes and oil colors (for covers and certain double-page cartoons). His style was one of realism, and his themes, like those of fellow cartoonist-in-paints Angus MacDonall, were often wistful, sentimental and gently humorous.

R.M.

OMOITSUKI FUJIN (Japan) *Omoitsuki Fujin* was a Japanese newspaper cartoon drawn by Fusato Hirai that began in 1938 and was popular during the early years of World War II. The title translates as "The Idea Woman," and that was precisely the theme of the cartoon—the introduction of clever time- and money-saving practices that were most likely intended as helpful hints to aid the war effort. The main character was a housewife who, clad in her white apron, found uses for otherwise old and seemingly functionless items. Each cartoon introduced a new idea such as using an old, beat-up thermos to keep a baby's formula warm for emergencies or using old rags to stuff new quilts.

From the perspective of our age of electronic conveniences, the "clever ideas" of *Omoitsuki Fujin* seem rather laughable, but as an indicator of the social consciousness of prewar Japan, this cartoon takes on added significance. Not only were readers eager to learn how they might make their yen go further in an age of depression, but they were also strongly encouraged to economize in the home so that the money and energy they saved could be collectively used for the goals of Imperial Japan. In a sense, *Omoitsuki Fujin* is a good example of an early wartime propaganda cartoon. During the years in which it ran, most of the newspaper cartoons in Japan became propaganda tools of the military government. Three years after the appearance of *Omoitsuki Fujin*, Koshi Ota, one of the founders of a popular, outspoken cartoon/humor magazine called *Karikare*, was imprisoned for "harboring subversive thoughts." *Omoitsuki Fujin*, therefore, represents a state of mind that was encouraged and eventually demanded by the wartime Japanese authorities.

J.C.

ONFROY DE BRÉVILLE, JACQUES (1858-1931) French cartoonist and illustrator born in eastern France on November 25, 1858. While serving in the army, Onfroy de Bréville developed an eye for detail in depicting uniforms and weapons, a talent he used not only in his early military paintings but in his cartoons also. Under the pen name "Job," he contributed from 1892 on to most of the important humor journals, principally to *L'Illustration*, *La Vie Militaire*, *La Caricature*, *Scribner's Magazine* and *Pick-Me-Up* (London). He also illustrated his own books, amusing works titled *Mémoires de César Chabrac* (1892) and *Les Epées de France* ("Swords of France"), as well as other writers' novels dealing with war, history, military life: *Histoire d'un Bonnet à Poil* ("History of a Bearskin," 1893), *Le Grand Napoléon des Petits Enfants* ("The Great Napoleon of Little Children," 1893), *L'Epopée du Costume Militaire Français* ("The Epic of French Military Uniform," 1898), *Bonaparte* (1910) and *Washington the Man of Action* (1914). In addition, he designed costumes and weapons for the theater. He died in Paris in September 1931. Job's sketches, well-drawn and full of verve, capture with good-natured irony human foibles both in and out of the army.

P.H.

ONO, SASEO (1905-1954) Japanese cartoonist born in Yokohama, Japan, in 1905. Saseo Ono is best remembered today for his skill at rendering the female form in his uniquely erotic sketches. From an early age he entertained himself and his friends with drawings both erotic and humorous. He graduated from the prestigious Ueno Art School in Tokyo in 1930 and thereafter regularly submitted his works to *Tokyo Puck*. At the time this magazine was edited by Kenichiro Shimada and had the unique distinction of uniting what would normally be considered two irreconcilable genres—proletarian and erotic art. While the socialist-leaning faction was led by such artists as Masamu Yanase, Fumio Matsuyama and Keiichi Suyama, Ono soon took command over the latter group with the help of his mentor, Oten Shimokawa.

Ono's women were typified by the Japanese "flapper" girls of the time. Western fashions were the rage among the more social young people, who were referred to as *moga-mobo*, a derivation from the English words "modern girl" and "modern boy." Ono's work depicted this somewhat decadent/progressive group in the cafés, bars and theaters of Tokyo. His cartoons rarely contained much in the way of a direct social statement or catchy ideas; rather, they were subtle illustrations of the society he loved. There were exceptions, however, such as "Mannequin Byo" ("Mannequin Disease"), which appeared as the back cover illustration for *Tokyo Puck* in 1936. It showed a starving young former college student working in a women's lingerie store, a humorous parody of the thousands of college graduates then unable to find work to their liking.

In 1941 Ono became a correspondent for the Imperial Army, as did many of his cartoonist compatriots. He was sent to Java, where he drew for the propaganda campaign then in progress. In 1946, after the end of the war, he was finally repatriated to Japan and soon resumed his work, concentrating ever more on depicting sensual women. Ironically, at a time when most Japanese were having trouble finding enough to eat, Ono's women became increasingly full-bodied and voluptuous—almost Western in their proportions. This indirectly contributed to Ono's popularity, and he soon became widely known by the familiar term *Ono-chan*. He joined the new Manga Shŭdan ("Cartoonists' Group"), and in 1951 he acted as judge, along with Hidezo Kondo and Kon Shimizu, for

the popular Nikaten exhibit held in Tokyo. His own work, "Carnival," was also greatly acclaimed at this time.

In real life Saseo Ono was apparently something of a character. Not only was he a true connoisseur of the female form, but according to one source, he was also quite a dandy, insisting that all his clothes be made by a favorite tailor who could create the Chicago gangster look he preferred. On February 1, 1954, Ono suddenly (but somehow fittingly) collapsed on his way to an appearance by Marilyn Monroe at Tokyo's famous Nichigeki Theater. His loss came as a shock to the many cartoonists and fans who loved and admired him. Today, however, his tradition is carried on by Koh Kojima in the cartooning field, and also by his son, Kosei Ono, who is presently one of Japan's foremost comics and film critics, specializing in the introduction of American comics into Japan.

F.S.

OPISSO Y SALA, RICARD (1880-1966) Spanish cartoonist born in Tarragona, Spain, in 1880. Ricard Opisso had his first cartoons published in the magazine *Luz* in 1898. As a young man he went to live in Paris and at the turn of the century contributed cartoons to the French magazines *Le Rire*, *Frou-Frou* and *Fantasio*. Later Opisso moved to Barcelona, where he was highly productive. He created many comic strips for *Els 4 Gats*, *Papitu* and the children's newspapers *Joventut*, *El Senyor Canons* and *TBO*. His single-panel cartoons appeared mainly in *Cu-Cut* (1902-12), *Xut!* (1922-36) and *L'Esquella de la Torratxa* (until 1939). In *L'Esquella de la Torratxa* he published his famous cartoons depicting large gatherings of people with distinct personalities making a wide variety of commentaries.

Opisso was one of the most internationally renowned 20th-century Spanish cartoonists. His drawings of crowd-packed scenes are particularly well known. He was also noted for the masterful use of color in his drawings. He died in Barcelona in 1966.

J.M.

OPITZ, GEORG EMANUEL (1775-1841) German painter, draftsman and printmaker born in Prague, Bohemia (then part of the Hapsburg empire, now in Czechoslovakia), in 1775.

In the late 18th and early 19th centuries, German humorous art was chiefly in the hands of universal draftsmen who included humor as one aspect of their widespread illustrative activities; Chodowiecki, Voltz and Opitz (also spelled Opiz) are the important representative examples.

After art study in Dresden with Giovanni Battista Casanova (a younger brother of the famous adventurer), Georg Opitz worked as a portraitist. About 1801, he wandered to Vienna, where he started gaining a reputation for his characteristic scenes of folk life; humor was always an element in print series of this kind. His gift for observation and his readiness to record all that met his eye resulted in paintings, prints and drawings of Paris when he accompanied the duchess of Courland there in 1814, upon the (first) capture of Napoleon; outstanding among these Paris productions were two large etchings, one depicting the removal of Napoleon's statue from the column in the Place Vendôme, the other showing Cossacks encamped on the Champs-Elysées.

Opitz spent some time in Heidelberg and Altenburg,

Saseo Ono, cover for "Tokyo Puck." © *Tokyo Puck.*

too, before finally settling down in Leipzig in 1820 to become the city's artistic chronicler. In that European crossroads, periodically enlivened by the great trade fair (*Leipziger Messe*), Opitz created what has been called "one of the most amusing and instructive cultural documents of Leipzig in the Biedermeier period." In addition to specific scenes of the fair, Opitz drew street cries of Leipzig; a series of German national and military costumes; scenes of the revolutionary activities of 1830 (waves of unrest shook Europe after Charles X was driven from the French throne during the "three glorious days" of July); such eternally popular print-series subjects as the "times of day"; theatrical and other genre scenes; and numerous views of many other European cities and resorts (such as Carlsbad).

Opitz worked up these scenes mainly in watercolor; they were marketed as aquatints or as contour etchings (also available with hand coloring). Sold at the fair, these eventually reached every corner of Europe, exerting a great influence on the image-mad bourgeoisie and the artists who were then rushing to supply that market. Opitz is said to have drawn some three thousand sheets, but the specific subjects of only about one tenth of these can be reconstructed today. He died in Leipzig on July 12, 1841.

S.A.

OPS
See Rábago, Andrés.

OREHEK, DON (1928-   ) American magazine gag cartoonist born in Brooklyn, New York, on August 9, 1928. The son of a former Austrian cavalry officer,

"Remember 'It's a Long Way to Tipperary'?
Well, it's a long way back too!"

Don Orehek. © Saturday Review.

Don Orehek served a tour of duty in the U.S. Navy after high school, and while in the service, he created the comic strip *Cyphers* for navy newspapers. In 1950, while a student at the School of Visual Arts in New York City, he sold his first cartoon professionally. From 1952 to 1956 he worked for Crestwood Publications in New York City. Crestwood published a series of inexpensive newsprint magazines featuring gag cartoons.

Don Orehek became a full-time freelance cartoonist in 1956 and has since become best known for his fluid illustrative style featuring beautiful women and risqué gags. His work is regularly published in *Playboy, Playgirl, Cosmopolitan, Penthouse* and other similar magazines. However, Orehek is a skilled master of magazine cartoons for general readership. The *Saturday Evening Post, Readers' Digest, Ladies' Home Journal* and the *Saturday Review* have often published his cartoons. He is also a regular contributor to *Cracked,* a teenage humor magazine. In 1973 Don Orehek received the National Cartoonists Society's award for Best Magazine Gag Cartoonist.

Even as a child, Orehek preferred magazine cartooning to comic strips and comic books. His work is more strongly influenced by classical illustration techniques than by anything else. His drawing was considerably tighter in the 1950s and blossomed in the 1960s into the flowing pen lines that are his trademark. Two elements of his style are the use of action in the drawing to promote the gag in the punch line, and the use of detail to qualify the characters of the people in his cartoons. The combination of quick fluid lines, action and detail gives Don Orehek's cartoons a distinctive look.

Gags in a historical setting are a favorite Orehek device. He also favors gags about doctors, lawyers and other professionals. For the past decade he has been showing his humorous watercolor paintings at the Washington Square Outdoor Art Exhibit in New York City. Don Orehek has illustrated two cartoon paperback books, *101 Pickle Jokes* and *Yankee Doodle Dandies.*

B.C.

ORLOV, DIMITRY STAKHIYEVICH (1883-1946) Soviet cartoonist and poster designer born in Novocherkassk, Russia, a city near the river Don, on November 3, 1883. Dimitry Orlov finished his high school studies in Rostov, then went to study art at the University of Moscow. He began drawing political cartoons for antigovernment publications such as *Budel'nik* at the time of the abortive 1905 revolution. After the 1917 revolution he emerged as one of the leading poster artists of the period. He also contributed cartoons to Orkna ROSTA (the Soviet organization responsible for putting up displays in telegraph-office windows all around Russia) as well as to the *Krasnoarmeyets* newspaper. It was around this time that he took up the pseudonym "D.S. Moor," under which he was to become famous.

D.S. Moor made his mark in the 1920s and 1930s, contributing widely acclaimed cartoons to all the leading Soviet publications, from *Pravda* and *Izvestia* to the humor magazines *Krokodil* and *Bezbozhnik u Stanka.* During World War II he went back to designing posters with strongly anti-Nazi and anti-Italian themes. D.S. Moor also did a number of book and magazine illustrations. He was made an Honorable Worker of the RSFSR (Russian Republic) in 1932 and also garnered a

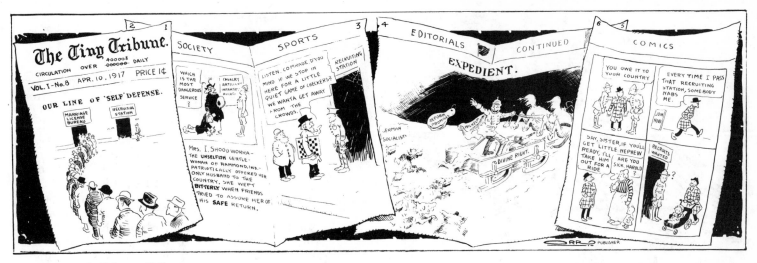

Carey Orr. © Chicago Tribune.

great many other honors. He died in Moscow on October 24, 1946.

M.H.

ORLOWSKI, ALEKSANDER (1777-1832) Polish cartoonist and painter born in Warsaw, Poland, on March 9, 1777. Aleksander Orlowski was born into a noble, if impoverished, Polish family. At the age of 16 he took part in the 1793 uprising against the Third Partition of Poland, and he painted and sketched some of the battle scenes in Raclawice and Warsaw. He then took up formal art studies with the noted painter J.P. Noblin. In addition to a number of fine paintings, Orlowski did a great many humorous sketches and cartoons directed against Prussia (which was then the occupying power). Some of these cartoons roused the ire of the Prussian authorities, and the artist found it prudent to move to Russia in 1802.

Settling in St. Petersburg, Orlowski soon became a successful artist, turning out innumerable genre, heroic and romantic paintings attuned to the temper of the times. His fame spread so rapidly that he was named a member of the Russian Academy of Arts in 1809. He also did caricatures of leading personalities and cartoons full of robust humor. These were not only published in Russian magazines and almanacs but were also reprinted in the rest of Europe, and they alone assured Orlowski's enduring fame. The latest edition of *The Great Soviet Encyclopedia* characterizes his work thus: "Orlowski's precisely drawn cartoon-portraits and caricatures have earned him recognition as one of the founders of the satirical genre in Russia." Orlowski died in St. Petersburg on March 13, 1832.

M.H.

ORR, CAREY (1890-1967) American artist born in Ada, Oklahoma, in 1890. The first 13 years of Carey Orr's life were spent on his grandparents' farm, where a tramp cartoonist one day inspired him to a career with the pen. His lumberjack father then took him to Spokane, Washington, where he attended high school and worked for a time at a lumber mill. Although he was receiving instruction in engineering, it was professional baseball that next loomed large in his life. Playing for a Canadian team, he earned enough money to pursue his first love, cartooning. He enrolled at the Chicago Academy of Fine Arts. His only other instruction was through the W.L. Evans Cartoon Correspondence Course, which he took at his home in Hillyard, Washington, and valued highly.

Soon, in 1911, Orr secured a cartooning job with Hearst's *Chicago Examiner* and the next year succeeded Charles Sykes on the *Nashville Tennessean*. Here he matured and drew handsome, clever cartoons that attracted national attention. As the South's premier cartoonist, he was widely reprinted, and in 1915 several papers, including the *St. Louis Post-Dispatch*, attempted to lure him away. Orr signed a much-publicized two-year renewal with the *Tennessean*, but at the end of that contract he accepted an offer from the *Chicago Tribune*, joining John McCutcheon and Frank King (and freeing King, incidentally, for general, non-editorial cartoon work). There he remained for 46 years.

Carey Orr became one of America's most potent conservative and patriotic cartoon voices; he was anti-interventionist concerning foreign war and opposed the New Deal as a threat to freedom. His cartoons, reminiscent of the Billy Ireland style and relying on realism rather than broad caricature, often appeared on the front page of the *Tribune*, almost always in color beginning on March 5, 1932.

In the 1910s his *Tiny Trib*, an elongated panel dealing with topics in the news, was a signal success, and the concept was adopted by other papers (which replaced the *Tribune*'s logo with theirs). For years Orr taught cartooning at the Chicago Academy and put a whole generation of successful cartoonists in his debt; his niece, Martha Orr, created the pioneer soap-opera comic strip *Apple Mary*. Orr won a Pulitzer Prize in 1961—an honor long overdue—and died in 1967.

R.M.

OSRIN, RAYMOND H. (1928-   ) American political cartoonist born in Brooklyn, New York, on October 5, 1928. Ray Osrin studied at the High School of Industrial Art in New York and at the Art Students League. His early influences were the strip cartoonists Milton Caniff and Frank Robbins and political cartoonists Herblock, Paul Conrad and many others.

From 1945 to 1957, Osrin served in various capacities in the art field as a comic book inker and as an illustrator. He worked in television animation in 1957 and 1958 and was a newspaper staff artist thereafter until 1966, when he succeeded Ed Kuekes as chief political cartoonist of the *Cleveland Plain Dealer*.

The politically Democratic-independent Osrin has altered his drawing style through the years, but he stands head and shoulders above the gaggle of horizontal-

"An army marches on its stomach."

Raymond Osrin. © The Plain Dealer.

format, tone-shading artists by virtue of his concepts; he is one of the most forceful political cartoonists drawing in the United States today. Osrin's awards have included the 1970 National Headliners Award, several Freedoms Foundation citations, and awards for his freelance advertising work.

R.M.

OSVALDO
See Navarro, Osvaldo.

OSWALD THE RABBIT (U.S.) In 1927, with the encouragement of his distributor, Charles Mintz, Walt Disney created a new character to replace the played-out *Alice in Cartoonland* series. They settled on a rabbit, and legend has it that Mintz picked a name for it out of a hat. Such was the birth of Oswald the Lucky Rabbit. With the help of his small team of animators (Ub Iwerks, Hugh Harman and Rudolph Ising prominent among them), Disney developed the floppy-eared rabbit into a well-rounded personality. With his propensity for getting into situations which he then helped solve, Oswald prefigured Mickey Mouse.

The cartoon series (released by Mintz through Universal) was popular enough to attract merchandising tie-ins, so it came as a shock to Disney when Mintz tried in 1928 to force him into accepting a smaller return for his shorts. Having been turned down by Disney, Mintz, who owned rights to the character, set out to produce *Oswald the Rabbit* cartoons (the "Lucky" having been dropped in the meantime) independently, with the help of Rudolph Ising and Hugh Harman, whom he had lured away from Disney. Within a year they had both left Mintz to strike out on their own (thus fulfilling a Disney prophecy, by the way).

Oswald the Rabbit was then farmed out to Walter Lantz; the 1929 "Amateur Nite" started the new series, which did not prove overly successful. Under Lantz's direction Oswald became sprightlier and cuddlier but did not succeed in establishing a strong personality. He seems to have disappeared in the 1940s (in comic books, however, he lasted until 1962).

Oswald was Disney's first effort at full-fledged animation. The lessons (both artistic and commercial) that he learned with the "lucky rabbit" were to serve him well in later years, especially in the making, developing and marketing of Mickey Mouse.

M.H.

OUTDOOR SPORTS
See Indoor/Outdoor Sports.

OUT OF THE INKWELL (U.S.) Max Fleischer conceived the idea for *Out of the Inkwell* in 1915, but it took him one year before his first cartoon short was released in 1916. Fleischer had used a conventional movie camera, which necessitated a separate drawing for each frame: only with the invention of the rotoscope camera (which he patented in 1917) could Fleischer produce his cartoons in sizable quantities.

The concept of the series was simple: the opening shots showed Max Fleischer (in live action) trying to think up an idea for his next cartoon; then a character in a clown costume would pop up from the inkwell (in animation) and get involved in all kinds of pranks before going back into the inkwell. "We used the title *Out of the Inkwell* for want of a better one," Fleischer later admitted. "The pictures were done in pen and ink. In addition there are so many things that can come out of an inkwell."

Fleischer produced his first cartoons at the J.R. Bray studios for release through Paramount. In 1919 he left Bray to set up Out of the Inkwell Films with his brother Dave. The little clown became so popular that in 1923 the Fleischers finally decided to bestow a name upon him: he was christened Ko-Ko the Clown. Later Ko-Ko was given a dog companion by the name of Bimbo, and the frolicsome pair became known as the Inkwell Imps.

While the *Out of the Inkwell* gags were often crude and the animation (done by Dave Fleischer and Dick Huemer) now seems rudimentary, the series enjoyed tremendous success in the 1920s. It became even more of a hit when Max introduced the famous bouncing ball to coax the audience into singing along with the cartoon characters to the accompaniment of the movie-house organ. (The first such "song car-

"*Oswald the Rabbit.*" © Walter Lantz.

"Out of the Inkwell." © *Max Fleischer.*

tune" was released in 1924, to the music and lyrics of Gus Kahn and Ted Fiorito's "Oh, Mabel.")

When sound came to the movies, the Fleischers discontinued *Out of the Inkwell* (the last cartoon in the series, "Chemical Ko-Ko," appeared in 1929). Ko-Ko's career ended there, for all practical purposes, but Bimbo continued well into the 1930s, first in the *Talkartoons* series, then as Betty Boop's companion.

In 1961, at the urging of one of his former animators, Hal Seegar, Max did a new series of cheaply produced *Out of the Inkwell* cartoons for television.

M.H.

OZ (U.S.) L. Frank Baum wrote *The Wonderful Wizard of Oz* in 1900. The book met with such success that it gave rise to scores of additional *Oz* stories written by Baum himself and by his successors; these in turn were adapted to the stage, comic strips, puppet shows, live-action films and animation. The first animated version of *The Wizard of Oz* was reportedly produced in 1933 by Ted

Eshbaugh; due to legal difficulties, however, it was never released. An animated cartoon series, *Tales of the Wizard of Oz*, was effectively produced by Videocraft in 1960-61 and syndicated for Saturday morning telecast. In 1964 NBC-TV broadcast another Videocraft effort, *Return to Oz*, one of the most inept cartoon films ever made.

On a higher technical and artistic level, Filmation brought out *Journey back to Oz*, which was released in 1972 in Britain and Australia, but not until 1974 in the United States; it was well directed by Hal Sutherland from a screenplay by Fred Ladd and Norman Prescott. The voices were done by an all-star cast including Liza Minelli (Dorothy), Mickey Rooney (Scarecrow), Danny Thomas (Tin Man) and Milton Berle (Cowardly Lion); Margaret Hamilton, who played the Wicked Witch in the celebrated 1939 movie version, was Mem in this one. The film was later shown on ABC-TV. A new animated version of *The Wizard of Oz* is rumored to be in the works in Italy.

M.H.

W.W. Denslow's illustration for "The Wonderful Wizard of Oz," 1900.